THIRD EDITION

Introduction to Counseling

An Art and Science Perspective

Michael S. Nystul

New Mexico State University

Boston   New York   San Francisco
Mexico City   Montreal   Toronto   London   Madrid   Munich   Paris
Hong Kong   Singapore   Tokyo   Cape Town   Sydney

Executive Editor: Virginia Lanigan
Series Editorial Assistant: Scott Blaszak
Marketing Manager: Kris Ellis-Levy
Production Editor: Gregory Erb
Editorial Production Service: Argosy Publishing
Composition Buyer: Linda Cox
Manufacturing Buyer: Andrew Turso
Electronic Composition: Argosy Publishing
Cover Designer: Linda Knowles

For related titles and support materials, visit our online catalog at www.ablongman.com.

Between the time Web site information is gathered and then published, it is not unusual for some sites to have closed. Also, the transcription of URLs can result in typographical errors. The publisher would appreciate notification where these errors occur so that they may be corrected in subsequent editions.

Library of Congress Cataloging-in-Publication Data
Nystul, Michael S.
    Introduction to counseling : an art and science perspective / Michael S. Nystul.—3rd ed.
        p. cm.
    Includes bibliographical references and indexes.
    ISBN 0–205–46410–6
    1. Counseling. 2. Psychotherapy. I. Title.

    BF637.C6 N97 2005
    158'.3—dc22

                                                                    2005047671

Text credits appear on page 532, which constitutes a continuation of this copyright page.

This book is dedicated to my incredible wife, Laura,
whose love, beauty, and charm make my world go around.
And whose warm smile says it all.

CONTENTS

8 Experiential Theories and Approaches   204

12 Group Counseling   341

PREFACE

This book provides an overview of the counseling profession. It is written from the perspective of counseling and psychotherapy as both an art and a science. This theme is extended throughout the book in an effort to create a balance in terms of the subjective and objective dimensions of counseling. The art and science are reflected in the book in a number of ways. For example, I provide an objective overview of the major topics emerging in the field of counseling. I also attempt to balance this science perspective with the art of counseling as reflected in a number of *Personal Notes,* which are based on over 35 years of clinical experience.

The first part of the book presents an overview of counseling and the counseling process. It attempts to provide a conceptual framework for understanding what counseling and the counseling process are. Chapter 1 presents several models that can be used to conceptualize counseling. These models include the art and science of counseling and psychotherapy, formal versus informal helping, counseling from a historical perspective, and various trends in counseling. Chapter 2 provides information about professional preparation and legal-ethical issues. Chapter 3 presents an overview of the counseling process and a description of the art of listening skills. Chapters 4 and 5 cover the art and science of assessment, diagnosis, research, and evaluation.

The second part of the book provides information on formulating a personal approach to counseling with a multicultural perspective. Chapter 6 offers specific guidelines for developing a counseling approach. Chapters 7, 8, and 9 address major counseling theories that can be utilized in one's counseling approach. Special attention is paid to the need to create a multicultural perspective in conceptualizing and implementing counseling theories and procedures. The importance of considering emerging trends such as spirituality, diversity, multiculturalism, postmodernism, and brief counseling is also addressed.

The third part of the book includes Chapters 10 through 15, which address special approaches and settings for counselors. After counselors have gained fundamental knowledge and skills in counseling, it is common to begin to develop expertise in working with special populations and settings, such as counseling children and adolescents in a school setting or working with mental health issues in clinics, hospitals, and private practice. Special approaches to counseling, such as marriage and family, child and adolescent, group, and career counseling can be useful modalities for counselors working with clients to promote optimal development across the life span. Numerous challenges and rewards are associated with developing these special skills and practices associated with the counseling profession.

As stated above, I have attempted to incorporate emerging trends such as postmodernism (which focuses on relational-contextual issues), evolving perspectives on multiculturalism (including spirituality and religion), and brief-solution-focused counseling. Together these emerging perspectives offer opportunities for major paradigm shifts that can redefine important elements of the theory, research, and practice of counseling. The ultimate goal of these changes appears to be developing models of helping that are more inclusive and adaptive as opposed to culturally encapsulated and can be translated into effective, efficient methods of helping in an environment of decreasing resources. It is indeed an exciting and rewarding time to be exploring the field of counseling.

Acknowledgments

I would like to recognize a number of individuals who have provided valuable input, ideas, and encouragement. Special thanks are extended to Gerald Corey, Gerald Becker, Frank Zeran, Jon Carlson, Richard Watts, Ray Short, Michael Waldo, Eve Adams, and Martin Greer. I would also like to thank the reviewers of the Third Edition of this book: Gregory Allinson, Beaufort County Community College; Amy Ginsberg, Long Island University; Henry L. Harris, Texas A&M University; David M. Kleist, Idaho State University; and Jeannette Seaberry, University of Nebraska at Omaha. In addition, I would like to extend a very big expression of gratitude to Virginia Lanigan, Executive Editor at Allyn and Bacon, for her insightful ideas and encouragement. Others in the Allyn and Bacon organization and elsewhere who provided key input and assistance include Greg Erb, Scott Blaszak, Shannon Leuma, and Scott Harris. Last, but certainly not least, I would like to thank my wife, Laura, for her encouragement and support.

ABOUT THE AUTHOR

Michael S. Nystul received his Ph.D. in counseling from Oregon State University in 1974. He holds the position of professor in the department of counseling and educational psychology at New Mexico State University. Professor Nystul is a licensed psychologist, clinical mental health counselor, and school psychologist. He has worked in a variety of clinical settings such as schools, hospitals, community mental health centers, university counseling centers, and private practice. His first position was an elementary school counselor with the Bureau of Indian Affairs in 1970, and he continues to be very interested in working with children in counseling. Professor Nystul has more than 100 publications to his name, including journal articles, book chapters, and books. He has three daughters and five grandchildren and relies on his wife, Laura, to maintain a sense of balance in life.

PART ONE

An Overview of Counseling and the Counseling Process

Part One provides a conceptual framework for understanding what counseling is and the counseling process. The following five chapters are covered in Part One.

1. An overview of counseling
2. Professional preparation and ethical and legal issues
3. The counseling process
4. Assessment and diagnosis
5. Counseling research and evaluation

1

An Overview of Counseling

CHAPTER OVERVIEW

This chapter provides several models that can be used to conceptualize counseling. Highlights of the chapter include

- The art and science of counseling and psychotherapy
- Counseling as storytelling
- Counseling versus psychotherapy
- Formal versus informal helping
- Personal qualities of effective helpers
- The helping profession
- Counseling from a historical perspective
- Future trends in counseling

Welcome to the Field of Counseling

The field of counseling can be of interest to you even if you do not want to become a professional counselor. It offers tools for understanding, connecting, and helping that can be used to promote self-awareness and self-improvement and to enhance all aspects of life, including interpersonal relations, coping with stress, and problem solving.

Counseling as a career can be exciting and rewarding, and there are many reasons for becoming a counselor. You may think that helping a client work through a crisis or develop a more effective and meaningful lifestyle will be personally gratifying. Perhaps you find people interesting, or you are curious about how the mind functions, or even fascinated by abnormal conditions such as schizophrenia. You may view the challenge of working in a relatively new profession as appealing. Counseling offers numerous opportunities for its practitioners to make a significant contribution to the profession. You can develop new approaches to counseling or become involved in professional issues such as licensure. There are many ways to involve yourself in the counseling profession, and this book tries to help you identify some facet of counseling you would like to explore.

What Is Counseling?

No simple answer addresses the question, What is counseling? Counseling can more appropriately be understood as a dynamic process associated with an emerging profession. It involves a professionally trained counselor assisting a client with particular concerns. In this process, the counselor can use a variety of counseling strategies such as individual, group, or family counseling to assist the client to bring about beneficial changes. These strategies can generate a variety of outcomes. Some of these are facilitating behavior change, enhancing coping skills, promoting decision making, and improving relationships.

This chapter provides several conceptual models through which the different facets of counseling can be understood. Counseling is described first as an art and a science, then from the perspective of narrative psychology or storytelling. The chapter also differentiates counseling from psychotherapy and formal from informal helping, describes the personal qualities of effective helpers, identifies members of the helping profession, and provides information on past and future trends in counseling.

The Art and Science of Counseling and Psychotherapy

Counseling is essentially both an art and a science. The art-and-science model promoted throughout the book suggests that counseling is an attempt to balance the subjective and objective dimensions of the counseling process. From this perspective, the counselor, like an artist, can sensitively reach into the world of the client, yet on some level maintain a sense of professional and scientific objectivity.

The theoretical origins of the art and science of counseling and psychotherapy can be traced to the scientist-practitioner model set forth in Boulder, Colorado, in 1949. The scientist-practitioner, or Boulder, model (Raimy, 1950) suggests that science should provide a foundation for clinical practice. The Boulder model continues to have a major influence over the structure of university programs in the helping professions (Bernstein & Kerr, 1993; Peterson, 1995). Beutler, Williams, Wakefield, and Entwistle (1995) noted that there is increasing discontent among practitioners with traditional research methodologies and a movement toward alternative research approaches that are more directly linked with everyday clinical practice.

The art and science of counseling and psychotherapy represents an extension of the scientist-practitioner model. From this perspective, the science of counseling generates a knowledge base that has been shown to promote competency and efficacy in counseling. The art of counseling involves using this knowledge base to develop skills that can be applied sensitively to clients in a multicultural society. In addition, the art of counseling relates to the subjective dimension and the science of counseling reflects the objective dimension. The focus of counseling can shift back and forth between these two dimensions as one proceeds through the counseling process. For example, during the initial sessions, the counselor may function more like an artist, using listening skills to understand the client. Later the focus might shift to the science of counseling as the counselor uses psychological tests to obtain an objective understanding of the client. Together, the art and science can create a balanced approach to counseling. A more detailed description of these two dimensions to counseling follows.

The Art of Counseling.   To a large degree counseling is an art. To call counseling an art suggests it is a *flexible, creative process* whereby the counselor adjusts the approach to the unique and emerging needs of the client. The first *Personal Note* that follows provides an illustration of how a counselor can be flexible and creative in working with a client.

Another aspect of the art of counseling is the concept of giving of oneself in counseling. This concept is derived from humanistic psychology and emphasizes the importance of counselors being authentic and human in the counseling approach.

Counselors can give of themselves on many levels. They can give concern and support as they empathize with their client. A more intense form of giving is an existential encounter, which involves the process of self-transcendence. In this experience, the counselor moves beyond the self and feels at one with the client (Nystul, 1987a). The experience can help a client overcome feelings of aloneness and alienation.

Giving of oneself in counseling may be especially appropriate in situations that involve working with neglected and abused children. These children may be wards of a court, without parents or significant others. They may feel unloved and lost, lacking a reason to live. In these cases, the counselor may attempt to communicate compassion, kindness, tenderness, and perhaps even love. The second *Personal Note* that follows illustrate the concept of giving of oneself in counseling.

A Personal Note

As a psychologist working for the Public Health Service on a Navajo Indian Reservation, I was asked to work with an autistic child as part of my consultation with the public schools. School personnel had placed the young girl in a classroom for the mentally retarded, not knowing she was autistic. The child was referred to me for counseling and self-concept development. When she came into my office, I had some puppets ready to use with her. These puppets were part of a self-concept program called Developing an Understanding of Self and Others (DUSO) (Dinkmeyer & Dinkmeyer, 1982). I soon realized that she seemed oblivious to me and the puppets. My counseling plans appeared to be useless.

I wanted to make contact with the child and find a way to reach into her world and develop a special relationship with her. I decided to let her be the guide, and I would follow. She walked over and threw the puppets into a neat pile. If she missed the pile, she threw it until it landed right on top of the others. She was very good at throwing puppets into a pile, and she seemed to enjoy doing it. I had identified one of her assets—something she felt good about, something she felt secure with. It was an extension of her world, her way of doing things. It made sense to her.

I wanted to become part of her world by reaching into it. I walked over and put my arms around her pile of puppets, becoming a puppet-basketball net. She continued to throw her puppets on the pile and through my net. For the next 20 minutes, the child threw the puppets into a pile. When she ran out of puppets, she would gather them up and start over, throwing them into a new pile. I would move the "net" as necessary. During this time, she never made eye contact with me or said a word. I became discouraged and walked back to my seat. As I did, I noticed that her eyes followed my movement. At that instant, I knew I had made contact. I had found a way into her world.

Over the next year, she let me further into her world. For the most part, she was the guide and I the follower—a guest in her home. As the relationship grew stronger, she became willing to explore my world. Through our relationship, I helped her reach out into the world of others. For example, I helped her with language development and encouraged her to move away from her ritualistic behavioral patterns. (A more detailed description of this case can be found by referring to Nystul, 1986.)

A Personal Note

A five-year-old child was abandoned by her parents and placed in a residential facility for neglected and abused children. On one occasion, the caretakers of the institution became concerned when the child stayed up all night crying and vomiting. They brought her to a hospital the next morning. A pediatrician found nothing physically wrong with the child and referred her to me for mental health services.

After introducing myself to the child, I asked her how she was feeling. She sat down, put her face between her legs, and began to cry. It was the most deep-sorrowful sobbing I had ever heard. I leaned forward and gently touched her head, trying to comfort her. I could feel her pain. She looked up at me and appeared frightened and alone. I reached over and held her hand and told her I wanted to help her feel better. My heart reached out to her. I looked at her and said I thought she was a beautiful person, and I wanted to work with her every day. She nodded in agreement. I worked with her in play therapy for several weeks. During that time, her depression gradually lifted.

Counselors must use safeguards when expressing intense feelings to a client. They must clearly establish their role as a counselor and not a parent. They must avoid becoming overly involved to the point where they lose professional objectivity. Counselors must also be aware that excessive concern or worry about a child could lead to burnout. Giving of oneself in counseling is a very delicate process. It can be enriching and rewarding for the counselor and the child, but it can also be exhausting. Communicating intense emotion may not be practical for some counselors. For others, it is an art that must be developed over time.

The Science of Counseling. The science of counseling provides a balance to the art of counseling by creating an objective dimension to the counseling process. Claiborn (1987) noted that science provides an important aspect to the identity of counselors in that it can differentiate professional counselors from nonprofessional helpers. He suggested that counselors should strive to be counselors-as-scientists (that is, someone who functions as a counselor and thinks as a scientist). Thinking as a scientist requires the counselor to have the skills to formulate objective observations and inferences, test hypotheses, and build theories (Claiborn, 1987).

Claiborn (1987) also suggested that the scientist-practitioner model, set forth by Pepinsky and Pepinsky (1954), could provide useful guidelines for contemporary counselors. Pepinsky and Pepinsky's model conceptualizes science and practice as integrated, mutually dependent, and overlapping activities. The interrelationship between theory, research, and practice provides an illustration of the complementary nature of science and practice. For example, practice can test a counseling theory that can, in turn, be evaluated by research.

The science of counseling also proposes that counselors develop skills that can promote professional objectivity in the counseling process. These include the observation, inference, hypothesis-testing, and theory-building skills that Claiborn (1987) suggested are necessary for counselors to think as scientists. Other strategies include the use of psychological tests, a systematic approach to diagnosis, and research methods to establish counseling accountability and efficacy. We should not view these as separate entities of counseling. Instead, counselors should integrate these skills and strategies into their overall role and function.

Counseling as Storytelling

Counseling as storytelling is an emerging conceptual model. Howard (1991) and Sexton and Whiston (1994) suggested that narrative (or storytelling) methods for understanding human behavior have become increasingly popular in psychology. For example, identity development can represent life-story construction, and psychopathology can be related to dysfunctional life stories and can involve story repair (Howard, 1991).

Narrative psychology and its application to counseling as a form of storytelling are related to two emerging and complementary trends in counseling. These trends are the theories associated with postmodernism and brief-solution-focused counseling approaches (additional information regarding these trends are provided throughout the text). Narrative approaches to counseling attempt to simplify and demystify counseling by focusing on the client's own language as opposed to psychological jargon (Eron & Lund, 1993). The role of the counselor is to engage in a collaborative, nonimpositional relationship with the client (Eron & Lund, 1993). In this process, the counselor and client work together to create new narratives (or alternative stories) as a means of enhancing the client's well-being.

Howard (1991) goes on to provide a more detailed description of the role of storytelling in counseling.

> In the course of telling the story of his or her problem, the client provides the therapist with a rough idea of his or her orientation toward life, his or her plans, goals, ambitions, and some idea of the events and pressures surrounding the particular presenting problem. Over time, the therapist must decide whether this problem represents a minor deviation from an otherwise healthy life story. Is this a normal, developmentally appropriate adjustment issue? Or does the therapist detect signs of more thoroughgoing problems in the client's life story? Will therapy play a minor, supportive role to an individual experiencing a low point in his or her life course? If so, the orientation and major themes of the life will be largely unchanged in the therapy experience. But if the trajectory of the life story is problematic in some fundamental way, then more serious, long-term story repair (or rebiographing) might be indicated. So, from this perspective, part of the work between client and therapist can be seen as life-story elaboration, adjustments, or repair. (p. 194)

Meichenbaum and Fitzpatrick (1992) provide additional information on storytelling in terms of how people cope with stress. According to Meichenbaum and Fitzpatrick,

- People organize information in terms of stories about themselves.
- Negative, stressful life events affect people's belief systems, thereby altering the nature of their stories.
- How people rescript their stories (that is, engage in narrative repair) will influence how well they cope with stress.
- The literature is beginning to identify what are adaptive and maladaptive narratives, and how stress-inoculation training can be used to help clients construct adaptive narratives to stressful life events.

Counseling as storytelling is an intriguing concept that appears to offer much promise to understanding counseling. Russell and Lucariello (1992) note that there is a great need for empirical research to investigate the impact of storytelling on the counseling process.

The following *Personal Note* provides an illustration of the role of storytelling in counseling.

Counseling and Psychotherapy

In order to understand what counseling is, it is important to understand key terms and concepts such as *counseling* and *psychotherapy*. The counseling literature has not made a clear distinction between counseling and psychotherapy (Corsini & Wedding, 2000), perhaps because the two processes are more similar than different. We can probably best understand their relationship within a continuum, with counseling at one end and psychotherapy at the

A Personal Note

It seems as if everyone has a story to tell if one is willing to listen. I remember a mailman (whom I did not even know) who stopped me when I was walking around in my backyard. He was visibly angry and proceded to tell me how a policeman had blocked his way on the road while he was giving a ticket. The mailman said, "I asked him to let me by, so I could do my job. But he wouldn't, so I went by anyway driving onto the shoulder. Good grief, some people only think of themselves."

As he talked on, I thought this is a story that this man must tell someone, anyone, to ventilate and to feel understood. I can think of many other examples (such as some plane and bus trips I've had) where people have expressed their desire to tell their stories. I have also been in need of telling my own stories from time to time.

Lately I have become more aware of the role of storytelling in counseling. It has been my experience that most clients have stories to tell. Many of these clients have told their stories to others (such as friends or family members) with disappointing results. In counseling, the clients, stories will hopefully be shown the respect and care they deserve.

One example of a client's story that stands out for me is one of pain, struggle, and courage. Pat was a forty-year-old Anglo single parent of four children. She had been in a serious car accident a year before I had my first counseling session with her. Much of our first sessions involved Pat sharing her story of the accident and her anger at the drunk driver who hit her and the lack of support she was feeling from her insurance company.

Pat's story was also one of struggling for her physical and emotional survival. She had to endure numerous operations for her physical injuries, was unable to go back to work due to physical limitations, and had multiple psychological problems that included insomnia, depression, and anxiety. It was therefore necessary to work closely with a psychiatrist to include medication in conjunction with counseling in her treatment program.

Fortunately Pat had a very strong support system, including friends and family members who helped her feel safe and encouraged, which helped her overcome some of her feelings of anxiety and depression. Gradually, Pat was able to work her way out of her sadness and depression and see some hope and possibilities for a better tomorrow. As she struggled to gain control of her life, she appeared to be engaging in a process of narrative repair, replacing words of gloom with feelings of hope.

other. A counselor may actually do both counseling and psychotherapy in one session. The two processes can therefore blend.

We can identify some subtle differences between these two processes. The main difference is that counseling addresses the conscious mental state, whereas psychotherapy also ventures into the client's unconscious processes. An example of relating to unconscious processes is providing insight to a client. Several other differences exist between counseling and psychotherapy in terms of focus, clients' problems, goals, treatment, and setting. These differences are shown in Table 1.1.

As depicted in Table 1.1, the focus of counseling tends to be developmental in nature, whereas psychotherapy has a remediative emphasis. Counseling attempts to empower clients with tools they can use to meet the normal developmental challenges of progressing through the life span. Counseling is therefore preventative in nature and growth facilitating. Psychotherapy, on the other hand, is directed at helping clients overcome the pain and suffering associated with existing problems such as anxiety and depression. Counseling is used with clients whose problems do not stem from a serious mental disorder such as a major depression. Instead, it is more appropriate for clients who have "problems of living," such as parent-child conflicts or marital difficulties. Goals of counseling tend to focus on resolving immediate concerns such as helping clients work through a relationship difficulty or make a career decision.

TABLE 1.1   Comparison of Counseling and Psychotherapy

	Counseling	Psychotherapy
Focus	Developmental—fosters coping skills to facilitate development and prevent problems.	Remediative—aimed at helping clients overcome existing problems, such as anxiety and depression.
Clients' Problems	Clients tend to have "problems of living," such as relationship difficulties, or need assistance with specific problems, such as career choice.	Clients' problems are more complex and may require formal diagnostic procedures to determine whether there is a mental disorder.
Goals	The focus is on short-term goals (resolution of immediate concerns).	The focus is on short- and long-term goals. Long-term goals can involve processes such as helping the client overcome a particular mental disorder.
Treatment Approaches	The treatment program can include preventative approaches and various counseling strategies to assist with the client's concerns.	Psychotherapeutic approaches are complex. They utilize strategies that relate to conscious and unconscious processes.
Setting	Counseling services can be provided in a variety of settings such as schools, churches, and mental health clinics.	Psychotherapy is typically offered in settings such as private practice, mental health centers, and hospitals.

Treatment programs in counseling vary according to the client's concern. For example, counseling might involve a parent education program to help parents learn how to establish a positive relationship with their child. Other counseling strategies might help a client work through marital difficulties. Counseling approaches are usually short-term, involving one session each week for three to twelve weeks. Counseling services may take place in a variety of settings such as schools, churches, and mental health clinics.

Psychotherapy is a process that can be used to assist a client who is experiencing more complex problems such as a mental disorder. Psychotherapy can involve both short- and long-term goals. The focus of short-term goals may be similar to problems addressed in counseling, for example, dealing with marital problems. Long-term goals relate to more deep-seated or involved problems such as depression or schizophrenia.

Psychotherapy is complex and relates to both conscious and unconscious processes. Hypnosis, projective tests, and dream analysis are all examples of techniques that relate to unconscious processes. Psychotherapy requires expertise in several areas such as personality theory and abnormal psychology. Psychotherapeutic approaches are usually long-term, occurring once each week for three to six months, and sometimes even longer. Typical settings for psychotherapy are private practice, mental health centers, and hospitals.

Differentiating Formal from Informal Helping

Another way to answer the question, What is counseling? is to differentiate counseling from the informal helping that can take place between friends. Some individuals who have had no formal training in counseling can provide valuable assistance. These informal helpers usually have some of the personal qualities associated with effective counselors, such as being caring, nonjudgmental, and able to utilize listening skills. Professional counselors may differ from informal helpers in a number of ways.

First, counselors can maintain a degree of objectivity because they are not directly involved in the client's life. Though there are exceptions, informal helpers usually have a personal relationship with the individual, so the assistance they provide is likely to reflect a personal bias. A related fact is that counselors usually do not have a preconceived idea of how a client should behave. Having no previous experience with the counselor, the client is free to try new modes of behaving and relating. This often does not occur with informal helpers, who may expect the person they are trying to help to act in a certain way. The person being helped might easily fall into the habits established in the relationship. This can create a restrictive environment.

Second, counselors are guided by a code of ethics, the American Counseling Association (ACA) *Code of Ethics and Standards of Practice* (1995), that is designed to protect the rights of clients. For example, the information that a client presents to a counselor must be held in confidence, except in extreme circumstances such as when the client plans to do serious harm to self or others. Knowing this, a client might feel more free to share thoughts and feelings with a professional counselor than with an informal helper.

Third, formal counseling can be an intense and emotionally exhausting experience. After establishing a rapport, the counselor may find it necessary to confront the client with painful issues. Informal helpers may avoid confrontation to avoid jeopardizing the friendship. They often play a more supportive and reassuring role, at times even attempting to rescue the person they are helping. In doing so, the helper, despite good intentions, does not communicate the all-important belief that the client is a capable person. The helper may also rob the individual of an opportunity to get in touch with feelings.

A final difference lies in the repertoire of counseling strategies and techniques available to professional counselors and their ability to systematically utilize these strategies and techniques to promote client growth. For example, a client may have a phobia such as a fear of heights. The counselor may use a behavioral technique called systematic desensitization, which helps the client replace an anxiety response to heights with a relaxation response. Some clients may not be able to stand up for their rights or state their opinions and could therefore benefit from assertiveness training. Other clients may have marriage or family problems, and the professional counselor may utilize the various schools of marriage and family therapy. Lacking formal counselor training, informal helpers are unfamiliar with and thereby unable to utilize these strategies. Instead, they typically rely on advice giving as their main method of helping.

Personal Qualities of Effective Helpers

The following *helping formula* developed by Brammer (1999) provides yet another conceptual model for answering the question, What is counseling?

$$\begin{array}{ccccccc} \text{Personality} & + & \text{Helping} & = & \text{Growth-Facilitating} & \rightarrow & \text{Specific} \\ \text{of the Helper} & & \text{Skills} & & \text{Conditions} & & \text{Outcomes} \end{array}$$

This formula suggests that taking the personality of the helper and adding some helping skills like counseling techniques can generate growth-facilitating conditions. A feeling of mutual trust, respect, and freedom between the counselor and client characterize these growth-facilitating conditions (Brammer, 2002). When such conditions exist, desirable outcomes tend to emerge from the counseling process.

The helping formula emphasizes the importance of the personality of the helper (Brammer, 2002). There is emerging evidence to suggest that the personal characteristics of the counselor play a critical role in the efficacy of counseling (Corey, Corey, & Callanan, 2003; Herman, 1993). As early as 1969, Combs et al. (1969) suggested that the central technique of counseling is to use the "self as an instrument" of change. In other words, counselors use their personality to create a presence that conveys encouragement for, belief in, and support of the client. Rogers (1981) also comments on the importance of the counselor's personal qualities. He notes that the client's perception of the counselor's attitude is more important than the counselor's theories and methods. Rogers' point underscores the fact that clients are interested in and influenced by the personal style of the counselor.

A number of attempts have been made to identify the personal characteristics that promote positive outcomes in counseling. Strong (1968) suggests that clients be perceived as expert, attractive, and trustworthy. Corey, Corey, and Callanan (2003) contend that effective counselors present a positive model for their clients by being actively involved in their own self-development, expanding their self-awareness as they look honestly at their lives and the choices associated with personal growth and development. Beutler, Machado, and Neufeldt (1994) found some empirical support for other counselor characteristics such as emotional well-being, self-disclosure, and optimism.

It would not be realistic to imply that an effective counselor must be a certain type of person. At the same time, the literature does suggest certain basic qualities tend to be important to the counseling process. I have incorporated these basic qualities into what I believe are the 14 personal characteristics of an effective counselor.

1. *Encouraging.* Being encouraging may be the most important quality of an effective counselor. Encouragement helps clients learn to believe in their potential for growth and development. A number of Adlerian counselors have written about the power of encouragement (e.g., Dinkmeyer & Losoncy, 1980).

2. *Artistic.* As mentioned, effective counselors tend to be sensitive and responsive to their clients. Being artistic implies being creative and flexible and adjusting counseling techniques to the unique needs of the client. Just as true artists give something of themselves to each thing they create, counselors must give of themselves to the counseling process. Effective counselors cannot insist on maintaining an emotional distance from the client if such a distance inhibits client growth. If necessary, counselors must allow themselves to experience the client's world directly and be personally affected by the counseling process, as they bring their humanness and vulnerability to the moment. Counselors who allow themselves to be human may also promote authenticity and genuineness in the counseling process.

3. *Emotionally stable.* An emotionally unbalanced counselor will probably do more harm than good for the client. Unfortunately, some counselors enter the counseling profession in an attempt to work through serious mental problems. These counselors may attempt to meet their own needs at the expense of their clients. Langs (1985) goes so far as to suggest that a substantial number of clients spend much of their energy adjusting to the mood swings of their counselor. In some instances, clients might even believe they have to provide temporary counseling for the counselor (Langs, 1985). Role reversals of this type are obviously not in the best interest of the client. An inconsistent counselor will not only waste valuable time but create confusion and insecurity within the client.

4. *Empathic and caring.* Effective counselors care about people and have the desire to help those in need. They are sensitive to the emotional states of others and can communicate an understanding of their struggles with life. Clients experience a sense of support and kindness from these counselors. This can help the client have the courage to face life realistically and explore new directions and possibilities.

5. *Self-aware.* Being self-aware enables counselors to become aware of their limitations. Self-awareness can also help counselors monitor their needs, so they can gratify those needs in a manner that does not interfere with the counseling process. Self-awareness requires an ongoing effort by the counselor. The various ways counselors can promote their self-awareness include using meditation techniques and taking time for personal reflection.

Self-awareness appears to be related to a number of other concepts related to the "self" such as self-acceptance, self-esteem, and self-realization. In this regard, as people become more aware of themselves, they are in a better position to accept themselves. Self-acceptance can then lead to enhancement of one's self-image or self-esteem, which in turn can free a person to move toward self-realization.

6. *Self-acceptance.* Self-acceptance suggests that counselors are comfortable with themselves. Although hopefully they will be working on improvement in their personal growth and development, the discrepancy between the real self and the ideal self is not so great to cause undue anxiety.

7. *Positive self-esteem.* A positive self-esteem can help counselors cope with their personal and professional lives and maintain the emotional stability that is central to their job. Also, counselors who do not feel positive about themselves may look for the negative in their clients. Even worse, such counselors may attempt to degrade the client to enhance their own self-image.

8. *Self-realization.* Self-realization is the process of actualizing one's potential. It represents a journey into personal growth and discovery. Effective helpers reach out in new directions and explore new horizons. As they do, they realize that growth requires commitment, risk, and suffering. In this process, they model for their clients that one must stretch to grow. Counselors welcome life experiences and learn from them. They develop a broad outlook on life that can help their clients put their problems in perspective. Being alive also means counselors have an enthusiasm for life. This enthusiasm can create energy and optimism that can energize and create hope for a client.

9. *Self-disclosure.* Effective counselors are constructively open with their thoughts and feelings. When counselors model openness, they encourage their clients to be open. The resulting candidness can be critical to the counseling process.

10. *Courageous.* Although it is important for clients to perceive their counselors as competent, counselors are not perfect, and they should not be viewed as perfect. Instead, they should try to model the courage to be imperfect (Nystul, 1979c). Counselors with the courage to communicate their weaknesses as well as their strengths are disclosing an authentic picture of themselves. They are also presenting a realistic view of the human condition and can help clients avoid self-defeating, perfectionist tendencies. Another facet of the courage to be imperfect is the willingness of counselors to seek out counseling services for themselves if the need arises. Counselors should not feel that they are too good for counseling or they may develop a condescending attitude about counseling that could result in looking down on their clients. Obtaining counseling can also help counselors understand what it feels like to be in the role of client, contributing to a better understanding of the counseling process.

11. *Patient.* Being patient can be valuable in the counseling process. Helping someone change is a complex process and requires significant effort. Clients may make some progress and then regress to old habits. Counselors must be patient with the goal of achieving overall positive therapeutic movement.

12. *Nonjudgmental.* Counselors must be careful not to impose their values or beliefs on the client, even though they may wish to expose clients to new ideas at times. Being nonjudgmental communicates a respect for clients and allows them to actualize their unique potential.

13. *Tolerance for ambiguity.* This can be an important characteristic of effective counselors. Ambiguity is often associated with the art of counseling. For example, the counselor never knows for sure what the best technique for a client is or exactly what was accomplished during a session. Although the science of counseling can contribute to the objective understanding of the counseling process, counselors must be able to tolerate some ambiguity.

14. *Spirituality.* Spirituality is an emerging trend in counseling. In this sense, the value of addressing and utilizing spiritual-religious processes in the helping process is being recognized. Characteristics of spirituality include capacities such as being sensitive to religious-spiritual issues in oneself and others (such as morality and the soul) and being able to function from and relate to the spiritual world as distinct from the material world.

The Helping Profession

Counseling can also be understood within the context of the helping profession. The term *helping profession* encompasses several professional disciplines, including psychology, counseling, and psychiatry. Each discipline can be distinguished by its unique training programs and resulting specialties. Many individuals from these various groups provide similar services, such as counseling and psychotherapy.

Members of the helping profession often work together on multidisciplinary teams. For example, school counselors and school psychologists join forces to provide counseling services in school settings. Psychiatrists, psychiatric nurses, psychiatric social workers, psychologists, and mental health counselors blend their specialized skills to provide a comprehensive treatment plan in mental health settings. An overview of the degree requirements, specialized skills, and work settings for the members of the helping profession is provided in Table 1.2.

Counseling: Past, Present, and Future

The counseling profession has been characterized by a dynamic evolution. This section describes some of the key individuals and events as well as attempting to predict some future trends in counseling.

Counseling from a Historical Perspective

Kottler and Brown (2000) traced the history of counseling to noted individuals from an ancestral past. These classic scholars provided insights into the human condition that continues to influence the evolution of counseling and modern clinical practice.

- Hippocrates (400 B.C.) developed a classification system for mental illness and personality types.

TABLE 1.2 Types of Professional Helpers

Type of Helper	Licensure and Degree Requirements	Skills and Responsibilities	Work Setting
Mental health counselor	Master's degree in counseling or related field. Most states require licensure.	Use of counseling and psychotherapeutic strategies.	Community mental health centers, hospitals, and private practice.
Marriage, child, and family counselors	Usually a master's degree in marriage, child, and family counseling or related field. An increasing number of states require licensure.	Marriage, child, and family counseling.	Private practice.
Psychiatric social worker	Usually a master's degree in social work. Most states require licensure.	Counseling and psychotherapy, usually from a family perspective; knowledge about psychiatric service; ability to assist with social services (food, shelter, child abuse and neglect, foster and nursing care).	Most work in hospitals and social service agencies. Some have their own private practice.
Pastoral counselor	Master's degree in counseling or related field. Some states require certification or licensure.	Counseling and psychotherapy from a religious perspective. Some focus on issues pertaining to marriage and the family (for example, marital enrichment).	Churches or agencies with church affiliation.
Clinical and counseling psychologist	Psy.D., Ph.D., or Ed.D. (doctor of psychology, philosophy, or education). All states require licensure or certification.	Counseling and psychotherapy, psychological testing, and mental health specialist.	University counseling centers, community mental health centers, hospitals, and private practice.
Psychiatrist	M.D. (medical degree) and 3–4 years specialized training in psychiatry in a full residency program. All states require licensure.	Treatment of serious mental disorders usually involving the use of medications, some counseling and psychotherapy, and consultation. Supervision of other mental health workers is usually involved.	Hospitals, community mental health centers, and private practice.
Psychiatric nurse	R.N. (registered nurse degree). All states require licensure.	Assist in the psychiatric treatment of mental disorders by monitoring medication and providing counseling and psychotherapy.	Hospitals and community mental health centers.
School counselor	Many states require a master's degree in counseling. All states require certification or licensure in school counseling.	Personal and career counseling and consultation with school staff and parents.	Elementary, middle, and high schools.
School psychologist	Many states require a master's degree in school psychology or related field. All states require certification or licensure as a school psychologist.	Psychological testing, counseling, and consulting.	Elementary, middle, and high schools.

- Socrates (400 B.C.) posited that self-awareness was the purest state of knowledge.
- Plato (350 B.C.) described human behavior as an internal state.
- Aristotle (350 B.C.) provided a psychological perspective of emotions including anger.
- St. Augustine (A.D. 400) suggested that introspection was necessary to control emotions.
- Leonardo da Vinci (1500) described the human condition in terms of art and science.
- Shakespeare (1600) created psychologically complex characters in literary work.
- Phillippe Pinel (1800) described abnormal conditions in terms of neurosis and psychosis.
- Anton Mesmer (1800) used hypnosis to treat psychological conditions.
- Charles Darwin (1850) proposed that individual differences are shaped by evolutionary events relating to the survival of the species.
- Søren Kierkegaard (1850) related existential thought to personal meaning in life.

A number of other prominent individuals have made unique and lasting contributions to the counseling profession. The pioneering work of Freud, Adler, and Jung (see Chapter 7) can be credited with establishing the foundation for modern clinical practice. These three men were colleagues in Vienna in the early 1900s, and each went on to develop a unique school of counseling and psychotherapy.

Freud developed psychoanalysis, which emphasizes the role of sexuality in personality development. Adler developed his own school of psychology called *individual psychology,* which emphasizes the importance of social interest in mental health. Jung is credited with originating the school of psychology called *analytic psychology.* Jung's work was influenced by various disciplines, including theology, philosophy, and anthropology. His theory is probably best known for its recognition of a collective unconscious, which suggests that all people share some common memories.

Numerous other schools of counseling have emerged since the pioneering work of Freud, Adler, and Jung. Perhaps more than any other theorist, Rogers has influenced the development of contemporary counseling approaches. His person-centered approach was a testament to the belief in the dignity and worth of the individual (Rogers, 1981). Rogers's approach has held wide appeal among individuals in the helping professions. He was particularly influential in the development of the third force, or humanistic school of counseling and psychotherapy. Cognitive behavioral approaches such as those developed by Albert Ellis (1994) and Aaron Beck (1993) are becoming increasingly popular theories of counseling. These approaches are welcomed by managed care because they tend to focus on symptom relief (such as anxiety or depression) and can be accomplished in a time-limited format.

Recent trends in counseling are reflected in the postmodern theories of constructivism (Mahoney, 1995a) and social constructionism (Gergen, 1994b); brief-solution-focused approaches to counseling (de Shazer, 1994); and empirically supported treatments (Norcross and Hill, 2003). Postmodern theories create an opportunity for a paradigm shift that recognizes the roles cognition, language, and narratives play in defining truth, knowledge, and reality. Brief-solution-focused approaches create another potential paradigm shift toward a focus on strengths and solutions as opposed to problems, weakness, and pathology.

Key Historic Events.   Several historic events have played important roles in the evolution of counseling. Among these are the vocational guidance movement, the standardized testing movement, the mental health movement, and key legislative acts.

The vocational guidance movement had its inception in the efforts of Frank Parsons, a Boston educator who started the Vocational Bureau in 1908. Parsons contended that an individual who took the time to choose a vocation, as opposed to a job, would be more likely to experience success and work satisfaction (Brown & Brooks, 2002). Career counseling, which focuses on helping clients explore their unique potential in relation to the world of work, evolved from the vocational movement.

The standardized testing movement can be traced to Sir Frances Golton, an English biologist, and his study of heredity. Golton developed simple tests to differentiate characteristics of genetically related and unrelated people (Anastasi & Urbina, 1997). Many others have made significant contributions to the testing movement. Cattel set forth the concept of mental testing in 1890 (Anastasi &Urbani, 1997), and Binet developed the first intelligence scale in 1905.

World Wars I and II played important roles in the testing movement. The army's need to classify new recruits for training programs resulted in the development of mass intelligence and ability testing. Examples are the Army Alpha and Army Beta tests during World War I and the Army General Classification test in World War II. After World War II, the use of tests proliferated throughout American society. Testing soon became an integral part of the public school system. Tests were also used in a variety of other settings, including mental health services and employment agencies. The testing movement slowed to some extent during the 1960s, when it became apparent that many standardized tests reflected a cultural bias (Minton & Schneider, 1981). Since that time, there appears to be an increased sensitivity to multicultural issues pertaining to the use of tests.

The mental health movement resulted from the contributions of several forces. In 1908, Clifford Beers wrote *A Mind That Found Itself,* describing the horrors of his three years as a patient in a mental hospital. Beers's efforts resulted in an increase in public awareness of the issues relating to mental disorders. Beers later formed the Society for Mental Hygiene, which promoted comprehensive treatment programs for the mentally ill (Baruth & Robinson, 1987).

Another major factor in the mental health movement was the development in 1952 of medications that could treat serious disorders such as schizophrenia (Rosenhan & Seligman, 1995). Today, it is uncommon for psychiatric patients to remain in a hospital for more than one or two months. Although these medications do not cure mental disorders, they often can control symptoms to the degree that a person can function in society.

Unfortunately, it has been difficult to develop effective follow-up programs for psychiatric patients after their discharge from a hospital. The result has been an alarming number of mentally disturbed people wandering the streets as homeless "street people." Several studies have estimated that 25–50 percent of homeless people are mentally ill (Frazier, 1985; Ball & Harassy, 1984). Many mental health professionals are attempting to develop more effective follow-up and outreach services for the chronically mentally ill.

Key legislative acts have also contributed to the evolution of the counseling profession, in particular, the National Defense Education Act (NDEA) of 1958. This act was designed to improve the teaching of science in public schools, motivated by a popular belief that the United States was lagging behind Russia's achievements in science. This belief developed after Americans learned of the Soviet Union's success in launching the first space satellite, *Sputnik*. The NDEA had a major impact on the counseling profession by providing funds to train school counselors, resulting in a marked increase in the number of counselors employed in U.S. schools.

Present Trends

This section goes beyond describing what counseling is and attempts to predict what directions it may take in the future. Several researchers have identified trends in research, ethics, multicultural counseling, managed mental health services, empirically supported treatment, brief-solution-focused counseling, mental disorders, postmodernism, spirituality, cybercounseling, technology, and problematic-impaired students.

Research. Gelso and Fassinger (1990) provided a comprehensive review of the counseling research conducted during the 1980s. They noted that the decade was characterized by increased interest in alternative research methodologies that incorporate more field-based and fewer laboratory-based designs. These authors suggested that the interest in alternative research designs would continue, along with "a trend toward the use of more refined methodological strategies and, in particular, advanced statistical procedures" (p. 374).

There appears to be increasing discontent with the scientist-practitioner model of counseling, which emphasizes the importance of clinicians integrating research into their clinical practice (Stricker & Trierweiler, 1995). The split between science and practice does not appear to be owing to a lack of interest by practitioners but rather that current research tends to offer little use or relevance to the day-to-day practice of counselors (Edelson, 1994; Havens, 1994).

Maling and Howard (1994) suggest that the statistical abstractions associated with quantitative research are of little use for counselors who are struggling with the individualized issues of clients. Alternative (qualitative) research methodologies are gaining increasing interest. They tend to focus on the use of interviews to discover with the subject (client) clinically relevant information (a process that parallels counseling). Qualitative methods appear to represent a blend of the art and science of counseling by providing information on the subjective and objective dimensions of the counseling process.

Ethical-Legal Issues. Lawrence and Kurpius (2000) note that ethical-legal issues regarding counseling minors is an emerging area of concern in counseling. Counseling children and adolescents is a specialty that requires unique competencies in clinical practice such as ethical-legal decision making. Ethical-legal issues relating to confidentiality, informed consent, and reporting child abuse and neglect raise particular challenges for counselors. For example, parents typically must provide informed consent for minors to receive counseling. There are some exceptions to this; some states allow minors to obtain counseling without their parents' permission when seeking substance abuse counseling or counseling relating to decisions regarding pregnancy. The issue of confidentiality is unique when providing counseling to minors. In these instances, parents "own the confidentiality" and therefore have legal access to what is discussed. At the same time, counselors need to create a means of sharing confidential information that is in the child's or adolescent's best interests. In addition, child abuse and neglect creates exceptions to parents' rights regarding confidentiality.

Multicultural Counseling.   Multicultural counseling can be considered the fourth force in psychology, following psychodynamic, existential-humanistic, and cognitive-behavioral forces (Pedersen, 1991a; Sue, Ivey, & Pedersen, 1996). The multicultural counseling movement is directed at reconceptualizing traditional counseling theory and practice. In this regard, Sue et al. (1996) argue that "current theories of counseling do not adequately address issues of diversity and must therefore be expanded to include a multicultural perspective.

Current trends in multicultural counseling do not suggest that traditional theories of counseling have been abandoned (McFadden, 1996; Patterson, 1996). The spirit of this movement appears to be directed at a more comprehensive integration of multiculturalism into all phases of the counseling process from establishing the relationship, to termination, and research and evaluation.

Multicultural counseling and therapy (MCT) (Sue et al., 1996) provides an example of this emerging trend in counseling. It can be used as a "lens" to conceptualize multicultural issues throughout the counseling process. As multicultural issues are identified, counseling theories, strategies, and other facets of the counseling process can be adjusted as necessary to meet the unique and emerging needs of clients (see Chapter 6 for a description of MCT and other multicultural perspectives).

Managed Mental Health Services.   Managed care for mental health services began in the late 1980s (Freeman, 1995) and continues as a major thrust in contemporary health care. Managed care focuses on managing care rather than managing benefits (Freeman, 1995). It typically involves health maintenance organizations (HMOs), managed mental health care organizations (MMHCOs), independent provider organizations (IPOs), and employer assistance programs (EAPs). It is becoming increasingly important for mental health practitioners to affiliate themselves with these organizations in order to be part of the health care system and be able to provide services.

A number of major concerns have been raised about the managed-care movement, such as reduced number of visits (usually three to seven sessions), problems with confidentiality, depersonalization, questionable training for those screening mental health problems, and restricted choice of mental health providers (Solomon, 1996). Rupert and Baird (2004) have assessed the impact of managed care on independent practice of psychology. Their study shows that managed care is a source of stress for practitioners, especially in terms of paperwork and external constraints such as issues relating to reimbursement. Degree of involvement with managed care is also related to stress and burnout with those highly involved in managed care being at risk for stress-related burnout.

Empirically Supported Treatment.   Norcross and Hill (2003) have noted that there is an international movement in the health care professions toward empirically supported treatments (EST). Managed-care organizations have recognized the merits of empirically supported interventions as a means to identify approved treatment protocols associated with diagnostic conditions (Wampold, Lichtenberg, & Waehler, 2002).

The APA Division of Clinical Psychology (Task Force, 1995) was an attempt to identify EST associated with mental health disorders and to communicate this information to the public and members of the helping professions. There has been considerable debate regarding what constitutes evidence of effective treatment (Wampold et al., 2002). Numerous models have evolved to evaluate treatment modalities. For example, Wampold et al. (2002) identified seven principles that could be used to review evidence of empirically supported interventions. Chwalisz (2003) suggested that evaluation of EST should be expanded to include consideration of philosophical, political, and social issues.

Norcross and Hill (2003) note that the EST movement does not consider personal issues such as counselor or client characteristics and the nature of the therapeutic relationship in evaluating counseling efficacy. They posit that the EST lists and guidelines are void of the human dimensions involving "disembodied therapists performing procedures on discrete Axis I disorders" (p. 22). Norcross and Hill (2003) have developed empirically supported (therapy) relationships in an attempt to determine what relationship variables work and how they can be adjusted to enhance treatment outcomes for individual patients.

EST appears to have much promise in terms of mental health services, although it can promote accountability and provide a recognized protocol for research and development of mental health treatments. The art and science of EST recognizes the need for balance between objective understanding and the need to consider human factors in determining treatment efficacy.

Brief-Solution-Focused Counseling.   The brief-solution-focused counseling movement appears to be gaining significant momentum. The pressures of budgetary and time constraints and the shift toward managed care have contributed to the increased interest in brief-counseling approaches. Many of the major counseling theories are being reinterpreted from a brief-counseling perspective (Friedman, 1997). In addition, some brief-counseling models have focused on problem solving (Nystul, 1995), while others are solution-focused (de Shazer, 1994). Brief-counseling models provide opportunities to reconceptualize counseling theories and practice from a strengths perspective. There is little doubt that the trends toward brief-solution-focused counseling models will play a major role in the future of counseling.

Mental Disorders.   Yager (1989) and Pincus et al. (1989) made projections about the impact of advances in science on the diagnosis and treatment of mental disorders. These projections continue to accurately predict future trends in the treatment of mental disorders. A summary of their predictions follows.

- Genetics will play an increasingly important role in the diagnosis and treatment of mental disorders. For example, scientists could use genetic engineering to alter the gene structure to prevent or treat mental disorders, and clinicians will be able to identify children who are at risk to develop mental disorders.
- Neurobiologists will gain a more complete understanding of the role of neurotransmitters, or agents that facilitate communication between neurons, in the development and treatment of mental disorders.
- Psychopharmacology researchers will develop more effective medications with fewer unwanted side effects to treat mental disorders. Scientists will also develop new medications that will successfully treat mental disorders previously unresponsive to medication. Examples are substance abuse disorders, including alcoholism, personality disorders, and sexual disorders.

- Sociobiologists will identify factors that trigger the onset of mental disorders.
- Advances in computer technology and software development will enable clinicians to make better use of computers in the diagnosis and treatment of mental disorders.

Postmodernism.   Postmodernism could have major implications for theory development and paradigm shifts in counseling. Postmodernism recognizes that truth, knowledge, and reality are reflected contextually in terms of social, political, cultural, and other forces that can have an impact on personal experience. Postmodernism therefore appears to offer opportunities for integrating diversity issues such as the role of culture and economic forces in mental health and counseling. Postmodernism is also associated with an evolving view of the self (Gergen, 1994b; M. B. Smith, 1994). Postmodernism suggests there is a movement away from the autonomous integral self to a social-community self that extends beyond the individual to all aspects of society.

Postmodern trends are associated with the emergence of two psychological theories (constructivism and social constructionism) that could have major implications for reconceptualizing the counseling process. Constructivism (Mahoney, 1988) emphasizes the role of cognition in interpreting external events, whereas social constructionism (Gergen, 1994b) stresses the impact of social forces in constructing reality. Both theories recognize the role that narratives play in creating stories that individuals utilize in defining personal meaning in life. Postmodern trends appear to offer multiple opportunities for theory building, especially in terms of infusing diversity issues in counseling. The implications of these new trends must be carefully investigated through research to determine their usefulness in counseling.

Spirituality.   Spirituality is an emerging trend in counseling that represents an important dimension to diversity, multiculturalism, and the counseling process (Richards & Bergin, 1997, 2004). Spirituality can be broadly conceptualized as the "invisible phenomena associated with thoughts and feelings of enlightenment, vision, harmony with truth, transcendence, peak experiences, and oneness with God, nature, or the universe" (Richards & Bergin, 1997, p. 77). From this perspective, all people are believed to recognize the spiritual (but not necessarily religious) realm of existence (Ingersoll, 1995). A number of factors are contributing to the increased interest in the spiritual domain of counseling. Spirituality can be conceptualized as a universal quality of humans as reflected in their search for meaning in their existence (Haase, Britt, Coward, Kline, & Penn, 1992; Ingersoll, 1995). In this regard, one does not have to be religious to be spiritual. Religion can play an important role in spirituality, with 90 percent of the residents of the United States believing in God (Kroll & Sheehan, 1989). Spirituality and religion are interrelated terms, with the religion realm providing a framework in which spirituality can be expressed. This conceptualization suggests that "spirituality becomes an organismic, developmental dimension and religion, a 'culturally flavored' framework that helps develop the organismic spiritual potential" (Ingersoll, 1995, p. 12). From this perspective, spirituality and religion also represent a multicultural-diversity consideration (Pate & Miller-Bondi, 1995).

Aside from the widespread appeal of spirituality, it is recognized as a neglected yet valued dimension to the counseling process (Miranti & Burke, 1995). It is conceptualized as an important force in all phases of the counseling process from establishing a relationship through assessment, goals setting, and treatment (Richards & Bergin, 1997). The spiritual perspective in counseling is also consistent with the movement toward brief-solution-focused counseling in terms of utilizing a strengths perspective. For example, it is common for people to turn to prayer and other forms of spirituality during times of great need to gain strength and support to promote recovery and healing (Miranti & Burke, 1995).

The counseling literature is beginning to provide more empirical support for considering the spiritual domain in counseling. Many clients are indicating that they cannot be effectively helped in counseling unless their spiritual issues are addressed sensitively and capably (Richards & Bergin, 1997, 2004; Shafranske, 1996). In addition, there is increasing evidence to suggest that spiritual health plays an important role in physical and psychological health and well-being (Bergin, 1991; Richards & Bergin, 1997, 2004). Studies such as these appear to be giving spirituality the scientific credibility that will help propel it into the mainstream of counseling in the twenty-first century and beyond.

Cybercounseling. Cybercounseling (counseling on the Internet) is becoming an increasingly popular means of providing counseling services (Wiggins-Frame, 1998). Cybercounseling can take many forms but often involves counselors creating Web sites such as Psych Central on the Web (Hannon, 1996). Counseling on these sites is done with e-mail and typically involves clients submitting questions of up to 200 words to the counselor and the counselor responding to the client in one to three days (Wiggins-Frame, 1998).

Haley (2005) identified a number of emerging forms of cybercounseling, including

- **E-mail counseling.** The counselor and client use e-mail as a forum for counseling.
- **Bulletin board counseling.** Clients post questions on a bulletin board, typically using pseudonyms such as "Goofy" to ensure confidentiality. A mental health professional then posts a response that is visible to all users.
- **Chat room counseling.** Clients and counselors engage in real-time (synchronous) communication over the Internet in a chat room.
- **Web-telephony counseling.** The client and counselor use a microphone and speakers to talk over the Internet (e.g., while in a chat room).
- **Computer-assisted or stimulated counseling.** Computer-generated counseling answers clients' concerns.
- **E-coaching.** Counselors provide guided activities for clients regarding specific problems such as how to cope with anxiety or depression. Clients are often given information and tasks associated with these topics and then receive feedback from the counselor.

Counselors appear to express guarded interest in participating in cybercounseling. Kirk (1997) conducted a survey that showed that 30 percent would never engage in cybercounseling; 25 percent would consider using it; and 45 percent would use it as an adjunct to face-to-face counseling.

Wiggins-Frame (1998) identified potential benefits and hazards of cybercounseling. Benefits include providing counseling services to individuals who otherwise might not be able to receive services (such as those who live in rural areas). Cybercounseling may also be more attractive to individuals with disabilities such as the hearing impaired. Hazards include a number of potential ethical problems such as difficulty ensuring confidentiality and client welfare and providing adequate informed consent.

Heinlen, Welfel, Richmond, and Rak (2003) provided additional information regarding cybercounseling. They surveyed 136 Web sites offering counseling services via chat rooms and e-mail. Results of their study showed a wide range of services, fee schedules, and credentials of providers. Results of the survey showed credentialed providers maintained significantly higher levels of compliance with ethical standards than noncredentialed providers. Cybercounseling was also found to be an unstable source of counseling with over a third of the Web sites no longer in existence eight months after the study was initiated. Heinlen et al. expressed concern over what appeared to be widespread ethical violations (especially among noncredentialed providers) that should be investigated. Concerns also related to the quality and scope of services provided and the instability regarding the Web sites.

Technology.   Haley (2005) provided an overview of technology and counseling. She suggested that by the year 2008, 90 percent of counselors will be using technology in 92 percent of their work. Haley noted that in addition to cybercounseling, technology is being used in a wide variety of counseling tasks. Tasks identified by Haley include the following.

■ **Computers as counselors.** The earliest example of computers as counselors occurred 30 years ago when Joseph Weizenbaum developed a computer program called Eliza. Eliza was a nondirective Rogerian type of counselor that responded to clients' concerns.

■ **Voice-activated computer systems.** This exciting new form of counseling involves state-of-the-art technology such as virtual reality to systematically desensitize clients from their phobias.

■ **Online testing.** Online testing (including test interpretation and scoring) is widely used for virtually all types of standardized testing (e.g., interest inventories, personality assessment, and career assessment).

■ **Databases.** Databases have been developed to assess clients on a variety of topics such as degree of risk for homicidal or suicidal behavior. Databases typically require responses to approximately a thousand questions relating to variables associated with specific areas of assessment. For example, databases relating to predicting violence could include questions on past history of violence, family background, and personality tendencies.

■ **Client intervention aides.** Counselors can turn to the Internet to obtain materials for therapy. For example, http://www.kn.pacbell.com was developed to help child trauma victims create a virtual world in which they could safely address difficult life situations.

■ **Information services and forums.** Numerous sites on the Internet provide information on all aspects of counseling from the latest treatment regimens for specific mental disorders (such as empirically supported treatments for childhood depression). Forums can allow for joint communication regarding developments such as the role of informed consent in legal-ethical decision making.

■ **Virtual self-help groups.** Internet self-help groups using e-mail, chat rooms, and other forms of electronic communication are becoming increasingly popular. Self-help groups find the Internet a convenient way to address a wide range of problems (e.g., attention deficit hyperactivity disorder). These Web sites often include guidance and other forms of support for the participants.

■ **Client-therapist referrals.** Many Web sites provide information on what counseling is (e.g., http://helping.apa.org) and how to receive assistance for obtaining counseling services (e.g., http://www.psyfidential.com).

■ **Counselor supervision.** Supervision is quickly integrating sophisticated forms of technology into the process of supervision. Some examples of this include online supervision with student counselors (e.g., providing group chat room supervision sessions). Another form of technology used in supervision is electromyography, which helps supervisors monitor student counselors' emotional state via changes in skin temperature and skin conductance levels, and process this information during videotaped replay or live supervision.

Problematic-Impaired Students. There appears to be an increased interest in "gate-keeping" issues relating to students who demonstrate professional deficiencies such as emotional problems, inappropriate interpersonal relation skills, and unethical behavior (Johnson & Campbell, 2004). Although other professions, such as law, have an established history of considering issues such as character and fitness, the same rigor has not been applied in the helping professions (Johnson & Campbell, 2004). Vacha-Haase, Davenport, and Kerewsky (2004) provide an overview of terms such as *problematic* and *impaired,* which are used to describe the personal issues of students in training programs. *Impairment* relates to mental illness, emotional distress, and other personal conflict that can undermine professional function. *Problematic* relates to behaviors that are unacceptable, such as inappropriate interpersonal behavior during academic training or clinical practice.

Vacha-Haase et al. (2004) recommend that training programs provide guidelines for what could be considered acceptable and problematic (unacceptable) behavior and what should be done when students engage in unacceptable behavior. Issues regarding what is developmentally normal (such as counselors in training experiencing anxiety when they first see clients) should be differentiated from abnormal emotional responses. Problematic student behavior must also be differentiated from impairment relating to disabilities defined by the American Disability Act of 1990. Elman and Forrest (2004) went on to provide guidelines for psychotherapy in the remediation of students in training programs. They noted a number of challenges in this process, including the balance between protecting the student's confidentiality in therapy to being informed on progress relating to student issues that needed to be addressed.

Summary

Counseling is a complex process that does not afford a simple definition. For example, counseling is both an art and science, emphasizing the importance of the subjective and objective dimensions. Counseling also has its basis in narrative psychology, or counseling as a form of storytelling.

Counseling is differentiated from psychotherapy in terms of clients, goals, treatment, and settings. It is also part of the helping profession, which includes psychiatrists, psychologists, mental health counselors, and school counselors.

Trends in counseling include managed mental health services, empirically supported treatment, brief-solution-focused counseling, postmodernism, spirituality, cybercounseling, increased use of technology, and how to address problematic-impaired students.

Personal Exploration

1. What interests you about counseling?
2. Do you think you would ever want to be a counselor and if so why?
3. Who are the people you are intrigued by in terms of the evolution of counseling and what fascinates you about these people?
4. What are some personal qualities that you have that you believe would help make you an effective counselor and why are these qualities important?

Web Sites for Chapter 1

American Counseling Association. (2002). *Consumers.* Retrieved March 3, 2005, from
   http://www.counseling.org/am/consumers.html
   Defines counseling and provides other resources for consumers.
The George Washington University. (2004). *Counseling.* Retrieved March 3, 2005, from
   http://www.gwu.edu/gelman/guides/social/counseling.html
   Provides resources, links, and definitions of counseling.
Henson, J. (unknown). *Counseling versus psychotherapy: An explanation.* Retrieved March 3,
   2005, from http://www.clinicalsolutions.org/Counseling_vs_Psychotherapy.html
   Briefly describes the differences between counseling and psychotherapy.
Hevern, V. W. (2004). *Narrative psychology: Internet and resource guide.* Retrieved March
   3, 2005, from http://web.lemoyne.edu/~hevern/narpsych.html
   Provides background information on narrative psychology.
Metanoia. (unknown). *ABC's of Internet Therapy.* Retrieved March 3, 2005, from
   http://www.metanoia.org/imhs/issues.htm
   Provides a brief overview of Internet therapy.

Professional Preparation and Ethical and Legal Issues

CHAPTER OVERVIEW

This chapter provides an overview of professional issues in counseling. It covers important aspects of becoming a professional counselor and major ethical and legal issues. Highlights of the chapter include

- Becoming a professional counselor, including formal study and professional affiliation, certification, and licensure; continuing education; and professional involvement
- Ethical issues, including client welfare, informed consent, confidentiality, and dual relationships
- Legal issues, including privileged communication and malpractice
- Special ethical and legal issues relating to marriage and family counseling, child counseling, group counseling, and AIDS
- Ethical-legal decision making, including clinical examples
- Diversity issues

Some of the major issues associated with becoming a professional counselor include certification and licensure, professional organizations, and ethical and legal issues. Guidelines for ethical decision making and clinical examples can illustrate some applications of ethical and legal principles.

Becoming a Professional Counselor

Deciding to undertake formal study in counseling constitutes the first step toward becoming a professional counselor. Being a professional counselor is an ongoing process that involves work, study, and commitment. This section describes four building blocks that characterize this process, as shown in Figure 2.1.

Formal Study and Professional Affiliation

Formal study in counseling usually involves working toward a master's or doctoral degree in the counseling field. There has been increasing pressure for graduate programs offering these degrees to obtain accreditation from one or more organizations: the Council for the Accreditation of Counseling and Related Problems (CACREP); the American Counseling

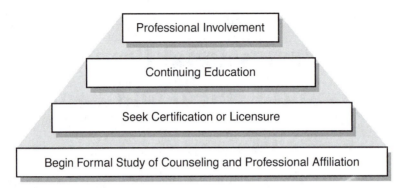

FIGURE 2.1   The Building Blocks of Professional Counseling

Association (ACA); of the American Psychological Association (APA); and, in some instances, the American Association of Marriage and Family Therapy (AAMFT). Accreditation helps ensure that the programs will maintain an acceptable level of standards. In addition, some certification processes in counseling or psychology require a degree from an accredited program. A current list of graduate programs approved by the ACA, APA, and AAMFT can be obtained by writing directly to each organization at the following addresses.

The ACA: 5999 Stevenson Ave., Alexandria, VA 22304
The APA: 750 1st St., N.E., Washington, DC 20002-4242
The AAMFT: 112 S. Alfred St., Alexandria, VA 22314-3061

Master's degree programs provide the necessary foundations for a career as a professional counselor. Students can also benefit from joining a professional organization such as the ACA or APA as a student member. Student members can attend conventions and involve themselves in professional issues facing counselors and psychologists. They also receive journals and newsletters that address important counseling issues and receive a copy of the code of ethics that guides clinical practice.

The ACA and APA each have numerous divisions that may be of interest to counselors and psychologists. Selected divisions are listed in Table 2.1.

Certification and Licensure

Certification and licensure are important to all professions, including counseling. They provide professional recognition as well as enable members of the helping profession to utilize third-party insurance to help clients pay for counseling services. Licensed counselors can access some form of third-party insurance in all states requiring counseling licensure.

Certification and licensure are similar processes in which the applicant must meet certain requirements in education, training, experience, and clinical competence. Forester (1977) identified several differences between certification and licensure. Certification recognizes the competence of practitioners by authorizing them to use the title adopted by the profession. Unlike certification, licensure is authorized by state legislation and regulates

TABLE 2.1 Selected Divisions and Affiliates of the ACA and APA

ACA	APA	
American College Counseling Association (ACCA)	Adult Development and Aging	Psychological Hypnosis
American Mental Health Counselors Association (AMHCA)	American Psychology-Law Society	Psychologists in Independent Practice
American Rehabilitation Counseling Association (ARCA)	American Society for the Advancement of Pharmaco-therapy	Psychologists in Public Service
American School Counselor Association (ASCA)	Applied Experimental and Engineering Psychology	Psychology and the Arts
Association for Adult Development and Aging (AADA)	Behavioral Neuroscience and Comparative Psychology	Psychology of Religion
Association for Assessment in Counseling (AAC)	Child, Youth and Family Services	Psychology of Women
Association for Counselor Education and Supervision (ACES)	Clinical Child Psychology	Psychopharmacology and Substance Abuse
Association for Counselors and Educators in Government (ACEG)[1]	Clinical Neuropsychology	Psychotherapy
Association for Gay, Lesbian, and Bisexual Issues in Counseling (AGLBIC)	Clinical Psychology	Rehabilitation Psychology
Association for Humanistic Education and Development (AHEAD)	Consulting Psychology	School Psychology
Association for Multicultural Counseling and Development (AMCD)	Counseling Psychology	Society for Community Research and Action: Division of Community Psychology
Association for Specialists in Group Work (ASGW)	Developmental Psychology	Society for Consumer Psychology
Association for Spiritual, Ethical, and Religious Values in Counseling (ASERVIC)	Division of Addictions	Society for Industrial and Organizational Psychology
Counseling Association for Humanistic Education and Development (CAHEAD)	Division of Behavior Analysis	Society for Pediatric Psychology
Counseling for Social Justice (CSJ)	Educational Psychology	Society for the Psychological Study of Ethnic Minority Issues
International Association of Addictions and Offender Counselors (IAAOC)	Evaluation, Measurement, and Statistics	Society for the Psychological Study of Lesbian, Gay and Bisexual Issues
International Association of Marriage and Family Counselors (IAMFC)	Exercise and Sport Psychology	Society for the Psychological Study of Men and Masculinity
National Career Development Association (NCDA)	Experimental Psychology	Society for the Psychological Study of Social Issues
National Employment Counseling Association (NECA)	Family Psychology	Society for the Study of Peace, Conflict, and Violence: Peace Psychology Division
	General Psychology	Society for the Teaching of Psychology
	Group Psychology and Group Psychotherapy	Society of Personality and Social Psychology
	Health Psychology	State Psychological Association Affairs
	History of Psychology	Theoretical and Philosophical Psychology
	Humanistic Psychology	
	International Psychology	
	Media Psychology	
	Mental Retardation and Developmental Disabilities	
	Military Psychology	
	Population and Environmental Psychology	
	Psychoanalysis	

[1]Denotes organizational affiliate status

the practice and title of the profession. Since licensure is a legal process, legal sanctions can be imposed on an individual who is licensed. Licensure also has more specific and comprehensive regulations, necessitating greater training and preparation than in the certification process (George & Cristiani, 1995).

Historically, most states have offered school counselors opportunities to be certified or licensed. Along with other school personnel, school counselors are traditionally certified by a state board of education. Most states also require counselors to be certified as teachers. Since 1977, all states have required that psychologists be either certified or licensed by a state board of psychologist examiners (Cummings, 1990).

More recently, there has been a trend to provide certification or licensure for counselors who wish to practice outside the school setting, for example, in mental health clinics, hospitals, or private practice. The counseling profession has made progress in passing legislation at the state level requiring certification or licensure. As of 2004, 49 states and the District of Columbia, Guam, and Puerto Rico have passed certification or licensure laws for counselors, as listed in Table 2.2. Certification or licensure in counseling requires 30 to 60

TABLE 2.2   States That Have Passed Certification or Licensure Laws for Counselors

State	Law Passed (Year)	State	Law Passed (Year)
Alabama	1979	Missouri	1985
Alaska	1999	Montana	1985
Arizona	1988	Nebraska	1988
Arkansas	1979	New Hampshire	1992
California	1989	New Jersey	1993
Colorado	1988	New Mexico	1993
Connecticut	1997	New York	2003
Delaware	1987	North Carolina	1983
District of Columbia	1994	North Dakota	1989
Florida	1981	Ohio	1989
Georgia	1987	Oklahoma	1985
Hawaii	2004	Oregon	1989
Idaho	1982	Pennsylvania	1998
Illinois	1993	Rhode Island	1987
Indiana	1997	South Carolina	1985
Iowa	1991	South Dakota	1990
Kansas	1987	Tennessee	1987
Kentucky	1996	Texas	1981
Louisiana	1987	Utah	1994
Maine	1989	Vermont	1988
Maryland	1985	Virginia	1976
Massachusetts	1987	Washington	1987
Michigan	1988	West Virginia	1986
Minnesota	2003	Wisconsin	1992
Mississippi	1985	Wyoming	1987

graduate hours, depending on the state; a master's degree in counseling or a closely related field; 2 to 4 hours per week of supervised counseling experience, depending on the state; and passing an examination. There is some concern that current examination processes do not assess an applicant's clinical skills and are therefore in need of modification (Brooks & Gerstein, 1990).

The ACA has taken an active role in certification and licensure for counselors at the state and national levels (Brooks & Gerstein, 1990). For example, the ACA helped create the National Board for Certified Counselors (NBCC) in an attempt to identify national standards for professional counselors. Individuals wishing to obtain recognition as an NBCC counselor must have a master's or doctoral degree in counseling or a closely related field, have at least two years of supervised professional counseling experience, and successfully complete a certification exam. There is some indication that the ACA may be going too far to promote licensure. Heppner, Casas, Carter, and Stone (2000) note that the ACA appears to have shifted its emphasis from being a learned society to a trades association focusing on professional credentialing and accreditation at the masters and doctoral levels.

Counselors may also pursue certification in a specialty field. Some examples are National Certified Career Counselors, Certified Clinical Mental Health Counselors, and Certified Rehabilitation Counselors (Brooks & Gerstein, 1990).

Some animosity has developed among the members of various helping professions over the proper qualifications. In this debate, members of specialties such as psychiatry, psychology, and counseling emphasize the merits of their respective fields. For example, psychiatrists promote the need for medical training. Unfortunately, the real issue appears to be gaining dominance and control. Some examples of this lack of cooperation are psychiatry's failure to support psychology, psychology's contempt for mental health counselors, and the counseling profession's (represented by the ACA) refusing to recognize the standards of the AAMFT as necessary to practice as marriage and family counselors (Cummings, 1990; Everett, 1990a). Clearly, there is a need for more cooperation among the helping professions and less concern with special interests (Brooks & Gerstein, 1990; Cummings, 1990).

Continuing Education

Some form of continuing education is essential for the ongoing development of professional counselors. Most certification and licensure regulations also require counselors to take continuing education courses to maintain their professional credentials. This usually involves attending workshops or presentations at conferences or taking courses that have been approved for continuing education credits.

Other professional development activities can help counselors remain current and refine their clinical skills. Some of these are reading professional journals and books, attending inservice training programs, cocounseling with an experienced clinician, seeking ongoing supervision, and attending institutes for advanced training in a counseling specialty.

Professional Involvement

As mentioned, being a professional counselor requires ongoing work and effort. As individuals embark on a career in counseling, they initially draw help and guidance from the profession.

As they advance in the profession, they find themselves in a position to make a contribution. Some ways that counselors can contribute include taking an active role in professional organizations, supporting efforts for certification and licensure, and writing in professional journals.

Professional involvement helps support and maintain the profession, but it also enriches the counselor. As counselors become professionally involved, they develop a network of friends who can often become an important support system. The experience can also diversify their interests and professional activities, which can be stimulating and professionally rewarding.

The following *Personal Note* speaks to the importance of professional involvement in counseling.

A Personal Note

I've noticed that colleagues of mine who are active in professional organizations tend to be happier, more productive, and less prone to burnout than those who don't take an active role in professional organizations. It seems as if those who aren't as active tend to get frustrated more easily, have a more negative view about their jobs, and get tired and give up more easily than those who are professionally active. Perhaps one reason for these differences between the professionally active and inactive counselor is that professional organizations provide counselors with a broader sense of the counseling community and help keep things in perspective.

I've made a lot of friends through my involvement in professional organizations and activities. These friends have created an important network and have been helpful in many ways. I've felt a sense of support and encouragement from these people. I've also experienced a number of career opportunities, such as reviewing one of my colleagues' books for a book company, which resulted in my obtaining my own book contract. Professional involvement has also been a way for me to contribute to the profession. It has been personally rewarding to give of my time and energy and to participate on committees, editorial boards, and other aspects of the various professional organizations with which I've been affiliated.

Ethical-Legal Issues

The Art and Science of Ethical-Legal Issues

Ethical-legal issues reflect on both the art and science of counseling. To a large degree ethical codes and legal statutes are not written in black-and-white terms but serve as principles to guide one's clinical practice. The art of counseling suggests that practitioners engage in creative approaches to ethical-legal decision making that are sensitive to multicultural issues. The science of counseling also recognizes that ethical codes and legal statutes also have some clear statements as to what constitutes ethical-legal behavior for a practitioner. For example, there are legal reporting duties when child abuse or neglect is suspected.

Meara, Schmidt, and Day (1996) conceptualize ethics in a manner that complements the art and science of counseling. They suggest that there are two dimensions to ethical decision making: principle ethics and virtue ethics. Principle ethics (like the science of counseling) are the overt ethical obligations that must be addressed in clinical situations such as the duty to warn and protect when a client becomes homicidal. Virtue ethics (like the art of counseling) suggest that practitioners go beyond the *obligatory* and strive toward the *ideals* to which professionals aspire. Central to this task is the development of virtuous character traits such as sensitivity to the cultural milieu, which can have an impact on ethical decision making. These authors go on to suggest that principle ethics and virtue ethics be integrated to create a balance in ethical decision making that is not only ethically and legally correct but also in the best interest of society as a whole.

Ethical-legal issues are becoming increasingly prevalent in the day-to-day practice of the professional counselor. This is as true for school counselors as it is for mental health counselors and other practitioners in the helping profession. The emergence of these issues represents a response to the increased risk of malpractice suits against counselors (Corey, 2001) and to the ACA's 1995 statement that counselors should "respect the integrity and promote the welfare of clients" (Section B.1). It is therefore imperative that counselors have the necessary knowledge and skills to integrate legal and ethical issues into every aspect of the counseling profession. The following *Personal Note* illustrates the importance of considering ethical-legal issues in one's practice.

A Personal Note

For the past twelve years, I've been working one day a week as a school psychologist for a local school district. In this job I've provided psychological services (which include assessment, consultation, and counseling) to six different elementary schools. It seems like each new year brings more and more legal and ethical issues that affect how I must do my job.

An error in the ethical or legal domain can have disastrous effects for the students, staff, and parents who I serve, as well as the school district and myself. For example, if I tell a parent that his or her child needs to be hospitalized for treatment of a mental disorder, the school district may have to pay for it. Since the bill for a mental health hospitalization can be $20,000 or more per month, such a decision on my part will not win any friends in the superintendent's office or on the school board. To avoid this dilemma, I work closely with the community mental health center, and when necessary arrange for them to refer students for hospitalization.

Ethical Issues

Ethical codes and standards of practice have been formulated by the ACA and the APA. The ACA (1995) code of ethics relates to issues such as general topics of concern, the counseling relationship, measurement and evaluation, research and publication, consulting, private practice, personnel administration, and preparation standards.

The various ethical standards are guidelines for what a counselor can or cannot do. Each clinical situation is unique and may require an interpretation of the particular code of ethics. In this regard, the standards can be viewed as guiding principles that counselors can use to formulate their clinical judgment. In addition, Mabe and Rollin (1986) note that the codes of ethics provide a framework for professional behavior and responsibility and serve as a means for establishing professional identity.

Baruth and Huber (1985) identify three major ethical issues that influence clinical practice: client welfare, informed consent, and confidentiality. An additional major ethical issue relates to dual relationships. An overview of these four ethical issues follows.

Client Welfare.   The counselor's primary responsibility is the welfare of the client. In this regard, the ACA and APA codes of ethics suggest that the client's needs come before the counselor's needs, counselors should practice within their area of competence, and counselors should terminate or refer a client who is no longer benefiting from the service.

Table 2.3 provides excerpts from the ACA and the APA regarding client welfare and conditions relating to client referral.

Informed Consent.   The ethical guidelines relating to informed consent require counselors to provide each client with an overview of what counseling will entail so that the client can decide whether to participate. Table 2.4 lists excerpts on this topic from the ACA and the APA. Mardirosian, McGuire, Abbott, and Blau (1990) note that counselors can assist a client in making an informed consent by providing information on policies, goals, and procedures. In controversial issues such as pregnancy counseling, the authors suggest that counselors should inform the client of their moral-value position.

One way to give a client information to assist with informed consent is by providing a professional disclosure statement. McFadden and Brooks (1983) have provided an example

TABLE 2.3   Ethical Considerations Relating to Client Welfare and Referral

Client Welfare	Client Referral
ACA (1995) *Primary Responsibility* The primary responsibility of counselors is to respect the dignity and to promote the welfare of clients. **APA (2003)** Psychologists strive to benefit those with whom they work and take care to do no harm. In their professional actions, psychologists seek to safeguard the welfare and rights of those with whom they interact professionally. . .	**ACA (1995)** If counselors determine an inability to be of professional assistance to clients, they avoid entering or immediately terminate a counseling relationship. Counselors are knowledgeable about referral resources and suggest appropriate alternatives. If clients decline the suggested referral, counselors should discontinue the relationship. **APA (2003)** Psychologists provide services, teach, and conduct research with populations and in areas only within the boundaries of their competence, based on their education, training, supervised experience, consultation, study, or professional experience. Psycholologists have or obtain the training, experience, consultation, or supervision necessary to ensure the competence of their services, or they make the appropriate referrals.

TABLE 2.4 Ethical Considerations Relating to Informed Consent

Informed Consent

ACA (1995)

When counseling is initiated, and throughout the counseling process as necessary, counselors inform clients of the purposes, goals, techniques, procedures, limitations, potential risks . . . and benefits of services to be performed, and other pertinent information.

APA (2003)

When psychologists conduct research or provide assessment, therapy, counseling, or consulting . . . they obtain the informed consent of the individual or individuals using language that is reasonably understandable to that person or persons.

Source: ACA excerpts reprinted from *Code of Ethics and Standards of Practice* (1995). © ACA. Reprinted by permission. No further reproduction authorized without written permission of the American Counseling Association. APA excerpts from *Ethical Principles of Psychologists and Code of Conduct.* Copyright © 2003 by the American Psychological Association. Reprinted by permission.

of such a statement, which has been incorporated into the professional disclosure statement shown in Table 2.5. The professional disclosure statement in Table 2.5 can be adjusted to reflect the counselor's professional identity and special theoretical orientation. For example, school counselors might mention that their approach includes consultation with parents and teachers and counseling with students individually and in small and large groups. In terms of theoretical orientation, school counselors might explain the importance of a developmental perspective in addressing the developmental tasks of children at different grade levels.

Confidentiality. Confidentiality is a critical condition in counseling and psychotherapy (Paradise & Kirby, 1990). The client must feel safe in disclosing information to the counselor for the counseling process to be effective (Reynolds, 1976). Denkowski and Denkowski (1982) identify two purposes of confidentiality in counseling: (a) protecting the client from the social stigma often associated with being in therapy, and (b) promoting the client's vital rights that are integral to the client's welfare. The ACA and the APA provide guidelines relating to confidentiality, as shown in Table 2.6. The major exception to the principle of confidentiality is when clients pose a clear and imminent danger to themselves or others, such as a client who threatens to commit suicide or kill someone (Gross & Robinson, 1987). It is important to ensure that clients are aware of the limits regarding confidentiality before they begin counseling. This can be accomplished in several ways, including the use of a professional disclosure statement.

Dual Relationships. Dual (or multiple) relationships involve counselors engaging in more than one relationship with a client (Corey, Corey, & Callanan, 2003), for example, a professor also being a student's counselor. Dual relationships can be problematic and violate ethical and legal standards when professional roles conflict (for example, a counselor dating a client). Table 2.7 provides excerpts from the ACA and APA regarding dual relationships.

TABLE 2.5   Professional Disclosure Statement

Professional Disclosure Statement

(LETTERHEAD)

Milton H. Counselor, Ph.D.
333 Maple Street
Littletown, Alabama 36501
(205) 555-5347
Hours by Appointment

STATEMENT OF PROFESSIONAL DISCLOSURE

Ph.D., Counseling—Bigname State University, 1981
B.A., Group Communication/Psychology—Bigname State University, 1973
B.S., Psychology—Bigname State University, 1972

Certified Clinical Mental Health Counselor, 1980
Certificate #609
Licensed Professional Counselor, 1980, License #576

Philosophical Base

I utilize a cognitive approach that emphasizes cognitive restructuring to alter affective states. This means that the way we feel and the way we behave are directly related to how and what we are thinking. The past and the future are not as important as living one's life to the fullest in the present. I view counseling as a process by which I facilitate my clients in exploration, clarification, and identification of their needs and help them make changes in their behavior that will result in the attainment of life satisfaction and self-acceptance.

Therapeutic Approach

I use an integrative approach. My core theory is Adlerian. I also utilize techniques and counseling procedures from other schools of counseling to meet the needs of my clients. In addition, I try to be especially sensitive to multicultural issues that may arise in counseling.

In individual counseling, I attempt to help clients focus their awareness on strengths rather than liabilities. Clients are encouraged to accept responsibility for initiating and maintaining change in their lives as those changes are identified through the counseling process. In marriage counseling, I focus on developing a healthy independence and interdependence.

This is accomplished by using the techniques that help to develop self-awareness as well as improving the communication skills of both partners. I view group counseling as an adjunct to individual counseling rather than as a substitute for it. In my work in family counseling and the management of behavioral problems of children, I use an approach that involves encouragement, rational thinking, logical consequences, understanding misdirected goals, and improved parent-child communication. In all cases, I stress the effect of cognition on behavior and emotions and the need to develop control over this function.

continued

TABLE 2.5 Continued

Areas of Competency

Individual counseling	Drug abuse counseling
Marriage counseling	Career counseling
Family counseling	Values clarification and life planning
Child counseling	Organization development
Group counseling	Biofeedback and relaxation training

Ethical Standards

I subscribe to the codes of ethics of the following organizations. Copies are available and will be discussed with the client upon request.

American Counseling Association
American Mental Health Counselors Association
National Academy of Certified Clinical Mental Health Counselors
Alabama Board of Examiners in Counseling

Limits to Confidentiality

All information discussed in counseling will be treated as confidential except in instances when the client becomes a serious threat to self (for example, suicidal) or others (for example, homicidal) or when mandated by law (for example, reporting of child abuse and neglect).

Professional Memberships

American Counseling Association
American Mental Health Counselors Association
Association for Specialists in Group Work
Alabama Association for Counseling and Development
Alabama Mental Health Counselors Association

Fees

Individual, marriage, or family counseling	$75 per session
Group counseling	$40 per session
Career counseling	Fees vary according to tests and services required.

(Ordinarily the above fee schedule will apply. Please feel free to discuss fees and special circumstances regarding fee payments at our first session.)

Please discuss any concerns about the counseling services you receive with me. If these concerns cannot be resolved between us, contact the Alabama Board of Examiners in Counseling, c/o Donald Schmitz, Chairman, Jacksonville State University, Jacksonville, AL 36265, or National Academy of Certified Clinical Mental Health Counselors, Two Skyline Place, Suite 400, 5203 Leesburg Pike, Falls Church, VA 22041.

Source: Reprinted from *Counseling Licensure Action Packet* by J. McFadden and D. K. Brooks, 1983, Alexandria, VA: AACD. © AACD. Reprinted by permission. No further reproduction authorized without written permission of the American Association of Counseling and Development.

TABLE 2.6   Ethical Considerations Relating to Confidentiality

Confidentiality

ACA (1995)
Counselors respect their clients' right to privacy and avoid illegal and unwarranted disclosures of confidential information.

APA (2003)
Psychologists have a primary obligation and take reasonable precautions to protect confidential information. Psychologists discuss with persons . . . the relevant limits of confidentiality.

Source: ACA excerpts reprinted from *Code of Ethics and Standards of Practice* (1995). © ACA. Reprinted by permission. No further reproduction authorized without written permission of the American Counseling Association. APA excerpts from *Ethical Principles of Psychologists and Code of Conduct.* Copyright © 2003 by the American Psychological Association. Reprinted by permission.

TABLE 2.7   Ethical Considerations Relating to Dual Relationships

ACA (1995)
Counselors are aware of their influential positions with respect to clients, and they avoid exploiting the trust and dependency of clients. Counselors make every effort to avoid dual relationships with clients that could impair professional judgment or increase the risk of harm to clients. (Examples of such relationships include, but are not limited to, familial, social, financial, business, or close personal relationships with clients.) When a dual relationship cannot be avoided, counselors take appropriate professional precautions such as informed consent, consultation, supervision, and documentation to ensure that judgment is not impaired and no exploitation occurs.

APA (2003)
A multiple relationship occurs when a psychologist is in a professional role with a person and (1) at the same time is in another role with the same person, (2) at the same time is in a relationship with a person closely associated with or related to the person with whom the psychologist has the professional relationship, or (3) promises to enter into another relationship in the future with the person or a person closely associated with or related to the person. A psychologist refrains from entering into a multiple relationship if the multiple relationship could reasonably be expected to impair the psychologist's objectivity, competence, or effectiveness in performing his or her functions as a psychologist, or otherwise risks exploitation or harm to the person with whom the professional relationship exists. Multiple relationships that would not reasonably be expected to cause impairment or risk exploitation or harm are not unethical. If a psychologist finds that, due to unforeseen factors, a potentially harmful multiple relationship has arisen, the psychologist takes reasonable steps to resolve it with due regard for the best interests of the affected person and maximal compliance with the Ethics Code.

Source: ACA excerpts reprinted from *Code of Ethics and Standards of Practice* (1995). © ACA. Reprinted by permission. No further reproduction authorized without written permission of the American Counseling Association. APA excerpts from *Ethical Principles of Psychologists and Code of Conduct.* Copyright © 2003 by the American Psychological Association. Reprinted by permission.

Lamb, Catanzaro, and Moorman (2004) provide information on how psychologists identify, assess, and respond to potential dual relationships with clients, supervisees, and students. Their research finds that relationships with supervisees in social situations is the most commonly discussed area of concern regarding nonsexual dual relationships. These researchers also note that the main reason cited by psychologists for not engaging in sexual dual relationships is concerns regarding ethics, values, and morals.

Sexual Relationships.   Sexual relationships between counselors and clients have become an important area of ethical-legal activity. Kitchener and Anderson (2000) provide an overview of the issues associated with sexual relations in counseling. Their recent surveys suggest that 1 percent to 9 percent of male therapists and .04 percent to 2.5 percent of female therapists have sex with their clients. Professional organizations have voiced strong prohibitions against sexual relationships between counselors and clients or even implying that they are a possibility. Sexual feelings towards clients occur for approximately 87 percent of psychologists. It is not considered unethical for a counselor to have sexual feelings, but acting on them can result in ethical and legal problems.

Ethically, sexual relations with clients can have adverse effects on the clients' welfare in that counselors may compromise their ability to maintain the clients' best interests because counselors are concurrently attempting to meet their own needs. Clients' trust in the counseling process can also be undermined if the post-counseling relationship does not work out. Dual relations is another ethical issue related to sexual relationships. The unequal power differential associated with the counseling relationship can result in clients being sexually exploited by counselors. Ethical codes (such as the 2003 APA Ethics Code) prohibit psychologists from entering into a sexual relationship with clients for at least two years following termination. In addition, it is incumbent on the psychologist to prove that there has been no sexual exploitation as a result of the sexual relationship.

Emerging Issues in Dual Relationships.   Corey et al. (2003) suggest that dual relationships can best be understood within the context of boundary and role issues. These scholars note that there is an emerging controversy regarding how boundaries and roles between practitioners and clients are defined. Lazarus (1998, 2001) contends that practitioners should take a reasonable nondogmatic approach regarding boundary and role issues. He believes that under some conditions, nonsexual dual relationships can have therapeutic value, and rigid interpretation of ethical standards can undermine clinical decision making. Borys (1994) disagrees with Lazarus, noting that refraining from dual relationships does not imply rigidity in clinical decision making. Gabbard (1994) goes further, noting that failure to establish and maintain clear boundaries is a recipe for disaster.

Younggren and Gottlieb (2004) note that some dual relationships cannot be avoided and in fact can be obligatory, such as in the military. They identify a risk management plan that can be used to assess the appropriateness of entering into a dual relationship. Questions that can be asked to promote risk management include

- Is it necessary to enter into a dual relationship with the client?
- To what degree can a dual relationship cause harm or benefit to the client?
- Would the dual relationship undermine the counseling relationship?
- Can the practitioner maintain objectivity after entering into a dual relationship?

- Is there informed consent from the client regarding entering into a dual relationship (including identifying potential risks)?
- Has decision making regarding entering into a dual relationship been documented in the treatment records?
- Is there documented evidence of ongoing consultation?
- Is the decision making based on the client's welfare, including consideration of issues relating to diagnostic and treatment issues?

Addressing dual relationships in counseling is a challenging and complex process. Clearly, entering into a dual relationship should occur only after careful consideration of risk management questions and careful ethical-legal decision making.

Legal Issues

Legal problems can result when counselors engage in sexual relationships with clients. For example, many states consider it a felony for professional helpers to be concurrently having sexual relationships with their clients. All things considered, it is not surprising that professional organizations strongly discourage counselors to ever engage in sexual relationships with clients.

Several legal issues that affect the practice of counseling relate to confidentiality. As mentioned, counselors are ethically obligated to maintain confidentiality unless clients pose a clear and imminent danger to themselves or others. A legal precedent for counselors to take decisive action to protect human life was set in the landmark case of Tarasoff versus the Board of Regents of the University of California (1974, 1976). The case involved a psychologist at the University of California at Berkeley who provided counseling services to a student. After the student threatened to kill his girlfriend, Tatiana Tarasoff, the psychologist failed to warn her of the threat. Two months later, the client killed the girl. Her parents filed suit against the university and won on the basis that the psychologist had been irresponsible.

The California Supreme Court went on to determine that there was also a duty to protect in Tarasoff cases. This typically involves arranging for clients to be hospitalized when they become homicidal. The following *Personal Note* describes some of the difficulties associated with the duty to warn and the duty to protect.

Monahan (1993) provides additional guidelines regarding the duty to warn and the duty to protect. Monahan emphasizes that the single best predictor of violence is a past history of violence. It is therefore imperative that an in-depth history be taken, including reviewing past hospitalizations and other forms of treatment as well as gathering information from significant others if necessary. Follow-up is also important to ensure that a homicidal client received the necessary treatment to prevent harm to self or others. In addition, Monahan stresses the importance of documentation and consultation.

Corey (2001) identifies three other situations in which counselors are legally required to report information: (a) when the counselor believes that a client under the age of 16 is the victim of child abuse, sexual abuse, or some other crime; (b) if the counselor determines that a client is in need of hospitalization; and (c) if information is made an issue in a court action.

The following *Personal Note* provides information on some of the stressors associated with legal issues in counseling.

A Personal Note

As society becomes increasingly violent, it is not surprising that counselors such as myself are dealing with a heightened number of potentially violent situations. I therefore find myself in numerous clinical situations that require instituting the Tarasoff ruling by warning and protecting my client's intended victim. One method that I've used to help determine whether a client presents a serious threat to others is the MMPI (not the test but an acronym for means, motive, plan, and intent). Other factors to consider are past histories of violence, abuse of alcohol and drugs, mental stability, and overall mental status. Consultation with a supervisor or colleague such as a psychologist or psychiatrist can also be helpful in determining whether someone represents a homicidal threat.

I have found the actual process of instituting the Tarasoff litigation in a clinical situation to be a very stressful experience for all involved. These situations typically have one or more lives at risk and also involve my client's welfare (including the client's mental health, career, family, and legal status). I find it very stressful to contact the intended victims and inform them that my client appears to be planning to kill them. It is also stressful to attempt to protect the client by taking the necessary steps, which often involve arranging for hospitalization. Having a client admitted voluntarily or involuntarily to a hospital is often a very difficult and time-consuming process. I'm also amazed at how quickly some of these hospitals discharge these patients back into the community, often creating additional legal-ethical dilemmas and stress for all involved.

Privileged Communication.   Another legal issue that pertains to confidentiality is the notion of *privileged communication.* This term refers to a legal protection for clients, preventing a counselor from disclosing confidential communication in court without their permission (Herlihy & Sheeley, 1987). The privilege exists to protect the rights of the client and not the counselor. The client owns and controls the privilege (Herlihy & Sheeley, 1987) and can therefore determine whether a counselor may disclose confidential information in a court of law.

Corey et al. (2003) have identified the following exceptions in which a client does not own and control the privilege and the counselor must provide information to the court. These instances are when:

- A counselor is acting in a court-appointed capacity, such as conducting a psychological examination (Remley, 1991)
- A counselor determines that a client has a high risk of suicide (Bedner, Bedner, Lambert, & Waite, 1991)
- A client initiates a lawsuit against a counselor (Denkowski & Denkowski, 1982)
- A client uses a mental condition as a claim or defense in a civil action (Leslie, 1991)
- A counselor suspects that a client under the age of 16 is the victim of a crime such as child abuse or neglect (Everstine et al., 1980)
- A counselor determines that a client requires hospitalization for a mental or psychological disorder (Bedner et al., 1991)
- A client reveals an intent to commit a crime or is assessed to be dangerous to the self or others (Bedner et al., 1991)

Laws relating to privileged communication between a client and a member of the helping profession vary considerably from state to state (Herlihy & Sheeley, 1987). Some states recognize privileged communication between psychologists and their clients but not between licensed counselors and their clients. Practitioners must therefore be aware of their state's laws regarding privileged communication.

Legal Issues in Managed Care.   Some form of managed care is currently present in all forms of health care (Appelbaum, 1993). A number of legal issues have emerged in conjunction with this movement toward managed care. Appelbaum (1993) identifies legal issues associated with managed care that affect practitioners and providers. Practitioners have several legal responsibilities associated with managed care. Some of these are the duty to appeal adverse decisions, the duty to disclose, and the duty to continue treatment. The duty to appeal adverse decisions relates to the necessity to write to the managed care provider and appeal a decision to limit or decline services if the counselor believes that it is not in the best interest of the client (for example, the client is suicidal or homicidal). The duty to disclose involves informing clients about the financial limitations of managed care (in terms of payment for therapy being stopped before the counselor or client believes that the goals of therapy have been reached) and the problems associated with confidentiality regarding the provider having access to personal information that the client has disclosed during counseling. There are legal and ethical issues relating to the duty to continue treatment. It is not considered ethical or legal to "abandon" clients who no longer have the financial means for counseling (for example, managed care refuses to pay). Counselors should attempt to refer the client to free or affordable services, see the client for free, or move toward an appropriate termination (Appelbaum, 1993).

Providers also have legal responsibilities regarding managed care. These include the duty to review appeals and other pertinent information regarding the care of clients, the duty to disclose to clients the limits of coverage, and the duty to select qualified providers (Appelbaum, 1993). Practitioners and providers must work closely together to ensure that clients receive appropriate care and services.

Malpractice.   Counselors have an increased risk of being sued for malpractice (Corey, 2001). It is therefore important for counselors to understand what malpractice is and what they can do to prevent legal difficulties.

Knapp (1980) defines malpractice as an act or omission by a counselor that is inconsistent with reasonable care and skill used by other reputable counselors and that results in injury to the client. Knapp (1980) notes that courts do not assume that malpractice exists if a counselor has made a mistake in judgment, since it is possible to make such a mistake and still exercise reasonable care. Keeton (1984) identifies four conditions that must exist for malpractice to have occurred. Applied to a counseling situation, these are (a) the counselor had a duty to a client, (b) the duty of care was not met, (c) the client sustained an injury, and (d) there was a close causal relationship between the counselor's failure to provide reasonable care and the resulting injury.

DePauw (1986) provides guidelines for avoiding ethical violations at each phase of the counseling process. These guidelines can minimize the risk of harm to clients and the incidence of malpractice suits for counselors.

Precounseling. Issues during this phase include accurately advertising services, making advance financial arrangements that are clearly understood and serve the best interest of the client, providing services within the counselor's parameters of competency, facilitating the client's informed choice of services, avoiding dual relationships, clearly indicating experimental treatment approaches and taking appropriate safety precautions, and identifying the limits to confidentiality.

Ongoing Counseling. Issues include maintaining confidentiality, seeking consultation as necessary, maintaining adequate client records, taking necessary action regarding clients who pose a clear and imminent danger to themselves or others, and complying with laws that relate to reporting child abuse and neglect.

Termination Phase. Issues at this point include being sensitive to the client's termination and post-termination concerns, initiating termination or referral if the client is no longer benefiting from services, and evaluating the efficacy of counseling services.

Special Ethical and Legal Issues

This section addresses some of the special ethical and legal issues associated with marriage and family therapy, child counseling, and group counseling. Information is also provided on ethical and legal issues relating to acquired immunodeficiency syndrome (AIDS).

Issues Relating to Marriage and Family Therapy. Gladding, Remley, and Huber (2001) identify ethical and legal issues in marriage and family therapy in terms of client welfare, confidentiality, informed consent, and dual relations.

Client Welfare. The following is AAMFT's (2001) ethical position relating to client welfare:

> Marriage and family therapists advance the welfare of families and individuals. They respect the rights of those persons seeking their assistance, and make reasonable efforts to ensure that their services are used appropriately.

The issue of client welfare can become complex in marriage and family therapy because the counselor is working with more than one client. Margolin (1982) notes that there can be a conflict in the goals of individuals seeking marriage and family therapy. This can occur in marriage therapy, for example, when one person wants a divorce and the other does not. Gladding et al. (2001) suggest that a counselor can avoid these problems by utilizing a systems perspective rather than focusing on the problems of individual clients.

Confidentiality. The following is AAMFT's (2001) ethical position on confidentiality:

> Marriage and family therapists have unique confidentiality concerns because the client in a therapeutic relationship may be more than one person. Therapists respect and guard confidences of each individual client.

Respecting the confidence of clients in marriage and family therapy can often create an ethical dilemma, for example, being asked to keep information about a client's affair from the client's spouse.

Margolin (1982) notes that counselors tend to take one of two positions regarding confidentiality when working with couples and families. One position involves the counselor viewing each marital partner or family member as an individual client. In this approach, the counselor may routinely see the clients individually before seeing them together in couples or family therapy. A counselor who utilizes this approach needs to develop a clear position on confidentiality and to communicate it to the clients. Typically, the counselor will either reserve the right to use professional judgment to maintain individual confidence or avoid disclosing sensitive information unless the client gives permission.

A second approach to confidentiality that Margolin (1982) describes is based on nonsecrecy. From this perspective, the counselor does not feel any obligation to withhold information from the other marital partner or family member. A counselor who utilizes this position usually avoids seeing the clients individually. In addition, the counselor should inform the clients of the policy on confidentiality before they commence counseling.

Confidentiality can also vary in marriage and family therapy in terms of privileged communication. Gladding et al. (2001) note that the concept of privileged communication was originally developed within a context of one-to-one relationships, for example, doctor-patient and attorney-client. It is therefore not surprising that there have been conflicting legal precedents when this concept has been applied to situations involving more than one client.

Several legal cases have tested the validity of privileged communication for clients involved in marriage counseling. Herrington (1979) notes that a Virginia judge ruled that there was no confidentiality because statements were not made in private to a doctor but were made in the presence of a spouse. Another case reported by Margolin (1982) provides support for privileged communication in marriage counseling. This case involved a man who decided to divorce his wife. He had his counselor subpoenaed to testify in court about statements his wife had made during their conjoint sessions. In this case, the husband was waiving his right of privileged communication, but the wife was not waiving hers. The judge ruled in favor of protecting the wife's right to confidentiality. In view of the varying litigation on this subject, it is important for counselors to determine the laws in their state regarding privileged communication in multiperson therapies (Gumper & Sprenkle, 1981).

Informed Consent.   The AAMFT (2001) provides the following ethical position relating to informed consent:

> Marriage and family therapists respect the right of clients to make decisions and help them to understand the consequences of these decisions. Therapists clearly advise the clients that they have the responsibility to make decisions regarding relationships such as cohabitation, marriage, divorce, separation, reconciliation, custody, and visitation.

Applying the concept of informed consent can be more difficult in marriage and family therapy than in individual counseling. Margolin (1982) notes that the individuals who undergo marriage and family therapy together do not always begin therapy at the same time. It may therefore be necessary to repeat the procedures associated with informed consent as new clients begin the counseling process.

Dual Relationships.   The AAMFT (2001) provides the following ethical position on dual relationships:

> Marriage and family therapists are aware of their influential position with respect to clients, and they avoid exploiting the trust and dependency of such persons. Therapists, therefore, make every effort to avoid dual relationships with clients that could impair their professional judgment or increase the risk of exploitation. When a dual relationship cannot be avoided, therapists take appropriate professional precautions to ensure judgment is not impaired and no exploitation occurs. Examples of such dual relationships include, but are not limited to, business or close personal relationships with clients. Sexual intimacy with clients is prohibited. Sexual intimacy with former clients for two years following the termination of therapy is prohibited.

Dual relationships can pose problems in all types of counseling, including marriage and family counseling. One potential problem in marriage and family counseling is providing individual counseling and marriage counseling to the same individual and attempting to ensure that confidentiality is maintained.

Issues Relating to Child and Adolescent Counseling.   Child and adolescent counseling can involve special ethical and legal issues in terms of informed consent, confidentiality, and reporting laws that relate to child abuse.

Informed Consent.   Corey et al. (2003) note that most states require parental consent for minors to receive counseling services. Some states permit minors to enter into a counseling relationship without parental permission in crisis situations, such as those involving substance abuse (Corey et al., 2003). Counselors should therefore be aware of the laws relating to informed consent in their state.

Confidentiality.   Ansell (1987) describes confidentiality with minors as a gray area that requires the counselor to proceed with caution. Conflicts can result from the counselor's legal responsibility to respect a parent's right to be informed of counseling services and the ethical responsibility to maintain the confidentiality of the minor (Huey, 1986).

Ansell (1987) suggests that counselors establish guidelines with the parents and the minor regarding the nature of information that can be released to parents. The ACA's (1995) ethical code can be used to structure these guidelines: "When counseling minors or persons unable to give voluntary informed consent, counselors act in these clients' best interest" (Section A:3). The counselor can therefore suggest that confidentiality information will be released to parents when the counselor believes it is in the child's best interest.

Parents are also legally entitled to have access to their child's or adolescent's confidential records (Thompson & Rudolph, 2003). Personal notes are exempt from this requirement when they are kept separate from institutional files; when they are not seen by anyone, including clerical staff; and when they were not discussed with anyone in the process of decision making (Thompson & Rudolph, 2003).

Child Abuse.   All states have laws relating to child abuse (Thompson & Rudolph, 2003), and most require counselors to report suspected abuse (Congdon, 1987). These laws usually "include penalties for failure to report and provide immunity for the reporter from criminal and civil liability" (Congdon, 1987). Counselors should limit their reporting of information to that which is required by law. Reporting additional information can make the counselor guilty of releasing privileged information (Congdon, 1987).

Issues Relating to Group Counseling.   The Association for Specialists in Group Work (ASGW) replaced its 1990 ethical standards in 1998 with the *Best Practices Guidelines for Group Workers*. These guidelines (Rapin & Keel, 1998) endorse the ethical code of the American Counseling Association (ACA), the parent organization of ASGW. In addition, the *Best Practices Guidelines* provide clarification regarding the practice of group work in terms of professional standards and ethical conduct. The guidelines address professional issues relating to planning, performing, and processing groups. Highlights of the ASGW *Best Practices Guidelines* are as follows:

Planning.   Group workers are able to utilize the ACA code of ethics and other pertinent guidelines regarding professional standards and practice. Group workers engage in professional practice that is consistent with their training and competence. In addition, group workers screen prospective members to ensure that they are appropriate for group experiences, provide informed consent, and engage in professional development.

Performing.   Group workers utilize appropriate skills and interventions to promote positive growth and development for group members. Group workers are sensitive to issues of diversity and attempt to develop the knowledge and skills necessary to address issues of diversity. Group workers are engaged in ongoing evaluation of their own strengths and weaknesses and the efficacy of the groups they lead. Group workers also utilize ethical decision-making models in their group work.

Processing.   Group workers process group issues such as the dynamics between group members within the group with group members and outside the group with supervisors, coleaders, and other colleagues as necessary. Group workers attempt to synthesize theory and practice to enhance the efficacy of group work. Group workers also evaluate group experiences to assist in program development. Follow-up services are utilized to assess whether group members need additional services.

Paradise and Kirby (1990) identify several legal issues relating to group counseling. They suggest that group counselors should take extra precautions regarding confidentiality. It is especially important to clarify the limits to confidentiality and privileged communication for members during pregroup orientation or the first session. Counselors can be sued for negligence if they have given the impression that confidentiality was guaranteed. In addition, group counselors should have all members sign a contract requiring confidentiality and stating that breach of confidentiality will result in the member being dropped from the group (Paradise & Kirby, 1990).

Legal problems in group counseling can also arise from issues relating to a counselor's duty to protect. As noted earlier in this chapter, the Tarasoff litigation (Tarasoff v. Board of Regents of the University of California, 1974, 1976) mandated that counselors have a legal responsibility to warn anyone who is the subject of a serious threat.

Corey, Corey, Callanan, and Russell (1982) note that the incidence of verbal abuse and subsequent casualties is higher in group counseling than in individual counseling because of the intensity of group work and interaction between members. Paradise and Kirby (1990) therefore suggest that group counselors screen out potentially dangerous clients and continuously monitor clients to ensure their physical and psychological safety.

Multicultural Issues.   Corey, Williams, and Moline (1995) emphasize the importance of recognizing multicultural issues in group counseling. They provide several guidelines for addressing diversity issues in group counseling. These are summarized as follows: group leaders must be respectful and sensitive to multicultural issues in groups, including differences in religious and spiritual issues of group members. Leaders need to be aware of social cultural forces such as racism and help group members recognize when their problems stem from external forces. In addition, leaders must be aware of their own biases and prejudices and work through them so they do not have an adverse effect on the group process.

Legal Issues in Group Counseling.   Corey et al. (1995) provide an overview of legal issues in group counseling. They note that the best way to avoid malpractice suits is to practice within the boundaries of one's competency and to practice in a *reasonable, ordinary, and prudent* manner. In addition, they suggest that group counselors (1) understand state laws and how they affect confidentiality and privileged communication, (2) use written contracts with members to ensure informed consent, (3) secure permission from legal guardians when working with minors, and (4) ensure the rights and safety of group members.

Issues Relating to AIDS.   Many authors have addressed ethical issues that relate to providing counseling services to clients infected by the AIDS virus (HIV) (Cohen, 1990; Gray & Harding, 1988; Melton, 1988). The main ethical question that emerges from the literature is, What should a counselor do when a sexually active client has tested positive for the AIDS virus and has not informed any partners of the illness? In these instances, the counselor's ethical dilemma is whether to maintain confidentiality or inform the client's sexual partners that they are being exposed to the AIDS virus.

Gray and Harding (1988) believe that there are both ethical and legal precedents for breaking confidentiality in these cases. In terms of ethics, the ACA ethical standards (1995) states that confidentiality can be breached when there is a "clear and imminent danger" to self or others (Section B.1.c). In addition, the ACA (1995) code of ethics (Section B.1.d) state "a counselor who receives information confirming that a client has a disease commonly known to be both communicable and fatal is justified in disclosing information to an identifiable third party, who by his or her relationship with the client is at a high risk for contracting the disease." The Tarasoff case also sets forth a legal precedent regarding "duty to warn" (Tarasoff v. Board of Regents of the University of California, 1974, 1976). As a result of the Tarasoff case, professional counselors have a legal duty to warn a person if their client poses a serious threat.

Naturally, counselors should not arbitrarily break confidentiality in cases involving clients who have tested positive for HIV. Instead, they should only do this as a last resort. Gray and Harding (1988) and Cohen (1990) provide several guidelines that can assist counselors in dealing with these sensitive ethical dilemmas. The following is a summary of their recommendations:

- Clients should be made aware of the limits to confidentiality before they begin counseling.
- Clients who have contracted the AIDS virus should be informed how the virus is spread and what precautions they can take to prevent its spreading.
- Clients should be encouraged to inform any sexual partner that they may have been exposed to the virus.
- If a client is unwilling to inform any partner who may be at risk, the counselor should first alert the client of the need to break confidentiality and then inform the sexual partner in a timely fashion.
- Counselors should limit disclosure of information to general medical information regarding the client's disease.
- Disclosures should only be made to the party at risk or to a guardian in the case of a minor.
- Disclosures should communicate willingness to provide counseling services to the client.
- Medical consultation and referral should be arranged as necessary.

Stanard and Hazler (1995) provide additional information regarding the implications of Tarasoff in HIV/AIDS cases. They suggest that each case needs to be carefully evaluated for its own unique circumstances. When the case presents medical evidence of the AIDS virus, when there is a high-risk relationship, and when there is little likelihood of the client's self-disclosure, "counselors are directed to seek consultation, to make sure no reasonable alternative can be utilized, and even then to release only information that is necessary, relevant, and verifiable" (Stanard & Hazler, 1995, p. 97). In addition, they stress the importance of working with clients to prevent the infection of present and future individuals.

Ethical-Legal Decision Making

Ethical-legal decision making provides a structure for addressing ethical-legal issues that have an impact on counseling. It must be emphasized that throughout the decision-making process, it is critical to consult when necessary and to document all significant activities and events such as consultation and treatment efforts (for example, phone calls to a suicidal client). The following four-step process can be useful in providing a structure for ethical-legal decision making.

Step 1: Determine Whether an Ethical-Legal Issue Needs to Be Addressed. Gladding et al. (2001) suggest that the first step in ethical-legal decision making is to determine whether an ethical-legal decision needs to be made. The four ethical "guiding principles" discussed in this chapter can be used to alert the counselor to potential ethical issues (i.e., client welfare, informed consent, confidentiality, and dual relationships). Important legal issues that may also need to be addressed in ethical-legal decision making include counseling minors, Tarasoff legislation, privileged communication, and laws relating to reporting child abuse and neglect.

Step 2: Address Contextual Issues Such As Culture and Personal Bias. Kelly (1999) suggests that the contextual perspective represents two basic assumptions. First, change is inevitable and ongoing. The second assumption recognizes the systemic nature of change, with change in one context influencing change in another context. Postmodern theories such as social constructivism emphasize the contextual nature of human experience.

Cottone (2001) proposes a social constructivist perspective for ethical-legal decision making. Social constructivism recognizes the contextual nature of decision making and the role that social-cultural forces play in constructing reality. Social-cultural forces that may undermine ethical-legal decision making include racism, prejudice, stereotyping, and oppression. For example, if counselors believe that a particular culture is prone to problems with alcoholism and child neglect, they may inadvertently make false charges of neglect with this population. Oppression can also interfere with ethical-legal decision making. Oppression can contribute to overly zealous ethical-legal action toward individuals who are targets of prejudice and racism (e.g., professionals who want to keep other professionals "in their place" by filing unwarranted ethics charges).

Meara, Schmidt, and Day (1996) provide another perspective for integrating social constructivism into ethical-legal decision making. They note that virtue ethics attempt to broaden ethical decision making beyond the self to reflect the interest of community and culture. These authors go on to suggest that "virtue ethics, rooted in the narratives and aspirations of specific communities, can be particularly helpful to professionals in discerning appropriate ethical conduct in multicultural settings and interactions" (p. 4). From this perspective, virtue ethics appear to parallel social constructionism's in terms of broadening the self to include sensitivity to the cultures reflected in the stories that clients tell.

Meara et al. (1996) also note that ethical-legal decision making evolved from a European-American perspective. A number of biases associated with ethnocentrism must therefore be addressed. These authors cite Carol Gilligan's (1982) seminal work on the role of gender in moral development as an example of the importance of considering diversity issues in ethical-legal decision making.

Gladding et al. (2001) also suggest that counselors need to address issues of personal bias during ethical-legal decision making. Ethical-legal decisions are not made in a vacuum. Decisions are better understood contextually in terms of relationships with others and within the context of where one works (Cottone, 2001). Gladding et al. (2001) posit that the relational aspects of ethical-legal decision making can create personal bias that can undermine professional objectivity. These scholars recognize that a counselor's personal and professional values may be in conflict, thereby inhibiting appropriate action. For example, a counselor may have a colleague who is also a close friend. The counselor may become aware of unethical behavior on the part of the colleague but may not want to take action because of their friendship. Another example of personal bias is a reluctance to report ethical-legal problems where one works for fear of adverse consequences, for being considered a "whistle blower." One way for counselors to overcome this personal bias is to remember that they will be acting unethically if they do not take constructive action.

Step 3: Formulating an Ethical-Legal Course of Action.   Once counselors establish that an ethical-legal dilemma exists, they must determine what form of action to take. Consultation with a legal advisor and/or one's supervisor can be an important first step in formulating a course of action. Legal consultation can be useful to identify potential legal issues and the appropriate action associated with a case. Supervisors can also play a vital role in formulating a course of action. Kitchener (1984, 1985) has identified two levels of ethics that can be used to formulate a course of action: intuitive and critical-evaluative. The intuitive level addresses immediate feelings in response to the situation. An intuitive reaction can be useful in situations that require immediate action, such as crisis intervention.

The critical-evaluative level of ethical reasoning can be used in situations that do not require immediate action. Most situations requiring an ethical decision are complex, with no clear right or wrong way of proceeding. Kitchener (1984, 1985) suggests a three-tiered approach to critically evaluate a particular situation. The first tier relates to principle ethics, whereas the second and third tiers relate to virtue ethics. The first tier for evaluating an ethical dilemma involves referring to the code of ethics for guidelines pertaining to the ethical situation. If these guidelines are insufficient, counselors can move on to the second tier and determine the philosophical foundations on which the ethical guidelines were based, such as the right to privacy or the right to make free choices. When counselors are still uncertain, they can proceed to the third tier and apply the principles of ethical theory. There are several noted ethical theorists who can help provide a rationale for ethical action (Ableson & Nielson, 1967; Baier, 1958). Gladding et al. (2001) have surveyed these theorists and identify suggestions that could be of help in ethical decision making. For example, counselors should do what they would want for themselves or significant others in a similar situation, or they should do what would result in the least amount of harm.

Step 4: Implementing an Action Plan.   Once counselors have determined a course of action and have overcome possible personal-professional conflicts, they are in a position to implement an action plan. This will require courage and the willingness to accept personal responsibility for their actions. After implementing a plan of action, counselors may wish to follow up and evaluate their professional functioning. Van Hoose (1980) has provided the following guidelines that counselors can use to determine whether their actions are ethically responsible. Counselors have probably acted ethically if they have maintained personal and professional honesty; had the client's best interest in mind; acted without malice or personal gain; and can justify their action as the best judgment according to the current state of the profession.

Clinical Examples

The following clinical examples provide an opportunity to practice ethical decision making. Four ethical dilemmas are presented that relate to a variety of clinical situations. There is no right or wrong way of responding to these examples; counselors should simply attempt to develop a response that reflects sound clinical judgment. Each example is followed by a description of the way I would respond.

Clinical Example #1.   You are a counselor at a community mental health center. A young woman was convicted of drunk driving and told by the judge that she must attend your alcohol treatment program to keep her driver's license. You are concerned about the issue of informed consent. What would you do in this situation if you were the counselor?

My Response.   Any situation that involves a client who has been court-ordered to undergo counseling creates an ethical dilemma. The ethical code regarding informed consent requires that this client must not be forced to attend counseling. In addition, the client should feel free to terminate counseling whenever she chooses. At the same time, the counselor must inform the judge if the client does not complete the alcohol program. Technically, the client is free to choose counseling and keep her driver's license or choose no counseling and lose her license. At the very least, if the client chooses counseling, she may be doing so under duress.

As the counselor, I would first discuss with the client what the alcohol treatment program entailed and give her a professional disclosure statement. The statement would provide information such as my background, my definition of counseling, and the limits to confidentiality. I would then explore with her the available options, that she may either lose her license or attend the alcohol program. If she did decide to participate in the alcohol program, I would recognize the duress she must be feeling and suggest that we both try to make the best of a difficult situation. I would tell her that she is free to terminate her participation in the program at any time. I would also emphasize that if she decided to do so, I would unfortunately be obligated to inform the judge that she did not complete the program successfully.

Clinical Example #2. You are an elementary school counselor. After working at the school for a month, you identify several policies that conflict with your ethical code. Two examples of these policies are (1) you are told you must provide counseling services for certain students even if they don't want them; and (2) you are not allowed to maintain confidentiality because you must inform the principal about what certain students tell you during their sessions.

My Response. The ACA (1995) code of ethics suggests that when an institution functions in a manner that conflicts with the counselor's code of ethics, the counselor should attempt to resolve the differences with the institution. In this process, counselors can note that following recognized standards of practice (such as promoting the client's welfare) would be in the best interests of the institutions, the clients, and the staff. Counselors should also note that not following standards of practice can create litigative opportunities that could adversely affect the institution. If the institution in this example is not willing to make the necessary changes, counselors can consult with the personnel department and if necessary file charges against the organization (e.g., for promoting a hostile work environment). At no point in this process should a counselor engage in unethical acts. It is important to consider that even when an institution asks you to act unethically, you cannot defend your action later by saying, "My supervisor told me to do it." In extreme instances, a counselor may be forced to seek employment elsewhere.

Clinical Example #3. You are a mental health counselor in a community mental health center. After the second session with a male client, you decide he may be suffering from a serious mental disorder. You don't feel comfortable providing counseling services because you think the client requires help beyond your area of competence. You decide to refer the client to a psychiatrist or other mental health professional. The client refuses to accept your suggestion and insists instead that you continue seeing him. What would you do if you were the counselor?

My Response. The ACA (1995) and APA (2003) codes of ethics regarding client welfare suggest that a counselor has an ethical responsibility to refer a client who requires help beyond the counselor's level of competency. If the client is reluctant or resistant to pursue a referral, the counselor can help the client overcome these impasses. The counselor may also wish to consult with a supervisor to gain ideas to facilitate the referral process. In addition, the counselor should document all attempts to assist with the referral to provide a "paper trail." This could be useful to be able to document that the counselor did not commit an ethical violation in terms of abandoning the client.

Clinical Example #4.   You have a private practice specializing in marriage, family, and child counseling. You are seeing a married couple, Dan and Mary, in marriage counseling. Your approach to marriage counseling is to see the marital partners individually for 15 minutes each and then together for 30 minutes.

During the initial session, you first talk with Dan. He informs you that he and Mary have been married for two years. Before the marriage, he was an intravenous drug user, "shooting up" heroin at least twice a day for several years. During this time, he tested positive for HIV. Dan says that Mary does not know that he tested positive for HIV, and he does not want to tell her because he is convinced that she would leave him. What would you do in this situation if you were the counselor?

My Response.   This case has several ethical issues (client welfare and confidentiality) and one legal issue (relating to the Tarasoff ruling). In terms of client welfare, I would be concerned for Dan regarding his drug problem, for Mary regarding the potential of her contracting the AIDS virus, and for the two of them regarding their marriage. I would also have some ethical and legal concerns regarding confidentiality. Ethically, I need to do whatever I can to ensure my clients' safety when they are in imminent danger (including breaking confidentiality). In addition, the ACA (1995) code of ethics (Section B.1.d) states "a counselor who receives information confirming that a client has a disease commonly known to be both communicable and fatal is justified in disclosing information to an identifiable third party, who by his or her relationship with the client is at a high risk for contracting the disease." The Tarasoff ruling of the duty to warn and protect also may require me to break confidentiality and take the necessary steps to ensure Mary's safety regarding contracting the AIDS virus from Dan.

As a counselor, I would be especially concerned about the possibility that Dan could infect Mary with the AIDS virus. In this regard, I would insist that Dan tell Mary, before the end of the counseling session, that he tested positive for HIV to minimize her risk for contracting the virus. If Dan refused to inform Mary, I would breach confidentiality on the basis that his illness presents a clear and imminent danger to Mary. At this time, I would also review with Mary and Dan the risk of having sexual intercourse so that she could make an informed decision as to what behaviors she would engage in with Dan. I would also encourage Dan to obtain necessary medical treatment, encourage him to enter into a drug rehabilitation program, and continue marital therapy as necessary.

Diversity Issues.   Diversity issues such as culture and spirituality affect all phases of the counseling process, including ethical-legal decision making. Pedersen (1997) provides a scholarly review of the ACA code of ethics in terms of culture. He concludes that the ACA code of ethics contains cultural bias, favors the dominant culture, and fosters cultural encapsulation. These problems are reflected in the ethical codes' failure to consider the world views of clients and the utilization of a unidimensional (instead of multidimensional) cultural perspective.

Spirituality is an emerging diversity issue that is being incorporated into a multicultural perspective (Bishop, 1995). Spiritual issues in counseling are recognizing the role that values and morality play in ethical-legal decision making and the necessity of addressing these issues from a multicultural perspective (Grant, 1992; Schulte, 1992). This literature suggests that counseling, by its very nature, is a value-laden process (Grant, 1992), whereby clients are aware of their counselors' value systems and counselors help clients explore value-laden issues (Patterson, 1992). Ethical-legal decision making must therefore take into consideration the multiple voices that define what is moral-ethical behavior. In this process counselors can attempt to understand clients' values (including morality) from their world view and guard against imposing universal unidimensional definitions of morality (Pedersen, 1997).

Summary

Counselors face many professional issues. Exploring the four building blocks of professional counseling—formal study of counseling and professional affiliation, certification or licensure, continuing education, and professional involvement—encourages students to become involved in professional issues as soon as possible.

Counselors and psychologists have codes of ethics such as the ACA, APA, and AAMFT to help guide their clinical practice. These ethical codes are not written in black-and-white terms but must be interpreted and applied to each particular clinical situation. Major ethical issues for counselors include client welfare, informed consent, confidentiality, and dual relationships. Special ethical issues relate to marriage and family therapy, child counseling, group counseling, and patients who are infected with the AIDS virus.

Several legal issues concern members of the counseling profession. For example, a counselor must break confidentiality when a client poses a clear and imminent danger to self or others. Privileged communication exists to protect the rights of clients in terms of confidentiality in a legal proceeding. This privilege belongs to the client and not the counselor.

Clinical examples provide opportunities to apply various ethical and legal principles. Counselors must also be aware of the diversity issues in ethical-legal decision making.

Personal Exploration

1. How can involvement in professional organizations be important to your career?
2. What intrigues you about legal-ethical issues in counseling?
3. What is malpractice and what steps can be taken to avoid a lawsuit?
4. Do you think a parent should be legally responsible for his or her child's behavior? If so, why?

Web Sites for Chapter 2

American Psychological Association. (2003). *Ethical principles of psychologists and codes of conduct.* Retrieved March 3, 2005, from http://www.apa.org/ethics/code 2002.html
Provides a comprehensive listing of the 2002 ethics code for the American Psychological Association.

Buckner, F., & Firestone, M. (2000). "*Where the public peril begins": 25 years after Tarasoff.* From the *Journal of Legal Medicine,* 21. Retrieved March 3, 2005, from http://cyber.law.harvard.edu/torts01/syllabus/readings/buckner.html
Provides a comprehensive and somewhat current article on the Tarasoff rulings by two medical doctors.

CHAPTER
3

The Counseling Process

CHAPTER OVERVIEW

This chapter provides an overview of the counseling process as well as a description of some of the common problems that beginning counselors experience. It explores what can occur in a counseling session and some of the special skills utilized in counseling. Highlights of the chapter include

- The art and science of the counseling process
- The six stages of the counseling process
- Listening skills
- Recent trends in the counseling process
- Brief-counseling approaches
- Common problems for beginning counselors
- Diversity issues

The Art and Science of the Counseling Process

The counseling process is both an art and a science. For example, it is an art to really listen to a client and to communicate caring and compassion. Through the art of listening, a counselor attempts to enter into the client's world and see things from the client's perspective. The art of counseling requires the counselor to reach sensitively into the world of clients and help them become aware of their strengths and hidden beauty. The art of counseling also recognizes the importance of tuning into and reacting appropriately to diversity issues such as culture, gender, and spirituality. All these issues play important roles in addressing the theory, research, and practice of counseling.

The science of counseling creates an important balance, providing an objective dimension to the subjective art of counseling. Counselors must be able to utilize scientific tools to gain an objective understanding of what is occurring during the various stages of the counseling process, from formulating a counseling relationship to termination and follow-up and research and evaluation. For example, the counseling literature has identified a number of factors associated with establishing a positive counseling relationship, such as core conditions (for example, empathy, respect, genuineness, and immediacy). There are numerous other examples of the role of science in counseling from the use of standardized tests in assessment to research methodology for evaluating efficacy in counseling.

Counseling is not a fixed entity but a fluid process in which the counselor continually tries to adjust course to accommodate the unique and emerging needs of clients. The art and science of counseling should provide a point of reference to chart an effective course through the counseling process.

The Six Stages of the Counseling Process

Most counseling sessions last approximately 50 minutes (Linder, 1954). A counseling session is therefore sometimes referred to as the 50-minute hour. What actually takes place in a session depends on the client's needs and the counselor's personal approach to counseling. Although there is some variation during a session, there is a basic structure that most counseling approaches have in common. This structure is described by Cormier and Hackney (1993) as a five-stage process: relationship building, assessment, goal setting, interventions, and termination and follow-up. These stages have been expanded into the following six-stage model of the counseling process.

Stage one: Relationship building
Stage two: Assessment and diagnosis
Stage three: Formulation of counseling goals
Stage four: Intervention and problem solving
Stage five: Termination and follow-up
Stage six: Research and evaluation

A typical counseling session can involve all six stages except termination. The focus of counseling may shift as the counseling process progresses over time. For example, during the first few sessions with a client, a counselor may place the primary emphasis on building a positive counseling relationship, assessment and diagnosis, and formulating counseling goals. During the later phase of the counseling process, the counselor may shift the emphasis to intervention and problem solving, termination and follow-up, and research and evaluation. A more complete description of these six stages follows.

Stage One: Relationship Building

The counseling relationship is the heart of the counseling process. It supplies the vitality and the support necessary for counseling to work. It is the critical factor associated with successful outcomes in counseling (Kokotovic & Tracey, 1990). Sexton and Whiston (1994, p. 6) commented on the importance of the counseling relationship when they noted that "the quality of the counseling relationship has consistently been found to have the most significant impact on successful client outcome."

Although there appears to be a general consensus that the counseling relationship is important, it is less clear how important it is and in what way (Gelso & Carter, 1985). Research efforts that have attempted to address these issues can be grouped into two general categories: counselor-offered conditions and counselor- and client-offered conditions.

Counseling can be conceptualized as a series of stages or steps that lead one through the counseling process.

Counselor-Offered Conditions.　　Counselor-offered conditions relate to how the counselor influences the counseling process. The majority of the literature on the counseling relationship has focused on counselor-offered conditions relating to core conditions for effective counseling and the social influence model. An overview of the issues associated with these two important topics follows.

Core Conditions.　　Rogers (1957) identified what he believed were core conditions for successful counseling: empathic understanding, unconditional positive regard, and congruence. Rogers (1957) suggested that these core conditions were necessary and sufficient for constructive personality change to occur. No other conditions were necessary. Later, Carkhuff (1969, 1971) expanded the core conditions to include respect, immediacy, confrontation, concreteness, and self-disclosure. Carkhuff (1969, 1971) also pioneered the development of listening skills that could be used to promote these core conditions. An overview of the eight conditions is provided in Table 3.1. This table is followed by a description of each of these core conditions.

Empathy.　　Empathy is considered the most important core condition in terms of promoting positive outcomes (Orlando & Howard, 1986). Gelso and Fretz (2001) observe that virtually all major schools of counseling note the importance of empathy in the counseling process.

　　Egan (2002) describes empathic understanding as a process that involves listening, understanding, *and* communicating that understanding to the client. Carl Rogers emphasizes the experiential nature of empathy. He vigorously rejects mechanistic explanations of empathy that focus on techniques such as reflection of feeling (Raskin & Rogers, 2000). According to Rogers, empathy involves entering into and experiencing the client's phenomenological world. It is an active, immediate, and ongoing process in which the counselor becomes aware of the client's feelings, experiences those feelings, and creates a mirror through which clients can explore and discover deeper meanings associated with their feelings (Raskin & Rogers, 2000).

TABLE 3.1   Core Conditions

Core Conditions	Description	Purpose
Empathy	Communicating a sense of caring and understanding	To establish rapport, gain an understanding of the client, and encourage self-exploration in the client
Unconditional positive regard	Communicating to clients that they have value and worth as individuals	To promote acceptance of the client as a person of worth as distinct from accepting the client's behavior
Congruence	Behaving in a manner consistent with how one thinks and feels	To be genuine (not phony) in interactions with the client
Respect	Focusing on the positive attributes of the client	To focus on the client's strengths (not weaknesses)
Immediacy	Communicating in the here-and-now about what is occurring in the counseling session	To promote direct mutual communication between the counselor and client
Confrontation	Pointing out discrepancies in what the client is saying and doing (between statements and nonverbal behavior), and how the client is viewed by the counselor and client	To help clients clearly and accurately understand themselves and the world around them
Concreteness	Helping clients discuss themselves in specific terms	To help clients focus on pertinent issues
Self-disclosure	Making the self known to others	To promote increasing counseling-relevant communication from the client, enhancing the client's evaluation of the counselor, and increasing the client's willingness to seek counseling

Empathic understanding can be understood as a multistage process (Barrett-Lennard, 1981, 1997; Gladstein, 1983) consisting of different types of empathy. Gladstein (1983) identifies the following stages of empathy: the counselor has an emotional reaction to the client's situation, the counselor attempts to understand the client's situation from the client's perspective, the counselor communicates empathy to the client, and the client feels a sense of caring and understanding from the counselor.

Several kinds of empathy have also been identified, for example, primary and advanced empathy (Egan, 2002). Egan describes primary empathy as a process that involves the counselor attending, listening, and communicating accurate perceptions of the client's messages. Advanced empathy involves the characteristics associated with primary empathy as well as utilizing the skills of self-disclosure, directives, or interpretations. The following *Personal Note* provides additional information on empathy.

Unconditional Positive Regard.   Unconditional positive regard involves the counselor communicating to clients that they are of value and worthy as individuals. This concept has

A Personal Note

Dr. Ernest Flores, a psychiatrist I respect very much, once gave a presentation to my Introduction to Counseling class on "What Is Counseling." He said, "I don't know what Professor Nystul says counseling is, but I have this to say about it: Counseling can be summed up in one word: 'empathy'—showing that you care." I believe there is much truth to this statement. Without a caring counseling relationship, there is very little chance of anything positive happening in the counseling process.

I believe an important point regarding empathy is that it involves not only actually caring about someone, but being perceived as being caring. For example, a father who never tells his children he loves them can feel love towards his children but may not be perceived as being loving. Children often need to hear the words of love to feel loved.

As a counselor educator, I have conceptualized empathy in terms of three levels of intensity. Level one involves using listening skills to phenomenologically understand the client's feelings and reflect the feelings back to the client in a manner that is perceived as caring.

Level two involves advanced empathy, which I define as "listening with a third ear" or "listening between the lines of communication." This type of listening can trigger off a "journey into self" whereby the client experiences a deeper level of emotional understanding. For example, when a client says to the counselor, "I am picking up a contradiction" (in terms of what you are telling me)," the counselor can respond to the client by saying, "Perhaps you are feeling a contradiction on some level also." Something similar to this occurred during the "Three Approaches to Psychotherapy" series when "Gloria" was asking Carl Rogers for advice regarding being honest with her daughter about sex.

The third level of empathy is what I refer to as "self-transcendence and the existential encounter." The existential encounter involves moving beyond the subject-object dichotomy, feeling at one with the client, and directly experiencing the client's innermost emotional state. Counselors can use the four stages of Multimodality Creative Arts Therapy such as music therapy to move beyond hearing about the client's blues to directly experiencing the client's emotional expression (see Chapter 8).

---

been referred to by several other names, including nonpossessive warmth, acceptance, prizing, respect, and regard. There has been some controversy regarding the core condition of unconditional positive regard. Gelso and Fretz (2001) contend that this concept is neither desirable nor obtainable. Martin (1989) counters the critics by suggesting that the concept has been misunderstood. According to Martin, unconditional positive regard does not imply that the counselor reacts permissively, accepting all the client's behavior. Instead, it means that the counselor's unconditional positive regard involves acceptance of the client while setting limits on certain behaviors (see Rogers, Gendlin, Kiesler, & Truax, 1967, for additional information on unconditional positive regard).

Congruence.   Congruence involves counselors behaving in a manner consistent with how they think and feel. This condition has also been referred to as genuineness. An example of not functioning congruently is a counselor who says "I'm glad to see you" when a client arrives for an appointment, even though the counselor does not like the client.

Respect.   Respect is similar to unconditional positive regard in that it focuses on the positive attributes of the client. Counselors can communicate respect by making positive statements about the client and openly and honestly acknowledging, appreciating, and tolerating individual differences (Okun, 2002).

Immediacy.   Carkhuff (1969, 1971) developed the concept of immediacy, which is similar to Ivey's (1971) notion of direct, mutual communication. Immediacy involves communication between the counselor and client that focuses on the here and now. It allows the counselor to directly address issues of importance to the counseling relationship. Immediacy can involve counselors describing how they feel in relation to the client in the moment. For example, if a client does not appear interested in counseling, the counselor might say, "I'm getting concerned that you're not finding our sessions meaningful. How are you feeling about what is going on in counseling now?"

Confrontation.   The core condition of confrontation involves the counselor pointing out discrepancies in what a client is saying. There can be discrepancies between what the client is saying and doing (Gazda, Asbury, Blazer, Childress, & Walters, 1979), between statements and nonverbal behavior (Ivey, 1999), and between how clients see themselves versus how the counselor sees them (Egan, 2002).

Confrontation is a difficult and risky counseling technique that is used most effectively by high-functioning counselors (Berenson & Mitchell, 1968). Confrontation can have a negative effect on the counseling process, for example, when a client misreads the confrontation and feels attacked or rejected by the counselor (Egan, 2002).

Concreteness.   Concreteness refers to the counselor helping clients discuss their concerns in specific terms. Clients can feel overwhelmed with their problems and have difficulty putting things into perspective. When this occurs, concreteness can help the counselor create a focus for the client in the counseling process.

Self-Disclosure.   Jourard (1958) developed the concept of self-disclosure, which involves making the self known to another. Danish, D'Augelli, and Brock (1976) differentiate two types of self-disclosure statements: self-disclosing and self-involving. In self-disclosing statements, counselors disclose factual information about themselves. In self-involving statements, counselors describe what they are experiencing in relation to the client in the counseling process.

A review of the literature suggests support for both types of self-disclosure, with some studies favoring the merits of self-disclosing statements and other studies recognizing the value of self-involving statements in the counseling process (Sexton & Whiston, 1994). In addition, Collins and Miller (1994) conducted a meta-analytic review of the literature on self-disclosure and liking. These researchers found that people are liked more when they engage in intimate self-disclosure (as compared to people who self-disclose at less intimate levels of self-disclosure), self-disclosure increases when people like each other, and people like each other more when they engage in self-disclosure. Current research trends on the various facets of self-disclosure show it to be a complex process subject to influence from mediating variables such as gender, culture, and disability (Collins & Miller, 1994; Sexton & Whiston, 1994). For example, Mallinckrodt and Helms (1986) found that counselors are perceived as being more attractive when they disclose having a disability that is not apparent to the client. Regarding culture, African-American clients favor self-disclosure in their counselors more than Caucasians in terms of their counselors disclosing information relating to sex, personal and professional information, and success and failure in counseling (Cashwell, Shcherbakova, & Cashwell, 2003). Another study found that East Asian American clients prefer self-disclosure that provides structure to the counseling session over disclosures that relate to approval/reassurance, facts/credentials, and feelings (Kim, Hill, Gelso, Goates, Asay, & Harbin, 2003).

Research on Core Conditions. As mentioned, Rogers (1957) contends that the core conditions are all that is necessary or sufficient for constructive personality change. Many researchers have conducted studies to evaluate this premise. The early research of Truax and Carkhuff (1967) and Truax and Mitchell (1971) provided support for Rogers's theory. During the 1970s, researchers began to report negative results with criticism of earlier studies for methodological flaws or failure to test the efficacy of core conditions in non-Rogerian approaches (Garfield & Bergin, 1971; Mintz, Luborsky, & Auerbach, 1971; Sloane, Staples, Cristol, Yorkston, & Whipple, 1975).

More recent research has overcome many of the methodological flaws and is showing overall support for the importance of the core conditions for enhancing the counseling relationship and fostering positive outcomes in counseling (Beutler, Machado, & Neufeldt, 1994; Sexton & Whiston, 1994). Gelso and Fretz's (2001) review of the literature on core conditions concludes that core conditions are not necessary and sufficient as Rogers suggests but do facilitate positive outcomes in counseling. The recent research trend also suggests that the relationship between the core conditions and the counseling process is more complex than previously believed. It appears to be not so much a counselor-offered condition but a set of variables (such as empathy and respect) that are dependent on both the counselor and client (Beutler et al., 1994).

Rogers and Wood (1974) object to the reductionist approach utilized by counselor educators regarding core conditions (for example, microtraining methods that equate reflection of feeling with empathy). From this perspective, core conditions are not discrete entities but are interrelated into the flow of the counseling session. Wickman and Campbell (2003) provide an analysis of how Carl Rogers implemented core conditions in his counseling session with "Gloria" (see Shostrom's "Three Approaches to Psychotherapy" film series, 1965). They conclude that Rogers's conversational style did incorporate his core conditions in a manner consistent with his client-centered theory.

Social Influence Model. Strong's (1968) social influence model is another theory that emphasizes the importance of counselor-offered conditions in the counseling process. Strong's model has two stages, representing an integration of social psychology into counseling theory. During the first stage, the counselor attempts to be perceived by the client as expert, attractive, and trustworthy. When this occurs, the counselor establishes a power base. In the second stage of Strong's model, the counselor uses the power base to exert positive influence on the client within the counseling process. Extensive research efforts have been conducted to test both stages of Strong's model (see Corrigan, Dell, Lewis, & Schmidt, 1980; Heppner & Dixon, 1981; and Heppner & Claiborn, 1989, for literature reviews). For example, Heppner and Claiborn provide an overview of studies that have evaluated each stage of Strong's model.

Studies evaluating the first stage of Strong's model attempt to identify what factors promote the client's perception of the counselor as expert, attractive, and trustworthy.

Counselors tend to be perceived as *expert* when they have objective evidence of training and utilize prestigious cues (Angle & Goodyear, 1984; Littrell, Caffrey, & Hopper, 1987); use frequent, consistent, and responsive nonverbal behavior such as touch, smiling, and body leans (Roll, Crowley, & Rappl, 1985; Strohmer & Biggs, 1983; Tyson & Wall, 1983); and use narrative analogies and empathic responses (Suit & Paradise, 1985). Counselors are perceived as *attractive* when they have objective evidence of training (Angle & Goodyear, 1984; Paradise, Conway, & Zweig, 1986), have status (McCarthy, 1982), and are self-disclosing (Andersen & Andersen, 1985; Curran & Loganbell, 1985). Counselors appear more *trustworthy* when they use credible introductions and reputational cues (Bernstein & Figioli, 1983; Littrell et al., 1987), responsive nonverbal behavior (Hackman & Claiborn, 1982), and verbal and nonverbal cues associated with confidentiality (La Fromboise & Dixon, 1981; Merluzzi & Brischetto, 1983).

As noted, the second stage of Strong's model suggests that once counselors establish a power base by appearing expert, attractive, and trustworthy, they can exert a positive influence on the client. The majority of the studies reviewed by Heppner and Claiborn (1989) provide support for the second stage of Strong's model. For example, expertness, attractiveness, and trustworthiness are related to client satisfaction (Heppner & Heesacker, 1983; McNeill, May, & Lee, 1987), changes in the client's self-concept (Dorn & Day, 1985), favorable counseling outcomes (La Crosse, 1980), and less-premature terminators (McNeill et al., 1987).

Counselor- and Client-Offered Conditions.   The working alliance is another concept that can be used to describe the counseling relationship. It goes beyond focusing on counselor-offered conditions and includes counselor- and client-offered conditions. Several models of the working alliance have emerged from the literature (Bordin, 1979; Gelso & Carter, 1985; Greenson, 1967). Bordin's model has received considerable attention (Kokotovic & Tracey, 1990). Bordin (1979) suggests that the working alliance is composed of three parts: agreement between the counselor and client in terms of the goals of counseling, agreement between the counselor and client in terms of the tasks of counseling, and the emotional bond between the counselor and client.

Research has suggested that positive outcomes in counseling are enhanced if the working alliance is established early in counseling (Kivlighan, 1990). Al-Darmaki and Kivlighan (1993) also note that the literature suggests that the working alliance is dependent on four factors: client precounseling characteristics such as motivation and interpersonal skills, counselor's personal characteristics, counselor's skills, and the match between the client's needs and the counselor's skills and resources. Gelso and Fretz (2001) and Lazarus (1993) have commented on the fourth factor (the importance of the counselor-client fit). Gelso and Fretz suggest that the strength of the working alliance depends on the degree of agreement relating to goals and tasks of counseling and the level of emotional attachment between the counselor and client. Lazarus (1993) goes on to note that the counseling relationship should be characterized by counselors functioning like "authentic chameleons," adjusting their therapeutic style to the unique and emerging needs of clients.

Stage Two: Assessment and Diagnosis

Assessment and diagnosis contribute to several important aspects of the counseling process. They can help a counselor develop an in-depth understanding of a client and identify mental disorders that require attention. This understanding can facilitate goal setting and also suggest types of intervention strategies.

Assessment procedures can be divided into two categories: standardized and nonstandardized measures (Kottler & Brown, 2000). Standardized measures include psychological tests that have a standardized norm group. Nonstandardized measures do not have a standardized norm group and include strategies such as the clinical interview and assessment of life history.

Diagnosis is a medical term that means "identification of the disease-causing pathogens responsible for a physical illness" (Nathan & Harris, 1980, p. 110). Rosenhan and Seligman (1995) identify four reasons for making a diagnosis: facilitating communication shorthand, indicating possible treatment strategies, communicating etiology, and aiding in scientific investigation. Additional information regarding assessment and diagnosis can be found in Chapter 4.

Stage Three: Formulation of Counseling Goals

Cormier and Hackney (1993) describe three functions that goals serve in the counseling process: motivational, educational, and evaluative.

First, goals can have a motivational function, especially when clients are involved in establishing the counseling goals. Clients appear to work harder on goals they help create (Cormier & Hackney, 1993). They may also be more motivated when they have specific, concrete goals to work toward. Concrete goals can help clients focus their energy on specific issues. It is also important for counselors to encourage clients to make a verbal commitment to work on a specific counseling goal. Clients tend to be more motivated to work when they have made a commitment to do so (Strong & Claiborn, 1982).

The second function of a counseling goal is educational. From this perspective, clients can learn new skills and behaviors that they can use to enhance their functioning. For example, a counseling goal might be to become more assertive. During assertiveness training, clients can learn skills to enhance their functioning in interpersonal situations.

The third function of a counseling goal is evaluative. Clear goals allow the counselor and client an opportunity to evaluate progress. Goals can also be useful in implementing research strategies, and they provide a means for counselor accountability.

We can also conceptualize counseling goals as either process or outcome goals (Cormier & Hackney, 1993). *Process goals* establish the conditions necessary to make the counseling process work. These goals relate to the issues of formulating a positive relationship by promoting the core conditions, as described earlier in this chapter. Process goals are primarily the counselor's responsibility. *Outcome goals* specify what the client hopes to accomplish in counseling. The counselor and client should agree on these goals and modify them as necessary. George and Cristiani (1995) identify five types of outcome goals: facilitating behavior change, enhancing coping skills, promoting decision making, improving relationships, and facilitating the client's potential. The following overview expands on these five outcome goals.

1. *Facilitating behavior change.*　Some form of behavior change is usually necessary for clients to resolve their concerns. The amount of change necessary varies from client to client. For example, one client might need counseling to learn how to deal effectively with a child, whereas another might require psychotherapy to change an unhealthy, stressful lifestyle.

2. *Enhancing coping skills.* Erikson (1968) identified several developmental tasks and associated coping mechanisms unique to the various stages of development. Blocher (1974) later created a developmental counseling approach that identified coping skills necessary to proceed through the life span. For example, intimacy and commitment are developmental tasks of young adulthood. Coping behaviors necessary to meet these developmental tasks include appropriate sexual behavior, risk-taking behavior, and value-consistent behavior such as giving and helping. In more general terms, many clients may require help coping with life. They may have problems dealing with stress, anxiety, or a dysfunctional lifestyle. In these situations, clients may benefit from a stress management program that includes relaxation, meditation, and exercise.

3. *Promoting decision making.* Some clients have difficulty making decisions. They may feel that no matter what they decide, it will be wrong. They may even think they are "going crazy." Difficulty making decisions is often a normal reaction to a stressful life situation such as a recent divorce. In these situations, the counselor may want to reassure clients that they are not going crazy. Helping clients feel normal can encourage them and alleviate unnecessary worry. For clients who need help developing decision-making skills, the counselor may wish to take a more active role. It may be appropriate to involve family members if the client is suffering from a serious mental disorder such as an organic brain syndrome.

4. *Improving relationships.* Adler (1964) once suggested that the barometer of mental health is social interest. He believed that a person who did not have a close relationship with anyone was at risk for mental problems. Glasser (1965) supported this notion when he noted that all people need one or more reciprocal relationships in which they feel loved and understood and experience a sense of caring. Counselors can use a variety of counseling strategies to help clients improve their interpersonal relations. These strategies include social-skill training programs (Argyle, 1981), group counseling that focuses on interpersonal relations (Rogers, 1970), couples therapy (Sager, 1976), and marital therapy (Humphrey, 1983).

5. *Facilitating the client's potential.* Goals in this category are more abstract and relate to the concepts of self-realization and self-actualization. Self-realization implies helping clients become all they can be as they maximize their creative potential. There can be roadblocks to self-realization that require the counselor's attention. For example, clients may become discouraged and want to quit at the first sign of failure. In these instances, the counselor can help clients gain a more realistic understanding of what is required to be successful. Maslow (1968) developed the concept of self-actualization, which relates to the need to fulfill one's potential. He believes that as people's basic needs are met, they will move toward self-actualization. Rogers (1981) incorporated the concept of self-actualization into his person-centered counseling approach. He believes that if the counselor establishes certain conditions, such as communicating nonpossessive warmth, unconditional positive regard, and empathy, then the client can move toward self-actualization and become a healthy, integrated person.

Stage Four: Intervention and Problem Solving

Once the counselor and client have formulated a counseling goal, they can determine what intervention strategy to implement. They may choose from a variety of interventions, including individual, group, couples, and family counseling. It may be best to begin with individual counseling for clients with problems of an intrapersonal nature. As clients become more secure, they may be able to benefit from the open dialogue that often characterizes group counseling. Couples or family counseling may be more appropriate for clients with difficulties of an interpersonal nature, as in a marital or parent-child conflict.

Involving clients in the process of selecting intervention strategies has some advantages. For example, Devine and Fernald (1973) note that this approach can help counselors avoid using strategies that a client has already tried without apparent success. Instead, the counselor and client together can select a strategy that seems realistic in terms of its strengths and weaknesses.

Cormier and Cormier (1998) provide the following guidelines, which encourage client involvement in selecting the appropriate intervention strategy. The counselor should provide an overview of the different treatment approaches available, describe the role of the counselor and client for each procedure, identify possible risks and benefits that may result, and estimate the time and cost of each procedure. In addition, it is important for the counselor to be sensitive to client characteristics such as values and beliefs when selecting an intervention strategy (Cormier & Hackney, 1993). This sensitivity should extend to multicultural issues. Counselors should also be aware of a client's personal strengths and weaknesses in selecting a counseling approach. For example, counselors should determine whether a client has the necessary self-control or ego strength to utilize a counseling strategy (Cormier & Hackney, 1993).

Problem-Solving Strategies. One way to conceptualize intervention is within the framework of problem solving. Dixon and Glover (1984) suggest that all counseling or psychotherapy is a problem-solving process, whether it involves individual, group, marriage, or family counseling. They note that since the counseling process is focused on helping a client resolve problems, counselors should develop a systematic approach to problem solving. Dixon and Glover also believe that counselors should attempt to teach clients how to use problem-solving skills in their daily lives. This approach would enable clients to learn skills that could contribute to their personal autonomy.

Several problem-solving approaches can be used in the counseling process (for example, Heppner & Krauskopf, 1987; Kanfer & Busemeyer, 1982). Kanfer and Busemeyer identify a six-stage model for problem solving: problem detection, problem definition, identification of alternative solutions, decision making, execution, and verification. This model is a behaviorally oriented approach that involves describing a particular problem in behavioral terms, identifying possible solutions associated with the problem, deciding on a course of action relative to the various alternative solutions, implementing the decision, and verifying whether the outcome is consistent with the expected outcome.

Heppner, Witty, and Dixon (2004) have identified the following as variables associated with problem solving and adjustment:

- Effective counseling is associated with resolving clients' problems and enhancing problem-solving abilities (for example, the number of alternatives generated in problem solving is associated with adjustment).
- Effective problem solvers are flexible, adaptive, and can handle stress. They can also develop strategies to reach their goals and satisfy their needs.
- Ineffective problem solvers have difficulty solving problems and coping with environmental stressors.
- Problem-solving appraisal is related to how well clients are able to address a wide array of life's challenges.

Heppner et al. (2004) contend that problem-solving appraisal has become an increasingly important aspect of the problem-solving process. Problem-solving appraisal has to do with clients' perceptions of their problem-solving ability (for example, how and whether the person can solve the problem). Butler and Meichenbaum (1981) suggest that appraisal of problem-solving skills influences problem-solving performance and outcomes of the problem-solving process. Bandura's (1986) self-efficacy theory provides support for the notion that belief in one's ability is related to performance outcomes.

Heppner and Petersen (1982) developed the Problem Solving Inventory (PSI) to provide a means of investigating the role of appraisal in problem solving. Heppner et al. (2004) reviewed over 120 studies that investigated problem-solving appraisal and human adjustment. They concluded that the PSI is a robust instrument that has been used to investigate a wide variety of issues, such as mental and physical health, coping with stress, and educational and vocational issues. For example, clients who do not believe they have effective problem-solving skills are more prone to depression.

Heppner et al. (2004) suggest that the PSI can be used in clinical practice to assess problem-solving styles, to create goals associated with problem-solving deficits (including issues relating to appraisal), and to identify appropriate problem-solving interventions to address these goals. For example, clients with negative problem-solving appraisal and hopelessness and depression tend to be at higher risk for suicide than are clients who are depressed but who have more positive appraisals of their problem-solving skills.

Problem-solving strategies can also be used in conjunction with counseling theories. Nystul (1995, 1999) developed a four-step problem-solving model based on Adler's and Glasser's theories. This problem-solving model can be used with children, adolescents, or adults and has a built-in mechanism to enhance clients' motivation for involvement in counseling and minimize client resistance. This model can be especially useful in brief-counseling approaches. An overview of the Nystul problem-solving model is as follows.

1. Step 1 is based on Glasser's theory (Glasser, 1989). It explores what the client is doing that is problematic and adding an "ing" to it to help the client realize the control he or she has over what he or she is doing (for example, angering).
2. Step 2 is based on Adlerian psychology (Adler, 1969) and involves exploring the purpose or psychology of use of the client's behavior. This process involves asking the client, "I'm sure your angering [or whatever it is that is problematic] has served some purpose and has been useful to you or you would not be doing it. I wonder when it all began, . . . when you first remember using angering." Together the counselor and

client can then explore some early memories in terms of what needs the client may have met while engaging in the problematic behavior. Maslow's hierarchy of needs can be used to help identify possible needs that were met.

Step 2 is the most important phase of the problem-solving approach. It is respectful in that it recognizes that the problematic behavior must be useful or the client would not be doing the angering (or other behavior). This is in contrast to many approaches that simply say things such as "I hear a lot of shoulds and musts in your statements. These sound irrational and can be the cause of your problems." By showing respect to the psychology of use of the client's inefficient approach, the counselor can minimize resistance to the change process and maximize motivation for change.

3. Step 3 involves helping the client realize the cost of not changing. It is based on Homans' (1962) social exchange theory (from social psychology), which suggests that people will change when they realize that the behavior they are engaged in is costing more than it is getting them. During this step, the counselor can help clients realize that what they did to meet their needs as children does not work to meet their needs as adults. This realization can be a paradoxical point in therapy, shifting the client's motivation toward increased involvement in the change process.

4. Step 4 involves helping the client develop a new approach that meets the needs identified in step 2 without the costs associated with step 3. This may involve helping the client learn new coping skills and other strategies necessary to be successful in his or her new approach.

A Case Example. A brief case example can be used to illustrate the four steps of the Nystul problem-solving method. Tom was a 45-year-old physician who had lost two jobs because of angry outbursts in front of his supervisors and had recently been given an ultimatum from his fiancée that he either get his anger under control or she "will be history." During step 1 of the problem-solving approach, the counselor and Tom identified angering as the problem that he needed help with. Tom liked the idea of adding the "ing" to anger because it gave him a feeling of control over his problematic behavior.

Step 2 involved exploring the psychology of use of his angering. Tom recalled several early memories that related to when he first engaged in angering. For example, his first early memory was of when he had just moved to a new city and had no friends. On the first day of school, he got into a fight and broke another boy's nose. Blood was everywhere, and people gathered around and said he was "one tough guy." After the fight, several other boys wanted to be his friend. Tom's initial experience with angering resulted in enhancing his self-esteem and belonging needs.

Step 3 involved helping Tom become aware of the cost of his angering. In this process, Tom and his counselor did a cost-benefit analysis of his angering (what he gets from it versus what it is costing him). Quickly it became clear that his angering worked for him when he was a child to meet his basic needs of self-esteem and belonging, but it did not work for him as an adult. In fact, angering was having an opposite effect in that it was driving people away and making them think he was immature and "infantile" in his behavior. Recognition of the paradoxical effect of angering helped Tom increase his motivation for letting go of his angering and developing more efficient means of meeting his needs.

The counselor then provided Tom insight into his problematic behavior by noting that what works for people as children often does not work for adults (that is, the primitive tools children use such as angering are not acceptable in adult relationships). However, people continue to use these primitive tools because their private logic (which is primarily unconscious) tricks them into thinking that they must use these tools to meet their needs. Providing Tom with this insight seemed to help normalize his angering and minimize his resistance to working through his problem.

Step 4 involved helping Tom learn a new approach to use to meet his needs without the cost associated with angering. Tom saw angering as reactive to conflict situations, and he wanted to be more proactive. Together the counselor and he decided that encouragement could be an approach to avoid conflict and work through conflict from a more positive perspective. Encouragement was also seen as an excellent tool to meet needs such as self-esteem and belonging. The counselor and Tom then spent two sessions helping him develop and implement his new approach, which they called encourag*ing,* to help him realize the control he had with this approach.

Stage Five: Termination and Follow-Up

Perhaps the ultimate goal in counseling is for counselors to become obsolete or unnecessary to their clients. This result can occur when clients have worked through their concerns and are able to proceed forward in their lives without the counselor's assistance. At this point, counseling can be terminated. It is usually best for the counselor and client to agree on a termination date, reducing the chance of premature termination or feelings of ambivalence.

Quintana and Holahan (1992, p. 299) note that research has identified four components of termination that are associated with positive outcomes in the counseling process. These components are discussion of the end of counseling, review of the course of counseling, closure of the counselor-client relationship, and discussion of the client's future post-counseling plans. Based on the literature, it is clear that counselors should attempt to address these four components to prepare clients appropriately for termination (Lamb, 1985). In this process, clients can explore what they have learned in counseling and identify how they will apply that knowledge to enhance their psychological functioning. In addition, clients and counselors can process their feelings regarding the counseling relationship and work toward closure regarding potential affective issues. Counselors can also arrange with clients to have a brief follow-up counseling session (for example, several weeks after the last formal session) to see how they are doing and provide additional counseling services as necessary.

Stage Six: Research and Evaluation

Research and evaluation can occur at any time during the counseling process or after termination. Some behavioral approaches utilize single-case or small-group research designs that require counselors to evaluate counseling whenever they implement an intervention strategy. These research procedures involve face-to-face interaction between the counselor and client. Other research procedures that may or may not involve direct interaction between counselor and client are empirical research involving hypothesis testing and alternative methodologies such as the discovery approach. These procedures may be used before or after a client has terminated (see Chapter 5 for a description of research methods).

Research and evaluation are an integral part of the counseling process. They contribute to the science dimension of counseling by promoting an objective understanding of what is occurring in counseling. Counselors can also use research and evaluation to communicate accountability.

Listening Skills

Listening skills play a vital role in virtually all aspects of counseling. Listening is a procedure that helps clients tell *their* story and feel connected and understood by a caring and interested person. It is a complex process that involves a number of strategies. Some of these strategies include attending (or tuning into) the verbal and nonverbal messages of clients, encouraging clients to freely express themselves, developing a phenomenological understanding of clients, and responding in an appropriate manner.

Listening skills can play an important role in all stages of the counseling process. Listening is especially important in terms of establishing a positive counseling relationship because the counselors can communicate care and understanding through listening-skill responses. Listening skills can be used in assessment, diagnosis, and goal setting as the counselor attempts to gain a phenomenological understanding of the client (seeing the client's concern from the client's perspective). Listening skills are useful interventions in the sense that talking in and of itself can have a healing power. This can occur when clients have their thoughts and feelings validated or normalized or can simply result from the letting go of feelings in the process of catharsis. Listening can also be an important tool for counselors during termination and follow-up and research and evaluation to determine how clients conceptualize their progress and the efficacy of counseling.

Listening skills can be conceptualized in terms of primary and secondary skills. Primary listening skills focus on generating the phenomenological understanding of the client and include open-ended questions, paraphrasing, reflection of feeling, minimal encouragers, clarifying remarks, summarizing, and perception check. Secondary listening skills do not promote a phenomenological perspective but can be facilitative (in terms of the counseling process) while the counselor is utilizing listening skills. Secondary skills include normalizing, structuring, and probing. An overview of listening skills follows, along with a brief counseling vignette to illustrate these skills.

Primary Listening Skills

Open-Ended Questions. These are questions such as, "What would you like to talk about?" or "How does this affect you?" These questions cannot be answered with a simple yes or no but instead encourage the client to elaborate on responses.

Paraphrasing. This can be useful after a client has talked at some length about a particular situation or problem. Paraphrasing allows the counselor to communicate that he or she has not only heard the client but understands what has been said. A paraphrase should be "tentatively" worded so the client can correct the counselor if necessary. Paraphrasing, like so many things, takes practice. A key to good paraphrasing is to keep it simple.

Paraphrasing often involves taking one or two key words that the client has said and finding analogous words. For example, if the client says, "I enjoy taking a run with my dog after work," a possible paraphrase is, "You like to jog with your dog." In this example, the counselor has found analogous words for enjoy (like) and run (jog). Another way to paraphrase is to repeat the client's overall message using slightly different words. For example, the client may say, "I like to take a jog after a stressful day because it helps me unwind." A possible paraphrase would be, "Jogging is a good stress release for you."

Reflection of Feeling.   This involves the counselor reflecting what he or she senses the client is feeling. It communicates that the counselor not only understands how the client is feeling but also empathizes with the client. For example, if a client tells the counselor how her husband insults her in public, the counselor could respond by saying, "This really makes you mad." Again, as in paraphrasing, it is important to phrase the reflection of feeling statement tentatively so the client can correct the counselor if necessary.

It is also important to be specific in attempting to reflect the client's feelings. For example, the word "upset" is usually too general and may not communicate a clear understanding of the client's feelings. It is therefore useful for counselors to develop a broad repertoire of words associated with various emotional states. Adler and Towne (1996) have provided a comprehensive list of words depicting various emotions (see Table 3.2).

Minimal Encouragers.   This technique allows the counselor to facilitate what the client is saying without changing the client's line of thought. Minimal encouragers include such words of acknowledgment as "yes," "yeah," "oh," "ah-ha," and so forth.

Clarifying Remarks.   This technique can be used when the counselor either did not hear or does not understand what the client has said. For example, the counselor could say "I didn't understand that," or "Could you go through that again?" Through the use of clarifying statements, the counselor communicates that he or she genuinely wants to understand what the client is saying.

Summarizing.   This involves restating some of the major concerns the client has mentioned during a particular session. Obviously this helps identify the client's areas of concern. Summarizing can also lead to a "perception check" and to the development of problem-solving strategies.

Perception Check.   This technique helps the counselor determine what the client wants to work on. It follows the summary statement as illustrated in the following example: "You seem to be worried about your performance at school, your relationship with your wife, and your lack of money (the summary statement). I know all these problems concern you. I was wondering if you would like to focus on one of these areas, or is there something else that you haven't mentioned that you would like to talk about?"

TABLE 3.2 **Words Depicting Feelings**

afraid	disappointed	hurried	protective
aggravated	disgusted	hurt	puzzled
amazed	disturbed	hysterical	refreshed
ambivalent	ecstatic	impatient	regretful
angry	edgy	impressed	relieved
annoyed	elated	inhibited	resentful
anxious	embarrassed	insecure	restless
apathetic	empty	interested	ridiculous
ashamed	enthusiastic	intimidated	romantic
bashful	envious	irritable	sad
bewildered	excited	jealous	sentimental
bitchy	exhausted	joyful	sexy
bitter	fearful	lazy	shaky
bored	fed up	lonely	shocked
brave	fidgety	loving	shy
calm	flattered	lukewarm	sorry
cantankerous	foolish	mad	strong
carefree	forlorn	mean	subdued
cheerful	free	miserable	surprised
cocky	friendly	mixed up	suspicious
cold	frustrated	mortified	tender
comfortable	furious	neglected	tense
concerned	glad	nervous	terrified
confident	glum	numb	tired
confused	grateful	optimistic	trapped
content	happy	paranoid	ugly
crazy	harassed	passionate	uneasy
defeated	helpless	peaceful	vulnerable
defensive	high	pessimistic	warm
delighted	hopeful	playful	weak
depressed	horrible	pleased	wonderful
detached	hostile	possessive	worried
devastated	humiliated	pressured	

Source: From *Looking Out/Looking In* (8th ed.) by R. B. Adler and N. Towne, Harcourt/Brace, 1996.

Secondary Listening Skills

Normalizing. Normalizing involves helping clients understand that what they are going through is a normal reaction to life (Nystul, 1994). Normalizing can alleviate unnecessary stress and anxiety so that clients can focus their energy on recovery. The opposite of normalizing could be called *pathologicalizing,* which involves overdiagnosing or engaging in other activities with clients that make them feel sicker or discouraged. An example of normalizing is to tell someone whose husband just died and is very sad and indecisive that it is normal to have intense feelings of depression and to have difficulty making decisions after a loved one has died.

Structuring.   Structuring involves describing the role and function of the counselor and client and provides a rationale for what the counselor is doing in counseling (Nystul, 1994). It helps clients understand what is going on in counseling, increasing their motivation and enabling them to take an active role in the counseling process. Structuring can also help them learn how to be their own self-therapist since they are assisted in understanding some of the dynamics of the counseling process.

Probing.   Probing involves asking for specific information such as questions relating to a suicidal assessment. Probing may be necessary during the use of listening skills to obtain specific information that is critical to understanding the client. It is important to minimize the use of probing while using listening skills because it takes the perspective away from the client's phenomenological field and forces the client to respond to the counselor's frame of reference.

Counseling Vignette

The following brief counseling vignette provides an illustration of how the primary and secondary listening skills can be used.

COUNSELOR: What would you like to talk about today? (open-ended)

CLIENT: My daughter has me really worried.

COUNSELOR: About what? (open-ended)

CLIENT: She's dating someone who is 15 years older than her.

COUNSELOR: That could worry anybody. (normalizing)

CLIENT: I just feel that in some ways he seems old enough to be her father.

COUNSELOR: This really does bother you. (reflection of feeling)

CLIENT: Yes, it does.

COUNSELOR: Could you tell me more how you feel about this? (open-ended)

CLIENT: I really don't know where to begin.

COUNSELOR: Perhaps you could start by telling me the age of your daughter. (probing)

CLIENT: Sure, she's 17 years old.

COUNSELOR: How does it make you feel for your 17-year-old daughter to be dating this 32-year-old man? (open-ended)

CLIENT: I feel like he's taking advantage of her and there is something immoral about it.

COUNSELOR: You are really worried about her. (reflection of feeling)

CLIENT: The whole thing just doesn't make sense to me.

COUNSELOR: Things don't add up. (paraphrase)

CLIENT: It's a crazy world.

COUNSELOR: I don't quite understand what you mean. Could you run that one by me again? (clarifying)

CLIENT: Sometimes I think she's just looking for a father figure.

COUNSELOR: Searching for something she is missing? (paraphrase)

CLIENT: I guess I just feel inadequate.

COUNSELOR: Ah-ha. (minimal encourager)

CLIENT: Yeah, like I'm one big zero.

COUNSELOR: You really do have some strong negative feelings about yourself. (reflection of feeling)

CLIENT: Yes, I could write a book on that one. My ex-wife said I had a BIG inferiority complex.

COUNSELOR: There really is a lot going on there. (paraphrase)

CLIENT: I guess my life is one big mess. I'm probably only supposed to talk about one problem at a time.

COUNSELOR: No, in counseling we want to get an overview of your concerns—especially during the initial stages of counseling. (structuring)

CLIENT: So what do we do now?

COUNSELOR: Well, so far we have identified some concerns about your daughter and her older boyfriend and your feeling about yourself. (summary)

CLIENT: Right.

COUNSELOR: Is there anything else you would like to tell me that you think I should know, or would you like to focus in on one of these concerns? (perception check)

Effective Listening "Don'ts"

This section provides some helpful guidelines for effective listening. Dinkmeyer and McKay's (1997) "roadblocks to effective listening" have been incorporated into the following list of things to avoid.

Avoid Moralizing or Being Judgmental.   Imposing one's belief system onto the client can cause defensive reactions and be a demoralizing, dehumanizing experience.

Avoid Premature Analysis.   Premature analysis involves identifying meaning behind the message, such as motivational forces associated with a particular action. It can occur when the counselor uses the word "because" in his or her paraphrase. For example, if the client says, "No matter what I do, nothing seems to go right," a counselor engaging in premature analysis might respond with, "Nothing is going right because you lack confidence in yourself."

When a counselor responds in this manner, the client may respond to the counselor's hunches (for example, "Is nothing going right because I lack confidence?"). This may result in redirecting the line of thought from client to the counselor. Once a counselor has gained a phenomenological understanding of the client, he may find it appropriate to analyze the content of the client's message and provide insights to the client (for example, suggest that a lack of self-confidence may be a problem for the client).

Avoid "Parroting."   Parroting means repeating exactly what the client has said, just changing the order of the words. This communicates what the counselor has *heard* but may not understand (like a parrot). For example, if the client says, "I really like to jog after work," the counselor responding like a parrot might say, "After work, you really like to jog."

Avoid "Gimmicky" Phrases.   Some counselors get into the habit of using a "lead in" phrase such as "Did I hear you say" each time they paraphrase. This often sounds "gimmicky" to a client.

Effective Listening "Do's"

Decide to Be in the Role of the Listener.   Effective listening is a skill the counselor must *decide* to take on. It involves utilizing a series of skills: attending and focusing on the client, encouraging the client to freely express him- or herself, attempting to develop a phenomenological understanding of the client, and implementing an appropriate response.

Try to Sense the Client's Inner Message.   Communication is a complex process. It is important to learn to listen with a "third ear." The counselor needs to learn to go beyond the spoken word and try to listen to what is really being communicated.

Be Aware of Nonverbal Communication.   A large percentage of communication is nonverbal. It often provides the most authentic indicator of the client's emotional state.

Allow Yourself to Correct Impressions.   Being in the role of listener is a tentative process. It is a joint effort in which the counselor works with the client until he or she gains a clear understanding of the client's situation.

A Final Thought Regarding Listening Skills

Becoming an effective listener is an art that takes time to develop. One of the best ways to learn listening skills is to obtain a videotape critique of one's work from an experienced counselor. It can also be helpful to do cocounseling with an experienced counselor and obtain feedback from the counselor regarding one's counseling approach.

Developing listening skills can be discouraging. At times a counselor may even feel he or she is becoming a less effective communicator. During these times, the counselor could consider that he or she is in the process of becoming a more effective communicator. With practice, these new skills will become integrated into the counselor's natural mode of responding.

Recent Trends in the Counseling Process

This section addresses three emerging trends that provide paradigm shifts for conceptualizing the counseling process. The first trend explores the role of emotions in the counseling process. For instance, emerging theories of emotions such as emotional balancing can provide clients with a "road map" to their emotions and guidelines for obtaining emotional balance in interpersonal relationships. Postmodernism and brief-counseling approaches represent two other emerging trends in counseling. These trends appear to be complementary to one another in that they recognize the role that narratives and storytelling can play in the counseling process. An overview of these three emerging trends follows.

Emotions

To a large degree, counseling is a process that focuses on helping clients with feelings such as shame, guilt, and anger. Unfortunately, there has been little emphasis on the role of emotions in counseling. Historically, emotions have taken a back seat in terms of conceptualizing major schools of counseling. For example, Ellis's (2005) rational-emotive behavior therapy emphasizes cognitions and behavior over emotions (i.e., emotions can be changed by focusing on changing cognitions and behaviors). The pendulum may be swinging toward emotions. For instance, there is some evidence that Beck (1996) has elevated the importance of emotions in cognitive therapy.

Warwar and Greenberg (2000) provide an overview of the role of emotions in counseling. These scholars suggest that emotions serve an adaptive–survival function enabling people to meet basic needs and derive personal meaning in life. They contend that adaptive emotions should be developed and utilized in counseling to facilitate problem solving and maximize positive change. Dysfunctional emotions should be addressed to help clients overcome impasses to change. For example, clients may experience problems with emotional processing such as an inability to consider and integrate emotional experiences.

Greenberg and Paivio (1997) describe three phases associated with the use of emotions in the counseling process. The first phase is the *bonding* phase, which involves emotional validation to enable clients to assess their emotions. *Evoking* is the second phase and involves activating emotional expressions associated with counseling issues. The evoking phases involves exploring and differentiating emotional expressions such as the relationship between primary emotions, needs, and thoughts. The third phase is referred to as *restructuring*. Restructuring involves working through dysfunctional emotions and faulty self-perceptions and creating adaptive emotions and a positive self-concept. For example, an adult who was sexually abused has problems with feelings of shame and thoughts of being worthless. Restructuring could involve helping the client work through the shame by unleashing unresolved anger and restructuring self-perceptions to "I'm worthwhile regardless of what others do."

Emotional balancing (Nystul, 2002a, 2002b) represents a theory of emotions based on the earlier work of Minuchin (1974). This theory of emotions can be used in counseling or as a self-help method to create a "road map" to one's emotions and to facilitate emotional balance in interpersonal relationships. Emotional balancing conceptualizes emotions on a continuum from emotional disengagement at one end, emotional balance in the middle, and emotional enmeshment at the other end of the continuum.

Emotional disengagement is characterized by high levels of independence and separateness. Emotional disengagement represents an extreme emotional position in which a person no longer attempts to maintain any form of a relationship with another person. An example of emotional disengagement could be a parent who disowns an adolescent for repeated acts of belligerence.

Emotional enmeshment is characterized by diffuse boundaries and a lack of individualization between people. Emotional enmeshment represents an emotional extreme whereby emotions interfere with one's ability to effectively relate to others. Emotional enmeshment can occur when a parent's emotions undermine choice and responsibility during disciplining. For example, a father attempts to discipline his daughter for staying out late and drinking and driving. While discussing the incident with the teen, the father loses his temper, yells at the teen, and grounds her for six months. The parent's emotional enmeshment allows the teen to shift her focus from taking responsibility for her bad choices (drinking and driving) and instead focus on how "crazy" and unreasonable she believes her parent is behaving.

Emotional balance is characterized by clear boundaries, autonomy, intimacy, and a moderate degree of connection and cohesion between people. Emotional balance represents a healthy emotional state whereby a person is able to maintain some degree of emotional contact with others in a manner that maximizes psychological functioning. An example of emotional balance would be a parent maintaining a line of communication versus utilizing ultimatums with a troubled teen. Guidelines for promoting emotional balance include the following:

- Emotional balance can be maintained on different levels of emotional intensity by using appropriate communication strategies such as *I* messages versus *You* messages (see Dinkmeyer and McKay, 1997, for a description of *I* messages).
- Consider systemic issues to identify impasses to emotional balance (for example, when one parent becomes emotionally enmeshed, the other parent may become emotionally disengaged).
- Utilize the core conditions of empathy, respect, concreteness, and self-disclosure counseling developed by Carl Rogers (1961) and others to promote healthy, functional relationships and emotional balance.
- Develop a plan of action by utilizing the emotions continuum to determine where one is emotionally, where one would like to go, and how to get there.

There appears to be much promise in terms of the role of emotions in counseling. Additional research and development is necessary regarding integrating theories of emotions into the counseling process.

Postmodern Trends

As noted in Chapter 1, postmodernism represents an emerging trend in counseling. It is contributing to a potential paradigm shift that is creating new opportunities for conceptualizing the counseling process. Bitter and Corey (1996) differentiate modern from postmodern in terms of different ways of viewing reality. Modernists believe in an objective reality that is independent from the observer, whereas postmodernists contend there is a subjective reality that varies contextually in relation to the observer. The modernist position is similar to the behaviorist theory, which focuses on overt measurable behavior such as recognizing the state of depression when a person has problems with sleep and appetite, loses interest in things that used to be fun, and so forth. The postmodernist position parallels experiential theories and contends that people are depressed when they experience depression as defined within the context of social-cultural forces such as language and narratives internalized by the individual.

Constructivism and social constructionism are two psychological perspectives that have evolved from postmodernism. Constructivism is primarily associated with cognitive behavioral approaches (see Neimeyer & Mahoney, 1995), and social constructionism has become an important dimension of marriage and family counseling (see Anderson & Goolishian, 1992). Gutterman (1996a) contrasts constructivism and social constructionism by noting that constructivists contend that knowledge is based on the subjective cognitions of the individual, whereas social constructionists hold that reality is constructed from the conversations of people.

The postmodern theoretical perspectives of constructivism and social constructionism appear to have more in common than they have differences. Both are concerned with issues relating to epistemology, "the theory of knowledge, or how we know what we think and what we think we think" (Durrant, 1995, p. 3). These theories appear to suggest that human experience is a highly individualized process based contextually on the interactions of cognition, social-cultural forces, language, and narratives. Knowledge and the concept of "truth" are therefore subjective and generate the possibility of multiple realities best understood from a phenomenological perspective. Postmodernists also emphasize the role that narratives and storytelling play in psychological functioning. According to this theory, people are constantly constructing stories about their lives, creating "storied lives" (Bitter & Corey, 1996).

The process of counseling and psychotherapy is therefore one of exploring life stories to gain insight into how clients generate personal meaning. When necessary, counselors can help clients engage in narrative repair, reauthoring life stories to help clients create opportunities to cope effectively and generate new meaning to life. Other goals of counseling include helping clients generate solution-focused approaches to problem solving and enhancing awareness of the effects of the dominant culture on human life (Bitter & Corey, 1996).

Bitter and Corey (1996) and Carlsen (1995) have identified techniques associated with postmodern counseling theories. These are summarized as follows.

Listening with an Open Mind. The counseling relationship is characterized as one of equality. Counselors avoid preconceived ideas or taking a judgmental position. The counselor attempts to empower clients by conveying optimism and encouragement and respecting and giving voice to the client's stories. The process is similar to qualitative research, where the counselor and client are coinvestigators attempting to discover meanings reflected in their stories and narratives.

An example of listening with an open mind is using listening skills to obtain a phenomenological understanding of the client. In this process, the counselor can convey a nonjudgmental position, encouraging clients to tell their story from their perspective.

Questions That Make a Difference. The counselor engages the client in dialogues or conversations that help clients address questions that can make a difference in terms of positive change. Questions tend to be circular or relational as reflected in the systemic concept of circular causality (for example, exploring the interrelationship between current and past problems).

An example of a question that could make a difference is a counselor asking the client, "Describe what it's like when you don't have this problem?" This type of question can make a difference by getting the client to focus on what works as opposed to what does not work, thus replacing a cycle of defeatism with one of hope.

Deconstruction and Externalization.   Externalization can be used to help clients deconstruct problems associated with their storied lives in two ways. Counselors can help clients gain valuable insights and minimize resistance by having them remove themselves from the problems associated with their storied lives. In the role of external observer, clients may be more open to engage in an adversarial relationship with their problems (deconstruction) and develop new methods for problem resolution (reconstruction). Another technique for deconstruction is similar to that used by feminists. It involves scientifically examining problematic narratives from the dominant culture (such as patriarchy) to provide evidence that refutes (deconstructs) the dominant culture's position.

An example of externalizing could be to ask a client named Sam, "How does this affect Sam?" This process can minimize resistance by providing an indirect voice for Sam to express his concerns. Externalizing techniques such as this also facilitate story deconstruction, since Sam may feel more free to be critical of his story with "Sam" being referred to in the third person.

Alternative Stories, Reauthoring, and Narrative Repair.   Clients are encouraged to rewrite their storied lives, creating alternative stories that are more consistent with their goals and aspirations. Reauthoring and narrative repair can be reflected in numerous ways, such as clients who begin to focus on solutions rather than problems.

Alternative stories, reauthoring, and narrative repair are terms that mean essentially the same thing (they help clients develop more functional or meaningful life stories). For example, a client's story may be one of sorrow, loss, and despair owing to the death of a family member. In time, the client can learn to engage in narrative repair and reauthor an alternative story that reflects purpose and hope in life. The following *Personal Note* describes the "Columbo" technique as a method of helping clients with the process of narrative repair and reauthoring.

Use of Metaphors.   A metaphor is a figure of speech that suggests that one idea is similar or analogous to another idea or concept. Metaphors can be client generated or counselor generated. An example of a client-generated metaphor would be an individual saying his marriage is like a "leaky boat." Wickman, Daniels, White, and Fesmire (1999) suggest that it is important to be aware of the metaphors that clients use during counseling. For example, the "leaky boat" metaphor could tell the counselor that the client feels that no matter what is addressed in marriage counseling, other problems will emerge. Counselor-generated metaphors can be used to help clients look at their problems from a different perspective. For example, in the following *Personal Note,* I use the metaphor of "going with the flow" to help children understand that cooperating with their teacher can be like going with the current of a river.

Metaphors are especially useful to overcome resistance by providing an indirect means of exploring painful issues and identifying alternative means of overcoming problems. In this regard, clients may not even be aware of the salient messages conveyed by metaphors as they "have a way of dropping below the surface of awareness to influence us in ways that we may not fully acknowledge or understand" (Carlsen, 1995, p. 131).

A Personal Note

I find the postmodern theories of constructivism and social constructionism very interesting. They offer exciting opportunities for developing creative counseling techniques. The "Columbo" technique and the use of metaphors in counseling are two examples of techniques that I have found useful in counseling. I developed the "Columbo" technique as a means of helping clients engage in narrative repair, or coauthoring more meaningful stories. The "Columbo" technique involves having the counselor act like the TV detective Columbo, who appears to lose track of a thought or need help from the suspect to clarify a point that he was confused about. In this process, the counselor can do such things as stop in mid-sentence and let the client finish the sentence, such as "You are really trying to. . . . " The client may respond by saying, "get my act together" and in doing so take responsibility for reauthoring his or her story in a more positive manner. Another "Columbo" technique is when the counselor says to the client, "I got the part about how you are convinced you are such a terrible parent. I'm just a bit confused about how a terrible parent is someone who has always been there for his children financially and emotionally and seems to care so much for his children's welfare. Perhaps you can help me understand that a bit better." As the parent offers his or her explanation, it will help him or her construct cognitions that foster more realistic, healthy narratives.

Metaphors are another counseling technique that are generating increased interest in counseling. I find the use of metaphors to be especially useful in working with children and adolescents. Metaphors involve the use of similes, or implied comparison, to symbolically represent an idea or a concept. An example of a metaphor that I am currently using with some of my students in Special Education is "going with the flow." In this metaphor, I suggest that life is like a river. I have the student visualize a river that he or she has seen, such as when going fishing. I have the student try to remember what the river was like and what the student saw floating down the river (such as leaves and so forth). I ask the student if the leaf had a motor to move it down the river, and the student says "no." I say, "You're right, leaves don't need motors to go down the river; they use the current of the river and 'go with the flow.'" I tell my students that they also can go with the flow when they listen to their teacher, follow instructions, get their work done, and try to get along with others in a polite and caring manner. Students that do not follow the rules will have their problems mounting up on them, and life for them will be like swimming against a current. I then have them imagine how it would feel to swim upriver against a current . . . against the flow of life.

Evaluation of Postmodern Trends. Postmodern trends and theories such as constructivism and social constructionism offer much promise in terms of conceptualizing the counseling process. They create opportunities to recognize the role that narrative psychology and diversity issues such as language and culture play in counseling. The postmodern perspective could provide another dimension to the multicultural counseling evolution.

Sexton and Whiston (1994) identify some concerns about postmodern trends such as social constructivism. For example, they note that social constructivism appears to be a theory that does not connect to any specific research methodology. Sexton and Whiston (1994) also suggest that social constructivism may be nothing more than "a call for relativism in which anything goes" (p. 69). Additional research is necessary to evaluate the postmodern theories and determine how they can be successfully integrated into counseling theory, research, and practice.

Brief-Counseling Approaches

Brief-counseling approaches are becoming increasingly popular and appear to characterize the counseling wave of the future. Koss and Shiang (1994) identify some of the factors that have contributed to the popularity of brief-counseling approaches. These are summarized as follows.

1. People seek counseling for help with specific problems and are only willing to commit to a few counseling sessions to resolve their problems. The mean number of sessions (regardless of theoretical orientation or if counseling is considered brief or nonbrief) is six to eight sessions, and 75 percent of those who are helped by counseling do so during the first six months they are in counseling.
2. Research has shown that brief counseling has efficacy rates similar to traditional approaches to counseling, especially when treating certain types of clients with certain types of disorders. Brief counseling is particularly effective for clients who relate well, are motivated, desire symptom relief, and suffer from a minor problem such as a mild depression or a severe stress reaction such as experiencing a natural disaster.
3. The popularity of brief counseling has to some degree evolved in response to managed care and its emphasis on time-limited, solution-focused counseling. Brief counseling is perceived to be a cost-effective alternative to traditional methods of counseling.

The origins of brief-counseling models can be traced to Milton Erickson (1954a), who was one of the most influential pioneers of brief counseling. Erickson was a genius at using paradoxical techniques and hypnosis (in as few as one session) to generate solutions to clients' problems. A number of other individuals have contributed to the movement toward brief approaches to counseling. Some of these are Haley (1984), De Shazer's solution-focused brief therapy (1985, 1991), O'Hanlon and Weiner-Davis (1989), and the Brief Therapy Project at the Mental Research Institute (Fisch, Weakland, & Segal, 1982). Forms of brief counseling have also been adapted to most of the major traditional schools of counseling (see Koss & Shiang, 1994; Steenbarger, 1992).

Littrell, Malia, and Vanderwood (1995) identify three main assumptions associated with brief approaches to counseling. The first assumption is that the problem clients present in counseling is the real problem. Although the problem can be related to some unknown deep-seated issues, simple straightforward methods are used whenever possible. The second assumption is that clients are capable of solving their own problems. Counselors need to help clients become aware of their strengths and how they can use them effectively. The third assumption is that change does not need to be large to make a significant difference. Small steps toward change may be all that is necessary to break self-defeating cycles and contribute to problem resolution. Durrant (1995) has identified a number of other assumptions associated with brief-counseling models, which are summarized as follows.

1. All problems have examples of exceptions, such as a person who has a problem with heights but on one occasion was able to go climb a historic landmark with friends.
2. Problems can be reframed in solution-focused terms.
3. If it's not broken, don't fix it. Do what is working more and stop doing what is not working.

4. It's not important to know what the problem is but what things will be like when the problem is solved.

These assumptions taken collectively suggest that brief counseling utilizes a strengths perspective that helps clients solve their problems as quickly and directly as possible.

Brief-Solution-Focused Counseling

The brief-solution-focused counseling model proposed in this text has four stages and is based primarily on brief-counseling models described by Durrant (1995), Koss and Shiang (1994), and Thompson (1996), as well as some of the techniques and procedures associated with postmodern theories of counseling.

Stage One: Establishing the Relationship and Defining the Problem. The counselor and client enter into a collaborative relationship. The counselor offers encouragement and hope and attempts to gain a phenomenological understanding of the client's life. Clients are encouraged to function as cocounselors and are empowered to take an active role in the counseling process from assessment through intervention and follow-up.

Problems are defined in simple direct terms void of complicated psychological jargon. When possible, counselors normalize the client's problems and experience and communicate "wellness" as opposed to using psychological labels that communicate "sickness." Expectations for change and positive action are communicated to foster a positive self-fulfilling prophecy. In addition, most brief counseling is practiced within a time-limited framework. This usually requires that the counselor and client determine as quickly as possible how many sessions will be required (or authorized by managed care) to resolve the problems.

Stage Two: Assessment and Establishing Treatment Goals. Rapid and early assessment is crucial in brief counseling. Assessment procedures serve a number of purposes such as determining whether a client is appropriate for brief counseling (for example, it is contraindicated for people with severe problems such as personality disorders, substance abuse, and psychosis), and it can also be used to obtain an overall understanding of clients and the nature of their problems. Assessment procedures can be directed at intrapsychic perspectives (within the person) as well as ecological perspectives (outside of the person). Assessment tends to focus on the here and now and avoid exploration of early life events. Another key aspect of assessment in brief-solution-focused counseling is assessing for strengths and resources and how clients can use these assets to resolve problems.

Standard traditional assessment procedures can be used in conjunction with assessment procedures unique to brief-solution-focused counseling. One commonly used assessment method in brief-counseling approaches is the scaling technique. This procedure involves having a client rate his or her problems on a 1 to 10 scale, with 10 representing resolution of the problem. Scaling questions are used that emphasize change, exceptions to the problem, and future aspirations. For example, a counselor could ask, "So you're a 3 now in terms of your anger management. When were you more than a 3, what was that like, what were you doing then, and how were things different?"

Counseling goals are established that are concrete, observable, and measurable. They allow for ongoing evaluation of the counseling process and establish a point of termination. Goals must be flexible and interface effectively with intervention strategies. Thompson (1996, p. 19) identifies the following key questions associated with counseling goals.

- What will be the very first sign that things are moving in the right direction?
- Who will be the first to notice?
- Are there small pieces of this that are already happening?
- What do you need to do to make it happen more?
- What else will you be doing differently when you no longer have this particular problem?

De Shazer's (1991) "miracle question" can be useful in generating counseling goals. The miracle question involves asking the client to imagine that a miracle occurred while he or she was asleep that solved the client's problem. What would be different in the client's life and how would he or she know that the miracle happened?

Stage Three: Designing and Implementing Interventions.   Interventions are designed to disrupt patterns of problematic behavior by introducing alternative ways of reacting to the problem. Some form of change (no matter how small) is a central component of intervention strategies. A focus on strengths or assets is another key concept associated with interventions used in brief-solution-focused counseling. Using this concept, counselors help clients discover what is working for them and how to use their strengths to overcome their problems.

The four interventions that are commonly used during the intervention stage are reframing, utilization, encouragement, and narrative repair. *Reframing* is a cognitive process that involves helping clients "frame" their problems in terms of what is right with their situation as opposed to what is wrong. *Utilization* involves helping clients find solutions within their problems. Solutions can be developed from the exceptions to the problem (for example, times when the client did not get anxious with heights) or from developing alternative methods of problem solving. *Encouragement* helps clients to believe in themselves, thus promoting self-efficacy and the "can-do" spirit. Encouragement helps overcome self-doubt and fosters a self-fulfilling prophecy for positive change. *Narrative repair* involves helping clients reauthor their stories to reflect a positive-strength perspective as opposed to a pathological-defeatist perspective.

Brief-solution-focused counseling is a task-action-results–oriented process whereby counselors and clients perceive their role as "doers" and not just "talkers." Clients are provided opportunities to learn solution-focused strategies and are encouraged to apply these strategies to their problems between sessions. Adjustments are made as necessary at the start of each session to ensure that clients can effectively make progress toward positive change.

Lewis and Osborn (2004) suggest that motivational interviewing (MI) can be used in conjunction with solution-focused counseling to facilitate the change process. MI is designed to instill hope, increase intrinsic motivation, enhance self-efficacy, and minimize resistance to change. The use of empathy is considered a key aspect of the MI approach. Two MI techniques are "change talk" and "roll with resistance." *Change talk* involves encouraging clients to engage in self-motivational statements associated with change. *Roll with the resistance* avoids an adversarial response to resistance. This technique recognizes that not all resistance is negative and may in fact be a self-protective response to avoiding unwanted change.

Stage Four: Termination, Follow-Up, and Evaluation. Once clients' problems have been resolved satisfactorily, they can terminate formal counseling. Brief-solution-focused counseling also encourages clients to become their own self-counselor and apply their problem-solving skills to new and emerging problems. In addition, the science of counseling suggests that research procedures can be used to evaluate the efficacy of the counseling experience. During the counseling process, clients can be provided opportunities to take an active role in the research process. In this regard, they can function as coinvestigators with counselors in an ongoing journey of discovery. Clients should be encouraged to continue to take an active role in self-evaluation after termination through processes such as self-monitoring and self-reflection.

Research on Brief Counseling. Koss and Shiang (1994) provide a comprehensive overview on the research that has been conducted on brief counseling. Results of their findings are summarized as follows. Brief-counseling approaches are being successfully applied to individual, group, and marriage and family counseling. Initial research efforts suggested that brief counseling was only suited for less severe problems such as adjustment reactions. More recent research indicates that brief counseling can be used successfully with a wide range of problems, including severe and chronic problems, if the treatment goals are reasonable. Some of the problems that brief counseling has been able to successfully treat are depression (Dobson, 1989), panic disorders (Beck, Sokol, Clark, Berchick, & Wright, 1992), and posttraumatic stress disorder (Foa, Rothbaum, Riggs, & Murdock, 1991).

Research efforts have also been directed at determining the client characteristics that are best suited for brief counseling. Koss and Shiang (1994) review this literature and indicate that individuals who appear to benefit most from brief counseling are those whose problem had a sudden or acute onset, were previously reasonably well adjusted, could relate well with others, and had high initial motivation when entering counseling.

Research suggests that brief counseling may be counterindicated for individuals whose personal characteristics are in contrast to those noted above and for some types of psychological disturbances such as substance abuse, psychosis, and personality disorders (Koss & Shiang, 1994). Additional research is necessary to gain a clearer understanding of how brief counseling can be effectively integrated into the counseling process with various traditional and nontraditional counseling theories and techniques.

Common Problems for Beginning Counselors

Beginning counselors tend to experience similar problems in counseling. These problems can manifest themselves as roadblocks to the counseling process. In this section, 15 typical roadblocks that can impede counseling effectiveness are discussed, with suggestions for overcoming each problem.

Focusing on the First Issue in a Session

Some beginning counselors tend to focus on the first problem the client presents in a session, even though a client may not want to work or be capable of working on this problem. The counselor may then spend the rest of the session trying to help the client resolve this particular problem. Counselors can overcome this roadblock by first obtaining an overview of the client's concerns and then selecting a counseling goal with the client.

Overlooking Physical or Medical Issues

Beginning counselors may assume that when a client seeks their services for counseling, counseling is all the client needs (Nystul, 1981). For example, a client may seek counseling to obtain stress management to help alleviate migraine headaches. In this instance, it would be important for the counselor to ensure the client has had a recent physical examination. This will enable the counselor to rule out possible organic causes of the headache such as a brain tumor. A substance abuse problem may be another medical issue that counselors may overlook. A counselor may assume that clients do not have substance abuse problems if they do not raise the issue. Counselors can avoid this problem by obtaining a history of alcohol and drug use when they gather other important background information.

Wanting to Rescue Clients from Their Unhappiness

Some beginning counselors have a naive notion that counseling is a process that makes clients feel happier. It is true that a major goal of counseling can be self-realization and inner peace. The road to that goal, however, will undoubtedly have ups and downs and emotional highs and lows.

Counseling is a process that requires the client to take risks and have the courage to face difficult issues. For example, a client may need to become aware of personal inadequacies or self-defeating patterns of behavior. This can make a client feel uncomfortable or sad and may even result in the client crying. Counselors may falsely conclude that since their client cried, they must have done something wrong. When this occurs, the counselor should consider that helping a client get in touch with inner feelings is an important part of the counseling process.

There are several ways that a counselor may rescue a client. The following are three common examples:

- *Reassuring clients.* When clients feel bad about their situation, the counselor may be tempted to say, "Don't worry, things will get better." It is important, however, for the counselor and client to have a realistic view of the counseling process. If the client does not make necessary changes, things probably will not get better. In fact, the client's situation may worsen.
- *Offering instant advice.* When clients are uncomfortable with their situation, the counselor may attempt to rescue the client by offering advice. In counseling, giving advice is usually unproductive, can foster dependency, and can be a superficial solution to a complex problem.

■ *Rescuing clients from intense emotions.* Some beginning counselors tend not to allow clients to experience any intense emotions. When clients express intense emotions such as anger or grief, the counselor may want to calm them or get them to think about something else. This type of rescuing prevents clients from getting in touch with and working through their feelings.

Having Perfectionist Tendencies

Some beginning counselors may have perfectionist tendencies. They may fear making mistakes or looking bad. These tendencies may cause several problems, including counselors being reluctant to explore a new idea or technique because they fear not learning or using it correctly, avoiding supervision because they believe seeking assistance might reflect their inadequacy, and being hesitant to refer a client because they think a referral might imply they could not handle the situation.

The following *Personal Note* provides some suggestions for helping beginning counselors overcome perfectionist tendencies.

Having Unrealistic Expectations

Some beginning counselors have unrealistic expectations for their clients. They may therefore become frustrated when their client does not make steady progress. When a client has a setback and regresses to old negative patterns of behavior, counselors may feel they have

A Personal Note

I have found several ways to help counselors overcome perfectionist tendencies. First, counselors should avoid absolutistic, or right-versus-wrong, views of the counseling process. Once counselors realize there is no right or wrong way of doing counseling they can stop worrying about making mistakes. The model of counseling as an art maintains a realistic, pragmatic view of counseling. This model suggests that when the client seems to be making progress, the counselor and client should continue using that counseling approach. When the client does not appear to be making gains in counseling, the counselor and client should make the necessary adjustments to the counseling process.

I identified the "monkey on the back" phenomenon as another way to help student counselors overcome perfectionist tendencies. The "monkey on the back" symbolizes why it is not productive to try to look perfect while learning new counseling skills. I begin by explaining to students that a counselor training program is in some ways like having a "monkey" put on their back. The "monkey"—instructions from the professor—may tell students to do some things differently from what they would ordinarily do. For example, the instructions might be to use open rather than closed questions during active listening.

When the "monkey" suggests that students stop to consider different ways of responding, they may feel the "monkey" is interfering with their spontaneity. If they focus on their professor perceiving them as spontaneous, they may avoid trying new behaviors. Unfortunately, these students will also not learn much from their counseling program.

I tell students that the feeling of the "monkey" interfering with their spontaneity is a good sign. It indicates that they are trying some new skills and are in the process of becoming a more effective counselor. In time, the new skills will become integrated into their natural way of working with clients and their spontaneity will be restored.

failed the client. In time, the counselor may project these negative feelings onto the client (Nystul, 1979b). The art-of-counseling model suggests that counselors develop a balanced set of expectations blending optimism with realism. These expectations involve believing that clients can improve and realizing that change can take time.

Getting Carried Away with the Latest Technique

Some beginning counselors tend to get carried away after learning a new technique, wanting to use this technique with all clients (Nystul, 1981). For example, after attending an extensive training program in hypnosis, a counselor may believe that every client could benefit from hypnosis. This enthusiasm may continue for a period of time until the counselor gets excited about another new technique.

It is important for counselors to get excited and be enthusiastic about their education. At the same time, they must learn to channel these energies into a positive direction rather than imposing their current interest on the client.

Getting Lost in the Counseling Process

Clients often feel overwhelmed with issues when they begin counseling. Each time they come to a counseling session, they may talk about many different concerns. They may describe these concerns in a very interesting manner, and the concerns may begin to seem like an ongoing soap opera from television.

As counselors hear these stories, they may find themselves taking a passive role in counseling. I call this the *popcorn syndrome* (Nystul, 1981). It is as if counselors are eating popcorn at the movies, listening to their client's latest struggle with life. Counselors who find themselves with the popcorn syndrome usually enjoy the counseling sessions, but they often have the feeling they are not accomplishing much. When this occurs, counselors can feel lost in the ongoing storytelling. To overcome this problem, the counselor can create a focus in the counseling process by exploring with the client what has happened in counseling—where they have been, what they are currently working on, and where they seem to be headed. Together they can make the necessary adjustments for future sessions. If the popcorn syndrome is occurring, the counselor may also want to create more of a shared responsibility in the counseling process and work toward clearer counseling goals.

Using Inappropriate Phrases

Although I contend there are no right or wrong ways to approach counseling, I believe that certain phrases are usually inappropriate and unproductive in counseling. The following are three examples:

- *"Why" questions.* "Why" questions usually provoke a defensive response, causing people to believe they need to justify their behavior. Instead of asking, "Why did you and Tim break up?" the counselor might ask, "Could you tell me what happened regarding your breakup with Tim?"
- *I know how you feel.* Counselors may use this phrase to show that they have been through a similar situation and can therefore understand the client. Actually, no two

people have exactly the same reaction to a situation. For example, take the varied reactions to a house burning down. One person might feel relief at the prospect of insurance money, whereas another might be heartbroken because of losing priceless family mementos. A client may have negative reactions to a counselor saying "I know how you feel." The client may think, "No, she does not. She is not me. Who does she think she is?" Another client might react by thinking, "If this counselor knows how I feel, why bother exploring my feelings with him?"

- *Let me tell you what I would do.* This phrase can lead to instant advice. As mentioned earlier, advice giving usually does not promote positive outcomes in counseling.

Having an Excessive Desire to Help

Many students are drawn to counseling because they truly want to help others. Wanting to help can be beneficial to the counseling process because it communicates enthusiasm, desire, and caring. Some counselors can be excessive in their need to help, however, to the point of being overly invested in the counseling process. A useful indicator that counselors may have gone too far in wanting to help is when they feel they are working harder than the client. Students should also explore their motives for wanting to become counselors. A positive motive would be to enjoy helping a client overcome self-defeating forces to move toward self-realization. A negative motive would be an excessive desire to feel needed by someone. This desire could foster unnecessary dependency in the counseling relationship. Another negative motive would be a need to feel power or control over others. This need could lead to a counselor intimidating clients, undermining their self-esteem, and fostering dependency. When counselors discover they have inappropriate motives for providing counseling services, they should refer the client and seek counseling for themselves.

Having an Excessive Need to Be Liked

Most people, including counselors, enjoy being liked. At times, however, the counselor may need to do things that could make the client angry or unhappy, such as during a confrontation. It is therefore not necessary for the client always to like the counselor. Instead, it is essential to establish mutual respect to maintain a rapport throughout the counseling process.

Getting Too Emotionally Involved

Some beginning counselors tend to get too emotionally involved with the counseling process. There can be many reasons for developing this tendency. One is what I call the *stray cat syndrome,* which involves counselors wanting to take responsibility for the client's welfare. These counselors may have tendencies to want to go out of their way to help all living creatures—including stray cats—that appear to need assistance. As a result, whenever they see a client suffering, they want to find a way to take away the pain and fix things, leading to the rescuing process described earlier.

Counselors can become so emotionally invested in their clients that they lose professional objectivity. They can also become emotionally exhausted and burned out. The art-of-counseling model suggests that for counseling to be effective, the counselor must be affected. At the same time, counselors should not assume ownership of the client's problems. They should instead help clients become capable of resolving their own problems.

Taking Things Too Personally

Beginning counselors may take things too personally when a client expresses intense emotions. For example, a client may react as if the counselor were another person with whom the client has had a close relationship, for example, a father or mother figure. During this process of transference, the client may become angry with the counselor. It would be inappropriate for the counselor to take this personally and retaliate against the client. Instead, the counselor should view the transference as an important part of therapy. For example, Freudian psychoanalysis contends that transference is therapeutic in that it allows the client to work through unresolved emotional trauma (Freud, 1969).

Having Difficulty Differentiating Between Normal and Abnormal

Beginning counselors often have a difficult time deciding whether clients suffer from some form of psychopathology. For example, a counselor may wonder if a client is acutely suicidal and needs hospitalization or mildly suicidal and only requires monitoring. Another dilemma may be differentiating a clinical depression, such as a major depression, from a normal depressive reaction to a life event relating to the death of a loved one.

The reason some beginning counselors have trouble differentiating between normal and abnormal may be their lack of exposure to psychopathology. Student counselors may overcome this obstacle by taking advantage of internships and other clinical placements during their educational placement to obtain experience working with clients who suffer from mental disorders.

Being Uncertain About Self-Disclosure

Another problem that beginning counselors commonly experience is determining how much they should self-disclose. Although there are no hard-and-fast rules on this issue, the following suggestions may be useful:

- Answer questions about yourself that you feel comfortable with—just answer the questions without elaborating. Feel free to offer information about your professional qualifications. Be willing to share immediate reactions to what is taking place in the session.
- Don't tell your life story to your clients—they are there to tell you their story, not listen to yours. Don't say, "This is how I handled it." It could lead to ineffective advice giving.

Being Uncertain About Confidentiality

Many beginning counselors are unclear about the limits of confidentiality. One of the most common sources of confusion relates to the question, "With whom can I discuss a client, and what information can I disclose?" The following are some suggestions regarding this issue: A counselor may discuss a case with a supervisor or when required by law, such as reporting child abuse or neglect. It is also permissible to break confidentiality when clients pose a serious threat in terms of harming themselves or others. It is not appropriate to discuss a case with a secretary, friends, or family members, even if you change the name of the client.

Diversity Issues

Gilbert (1992) and Sue, Zane, and Young (1994) provide an extensive overview of the literature on diversity and the counseling process. These reviews provide specific information on diversity issues such as culture and gender as well as a description of how multicultural issues affect the counseling process. Research topics that are attracting much interest include the impact of similarity and difference between the counselor and client on the therapeutic alliance, how tests and diagnostic processes can be culturally biased, and how diversity serves as a mediating variable in assessing counseling interventions and outcomes.

Spirituality (including religion) is an emerging area of diversity in the literature that has vast potential for integration into counseling (Bishop, 1995). Spirituality can be broadly defined as "attunement with God, the Spirit of Truth, or the divine intelligence that governs or harmonizes the universe" (Richards & Bergin, 1997, p. 77). From this perspective, all people are believed to recognize the spiritual (but not necessarily religious) realm of existence (Ingersoll, 1995). Richards and Bergin (1997) refer to spiritual trends in counseling as the New Zeitgeist (spirit of our times). This recognition of the role of spirituality in counseling is reflected in the increased interests in the healing power associated with spirituality and holistic health (Richards & Bergin, 2004; Witmer & Sweeney, 1995).

Historically, counseling and spirituality have to a large degree been kept separate. More recently, the counseling literature is suggesting that spirituality is another form of diversity that should be carefully and sensitively addressed to obtain an accurate understanding of a client's world view (Bishop, 1995). Miranti and Burke (1995) suggest that recognition of the spiritual domain in counseling enables counselors to relate to the core essence of a client's being. Spirituality and religion provide strength and support that many people turn to during times of crisis to derive meaning from life. This is especially true for people as they get older (Smith, 1993).

A number of individuals are beginning to provide a structure for how spirituality and religion can be integrated into the counseling process (Ingersoll, 1995; Richards & Bergin, 1997). Ingersoll suggests that counselors should attempt to recognize and affirm clients' concepts of spirituality, enter the clients' spiritual world views to gain a phenomenological perspective, and consult with other "healers" in clients' lives as necessary. Richards and Bergin (1997) provide extensive guidelines such as assessment and intervention for addressing spiritual issues throughout the various phases of the counseling process. For example, spiritual forms of intervention can require special training and may include such strategies as cognitive restructuring of irrational religious beliefs, methods to foster forgiveness, and meditation and prayer.

The spiritual domain of counseling appears to represent a vast, largely untapped reservoir of potential. Additional theory, research, and practice will be necessary to facilitate a meaningful evolution of this important dimension into the counseling process.

Summary

A six-stage approach to counseling involves relationship building, assessment and diagnosis, goal setting, intervention and problem solving, termination and follow-up, and research and evaluation.

Current trends in the counseling process such as postmodernism and brief counseling offer new ways of conceptualizing the counseling process in terms of narrative psychology and counseling as storytelling and brief-solution-focused approaches to counseling. These counseling trends appear to offer special promise for addressing issues in multicultural counseling and managed care. Diversity issues and the emerging trends in the counseling literature, such as spirituality and religion, offer much hope and promise in terms of enriching the counseling process.

Problems that beginning counselors experience include focusing only on the first issue in a session, overlooking medical issues, wanting to rescue clients, having perfectionist tendencies or unrealistic expectations, getting carried away with the latest technique learned, getting lost in the counseling process, using inappropriate phrases, having an excessive desire to help or to be liked, getting too emotionally involved or taking things too personally, and being uncertain about psychopathology issues, self-disclosure, or confidentiality.

In the final analysis, counseling is a process that varies in length and content according to the concerns of the client. In this process, the client may appear to make some progress and then regress to self-defeating habits. When things appear to be going wrong, the counselor, like a navigator on a ship, can adjust course. Counseling may be considered successful when the overall direction of therapy is positive.

Personal Exploration

1. How would you assess your listening skills, and how can the listening skills in this chapter facilitate your ability to listen?
2. Why is the phenomenological perspective important in listening?
3. How can you use Strong's social influence model to enhance your ability to influence others?
4. What are some common problems of beginning counselors that you can identify with, and why might these be issues for you?

Web Sites for Chapter 3

Freedman, F. K. (1999). *Multicultural Counseling.* Retrieved March 3, 2005, from
   http://www.alaska.net/~fken/Multiculture.htm
   *Provides a fairly current and solid paper on multicultural counseling using D. W.
   Sue and D. Sue's (1990) text (*Counseling the Culturally Different: Theory and Practices, *2nd Edition) as a primary resource.*

Lobovits, D., Epston, D., & Freeman, J. (2004). *Welcome to narrative approaches.com.* Retrieved March 3, 2005, from http://www.narrativeapproaches.com
Provides a variety of materials and resources for those interested in narrative therapy. (Make no mistake though, this page is about selling products as well.)

White, M. (unknown). *Narrative therapy.* Retrieved March 3, 2005, from http://www. massey.ac.nz/~alock/virtual/white.htm
Provides a brief and accessible point-by-point overview of Michael White's narrative therapy.

4 Assessment and Diagnosis

CHAPTER OVERVIEW

This chapter provides an overview of assessment and diagnosis. Highlights of the chapter include

- The art and science of assessment and diagnosis
- Evaluation of tests
- Administration and interpretation of tests
- Test bias
- Types of tests
- Historical perspective of diagnosis
- Uses of diagnosis
- The DSM-IV-TR
- Treatment planning
- Diversity and postmodern issues in assessment and diagnosis

The Art and Science of Assessment and Diagnosis

The art of assessment and diagnosis is an emerging dimension of the counseling process. The counselor-as-artist recognizes there are infinite methods and procedures to discover overt and salient aspects of clients. From this perspective, counselors adjust assessment and diagnostic procedures to accommodate the unique and emerging needs of the client. Examples of these procedures include the use of projective techniques to help a resistant client have a less-threatening means of self-disclosure and adjusting test procedures to accommodate issues of diversity.

Assessment and diagnosis represent an important dimension of the science of counseling and psychotherapy. They provide standardized methods such as intelligence and personality tests to obtain an objective understanding of the client's overall psychological functioning. The counselor-as-scientist emphasizes the necessity of comprehensive ongoing education in psychological testing. This training is a prerequisite for accurately administering, scoring, and interpreting tests. In addition, continuing education is necessary to keep up with the revision of tests and the complete revamping of the procedures used in tests (such as the Exner system for the Rorschach inkblot test).

Virtually all aspects of assessment and diagnosis relate to the art and science of counseling. For example, treatment planning is an art that requires the counselor to creatively integrate vast amounts of information from different sources into a meaningful composite of the client. Treatment planning is also a science that involves organizing this information into a cohesive, effective program that provides structure and direction to the counseling process. Together the art and science of assessment and diagnosis create a balance, bridging the subjective and objective underpinnings on this important aspect of the counseling process.

Assessment and Diagnosis

Hohenshil (1996) notes that assessment and diagnosis tend to be interrelated processes, with assessment providing the necessary information to make a diagnosis. All counselors use some form of assessment to obtain an overall understanding of clients. Most counselors also incorporate diagnosis in their counseling process. Some theoretical perspectives such as reality therapy and person-centered counseling tend to abstain from the diagnostic process because they promote inaccurate and harmful labels. Most counselors find diagnosis essential to formulating treatment strategies and as a means of communication shorthand (Hohenshil, 1996). Key publications associated with diagnosis are also attempting to be more sensitive about the labeling process by referring to someone as a person with mental retardation or schizophrenia and so on instead of saying that someone is mentally retarded or schizophrenic (Hohenshil, 1996). This certainly makes sense, as no one would be referred to as "a cancer" or "a broken bone." They would be referred to as someone with cancer or with a broken bone.

Hohenshil (1996) suggests that in reality all counselors (regardless of their theoretical orientation) engage in some form of diagnosis. For example, when a person-centered counselor decides that a client has psychopathology that requires the attention of a psychologist or psychiatrist, the counselor is making a diagnosis (Hohenshil, 1996). Hamann (1994) goes on to note that most counselors are actively involved in making diagnoses so that they can communicate effectively with other professional helpers and provide the necessary information to insurance companies, and so forth. Although counselors utilize diagnostic procedures on a regular basis, they often have not had the appropriate training to do so, resulting in serious potential ethical problems (Hamann, 1994).

Assessment

Sundberg (1977) notes that *assessment* first appeared as a psychological term in *Assessment of Men* (Office of Strategic Services, 1948). The term was used to describe the process of selecting men to serve on special missions in World War II. Since that time its meaning has broadened to include a wide range of techniques and processes. These include standardized psychological tests, interviewing and observation strategies, sociocultural assessment, behavioral assessment, and environmental assessment. This section provides a description of these assessment procedures as well as information on evaluating tests and the administration and interpretation of test results.

Evaluation of Tests

Anastasi and Urbina (1997) describe several sources of information that provide valuable means of evaluating tests:

- *Mental Measurement Yearbook,* edited by Burros, provides information on most tests as well as a critique of each test.
- *Test Collection Bibliographies,* produced by the Educational Testing Service, provides information on tests pertaining to a particular content, such as physical disabilities.
- *Test and Microfiche,* distributed by Test Collection, Educational Testing Service, provides important information about tests, such as reliability and validity.
- *The APA's Standards for Educational and Psychological Testing* provides guidelines for proper test use and interpretation of test results.

Three concepts are especially important in evaluating tests: validity, reliability, and norms.

Validity.   Validity is the degree to which a test measures what it is intended to measure (Anastasi & Urbina, 1997). According to Anastasi and Urbina (1997), validity is the most important characteristic of a test and provides a check on how well the test fulfills its intended function. For example, the Graduate Record Examination (GRE) could be used to help select students for Ph.D. programs in counseling psychology. The test would have a high validity only if the students who scored high were also successful in their graduate programs.

The three major types of validity are content, construct, and criterion-related. Anastasi and Urbina (1997) provide a description of these types of validity:

1. *Content validity* involves the examination of a test's content to determine whether it covers a representative sample of the behavior to be measured. Content validity is often used in achievement tests to determine whether the test content is representative of the information that an individual was exposed to (for example, biology concepts in a biology course).
2. *Construct validity* refers to the degree to which a test measures a theoretical construct or trait such as neuroticism or anxiety.
3. *Criterion-related validity* provides an indication of how well a test predicts an individual's performance on a particular criterion. For example, a mechanical aptitude test might be used to predict how well a person will perform as a machinist. There are two types of criterion-related validity. *Concurrent validity* is determined when the criterion is available at the time of testing. *Predictive validity* can be assessed when the criterion is available only after the testing has occurred.

Reliability.   Reliability is another important factor that should be considered in test evaluation. It refers to the "consistency of scores obtained by the same persons when they are reexamined with the same test on different occasions, or with different sets of equivalent items, or under variable examining conditions" (Anastasi & Urbina, 1997, p. 84). Reliability can be determined by the following three methods:

1. *Test-retest reliability* involves administering the same test again to an individual.
2. *Alternate-forms reliability* refers to administering equivalent forms to the individual on separate occasions.
3. *Split-half reliability* involves dividing a test into two equivalent halves and administering each half to the individual. It provides a measure of the test's internal consistency.

Norms.   Sundberg (1977) notes that to understand an individual's score on a test, it is necessary to have information on the scores of other people who have taken the test (that is, the norm group). In evaluating the norms used in a test, it is important to determine whether the norm group is representative of the population for whom the test was designed (Sundberg, 1977). For example, a test with norms derived from an upper-class white group may be inappropriate to use with minority clients.

Administration and Interpretation of Tests

Only qualified individuals should administer and interpret tests. Many tests such as the Wechsler intelligence test require specialized training in test administration and interpretation. In addition, counselors should carefully review the test manual to determine procedures to use in test interpretation. For example, it is important to determine the strengths and limitations of the test and whether the norm group is representative of the individual being tested.

Miller (1982) provides the following guidelines for interpreting test results to clients:

- The counselor should explore how the client felt about taking the test.
- The counselor should review the purpose of taking the test and provide information necessary for test interpretation (for example, norms and percentiles).
- The counselor and client should examine the test results and discuss what the results mean to the client.
- The counselor should help the client integrate the test scores into other aspects of the client's self-knowledge.
- The counselor should encourage the client to develop a plan to utilize the test results.

Goodyear (1990) suggests that counselors should introduce test materials and interpretations in response to specific concerns raised by the client throughout the counseling process rather than at one particular point in counseling. Goodyear contends that a client will achieve better assimilation of information from an approach to interpretation that occurs at various phases of the counseling process.

Several research studies provide useful information regarding interpretation. Jones and Gelso (1988) have found that clients perceive tentative interpretations as more helpful than absolute interpretations. Clients are also more willing to see counselors who use tentative interpretations. Goodyear (1990) cites a study by Taylor and Brown (1988) that found that mentally healthy individuals were more likely to harbor unrealistic positive self-perceptions. Based on these findings, Goodyear warns that clients may be prone to distort test interpretations in an unrealistically positive manner. Other studies have shown that clients prefer individual test interpretations over group interpretations in terms of clarity (Miller & Cochran, 1979), favorability (Oliver, 1977), and helpfulness (Wilkerson, 1967).

Rawlins, Eberly, and Rawlins (1991) note that counselors are ill-prepared to deal with the wide array of potential problems in testing and are in need of better training in measurement. These authors suggest that counselors could overcome some of their problems with testing by infusing counseling skills in test interpretation. Rawlins et al. (1991) suggest that neuro-linguistic programming (NLP) can be integrated with counseling technique and theory to facilitate test interpretation. For example, counselors can use the NLP technique (such as pacing) to gain insight into what the client is experiencing regarding the test interpretation. Pacing involves staying with the client's experience by using counseling techniques (such as listening skills) to determine what sensory modality the client is functioning from (for example, visual, auditory, or tactile), and then matching predicates (such as "I see your point" with a visual learner) and mirroring bodily states (such as breathing rates) to facilitate rapport and understanding in the test interpretation process. In this regard, the use of NLP and other counseling strategies facilitates the art of counseling and test interpretation by helping counselors adjust to the unique and emerging needs of clients.

Computer-based test interpretation (CBTI) is an increasingly popular resource for testing and assessment (Sampson, 1990). A variety of computer software programs have been designed to assist counselors in interpreting the most commonly used tests, such as the Minnesota Multiphasic Personality Inventory (MMPI-II) and the Wechsler intelligence scales. CBTI systems are not intended to replace the counselor's role in the assessment process. Instead, counselors should view CBTI as a basic framework to aid in assessment, diagnosis, and treatment planning (Sampson, 1990).

Test Bias

Watkins and Campbell (1990) note increasing concern in the literature regarding the fairness of tests and assessment methods for clients of culturally diverse backgrounds. Evidence of cultural bias has been found in numerous assessment procedures such as projective techniques, intelligence tests, and self-report measures (Jewell, 1989). Reynolds (1982) identifies the following factors often associated with test bias:

- *Inappropriate content.* Test content is biased toward the values and experiences of white, middle-class individuals.
- *Inappropriate standardization samples.* Most norm groups, which tend to be underrepresented by ethnic minorities, are not realistic reference groups for minorities.
- *Examiner and language bias.* Psychologists tend to be white and speak only standard English. As test examiners, they can therefore intimidate ethnic minorities and create communication barriers, which can account for lower performance on tests.

- *Inequitable social consequences.* Ethnic minorities receive unfair labels from tests (for example, low intelligence), which can relegate them to dead-end educational tracks.
- *Measurement of different constructs.* Tests measure significantly different attributes when used with ethnic minorities (for example, the degree of their adherence to the value system of the dominant culture).
- *Differential predictive validity.* Although tests can accurately predict outcomes such as academic attainment for whites, they are much less effective at predicting outcomes for ethnic minorities.

In response to the potential problems in multicultural assessment, Anastasi and Urbina (1997) suggest that testing should be conceptualized within a multicultural perspective. Culture-fair tests have been developed in an attempt to overcome the problems associated with test bias. Penrose and Raven (1936) developed one of the first culture-fair intelligence tests, called the Raven Progressive Matrices Test. This test has three versions, allowing for the evaluation of mentally retarded individuals up to normal adults. Each version consists of a nonverbal test in which the examinee must choose which matrix completes a particular pattern. Cattell (1949) developed another culture-fair intelligence test called the Cattell Culture-Fair Intelligence Test. The test is primarily nonpictorial and nonverbal and can be used with individuals from age 4 through adult.

The System of Multicultural Pluralistic Assessment (SOMPA), developed by Mercer (1977), can be used to promote culture-fair assessment with children from 5 to 11 years of age. The SOMPA approach has several unique qualities. First, the child is administered several tests, including the Wechsler Intelligence Test for Children—Fourth Edition (WISC-IV). Second, an interview is conducted with the child's primary caregiver to obtain information on how the child functions in various activities and settings (McMillan, 1984). The WISC-IV score is then "corrected" after consideration of other test scores and the interview. Mercer contends that the "uncorrected" test scores can be useful in making educational and instructional decisions, but the "corrected" score more accurately reflects the child's intellectual aptitude (McMillan, 1984).

Ridley, Li, and Hill (1998) developed the Multicultural Assessment Procedure (MAP) as a means of addressing the challenges associated with multicultural assessment and diagnosis. The Multicultural Assessment Procedure has four phases that can be used as a framework to create a multicultural framework for assessment and diagnosis:

1. *Identifying cultural data.* Objective and subjective assessment procedures are used to identify cultural data. Listening skills, encouraging clients to tell their story, and the clinical interview can be used as a starting point to obtain this information. For example, clients can report cultural data such as experiences of racism at work that appear to be related to their depression.

2. *Interpreting cultural data to formulate a working hypothesis.* MAP contends that assessment and diagnosis involves creating a working hypothesis that can be used to interpret cultural data. A central task in this process is differentiating cultural data from idiosyncratic data (i.e., determining to what degree the information is specific to the client's culture or unique to the client). For example, a working hypothesis could be that a client's depression may be due in part to racism at work and conflicts with his/her identity development (cultural specific data), and may also be associated with alcoholism (idiosyncratic or specific to the individual).

3. *Incorporating cultural data to test the working hypothesis.* The third phase of MAP involves utilizing a comprehensive assessment and diagnostic approach to test the working hypothesis. This process involves integrating culturally relevant information with commonly used clinical procedures such as medical examinations, psychological testing, and the use of the *Diagnostic and Statistical Manual of Mental Disorders* (DSM). For example, counselors can utilize cultural considerations in the DSM to strive for cultural sensitivity in the diagnostic process.

4. *Arriving at a sound assessment decision.* The final phase of MAP involves creating a comprehensive, culture-inclusive assessment profile of clients from which clinical decisions can be made. Diagnostic decisions are finalized (in terms of the DSM) and cultural-relevant treatment programs can be formulated.

Types of Tests

Assessment procedures can be divided into two major categories: standardized and non-standardized measures (Kottler & Brown, 2000). *Standardized measures* are tests that have a standardized norm group. This category includes a wide variety of psychological tests such as intelligence tests, personality tests, interest tests, aptitude tests, achievement tests, and neuropsychological tests. Nonstandardized measures do not have a standardized norm group and include procedures such as observations, behavioral assessment, and environmental assessment.

Each form has advantages and disadvantages. Standardized assessment procedures provide the counselor with objective information regarding the client. In addition, these tests contain information on validity and reliability, which can be used to evaluate the results. The disadvantages include potential cultural bias, promoting harmful labels, and producing scores that may be oversimplified or misleading.

Testing can provide counselors with objective information regarding the client's psychological functioning.

Nonstandardized assessment procedures also have inherent strengths and weaknesses. One strength of these measures is providing a flexible and individualized approach, which yields information unique to the individual. They can also be easily modified to accommodate individual differences, thereby minimizing cultural bias. Weaknesses include a lack of information on reliability and validity to evaluate the assessment procedures and a lack of objectivity in terms of test results. The advantages and disadvantages of standardized and nonstandardized assessment procedures are summarized in Table 4.1.

Standardized Measures.   Standardized measures include a wide range of psychological tests. Anastasi and Urbina (1997) define a psychological test as "an objective and standardized measure of a sample behavior" (p. 4). "Standardization implies *uniformity of procedure* in administering and scoring the test" (Anastasi & Urbina, 1997, p. 6). Psychological tests can be administered to an individual or a group to assess a wide range of traits and attributes such as intelligence, achievement, aptitude, interest, personality, and neuropsychological impairment. Some commonly used tests in these domains are intelligence tests, achievement tests, aptitude tests, interest inventories, personality inventories, projective techniques, and neuropsychological tests.

Intelligence tests provide information regarding the client's intellectual functioning. The most common individually administered intelligence tests are the Stanford Binet and three Wechsler scales: the Wechsler Pre-School and Primary Scale of Intelligence—Third Edition (WPPSI-III), the Wechsler Intelligence Scale for Children—Fourth Edition (WISC-IV), and the Wechsler Adult Intelligence Scale—Third Edition (WAIS-III). Two of the more commonly used group-administered intelligence tests are the Otis-Lennon Mental Ability Test and the California Tests of Mental Maturity. Nonverbal intelligence tests are

TABLE 4.1   Comparison of Standardized and Nonstandardized Measures

Type of Test	Advantages	Disadvantages
Standardized	1. Provides objective information regarding the client	1. Is prone to cultural bias
	2. Provides specific information about a client relative to a norm group	2. Often results in "labels"
	3. Contains information on validity and reliability that can be used to evaluate the test	3. Can lead to oversimplified and misleading test results (for example, IQ scores)
Nonstandardized	1. Provides a flexible, individualized approach that yields information unique to the individual client	1. Lacks information on validity and reliability
	2. Fosters an active role for the client in the assessment process	2. Lacks objectivity and ability to generalize to a reference group
	3. Can be easily modified to accommodate individual differences	3. Lacks specific scores and reference groups, which may make assessment results appear confusing to clients

also available, such as the Raven Progressive Matrixes and the Test of Nonverbal Intelligence (TONI). These are especially useful in multicultural testing to overcome language barriers. They can also be used if the counselor has limited time available and only needs to have a rough estimate of the client's intellectual level (Anastasi & Urbina, 1997).

Achievement tests are used primarily in school settings. They provide information on what a person has learned. Three of the more popular achievement tests are the Iowa Test of Basic Skills, the Wide Range Achievement Test, and Woodcock Johnson Psycho-Educational Battery (Anastasi & Urbina, 1997).

Aptitude tests focus on the client's potential in an attempt to predict success. As mentioned, the GRE is an example of an aptitude test designed to predict whether a person will be able to successfully complete graduate study. Another example is the Differential Aptitude Test, which counselors use frequently in educational and vocational counseling of students in grades 8 through 12 (Anastasi & Urbina, 1997).

Interest inventories help the counselor determine where the client's interests lie. This information can be especially useful to career counselors. Three of the most commonly used interest inventories are the Kuder Preference Record, the Career Assessment Inventory, and the Strong Campbell Interest Inventory.

Personality inventories provide information about personality dynamics and can also be part of the diagnostic process to determine a client has a mental disorder. The two types of personality tests are objective and subjective. Objective tests require more rigid responses, such as true-false or multiple-choice responses. The most widely used objective personality test is the MMPI-II. It is especially useful in identifying certain mental disorders, such as depression or schizophrenia. Two popular objective personality tests that provide an overview of the personality are the California Psychological Inventory (CPI) and the 16 Personality Factors Questionnaire (16 PF).

Projective techniques are subjective tests that require clients to project their thoughts and feelings into a variety of ambiguous stimuli, such as the inkblots of the Rorschach test or pictures in the thematic apperception test. Projective tests are sometimes more appropriate in multicultural settings since they minimize the use of words, thereby decreasing tendencies toward cultural bias. Two other commonly used examples are the Draw-a-Person and House-Tree-Person tests. Clark (1995) suggests that projective tests are underutilized by counselors and can provide a valuable means of enhancing the counseling process. Clark notes that projective tests have a variety of uses in counseling, such as overcoming resistance, obtaining a phenomenological understanding of the client, identifying goals, and establishing a treatment plan.

Neuropsychological tests "are used to evaluate the neurologically impaired patients' cognitive, behavioral, and psychological strengths and weaknesses and to determine their relationship to cerebral functioning" (Newmark, 1985, p. 383). Several popular neuropsychological tests and test batteries are in use. One example is the Bender-Gestalt Test, which involves having the client copy nine separate designs. This test can be scored by subjective intuitive means or by utilizing an objective scoring procedure (Anastasi & Urbina, 1997). Another neuropsychological test that clinicians use is the Benton Visual Retention Test, which requires the client to reproduce 10 different geometric figures. Although these two tests can provide an indication of brain damage, they should not be used as a sole means of making a diagnosis. Bigler and Ehrfurth (1981) even suggest that the Bender should be banned as a single neuropsychological technique.

Several neuropsychological test batteries have been developed in an attempt to create a more comprehensive approach to assessment and diagnosis. The two most popular test batteries are the Halstead-Reitan Neuropsychological Test Battery and the Luria Nebraska Neuropsychological Battery. The Halstead-Reitan Neuropsychological Test can be used with individuals age 15 and older. It is technically comprised of 10 tests, two of which are considered allied procedures (Newmark, 1985). The main battery is comprised of the Category Test, Speech-Sounds Perception, Seashore Rhythm, Tactual Performance Test (TPT), Finger Oscillation, Trail Making A and B, Aphasia Screening, and Sensory Perceptual Examination. The allied procedures are the WAIS-III and the MMPI-II. Compared with the Halstead-Reitan, the Luria Nebraska Battery requires less time to administer (2 $\frac{1}{2}$ hours as opposed to 6 or more hours), is more highly standardized, and provides a fuller coverage of neurological deficits (Anastasi & Urbina, 1997).

Nonstandardized Measures. Goldman (1990) refers to nonstandardized measures as qualitative assessment, noting that for the most part these forms of assessment do not yield quantitative raw scores as are found in standardized measures. Goldman suggests that qualitative assessment has a number of advantages over standardized approaches. The following are some advantages of qualitative assessment procedures:

- They foster an "active role for the client in the process of collecting and teasing meaning out of data, rather than the role of a passive responder who is being measured, predicted, placed, or diagnosed" (Goldman, 1990, p. 205).
- They emphasize "the *holistic study* of the individual rather than the isolation and precise measurement of narrowly defined discrete elements of ability, interest, or personality" (Goldman, 1990, p. 205).
- They encourage clients to learn about themselves within a developmental framework.
- They are especially effective in group work, in which clients can learn about individual differences as well as gain an understanding about themselves in relation to others in the group.
- They reduce the distinction between assessment and counseling by stimulating rather than hampering counseling methods, as can be the case with standardized assessment.
- They can be easily modified to accommodate individual differences such as cultural diversity and gender since they do not attempt precise measurements from normative samples.

A variety of nonstandardized measures can be used in the counseling process. These include observation skills, behavioral assessment, and environmental assessment. A description of each of these procedures follows.

Observation Skills. The power of observation can be a very revealing aspect of clinical assessment. Freud attested to the power of observation when he said, "He that has eyes to see and ears to hear may convince himself that no mortal can keep a secret. If his lips are silent, he chatters with his fingertips; betrayal oozes out of him at every pore" (Freud, 1953, pp. 77–78). As Freud noted, the skilled clinician can learn much from observing what occurs during the counseling session.

Ivey (1999) and Baruth and Huber (1985) provide a description of how nonverbal behavior can provide valuable information regarding clients. These observations have been incorporated into the following overview. In reviewing these facets of nonverbal behavior, it is important to consider how diversity issues such as culture and gender can contribute to variation in communication.

- *Touch.* The amount and nature of the physical contact (in terms of touch) can provide information on such things as interpersonal comfort and closeness, capacity for empathic responding, and so forth.
- *Proxemics.* Proxemics is the study of physical space or distance between people. For example, people who seek close physical distance between each other could suggest intimacy, and those that desire more space could be seeking to meet needs such as solace or safety.
- *Kinesics.* Kinesics relates to how body movements contribute to communication. Much can be learned from a client's body language. For example, crossing the arms can suggest reluctance or resistance; leaning forward can imply interest; and leaning away can imply fear or boredom.
- *Autonomic physiological behavior.* Autonomic responses are very expressive and provide uncensored information about the client. For example, rapid breathing can suggest anxiety or nervousness, and blushing can indicate embarrassment.
- *Vocal qualities.* A client's voice quality can provide important information to the counselor. Changes in rate, volume, or pitch can communicate different messages. For example, hesitations and breaks can suggest confusion or stress.
- *Facial expressions.* Grimaces, frowns, smiles, and raised eyebrows all communicate something important about the client's emotional state.
- *Eye contact.* Pupils tend to dilate when clients are discussing an interesting topic and contract when they are bored or uncomfortable. In addition, clients tend to look away when discussing something that is depressing or disturbing.

Counselors can also learn from observing clients in their natural habitat. Goldman (1990) refers to this process as *shadowing,* which he defines as "following someone through a day or part of a day to observe how the person acts and reacts in various places and in various interactions" (p. 210). Shadowing can provide information on how the client functions in a real-life situation. Numerous possibilities exist for making observations in the field. Some examples include observing a student in a classroom, on a school bus, or on a playground to assess the child's interpersonal skills; observing a mother or father with a newborn to determine the degree of bonding; conducting a marriage or family session in a client's home to observe the family in their natural habitat; and observing a manager role-playing administrative functions in an organizational setting.

Sundberg (1977) identifies systematic methods for observing and recording behavior in organizational settings. These methods include the situational test, in-basket test, and critical incidence technique.

- The *situational test* involves a contrived situation in which the subject is given a task to accomplish, for example, as a perspective policeman attempting to find a person who has mysteriously vanished. Specific measures of observation are identified to facilitate accurate recording of information.

- The *in-basket test* is a method used to select and train managers and executives (Bray, Campbell, & Grant, 1974; Lopez, 1966; Vernon & Parry, 1949). This test entails observing an individual role-playing various administrative tasks. Systematic procedures are then identified for observing and recording behavior.
- The *critical incidence technique* involves an observer recording instances of behavior that indicate good or poor performance. From this information procedures are identified to chart performance or plan training.

Behavioral Assessment.   Behavioral assessment, which evolved from behavioral psychology, involves the systematic measurement of behaviors broadly defined to include attitudes, feelings, and cognitions (Sundberg, 1977). In behavioral assessment, counselors may use a wide variety of procedures, including direct observation in the natural environment, problem checklists, self-reports, and record-keeping (Anastasi & Urbina, 1997; Sundberg, 1977).

Behavioral assessment can be tied directly into treatment by using single-subject designs, such as A-B and A-B-A designs. The A phase involves obtaining a baseline of a problem behavior before treatment. The B phase assesses behavior after treatment. The behaviors recorded during the A and B phases are usually graphed to provide a measure of behavior change before and after treatment. Additional information on single-subject designs such as A-B and A-B-A can be found in Chapter 5.

Environmental/Ecological Assessment.   Environmental assessment (also referred to as ecological assessment) involves consideration of environmental factors such as sociocultural forces in the assessment of psychological functioning. It shares common characteristics with other theories such as family therapy, interpersonal psychotherapy, and postmodern theories. Family therapy recognizes the need to assess people from a systemic or systems perspective. Interpersonal psychotherapy is similar to family therapy in that it emphasizes the role of interpersonal relationships in mental health. Postmodern theories such as social constructionism also emphasize the role of sociocultural forces in assessment. Central to this position is a redefining of the self from being an autonomous self to a social self that extends beyond the individual to all aspects of society (Gergen, 1994a). Alfred Adler's concept of social interest as the barometer of mental health is an excellent example of the relationship between social embeddedness and psychological functioning (Jones, 1995).

Walsh (1990) observes that any assessment is incomplete without some assessment of the environment. Walsh suggested that counselors include an environmental assessment to determine how clients perceive their environment and how these perceptions influence their behavior. Environmental assessment can be particularly important when determining the etiology, or cause, of psychopathology. A counselor who does not consider environmental factors may attribute a mental disorder to intrapsychic forces, that is, forces within the person, instead of considering environmental factors such as living in poverty.

As counseling becomes increasingly multicultural, it is particularly important to include an assessment of sociocultural factors when conducting an environmental assessment. Social forces that may warrant attention include how clients feel about where they live and with whom they live and their attitudes toward their job, family, and friends. Topper (1985) identifies cultural factors that counselors should address during the assessment process. He notes that it is particularly important to evaluate the client's level of acculturation to determine whether traditional Western counseling approaches will be appropriate.

In addition, he suggests that it would be advantageous to determine how the client's condition will be viewed by members of the client's culture and then evaluate the client in terms of patterns of psychological development that are normative to that culture.

Hershenson, Power, and Waldo (1996) provide additional information regarding environmental assessment. These authors note that there has been an increased interest in the role of the environment in psychological functioning. They contend that in many instances, the environment is both the primary source of a client's problem and the potential target for an intervention in counseling. They go on to describe theories and strategies for environmental assessment. Theories include the behavior-setting approach (the environment shapes behavior), need-press theory (the relationship between needs and environmental presses), human aggregate model (the match between the individual and the environment), and social climate models (a systems perspective that also considers the person's perception of environmental events). These theories describe a complex interaction between each individual and the environment. Environments represent numerous tasks of life such as work, marriage and family, social environment, and spiritual environment and are influenced by various forces such as war and peace, poverty and affluence, and oppression and mutual respect. These environmental forces can be reinforcing to an individual and contribute to need fulfillment or be a source of stress and discontent. Individual perceptions of the environment play a key role in what is actually experienced. For some, a disorganized work setting is perceived as a challenge and for others a major source of stress.

Strategies for environmental assessment are directed at identifying the ultimate client-environment fit. In this process it is important to assess how the various environmental forces affect each other, such as stresses at work and functioning at home, and to obtain an accurate reading of individual perceptions of these forces. Hershenson et al. (1996) adapted information from Huebner (1980) in making the following guidelines for environmental assessment:

1. All aspects of the environment must be assessed independently and in relation to each other.
2. Instruments used in assessment should provide information on the sources of pressure within the environment.
3. Locally developed instruments should be considered in intervention planning.
4. Multiple strategies and procedures should be utilized when assessing complex person-environment relationships.
5. The relationship between the objective and perceived environment should be differentiated.
6. Assessment instruments should be reliable and valid for the purpose they are to be used.

Environmental assessment appears to offer another important dimension of the assessment process. It expands the horizons of assessment beyond the individual to include the assessment of people within the context of their social milieu. Environmental assessment appears to offer much promise in terms of generating information on the role of sociocultural forces in psychological functioning.

Diagnosis

Historical Perspective

Nathan and Harris (1980) provide information that shows that the process of diagnosis can be traced to the preclassical period in Greece. The Greeks were able to identify the behavioral consequences associated with the aging process and the mental health consequences of alcoholism. Somewhat later during classical times, the Greeks went on to identify and describe psychological disorders that are still recognized today, such as mania, melancholia, and paranoia.

It was not until much later that a formal classification of psychological disorders was developed. Rosenhan and Seligman (1995) identify several key individuals who contributed to this process. Philippe Pinel (1745–1826), the psychiatric reformer, divided psychological disorders into melancholia, mania (with and without delirium), dementia, and idiotism. In 1896, Emil Kraepelin (1856–1926) developed the first comprehensive system of classifying psychological disorders. He based this system of diagnosis on a medical model. In this regard, Kraepelin believed that all medical disorders had a physical origin and that diagnosis required a careful assessment of symptoms. Rosenhan and Seligman identify several other individuals, such as Eugen Bleuler and Adolf Meyer, who proposed their own systems of diagnosis.

Although there are merits in the various diagnostic systems, the need for one coherent system of diagnosis became apparent. This led to the development of the *Diagnostic and Statistical Manual of Mental Disorders* (DSM) in 1952. The DSM has undergone several revisions since that time, with the DSM-IV-TR being published in 2000.

Uses of Diagnosis.　Diagnosis is an important aspect of the counseling process. Rosenhan and Seligman (1995) describe four reasons for making a diagnosis:

1. *It provides communication shorthand among clinicians.* Diagnosis enables the clinician to incorporate the various symptoms of a client into a single diagnosis that other clinicians can easily understand.
2. *It suggests treatment possibilities.* Diagnosis can help clinicians narrow down the treatment possibilities. For example, a paranoid schizophrenic will usually not respond well to verbal therapies.
3. *It can communicate information about etiology.* Mental disorders are associated with different types of etiology. For example, one of the major causative factors associated with schizophrenia is an excess of the neurotransmitter dopamine in the brain.
4. *It aids scientific investigation.* Diagnosis helps group symptoms together so they can be systematically studied to determine etiology and treatment strategies.

Woody, Hansen, and Rossberg (1989) note that some counselors shy away from diagnosis because they believe it is a judgmental process that labels clients. These authors counter that diagnosis is more than a process of labeling. It also provides an analysis of the client's functioning to determine the most appropriate treatment.

The DSM-IV-TR

The DSM-IV-TR is a classification system of all recognized mental disorders. It is a multi-axial evaluation system that provides information on five separate axes.

Axes I and II.   These two axes comprise the entire system of mental disorders. All recognized mental disorders will be on either Axis I or Axis II. The DSM-IV-TR provides decision trees that describe the symptoms associated with various mental disorders. Clinicians can use decision trees to rule out certain disorders when conducting a differential diagnosis to determine whether a patient has a particular mental disorder.

Axis I is used for all mental disorders except for personality disorders and mental retardation, which are placed on Axis II. Axis I can also be used to record counseling problems that are not mental disorders but require professional attention or treatment. These are called V-codes and include many so-called problems of living, such as marital difficulty or parent-child problems. It is also important to note that multiple diagnoses can be recorded on both Axis I and Axis II. For example, a 54-year-old male with a history of alcohol abuse is currently experiencing a major depression. In addition, the patient has an antisocial personality disorder. These disorders can be recorded on each axis as follows:

Axis I	296.22	Major depression, single episode, moderate
	305.00	Alcohol abuse
Axis II	301.70	Antisocial personality disorder

Clinicians record the presence or absence of a diagnosis on Axis I and Axis II, as illustrated in the following examples.

A 12-year-old client who is mentally retarded can be recorded as follows:

| Axis I | V71.09 | No diagnosis or condition an Axis I |
| Axis II | 317 | Mild mental retardation |

A client who does not have a mental disorder but is receiving help for a marital problem can be recorded as follows:

| Axis I | V61.10 | Partner relational problem |
| Axis II | V71.09 | No diagnosis on Axis II |

Another factor for clinicians to consider when making an Axis I or Axis II diagnosis is to determine the principal diagnosis or condition. The principal diagnosis is the condition that is primarily responsible for the evaluation and will be the main focus of attention. When making two or more diagnoses on the same axis, the clinician should list the primary diagnosis first on that axis. When making diagnoses on both axes, the clinician should indicate which is the primary diagnosis, as illustrated in the following example:

| Axis I | 309.24 | Adjustment disorder with anxiety |
| Axis II | 301.20 | Schizoid personality disorder (principal diagnosis) |

The DSM-IV-TR also provides a mechanism for the clinician to indicate the degree of diagnostic certainty. There may be inadequate information to make a diagnosis on either Axis I or Axis II. When this occurs, the clinician can use the notation, "799.90 Diagnosis or condition deferred," on the appropriate axis, as illustrated in the following example:

Axis I	799.90	Diagnosis or condition deferred on Axis I
Axis II	799.90	Diagnosis or condition deferred on Axis II

The clinician can also make a provisional diagnosis on either axis. This enables the clinician to formulate a tentative diagnosis, which requires additional assessment before a final diagnosis can be made. The following example shows how the clinician indicates a provisional diagnosis:

Axis I	296.22	Major depression, single episode, moderate (provisional)

Axis III. Axis III allows the clinician to indicate whether there is a current medical disorder or condition that may be relevant to the particular case. For example, a person may be suffering from syphilis, which could be responsible for producing hallucinations. If this is the case, the clinician would record a diagnosis of untreated syphilis on Axis III.

Axis IV. Axis IV provides information relating to pertinent psychosocial and environmental problems, which can affect the diagnosis or treatment of a mental disorder. Generally these are problems that have occurred during the past year but can extend beyond that timeframe if the events appear to have a bearing on the current mental status of the client, such as being a Vietnam veteran. The DSM provides specific categories for reporting psychosocial and environmental problems such as educational problems or occupational problems. The clinician should use these categories to help describe the particular circumstances of the client. The clinician can list more than one problem area. For example, a client who is about to fail out of school and lose his part-time job can be recorded as follows:

Axis IV	Academic difficulties
	Threat of job loss

Some psychosocial and environmental problems can become so significant in the client's treatment that they may become the focus of the clinician's attention. When this occurs, they should also be recorded on Axis I as a V code (as noted earlier in the description of Axis I) as in the following example:

Axis I	V62.3	Academic problem
	V62.2	Occupational problem

Axis V. Axis V allows the clinician to indicate the client's overall level of functioning (in terms of psychological, social, and occupational functioning). A Global Assessment of Functioning (GAF) scale is provided to rate the client. The scale is rated from 0 to 100, with

100 indicating superior functioning and 1 indicating seriously impaired functioning. The clinician should record the GAF number and what time period it reflects (for example, current, highest level in past year, on admission, at discharge). A person with serious suicidal thoughts upon admission to a hospital could be recorded as follows:

Axis V   GAF = 50 (on admission)

A Case Study.   Spitzer et al. (2002) provide an excellent learning tool for counselors to gain expertise in using the DSM. For numerous case studies involving children, adolescents, and adults, the authors follow a format of describing each case study, giving a DSM-IV-TR diagnosis, and explaining the rationale for the diagnosis. The following excerpt from *The DSM-IV-TR Casebook* (Spitzer et al., 2002, pp. 323–325) provides an example of how to apply the DSM diagnostic process to a case (reprinted by permission).

"Sniper"

Leah, age 7, was referred by her teacher for evaluation because of her tearfulness, irritability, and difficulty concentrating in class. Two and a half months earlier Leah had been among a group of children pinned down by sniper fire on her school playground. Over a period of 15 minutes, the sniper killed one child and injured several others. After the gunfire ceased, no one moved until the police stormed the sniper's apartment and found that he had killed himself. Leah did not personally know the child who was killed or the sniper.

Before the shooting, according to her teacher, Leah was shy but vivacious, well-behaved, and a good student. Within a few days after the incident, there was a noticeable change in her behavior. She withdrew from her friends. She began to bicker with other children when they spoke to her. She seemed uninterested in her schoolwork and had to be prodded to persist in required tasks. The teacher noticed that Leah jumped whenever there was static noise in the public address system and when the class shouted answers to flashcards.

Leah's parents were relieved when the school made the referral, because they were uncertain about how to help her. Leah was uncharacteristically quiet when her parents asked her about the sniping incident. At home she had become moody, irritable, argumentative, fearful, and clinging. She was apprehensive about new situations and fearful of being alone and insisted that someone accompany her to the bathroom. Leah regularly asked to sleep with her parents. She slept restlessly and occasionally cried out in her sleep. She appeared always to be tired, complained of minor physical problems, and seemed more susceptible to minor infections. Her parents were especially worried after Leah nearly walked in front of a moving car without being aware of it. Although she seemed less interested in any of her usual games, her parents noticed that she kept engaging her siblings in nurse games, in which she was often bandaged.

When asked about the incident in the interview, Leah said that she had tried desperately to hide behind a trash can when she heard the repeated gunfire. She had been terrified of being killed, and was "shaking all over," her heart pounding and her head hurting. She vividly told of watching an older child fall to the ground, bleeding and motionless. She ran to safety when there was a pause in the shooting.

Leah described a recurring image of the injured girl lying bleeding on the playground. She said that thoughts of the incident sometimes disrupted her attention, though she would try to think about something else. Lately, she could not always remember what was being said in class.

She no longer played in the area where the shooting had occurred. During recess or after school, she avoided crossing over the playground on her way home from school each day and avoided the sniper's house and street. She was particularly afraid at school on Fridays, the day the shooting had occurred. Although her mother and father had comforted her, she did not know how to tell them what she was feeling.

Leah continued to be afraid that someone would shoot at her again. She had nightmares about the shooting and dreams in which she or a family member was being shot at or pursued. She ran away from any "popping noises" at home or in the neighborhood. Although she said that she had less desire to play, when asked about new games, she reported frequently playing a game in which a nurse helped an injured person. She began to watch television news about violence, and recounted news stories that demonstrated that the world was full of danger.

Discussion of "Sniper"

Leah experienced a traumatic event that involved actual or threatened death or serious injury to herself and to her classmates and evoked intense fear, helplessness, and horror. Within a few days of the trauma, she began to exhibit the characteristic symptoms of severe Posttraumatic Stress Disorder (DSM-IV-TR, p. 467). Because the duration of symptoms is less than 3 months, we further specify Acute.

Although adults sometimes have "flashbacks" in which they actually experience the situation as if it were currently happening, children rarely reexperience trauma in this way. As is typical for her age, Leah reexperienced the trauma in the form of recurrent, intrusive images and recollections of the event and recurrent, distressing dreams about it. She also incorporated themes from the event into repetitive themes in play.

Leah attempted to avoid thoughts and feelings associated with the trauma and places that reminded her of the event. This formerly vivacious little girl now exhibited numbing of general responsiveness. She became apathetic and uninterested in her schoolwork and detached from her former friends. She displayed persistent symptoms of increased arousal, including exaggerated startle reaction (to loud noises), irritability, difficulty concentrating, and sleep disturbance.

In making a multiaxial assessment, we check on Axis IV, "Problem Related to Interaction with Legal System/Crime" and specify "victim of sniper attack." Because of the serious symptoms and impairment in her social relationships and schoolwork, we assign a current Global Assessment of Functioning score of 45.

A DSM-IV-TR diagnosis for Leah is

Axis I	309.81	Posttraumatic stress disorder
Axis II	V71.09	No diagnosis on Axis II
Axis III		None
Axis IV		Problem related to interaction with the legal system/crime (victim of sniper attack)
Axis V		GAF: 45 (current)

The Clinical Interview

The clinical interview provides a structure for assimilating information pertaining to assessment and diagnosis. May (1990) notes that the clinical interview is one of the most widely used assessment procedures. It serves a variety of purposes such as providing information on the client's presenting problem and concerns; enabling the counselor to gain necessary historical information, including organic factors that could contribute to the client's condition; and aiding in the process of making a differential diagnosis to determine whether a client suffers from a particular mental disorder.

The clinical interview normally takes place early in the counseling process, usually during the first or second session. It allows the counselor to gain important background information and determine whether the client suffers from a mental disorder or is in a state of crisis that requires immediate attention. The clinical interview can be structured according to the counselor's theoretical orientation and the client's unique issues and concerns.

I have developed a four-stage model for the clinical interview: using listening skills, taking the client's history, conducting a mental status exam, and using standardized and nonstandardized measures. These four stages serve overlapping functions and should not be perceived as discrete entities. For example, a counselor may gain useful information about the client's history and mental status while using listening skills. An overview of these four stages follows.

Stage One: Using Listening Skills.   Counselors can begin the clinical interview by using listening skills to obtain a phenomenological understanding of the client. Counselors can also use listening skills to determine whether a client is self-referred, what prompted the appointment, and a description of the presenting problem and underlying concerns.

Stage Two: Taking the Client's History.   The counselor may take an in-depth history after clients have had a chance to discuss their situation with the counselor. The history can be divided into two parts. The first part involves the client providing background information regarding work, family, social relationships, health, and other areas of interest such as important turning points in the client's life. Counselors may develop or use forms to solicit information on these topics as an efficient method of gathering this part of the history. The second part of the history involves exploring the client's symptoms and concerns, such as difficulty sleeping, loss of appetite, or marital problems, in terms of onset, duration, and severity. This information can help the counselor gain a better overall understanding of the client's condition. It can also be particularly useful in diagnosis, since major systems of diagnosis such as the DSM-IV-TR require this information to make a differential diagnosis.

It is particularly important when conducting a history to explore possible organic factors that could contribute to mental disorders. These factors include the use of alcohol or drugs, prescription medications, and existing or past medical conditions. For example, excessive use of alcohol can create hallucinations, resulting in a mental disorder called alcohol hallucinosis. Many prescription drugs have been known to contribute to the symptoms associated with mental disorders (Othmer & Othmer, 1989). For example, estrogen can cause anxiety and depression; diuretics can produce irritability, restlessness, insomnia, and delirium; and insulin can induce psychosis and confusion. Medical conditions may also be accompanied by symptoms of psychological distress. For example, gout or brain tumors can produce depression; head injury can cause anxiety; and multiple sclerosis can foster anxiety, depression, and episodic psychiatric symptoms. Othmer and Othmer (1989) provide a more complete list of prescription drugs and medical conditions and their associated psychiatric symptoms.

Stage Three: Conducting a Mental Status Exam. Counselors can conduct a mental status exam to help make a differential diagnosis. For a client who reports hearing voices, a counselor may consider schizophrenia as a possible diagnosis. The counselor could then use the mental status exam to explore whether the client has other symptoms associated with schizophrenia, such as delusions, flat or inappropriate affect, and evidence of a thought disorder.

Trzepacz and Baker (1993) describe six components that should be addressed in a mental status exam:

1. *Appearance, attitude, and activity level.* Much can be learned from *appearance.* Bizarre dress and overall appearance can suggest disorientation and a mental disorder. Physical appearance can also provide some information regarding the person's physical health (for example, runny nose and so forth can suggest a cold or illness). *Attitude* relates to the individual's demeanor during the interview. This can range from cooperative to hostile and can provide indications of the person's interpersonal style and reaction to the counselor. *Activity level* relates to the quality and degree of physical and motor movement. Some clients are constantly pacing, suggesting possible explosive tendencies, whereas others are listless with little movement, which may suggest depression.

2. *Mood and affect.* *Mood* is the person's *internal* emotional state, such as happy, sad, or anxious. *Affect* is the *external* manifestation of how emotions are expressed. Affect is communicated verbally and nonverbally in numerous ways, such as facial expressions, tone of voice, laughter, and crying. Mood and affect can be congruent and appropriate (indicating mental health), such as laughing when one feels happy, or incongruent, such as laughing when one is sad (indicating a possible mental disorder).

3. *Speech and language.* *Speech* and *language* relate to verbal and written communication involving words, concepts, and ideas. Assessment of speech and language can help identify problems with fluency (such as stuttering), communication disorders (relating to information processing), and learning disabilities.

4. *Thought process, thought content, and perception.* *Thought processes* relate to *how* we are thinking, where as *thought content* is directed at *what* we are thinking. Normal thought processes tend to be connected (or linear), with one idea contributing to the next idea. Problems with thought processes can occur in schizophrenia when the individual has difficulty staying with one line of thought and instead jumps from one topic to another, unrelated topic. *Thought content* and *perceptions* can also suggest mental health or illness. For example, it is common in psychosis for clients to have problems with thought content (such as being delusional) and problems with perceptions (such as having hallucinations).

5. *Cognition.* *Cognition* relates to a wide array of intellectual functions, including memory, the ability to think and reason, problem-solving skills, and creativity. Assessment of cognition involves a variety of skills and abilities, such as determining a person's degree of orientation (for example, who they are and where they are) and a person's ability to attend, concentrate, remember, and use abstract thinking to solve complex problems. Failure to use basic mental facilities can suggest brain damage such as that found in Alzheimer's dementia.

6. *Insight and judgment.* *Insight* and *judgment* involve the use of a variety of higher-order functions that can be referred to as "emotional intelligence," or EQ. EQ can include such things as having self-awareness, being able to "read social situations" to determine appropriate interpersonal behavior, and utilizing decision-making skills necessary for sound judgment.

Stage Four: Using Standardized and Nonstandardized Measures.   Counselors can use standardized and nonstandardized measures to refine diagnostic considerations and plan treatment. For example, a client's MMPI-II profile might include elevated scales on 2 (depression) and 9 (mania), which could contribute to a diagnosis of manic depression. In terms of nonstandardized measures, environmental assessment might show that the client feels depressed about living on the East Coast, hates working in a retail job, and wants to go back to school. Information from the environmental assessment can be useful in terms of understanding the etiology, or cause, of the mental disorder as well as in planning treatment. In this example, the client could consider moving and going to school.

Treatment Planning

Treatment planning can be defined as "an organized conceptual effort to design a program *outlining in advance* the specific steps by which the therapist will help the patient recover from his or her presenting dysfunctional state" (Makover, 1992, p. 338). Linda Seligman (1998) conceptualizes treatment planning in terms of an hourglass. Initially, the counselor generates a large amount of information during the assessment phases (such as psychosocial and medical history). This information gets narrowed down, generating one or more diagnoses. The diagnosis then broadens into consideration of treatment goals and associated counseling techniques and strategies.

Seligman (1998) notes that it is important to consider counselor and client variables when formulating a treatment plan. Consideration of counselor and client characteristics can be useful in selecting treatment modalities for client problems and disorders. For example, there is some evidence to suggest that depressed individuals with low social dysfunction respond well to interpersonal therapy and those with low cognitive dysfunction respond well to cognitive-behavioral therapy (Shea et al., 1990). The literature provides a rich description of the client variables (Garfield, 1994) and the counselor variables (Beutler, Machado, & Neufeldt, 1994) on counseling outcomes that can provide additional information for treatment planning.

Treatment planning can be conceptualized from several perspectives, such as managed care, brief-solution-focused counseling, use of treatment planners, and curative factors that promote success in treatment planning. To a large degree, treatment planning must address the criteria acceptable by managed care organizations. For example, Kelly (1999) notes that managed care will continue to require empirically validated treatment models. Managed care also prescribes to the motto that quicker is better. Brief-solution-focused treatment planning has therefore become the rule and not the exception. For brief-solution-focused counseling, treatment planning tends to be narrow in nature, focusing on symptom relief and returning the individual to a functional state as quickly as possible. Traditional treatment planning is more comprehensive, with the goal of addressing as many clinical issues and client modalities as necessary to move the client toward optimal development.

All perspectives on treatment planning share some common elements. Young (1992) identifies two aspects of treatment planning that would seem to be useful for most theoretical perspectives. First, the counselor and client formulate mutually agreed on treatment goals, which are prioritized and associated with counseling strategies. A number of useful treatment planners are available that can be used to identify treatment goals and the associated counseling strategies for common counseling problems (such as anger management) and mental disorders (see Jongsma & Peterson, 1995). Second, the counselor utilizes curative factors to promote success in the treatment planning process. These curative factors are maintaining a positive counseling relationship, enhancing the client's self-efficacy and self-esteem, lowering and raising emotional arousal, increasing hope and expectations, and practicing behaviors and providing new learning experiences. Curative factors such as these appear to offer much promise for promoting efficacy in all phases of the counseling process and warrant in-depth research evaluation to determine the actual effect they have on different phases of the counseling process.

Several comprehensive treatment planning models have emerged from the literature. Seligman's (1998) model is based on the acronym DO A CLIENT MAP. DO A CLIENT MAP represents a comprehensive treatment planning model that addresses a number of clinical components, such as the overall diagnosis and treatment goals, nature of assessment procedures required, counselor characteristics that would be facilitative, types of interventions (such as individual or group counseling), and the prognosis regarding recovery. A description of each of the elements of Seligman's approach is provided in Table 4.2.

Arnold Lazarus's (1997, 2000) multimodal therapy (MMT) is both a separate school of counseling and a method that can be used in treatment planning. As a school of counseling, Lazarus's (2000) approach is based on social-learning theory, general systems theory, and group and communication theory. Lazarus (1997) notes that MMT has always been a brief form of therapy embracing the major trends in brief counseling such as problem-centered, solution-focused, and active-directive. Lazarus (1997) recognizes the pressures from managed health care and strengthens his brief therapy perspective as follows. Brief-MMT is characterized by the following:

- Active-directive strategies that include advice giving and homework assignment
- A didactic-educational focus (such as direct teaching and bibliotherapy) to help clients learn effective coping responses
- Use of the BASIC I.D. modalities in assessment, diagnosis, and treatment planning and to quickly identify key problems and counseling goals
- Use of "elegant solutions" (from sources such as Ellis's 1996 brief rational-emotive behavior therapy) to provide brief yet comprehensive approaches to problem resolution

TABLE 4.2   Overview of Seligman's DO A CLIENT MAP

Elements of the Model	Description
D Diagnosis	The overall diagnosis
O Objective	Treatment goals
A Assessments	Nature of assessment procedures required
C Clinician	Counselor characteristics that would be facilitative
L Location of treatment	Setting of treatment (for example, school or hospital)
I Interventions	Types of counseling strategies utilized
E Emphasis of treatment	Behavioral, cognitive, affective, supportive, directive, and so forth
N Nature of treatment	Individual, group, marriage and family, and so forth
T Timing	Frequency, duration, and number of counseling sessions
M Medications	Nature of medication needs
A Adjunct services	Types of additional services needed, such as human services
P Prognosis	Amount of improvement that is expected

According to Lazarus (1993), MMT is a form of technical eclecticism that utilizes a recognized theory along with counseling strategies from other theories. Lazarus (1993) contends that technical eclectic theories such as MMT have an advantage over other approaches in that they provide specific decision-making criteria for treatment planning.

The core of MMT is conceptualized in terms of the acronym BASIC I.D., which addresses seven modalities that provide a basis for treatment planning. Table 4.3 provides an overview of Lazarus's BASIC I.D.

Lazarus (1997) suggests that an assessment of all seven modalities provides an overview of the client's physical and psychological functioning. Additional assessment can be conducted in each modality as necessary to obtain a more in-depth understanding of the client. For example, an exploration of the nature and content of a client's cognition could

TABLE 4.3   Larazus's BASIC I.D.

Elements of Model	Description
B Behavior	Actions that people do (such as withdraw or avoid)
A Affect	Emotional states (such as depression and anxiety)
S Sensation	Feelings derived from the bodily senses (such as emptiness)
I Imagery	Visualizations (such as daydreaming and fantasizing)
C Cognition	Thoughts and ideas (such as *I wish I were dead*)
I Interpersonal relations	How people relate to each other (such as encouraging)
D Drugs	Biophysiological states (such as use of medication)

suggest a pattern of self-destructive behavior (such as statements like "I'm no good. My wife would be better off without me"). Once the modalities have been evaluated, the counselor is in a position to formulate treatment goals with the client.

Makover (1992) provides another model of treatment planning called *hierarchical treatment planning.* It is a very practical, easy-to-understand approach. Makover suggests that counselors and clients should work together on formulating a treatment plan. Makover goes on to note that agreement on a treatment plan can be facilitated if clinicians generate answers to three questions by the end of the first session. The three questions are: "Why did the client come here?," "Why did the client come now?" and "What does the client want?," These questions can help identify what precipitated the request for counseling, current stressors, and the overall aim of receiving counseling.

Hierarchical treatment planning is composed of a four-tier hierarchy that provides a mechanism for understanding the interrelationship between the counseling process and treatment planning. The hierarchical approach begins with an identification of the final outcome or overall aim of counseling (such as an enhanced marital relationship). The second tier of the hierarchy is the counseling goals (such as improved communication skills) associated with the overall aim. The third tier is the strategies (such as listening skills) that can be used to meet the goals. The fourth tier is the techniques (such as use of paraphrasing) that are associated with the counseling strategies. It must be emphasized that hierarchical treatment planning begins by identifying the overall aim of counseling and works downward to goals, strategies, and techniques. Counselors who emphasize techniques in counseling can essentially get treatment planning "backward," using a technique-oriented approach to generate what the final outcomes will become.

In the final analysis, all three models of treatment planning can be used collectively to provide a comprehensive approach to treatment planning. Together they provide useful information on the counseling process in terms of assessment, diagnosis, and treatment and the interrelationship between aims, goals, strategies, and techniques; they also provide information on client modalities such as affect, cognitions, and interpersonal relations. In this regard, treatment planning provides an organizational structure to promote a sense of direction for the counseling process.

Diversity and Postmodern Issues in Assessment and Diagnosis

It is important to use a multicultural perspective in all phases of counseling, including assessment, diagnosis, and treatment. A muticultural assessment helps counselors gain an accurate understanding of clients in terms of cultural, gender, religion/spirituality, and other issues of diversity. The following *Personal Note* provides an example of the importance of a multicultural perspective in assessment and diagnosis.

Fortunately, criteria for recognizing and describing mental disorders such as the *Diagnostic and Statistical Manual* (DSM) are beginning to address issues of diversity such as culture and spirituality. The trend toward cultural sensitivity began with the DSM-IV (Smart & Smart, 1997). The DSM-IV (as compared to the DSM-III-R) demonstrates significant improvement in incorporating cultural considerations in the diagnostic process. According to Smart and Smart (1997), the DSM-IV achieves its enhanced cultural

A Personal Note

The importance of considering diversity issues such as religion/spirituality and culture in assessment and diagnosis became very clear to me in a recent clinical case. The case involved "Jim," a tenth-grade Navajo student. Jim began experiencing anxiety and depression shortly after he witnessed his brother killed in a shark attack when his family was vacationing in Australia a year earlier. He had also been in the water but was able to get out and back on the boat. Since the accident, Jim's personality began to change. He was no longer the fun-loving outdoors person that seemed to be full of self-confidence and was interested in playing sports and hanging out with his friends. Instead, Jim became solemn and isolated himself from others. He also developed paranoia shortly after the accident, contending that others were out to get him. When Jim returned to the United States, he had panic attacks at school several times a week, interfering with his ability to attend class. On several occasions he lost consciousness during the panic attack, resulting in the school calling for an ambulance.

Jim had several evaluations and received a diagnosis associated with anxiety and depression such as posttraumatic stress disorder, panic disorder, and so forth. Several medications had been used along with cognitive behavioral therapy. When he did not respond to treatment, I was asked to provide consultation. In my clinical interview, I asked him several questions that related to culture and religion/spirituality that turned out to be quite helpful in terms of assessment, diagnosis, and treatment. These questions were as follows: From the perspective of the Navajo culture, how is mental health and mental illness conceptualized? How can your culture, religion, and spirituality be used to explain how you developed your mental health problems? How can your culture, religion, and spirituality be used to help you get better?

Jim's responses to these questions were quite interesting. He said that Navajo culture did not separate mental from physical health—they were interrelated. In addition, when a person had health problems, it was often associated with being out of synch with one's culture or "traditional ways." Jim noted that he had a warning that this was the case for him before his family went to Australia—a coyote ran in front of his parents' car on the way to the airport. According to Navajo culture, this is a sign that his family was "not right" with their culture and that they would need a ceremony as soon as possible. In addition, Jim said an Aboriginal man in Australia gave him "the evil eye" a week after the shark attack and put a "hex" on him. From that point he began to feel others were out to get him. Jim went on to say that for him to get better, he would need a ceremony to make his family "right" with their culture, and he would need a ceremony to help him get rid of his "hex." Shortly after the two ceremonies were arranged, Jim was able to overcome the paranoia and panic attacks and regain some self-confidence. At that point he was able to benefit from counseling to address the posttraumatic stress disorder and anxiety and depression associated with the loss of his brother. After six months of weekly counseling, he was able to work through most of the issues that were undermining his health and well-being.

perspective by including "(a) descriptions of specific cultural features that may be present in various disorders, (b) a glossary of 25 culture-bound syndromes, (c) an Outline for Cultural Formulation intended to help counselors in evaluating the impact of the client's cultural background, (d) a broader definition of Axis IV, and (e) the inclusion of new culturally sensitive 'V codes'" (p. 393). For example, the Outline for Cultural Formulation provides culturally relevant information that can be considered in formulating a multiaxial diagnosis, and examples of new "V codes" include V62.4, Acculturation Problem, and V62.89, Religious or Spiritual Problems.

Although the DSM is beginning to make advances in terms of addressing diversity issues, additional work is required to establish a realistic understanding of the diagnosis and description of mental disorders within a multicultural perspective (Smart & Smart, 1997).

Postmodern theories such as social constructionism emphasize the role of diversity in assessment and diagnosis. From this perspective, it is important to take into consideration the effects of culture, gender, age, environment, language, and the multiple realities that can be generated from each individual's unique world view. Assessment and diagnosis must therefore involve processes that move beyond the intrapsychic or self-analysis to include a consideration of diversity issues.

Numerous diversity issues are associated with assessment. For example, the importance of being aware of possible cultural bias is described earlier in this chapter. Environmental assessment and assessment of world view provide good examples of how a counselor can look beyond intrapsychic forces to gain a broader picture of the client's world.

Spirituality is an emerging dimension of multiculturalism, which should be considered during the assessment process (Richards & Bergin, 1997). Spiritual assessment is in its infancy stage of development, with few formal spiritual assessment instruments available. Richards and Bergin therefore recommend that spiritual assessment be done primarily during the initial history-taking and the clinical interview. Spiritual assessment can be used with all clients to obtain an understanding of their world view regarding spiritual issues (which may or may not include religious beliefs). It may be particularly useful to determine whether clients perceive spirituality as a source of strength and guidance and whether they turn to spiritual processes during times of personal difficulties. In these instances, spirituality can be used to foster a strengths perspective in counseling.

In some instances, counselors may also wish to determine whether clients' spiritual beliefs and values are healthy or unhealthy in terms of promoting mental health (Richards & Bergin, 1997). For example, Allport and Ross (1967) differentiate unhealthy and healthy religious practice in terms of extrinsic versus intrinsic motivation. Unhealthy religious practice is characterized by an extrinsic religious orientation and includes people who use religion as a way of impressing others with status and self-righteousness. Healthy religious orientation tends to be intrinsically motivated and is characterized by personal spiritual journeys with individualized goals and aspirations. Clients who have potentially unhealthy spiritual beliefs and values can address these issues in counseling or be referred to specialists for assistance.

Accurate diagnosis also requires sensitivity to issues in diversity. It is especially important for counselors to be aware of the cultural context of language when differentiating mental health from mental illness. What might be considered normal can vary dramatically from one culture to the next. Gergen (1994a) points out the role of language and culture in the etiology of mental disorders. He notes that some cultures have survived for centuries without any word or concept for depression, yet cultures that have a term for depression seem to find depression virtually everywhere.

Other important factors to consider in diagnosis include age and gender. Developmental psychopathology has identified how problems such as anxiety and depression manifest themselves differently according to age. For example, it is not uncommon for a child's or adolescent's depression to be "masked" by anger. Gender is also important to consider. For example, a woman who has just had a baby and becomes depressed could be experiencing a postpartum depression.

Summary

Assessment and diagnosis are important parts of the counseling process. They provide critical background information that is necessary before the counselor and client can establish counseling goals. Assessment and diagnosis also contribute to the science dimension of counseling by providing objective information regarding the counseling process.

Standardized assessment procedures include psychological tests that have a standardized norm group, such as the MMPI-II. Nonstandardized tests do not have standardized norm groups, are more subjective in nature, and include a variety of procedures such as observation and environmental assessment. Standardized and nonstandardized assessment procedures have their inherent strengths and weaknesses. For example, the major strength of nonstandardized measures lies in the ease of adjusting these procedures to the unique characteristics of the individual, thereby avoiding tendencies to induce test bias.

The DSM-IV-TR can be used to formulate a multiaxial diagnosis. The clinical interview is a valuable tool for counselors to use in assessment and diagnosis. Counselors can use the interview to establish positive relationships and provide a structure for assessment and diagnosis. The clinical interview can also help the counselor avoid overlooking important issues such as a medical condition, past history of alcohol or drug abuse, and symptoms associated with a mental disorder. Diversity issues such as culture, gender, age, and spirituality should also be considered in assessment and diagnosis.

Personal Exploration

1. What assessment procedures do you find interesting and what intrigues you about them?
2. What is your opinion regarding mental disorders?
3. How do issues of diversity, such as age, gender, and culture, influence the way mental disorders are diagnosed and treated?
4. What is your opinion of using drugs to treat mental disorders in children and adolescents?

Web Sites for Chapter 4

Franklin, D. J. (2000). *Psychological evaluations.* Retrieved March 3, 2005, from
   http://psychologyinfo.com/treatment/evaluations.html
   Describes the interview process in counselor assessment.
Franklin, D. J. (2000). *Psychological testing.* Retrieved March 3, 2005, from
   http://psychologyinfo.com/treatment/testing.html
   Describes psychological tests and various forms of testing used in the assessment process.

Counseling Research and Evaluation

CHAPTER OVERVIEW

This chapter provides an overview of the issues relating to counseling research and evaluation. In addition to discussing traditional research methodologies, particular attention is focused on field-based methodologies such as qualitative and single-subject research designs. These newer methodologies are attracting considerable attention in the literature as being particularly relevant to the practitioner. Highlights of the chapter include

- The art and science of research and evaluation
- The purpose of research and evaluation relative to theory and practice, counselor accountability, and the body of knowledge in the counseling field
- An overview of types of research such as qualitative research methodologies and single-subject designs
- Diversity and postmodern issues in research and evaluation

The Art and Science of Research and Evaluation

Counseling research is both an art and a science, providing subjective and objective means for understanding and evaluating counseling. Traditionally, counseling research has emphasized the science dimension by utilizing experimental/quantitative research methodology involving hypothesis testing and statistical analysis. Experimental/quantitative research continues to hold an important position in the science of counseling, providing counselors with an objective tool for understanding and evaluating techniques and procedures in counseling.

Unfortunately, few practitioners use experimental/quantitative research methods, creating an ever-widening gap between practice and research (Peterson, 1995; Reisetter, et al., 2004). Goldfried and Wolfe (1996) note that with the changes in health care delivery resulting from managed care, it is becoming increasingly important for clinicians to utilize some form of research to demonstrate accountability.

Recent trends in research have explored how the art of counseling research can be developed as a means of bridging the gap between practice and research. In this regard,

The section on single-subject design was written by Dr. Stephen W. Stile.

qualitative approaches have emerged that provide practitioners with methodologies that are less rigid and involve more clinical skills than are used in traditional research methodologies (Reisetter et al., 2004). For example, qualitative approaches may focus on the researcher/evaluator and participant functioning as coinvestigators attempting to discover important information relating to a particular subject. In this process, more emphasis is given to awareness and sensitivity to diversity and other social forces and less emphasis is directed at data gathering and statistical analysis.

Both quantitative and qualitative approaches to research and evaluation have their place in counseling. In time there may be an integration of these positions, creating a balance between the art and science of research and evaluation in counseling.

The Purpose of Research and Evaluation

Counseling research serves many functions in the counseling process. This section reviews several of these functions, such as evaluating the efficacy of a counseling approach through the interaction of theory, practice, and research; providing a means for communicating counselor accountability; and contributing to the body of knowledge in the counseling field.

Theory, Research, and Practice

The art and science of counseling and psychotherapy are similar to the scientist-practitioner model, which emphasizes the role that science plays in shaping clinical practice. Unfortunately, the science of counseling has not kept up with the art of counseling. Hill and Corbett (1993) note that practitioners tend to rely on clinical judgment rather than research to formulate which theories and techniques to use.

The art and science of counseling emphasize the interrelationship between theory, research, and practice. Postmodern theories such as social constructionism stress the role of theory in scientific investigation. In this regard, Gergen (1994a) suggests that theories are representations of language and culture and provide a paradigm to understand reality.

Figure 5.1 provides an illustration of the interrelationship between theory, research, and practice. It shows theory to be at the apex of a triangle, thus placing it in the uppermost

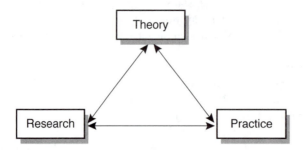

FIGURE 5.1 **The Relationship Between Theory, Research, and Practice**

position. The interrelationship between theory, practice, and research can be illustrated in the following example. The counseling theory of behavior therapy develops techniques such as assertion training. A counselor may use this technique in clinical practice and later implement research strategies to evaluate its effectiveness. The results of this research can provide useful information to refine the theoretical origins of assertion training.

Arrows in Figure 5.1 extend in both directions to depict the reciprocal influence of theory, research, and practice. For example, knowledge can flow up from practice to theory and vice versa in a circular rather than linear fashion. This model also recognizes the postmodern position regarding "action research" that suggests that practitioners and researchers are partners in the search for knowledge.

Research, Evaluation, and Counselor Accountability

Research and evaluation can also be used to communicate counselor accountability. One way to conceptualize how this occurs is through the interaction of research, evaluation, and accountability, as shown in Figure 5.2. This model suggests that counselors can use research strategies to evaluate their individual clinical skills or an entire counseling program. The information obtained from the evaluation process can then provide professional accountability. However, even though accountability has been established, the process is still incomplete. The counselor should then set up an ongoing accountability program. This may require additional research strategies to evaluate the various facets of one's professional activities.

Gibson (1977) and Hershenson, Power, and Waldo (1996) provide the following guidelines regarding evaluation research:

- *Determine the purpose of the evaluation.* It is necessary to identify what type of information needs to be generated from the evaluation. Should the evaluation focus on cost-effectiveness or other issues such as quality control?
- *Effective evaluation uses valid measuring criteria.* Once goals have been identified, criteria for measuring these goals must be established. For example, a goal in a mental health center might be to have all counselors initiate a follow-up contact with each client within one to two months after termination of counseling services. The

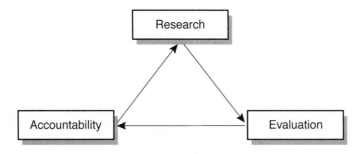

FIGURE 5.2 The Relationship Between Research, Evaluation, and Accountability

measuring criterion might be the percentage of clients whose follow-up activities were initiated.

- *Effective program evaluation depends on accurate application of the measuring criteria.* Appropriate research strategies should be used to collect and analyze the data.
- *Program evaluation should obtain input from all people involved in the program.* Opportunities for input from all levels of the organization should be provided. In a mental health center, for example, the evaluation might include information from administrators, clerical staff, counselors, and clients.
- *The evaluation should include feedback and follow-through.* Once the evaluation is complete, the results may be communicated to the staff in a clear and concise fashion. Recommendations should be included to facilitate future program planning and development.
- *Evaluation should be a planned and continuous process.* A program should have an ongoing evaluation process. This enables the staff to monitor strengths and weaknesses. Accountability does not imply that a program has only strengths. Rather, it implies also becoming aware of weaknesses and attempting to rectify them.
- Program *evaluations should be sensitive to the politics of the organization.* All organizational systems have unique political structures that impact the functioning of the organization. It is therefore important to take these political forces into consideration throughout the evaluation process.

Hershenson et al. (1996) go on to identify knowledge and skills necessary for effective evaluation. Effective evaluation requires knowledge of the particular program—its needs, resources, the population it serves, and how the evaluation process can be of use or benefit. Knowledge is also required about creating the best fit regarding program needs and evaluation procedures. Numerous skills are also facilitative, such as communication, interpersonal, organizational, and advocacy skills.

The Contribution of Research to the Counseling Field

Another purpose of conducting research is to contribute to the body of knowledge in the counseling field so that theories can be tested and practices refined.

Hill and Corbett (1993) identify the following future trends in research relating to process and outcome issues in counseling:

- "The overall goals of process and outcome research should be to develop new theories of therapy, to provide information for practitioners about how to intervene with clients at different points in therapy, and to develop training programs based on the empirical results of what works in therapy" (p. 16).
- Research should be directed at analyzing an entire model of the counseling process such as the one proposed by Hill (1992), which includes the therapist intentions, therapist response modes, client reactions, and client behaviors.
- Research should explore issues relating to competence in counseling (that is, what it means to be a good counselor).

- Research priorities should focus on first determining what the effective process components of counseling are, then developing and evaluating treatment models that emerge from this basic research.
- Additional research is necessary to determine similarities and differences between career and personal counseling.
- Measures need to be developed that can be used to evaluate the content of counseling (for example, interpersonal relations and cultural conflicts) and to measure the strength and healthy functioning of clients as opposed to their psychopathology.
- And finally, researchers across disciplines need to make more effort to work together to communicate methods and results.

Additional research will need to be conducted on these topics as well as others if counseling is to continue to evolve in a meaningful fashion. Counselors can play a vital role in contributing to their profession by engaging in an ongoing research program. The following guidelines can be used to formulate a research program:

1. Do research on topics that interest you rather than selecting a topic to impress someone else.
2. Develop some tenacity when doing research. Once you believe in a project, stick with it and follow it through. There will always be someone to tell you what you can't do. Your job is to tell yourself what you can do and will do.
3. Make a detailed outline before starting to write the research report. This will help you organize your ideas and make your paper easier to read and understand.
4. Don't get discouraged with the publishing process. Once you submit a paper to a journal, it may be accepted, accepted provisionally, rejected with suggestions for resubmission, or rejected. Don't give up if you are requested to revise and resubmit your paper. Only 4 percent of the articles submitted to American Counseling Association journals are accepted without necessary revisions (Seligman, 1986).
5. Finally, never assume your idea is so simple that someone must have published it already. There is a good chance that your idea has not been published, and your contribution might be valuable to the counseling profession.

In the following *Personal Note,* I share some of my personal rewards and struggles with the publishing process.

Overview of the Types of Research

Research can be classified in several ways. One classification system differentiates basic research from applied research. *Basic research* is usually conducted under controlled conditions in a laboratory setting, often in a university. Basic research usually involves university students acting as subjects. Although basic research studies tend to use rigorous research designs, it may be risky to generalize the results of this type of research to the real world. *Applied research* typically tests theories in a field setting. Applied research is therefore reflective of people in their natural habitat. Unfortunately, field studies are not always easy to control and may provide misleading results. Regardless of these limitations, applied research may provide a more realistic alternative for clinicians.

A Personal Note

I've had my share of ups and downs in conducting research. Some highs include having my first paper accepted for publication and feeling excited about contributing to an area of investigation. I was particularly pleased that this was a theoretical paper about a new dimension of social interest. I remember thinking, "Wow, now I'm part of the evolution of Adlerian theory development." I've also had my share of lows in conducting research. The letters of rejection and critical reviews of articles are still painful to receive today.

To survive the research and publication process, I've had to develop a lot of tolerance, patience, perseverance, and self-discipline. But it's been worth it. I've been able to gain a better understanding of a wide range of topics from stuttering to why children soil their pants. Research has also helped me continually develop my personal approach to counseling, as I carefully examine what occurred in a case study. In addition, research has been a helpful tool to communicate accountability. For example, I have used a single-subject design, a topic discussed later in this chapter, to assess what is occurring with a program I'm using to treat encopresis (soiling the pants).

Types of Research Methodologies

Research can also be classified in terms of design. Some of the more common types of research designs are as follows.

Survey Studies.   Survey research typically describes a variable in terms of its frequency in a population (Wilkinson & McNeil, 1996). For example, an investigator might survey a representative sample of professional counselors to determine which counseling approaches are used most often. An influential survey was published by *Consumer Reports* (1995, November). The *Consumer Reports* survey was reviewed by Seligman (1995). He concludes that the study showed that long-term therapy was superior to short-term therapy; therapy was as effective as medication and therapy; and psychologists, psychiatrists, and social workers were equally as effective as therapists and were more effective than marriage counselors and long-term family counseling. In addition, Seligman notes that clients whose length or choice of therapy were determined by managed care insurance did worse than those who were not so restricted. More recently, research suggests that the *Consumer Reports* findings may be too optimistic and too general (e.g., longer more intensive therapy is superior to short-term therapy) (Nielsen et al., 2004).

Seligman notes that although the *Consumer Reports* study has several methodological shortcomings, it should be taken seriously since it provides valuable information regarding counseling efficacy. VandenBos (1996) suggests that the *Consumer Reports* survey provides encouraging information on the public's perception of psychotherapy in terms of need and efficacy. The survey provides evidence that the public clearly values the use of psychotherapy as a form of mental health treatment. In addition, the survey is to a large degree supportive of previous empirical research. However, additional research appears necessary to address the issues posed by the *Consumer Reports* survey.

Correlational Studies.   Correlational studies are used to determine whether two factors are related. For example, a counselor may want to determine whether there is a relationship between gender and age of clients. A review of the counselor's clients over a two-year period may show that clients over 40 years of age tend to be female and those under 15 tend to be male.

Experimental Methods.   This methodology is also referred to as *quantitative research;* it involves evaluating a particular treatment under controlled conditions to determine whether a cause-and-effect relationship exists. For example, an investigator may wish to evaluate the effects of a parent education program on parental attitudes and parent-child behavioral interactions. Traditional experimental designs involve randomly assigning a group of subjects to a treatment group (subjects receiving parent education) and a control group (subjects who do not receive parent education). The two groups can then be compared before and after the program on attitudes, behaviors, or other measures. Statistical analysis is used to evaluate the degree of change in the particular measures to determine the effects of the parent education program.

Longitudinal Studies.   Longitudinal studies are designed to evaluate a particular group of subjects over an extended period of time. For example, a counselor may want to analyze how well a group of immigrants adjusts to American society. Using this research design, the counselor might periodically check on variables such as the percent who graduate from high school and college or tendencies toward physical or mental health problems.

Large-Scale Reviews.   This methodology involves reviewing many published research studies. It has usually been conducted in an attempt to assess the efficacy of counseling. Some of the early work of this type did much to challenge the efficacy of counseling. This was especially true for Eysenck (1965), who claimed that counseling was not effective and that people tended to get better regardless of whether they received counseling. Levitt (1957) also challenged the efficacy of counseling in a large-scale review of studies that evaluated the effectiveness of child counseling and concluded that Eysenck's findings were essentially correct.

Several large-scale reviews of outcome research provide support for the effectiveness of counseling and psychotherapy (Elkin et al., 1989; Garfield, 1983; Lambert, 1991; McNeilly & Howard, 1991; Smith & Glass, 1977; Smith, Glass, & Miller, 1980). These large-scale reviews often use a sophisticated form of statistical analysis called *meta-analysis* in an attempt to reduce some of the methodological problems that can result from grouping together numerous studies for analysis. Smith and Glass (1977) conducted the first large-scale review that demonstrated strong empirical support for the effectiveness of counseling. Their investigation of 400 studies shows that treated individuals were better off than 75 percent of those who did not receive counseling. Smith et al. (1980) reviewed 475 studies and found that treated individuals were better off than 80 percent of those who did not receive counseling. (See Lambert & Bergin, 1994, for additional information regarding the efficacy of counseling.)

Qualitative Methods.   This design attempts to understand people and events in their natural setting. It has therefore been referred to as a naturalistic approach. Qualitative methods are concerned with understanding the individual's point of view and the lived experience and perspective of the people under study (Silverman, 2004). Such methods typically employ nonstandardized measures such as interviews and observations as a means of collecting data. Qualitative methods are oriented to the discovery of insights rather than confirmation of hypotheses. Qualitative methods are also associated with postmodern concepts such as narrative psychology and social constructionism (Northcutt & McCoy, 2004; Reisetter et al., 2004).

Case Studies and Single-Subject Designs.   This method involves an intensive study of one individual or a group of individuals. Information is obtained from interviews, observations, and client self-reports (Wilkinson & McNeil, 1996).

Case studies can be expanded to incorporate some of the principles of experimental design. These designs are sometimes referred to as *single-subject designs* and are presented later in this chapter. They can increase the counselor's ability to evaluate counseling outcomes objectively. Case studies are also a popular means for counselors to illustrate new concepts in counseling theory and practice.

Shortcomings of Traditional Counseling Research

Although the scientist-practitioner model appears to be a goal in the counseling profession, it is not yet a reality. University programs have historically advocated the merits of the scientist-practitioner model, yet clinicians failed to integrate these positions (Peterson, 1995). Clinicians have essentially taken the position that research relates to statistical abstractions and not the average person and therefore has little relevance to the challenges of clinical practice (Beutler, Williams, Wakefield, & Entwistle 1995).

Beutler et al. (1995) make several recommendations that could help bridge the gap between science and practice. These are summarized as follows: (1) scientists need to become more knowledgeable about the issues of clinicians by maintaining ongoing relationships with clinicians, (2) the role of science in practice needs to be reevaluated, (3) new research methods must be developed to make research more relevant to clinicians, and (4) new vehicles are needed to communicate research findings to practitioners.

It is obvious that changes are required to make research more relevant to the needs of practitioners. Qualitative research methodologies represent an emerging force that offers much promise to practitioners and other researchers in the social sciences (Garfield & Bergin, 1994; Reisetter et al., 2004; Silverman, 2004).

Reisetter et al. (2004) describe several positive attributes of qualitative research described by graduate students in counseling:

- *Worldview congruence.* Students noted that the underlying philosophy of qualitative research and their worldviews were congruent (that is, both adhered to postmodern concepts such as the social construction of knowledge, the rejection of absolutes, and the phenomenological perspective).
- *Counseling theory and skills.* Students contended that the principles of qualitative research were consistent with the theories and skills of counseling (e.g., their open-ended, "not knowing" posture enables them to be used to generate personal meaning and opportunities for discovery).

■ *Research identity and professional viability.* Students believed that the qualitative paradigm provided an opportunity to make research an ongoing dimension of their professional identity.

■ *Holistic experience.* Students found that the qualitative perspective provided a useful structure for them to organize and conceptualize various roles in their lives (personal, counselor, and researcher).

Qualitative Research Methodologies. As mentioned, qualitative research methods have evolved in response to disillusionment with traditional basic research methodologies, which typically utilize experimental designs such as subjects and control groups. In addition, advocates of qualitative research methodologies suggest that basic research designs are unnecessarily restrictive and yield results that have little relevance to practitioners (Mahrer, 1988; Resisetter et al., 2004).

Hoshmand (1989) and Hill, Thompson, and Willams (1997) provide an extensive overview of qualitative methodologies. They present information relating to the purpose of qualitative methods, the roles of the researcher and participants, the process of inquiry, the types of inquiry, and data analysis. This information has been incorporated into the following overview:

■ *Purpose.* Qualitative research designs are characterized by the purpose of developing an understanding of the essence of human experience. They emphasize description and discovery rather than hypothesis testing. Qualitative research can also be used for theory construction and testing such as in Glaser & Strauss's (1967) Grounded Theory.

■ *Role of the researcher and participants.* The researcher takes a more active role in the research process than simply observing and recording data. This role may involve engaging in dialogue and interacting with the participants as a means of exploring and discovering significant events that the client has experienced. Participants also take a more active role, becoming coinvestigators in a collaborative and reciprocal relationship with the researcher. From this perspective, research activity is not controlled by the researcher. In addition, participants are consulted as to what they consider meaningful and relevant research questions and whether the interpretations and conclusions are valid for the participants. In this context, reality can be defined from the perspective of the participants.

■ *The process of inquiry.* Inquiry is characterized as an emergent, ongoing process that includes responsiveness to feedback from the participants. The course of inquiry is therefore determined by collaboration between the researcher and participant. The emphasis is also on process and outcome rather than outcome alone.

■ *Data gathering.* Data-gathering procedures vary according to the methodology employed. Typical methods include observation in the client's natural setting for extended periods of time, in-depth interviews from a phenomenological perspective, and oral histories such as recording myths and legends.

■ *Data analysis.* The methods of data analysis can be described as interpretive, with the goal of recognizing meaningful patterns. A number of comparisons can be made between qualitative and quantitative data analysis. Phenomena are described rather than manipulated; emphasis is on descriptions rather than explanations; focus is on emergence of concepts as opposed to relating findings to existing theories; results are expressed linguistically rather than numerically; scientific knowledge is viewed as tentative, not fixed; and data are conceptualized contextually, not as isolated controlled entities.

Types of Qualitative Research Methodologies. This section presents five types of qualitative methodologies: naturalistic-ethnographic, discovery-oriented, representative-case methods, interactive qualitative analysis, and consensual qualitative research.

Hoshmand (1989) describes *naturalistic-ethnographic* methodologies as involving the observation of participants in their natural context to obtain an understanding of the factors that influence human behavior. This approach requires prolonged contact and immersion in a particular setting to enable the researcher to obtain an understanding of the members in that setting. Data gathering may incorporate activities such as observation, interviews, oral histories, reviews of existing research documents and literature, and the use of critical incidence. Kidder, Judd, and Smith (1986) and Lincoln and Guba (1985) provide detailed descriptions of these procedures. The selection of a particular data-gathering procedure involves a consideration of how to relate effectively to the population under study. For example, one investigation used "rap" groups in a data-gathering method with mentally retarded adults (Hoshmand, 1985). Data analysis entails constant recording, categorizing, sorting, and re-sorting in an attempt to create emergent core categories of meaning. Field notes are transcribed verbatim and analyzed during repeated readings of the data to identify key phrases and concepts. Independent judges identify categories of meaning and sort them into themes to check for reliability. The researcher then collaborates with the participants for their opinion on the data that were generated.

McKenzie (1986) provides an example of a naturalistic-ethnographic study, which investigated the attitudes of West Indian American youths toward counseling. In the first phase of the study, a counselor spent six months immersing himself in the schools, homes, peer groups, and other activities of students under study. The researcher spent an average of forty hours with each student. During the second phase, the researcher conducted in-depth interviews with the students and counseling staff, exploring issues such as development and attitudes toward counseling and toward seeking help. The data were then analyzed to identify meaningful patterns. Results of the study showed that West Indian Americans had strong taboos against seeking counseling, their cultural background affected their career choices, and biculturalism induced conflict within their families.

Mahrer (1988) developed another type of qualitative methodology, which he calls *discovery-oriented psychotherapy research.* The purpose of the discovery-oriented approach is to take an in-depth look at psychotherapy and attempt to discover important aspects of what is occurring in counseling, such as what prompted a personality change in a client. Mahrer described the following method for using the discovery-oriented approach.

1. *Select the target of investigation.* Start off by identifying some aspect of counseling of interest, no matter how large or insignificant it may seem. Avoid getting sidetracked by technical jargon such as "transference" or "locus of control."

2. *Obtain instances of the target being investigated.* Obtain as many instances as possible of the target under investigation. For example, a researcher may be interested in what can be discovered about early childhood memories. The researcher can attempt to obtain examples of these memories in a variety of ways, such as video recordings of sessions and narratives provided by clients.

3. *Obtain an instrument to take a closer look.* Once incidences of target behavior are obtained, the researcher can develop an instrument to take a closer look at the target being investigated (for example, early memories). A category system can be used for this purpose. This can begin with a search of the literature. Next, a group of judges can review the sample incidences of the target under investigation (for example, videotapes) and continuously review this material until meaningful themes or categories of data emerge. The themes and categories obtained can provide the researcher with an instrument to systematically evaluate the target of investigation.

4. *Gather data.* This step involves obtaining the necessary data for the study and applying the instrument to the data. This may involve analyzing the original data obtained during step 2 or obtaining new examples of the target of investigation (for example, additional early memories).

5. *Make discovery-oriented sense of the data.* This step involves interpreting the data to determine what can be learned from the study. This process requires the characteristics associated with the art of counseling. The investigator must be sensitive to the discoverable by being open to what appears new, unexpected, challenging, or disconcerting in the data.

Gordon and Shontz (1990) have developed a case-study type of qualitative methodology called *representative-case research.* This method can be used to gain an in-depth understanding of people with various problems, such as children who are terminally ill, school dropouts, and single parents. Gordon and Shontz describe representative-case research as a process that involves carefully examining "chosen persons one at a time, in depth, to learn how each experiences and manages an event, situation, or set of circumstances or conditions that is important in human life" (p. 62).

Representative-case research is considered a qualitative methodology because it requires the active involvement of the client, who is considered to be an expert on the problem under study and a coinvestigator. It is a process that attempts to discover what a client has learned about a particular experience or set of circumstances. The assistance of supervisors or advisors can also promote objectivity and monitor different aspects of the research process. These individuals can help with various activities such as data analysis and interpretation. They can also assist with the relationship between the counselor and client—the investigator and coinvestigator.

Interactive qualitative analysis (Northcutt & McCoy, 2004) represents a new approach to qualitative research. It integrates a number of concepts and theories associated with qualitative research and establishes a set of procedures to facilitate data collection and analysis. In this regard, Northcutt and McCoy note, "There appears to be no other single work in the field of qualitative research methods that integrates a theory of epistemology with systems theory to produce an explicit set of protocols by which qualitative studies can be conducted and documented" (p. xxiv). Northcutt and McCoy go on to note that interactive qualitative analysis is influenced by postmodernism, grounded theory, action research, concept mapping, systems theory, and Kurt Lewin's field theory.

Interactive qualitative analysis is concerned with scientific rigor or, as Lincoln and Guba (1985) note, "truth value" in research. In this regard, interactive qualitative analysis addresses the relationship between the following questions:

- The ontological: What is real?
- The epistemological: How do we know?
- The ethical/moral: What is good?
- The systemic: What is reliability and validity?

Interactive qualitative analysis appears to have much promise as an emerging theory for qualitative research. It provides a protocol for unraveling the mysteries of data collection, observation, interpreting, analysis, and coding and integrates a number of theoretical perspectives associated with qualitative research. Additional research regarding this approach appears warranted.

Hill, Thompson, and Williams (1997) developed consensual qualitative research as a method that can provide structure and a degree of objectivity to qualitative research. This model attempts to maintain the central qualities associated with qualitative research. At the same time it offers systematic procedures that can add in teaching qualitative procedures and enable qualitative researchers to replicate studies. In addition, this model advocates the use of three to five investigators to engage in consensual decision making during data analysis to encourage diversification of opinions. One or two auditors are also employed to ensure that the investigators did not overlook important data.

Three general steps are utilized in consensual qualitative research:

1. Responses to open-ended questions from questionnaires or interviews for each individual case are divided into domains (that is, topic areas).
2. Core ideas (that is, abstracts or brief summaries) are constructed for all the material within each domain for each individual case.
3. A cross-analysis, which involves developing categories to describe consistencies in the core ideas within domains across cases, is conducted (Hill, Thompson, & Williams, 1997, p. 523).

Consensual qualitative research appears to be a step toward the integration of qualitative and quantitative research in terms of attempting to standardize some of the highly subjective procedures associated with qualitative research. An integrative, "middle ground" form of research methodology provides another valuable research alternative for the art and science of counseling.

Evaluation of Qualitative Methodologies.   Qualitative methods appear to offer much promise for practitioners as viable research methods, but they also pose some potential problems. One way to assess this new form of research is to relate it to nonstandardized measures, as described in Chapter 4. The same strengths and weaknesses apply to both, since qualitative research methods typically utilize nonstandardized measures, such as observation and environmental assessment.

In terms of weaknesses, both nonstandardized assessment and qualitative research methods lack objectivity, the ability to generalize to a reference group, and they can create confusing results and often lack acceptable levels of validity and reliability. The advantages common to both nonstandardized measures and qualitative research methods are that they provide a flexible, individualized approach, which generates information unique to the individual, can be easily modified to accommodate individual differences, and fosters an active role between the counselor (researcher) and the client (participant).

These advantages make qualitative research methods particularly attractive to multicultural counseling research (Helms, 1989). Another advantage of qualitative methods is that they require some of the same skills associated with effective counseling, as Goldman (1989) writes:

> . . . these new methods are not for the faint of heart. They demand imagination, courage to face the unknown, flexibility, some creativeness, and a good deal of personal skill in observation, interviewing, and self-examination—some of the same skills, in fact, required for effective counseling, but now systematically directed toward the education of principles and generalizations, rather than effective change in individuals. (pp. 83–84)

Although qualitative research has established its place as a major force in research, misconceptions and other challenges continue to undermine its usefulness. For example, clinicians may get the impression that qualitative research methods must involve a lengthy investigative process that includes living in the particular setting under study. These impressions could discourage active clinicians from considering this form of research. Clearer guidelines for data gathering and analysis would also facilitate the use of qualitative methods in research. At present, many of these procedures appear vague, lacking in structure, and confusing. Hopefully, new approaches such as integrative qualitative analysis will prove useful in terms of overcoming these challenges, including clarifying the protocols associated with data gathering and analysis.

Challenges associated with maintaining scientific rigor in qualitative research are addressed by Silverman (2001, 2004), who contends that qualitative research can be assessed by evaluating the quality of methods, data, and data analysis. In this process, "Silverman (2001) stresses the importance of adhering to sensible and rigorous methods for making sense of data even as we acknowledge that social phenomena are locally and socially constructed through the activities of participants" (in Markham, 2004, p. 120).

Single-Subject Designs. Single-subject experimental designs constitute another emerging form of research that offers much promise to the practitioner. These designs may be used with one client or a small group of clients. According to Lundervold and Belwood (2000), single subject (N = 1) designs have been developed for use in clinical settings to evaluate the counseling process, interventions, and outcomes. In addition, the authors contend that single-subject designs tend to be the best-kept secret in counseling, resulting in an underutilization of this valuable research tool.

Single-subject designs may be classified into three distinct families or groups: ABA or "withdrawal" designs, multiple baseline designs, and comparative treatment designs

(Stile, 1993). Table 5.1 describes eight major steps involved in applying single-subject design strategies to counseling research or evaluation. These steps are the same regardless of the design used.

ABA Designs.   This family of designs gets its name from the simplest single-subject experimental design, which requires *withdrawal* of a treatment in order to measure its effects when it is introduced and again when it is removed.

   The five most common ABA designs are the A, the B, the A-B, the A-B-A, and the A-B-A-B. The first three designs have been termed *preexperimental* (the A and B designs) and *quasi-experimental* (the A-B design) in relation to their abilities to establish cause-and-effect relationships. The A-B-A and A-B-A-B designs are classified as *experimental* designs since they can be used to establish cause and effect with single subjects or small groups.

The A Design.   This design has also been referred to as the *case study method.* According to Borg and Gall (1989), "the case study . . . involves an investigator who makes a detailed

TABLE 5.1   Steps in Applying Single-Subject Strategies

Step	Procedure
1. Identification	Identify which skills or behaviors will be targeted for change (for example, "irresponsibility").
2. Definition	Define the targeted skill or behavior in such a way that it can be observed and measured (for example, "staying out late" provides a more adequate unit of measurement than "irresponsibility").
3. Selection of dependent variable or measure	Select the characteristic of the behavior to be measured and the counseling objective. For example, the *number* of occurrences of staying out late can be measured in relation to a particular treatment. Zero occurrences may be established as the outcome.
4. Identification of independent variable or treatment	Identify the treatment (for example, counseling technique) to be applied to the dependent variable. For example, logical consequences may be applied to occurrences of staying out late.
5. Completion of planning	Complete all related planning. Decisions made at this step should include who will record the occurrence of the behavior (for example, staying out late) and how the occurrence of the behavior will be recorded (for example, tally marks on a simple recording instrument).
6. Training	Train (if appropriate) all other participants to consistently carry out data collection/treatment procedures. For example, all observers should practice collecting data until they reach close agreement on recording of the dependent variable.
7. Intervention and data collection	Intervene by withholding, applying, or withdrawing the treatment while continuously collecting data on the dependent variable (for example, number of occurrences).
8. Graphing	Graph the results of the treatment by plotting data points on graph paper and connecting the points to represent trends.

examination of a single subject or group or phenomenon" (p. 402). Although case studies have long been considered unscientific because of a lack of control and subjectivity, Borg and Gall have recently noted an increased acceptance of qualitative methods such as "ethnography and participant observation." The A design can be thought of as an extended period during which data are collected on the dependent variable—the behavior you hope to change—but treatment is withheld.

The B Design.　The B design is closely related to the A design. In this design, no baseline observations are made, but dependent variables are monitored throughout the course of a treatment. The B design is generally considered to be an improvement over the uncontrolled case study method.

The A-B Design.　The A-B design corrects for some of the weaknesses of the A and B designs. The inquirer begins by selecting a subject or subjects, pinpointing a problem, selecting a dependent variable, and choosing a treatment. Next, the dependent variable is measured during a minimum of three baseline (A) observations. In the second and final phase of this design, the investigator applies the treatment (B) and measures its effect on the dependent variable. In this design the baseline can be thought of as a control since it predicts future behavior without intervention. The major objection to this design is the possibility that some other variable may be operating simultaneously with the treatment to bring about change in skills or behavior.

The A-B-A Design.　The A-B-A design addresses objections to the A-B design by employing a second baseline (A2) as a control. If withdrawal of treatment results in trends in A2 that approximate A1, arguments for a cause-and-effect relationship between the independent and dependent variables gain considerable support.

The A-B-A-B Design.　The A-B-A-B design addresses the major shortcoming of the A-B-A design because it ends in a second treatment condition, or B2. The A-B-A design is rarely the original design of choice anymore. In fact, it is usually used only when attrition prevents the final phase of the A-B-A-B design. Since no limitation exists regarding the length of B2, a successful treatment may be left in place for a lengthy period to help ensure maintenance of change. The major shortcoming of the A-B-A design is that it often ends on a "negative note" (Borg & Gall, 1989) since a presumably effective treatment is withdrawn.

　　　The following case illustrates the steps in the application of a member of the ABA family of single-subject designs (the A-B) to evaluate the efficiency of a counseling program. The steps refer to those listed in Table 5.1. The A-B design was chosen because it is easy to apply. Beginning counselors may wish to use this design in a pilot study of a new counseling technique.

The Case of Ann.　Ann was a 17-year-old girl enrolled in a large urban high school. The target behavior identified (step 1 in Table 5.1) in this case was "school phobia." The school principal defined Ann's behavior (step 2) as often refusing to go to school or failing to remain there once she arrived. Ann was referred to the school counselor for assistance with this problem. Before seeing Ann, the school counselor examined her attendance records. These records showed that she had attended school for the entire day only 40 percent, 60 percent, and 20 percent of the time during the first, second, and third weeks of school, respectively. At this point, the counselor identified percent of attendance as the dependent variable and established the therapeutic objective (step 3) that Ann would attend school 95 percent of the time every week unless she had a legitimate excuse such as a family emergency. Next, the counselor identified a treatment package consisting of individual and group counseling sessions as the independent variable and completed all prior planning (steps 4 and 5). Since training (step 6) was not necessary in this case, the next step was to begin the intervention and data collection (step 7).

A behaviorally oriented approach was used in individual sessions. In these sessions, Ann was helped to understand how school had become threatening to her and how certain physical symptoms including nausea, diarrhea, and dizziness were related to her anxiety. After four sessions, Ann was able to enter the counselor's office and attend one class independently. She was then invited to attend weekly group sessions with the school's five other school-phobic students to discuss feelings toward school and related issues.

Over a four-month period, the counselor observed that Ann developed a caring attitude toward other group members. She met with them before school, and they often walked home together. Beginning with the first group session, Ann was asked to monitor her own school attendance. By the beginning of Christmas vacation (week 15), she reported to the group that her attendance (that is, the dependent variable) had increased to 100 percent. Periodic checks at monthly intervals revealed that her attendance remained at this level. The graph developed by Ann and her counselor (step 8) is shown as Figure 5.3.

Multiple-Baseline Designs.   A variation of the A-B design is the multiple-baseline design. Frequently, withdrawal designs such as A-B-A or A-B-A-B are inappropriate for a given behavior. For example, a counselor might be viewed as unethical for beginning a second

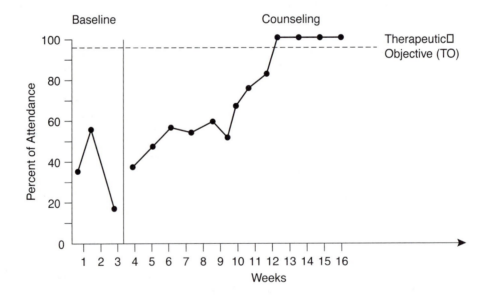

FIGURE 5.3   A-B Design for the Case of Ann

baseline phase when it appears that treatment (for example, self-monitoring) is associated with a significant reduction of aggressive behavior in the client. In such cases, multiple-baseline designs should be considered.

The three major multiple-baseline designs are multiple baseline across behaviors, multiple baseline across settings, and multiple baseline across subjects. All three may be thought of as extensions of the A-B design illustrated by the case of Ann.

Multiple Baseline Across Behaviors. This design is intended for use with single subjects or groups. When used with groups, arithmetic means are calculated and the group is treated as a single subject. When using the across-behaviors design, the inquirer is cautioned to select behaviors that are independent of one another. Borg and Gall (1989) explain as follows:

> Independence is demonstrated by a change in the target behavior to which the treatment is being applied while other target behaviors (or controls) maintain a stable baseline rate. If other behaviors change reliably from baseline, the multiple-baseline design is invalid. (p. 585)

Multiple Baseline Across Settings. The across-settings design is also intended for use with single groups or subjects. In this design, the effect of a treatment on a dependent variable is studied in independent temporal and/or physical settings.

Multiple Baseline Across Subjects. The across-subjects design is used for inquiry with matched groups. For example, Gardill and Browder (1995) use this methodology to examine the effectiveness of training students with severe behavior disorders and developmental disabilities to use money independently.

The following case illustrates the steps in implementing the design of multiple baseline across behaviors in a counseling situation. As shown in Figure 5.4, this design requires that the counselor apply a treatment (B) to a *succession* of behaviors that are being baselined (A). The steps refer to those shown in Table 5.1.

The Case of Drew. Drew was an 18-year-old college freshman living at home with his mother and father. The target behavior identified (step 1) by counselor and parents was "irresponsibility." Irresponsible behavior was defined as (a) staying out too late on school nights, (b) not parking the car in the garage, and (c) not putting his father's tools away after use (step 2). After closely observing these behaviors for five days, Drew's father established the number of occurrences of irresponsible behavior as the dependent variable and set zero occurrences of the behavior as the therapeutic objective (step 3). After a lengthy discussion, the counselor and family decided that logical consequences (Dreikurs & Soltz, 1964) would be the treatment approach used in response to Drew's irresponsible behaviors (step 4). Logical consequences involve experiencing the consequences of one's behavior, as in losing the use of a car if one gets a citation for driving while intoxicated. Planning was completed (step 5) when it was decided that Drew would experience a logical consequence immediately upon occurrence of an irresponsible behavior. In addition, application of the logical consequences would be applied sequentially as follows: (a) first only with staying out late; (b) second, it would be applied to inappropriate car parking; and (c) finally it would

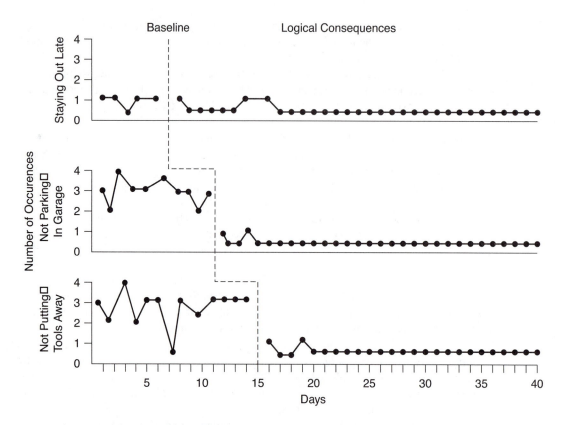

FIGURE 5.4 **Multiple Baseline Across Behavior Design for the Case of Drew**

be applied to all three behaviors (staying out late, parking the car, and not putting away the tools). Drew's father and mother were then trained by the counselor to tally occurrences of the three behaviors on a simple record-keeping instrument (step 6).

The treatment began (step 7) with Drew being told that he would lose the privilege of going out on school nights (Sunday through Thursday) if he came home after 11:00 P.M. After five more days, the logical consequence treatment was also applied to his parking the car. That is, if he did not park the car in the garage, he would be unable to use it. Finally, after an additional five days (day 16), the logical consequence strategy was applied to putting his father's tools away. If Drew failed to put his father's tools away after using them, he would be unable to borrow them. Thus beginning on day 16, the treatment was applied to all three behaviors with Drew's mother and father continuing observations and data collection. His father charted Drew's progress on a graph (step 8), as shown in Figure 5.4. The use of logical consequences appears to have resulted in the elimination of each of the problem behaviors targeted for change. In addition, the zero rate of occurrence was maintained until the treatment and monitoring were withdrawn after 40 days.

Evaluation of Single-Subject Designs. Single-case designs offer much value to the active clinician. They provide an objective means to evaluate what is occurring in the counseling process with one client at a time. A counselor can use this information to adjust the treatment program throughout the counseling process. It also can provide a useful tool to keep the client informed as to what is occurring in counseling. These designs have been used primarily in conjunction with behavioral approaches. Additional research and development are necessary to expand their use to accommodate other schools of counseling.

Diversity and Postmodern Issues in Research and Evaluation

All aspects of the counseling process (including research and evaluation) must be conceptualized from a multicultural counseling perspective. The multicultural perspective enables counselors, like artists, to sensitively navigate diversity issues that may have an impact on scientific investigations. For example, it is common to consider issues of gender, culture, and socioeconomic level when designing a research study.

Another issue relating to diversity and research is the role of white researchers in multicultural counseling. There appears to be some concern that the field of multicultural counseling has been dominated by white researchers at the expense of minority individuals (Mio & Iwamasa, 1993). Atkinson (1993) contends that the major issues in this debate relate to ethics and turf. The ethical issues are directed at determining who is in the best position to realistically evaluate multicultural counseling. The answer to this question will no doubt impact issues of turf. Pedersen (1993) contends that a central problem in the debate relates to an oversimplification and polarization of categories such as majority-minority and the need for all researchers to work toward a common ground characterized by shared interests.

Postmodern trends are based on a subjective view of reality and appear to parallel characteristics of qualitative research and the art of counseling. Case studies and in-depth interviews are examples of postmodern research since they provide opportunities to discover meanings from a participant's stories. Modernism adheres to an objective view of reality and therefore has more in common with quantitative research and the science of counseling. The modernism's fixed view of reality characterizes quantitative research. Quantitative research is characterized by statistically focused hypothesis testing, which attempts to seek out the "truth" in definitive black-and-white terms.

Gergen (1994a) posits a case for postmodern research and its subjective view of truth. Gergen contends that research that adheres to universal assumptions regarding reality and knowledge may convey inaccurate, misleading, and potentially harmful information about what is to be regarded as the truth. Gergen suggests that researchers should be aware of how sociocultural forces and language create multiple realities. For example, many Western cultures recognize depression, with millions being treated with antidepressant medications, whereas individuals from other cultures have survived for centuries without the concept of depression reflected in their language.

Summary

Research and evaluation are an ongoing facet of the counseling process. Research strategies serve several functions, such as offering a means to evaluate the efficacy of a counseling approach, communicate accountability, and contribute to the body of knowledge relating to the counseling profession. Research and evaluation can also be conceptualized as contributing to the science-of-counseling model by providing objective information regarding the counseling process. The practice of research and evaluation is both an art and a science, with approaches such as qualitative methodologies and single-subject designs encouraging clinicians to develop flexible, creative strategies of evaluation.

Personal Exploration

1. How is qualitative research similar to postmodern theory?
2. How do theory, research, and practice influence each other?
3. What type of research interests you?
4. How can issues of diversity such as culture, gender, and age have an impact on research?

Web Sites for Chapter 5

Berkowitz, J. (unknown). *Quantitative research design.* Retrieved March 3, 2005, from
   http://www.familypractice.ubc.ca/research/binderprojdesignl.html
   Provides a very basic outline of quantitative research design.
Boeree, C. G. (1997). *Qualitative methods workbook.* Retrieved March 3, 2005, from
   http://www.ship.edu/~cgboeree/qualmeth.html
   Provides an interesting but lengthy description ("workbook") of qualitative research methods.

Developing a Personal Approach to Counseling from a Multicultural Perspective

Part Two provides guidelines for formulating a personal approach to counseling within a multicultural perspective. The following four chapters are covered in Part Two.

6

Developing a Personal Approach to Counseling from a Multicultural Perspective

CHAPTER OVERVIEW

This chapter provides guidelines for formulating a personal approach to counseling and addresses issues relating to multicultural counseling. Highlights of the chapter include

- The art and science of developing a personal approach to counseling from a multicultural perspective
- Developing a personal approach to counseling
- An eight-stage model for developing a personal approach
- Multicultural counseling
- Potential challenges in multicultural counseling
- Suggestions for incorporating a multicultural perspective

The Art and Science of Developing a Personal Approach to Counseling from a Multicultural Perspective

Developing a personal approach to counseling from a multicultural perspective is both an art and a science. It is an art to draw together multiple factors such as personal preference, diversity issues, and client characteristics in developing and implementing a counseling approach. The art of counseling suggests that the process of developing a personal approach to counseling begins with self-assessment to identify strengths, weaknesses, attitudes, and beliefs that can promote or inhibit the counseling process. Counselors are then encouraged to work toward developing personal characteristics that promote optimal development in the client. The science of developing a personal approach relates to the importance of using research to determine the efficacy of theories and procedures to maximize the use of proven approaches throughout the counseling process.

The multicultural perspective contributes a critical dimension to a personal approach to counseling. It can be conceptualized as a lens that can bring multicultural issues into focus throughout the counseling process. The art of multicultural counseling is related to the counselor's skill in adjusting the multicultural lens to accurately assess and respond to diversity issues such as socioeconomic status, culture, gender, and sexual orientation. A related challenge in the art of counseling is learning how to adjust traditional counseling theories and procedures to meet the unique and emerging needs of clients from a multicultural perspective. This can involve recognizing the value of alternative methods to helping, including the use of traditional healers such as medicine men with American Indians. In addition, the art of counseling suggests that counselors create opportunities to experience and be enriched by multiculturalism. This can involve a wide variety of activities, from taking an interest in the traditional art of a culture (such as Navajo rugs) to exploring issues such as acculturation, world view, and identity development to gain an awareness of individual differences and relational-contextual issues that can affect clients.

The science of multicultural counseling is entering into an exciting phase in the evolution of counseling. Traditional schools of counseling and research methodology are being reassessed from a multicultural perspective in an attempt to overcome problems such as bias toward the white, middle-class, male model of counseling. Theories basic to counseling (such as developmental theories) are being modified to accommodate diversity issues such as gender and culture. Carol Gilligan's (1982) seminal work on female moral development is an excellent example of these exciting trends.

Hansen (2002) has identified postmodern implications for the art and science of counseling. He suggests that traditional counseling approaches are grounded in science, which can promote a career-long adherence to a particular approach. Hansen contends that when "approaches are conceptualized as narrative explanatory structures, beginning counselors can create less rigid professional identities that will naturally translate into more flexible client-centered practice" (p. 321). In this process, the counselor can help clients view their world from a creative new vantage point (which has been a hallmark of the arts). Hansen also notes that counseling is a persuasive art that helps clients transition from despair to hope and from helplessness to personal autonomy.

Hansen (2002) goes on to note that postmodern thought can be used for theory integration. In this regard, he posits that counseling approaches can be conceptualized as "meaning structures" that share common narratives. The features narratives have in common are "consistency with the values of society, an initial association with science and internal features that protect the narrative from being falsified, and client independence as a fundamental goal" (Hansen, 2002, p. 320).

Developing a Personal Approach to Counseling

All counselors and counselors in training have a personal approach to counseling. Some put a considerable amount of time and effort into the process, whereas others simply "do counseling." Using a personal approach that results from careful planning enhances the complex process of counseling.

Over the years, there has been a proliferation of counseling approaches. Lynn and Garske (1985) observed more than 130 different approaches, many of which they say were far from the mainstream and of questionable value. The authors believe there appears to be a shift in emphasis from more to fewer theories, creating an optimal climate for integrating theories.

Patterson (1989) and Lazarus and Beutler (1993) support this view, suggesting there is a trend toward integration and eclecticism. Norcross and Newman (1992) go on to identify several other factors that appear to be contributing to this trend. These factors are summarized as follows: (1) no one theory can possibly address the diversified needs of clients, (2) research has shown similar efficacy rates for counseling theories, and (3) trends for short-term counseling have required modification in how theories are implemented. With so many forces at work, it is not surprising that in surveys 30 to 50 percent of clinical and counseling psychologists consider themselves to be eclectic or integrative (Norcross & Newman, 1992) and 64 percent of counselors claim to be eclectic (Norcross, Prochaska, & Gallagher, 1989).

Numerous models of eclecticism and integration have emerged. Historically, eclecticism has been considered by some to be a disjointed approach, whereby a counselor utilizes various theories and techniques without the benefit of an internally consistent psychological frame of reference (Wachtel, 1991). Students of the eclectic approach often lack a clear sense of structure or direction in the counseling process and struggle with problems such as how to shift from one therapeutic modality to another (Wachtel, 1991). Lazarus and Beutler (1993) refer to this type of eclecticism as *unsystematic eclecticism* and contend that this smorgasbord approach to counseling lacks clinical precision and contributes to confusion in counseling.

Lazarus and Beutler (1993) go on to describe *technical eclecticism* as a practical and effective method of conceptualizing a personal approach to counseling. They summarize the basic tenets of technical eclecticism as follows:

> . . . technical eclectics select procedures from different sources without necessarily subscribing to the theories that spawned them; they work within a preferred theory (Dryden, 1987) but recognize that few techniques are inevitably wedded to any theory. Hence, they borrow techniques from other orientations, based on the proven worth of these procedures. (p. 384)

In addition, technical eclecticism favors the restriction of use of theories and techniques to those that have proven efficacy in research and those that contribute to systematic decision making in treatment planning. In this regard, Lazarus (2000) has developed a school of counseling called *multimodal therapy*. It is based on social-learning theory, general systems theory, and group and communication theory. Central to his approach is his concept of the BASIC I.D., which provides a conceptual model for treatment planning (see Chapter 4).

Theoretical integration represents another recognized model for formulating a personal approach to counseling. Norcross and Newman (1992) describe theoretical integration as an approach that involves the synthesis of two or more counseling theories. The recent trend toward integrating cognitive and behavioral counseling is an example of theoretical integration. Warwar and Greenberg (2000) suggest that complete integration of one school of counseling with another would be a daunting task. They also contend that future trends will represent an integration of elements of two or more counseling theories, such as the assimilation of cognitions into humanistic approaches and the newly emerging emphasis on emotions into cognitive therapy. Several other individuals have suggested that theoretical integration should be based on a core counseling theory such as Adlerian or existential to promote internal consistency and a sense of structure and direction for counseling (Ginter, 1988; McBride & Martin, 1990; Wachtel, 1991; Watts, 1993).

Utilizing the "core approach to theory integration" when developing a personal approach to counseling represents an integration of technical eclecticism and theoretical integration. The major feature of this approach is to first obtain an in-depth understanding of one counseling theory to establish a core theory. The classic theories of Freud, Adler, and Jung described in Chapter 7 are ideal for this purpose since they also have a comprehensive theory of personality to complement their theory of counseling. The core theory will help establish a degree of internal consistency in the personal approach. The counselor can then select components from other counseling theories to meet the unique and emerging needs of clients from a multicultural perspective. Techniques and procedures utilized should have support from research and lead to appropriate treatment planning.

An Eight-Stage Model for Developing a Personal Approach

The following eight-stage model can be used to develop a personal approach to counseling. The eight stages of this model are self-assessment, survey of supportive disciplines, overview of major counseling theories, intensive study of one (core) counseling theory, sensitivity to individual differences, integration of techniques from counseling theories, implementation, and research and evaluation.

Stage One: Self-Assessment

Self-assessment helps counselors understand their values, beliefs, strengths, and weaknesses. With self-awareness, counselors can avoid overreacting in counseling and use their strengths to maximize their effectiveness. Vontress (1988) notes that self-knowledge may be the best predictor of effective living because it provides a clear direction in life and is necessary to make meaningful decisions. Richardson and Molinaro (1996) go on to note that multicultural sensitivity can be enhanced by counselors engaging in self-awareness exercises that explore their values, cultural identity, and worldview. McWhirter (1994) expands on the need for multicultural self-awareness, noting that counselors should pay more attention to the *person of the counselor* in terms of how counselors can be vehicles of cultural oppression.

Counselors can undertake a self-assessment in numerous ways. Perhaps the most comprehensive approach is to obtain formal counseling. Through the use of tests and other counseling strategies, counselors can gain information about their self-concept, personality, interests, values, aptitude, and other important aspects of the self. Many training programs—for example, in psychiatry—require students to undertake analysis by a psychotherapist for one year or longer. The underlying belief in this requirement is that the experience can help provide students with personal insights necessary to become effective helpers.

Self-assessment through personal counseling or other procedures can generate an understanding of personal characteristics that may or may not be helpful in counseling. Chapter 1 provides an overview of the personal characteristics of effective counselors. These include qualities such as being encouraging, empathic and caring, patient, nonjudgmental, and flexible. These characteristics can enable counselors to use the "self as an instrument of change." In this regard, counselors can facilitate the counseling process by fostering core conditions such as unconditional positive regard, self-disclosure, empathy, and respect.

Stage Two: Survey of Supportive Disciplines

A variety of disciplines can contribute to the development of a personal approach to counseling, but psychology and medicine are perhaps the most relevant. Other disciplines that may be useful are philosophy, theology, anthropology, sociology, and literature. A brief description of each of these disciplines follows.

Psychology.   Psychology is vital as a discipline for counselors to draw from since it encompasses the major schools of counseling and psychotherapy, which are the topics of Chapters 7, 8, and 9. Psychology also has a number of specialties that can contribute to a counselor's personal theory. The following list summarizes the relevant aspects of some of these specialties:

- *Clinical and counseling psychology* investigates how psychological tests and other helping skills can be used in the counseling process.
- *Developmental psychology* helps counselors gain an understanding of how human growth and development take place over the life span. The counseling profession emphasizes the importance of utilizing a developmental perspective. This perspective enables counselors to adapt their approaches to the unique needs of clients progressing through the life span.
- *Experimental psychology* provides an important link to the science-of-counseling model by identifying research strategies to evaluate counseling approaches and processes.
- *Abnormal psychology* provides an overview of mental disorders and helps counselors learn how to use this information in the process of assessment and diagnosis.
- *Multicultural psychology* explores how psychology varies across cultures. This knowledge can be particularly important in developing a counseling perspective.
- *School psychology* focuses on the use of psychological tests in the school setting to assess personality, intelligence, aptitude, and achievement.
- *Physiological psychology* explores the physiological foundations of psychology. It can contribute a frame of reference for understanding physiological factors associated with behavior, cognition, and emotions.
- *Social psychology* explores psychology from a social perspective. It provides much promise to counseling research in terms of identifying paradigms relating to the social forces that influence the counseling process.

Medicine.   Medicine is another important discipline for counselors to study to develop some theoretical grounding. The mind and body are not separate entities but an interrelated whole. To understand one, it is essential to have some knowledge of the other. The following *Personal Note* illustrates how some physical illnesses can cause psychiatric symptoms such as hallucinations.

A Personal Note

A doctor suspected that a female patient had a schizophrenic disorder since she was having auditory hallucinations (was hearing voices), and referred the woman to me. My psychological evaluation of the patient did not suggest that she was suffering from schizophrenia. In reviewing her hospital chart, however, I noticed that she had been diagnosed as having syphilis more than 10 years earlier and that there was no record of her successfully completing treatment for the condition. I knew that syphilis can cause hallucinations, so I referred the patient back to the physician to begin medical treatment for syphilis. I also arranged for the patient to see a consulting psychiatrist, who gave her medication for the auditory hallucinations.

Psychiatry is a medical specialty that has direct relevance to counseling. The three "classic" theorists who will be discussed in Chapter 7 were all psychiatrists. Psychiatry is the study of human behavior from a medical perspective. Psychiatrists have a special interest in how pathology, or abnormality, in the brain and nervous system can cause mental disorders such as schizophrenia and major depression. They also have special training in the use of medications to treat these mental disorders. A basic background in psychiatry can help counselors differentiate a medical problem from a psychological problem so the client can receive the appropriate treatment. It can also assist counselors in understanding physiological factors associated with mental disorders.

Philosophy.   Philosophy can provide a valuable foundation for counselors in developing a personal approach. It can help them broaden and enrich how they see life and clarify their beliefs, attitudes, and values. The following issues may be useful to explore in undertaking a study of philosophy:

1. Do people have free will?
2. What is the purpose of anxiety in life? Is it something to be avoided at all cost?
3. In order to experience love and joy, must one also be able to bear pain and sorrow?
4. Are people inherently good or bad, or is their nature primarily determined by environmental forces?

The study of philosophy can help counselors explore these and other relevant issues. It can also help counselors become aware of personal biases to avoid imposing them on clients.

Existentialism is a major school of philosophy that may be particularly interesting to counselors. Existentialism contends that people are self-determined and have free will, which they can use to make choices in life. William Shakespeare summed up the spirit of existentialism when he wrote, "To be or not to be—that is the question."

The writings of several noted philosophers can be used to develop a philosophical perspective. A list of recommended reading is provided at the end of this chapter. One example is Kahlil Gibran's (1965) popular book *The Prophet,* which expresses philosophical views that are easy to understand. It covers a wide variety of topics from children to love. The following is an excerpt from the section on children:

> ### On Children
> And a woman who held a babe against her bosom said, Speak to us of Children. And he said: Your children are not your children. They are the sons and daughters of life's longing for itself. They come through you but not from you. You may give them your love but not your thoughts, for they have their own thoughts. You may house their bodies but not their souls, for their souls dwell in the house of tomorrow, which you cannot visit, not even in your dreams. You may strive to be like them, but seek not to make them like you. For life goes not backward nor tarries with yesterday. You are the bows from which your children as living arrows are sent forth. The archer sees the mark upon the path of the infinite, and he bends you with his might that his arrows may go swift and far. Let your bending in the archer's hand be for gladness; for even as he loves the arrow that flies, so he loves also the bow that is stable. (pp. 17–18)

Theology.   Theology is the study of spirituality and religion, and various schools of theology incorporate theories of philosophy. Theological concepts have traditionally not played a significant role in counseling. Most counselors have viewed religion as a personal, private matter that is not necessary or appropriate to explore with a client. An exception to this view is pastoral counseling, in which counselors practice from a particular religious perspective. In those situations, the client often seeks counseling from a religious orientation. Many churches employ counselors for this purpose.

Spirituality is an emerging trend in counseling that can be used to provide a theological foundation for a personal approach to counseling and that also represents an important diversity consideration in multicultural counseling (Bishop, 1995; Richards & Bergin, 1997). Spirituality is considered to be endemic to all people, whereas religion can be used to create a structure and focus for the spiritual realm (Ingersoll, 1995). Recognition of the strength and support people draw from spirituality is contributing to its acceptance as an important dimension of the counseling process (Miranti & Burke, 1995). When religious issues do come up in counseling, clients tend to expect counselors to be supportive of their religion or attend to psychological issues and not challenge their religious beliefs (Morrow, Worthington, & McCullough, 1993).

Worthington (1989) identifies five reasons why counselors should make more of an effort to include spiritual and religious considerations in formulating a counseling approach:

1. A high percentage of people in the United States are religious.
2. People often turn to religion during an emotional crisis.
3. Clients (especially religious clients) are reluctant to mention religious issues during secular therapy.

4. Counselors do not tend to be as religiously oriented as their clients.
5. Since many counselors are not as religiously oriented as their clients, they tend to be less informed about religion and are therefore less helpful to these clients.

Worthington (1989) provides guidelines for incorporating spiritual and religious issues into the counseling process. In these guidelines, he provides information on spiritual and religious faith across the life span in terms of implications for counseling and research.

Zinnbauer and Pargament (2000) identify four helping orientations to religious and spiritual issues in counseling: rejectionist, exclusivist, constructivist, and pluralist. Rejectionist and exclusivist represent two rigid, extreme positions and are not considered useful perspectives for counselors to use when relating to religious/spiritual issues. Rejectionists are essentially atheists rejecting the notion of God and religion and, therefore, restrict opportunities for addressing spirituality and religion in counseling. Exclusivists take an "orthodox" religious position, embracing a rigid definition of God and religion. Exclusivists contend that counselors and clients must share the same religion or spiritual worldview to be able to effectively work together in counseling.

Constructivists and pluralists are believed to be flexible, useful approaches to address religious/spiritual issues in counseling (Zinnbauer & Pargament, 2000). Constructivists do not believe that there is one ultimate reality and contend that individuals construct their own personal meanings and reality. Constructivists take a phenomenological perspective and attempt to communicate respect and understanding for whatever realities (including atheism) clients construct. Unconditional acceptance of clients' values and beliefs can be counterproductive for constructivists when those values and beliefs support self-defeating or destructive worldviews (for example, when parents use religion to justify excessive punishment of children). Pluralists, unlike constructivists, believe that there is an ultimate spiritual reality and that God does exist. While pluralists have a well thought-out religious orientation, they (unlike exclusivists) can also appreciate the value and merits of other religions.

Theological issues can have an impact on virtually all aspects of the counseling process. Smith (1993) suggests that it is especially important to explore the religious-spiritual needs of the dying. Smith notes that 79 percent of people surveyed believed that spiritual issues would play an important role in attaining a "healthy" death. In addition, 50 percent of people who were dying reported that they did not have an affiliation with an organized religion but felt the need to discuss religious-spiritual issues. Smith goes on to provide a description of theological counseling tools that can be used with dying clients. For example, the client can be asked to write a "healthy death story" in which the individual describes the ideal death. Smith recommends that counselors use these tools to explore clients' theological concerns, struggles, and resources.

Multicultural counseling provides another impetus for incorporating a theological perspective in counseling (Pate & Bondi, 1992). According to Pate and Bondi, spiritual and religious beliefs are related to clients' cultural background and should therefore be incorporated into a multicultural perspective. Multicultural counseling and therapy (MCT) (Sue, Ivey, & Pedersen, 1996) provides additional evidence of the need to address religious and spiritual issues in multicultural counseling. According to MCT, counselors need to modify conventional helping roles to accommodate various cultural groups. The need for alternative styles of helping that focus on spiritual issues appears especially important for non-Western cultures. In this regard, Lee, Oh, and Mountcastle (1992) surveyed 16 countries and found that the three main sources of healing were the use of communal groups and family, spiritualism and religion, and traditional healers (such as the medicine man with Native Americans). Counselors can effectively broaden their helping role by addressing these important sources of healing by providing interventions (such as family counseling and support groups), addressing theological issues, and recognizing the value of culturally relevant healers.

The holistic health movement also recognizes the value of addressing all aspects of the mind and body (including spiritual issues) in fostering health and wellness. In this regard, Westgate (1996) suggests that spiritual issues can contribute to a holistic approach to prevention and treatment of depression. According to Westgate, spiritual void is associated with depressive symptomology such as meaninglessness, emptiness, alienation, and hopelessness. The spiritually well person is able to draw strength from religion to gain meaning and a sense of direction in life. Westgate (1996) goes on to identify four spiritual dimensions that counselors can use to overcome problems with depression: "a sense of meaning in life, a transcendent perspective, an intrinsic value system, and a sense of belonging to a spiritual community of shared values and support" (p. 26).

Spirituality is a dimension of counseling that appears to offer many opportunities and challenges. It appears to fit emerging trends in counseling that use a strengths perspective, such as brief-solution-focused counseling. In this regard, counselors can encourage clients to use their faith (including, if appropriate, prayer) as a strength to help deal with the challenges they face. Unfortunately, many counselors appear to be unprepared to relate effectively to spiritual issues in counseling (Genia, 1994). According to Genia (1994), counselor educators can play an important role in enhancing the spiritual dimension to counseling by providing training on spirituality in counseling. This can include activities such as coursework on religion (for example, the psychology of religion) and supervised experience in counseling religious clients (Genia, 1994). Additional research on counseling and spirituality seems warranted.

Anthropology.   Cultural anthropology is the study of cultures. Mental health cultural anthropology is a specialty that investigates mental health issues unique to a particular culture. For example, Topper (1985) has explored Navajo alcoholism in terms of drinking, alcohol abuse, and treatment in a changing cultural environment. The mental health–cultural anthropology perspective can be particularly useful in addressing cross-cultural issues in counseling.

Sociology.   Sociology is the study of social group behavior. A basic premise is that behavior is primarily determined by a person's social interaction. For example, during the socialization process, a person is encouraged to conform to the norms and laws of society. Many different groups and institutions can exert a significant influence on personality development. Some of these are family, friends, church, the workplace, and school. A counselor may be interested in how these forces affect the client.

Literature.   The roads of literature and psychology have often crossed, creating new perspectives for understanding the psychology of people and exploring the counseling process. Adler emphasized the importance of literature in the development of individual psychology, as illustrated in the following excerpt:

Some day soon it will be realized that the artist is the leader of mankind on the path to the absolute truth. Among poetic works of art which have led me to the insights of Individual Psychology, the following stand out as pinnacles: fairy tales, the Bible, Shakespeare, and Goethe. (Ansbacher & Ansbacher, 1956, p. 291)

Numerous possibilities exist for exploring the implications for counseling to be found in literature. For example, Adlerian psychotherapy and lifestyle analysis have been related to the investigative strategies employed by Sherlock Holmes (Nystul, 1978a). Kopp (1971) provides another example of understanding literature from a counseling perspective in his analysis of *The Wizard of Oz*. He notes that Dorothy is similar to a client in search of herself, and the Wizard can be perceived as her counselor. As Dorothy journeys through the Land of Oz, she encounters the Scarecrow, the Tin Man, and the Cowardly Lion, who become her support system.

Kopp (1971) identifies several insights into life that Dorothy and her friends may have realized, as the following excerpt shows:

Acquiring wisdom involves risking being wrong or foolish; being loving and tender requires a willingness to bear unhappiness; courage is the confidence to face danger, though afraid; gaining freedom and power requires only a willingness to recognize their existence and to face their consequences. We can find ourselves only when we are willing to risk losing ourselves to another, to the moment, to a quest, and love is the bridge. (p. 98)

Bibliotherapy provides another example of how the roads of literature and counseling cross (see Chapter 8). Bibliotherapy involves having clients read books or other literary works to promote different outcomes associated with counseling, such as anxiety reduction and stress management. Gelso and Fassinger (1990) suggest that counselors should consider client characteristics to determine the appropriateness of self-help literature.

Stage Three: Overview of Major Counseling Theories

It is necessary to study the major schools of counseling to obtain an overview of the various counseling theories (see Chapters 7, 8, and 9). This understanding alerts counselors to the various theoretical perspectives that are available to use with different clients. One central or core theory can then be selected as the foundation of an integrative approach.

Stage Four: Intensive Study of One Counseling Theory

A solid foundation in theory is necessary for developing a personal approach. The importance of a theoretical foundation is evident in all disciplines. For example, music students usually benefit from studying music theory and learning to read music before creating their own musical composition. The same is true in counseling. After students have established an in-depth theoretical foundation, they are ready to develop their own personal style and approach.

Stage 4 suggests that counselors undertake an in-depth study of the particular school they have selected. The core theory should include a comprehensive theory of personality to provide an understanding of the dynamics of behavior. The theory should be a well thought-out approach to counseling that includes an understanding of the counseling process. The core theory can provide internal consistency in terms of how counselors understand and work with a client.

Counselors who do not have a well thought-out core theory are prone to superficial and fragmented personality assessment. They are likely to have a technique-oriented approach to counseling, thinking, for example, "With this client, I'll use this theory's suggested technique." It is important for counselors to read books and articles written by the founder of the school they have selected. Reading about an approach in a textbook will not provide an in-depth understanding. Training in an institute associated with the theory, such as the Gestalt Institute in Arizona, can also help counselors develop expertise in a particular school of counseling. It may be useful to join a professional organization associated with the chosen theory. An example is the North American Society of Individual Psychology for counselors interested in Adlerian psychology.

Stage Five: Sensitivity to Individual Differences

Counselors should not force a client to fit into their personal approach. I refer to this as "forcing square pegs into round holes" (Nystul, 1981). On the contrary, a counselor's approach should be adjusted to the unique and emerging needs of the client. In this regard, the counselor should be sensitive to the individual differences of clients. It is particularly important to address multicultural issues to make the counseling process relevant to the needs of the client. The next section of this chapter describes multicultural issues that can be used to formulate one's personal approach to counseling.

Recent trends in counseling have emphasized that counseling interventions must be matched with client characteristics (Warwar & Greenberg, 2000). These scholars suggest it is particularly important to match interventions with client needs, plans, and goals. Another way of matching interventions with client characteristics is in terms of how clients engage in problem solving regarding "spaces of perception." This theory suggests there are three spaces of perception: near-, mid-, and far-spaced (Nystul, 1981). *Near-spaced* clients tend to want a lot of detail in problem solving. For example, they want to know exactly what and how they are supposed to do something. These clients may be better able to utilize behavioral approaches that incorporate the monitoring of behavior with graphs and other objective procedures.

At the other extreme are *far-spaced* clients. These are people who hate to be pinned down with a lot of details. They do not want to be locked into a preconceived method of problem solving. An existential or humanistically oriented approach may be more in keeping with their mode of problem solving.

Mid-spaced clients are characterized by having difficulty making decisions. They tend to want others to make decisions and resolve problems for them. Reality therapy or Gestalt therapy may help these clients become aware of choices and accept responsibility for their behavior.

Garfield (1994) provides an extensive review of the literature on client variables in counseling and psychotherapy in terms of continuation in counseling and outcome. For example, clients from an upper socioeconomic status tend to stay longer in counseling and have less of a tendency to engage in premature termination. A number of variables have also been investigated in terms of outcome. There is some evidence to suggest that degree of disturbance is related to outcome, with extreme disturbance being negatively correlated with positive outcomes in counseling.

Stage Six: Integration of Techniques from Counseling Theories

To develop an integrative counseling approach, counselors may draw from different counseling theories to add to their repertoire of counseling techniques. In reviewing the various schools of counseling, students may find that these theories have more in common than they have differences. Subtle differences do exist, however, enabling counselors to adjust their approach to the particular problems that present themselves in the counseling session.

Stage Seven: Implementation

As counselors make the transition from theory to practice, they will begin to implement their approach. The application of one's approach is an art. It is a creative process that varies according to the particular clinical situation.

Stage Eight: Research and Evaluation

Research and evaluation enable counselors and counselors in training to determine the efficacy of their approach, use the literature to refine their approach, and contribute to the literature on a topic of interest. Chapter 5 provides information pertaining to this important topic.

Multicultural Counseling

The preceding discussion suggests that a personal approach to counseling should incorporate a multicultural perspective sensitive to the individual differences that reflect contemporary society. In this regard, Pedersen (1991a) contends that multicultural counseling has become a fourth force, which follows psychodynamic, behavioral, and humanistic counseling. It is relevant to all aspects of counseling as a generic rather than exotic perspective (Pedersen, 1991a).

This section describes key terms and concepts of some of the major issues in multicultural counseling. The next two sections provide an overview of multicultural counseling and therapy (MCT), identify potential problems associated with multicultural counseling, and provide guidelines for developing a multicultural perspective.

Terms and Concepts

Many terms relating to multicultural counseling can be difficult to differentiate and can therefore obscure its meaning. The following explanations help clarify some common terms and concepts:

- *Culture* is an ambiguous concept that defies definition. In a broad sense it can be thought of as "things a stranger needs to know to behave appropriately in a particular setting" (Pedersen, 1988, p. viii).
- *Race* "refers to a pseudobiological system of classifying persons by a shared genetic history or physical characteristics such as skin color" (Pedersen, 1988, p. viii).

- *Minority* "generally refers to a group receiving differential and unequal treatment because of collective discrimination" (Pedersen, 1988, p. viii).
- *Ethnicity* "includes a shared sociocultural heritage that includes similarities of religion, history, and common ancestry" (Pedersen, 1988, p. viii).
- *Cross-cultural counseling* is "any counseling relationship in which two or more of the participants differ with respect to cultural background, values, and lifestyle" (Sue et al., 1982, p. 47).
- *Multicultural counseling* has a broader definition of culture than implied in cross-cultural counseling. Pedersen (1988) defines multicultural counseling as "a situation in which two or more persons with different ways of perceiving their social environment are brought together in a helping relationship" (p. viii). Pedersen (1991b) prefers the broader definition of culture associated with multicultural counseling, because it "helps counselors become more aware of the complexity in cultural identity patterns, which may or may not include the obvious indicators of ethnicity and nationality" (p. 11).
- *Diversity* refers to variables such as age, gender, culture, spirituality, and sexual orientation, which are addressed within the context of multicultural counseling.

Theoretical Perspectives for Multicultural Counseling

Multicultural counseling and therapy (MCT) represents the first comprehensive theory of multicultural counseling (Sue et al., 1996). MCT was developed in an attempt to overcome multicultural limitations associated with contemporary counseling theory, research, and practice. According to Sue et al. (1996), the major problem with existing schools of counseling is that they are culture bound and do not adequately provide conceptual tools to incorporate a multicultural perspective. Sue et al. (1996) go on to suggest that a *culture-centered theory* is necessary to broaden the theoretical foundations of counseling to make it relevant to the needs of a multicultural society.

MCT can be used to provide a perspective or lens to conceptualize diversity issues such as gender, culture, age, and sexual orientation in all phases of counseling. Throughout the counseling process, the MCT lens must be continuously adjusted to promote a clear understanding of emerging multicultural issues. Once diversity issues are identified, counseling theories and procedures can be modified to reflect an MCT perspective.

Sue et al. (1996) identify six propositions for MCT that provide an overview of the basic assumptions from which this theory is based.

Proposition 1.   MCT can be used to provide an organizational framework for understanding Western and non-Western theories and methods of helping.

Proposition 2.   Counselors' and clients' identities are reflected in various levels of human experience (individual, group, system, and universal). Contextual issues in treatment must therefore be addressed as necessary.

Proposition 3.   Cultural identity development affects how the counselor and client view the self and others and how they formulate counseling goals and interventions. It is therefore important to be cognizant of how cultural identity development is affecting the counseling process, including being aware of the different sociocultural forces that influence its development.

Proposition 4. The efficacy of MCT is enhanced when counselors use procedures congruent with the values and experiences of the client. Counselors are encouraged to broaden their helping responses so that they demonstrate multicultural sensitivity throughout the counseling process.

Proposition 5. MCT encourages counselors to expand their helping roles to include conventional and alternative methods of helping as necessary to meet the cultural needs of clients.

Proposition 6. A fundamental goal of MCT theory is the liberation of consciousness from a relational-contextual perspective. In this regard, MCT attempts to provide opportunities to promote an awareness of how cultural and relational issues (such as self in relation to family) affect present concerns.

Potential Challenges in Multicultural Counseling

Many studies have identified potential challenges in multicultural counseling. This research addresses a wide range of topics, including counseling as a white middle-class activity, social class, gender, the intrapsychic perspective, sexual orientation, stereotyping, communication problems, faulty assumptions, test bias, prejudice, racism, and the efficacy of multicultural counseling.

Counseling as a White Middle-Class Activity

A major criticism of contemporary counseling is that its theories and techniques have been developed primarily by people from a white middle-class culture. As a result, contemporary counseling is not directly applicable to ethnic minorities because its theories and techniques do not address their specific issues and concerns (Sue et al., 1996). In addition, Ponterotto and Casas (1991) note that traditionally trained counselors are encapsulated in a culturally biased framework and consequently tend to engage in culturally conflicting and oppressive counseling approaches. It is therefore not surprising that counseling services are not utilized as much by minorities as by whites (Sue & Sue, 1999). In addition, the rate of dropping out of counseling after attending one session is 50 percent for ethnic minorities versus 30 percent for whites (Sue & Sue, 1999).

Social Class

Social-class differences may be more profound than cultural differences (Baruth & Manning, 1999). For example, whites in the lower socioeconomic class may have more in common with Hispanics in the same class than with whites in the middle or upper class.

Diagnostic and treatment bias is one concern that has been associated with social class. In one of the earliest studies on this subject, Lee (1968) found that clients from the lower socioeconomic class received a diagnosis of mental illness at a higher rate than clients from the upper socioeconomic class. Some evidence also suggests that counselors become more involved with clients from the upper class than with clients from the lower class (Garfield, Weiss, & Pollack, 1973). Considering these findings, it is not surprising that clients with a lower socioeconomic status tend to drop out of counseling after one or two sessions (Berrigan & Garfield, 1981; Weighill, Hodge, & Peck, 1983). With these concerns in mind, Atkinson, Morten, and Sue (1998) note that social class is an important variable to consider when formulating a treatment approach.

Gender

A proliferation of research has emerged suggesting that women's issues have not been adequately addressed in terms of the theory, practice, and research of counseling. Gender bias in theory begins with developmental theories (a theoretical foundation for counseling). In this regard, Carol Gilligan's (1982, 1991) seminal work on female moral development and identity development provides evidence of the need to create developmental theories that address men's *and* women's issues.

Feminists have also identified systematic bias in traditional counseling theories and theories of psychopathology (Enns, 1993). From a feminist's counseling perspective, counseling theories have been written from a white-male perspective, acknowledging values of autonomy and independence over relational considerations. In addition, assessment of psychopathology tends to ascribe causality to a lack of internal conditions (such as autonomy and independence) as opposed to a recognition of external forces (such as sociopolitical oppression from a male-dominated society). The practice of counseling can therefore be a process of cultural encapsulation, whereby women are controlled and manipulated to conform to expectations of a white-male counseling perspective. It is therefore not surprising that research evidence suggests that women tend to prefer women counselors to discuss relationship issues such as love, closeness, and sexual behavior (Snell, Hampton, & McManus, 1992).

Lucia Gilbert (1992, p. 387) also notes that "sexism and gender bias characterize psychological research and theory to the extent that unexamined assumptions about the sexes or untested distinctions based on gender enter into the hypotheses, rationale, norms of adjustment, or coverage of the field." Gilbert goes on to suggest that in order to overcome gender bias in research, it is essential to begin by accurately describing the experiences of men *and* women. In addition, Ballou (1996) posits that women's experiences deserve to be valued and recognized as offering alternative views of knowledge and reality. This postmodern perspective would include an understanding of relational-contextual issues that define women's existence and concept of "self" as important considerations for counseling research.

The Intrapsychic Perspective

The intrapsychic perspective focuses on internal forces such as the unconscious processes and endopsychic conflicts described by Freud (see Chapter 7). The multicultural counseling perspective suggests that traditional schools of counseling rely on an overemphasis of intrapsychic forces in conceptualizing the dynamics of behavior. The multicultural perspective suggests that external forces such as oppression, racism, and discrimination can also have a direct bearing on psychological functioning (Sue & Sue, 1999).

Postmodernism offers an alternative perspective for understanding the human condition. From a postmodern perspective, issues such as language and narratives provide a relational-contextual perspective for defining what truth, knowledge, and reality are. This can be particularly true in terms of gender and culture, since women tend to emphasize relational issues and minorities are directly affected by sociopolitical forces. A relational-contextual perspective can therefore provide an important frame of reference in counseling women and minorities.

Sexual Orientation

Sexual orientation is an important diversity issue in counseling. Fassinger (1991) defines several key terms associated with sexual orientation. Sexual orientation (or preference) refers to the complex set of behaviors, attitudes, and lifestyle factors associated with choosing a sexual partner. Homosexuality refers to sex with a same-sex partner, and the etiology of homosexuality is to a large degree considered to be genetic or biologically based. *Gay* and *lesbian* tend to be preferred terms (rather than *homosexual*) because they promote a more positive image that extends beyond sexual activity and includes the cultural considerations associated with gay/lesbian lifestyles. *Homophobia* is another common term associated with sexual orientation. It can be defined as the negative attitudes of fear and hatred that people may direct at gay and lesbian people.

The counseling literature has to some degree been negligent in addressing issues associated with gays and lesbians, even though these individuals represent 10–15 percent of the general population (Fassinger, 1991). Literature is beginning to emerge that provides models for conceptualizing developmental, treatment, and spiritual issues of gay and lesbian clients. Several gay-identity development models have been developed (for example, Cass, 1979; Minton & McDonald, 1984). According to Fassinger (1991), these models tend to have three central stages: recognition, acceptance, and affirmation. The process of "coming out" (sharing one's sexual orientation with friends and family) is perceived to be an important step in promoting a positive gay/lesbian identity and fostering optimal development (Fassinger, 1991). The process of coming out varies according to a number of factors such as age, gender, and culture. For example, in terms of age, younger individuals may have to be especially cautious in coming out because they are still financially dependent on their parents. Black and Underwood (1998) comment on additional issues associated with adolescents coming out. They note that when the circumstances are right, coming out can be a very positive experience, promoting self-acceptance and psychological well-being. Premature coming out can be associated with numerous problems such as rejection by friends and family. Adolescents should wait to come out until they have worked through self-doubt and have a clear sense of identity, feel self-worth, and have an established support system. It may be difficult to achieve some of these foundations for coming out since they are also associated as a consequence of coming out.

Browning, Reynolds, and Dworkin (1991) address treatment issues pertaining to lesbian women and Shannon and Woods (1991) provide information on counseling gay men. These scholars emphasize that it is important to look beyond sexuality when thinking about gays and lesbians and consider the special diversity and lifestyle issues that contribute to the unique features of this cultural group. For example, lifestyle considerations include career considerations, such as considering selecting careers where coming out could jeopardize job security and/or advancement (for example, the military). It is also important to help gays and lesbians adjust to same-sex relationships in a homophobic world. This can involve helping gay and lesbian clients work through feelings of isolation, oppression, abandonment, and anger. In addition, counselors should strive to develop an understanding of the unique relationship issues associated with gays and lesbians (for example, sexuality, communication, and parenting).

Ritter and O'Neill (1995) provide an overview of spiritual issues in counseling gays and lesbians. They note that traditional organized religion has offered little positive and much negative in terms of the psychological functioning and development of gays and lesbians. Essentially, most of the organized religions (for example, Judeo-Christian) have promoted the message that homosexuality is wrong, a sin, and a form of perversion. Obviously, the evidence that homosexuality is primarily determined by biological forces does not tend to be recognized by these religious groups (Ritter & O'Neill, 1995). A gay or lesbian person's only acceptable response to church doctrine tends to be conversion, repentance, celibacy, or an attempt to function in spurious heterosexual relationships (Ritter & O'Neill, 1995). Gays and lesbians who fail to measure up to church policy tend to receive little support or empowerment in terms of involvement in church functioning (for example, not being married as gays or lesbians in the church). Without access to church functions, it is also difficult to use the church as a source of strength and support during difficult times, such as working through loss due to death, divorce, and other adverse life events.

Ritter and O'Neill (1995) suggest that gays and lesbians experience numerous psychological and developmental problems resulting from exclusionary church doctrine and policy. On a psychological level, gay and lesbian people can struggle with negative feelings such as guilt, shame, and isolation, which in turn can interfere with self-acceptance and identity development. Feelings of isolation are endemic to gays and lesbians. It is therefore not surprising that they often feel like invisible people, living in an existential void beyond the recognized fringes of society. Counselors must take care to consider the vast array of special needs of gay and lesbian clients so that they can be afforded opportunities for spiritual development and enhancement.

Stereotyping

Stereotyping can be defined as "rigid preconceptions we hold about *all* people who are members of a particular group, whether it be defined along racial, religious, sexual, or other lines" (Sue & Sue, 1999). Examples of stereotyping are Native Americans have drinking problems and Asians are good at math. Stereotyping has negative effects on the counseling process (Sue, 1988). Some potential concerns are that stereotyping causes counselors to apply a perceived characteristic of a group to all members of that group without regard for individual differences, to fail to take logic or experience into consideration, and to distort all new information to fit preconceived ideas (Sue & Sue, 1999).

Communication Problems

Pedersen (1988) notes that much of the criticism directed at multicultural counseling relates to communication problems that interfere with the counseling process. Language differences can result in a variety of challenges in counseling (Sue, 1988). For example,

Vontress (1973) has found that counselors who experience language difficulties with a client have trouble establishing a positive counseling relationship with the client. Sue and Sue (1977) also warn that counselors who use only standard English with a bilingual client may make an inaccurate assessment of the client's strengths and weaknesses.

The style of nonverbal communication may also vary across cultures, creating communication problems. For example, African Americans tend to utilize more direct eye contact when speaking than whites and as a result have been labeled as more often angry (Sue & Sue, 1999). Native Americans tend to avoid direct eye contact when listening, causing them to be incorrectly perceived as inattentive (Sue & Sue, 1999). Herring (1990) notes the particular importance of counselors being able to assess nonverbal communication accurately, because this type of communication is more ambiguous and culturally bound than verbal communication.

Westwood and Ishiyama (1990) provide the following guidelines regarding the communication process in multicultural counseling:

1. Counselors should check with the client on the accuracy of their interpretation of nonverbal communication.
2. Counselors can promote catharsis by encouraging clients to use their own language to express a particular feeling when another language cannot accurately describe it.
3. Counselors should try to learn culturally meaningful expressions of the client to accurately describe the client's inner process.
4. Counselors should use alternative modes of communicating, such as art, music, and photography.

Faulty Assumptions

Pedersen (1987) identifies 10 faulty assumptions that can impede progress in counseling. Later in this chapter these assumptions are used to evaluate the appropriateness of counseling theory in multicultural counseling. These 10 faulty assumptions are summarized as follows.

Misconceptions of Normal Behavior. A tendency exists for people to assume that the definition of *normal* is universal across social, cultural, economic, and political backgrounds. Pedersen (1987) suggests that "what is considered normal will vary according to the situation, the cultural background of a person or persons being judged, and the time during which a behavior is being displayed or observed" (p. 17). Counselors can make an error of diagnosis if they fail to consider how the definition of normalcy can vary.

Emphasis on Individualism. Counselors with a traditional Western approach tend to emphasize the importance of the welfare of the individual. Self-awareness, self-fulfillment, and self-discovery are often used as indices of success in counseling. In addition, the task of the counselor is often perceived as "changing the individual in a positive direction even at the expense of the group in which that individual is a member" (Pedersen, 1987, p. 18).

This emphasis on the interests of the individual over the group may not be consistent with the value system of some cultures. In the Chinese culture, for example, it would be inappropriate to put the welfare of an individual before the welfare of that individual's family (Pedersen, 1987). Counselors should therefore take cultural issues into consideration before promoting the virtues of individualism in counseling.

Fragmentation by Academic Disciplines.   Some tendency exists for counselors to isolate themselves from related disciplines such as sociology, anthropology, theology, and medicine. This can result in a narrow view of people and an inability to understand individual differences. Cultural anthropology can be a particularly useful area for a counselor to study in terms of addressing multicultural issues.

Use of Abstract or Out-of-Context Concepts.   Many counseling principles contain abstract concepts, which can be easily misunderstood across cultures. In addition, the meaning of a concept will vary from one context or situation to another. It is therefore important to determine what a concept means as it relates to a particular client.

Overemphasis on Independence.   A common goal in counseling is to help clients become autonomous and independent. Pedersen (1987) warns that some cultures, such as the Japanese, believe that dependency is not only healthy but necessary. Some examples of relationships in which the Japanese culture views dependency as appropriate are those between employer and employee, mother and son, and teacher and student. Counselors should therefore be sensitive to cultural issues in determining whether a client's dependence is excessive.

Neglect of Client's Support System.   A client who enters counseling may want the counseling relationship to become a substitute for existing support systems. To ensure that this does not occur, counselors should include the client's support system in treatment planning. This can be especially important for a minority client who may already feel a high degree of isolation because of cultural differences.

Dependence on Linear Thinking.   Traditional Western counseling approaches tend to be characterized by linear thinking, whereby each cause has an effect and each effect has a particular cause. Some cultures are not tied to the linear model of analysis. The concept of Yin and Yang from Eastern culture does not differentiate between cause and effect but sees them as interrelated. In counseling it is therefore important to attempt to communicate in a manner that is consistent with the client's way of viewing the world.

Focus on Changing the Individual, Not the System.   "In many minority groups counseling has a bad reputation for taking the side of the status quo in forcing individuals to adjust or adapt to the institutions of society" (Pedersen, 1987, p. 22). To overcome this obstacle, counselors should broaden their intervention strategies to include a community psychology perspective. This can include trying to change the system if it appears the system is having a detrimental effect on the client. If a client's depression appears to be related to high unemployment in the community, the counselor may become active in efforts to create employment opportunities.

Neglect of History.   Counselors may focus only on the most recent precipitating events that led up to a crisis or mental disorder and fail to consider the client's problems from a historical perspective. For some minority clients, a historical perspective may be more appropriate because it can help the counselor understand sociocultural forces that have contributed to shaping a client's approach to problem solving and his or her outlook on life. Many African Americans, for instance, have experienced years of poverty, oppression, prejudice, racism, and exploitation. This can cause some to develop limited horizons and affect the way they view themselves and others, for example, with a sense of despair, helplessness toward self, or hostility or suspicion toward others.

Dangers of Cultural Encapsulation. *Cultural encapsulation* is a process in which counselors cannot see beyond their belief system and fail to address cultural issues with the client. Multicultural counselors must move beyond "parochial concerns and perspectives" and develop a comprehensive perspective that integrates contrasting assumptions from other cultures (Pedersen, 1987, p. 23).

Test Bias

Lonner (1985) provides a comprehensive overview of testing and assessment in multicultural counseling, identifying a variety of potential problems in multicultural testing that could contribute to test bias. These include difficulties in reactions to test-taking situations and problems that relate to validity, reliability, and norms.

Regarding test-taking situations, Lonner (1985) notes that there may be cultural differences in terms of use of time, language difficulties, and the manner of response to test questions. As an example of the effect of culture on an individual's manner of response, it may be culturally appropriate for some to agree with nearly every statement out of politeness. For others, it may be appropriate to give only socially desirable answers. Some individuals may view tests as unimportant and respond carelessly (Lonner, 1985).

Validity, reliability, and norms are critical in determining the use and effectiveness of tests, as discussed in Chapter 4. Validity may be the most important factor in evaluating a test. Construct validity is the extent to which a test measures a theoretical construct or trait such as intelligence and verbal fluency (Anastasi & Urbina, 1997). The meaning and importance of these constructs may vary from one culture to another (Lonner, 1985). Tests that utilize the same constructs across cultures may therefore have invalid construct validities.

Sociocultural factors may influence a test's reliability. Different opportunities in learning may vary across cultures, affecting a test's reliability. One culture may require formal education, for instance, whereas another may not (Lonner, 1985). It is therefore best to develop separate indices of reliability for each culture (Lonner, 1985).

Another potential problem in using psychological tests multiculturally relates to norms. Most standardized tests utilize a white, middle-class norm group in determining standards or points of comparison. These standards often vary considerably across cultures. The norms are therefore only relevant for the particular reference group or culture in which they were developed. If the test is to be used multiculturally, new norms should be established based on the population (Lonner, 1985).

It is also important to ensure that the test results are used in an appropriate fashion. Cronbach (1984) warns that the central issue in the test-bias controversy relates to decision making and how the inappropriate use of a test can create an unfair advantage for one culture over another. For example, using a culturally biased test in job selection could create an unfair advantage for some prospective employees. Culture-fair tests have been developed in an attempt to overcome some of the problems associated with test bias. Several of these tests are described in Chapter 4.

Prejudice

Sandhu and Aspy (1997) suggest that prejudice and prejudice reduction and prevention are important considerations in multicultural counseling. These scholars adapt Gordon Allport's (1954) definition of prejudice: "thinking ill of others without sufficient warrant" (p. 7). Prejudice is believed to emanate from a variety of individual, social, and political forces, such as oppressive attitudes (for example, stereotyping and racism), life-societal events (for example, loss of job due to foreign competition), and fear (Sandhu & Aspy, 1997). Geoseffi (1993) provides an alternative explanation for the etiology of prejudice, suggesting it can be traced to self-hatred. From this perspective, prejudice results from feelings of inadequacy that are projected onto others. Maslow's (1968) hierarchy of needs can also be used to understand prejudice. In this context, prejudice can be seen as a reflection of unmet needs (Sandhu & Aspy, 1997).

Prejudice can have adverse effects on the overall functioning of society and the peoples of the world, playing a major role in discrimination, oppression, violence, and even war. Sandhu and Aspy (1997) suggest that prejudice in the form of discrimination, cultural alienation, and restricted access to opportunities can also have detrimental effects on individuals' optimal development and self-actualization. In the final analysis, prejudice is a form of negativity that imparts a destructive force on anything in its path.

Sandhu and Aspy (1997) provide a comprehensive model for conceptualizing and addressing issues of prejudice in counseling (the multidimensional model of prejudice prevention and reduction [MMPPR]). From an MMPPR perspective, prejudice is the result of individual, social, and political factors. Although eclectic in nature, the model draws heavily from Maslow's (1968) hierarchy of needs theory (people tend to meet their needs in a hierarchical manner—that is, physiological, safety, love and belonging, and self-actualization needs). According to this theory, when people believe their need gratification is being interfered with, they attribute blame (in the form of prejudice) to the perceived source of the need inhibition. Conversely, people who have healthy need systems and can satisfy their needs tend to have self-actualizing tendencies such as harmony with self and others. The process of prejudice prevention and reduction, reduced to its most basic elements, is directed at helping clients meet their needs in a responsible manner. Sandhu and Aspy (1997) provide numerous assessment and intervention methods that can be used by counselors to address the complex individual, social, and political issues to overcome prejudice.

Prejudice prevention and reduction appear to offer much promise as an emerging dimension to the multicultural literature. It suggests that counselors become proactive and promote multidimensional roles and interventions in fighting the tide of prejudice. This can involve activities and initiatives such as addressing prejudice in all phases of the counseling process and becoming advocates for social reform regarding prejudice. Additional research and investigation are needed to determine how models for addressing prejudice can be effectively incorporated into multicultural counseling.

Racism

Racism represents another potential challenge to multicultural counseling. Thompson and Neville (1999) provide an in-depth analysis of racism and its relationship to mental health and psychotherapy. These scholars highlight several definitions of racism. Cox's (1959) model suggests that racism is "a social attitude propagated among the public by an exploiting class for the purpose of stigmatizing some group as inferior so that the exploitation of either the group itself or its resources or both may be justified" (p. 393). Cox sees racism as a way of justifying the domination and exploitation of one group of people over another group.

Chesler (1976) provides a sociological model of racism that suggests that racism has a political-institutional-ideological dimension. From this perspective, racism can often be traced to the ideology associated with political institutions whose laws maintain and propagate dominance and control of one group over another group.

Thompson and Neville (1999) describe a model of racism based on the earlier work of Cox and Chesler. This model contends the following:

- that racism has evolved across geographical regions over generations;
- that there are structural and ideological factors associated with racism; and
- that there are four forms of racism: individual, institutional, cultural, and environmental.

Thompson and Neville's model recognizes that racism in the United States has existed in different forms since the first settlers arrived. Originally, it was characterized by the dominance of European colonizers over Native Americans. Later the focus shifted to the domination of whites over blacks. Racism has taken different forms over time as reflected in structural and ideological factors. Structural factors relate to the political and organizational structures that maintain and perpetuate the domination/control and oppressive forces of minority groups. The civil war highlighted racial political views regarding the rights of blacks in America. Ideologies relate to belief systems such as prejudice that promotes racism. Racist ideologies express a misrepresentation of a cultural group that can be used to justify an oppressive behavior such as the use of slavery.

Thompson and Neville (1999) identify four forms of racism. Individual and everyday racism relates to such things as the insults and daily humiliation people experience as a result of their minority status (for example, an elementary school student with a disability being taunted by classmates). Institutional racism is reflected in the manner in which society creates favorable conditions for the dominant group over minority groups. An example of institutional racism is discriminatory hiring practices. Cultural racism is the practice of promoting the cultural beliefs and values of the dominant group and not recognizing the value of beliefs and customs of minority groups. Cultural racism in the United States occurs when individuals from the dominant culture contend their customs and beliefs are "American" and that the values and practices of minorities are not. Environmental racism is the fourth type of racism. It occurs when discriminatory laws result in minorities being exposed to unsafe environments such as living in housing projects with toxic levels of lead and high rates of violence.

Thompson and Neville (1999) also describe how racism can be related to mental health and psychotherapy. They suggest that healthy psychological functioning promotes the necessary strength and resiliency to stand up to racial oppression. Mental health and personality factors that are particularly important in overcoming racism include moral development, a stable identity, self-awareness, good coping skills, good interpersonal skills, and the ability to accurately perceive one's environment. Psychotherapy can be used to promote mental health and healthy, functional personalities. Thompson and Neville (1999) also suggest that issues relating to racism are often overlooked in psychotherapy. They contend it is important to explore how clients' problems (such as depression) can be related to issues of racism. For example, comprehensive treatment planning may entail addressing issues of racism such as racial discrimination and oppression in the work environment. In addition, therapists should assess how their counseling approach may foster racism. For example, therapists can attempt to identify problematic ideologies (such as prejudices) and determine how they may contribute to racial oppression within the counseling process.

Racism provides an important challenge to multicultural counseling. Thompson and Neville (1999) provide a useful model for conceptualizing racism within the counseling process. Models such as this can play a key role in assisting counselors in overcoming racial oppression. Additional research is necessary to provide further exploration and understanding of this complex phenomenon.

The Efficacy of Multicultural Counseling

After reviewing the potential challenges in multicultural counseling, one may wonder whether any counselor could overcome these barriers. Research in this area has tended to focus on the role of similarity between the counselor and client on the counseling process and counseling outcome. Atkinson and Thompson (1992) provide an overview of the literature on racial/ethnic similarity, attitude similarity, and educational dissimilarity. They note that clients tend to rate counselors as more attractive when they are similar to them, except when dissimilarity is valued (such as the counselor having more education than the client). Attitudinal similarity is found to be more important to perceived counselor attractiveness than ethnic/cultural similarity. The literature on ethnic/cultural similarity is conflicting, with some studies favoring similarity and others suggesting clients would prefer dissimilar counselors in terms of the ethnic/cultural status. There is some evidence that similar attitudes and counselor credibility are rated as higher priorities for clients than is ethnic/cultural similarity.

Cultural mistrust, level of acculturation, and stages of identity development may be variables that should be considered in determining preference for ethnic/cultural similarity. In terms of cultural mistrust, Atkinson and Thompson (1992) describe several studies that indicate that African-American clients who rated high on cultural mistrust engaged in premature termination when paired with white counselors and rated white counselors as less credible, accepting, expert, and trustworthy. Level of acculturation also appears to play a role in preference for similar ethnic/cultural counselors. A review of these studies shows clients rated low in acculturation prefer counselors who have similar ethnic/cultural status (Atkinson & Thompson, 1992). Stages of identity development provides another example of a variable that can influence clients' preference for counselors with similar ethnic/cultural status (Atkinson et al., 1998). This line of research is beginning to determine how clients' preference for counselors with similar ethnic/cultural status depends to some degree on their current stage of identity development.

Several other studies have investigated the relationship between personality similarity between counselor and client and the counseling process. Berry and Sipps (1991) researched the relationship between personality similarity, client's level of self-esteem, and premature termination. They found that clients who had low self-esteem tended to engage in premature termination when they also rated high on similarity with their counselor in terms of the Myers-Briggs Type Indicator. These researchers suggest that clients with low self-esteem may have a tendency to project their feelings of inadequacy onto their similar counselors, reducing these counselors' credibility and increasing tendencies toward premature termination. Towberman (1992) provides additional information on the relationship between personality similarity on the counseling process. She finds that similarity between the counselor and client (as measured by the California Psychological Inventory) is related to clients' positive perception of the counseling relationship in terms of degree of involvement, support, and expressiveness.

Beutler, Machado, and Neufeldt (1994) provide a review of the literature regarding gender similarity and counseling outcome. They note that the literature does not present a clear statement regarding the efficacy of male versus female counselors or whether gender similarity between the counselor and client promotes superior efficacy over diverse gender pairings in counseling. Research is beginning to differentiate styles of counseling between males and females, with males using counseling approaches that tend to be more directive and controlling than females (Nelson & Holloway, 1990; Wogan & Norcross, 1985). Feminist counselors are investigating issues such as male dominance and control and women's oppression in the counseling process (Enns, 1993). From a feminist perspective, it is not surprising that there is preliminary evidence to suggest that women prefer women counselors for assistance with relationship issues (Snell et al., 1992). Additional research seems required to gain a clearer understanding of the role of gender in the counseling process.

This literature, taken collectively, appears to suggest that clients first and foremost want a counselor who is credible (someone they believe can help them with their problems). Clients also place a high value on having a counselor who has a similar personality and attitudes (someone who they can relate to and feel comfortable with). Ethnic/racial similarity becomes important for clients who are experiencing high levels of cultural mistrust and low levels of acculturation and are processing issues of identity development. Gender also is an important variable, with women showing some tendency to prefer same-sex counselors to explore relationship issues. In addition, there appear to be some salient variables (such as self-esteem) that should be considered to gain a more in-depth understanding of the role of similarity in the counseling process.

The following *Personal Note* illustrates how a counselor can turn potential challenges in multicultural counseling into an advantage.

A Personal Note

I was surprised to discover that some of the barriers I envisioned in multicultural counseling turned out to be benefits. When I was a psychologist at a public health hospital on the Navajo Indian reservation, I was especially concerned about language barriers. I was told that I would need an interpreter since some Navajos could not speak English. This proved to be true in individual counseling with clients who did not speak English. In family therapy, however, I often found that some family members could not speak English but others were bilingual. In these situations, I would have the bilingual family members act as interpreters, so an "outside" interpreter was not necessary.

Several positive outcomes resulted from having clients act as interpreters. First, they seemed to listen very carefully since they did not know when I would ask them to interpret. These clients seemed to take their responsibility as interpreter very seriously. Perhaps it allowed them to show respect for what other family members said. Second, clients were taking an active role in the counseling process, since interpreting is basically paraphrasing.

I believe that many of the potential challenges in multicultural counseling can be overcome if the counselor develops a positive attitude and is sensitive to adjusting the approach to the unique needs of the client.

Suggestions for Incorporating a Multicultural Perspective

This section identifies suggestions for counselors to incorporate a multicultural perspective into their personal approach to counseling. It presents information on beliefs, knowledge, and skills necessary for multicultural counseling; discusses social justice; describes the concept of *worldview* as a construct that can be used to individualize multicultural counseling; provides an overview of identity development; presents methods for determining the appropriateness of traditional counseling theory; and provides general guidelines for implementing a multicultural approach.

Beliefs, Knowledge, and Skills

The Division of Counseling Psychology of the American Psychological Association (APA) established a taskforce (Sue et al., 1982) that identified cross-cultural competencies associated with beliefs and attitudes, knowledge, and skills of culturally skilled counselors. The following overview provides a summary of the taskforce's findings.

Beliefs and Attitudes.   To be effective in a multicultural setting, counselors should be aware of how their beliefs and attitudes may affect the counseling process. Sue (1981) notes that counselors who are not aware of their beliefs and attitudes may unknowingly impose their values and standards on others and engage in cultural oppression. It is therefore important to develop appropriate attitudes and beliefs. Sue et al. (1982) suggest that culturally skilled counselors

Gaining knowledge about a culture can be important to multicultural counseling.

- Are aware of and sensitive to their cultural heritage and have learned to value and respect differences
- Are aware of their own values and biases and how those attitudes may affect minority clients
- Are comfortable with differences that exist between themselves and their client in terms of race and beliefs
- Are sensitive to circumstances such as personal biases, stages of ethnic identity, and sociopolitical influences that may dictate a referral of a minority client to a counselor of the client's culture (Sue et al., 1982)

Knowledge. An effective multicultural approach to counseling requires some knowledge about the client's culture. In addition, Sue et al. (1982) note that culturally skilled counselors

- Have a good understanding of the sociopolitical system's operation in the United States with respect to its treatment of minorities
- Possess specific knowledge and information about a particular group they are working with
- Have clear, explicit knowledge and understanding of the generic characteristics of counseling and therapy
- Are aware of institutional barriers that prevent minorities from using mental health services

Skills. Some counseling strategies, such as being a good listener, are usually effective regardless of the culture. At the same time, as Sue (1981) warns, different cultural groups usually have different counseling goals and therefore require different counseling strategies to be effective. In addition, Sue et al. (1982) suggest that culturally skilled counselors

- Are able to generate a wide variety of verbal and nonverbal responses
- Are able to send and receive both verbal and nonverbal messages accurately

■ Are able to exercise institutional intervention skills on behalf of their clients when appropriate (Sue et al., 1982)

Recent Trends in Multicultural Competency

Sue et al.'s seminal work in multicultural competency (1982) has played a major role in the evolution of multicultural counseling over the past 20 years (Ridley and Kleiner, 2003). Sue, Arredondo, and McDavis (1992) issued a call to the profession, to identify standards of culturally competent counselors that should be addressed in education and incorporated into counseling practice. The Association for Multicultural Counseling and Development responded to the challenge by publishing the *Operationalization of the Multicultural Counseling Competencies* (Arredondo et al., 1996). Arredondo and Toporek (2004) report that the Arrendondo et al. (1996) document included 31 competencies and 119 explanatory statements that provide guidelines for clinical practice. Thomas and Weinrach (2004) note that the American Psychological Association and the American Counseling Association endorsed their own versions of multicultural competencies in 2002 and 2003, respectively (APA, 2002; ACA, 2003). Not all professional organizations have endorsed the competencies. For example, as of 2004, the American Mental Health Counseling Association has not endorsed or taken a position regarding multicultural competencies (Thomas & Weinrach, 2004).

Multicultural competency has become one of the most widely researched areas of the helping profession. Researchers have investigated the role of multicultural competency in education (Pope-Davis & Ottavi, 1994), case conceptualization (Constantine & Ladany, 2000), clients' perspective of counseling (Pope-Davis et al., 2002), and social justice (Vera & Speight, 2003). In 2002, the APA set forth guidelines on multicultural education, training, research, practice, and organizational change for psychologists (APA, 2002).

Social justice has become an emerging force in the field of counseling that is particularly well suited for integration into multicultural competency (Vera & Speight, 2003). Social justice involves addressing social-political forces such as cultural oppression that undermine human rights. Vera and Speight (2003) contend that multicultural competency should be grounded in a commitment to social justice. Social justice requires that counselors expand their role beyond counseling and psychotherapy to include social change. Feminist therapy (Brown, L. S., 1997; Enns, 1993) can be used to promote social justice by engaging in social-political action to overcome oppression and promote equality.

Although multicultural competency appears to have much promise, there has also been concern as to its validity as a proven method of advancing the practice of counseling. Weinrach and Thomas (2002) suggest that there is no empirical evidence that a counselor who masters the competencies set forth by Arredondo et al. (1996) would be better off than one who has not mastered the competencies. In addition, these authors contend there are flaws in the competencies regarding content and assumptions. In this regard, Weinrach and Thomas (2002) cite a personal communication from Vontress (Oct. 21, 1998):

> . . . the competencies are restricted in their development to the four national minority groups: African Americans, Native Americans, Asian Americans, and Latino Americans as if culture is owned by just these groups . . . . The writers of the multicultural competencies seem to take a racio-ethic view of culture with an emphasis on differences which bring people apart rather than on similarities which bring people together. (p. 24)

Patterson (2004) suggests that multicultural competencies are not necessary and can be misleading and counterproductive. He cites two problems associated with multicultural competencies. First, positive counseling outcomes are much more than a matter of knowledge and skills associated with multicultural competencies. Effective counseling includes a wide array of variables such as Rogers' (1957) core conditions and rapport between the counselor and client. Second, it is a mistake to assume that client differences are more important than their similarities and to therefore classify clients into discrete groups, each requiring their own counseling approaches.

Weinrach and Thomas (2004) posit that multicultural competencies have been a success on a symbolic level in that "they have successfully brought to professional counselors awareness of the importance of attending to the diverse counseling needs of visible minorities" (p. 91). They believe that multicultural competencies have been a failure on the applied level in that they have not provided persuasive evidence that multicultural competencies will result in enhanced counseling outcomes. In addition, Weinrach and Thomas contend that the greatest flaw of multicultural competency is its emphasis on deficits regarding clients and the counseling profession and not on clients' strengths.

On a more positive note, Arredondo and Toporek (2004) contend that multicultural competency is a living document subject to ongoing refinements, developments, and validation. They suggest that there is ample empirical evidence to support the adaptation of multicultural competencies, and that multicultural competencies provide an ethically and culturally responsive standard of practice. Clearly, additional research and investigation appear necessary to determine the efficacy of multicultural competencies.

Worldview

Although it is important to have a knowledge of the client's culture, it is also essential to be able to understand the client as a unique individual. Worldview, a concept with increasing recognition in the multicultural literature, is a construct that can be used to individualize the counseling process (Ibrahim, 1991; Sue, 1978, 1981).

Worldview, which extends beyond culture or ethnic group, can be defined as assumptions and perceptions regarding the world (Sire, 1976; Sue, 1978). World view is directly related to thoughts, feelings, and perceptions of social relations and the world (Ibrahim, 1991). It also has a direct effect on a client's ability to solve problems, make decisions, and resolve conflicts (Ibrahim, 1993). Knowledge of a client's world view can promote a better understanding of the client and can lead to more sensitive and effective counseling strategies (Ibrahim, 1991).

Ibrahim (1991) suggests that a client's worldview should be determined during the initial client assessment. One effective tool for determining a client's worldview is the Scale to Assess World Views (SAWV) (Ibrahim & Kahn, 1984, 1987). The SAWV assesses information regarding the client's view of human nature, social relations, relations with nature, time orientation, and activity orientation. The SAWV can help the counselor explore the client's values, beliefs, and assumptions; gain an understanding of the client's concerns; and differentiate between the client's worldview and cultural views (Ibrahim, 1991).

Trevino (1996) proposes a model for conceptualizing the change process that has a multicultural perspective. It is based primarily on the concept of worldview and also incorporates concepts from anthropology and research on the counseling process. Trevino's model of change recognizes both a general and specific worldview for both the counselor and client. According to this theory, it is advantageous for the counselor and client to have congruent general worldviews (one's basic understanding of the world in a broad abstract sense) and discrepant specific worldviews (more definite thoughts and opinions based on life experiences). Throughout the change process in counseling, similarity about general outlook on life is believed to promote empathy and foster a positive counseling relationship; discrepant specific world views promote alternative perspectives for problem solving.

Identity Development

Identity development is "a process of integrating and expanding one's sense of self" (Myers et al., 1991, p. 54). Establishing a positive self-identity can be difficult to attain (Myers et al., 1991). Helping clients clarify or enhance their self-identity can be a central task in counseling.

Identity development models have emerged as a means of understanding the process of identity formation and determining where clients are functioning in that process. Several models have emerged to describe the stages of identity development for racial-ethnic groups, such as those for African Americans (Cross, 1995), Hispanic Americans (Casas & Pytlulk, 1995), Asian Americans (Kim, 1981), white Americans (Helms, 1995; Rowe, Behrens, & Leach, 1995), and biracial Americans (Kerwin & Ponterotto, 1995).

Myers et al. (1991) note that racial-ethnic identity development models may have several limitations. For example, they may not take into account multiple oppressive factors such as socioeconomic status and minority status (for example, lower-class Mexican Americans) or multiracial backgrounds (for example, Amerasians). In an attempt to overcome some of these limitations, these authors developed the Optimal Theory Applied to Identity Development (OTAID) model. The OTAID model allows for consideration of multiple oppressive factors that can influence identity development. In addition, it is based on a worldview rather than being restricted to racial-ethnic considerations.

Myers et al. (1991) describe the OTAID model as a seven-phase process:

- *Phase 0: Absence of Conscious Awareness.* In this phase, individuals lack a sense of the self as a separate individual. Individuals do not develop self-awareness until 1 or 2 years of age (Dworetzky, 1996).
- *Phase 1: Individuation.* During this phase, individuals adhere to a personal identity that was generated by early familial and societal experiences. They utilize an egocentric view of themselves, which does not take into account the negative views of others.
- *Phase 2: Dissonance.* In phase 2, individuals begin to consider the opinions of others regarding who they are, even if these opinions are negative. Their perceptions of negative views from others create dissonance, and they begin to wonder who they really are.
- *Phase 3: Immersion.* Individuals who feel devalued by others may immerse themselves in the customs and way of life of the devalued group and react angrily toward the dominant group. For example, a 20-year-old Asian-American woman who had identified with Anglo customs now rejects those customs and immerses herself in Asian customs if she hears white people talking about her race in derogatory ways.

- *Phase 4: Internalization.* During this phase, individuals incorporate a number of salient aspects of the self in formulating their personal identity. This broadened self-image enables them to be more tolerant and accepting of the criticisms of others.
- *Phase 5: Integration.* As individuals gain deeper self-understanding, they begin to change their assumptions regarding the world. Their world view is broad and accepting of individual differences. At this point, they choose friends on the basis of shared values and interest instead of ethnic-racial criteria.
- *Phase 6: Transformation.* In the transformation phase, the self is redefined according to a world view that appreciates the interrelatedness of all aspects of life. This emerging personal identity incorporates a spiritual awareness regarding the order of life and the universe and fosters a sense of wholeness or completeness in the individual.

Methods to Evaluate Counseling Theories

To formulate a personal approach to counseling, it is necessary to determine the appropriateness of traditional counseling theory in multicultural counseling. Several methods can be used to assist with this process.

Acculturation Theory. Acculturation is a complex multicultural phenomenon that attempts to measure the extent of adaptation of the customs and values associated with the host culture. Kim and Abreu (2001) note that an individual's level of acculturation is associated with the degree of change (between the native and host culture) in terms of values and behaviors, cultural awareness, and cultural loyalty. Counselors can also estimate a client's level of acculturation by examining how much the client has assimilated into the mainstream society. Lee (1991) note that the factors that influence acculturation include educational level, socioeconomic status, length of time lived in the United States, and extent of exposure to racism.

Acculturation theories have been developed for different ethnic/cultural groups to obtain an understanding of the process of acculturation (for example, for American Indians, Choney, Berryhill-Paapke, & Robbins, 1995). In addition, acculturation scales are available for African Americans (Helms, 1986), American Indians (Hoffman, Dana, & Bolton, 1985), Asians (Suinn, Rickard-Figueroa, Lew, & Vigil, 1987), and Hispanics (Mendoza, 1989).

Acculturation theory appears to offer much promise to the counseling literature. Researchers are beginning to use this theory to explore issues that extend beyond evaluating the appropriateness of traditional counseling procedures with minority clients. For example, "acculturative stress" is being investigated by a number of researchers. Smart and Smart (1995) define acculturative stress as the "psychological impact of adjusting to a new culture" (p. 25). Moyerman and Forman (1992) provide a meta-analytic analysis of 49 studies of acculturation and adjustment and conclude that stress is more intense at the beginning of the acculturation process. Smart and Smart (1995) go on to identify health factors and counseling implications associated with acculturative stress of Hispanic immigrants. They find acculturative stress to be related to such phenomena as impaired physical health, decision making, occupational functioning, and utility of the counseling relationship. Acculturation theory will undoubtedly stimulate additional research activity on a wide range of issues relevant to counseling within a multicultural perspective.

Usher's Model.   Usher (1989) presents another method to evaluate the appropriateness of a theory. She suggests that the ten faulty assumptions identified by Pedersen (1987) can be used to determine whether a traditional counseling theory can be used in multicultural counseling. A counseling theory that appears to foster one or more of these faulty assumptions could either be modified or avoided in a multicultural context. Usher (1989) illustrates this method by using the ten faulty assumptions to evaluate Rogers's (1951) person-centered therapy. Her analysis shows Rogers's theory to have some strengths and weaknesses in terms of its use in multicultural counseling.

Usher (1989) identifies two facets of Rogers's theory that appear to promote multi-cultural counseling. First, since clients define the goals and determine the evaluation process, there is less chance of their being judged in terms of the dominant culture's view of normality. Second, Rogers's approach contains elements of circularity, allowing clients to express themselves within a framework that is nondirective and nonjudgmental.

Usher (1989) also identifies some potential problems with person-centered counseling in multicultural settings. One problem relates to Rogers's emphasis on individualism and independence from others. Rogers does not recognize the view of healthy dependencies that some cultures hold for authorities and family members. A second problem could arise from Rogers's belief that the locus of control and responsibility resides within the client. This position does not take into account environmental factors such as poverty, which can contribute to the client's growth process. Another potential problem relates to Rogers's emphasis on the here and now. Such a frame of reference may not be adequate to understand problems such as oppression that may affect culturally different clients.

Etic-Emic Model.   A third method that can be used to evaluate the efficacy of counseling theory in multicultural counseling involves the concepts of *etic* and *emic,* terms linked to linguistics (Lee, 1984; Ridley, Mendoza, & Kanitz, 1994). Etic relates to phonetics, which is something common to all languages. Etic is associated with concepts in counseling theory that are universal to all cultures. An example of an etic concept is the contention in rational emotive behavioral therapy (REBT) that irrational beliefs contribute to negative emotional consequences (Ellis, 2005). Emic relates to phonemics, which is something unique to that particular language. Emic is associated with concepts that emphasize individuality. An example of an emic concept is neuro-linguistic programming since it is an approach that varies with each individual (Bandler & Grinder, 1975).

There may be some advantages in using emic concepts as opposed to etic concepts in multicultural counseling. Emic concepts encourage the counselor to treat each client as an individual, thereby avoiding tendencies to engage in prejudice or stereotyping. Etic concepts, on the other hand, must be truly universal to be applied to different cultures without bias. Problems can surface with etic concepts when the theory assumes the concept is universal when in fact it is not. This could occur in REBT since it suggests that irrational thinking will generate emotional difficulties regardless of the culture (Bandler & Grinder, 1975). REBT does not appear to take into consideration the possibility that the definition of irrational ideas may vary from one culture to another. The efficacy of REBT would therefore be significantly reduced in situations in which a counselor was imposing inappropriate standards regarding what is rational, irrational, and self-defeating.

Fischer, Jome, and Atkinson (1998) provide a common factors model that can be used to address both etic (universal) and emic (culturally specific) perspectives in counseling. The common factors model contends that all counseling is multicultural and that a framework is needed to address universal health conditions in a culturally specific context. The model suggests there are four common factors that research supports as having universal healing value across cultures:

1. *The therapeutic relationship.* Across all cultures, the word *therapy* suggests a relationship between two people. A relationship of trust and caring is considered the heart of the counseling process.
2. *Shared worldview.* A shared worldview represents a common ground of understanding between counselors and clients. It acknowledges that although the worldviews of counselors and clients will vary, there is a communication of appreciation and mutual respect for their respective perceptions of the world.
3. *Client expectations.* For counseling to be beneficial, clients must believe that it will be of help. Faith in the benefits of counseling can be enhanced by counselors seeing clients in their own environments such as by having sessions in clients' homes or churches. In these instances, clients' expectations are enhanced when counselors communicate caring and understanding of clients' worldviews.
4. *Ritual or intervention.* Ritual or intervention relates to the importance of matching counseling procedures with culturally specific issues unique to the client. Culturally sensitive interventions require a strong knowledge base in diversity issues and individual differences. For example, Lewis (1994) emphasizes the importance of modifying common approaches, such as cognitive therapy, to incorporate the cultural milieu of the client. In this regard, Lewis notes that African-American clients placed a high value on family, religion, and spirituality. In these instances, Lewis suggests that counselors might consider framing cognitive restructuring within the context of biblical passages.

The model of Fischer et al. (1998) provides a framework in which to conduct all counseling from a multicultural perspective. Reduced to its simplest elements, the model suggests counselors use the following question to frame the counseling process: "How can I continue building relationships with my clients, understanding my clients' world views and perceptions of distress, raising my clients' expectations, and implementing culturally relevant interventions?" (Fischer et al., 1998, p. 569). The common factors model appears to offer much to the counseling literature in terms of bridging the gap between the etic and emic perspectives of multicultural counseling. Additional research is needed to evaluate the four common factors specifically as they pertain to multicultural counseling.

Guidelines for Multicultural Counseling

This section provides 10 guidelines for incorporating multicultural counseling strategies into a personal approach to counseling.

Establish Mutual Respect. Mutual respect forms the foundation for all relationships (Dinkmeyer & McKay, 1997). This may be especially important in multicultural counseling when a counselor from the majority culture counsels a minority client. In these situations, clients may feel they are being looked down upon and consequently resist participating in counseling.

Counselors can create opportunities to communicate respect to the client by honoring the client's unique way of perceiving and interacting with the world. Counselors can also communicate an acceptance of their client whenever possible. For example, some clients may become embarrassed because they have difficulty speaking English. When this occurs, the counselor can tell these clients that it is impressive that they are becoming bilingual when most people can speak only one language.

As clients experience acceptance and respect, they may become more relaxed with and accepting of their counselor. The resulting mutual respect can contribute to a relationship of equality in the counseling process.

Don't Impose Your Belief System. When working in multicultural counseling, it is important for the counselor to be nonjudgmental. Each culture has its own norms and value system. This may influence how clients see important issues pertaining to counseling, such as their understanding of mental health. For example, the Navajos do not differentiate between physical and mental health (Harrar, 1984). They see mental problems as being a result of a person being "out of harmony." with the traditional Navajo culture (Harrar, 1984).

Treat Clients as Unique Individuals First and as People from a Particular Culture Second. It is important to consider that all people are unique, even in terms of what it means to be part of a particular culture. Focusing on the unique characteristics of a particular client will help counselors overcome stereotyping and other self-defeating processes.

Determine Whether Traditional Counseling Approaches Would Be Appropriate for a Particular Client. The counselor can use the three methods described in this chapter to determine the appropriateness of traditional counseling theory in multicultural settings.

Provide Accessible, Dependable Services. It is important for counseling services to be adequately staffed so clients will know someone will be there if they come for help. This is especially important in rural areas, where a client may have traveled a long distance to come for counseling services. On the Navajo reservation, it was not uncommon that clients may have journeyed 100 miles and may have had to get a ride from a friend or hitchhike. It would not be very welcoming for these clients to be told that they would have to come back the next day or wait a long time to receive help. It is essential for the counseling center to develop a reputation for being reliable and responsive, or clients will stop coming.

Some clients may feel that their problems are not "big enough" to warrant counseling services. These are often the clients who need help the most. They need to be reassured that the counseling service is there for them to use and that they are not "in the way," as they might feel, but are welcome.

Use a Flexible Approach.   Counselors should adjust their approach to the client's unique needs in all cases, but flexibility is especially important in multicultural counseling. In many minority cultures, such as those of Mexican Americans, African Americans, and Native Americans, a high percentage of people are struggling against the elements of poverty. These individuals may therefore need assistance with basic needs such as food, shelter, and safety. When this occurs, counselors should adjust their approach to meet these needs, becoming more action-oriented and focused in the present (Sue, 1981). Counselors may even function to some degree as advocates for the client's basic rights. This may involve helping clients obtain benefits from social services or other agencies.

Be Perceived as a Doer, Not Just a Talker.   Counselors should show they are capable of accomplishing something concrete with the client as early as possible in the counseling relationship. A counselor who is perceived as a doer and not just a talker will be valued and sought after by clients, especially those struggling to fulfill basic needs.

Conduct an Environmental Assessment.   It is important to avoid an overemphasis on intrapsychic forces in assessment and diagnosis. An environmental assessment will enable the counselor to explore sociocultural factors that could also be contributing to the client's problems. This will not only contribute to more accurate assessment and diagnosis but also help the counselor and client identify realistic treatment goals.

Allow Yourself to Be Enriched by the Client's Culture.   Multicultural counseling can be rewarding and exciting. It can involve living and working in a different culture or simply providing a multicultural counseling service. Regardless of the degree of a counselor's multicultural experience, many opportunities exist for cultural enrichment. A counselor may soon discover some of the special facets of a culture such as types of food, styles of dress, differences in family life, and approaches to physical and mental health.

Each culture also has its special customs, beliefs, heritages, and creative arts. It may be helpful to study a culture to appreciate its special beauty. This can involve reading, going to art exhibits and other cultural events, and, of course, learning from clients.

You Don't Have to Be a Minority to Counsel a Minority.   There can be potential problems in multicultural counseling such as language barriers, stereotyping, and a lack of awareness of the value systems of a cultural group. At the same time, counselors can overcome these problems by being sensitive to the unique needs of the client and attempting to gain the beliefs, knowledge, and skills necessary to counsel in multicultural settings.

Summary

Developing a well thought-out personal approach to counseling creates the necessary structure to work within the counseling process. An eight-stage model, including the merits of using an integrative approach, provides guidelines for formulating a personal approach responsive to a multicultural society. This model suggests that counselors who utilize a central or core theory will have a solid foundation to approach the counseling process. This foundation will provide internal consistency for the counselor's approach.

Some of the potential challenges associated with multicultural counseling include a tendency for diagnostic and treatment bias. These concerns can be overcome when the counselor treats the client as a person first and a member of a particular culture second; sensitively relates to the special needs and circumstances of the client; and gains the necessary beliefs, knowledge, and skills associated with the populations the counselor intends to serve.

Personal Exploration

1. What is important to you in formulating your personal approach to counseling?
2. What intrigues you about multicultural counseling?
3. What is your position regarding diversity issues such as sexual orientation?
4. What guidelines would you follow regarding multicultural counseling?

Web Sites for Chapter 6

Carter, D. J. (1999). *Multicultural counseling.* Retrieved March 3, 2005, from
   http://idsdev.mccneb.edu/dcarter/stagesof.htm
   Presents a sample framework of stages of ethnic identity in multicultural counseling.
Cillo, L. (1998). *Multicultural issues.* Retrieved March 3, 2005, from
   http://members.aol.com/lacillo/multicultural.html
   Covers the basics of multicultural counseling and provides useful links.
Freedman, F. K. (1999). *Multicultural counseling.* Retrieved March 3, 2005, from
   http://www.alaska.net/~fken/Multiculture.htm
   *Presents a semi-current review of multicultural counseling, citing mostly D. W. Sue and D. Sue's (1990) text (*Counseling the Culturally Different: Theory and Practice, 2nd Edition*) on cross-cultural counseling.*
Green, D. (1997). *Multicultural counseling.* Retrieved March 3, 2005, from
   http://www.lausd.k12.ca.us/orgs/lasca/html/multicultural_counseling.html
   Provides an array of multicultural counseling resources and links.

7

The Classic Theories of Freud, Adler, and Jung

CHAPTER OVERVIEW

This chapter provides a description of the three classic theories of Freud, Adler, and Jung. Highlights of the chapter include

- The art and science of the three classic theories
- Background information regarding the three classic theories
- The theory of personality regarding the three classic theories
- The theory of counseling and psychotherapy regarding the three classic theories
- Contemporary issues for the three classic theories
- Brief-counseling approaches for the three classic theories
- Diversity issues for the three classic theories

The Art and Science of the Classic Theories

The art of counseling owes much to the classic theories. Freud was one of the first clinicians to really listen to clients' stories through processes such as free association and dream analysis. It was a creative process that involved reaching into the clients' world and attempting to discover hidden or symbolic content that could be interpreted to the client. Adlerian psychology provides another dimension to the art of counseling. Adler referred to the center or nucleus of the person as the creative self, emphasizing the creative capacity to interact with the world in a manner that reflects each person's uniqueness. Jung's theory more than any other counseling theory may capture the spirit of the art of counseling. He was a very sensitive individual who would adapt his approach to meet the needs of his client. For example, Jung found that by mirroring the gestures of his psychotic clients he could attempt to understand what they were trying to communicate (Douglas, 2005). In addition, Jung frequently used different modalities within the creative arts, such as having a client draw an image from a dream to provide additional means for analysis (Douglas, 2005).

The classic theories also provide a strong foundation for the science of counseling. From a science perspective, these theories have played an integral role in the evolution of current psychotherapies. Some of the concepts generated by the classic theorists that are commonly used by clinicians include the conscious-unconscious continuum, defense mechanisms, the importance of early life experiences on personality development, the therapeutic alliance, lifestyle, and the relationship between wholeness and psychological balance to psychological growth and self-healing.

There has been a wide array of research endeavors directed at the classic theories. Henry, Strupp, Schacht, & Gaston (1994) have reviewed research on Freud's theory and found that current trends in research are directed at gaining a better understanding of transference relationships, interpretation, and the therapeutic alliance. Adlerian theoretical constructs continue to receive interest in the literature (for example, birth order, Sullivan & Schwebel, 1996, and lifestyle, Kern, Gfroerer, Summers, Curlette, & Matheny, 1996). Current research trends in Jungian psychology include recognition of the importance of affect, feelings, and body awareness in the analytic process (Douglas, 2005).

As noted in Chapter 6, the art and science of counseling recommend using a multicultural perspective to conceptualize diversity issues throughout the counseling process. It is especially important to utilize a multicultural perspective with the classic theories because some concepts may appear dated and out of step with contemporary values and beliefs. The art and science of the classic theories involve making the necessary modification to these theories by utilizing multicultural research findings and maintaining a sensitivity to the evolving needs of clients.

An Overview of Freud, Adler, and Jung

The classic psychological theories of Sigmund Freud, Alfred Adler, and Carl Jung laid the foundation for modern clinical practice. Their influence transcended psychology, having a significant impact on the arts, education, child-rearing practices, and numerous other aspects of daily living.

Freud's (1972) masterpiece, *The Interpretation of Dreams,* which was originally published in 1900, caught the interest of Adler and Jung. Adler and Jung were colleagues of Freud who became central figures in the psychoanalytic organization. They eventually broke ranks with Freud when they believed he overemphasized the role of sexuality in personality development. Adler and Jung proceeded to develop their own psychological theories. The three distinct schools of psychology that evolved have a number of commonalities. Each emphasizes the importance of early life experiences on personality development and also views insight as an important prerequisite to change.

The Freudian, Adlerian, and Jungian schools of psychology can be considered the "classic schools" because each developed its own comprehensive theory of personality and approach to psychotherapy. They can be used as the central or core theory from which to develop an integrative counseling approach. Table 7.1 presents an overview of these three theories. This is followed by an overview of the three classic theories, each with background information on the theorist and information on his theory of personality and theory of counseling and psychotherapy. The chapter concludes by addressing diversity issues and brief-counseling perspectives of the classic theories.

TABLE 7.1 Freud, Adler, and Jung

Theory	Key Concepts	The Counseling Process	Techniques
Freud's psychoanalytic theory	Endopsychic conflicts resulting from the id, ego, and superego; defense mechanisms; the conscious-unconscious continuum; and the effects of traumatic experiences in childhood on personality development	Has the major aim of resolving intrapsychic conflicts to restructure the personality as necessary	Dream analysis and free association can be used to explore unconscious processes; confronting, clarification, and interpretation provide necessary insight
Adler's individual psychology	The creative self; behavior as goal directed and purposeful; social interest; striving for significance as a motivational force; and the family constellation	Is educationally oriented, provides information, guides and attempts to encourage discouraged clients	The lifestyle analysis as an assessment technique, motivation modification to modify underlying motivational forces, and techniques to reorient clients from basic mistakes
Jung's analytic psychology	The collective unconscious, archetypes, and personality types	Explores unconscious processes to help the self emerge so clients can be free to move toward self-realization	Analysis of the interrelationship of several dreams for their symbolic content and cues to the various systems of the personality

Freud's Psychoanalytic Theory

Background Information

Patterson (1986) describes some of the significant events of Freud's life. These observations have been incorporated into the following overview.

Sigmund Freud (1856–1939) was born in Freiberg, Moravia, a town in the Czech Republic. He was the oldest of eight children and moved with his family to Vienna when he was 4 years old.

Freud obtained a medical degree in 1881 from the University of Vienna. After graduation, he went to Paris to study with Jean-Martin Charcot, who was known for his work with hypnosis in the treatment of hysteria. Freud then returned to Vienna and married Martha Bernays. They had six children; the youngest was Anna, who later became a distinguished child analyst.

In 1882, Freud began a private practice in medicine, initially specializing in nervous diseases. He later broadened his practice into what is known today as psychiatry. At this point in his career, Freud became interested in the "talking cure," which was being developed by the prominent Viennese physician Joseph Breuer. Breuer believed that a client

Sigmund Freud

could be helped by simply talking about his problem. This concept contributed to Freud's free-association technique and is an important part of the evolution of the counseling profession.

The most creative period in Freud's life was also a period during which he experienced serious emotional problems. He was tormented by psychosomatic disorders and phobias such as an exaggerated fear of dying. At one point he was even afraid to cross the street. During this time Freud engaged in extensive self-analysis by studying his dreams. The insights Freud gained from his self-analysis became very influential in the development of his own theories, such as the Oedipus complex. He remembered that as a child he felt hostility toward his father, whom he perceived as an overbearing authority figure. On the other hand, Freud had sexual feelings for his mother, whom he remembered to be loving, attractive, and protective.

Freud's rise to prominence required perseverance and an ability to withstand severe criticism. As he developed his revolutionary theory, he was initially met with scorn and ridicule from all corners of the academic and scientific community. Alone, he forged on, typically working for 18 hours a day. Finally, with his publication of *The Interpretation of Dreams* in 1900, he became "respectable" again. Shortly thereafter, Freud was welcomed back to the intellectual community and regarded with great esteem.

In later years, Freud's struggles turned to his personal health. His fondness for cigars apparently contributed to the development of jaw cancer. During the last 20 years of his life, he was in almost constant pain and underwent 33 operations. Somehow, he still managed to maintain an active professional life. Hall and Lindzey (1978) note that Freud was a prolific writer, with his collective works filling 24 volumes. His work also stands out from a literary point of view. Freud's eloquent writing style did much to popularize his ideas.

Theory of Personality

Freud's theory of personality was well developed, providing information on how behavior manifests itself in terms of the id, ego, and superego; the unconscious-conscious continuum; defense mechanisms; and other useful psychological constructs.

View of Human Nature.   Freud had a deterministic view of human nature. He was convinced that behavior was determined by unconscious biological urges of sex and aggression and psychosexual experiences during the first six years of life.

Key Concepts.   Freud's theory of personality is characterized by several key concepts (Strachey, 1953–1974). Some of these are the structure of the personality, endopsychic conflicts, defense mechanisms, the conscious-unconscious continuum, and psychosexual stages of development. These concepts, as described by Freud (Strachey, 1953–1974), are incorporated into the following overview.

The Structure of the Personality.   In Freud's view, the personality is made up of three autonomous yet interdependent systems: the id, ego, and superego.

The *id* is the original system of the personality from which the ego and superego emerge (Hall & Lindzey, 1978). It is the reservoir of psychic energy, supplying energy to the other two systems. The id can be considered the "hedonistic branch" of the personality (Hall, 1954). It is driven by the pleasure principle, which attempts to reduce tension by gratification of sexual and aggressive impulses.

The *superego* is the other extreme of the personality. It can be considered the "judicial branch" and is concerned with moralistic issues determining what is right or wrong (Hall, 1954). It represents the values and ideals of society as handed down from parent to child. The superego has three purposes: to inhibit the impulses from the id, to alter the ego's orientation from realistic to moralistic, and to encourage the personality to strive for perfection.

The *ego* can be considered the "executive branch" of the personality (Hall, 1954). It is ruled by the reality principle, which attempts to exert a realistic, reality-based influence over the id and superego.

Endopsychic Conflicts.   An *endopsychic* conflict is a conflict within (from *endo*) the psyche. Endopsychic conflicts result from the interaction of the three parts of the personality: the id, ego, and superego. According to Freud, there is only so much "psychic energy" for the three parts of the personality to function. All three systems are therefore in constant competition for this energy to take control and dominate the personality. As the three parts of the personality compete for psychic energy, they create conflicts within the psyche, called *endopsychic conflicts.* These conflicts create anxiety, which the organism can attempt to alleviate by creating defense mechanisms.

Endopsychic conflicts always involve the ego and the id or superego (or both the id and superego). The following are possible examples of endopsychic conflicts:

- *Id versus ego:* (Id:) "I want to rape or murder." (Ego:) "If you do, you will go to jail."
- *Id versus superego and ego:* (Id:) "I want to rape or murder." (Superego:) "You shouldn't because it is wrong" and (Ego:) "You will go to jail."
- *Ego versus superego:* (Ego:) "I would like to go to bed with my lover." (Superego:) "Don't do it because it is a sin to have sex unless you are married."

Defense Mechanisms.   Freud's concept of defense mechanisms was one of his most important theoretical achievements. Defense mechanisms develop unconsciously when the ego feels threatened by an endopsychic conflict. When this occurs, defense mechanisms can be utilized to deny, falsify, or distort reality so the ego can cope. The role of the counselor can therefore be to help strengthen the client's ego to minimize stress from endopsychic conflicts and the resulting defense mechanisms. This process of strengthening can involve psychoeducational interventions that provide clients with information they can use to take a more realistic position regarding stresses in their environment.

Some of the more common defense mechanisms are projection, reaction formation, fixation, regression, and repression.

Projection is an attempt to attribute to another person one's own thoughts or feelings. For example, instead of saying you hate someone, you say, "That person hates me." In this example, projection occurs because the ego is threatened by aggressive id impulses. Projection can therefore be seen as an attempt to "externalize the danger."

Reaction formation is a way of coping by creating an extreme emotional response that is the opposite of how one actually feels. This results in a "falsification of reality." For example, a man may hate his wife and want a divorce. At the same time, he may have intense feelings of guilt since he believes divorce is morally wrong. If the man tells others how wonderful his wife is and how much he loves her, a reaction formation may be operating.

Fixation can occur if the demands of life become too threatening. In an attempt to avoid new responsibilities, a person can avoid growing up and fixate, or stand still, in terms of development. When this occurs during adolescence, the individual's personality remains like an adolescent for the remainder of life.

Regression is an attempt to cope by moving back to a point in one's development that was less threatening. For example, a person who has a major business failure may feel life is falling apart. In an attempt to cope, the person may try to escape these feelings of failure by moving back to a point in time that was not so threatening. When this occurs, the person may assume the role of a child to avoid adult responsibilities.

Repression is an attempt to cope by creating an avoidance response. In repression, the stressful situation is pushed from the conscious to the unconscious dimension of the mind.

The Conscious-Unconscious Continuum.   Freud was one of the first to explore the unconscious dimension of the human psyche. He believed it held the key to understanding behavior and problems within the personality. It is therefore not surprising that the majority of the techniques associated with psychoanalysis (such as free association and dream analysis) are used to explore unconscious processes.

Freud conceptualized conscious and unconscious processes in terms of a continuum. The analogy of the iceberg can be used to understand this continuum, as illustrated in Figure 7.1.

As shown in Figure 7.1, most of the psyche involves unconscious processes. The *conscious* dimension contains material that the person is aware of and can readily retrieve. The *preconscious* relates to material that the person is almost consciously aware of but that is just out of mental awareness (for example, almost being able to remember a person's name). The *unconscious proper* includes all memory traces that the person is not consciously aware of (for example, a repressed traumatic experience such as childhood incest).

Psychosexual Stages of Development.   Freud contended that personality development was determined to a large degree by early life experiences. His theory suggests that problems in the personality can result if the child has a traumatic experience or the child's basic needs are

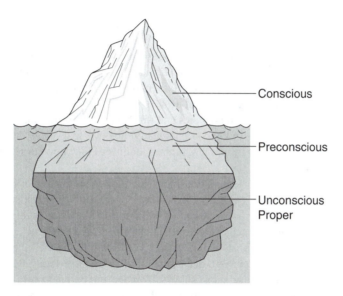

FIGURE 7.1   Iceberg Analogy

not met. When this occurs, the person could attempt to achieve indirect gratification by displacement or sublimation to restore equilibrium to the organism. Displacement is indirect gratification, such as a baby sucking his or her thumb when not allowed to eat. Sublimation is also indirect gratification, but it results in some form of social recognition. An example of sublimation is a sexually frustrated person creating a beautiful, sensuous painting.

Freud was one of the first theorists to identify stages of development that a person progresses through. He called them psychosexual stages, emphasizing the role of sexuality in the developmental process. Freud divided these stages into three periods: the pregenital period, which lasts until age 6; the latency period, which spans from age 6 to adolescence; and the genital period, which continues for the rest of a person's life.

The pregenital period is composed of the oral, anal, and phallic stages and the latency period. Freud believed that the *oral stage* occurs during the first 18 months of life. It is called the oral stage because the child appears preoccupied with oral functions (for example, sucking the mother's breast and exploring objects by putting them into the mouth). Problems that occur during the oral stage (such as extreme frustration of oral gratification) could result in the individual developing an oral personality as an adult. Adult nail-biting could be an example of displacement of latent oral needs. Becoming a teacher or orator could result from sublimation of oral needs.

The *anal stage* occurs from 18 months to 3 years of age. This stage emphasizes the impact of toilet-training on personality development. Problems that can occur during the anal stage may result in an anal-explosive or anal-retentive personality. The anal-explosive personality is an aggressive type of person. This style of personality could result when a child went to the toilet all the time as a means of keeping a parent's attention. The anal-explosive personality could develop skills in football or boxing as a form of sublimation. An anal-retentive personality could occur if a parent used severe punishment when the child had an "accident." Out of fear, the child could develop a pattern of not going to the toilet. An example of sublimation for the anal-retentive personality could be a person who is good at saving money.

The *phallic stage* occurs between the ages of 3 and 6. According to Freud, it is a time when male children become sexually interested in their mothers (the Oedipus complex), and female children become attracted to their fathers (the Electra complex). The boy eventually resolves his Oedipus complex out of fear of castration from his father. Problems could occur if a father had jealous tendencies and threatened to hurt his son if the boy did not stop "pestering mother." This threat could intensify the boy's fear of castration. According to Freud, this fear could then inhibit any future thoughts of the opposite sex, promoting homosexual tendencies.

Unlike the male child, the female does not have a dramatic means of resolving her Electra complex, such as fear of castration. Instead, she may resolve her sexual feelings by reacting to the realistic barriers that are established to prohibit incestuous relationships. A problem could result during this stage if a child felt emotionally rejected by her father, possibly causing her to avoid relationships with males in the future. On the other hand, if an incestuous relationship were allowed to occur, the child could experience even more profound difficulties in her personality, such as low self-image and perhaps promiscuity.

The *latency period,* which occurs between the ages of 6 and 12, is a period of relative calm. The child has emerged from the turbulence of the pregenital period with the basic structure of the personality largely formed. During this period, the child develops new interests to replace infantile sexual impulses. Socialization takes place as the child moves from a narcissistic preoccupation to a more altruistic orientation. Problems could occur during this period if the parents did not encourage the child's interest in establishing positive social relationships. As a result, the child might not be able to develop the social skills necessary for successful interpersonal relationships.

The *genital period* begins at puberty and continues for the rest of life. The focus of this period is an opposite-sex relationship leading to the experience of intimacy. Problems during this period could occur for an individual who was discouraged from socializing or began sexual relationships before being emotionally ready to handle them.

Theory of Counseling and Psychotherapy

Freud's approach to counseling and psychotherapy is called *psychoanalysis,* emphasizing the analysis of the mind. It is a time-consuming approach that can typically involve four one-hour sessions each week over a period of several years (Arlow, 2005).

The major aim of psychoanalysis is to restructure the personality by resolution of intrapsychic conflicts. The actual process of traditional psychoanalysis involves the client lying on a couch and engaging in free association, saying whatever comes to mind. In this process, the analyst is seated out of the client's view behind the couch and listens and reacts in a noncritical manner. Arlow (2005) describes four phases of psychoanalysis: the opening phase, the development of transference, working through, and the resolution of transference.

The Opening Phase.   During this phase, the analyst obtains important history from the client. Gradually, over a period of three to six months, the analyst obtains a broad understanding of the client's unconscious conflicts.

The Development of Transference.   During this phase, the client begins to experience a transference relationship with the analyst. This involves projecting thoughts and feelings onto the analyst that are associated with significant others such as a father or mother. Transference is encouraged during psychoanalysis. It plays a key role in bringing unresolved conflicts (which typically originated in childhood) to the surface, so they can be worked through and resolved within the safety and support of the therapeutic relationship.

Analysis of the transference is a cornerstone of the psychoanalytic process. It provides the client with insight into how past relationships and experiences are creating problems in present relationships. Analysis of transference also helps the client learn how to use insight to make appropriate, mature decisions regarding current relationships.

Countertransference may also occur in therapy and results when analysts unconsciously begin to see qualities in the client that remind them of someone from their past. Countertransference can interfere with the analyst's objectivity and destroy the therapeutic process. When this occurs, the analyst may need psychoanalysis to work through these tendencies.

Working Through.   This phase is essentially a continuation of the previous phase. It involves additional analysis of transference aimed at generating more profound insights and consolidating what can be learned from them.

The Resolution of Transference.   During the final phase of therapy, the analyst and client work toward termination. This can involve working through resistance from the client regarding termination or preparing the client to function independently once termination is complete.

Techniques

Freud developed many techniques that could be used in psychoanalysis (Strachey, 1953–1974). Their primary purpose is to make the unconscious conscious. The following are some of the more commonly used techniques:

- *Free association* is the primary technique used in psychoanalysis. As discussed earlier, it is used throughout the counseling process. Free association encourages the client to discuss whatever comes to mind, thereby overcoming his or her tendencies to suppress or censor information.
- *Dream analysis* is a technique Freud developed as a means to explore unconscious processes. He suggested that elements of dreams contained symbolic meaning, such as a screwdriver being a phallic symbol, representing a penis.
- *Confrontation and clarification* are feedback procedures to help the client become aware of what is occurring and in need of further analysis (Prochaska, 1984).
- *Interpretation* involves providing insight to the client regarding inner conflicts reflected in resistance, transference, and other processes.

Contemporary Issues

Contemporary Freudian psychology reflects several changes and modifications from Freud's original theory. These changes evolved primarily in response to what was considered to be his overemphasis on the role of sexuality in personality development and the excessive time required to complete psychoanalysis.

Strupp (1992) describes several trends in psychoanalysis:

1. The role of the analyst has shifted from the detached, impersonal classical Freudian position to the more humanistic interactive model associated with the therapeutic alliance.
2. The role of the Oedipus complex in psychopathology has been deemphasized, with earlier developmental periods playing a more central role in psychological dysfunction.
3. Treatment considerations have shifted from neurotic conditions such as obsessive-compulsive disorders and phobias to the treatment of personality disorders.
4. Transference and countertransference have been reconceptualized in terms of interpersonal theory, which emphasizes the dyadic quality of the counseling relationship. Within this context, the analyst and client continually contribute to transference and countertransference processes as a natural outcome of their ongoing relationship. Thus negative connotations of transference and countertransference have been replaced by a more robust and positive view of how the counseling relationship can provide opportunities for insights and analysis.

Strupp (1992) identifies several additional trends in psychoanalysis. They include a recognition of the importance of interpersonal relations in psychological health, a reassessment of the role of the ego in psychological functioning, and the movement toward time-limited psychoanalysis.

The Interpersonal Perspective.   The interpersonal perspective contends that psychoanalytic theory overemphasizes intrapsychic forces (such as inner conflicts over sexuality) and does not recognize the importance of environmental forces (such as the quality of interpersonal relationships). Interpersonal psychotherapy is an emerging form of psychotherapy based on the work of Harry Stack Sullivan (1968) and his collaborators (for example, Adolph Meyer, 1957, and John Bowlby, 1973). This approach recognizes the effect of early life experiences (such as the degree of parent-child attachment) on the quality of interpersonal relationships later in life and the role that interpersonal functioning plays in depression (Prochaska & Norcross, 2002).

Interpersonal theory suggests that people are motivated by interpersonal anxiety to avoid rejection and to maintain self-esteem (Schwartz & Waldo, 2003). Interpersonal psychotherapy involves identifying and working through parataxic distortions ("inappropriate ways of reacting to others . . . based on previous experiences, usually in the family of origin" (Schwartz & Waldo, 2003, p. 105). Interpersonal psychotherapy is a time-limited approach that focuses on enhancing social skills and improving interpersonal relationships (Prochaska & Norcross, 2002).

Chapter 9 provides additional information on interpersonal psychotherapy, with transactional analysis featured as an example of this school of counseling and psychotherapy.

Ego-Analytic Theory. The ego-analytic position incorporates theories associated with ego psychology and object-relations theory. Ego psychology is associated with the work of Erikson (1950) and Rapaport (1958) and represents a shift in focus from the id to the ego as the primary driving force of personality (Prochaska & Norcross, 2002). In this new role, the ego is viewed as capable of functioning independently from the id in its attempt to adapt to reality and master the environment (Prochaska & Norcross, 2002).

Object-relations theory, as proposed by Kernberg (1976) and Kohut (1971), emphasizes the self and objects (people) as the primary organizing force in personality functioning (Prochaska & Norcross, 2002). Object relations are intrapsychic structures based on the mental representations of the self and others (Prochaska & Norcross, 2002).

Baker (1985) identifies the following six characteristics of the ego-analytic position:

1. Noninstinctual factors are emphasized.
2. The ego is conceptualized as a separate autonomous structure that operates independently of the id.
3. The function of the ego has been expanded to include the role of adaptation to the environment by developing coping and mastery skills.
4. Psychosocial and interpersonal variables are emphasized over biological-instinctual variables.
5. Developmental stages that occur after puberty are considered as important as those occurring before puberty.
6. Psychopathology occurs as a result of not meeting the needs associated with developmental tasks and other forces that could cause defects in the personality structure of the individual.

Freudian Brief Approaches to Counseling

With the emergence of managed care, long-term open-ended psychoanalysis is a luxury that few individuals and insurance companies can afford (Strupp, 1992). There is therefore increasing pressure for all forms of psychotherapy (including psychoanalysis) to be directed toward the treatment of specific mental disorders within the context of a limited number of sessions (Strupp, 1992). Brief psychodynamic psychotherapy evolved as an alternative to classic psychoanalysis. Among the brief psychodynamic approaches are Malan's (1976, 1980) focal therapy, Mann's (1973, 1981) time-limited psychotherapy, Sifneos's (1979, 1984) short-term dynamic psychotherapy, and Davanloo's (1978, 1984) short-term dynamic psychotherapy. Garske and Molteni (1985) note that all brief psychodynamic approaches share several characteristics. The approaches are all based on psychoanalytic theory, suggest similar efficacy, and modify psychoanalytic procedures for use in a briefer format.

The aim of brief psychodynamic psychotherapy is to go beyond symptom relief and bring out necessary changes in the client's personality (Garske & Molteni, 1985). The number of sessions required in brief psychodynamic psychotherapy tends to be limited to 12 and depends on the nature of the client's problem and the type of therapy utilized (Garske & Molteni, 1985). Mann's (1973) time-limited model has a duration of between 1 and 12 sessions. Davanloo's (1978, 1984) short-term dynamic approach varies the number of recommended sessions from 2 to 5 sessions, 6 to 15 sessions, 16 to 25 sessions, or 26 to 40 sessions depending on the nature of the client's problem.

Garske and Molteni (1985) identify the following six factors seen to promote change in brief psychodynamic psychotherapy:

1. A contract is established with the client, which includes a description of the client's problems in psychoanalytic terms.
2. A statement of goals and objectives is established, along with a time limit on the number of sessions.
3. The analyst takes an active, probing approach, clarifying and confronting the client's resistance.
4. The analyst interprets the links between the client's current problems, relationship with the analyst and significant others, and past conflicts.
5. The time-limited aspect of therapy arouses issues relating to separation and individualization within the client.
6. The termination phase of therapy is characterized by working through problems associated with separation and individualization.

Research efforts have attempted to determine what factors contribute to efficacy of brief psychodynamic psychotherapy. Nergaard and Silberschatz (1989) found that high measures of shame and guilt (especially guilt), as measured by the Therapy Shame and Guilt Scale, correlated with positive therapy outcomes. Mills, Bauer, and Miars (1989) note that transference reactions should be addressed quickly and energetically by the therapist to maximize their impact.

Goldfried, Greenberg, and Mormar (1990) review the literature on brief psychodynamic psychotherapy. They note the approach has been effective for treating stress and bereavement disorders (Mormar & Horowitz, 1988); late-life depression (Thompson, Gallagher, & Breckenridge, 1987); and adjustment, affective, and personality disorders (Marziali, 1984). In addition, Barth et al. (1988) evaluated 34 short-term dynamic psychotherapy cases. They found significant gains in symptom relief, adaptive functioning, and personality change at termination and over a two-year follow-up period.

Summary and Evaluation

Sigmund Freud's place in history is secure. He is widely regarded as one of the most prominent intellectual figures of all time. His contributions to psychology and other fields are phenomenal. His most remarkable achievements include the concept of defense mechanisms as a means for coping with anxiety, the mapping of the conscious-unconscious continuum, and his methods for exploring unconscious processes in psychoanalysis. Weaknesses of Freud's theory are what has been considered his overemphasis of the role of sexuality in personality development and the excessive length of time required to achieve the aims of psychoanalysis. New advances in Freudian theory as reflected in the ego-analytic position and in brief psychodynamic psychotherapy are attempts to overcome these problems.

Adler's Individual Psychology

Background Information

Alfred Adler (1870–1937) received a medical degree from the University of Vienna in 1895. In 1902, he began what was to develop into a rather stormy relationship with Freud. Adler quickly took an active role in Freud's psychoanalytic society and was elected as its president in 1910. He and Freud cofounded and became coeditors of the *Journal of Psycho-analysis.* Shortly thereafter, Adler broke ranks with Freud over several important theoreti-cal issues. These differences culminated in Adler's resigning from his positions as president of the society and coeditor of the journal. At this point, Adler disassociated himself from the Freudian circle and founded his own school, which he called *individual psychology.*

After serving as a medical officer during World War I, Adler returned to practice medicine in Vienna. In 1922, he turned his attention to the problems of children and estab-lished a child guidance clinic in the Vienna public schools (Dinkmeyer & Dinkmeyer, 1985). Eventually more than 50 similar guidance clinics were opened before political tur-moil restricted the growth of Adlerian psychology in Europe (Dinkmeyer & Dinkmeyer, 1985). By 1935, political unrest forced Adler to flee Europe, and he settled in the United States. Adler died two years later while on a lecture tour in Aberdeen, Scotland.

Adler maintained a busy schedule throughout his career. He was particularly known for his extensive lecture tours, during which he would often work with a client in front of an audience. This was revolutionary at the time because therapy was not practiced with such openness (Dinkmeyer & Dinkmeyer, 1985). Today, Adlerians continue the tradition of demonstrating counseling strategies in front of live audiences.

Adler was a prolific writer, publishing more than 100 books and articles during his lifetime. *The Practice and Theory of Individual Psychology* (Adler, 1969) is an excellent introduction to Adlerian psychology.

Alfred Adler

Theory of Personality

Adler's theory of personality is a comprehensive in-depth analysis of how people function. It emphasizes the importance of early life experiences within the family of origin, or as Adler referred to it, the *family constellation.* From this perspective, factors such as birth order, sibling rivalry, and social interest played important roles in the formulation and functioning of the personality.

View of Human Nature.   Adler held an optimistic view of people. He believed people were basically positive, with the capability of self-determination. This view of human nature stimulated the development of the humanistic movement in psychology, which focuses on the dignity and worth of the individual. Adler also emphasized that behavior is holistic, or interrelated; teleological, in that it has a purpose and is directed toward a goal; and phenomenological, because it can best be understood from the client's frame of reference.

Key Concepts.   Adler (1969) and Ansbacher and Ansbacher (1956, 1964) have described a number of key concepts that make up the structure of Adler's theory of personality. The following 10 principles are central to this theory.

The Creative Self.   This concept was Adler's "crowning achievement as a personality theorist" (Hall & Lindzey, 1978, p. 165). It lies at the heart of the Adlerian theory of personality. The creative self is the center or nucleus from which all life movement generates (Ansbacher & Ansbacher, 1956). Freud called this center the ego. For Adler, the creative self emphasized that each person has the potential to creatively interact with the world. Adler expressed the potential for self-determined behavior when he said:

> . . . the important thing is not what one is born with, but what use one makes of that equipment . . . To understand this we find it is necessary to assume the existence of still another force, the creative power of the individual. (Ansbacher & Ansbacher, 1964, pp. 86–87)

The Concept of Teleological Movement.   Adler saw all behavior in terms of movement: nothing was static. This movement is teleological in nature since it has a purpose and is directed toward a goal. According to Adler, a person can move on the useful or useless side of life. Movement on the useful side is characterized by cooperative efforts, whereas movement on the useless side is narcissistic in nature (Ansbacher & Ansbacher, 1956).

Adler also believed that life movement was from a sensed minus to a sensed plus. According to their private logic, individuals will behave in a manner that appears to improve their position (Ansbacher & Ansbacher, 1956). This concept can be useful to understand the motivation behind misbehavior. For example, a child may move toward a goal of power to gain recognition. In this instance, the private logic may be, "I can be somebody if I fight with others."

Behavior Can Be Understood from an Interpersonal Perspective.   Adler emphasized that behavior can best be understood from an interpersonal perspective (Ansbacher & Ansbacher, 1956). This spirit was captured by the poet John Donne when he said, "No man is an island." Adler believed that people do not behave in isolation from others but in relation to others. This reasoning can be used to identify goals of misbehavior. For example, parents can develop a tentative hypothesis by asking themselves how they feel when their child misbehaves. Feeling annoyed could indicate their child has a goal of attention; feeling angry or threatened could suggest a goal of power; feeling hurt could indicate a goal of revenge; and feeling desperate or hopeless could suggest a goal of a display of inadequacy (Dinkmeyer & McKay, 1997; Dreikurs & Soltz, 1964).

The Psychology of Use.   Adler stressed that all behavior has a use or payoff that is usually unconscious in nature (Ansbacher & Ansbacher, 1956). Emotions serve a use in helping propel a person toward a goal. This concept can also be used to understand the symptoms associated with psychopathology, as the following *Personal Note* illustrates.

A Personal Note

Don was a 22-year-old assistant accountant. One day while he was working, his hand became numb and he was unable to move it. Don was taken to a hospital where I was the staff psychologist. The patient received a complete medical evaluation, including numerous neurological tests. After the doctors decided there was nothing physically wrong with the patient's hand, they referred him to me. When I asked Don how he liked his work, he said he hated it, largely because he wanted to go to medical school. After some additional assessment, I decided to hypnotize him. I told him he was a doctor and asked him to take my blood pressure. At this point, he was able to move his hand.

The psychology of use was quite apparent in this case since the patient's inability to move his hand could help him avoid a job he hated. It is important to point out that Don wasn't consciously aware of trying to avoid his job. He was actually relieved to discover there was nothing physically wrong with his hand.

Together, we decided that Don would try to go back to college so he could be doing something he wanted to do. With this in mind, I spent the next few sessions helping him apply for admission into college. It is interesting to note that Don could not voluntarily move his hand until he received a letter of acceptance from the college.

Don's disorder is known in the literature as a *conversion disorder.* It involves losing a bodily function such as the use of a hand or sight due to psychological, not physical, reasons. As illustrated in this case, the disorder can also be understood in terms of the psychology of use.

A Phenomenological Psychology.   The phenomenological perspective provides an understanding of clients from their internal frame of reference. Adler suggested that what individuals perceive is biased according to past experiences (Ansbacher & Ansbacher, 1964). He referred to this phenomenon as an *apperception.* A phenomenological perspective is therefore necessary to understand clients' interpretations of their experiences.

Emphasis on Social Interest.   Adler's term *Gemeinschaftsgefühl* has been translated into English as "social interest" (Ansbacher & Ansbacher, 1964). It refers to an inborn tendency to cooperate and work with others for the common good (Ansbacher & Ansbacher, 1964). Adler related this concept to mental health when he observed that social interest is the barometer of mental health (Ansbacher & Ansbacher, 1964). Glasser (1965) supports this position when he suggests that all people need love and affection to be fulfilled. Social interest is considered a major motivational force in Adlerian psychology.

The Lifestyle.   Hall and Lindzey (1978) suggest that lifestyle became the recurrent theme in Adler's later writings and the most distinctive feature of his psychology. "The term *life style* refers to the person's basic orientation to life—the set of patterns of recurrent themes that run through his or her existence" (Dinkmeyer & Dinkmeyer, 1985, p. 123). According to Adler, the lifestyle is relatively fixed by age 4 or 5. Once established, the individual's lifestyle guides the assimilation and utilization of future experiences (Hall and Lindzey, 1978).

A Holistic Psychology.   Adler's individual psychology means the individual is indivisible and undivided. It is therefore a holistic psychology that attempts to understand the overall lifestyle as a unified whole. Adlerians are interested in assessing how the person organizes the self as a whole person with interrelated and coherent beliefs, perceptions, and goals (Dinkmeyer & Dinkmeyer, 1985). This position is similar to the holistic health concept, which views the mind and body as an interacting system, not as separate entities.

Striving for Significance.   Adler believed that people have a basic tendency to avoid feelings of inferiority by striving for superiority (Ansbacher & Ansbacher, 1956). A person could therefore compensate for feelings of inadequacy in one area by excelling in another aspect of life. In this example, striving for superiority should not be viewed as an attempt to feel superior over others. Instead, it amounts to a striving for significance and worth as an individual and is a major motivational force (Dinkmeyer & Dinkmeyer, 1985).

The Family Constellation.   The family constellation encompasses many factors associated with a person's family of origin, such as birth order, family size, and the relationship between family members. Adler believed that each person's family constellation was unique and could therefore make a significant impact on the development of the lifestyle. Adler was particularly interested in birth order and how it affected a person's development (Ansbacher & Ansbacher, 1956). For example, first-born children tend to be bossy and talkative since they are used to telling their brothers and sisters what to do. They also tend to be conservative since they are born into a world of adults and therefore tend to affiliate with adults and adult values.

With the arrival of a second child, first-born children can feel temporarily dethroned since they have to share their parent's attention. This can cause them to be suspicious and tend to protect themselves from sudden reversals of fortune. Middle-born children tend to be very ambitious as they attempt to compete with the oldest. This can result in the "race-course syndrome," which can foster an achievement orientation in middle-born children. It can also promote sibling rivalry or competition between siblings, which is another Adlerian principle. In addition, middle-born children can grow up having difficulty feeling a sense of belonging since they don't have the special place of being the oldest or youngest. They also tend to be observers and mediators interested in what is going on between the siblings and willing to mediate when a conflict occurs.

The youngest child of the family is the "baby." Parents tend to be more lenient and give special favors to the baby. Youngest children usually appreciate these special considerations and learn early in life that other people will take care of them and protect them from life's difficulties.

Dinkmeyer and Dinkmeyer (1985) note that birth-order characteristics are only tendencies, which may or may not occur. Whether they manifest themselves depends on how parents relate to a child and how children interpret their ordinal position. When a person does not have the typical characteristics of a particular birth order, it can be interesting to determine what familial factors could account for the differences. For example, a middle-born female with three brothers and no sisters will usually not lack a sense of belonging because she feels special as the only girl. A middle-born male may act like a first-born child as a result of the first-born being disowned from the family because of doing something extreme, such as committing murder.

Theory of Counseling and Psychotherapy

Adlerian counseling and psychotherapy stresses the role of cognition in psychological functioning. It begins by using the lifestyle analysis to gain an understanding of the client. Through various techniques and procedures such as encouragement and acting as-if, clients are helped to reorient themselves toward more positive ways of functioning.

Adlerians attempt to go beyond overt behavior and understand the motivation behind the behavior (Nystul, 1985b). This approach is therefore more concerned with modifying motivation than with modifying behavior. Sonstegard, Hagerman, and Bitter (1975) elaborate on this position:

> The Adlerian counselor is not preoccupied with changing behavior, rather he is concerned with understanding the individual's subjective frame of reference and the identification of the individual's mistaken notion or goal within that framework. Indeed, the behavior of an individual is only understood when the goals are identified . . . (p. 17)

Mosak (2005) summarizes the major goals of Adlerian psychotherapy as the following:

- Increasing clients' social interest
- Helping clients overcome feelings of discouragement and reducing inferiority feelings
- Modifying clients' views and goals and changing their life scripts
- Changing faulty motivation
- Helping clients feel a sense of equality with others
- Assisting clients to become contributing members of society

The counseling process is educationally oriented, providing information, guiding, and attempting to encourage discouraged clients. The approach attempts to reeducate clients so they can live in society as equals, both giving and receiving from others (Mosak, 2005).

The counseling relationship is based on equality. Adlerians avoid placing the client in a subservient position as in a doctor-patient relationship. They consider a sense of mutual respect to be vital to all relationships, including the counseling relationship.

Dinkmeyer and Dinkmeyer (1985) identify four phases of Adlerian psychotherapy: establishing the relationship, performing analysis and assessment, promoting insight, and reorientation. The authors observe that these phases are not intended to be separate or distinct processes but instead tend to overlap and blend in clinical practice. This can be especially true in the process of establishing a positive relationship. Adlerians believe it is important to maintain a positive relationship throughout the counseling process.

Techniques

Adlerian techniques can be described in terms of the four phases of Adlerian psychotherapy.

Phase One: Establishing the Relationship. Adlerians utilize many techniques to establish a positive relationship. Three of these techniques are

1. *Use of listening skills.* Dinkmeyer and Sperry (2000) note that effective listening skills are necessary to promote mutual trust and mutual respect—two essential elements of the Adlerian counseling relationship.
2. *Winning respect and offering hope.* Nystul (1985b) suggests that a counselor can increase the client's motivation for becoming involved in counseling by winning the client's respect and offering hope.
3. *Encouragement.* Encouragement communicates a sense of support and can also help clients learn to believe in themselves. Dinkmeyer and Losoncy (1980) and Watts and Pietrzak (2000) identify important skills that are involved in the encouragement process. Some of these skills are focusing on progress, assets, and strengths; helping clients see the humor in life experiences; communicating respect and confidence; being enthusiastic; helping the client become aware of choices; combating self-defeating, discouraging processes; and promoting self-encouragement.

Watts and Pietrzak (2000) suggest that Adlerian psychotherapy is essentially a process of encouragement. In this process, clients can be assisted in restoring hope and vitality in life. For example, a client was asked what stood out for him in Adlerian psychotherapy. He responded that Adlerian psychotherapy helped him find the courage to go on living. Watts and Pietrzak (2000) note that the Adlerian concept of encouragement is similar to solution-focused brief therapy (de Shazer, 1985). Both theoretical perspectives are optimistic, focusing on strengths, solutions, and resources. They also parallel each other regarding how they conceptualize maladjustment, avoiding the medical model and focusing on overcoming discouragement (Adlerian) and identifying exceptions to the problems (solution-focused brief therapy).

Phase Two: Performing Analysis and Assessment. Adlerians typically do an in-depth analysis and assessment as early as the first session. This usually involves conducting a lifestyle analysis to explore how early life experiences can contribute to the adult personality.

Dream analysis can be a part of the lifestyle analysis (Mosak, 2005). Adlerians do not attempt to analyze dreams in terms of their symbolic content, as do Freudians. Instead, they see dreams as an attempt to deal with the difficulties and challenges of life. In this sense, dreams become a problem-solving activity, allowing the person a chance to rehearse for some future action (Mosak, 2005).

The lifestyle analysis can also be used to identify the client's strengths or assets that can be used to overcome the client's problems. It can also be used to identify faulty or irrational views that may interfere with the client's growth. These are referred to as *basic mistakes,* and the following descriptions of these statements by Mosak (2005) are listed with examples:

- *Overgeneralizations:* "People can't be trusted."
- *False or impossible goals of security:* "I must please everybody."

- *Misrepresentations of life and life's demands.* "I never get any breaks."
- *Minimization or denial of one's worth:* "I'm dumb."
- *Faulty values:* "It doesn't matter how you play the game as long as you win."

Phase Three: Promoting Insight.   Adlerians believe that insight is an important prerequisite to long-term change. Insight allows clients to understand the dynamics of self-defeating patterns so they can be corrected during the reorientation process. The main tool for providing insight is interpretation, which focuses on creating awareness of basic mistakes that are impeding the client's growth.

Counselors can use confrontation techniques during the insight process if they encounter resistance from clients. Shulman (1973) notes that confrontation can challenge a client to make an immediate response or change or to examine some issue. It can also foster immediacy in the relationship by enabling a client to know how the counselor is experiencing the client at the moment (Dinkmeyer & Dinkmeyer, 1985).

Phase Four: Reorientation.   The final phase of Adlerian psychotherapy involves putting insight into action. Clients are encouraged to make necessary changes in their life as they develop more functional beliefs and behaviors. Counselors can use the following techniques during the reorientation phase:

1. *Spitting in the client's soup.* This technique can be used when clients engage in manipulative games such as acting like a martyr. Spitting in their soup involves determining the payoff of the game and interpreting it to the client. For instance, a client may say, "My husband is such a drunk. I don't know why I put up with him." The counselor could respond by saying, "You must get a lot of sympathy from others because you have to put up with so much." As this client realizes that someone is aware of the payoffs she is receiving from her martyr syndrome, the game may seem less enjoyable.
2. *The push-button technique.* This technique is based on Ellis's (1962) rational-emotive therapy. It involves having clients concentrate on pleasant and unpleasant experiences and the feelings they generate (Dinkmeyer & Dinkmeyer, 1985). When clients discover that their thoughts influence their emotions, they recognize that they can take control of their emotional responses. The push-button concept symbolizes the amount of control clients can exert when they "push the button" and put a stop to self-defeating processes. They can then create a constructive way of reacting to their situation, producing a more positive emotional response.
3. *Catching oneself.* Clients can use this technique to avoid old self-defeating patterns. Initially, clients may catch themselves in the process of self-defeating behaviors, such as playing a manipulative game. Eventually, they can catch themselves just before they start playing the game. Clients can be encouraged to use humor when they catch themselves, learning to laugh at how ridiculous their self-defeating tendencies are.
4. *Acting as-if.* This technique involves clients acting as if they could do whatever they would like to do, such as being more confident or being a better listener. The technique promotes a positive "can-do" spirit and a self-fulfilling prophecy, which can help clients experience success.

5. *Task setting and commitment.* Adlerians do not believe that change occurs by osmosis. They believe instead that it takes work and effort to change. Task setting and commitment are therefore essential aspects of Adlerian psychotherapy. Homework assignments can be useful in this regard by providing a structure through which clients can try out new modes of behaving.

Contemporary Issues

Many contemporary Adlerian concepts derive from the work of Rudolph Dreikurs (1897–1972). Dreikurs was a student of Adler's. In 1939, just two years after Adler's death, Dreikurs moved to Chicago and established the Alfred Adler Institute of Chicago (Dinkmeyer & Dinkmeyer, 1985). In many ways, he picked up where Adler left off (Dinkmeyer & Dinkmeyer, 1985). He continued the development of Adlerian theory, especially in terms of parent education and child guidance. Dreikurs had a gift for taking Adler's writings and reworking them into concepts that are easy to understand and apply. In addition, he developed his own concepts based on Adlerian principles, such as the four goals of misbehavior (Dreikurs, 1949; Dreikurs & Soltz, 1964), encouragement (Dinkmeyer & Dreikurs, 1963), logical and natural consequences (Dreikurs & Soltz, 1964), and social equality (Dreikurs, 1971). Dreikurs maintained an active lecture tour during which he would demonstrate his approach. He is credited with having a great deal to do with the popularization and acceptance of Adlerian psychology as a major school of counseling and psychotherapy (Dinkmeyer & Dinkmeyer, 1985).

Don Dinkmeyer is another key individual in the evolution of Adlerian psychology. Dinkmeyer and his associates have incorporated a number of Adlerian and Dreikursian concepts into programs relating to children, adolescents, parents, and teachers. These programs have gained popularity among counselors and other members of the helping professions. Some of these programs are systematic training for effective parenting (STEP) (Dinkmeyer & McKay, 1997) and developing understanding of self and others (DUSO-R) (Dinkmeyer & Dinkmeyer, 1982).

Several other individuals have made significant contributions to contemporary Adlerian psychology. Ray Corsini (1977, 1979) developed an educational system based on Adlerian principles, which he called "individual education." Dreikurs, Corsini, Lowe, and Sonstegard (1959), Sherman and Dinkmeyer (1987), and Oscar Christenson have done much to promote the popularity of Adlerian family counseling.

There has been a movement toward integrating Adlerian psychology with other schools of thought. In this regard, Shulman suggested that Adlerian psychology needed to develop further to incorporate new advances in the field of child development, neurochemical processes in the brain, and cognitive psychology (Nystul, 1988). Watkins (1984) provides another example of integration in terms of similarities between Adler's theory and vocational counseling. For example, Watkins notes that Adler's construct of lifestyle and Holland's personality types (such as realistic and investigative) both acknowledge the role that individual difference plays in psychological functioning.

The movement toward integration has gained momentum among the Adlerian ranks. A special issue of *Individual Psychology: The Journal of Adlerian Theory, Research, and Practice* focused on exploring the issues relating to "beyond Adler." In this special issue, Carlson (Nystul, 1991) suggests that the Adlerian movement has become isolated, focusing too much on well-developed concepts such as the four goals of misbehavior and logical consequences. Carlson contends that broader, more permeable boundaries are needed for Adlerian psychology to become part of the mainstream of contemporary psychology (Nystul, 1991). Carlson also suggests that Adlerian approaches could be developed to reach nontraditional, non-YAVIS (young, attractive, verbal, intelligent, and sensitive) clients; clients who are victims of family violence; clients with HIV/AIDS; and clients who require sex therapy. Mosak (1991) echoes the call for change by noting that Adlerian theory focuses too much on the psychology of abnormalcy and not enough on the psychology of normalcy.

Some progress appears to be made regarding the infusing of new concepts and ideas into Adlerian psychology. Watts (2000) contends that Adlerian psychology is relevant as we enter the new millennium, suggesting that Adlerian psychology has a broad theoretical basis and is well suited for integrating. Watts contends that in its current form, Adlerian psychotherapy represents an integration of psychodynamic, cognitive, and systemic theories. Watts goes on to note that Adlerian psychology can also be easily adapted to emerging trends in counseling such as approaches that are directive, time-limited, present-centered, and problem-focused.

Schwartz and Waldo (2003) note that Adlerian psychology (Adler, 1969) and interpersonal theory (Meyer, 1957; Sullivan, 1968) share a social/interpersonal perspective that makes these two theories excellent candidates for integration. Common theoretical perspectives shared by these two theories include

- Early life experiences play a role in how people develop and maintain interpersonal relationships throughout life.
- Therapy involves reorienting people from inappropriate ways of reacting to others often based on early life experiences.
- People are motivated to establish and maintain meaningful interpersonal relationships.
- Mental health is associated with social interest and interpersonal functioning.

Adlerian Brief Approaches to Counseling

According to the Adlerian scholar Ansbacher (1989), Adlerian counseling and psychotherapy was the first form of brief counseling. Adler believed that time limits in counseling could be beneficial and typically restricted his sessions over a 10-week period with two sessions per week (Ansbacher, 1989). A number of Adlerian constructs are particularly relevant to brief-counseling theory and practice. For example, the use of encouragement and focusing on clients' assets is consistent with the strengths perspective advocated in contemporary brief-counseling models. Kurt Adler (Adler's son) suggested that although Adlerian counseling is a forerunner in brief-counseling methods, it is neither a short- nor long-term form of counseling but a flexible approach that can be adjusted to the unique and emerging needs of clients (Adler, 1972).

Contemporary Adlerians are making innovative advances in terms of developing brief-counseling approaches. Sperry (1987, 1989b) was one of the first Adlerians to set forth specific procedures for conducting brief counseling. He developed a simple cognitive map that clinicians can use to organize all forms of brief consultations, including "sidewalk consults" and emergency phone calls. Maniacci (1996) developed a brief-counseling model for treating personality disorders. He notes that Adlerian procedures such as the lifestyle assessment are particularly useful to understanding core personality issues.

Adlerian brief therapy is a relatively new Adlerian approach developed by Bitter and Nicoll (2004) that has a relational focus. These scholars contend that the therapeutic relationship and client change are interrelated. Adlerian brief therapy represents an integration of Adlerian theory and solution-focused therapy. Factors that help keep the approach brief include time limits, therapeutic focus, counselor directiveness and optimism, symptoms as solutions, and assignments of behavioral tasks.

Postmodern Trends and Adlerian Psychology

The postmodern trends of constructivism and social constructionism appear to have much in common with Adlerian psychology. Adlerian psychology has been recognized as laying the theoretical foundations for constructivism (Mahoney, 1991; Mahoney & Lyddon, 1988; Watts, 2000; Watts & Pietrzak, 2000). Jones (1995) and Scott, Kelly, and Tolbert (1995) identify several psychological constructs that constructivism and Adler's theory have in common. For example, both theories emphasize the role of cognition in psychological functioning, noting the active role people play in creating their own reality. In this regard, Adler contends that the creative self allows each person an opportunity to make a unique response based on one's past experiences and the capacity for self-determination.

Adlerian psychology also appears to share commonalties with social constructionism. Social constructionism stresses the role of social forces such as the narratives reflected in cultures in creating personal meanings or "storied lives." Adler's construct of social interests also reflects an ecological perspective. In this regard, Adler contends that mental health and meaning to life is to a large degree achieved through interest, concern, and involvement with others.

Summary and Evaluation

Adler was a man ahead of his time. His psychological insights stressed the importance of phenomenology, holism, and social interest. These concepts are incorporated into most contemporary counseling theories. Adlerian psychology is perhaps best known for concepts that can be used to understand individual differences such as lifestyle, family dynamics, birth order, and sibling rivalry. Another strength of Adlerian psychology is its influence on programs such as systematic training for effective parenting (STEP) and other guidance programs.

A criticism is that Adlerian counselors may be trying too hard to adhere to Adler's original concepts in terms of theory, research, and practice. As Shulman recommends, Adlerian psychology must be responsive to ongoing advances in counseling and psychology if it is to remain a viable theory for contemporary practitioners (Nystul, 1988).

Another criticism can be directed at Adlerian psychotherapy in terms of its narrow focus and use of the concept of basic mistakes (Nystul, 1994a). Jones (1995) notes that Adlerian psychology focuses on cognitions rather than behaviors, emotions, and cognitions. It would seem that a more comprehensive treatment program would focus on all three of these domains of psychological functioning.

There also appear to be problems in the manner in which cognitions are conceptualized in Adlerian psychotherapy. From an Adlerian perspective, cognitions are primarily conceptualized in terms of the concept of basic mistakes (Jones, 1995; Nystul, 1994a). Jones notes that basic mistakes are key to understanding lifestyle and emotional disorders. Nystul (1994a) goes on to suggest that to a large degree Adlerian psychotherapy involves reorienting clients from their basic mistakes. It is unfortunate that so much emphasis has been placed on the concept of basic mistakes because the concept may be inconsistent with Adlerian theory of personality and discouraging to clients (Nystul, 1994a).

Jung's Analytic Psychology

Background Information

Carl Gustav Jung (1875–1961) was born in Kesswil, Switzerland. His father was a pastor, which may have contributed to his fondness for religion. Jung's intellectual interests were by far the most varied of the three classic theorists. As a young man, he became intrigued by mythology, philosophy, religion, history, literature, and archeology. While Jung was struggling to decide what to study at the university, he had an unusual dream that somehow compelled him to pursue medicine (Hall & Lindzey, 1978). Jung went on to obtain a medical degree from the University of Basel in 1900, the same year Freud published *The Interpretation of Dreams*. Freud's work may have influenced his decision to specialize in psychiatry. Shortly thereafter, Jung obtained a position at the University of Zurich and worked under Eugene Bleuler, who was well known for his theories on schizophrenia. During this time, Jung was also fortunate to study with Pierre Janet, who was conducting research on hysteria and multiple personality disorders.

By 1907, Jung had his first meeting with Freud. They found many areas of common interest as they talked continuously for 13 hours. Freud believed that Jung was his crown prince and successor (Hall & Lindzey, 1978). It was therefore not surprising that in 1910 Jung became the first president of the International Psychoanalytic Association. Their initial compatibility was short-lived, however, as Jung began to differ with Freud on important theoretical issues. Like Adler, Jung became particularly disenchanted with Freud's emphasis on the role of sexuality in personality development. By 1914, Jung felt he could no longer participate in the Freudian movement and resigned from the presidency of the International Psychoanalytic Association.

At this point, Jung decided to develop his own school of psychology, which he called *analytic psychology*. It is interesting to note that some of Jung's most creative years occurred during a time of personal distress, between 1913 and 1916, as with Freud. Jung was able to make the most of difficult times. During this period, Jung did extensive self-analysis through the interpretation of his dreams. He obtained a number of insights that had a profound effect on the development of his theory. An example is the importance of gaining an understanding of unconscious processes during psychotherapy.

Jung's analytic theory was unique in its varied theoretical foundations. Jung was able to integrate his early interests in religion, mythology, archeology, literature, history, and philosophy into the study of psychology. This work resulted in what may be the most comprehensive understanding of the human condition (Hall & Lindzey, 1978). His collective works are extensive, filling 20 volumes (Read, Fordham, & Adler, 1953–1978). Jung's work holds particular interest for those who wish to integrate mystical ideas from the Far East with analytical concepts from the Western European and American traditions.

Carl Jung

Theory of Personality

Jung's theory of personality is very robust, incorporating elements from various disciplines such as Eastern philosophy, theology and religion, medicine, and psychology. Harris (1996) contends that Jung's ideas are becoming increasingly popular and can even be found in such best-selling books as Estes's (1992) *Women Who Run with the Wolves*. An overview of Jung's theory of personality follows.

View of Human Nature.   Jung (1928) had a positive view of the human condition, believing that people had inherent tendencies toward individualization—becoming unique individuals capable of wholeness and self-realization. This process of individualization is characterized by a union or integration of conscious and unconscious processes (Jung, 1928).

Key Concepts.   Jung identified the following concepts, which were associated with his theory of personality (Read et al., 1953–1978).

The Ego, the Personal Unconscious, and the Collective Unconscious.   According to Kaufmann (1989), Jung believed that the psyche is made up of autonomous yet interdependent subsystems of the ego, the personal unconscious, and the collective unconscious. The ego represents the conscious mind and the personal unconscious and collective unconscious make up the unconscious domain of the psyche.

The *ego* is the center of consciousness and is made up of conscious perceptions, memories, thoughts, and feelings (Kaufmann, 1989). It provides consistency and direction in people's lives (Fadiman & Frager, 1976).

The *personal unconscious* is similar to Freud's preconscious, containing thoughts based on personal experience just beyond the reach of conscious recall (Feist, 1985). It contains forgotten or repressed material that had once been conscious and could become conscious in the future (Hall & Lindzey, 1978). The information in the personal unconscious clusters around several complexes (Kaufmann, 1989). Complexes revolve around themes such as prestige or control, which can interfere with effective living (Corey, 1982). For example, a client could have a "mother complex," whereby he behaves as if he were under his mother's domination or control.

The *collective unconscious* is sometimes referred to as the transpersonal or non-personal unconscious since it is not associated with personal experiences. It is considered the most provocative yet controversial aspect of Jung's theory (Hall & Lindzey, 1978). The collective unconscious is made up of memory traces inherited from one's ancestral past. Jung called it *collective* because he believed that all people shared common images and thoughts regarding such things as mother, earth, birth, and death.

Jung referred to these universal thoughts as *archetypes*. He believed that the collective unconscious creates the foundation for the personality. Starting from birth, the collective unconscious guides an individual's life experiences, thereby influencing perceptions, emotions, and behavior. It is therefore the most powerful and influential aspect of the personality (Hall & Lindzey, 1978).

Jung suggested that the collective unconscious was not directly amenable to the conscious but could be observed indirectly through its manifestations in eternal themes in mythology, folklore, and art (Kaufmann, 1989). Jung visited numerous "primitive" cultures to test his theory in Africa and the American Southwest. He found that even though these cultures evolved independently, they shared intricate memories that could have been transmitted only by a collective unconscious.

Archetypes.   Jung discovered that several archetypes evolved so completely that they could be considered separate systems within the personality (Hall & Lindzey, 1978). These are the persona, the anima and animus, the shadow, and the self.

The *persona* is the public self one projects as opposed to the private, personal view of oneself. The persona is reflected in various roles such as work, marriage and family, and social situations. According to Jung, awareness of the persona has an inverse relation to awareness of one's personal self or individuality. For example, the more aware one is of the persona, the less aware that person will be of individuality and the private, personal self.

The *anima* and *animus* refer to the suggestion that people have both masculine and feminine dimensions to their personality. The anima is the feminine archetype in men, and the animus is the masculine archetype in women. Jung believed these archetypes resulted from years of men and women living together (Hall & Lindzey, 1978). Fadiman and Frager (1976) note that this archetype appears in dreams and fantasies as figures of the opposite sex and functions as the primary mediator between unconscious and conscious processes.

The *shadow* represents the negative or evil side of the personality that people do not want to recognize. The shadow is associated with thoughts that originate from animal instincts inherited through the evolutionary process.

The *self* is the center of the personality, including the conscious and unconscious parts of the mind (Feist, 1985). The self provides the personality with a sense of unity, equilibrium, and stability (Hall & Lindzey, 1978). The self cannot emerge until the other systems of the personality have fully developed, which is usually not until middle age (Corey, 1982). The emergence of the self occurs when the center of the individual shifts from the conscious ego to the midpoint between conscious and unconscious (Hall & Lindzey, 1978). This midpoint region becomes the domain of the self. It is not surprising that Jung discovered the existence of the self when he was studying Eastern meditation practices, which emphasize the interaction between conscious and unconscious processes.

Personality Types.   Jung noted that personality types could be differentiated in terms of attitudes and functions. He identified two types of attitudes: extroverted (or outgoing) and introverted (or introspective). According to Jung, people have both attitudes in their personality makeup. The dominant attitude is represented in the conscious mind and the subordinate attitude exists in the unconscious psyche (Hall & Lindzey, 1978).

Jung also described four functions that provide additional means to differentiate personality types. These functions include thinking, feeling, sensation, and intuition. Jung contended that although people rely on all these functions to react to events, the function that is the best developed will be relied on most and becomes the superior function.

Theory of Counseling and Psychotherapy

Jung's approach to counseling and psychotherapy is called *analytic psychotherapy.* It emphasizes the role of unconscious processes in psychological functioning. Through dream analysis and other procedures, the client becomes aware of unconscious processes and learns to use that understanding to maximize mental health and wellness.

The overall aim of analytic psychotherapy is to help the self emerge so the client can be free to move toward self-realization. For this to occur, the analyst must help the client develop the other major systems of the personality. Much of psychotherapy therefore involves exploring unconscious processes in order for clients to gain insight into the structure of their personality (Kaufmann, 1989). In time, clients can learn how to make the various systems develop to their fullest and function in a complementary fashion. For example, a client who describes himself as a real "macho-type" person seeks help for marital problems. The analytic psychotherapist may encourage the client to recognize the feminine (anima) dimension to his personality. According to analytic theory, this will help the client become a more fully functioning person and develop a better understanding of life.

Jung had a unique conception of psychopathology. He did not view it as a disease or abnormal state (Kaufmann, 1989). Instead, he believed the symptoms associated with psychopathology could be instructive for both the client and analyst (Kaufmann, 1989). They could serve as warning signals that something was wrong and could also provide clues into the functioning of the personality (Kaufmann, 1989). Jung was therefore reluctant to use medication to treat mental disorders because he was afraid it might mask important messages that symptoms could communicate.

The nature of the therapeutic relationship is also unique in analytic psychotherapy. Analysts are required to undertake their own analysis, which helps them gain a respect for what is involved in being a client. They do not see the counseling relationship as a healthy analyst treating a sick patient. Instead, Jungian analysts view therapy as one person who has journeyed into the unconscious helping another person develop a meaningful dialogue with unconscious processes (Kaufmann, 1989). The Jungian analyst also believes it is critical for the client to feel a sense of acceptance during therapy (Kaufmann, 1989).

Fadiman and Frager (1976) describe two major stages utilized in Jungian psychotherapy. In the *analytic stage,* clients attempt to identify unconscious material. This is followed by the *synthetic stage,* which initially involves helping clients use insight to formulate new experiences. The final phase of the synthetic stage is called *transformation,* in which clients engage in self-education and thus become more autonomous and responsible for their own development.

Techniques

Jung advocated a flexible approach to psychotherapy, believing that the method of treatment should be determined by the unique features of each client (Harris, 1996). His approach shares the characteristics associated with the art-of-counseling model described in Chapter 1 in that he recommended the analyst be creative and flexible in working with the client.

Jungian psychotherapy is a practical approach based on the guiding principle that anything goes, as long as it seems to work (Kaufmann, 1989). When one client complained of difficulty falling asleep, for example, Jung simply sang the client a lullaby (Kaufmann, 1989).

Jung was skeptical of using techniques in therapy because he thought they could be unnecessarily restrictive. At the same time, he believed dream analysis could be a useful vehicle for helping clients explore unconscious processes. Unlike Freud, Jung found little value in analyzing a single dream. He believed it was essential to investigate the interrelationship of several dreams recorded over a period of time. In this process, Jung would help the client understand the symbolic meaning of dreams and how they provide clues to the various systems of the personality.

Contemporary Issues

Harris (1996) suggests that an emerging trend is the conceptualization of Jungian psychology from a paradoxical perspective. According to Harris (1996), Jung's theory is founded on the concept of paradox, and paradox implies "ambiguity, a puzzle or dilemma, a tension between opposite poles of an issue, even incongruity between elements of a larger whole" (p. 4). She suggests that there are no simple answers in Jungian psychology. Instead, balance and wholeness can evolve from working with opposing paradoxical forces. In this regard, analytic psychotherapy involves helping clients seek out painful opposing forces in their lives to generate creative new solutions to old problems (Harris, 1996).

Additional trends in Jungian psychology are directed at diversification and integration. Samuels (1985) notes that there are three schools of Jungian psychology: classical, developmental, and archetypal. The classical school emphasizes the role of the self as the major personality construct, the developmental school focuses on the use of transference and interpretation to work through problems associated with childhood experiences, and the archetypal school relates primarily to issues pertaining to archetypes (Spiegelman, 1989). Samuels (1989) suggests that the emerging schools of Jungian psychology need not be viewed as a form of conflict. He believes differences should be encouraged to foster creative developments in Jungian psychology. Jungian psychology is also expanding its horizons in an attempt to incorporate other theories and approaches. Saayman, Faber, and Saayman (1988) provide an example of this by exploring how family systems theory could be integrated into Jungian marital therapy.

Jungian concepts have also been incorporated into other psychological theories and systems. Myers and McCaulley (1985) incorporate Jung's concept of attitudes and functions (for example, introvert, extrovert, thinking, feeling) into the development of the Myers-Briggs Type Indicator (MBTI). The MBTI has become a popular personality instrument for individuals who want to gain self-understanding and for use in organizational and industrial psychology (McCrae & Costa, 1989). Unfortunately, research evidence has emerged suggesting that Jung's theory was inaccurately incorporated into the MBTI and therefore should not be used to interpret test results (McCrae & Costa, 1989).

Jungian Brief Approaches to Counseling

Harris (1996) notes that analytic psychotherapy has traditionally been a long-term form of treatment directed at maximizing the functioning of the personality. Harris suggests that owing to the restrictions on length and nature of counseling imposed by managed care, Jungian clinicians must develop flexible practices and approaches. She contends that Jungian principles and strategies have been successfully adapted for use in time-limited counseling, focused on resolving specific problems with clients of various ages and socioeconomic status. Harris also notes that Jungian analyst use strategies such as sand-tray therapy, art therapy, and dance therapy, which can be valuable adjuncts to brief-counseling approaches. Harris also believes that Jungian long-term counseling and psychotherapy can also be valuable, especially in cases requiring personality restructuring. In these instances, the analyst may work with a client to provide the necessary services outside of the restrictions imposed by managed care.

Summary and Evaluation

The fundamental strength of Jung's approach lies in his comprehensive view of the human condition. In this regard, Hall and Lindzey (1978) observed:

> The originality and audacity of Jung's thinking have few parallels in recent scientific history, and no other person aside from Freud has opened more conceptual windows into what Jung would choose to call the "soul of man." (p. 149)

Jung has had a major influence on many aspects of contemporary thought, such as religion, art, music, literature, and drama (Douglas, 2005). For example, Jung's theories and interest in Eastern philosophy and spirituality such as yoga and mediation appear to be playing a key role in the emerging interest in holistic health. In this regard, Jung believed that wholeness and psychological balance occur when the conscious and unconscious mind learn to work in harmony. He also believed that people have the inherent capacity for psychological growth and self-healing (Douglas, 2005).

Jung's theories have also played a role in the evolution of psychological theories. For example, Jung's notion of individualization over the life span has been incorporated into life-span theories such as those of Gilligan, Erikson, and Kohlberg (Douglas, 2005). Jung's deep caring for his clients and sense of hope and optimism have also laid the foundation for the humanistic theories of Maslow, Rogers, and others (Douglas, 2005).

Jungian concepts have also played a role in counseling procedures, especially creative arts such as art therapy, dance therapy, and sand-tray therapy (Douglas, 2005). Jung utilized these creative arts modalities in his own therapeutic procedures. For example, he would encourage clients to express themselves through art or expressive movement and would also engage in these processes to better understand the client (Douglas, 2005). In his own self-analysis, Jung constructed a stone village as a means of working through some of his own issues (Douglas, 2005). This concept was later modified into what is currently known as sand-tray therapy (see Allan & Brown, 1993, and Carmichael, 1994, for more information on sand-tray therapy).

Several criticisms have been directed at Jungian psychology. The existence of a collective unconscious has been challenged more than any other. Glover (1950) insists that the concept is metaphysical and incapable of proof. Glover (1950) further suggests that Jung's theory lacks development concepts necessary to explain the growth of the mind. Hall and Lindzey (1978) observe that many psychologists have found Jung's writing to be "baffling, obscure, confusing, and disorganized" (p. 148).

The Classic Theories and Their Use in Contemporary Practice

The classic theories of Freud, Adler, and Jung may be criticized as outdated and of little use to clinicians. Concerns can be directed at the degree these theories have effectively kept up with recent trends such as brief counseling and diversity issues. Although these concerns have some validity (which needs to be taken into consideration in clinical practice), the classic theories also have some strengths that can be of use to practitioners. The following section provides a brief overview of the classic theories in terms of diversity issues and brief-counseling approaches.

Diversity Issues in the Classic Theories

The classic theories of Freud, Adler, and Jung pose special considerations in cross-cultural counseling. Freudian theory may have the most limitations from a cross-cultural perspective. Freud tended to overemphasize intrapsychic forces such as the endopsychic forces resulting from competition between the id, ego, and superego at the expense of understanding sociocultural forces that can play a role in human functioning. On the positive side, Freud was a genius for describing intrapsychic forces, and a recognition of these forces is essential to the understanding of people regardless of culture.

Adler and Jung appear to have achieved more of a balance between the intrapsychic and sociocultural perspective. This may be especially true for Adler, who emphasized cognitive processes (intrapsychic forces) and social interest (social embeddedness), both playing key roles in psychological functioning. Jung also sought out balance in his theory as he attempted to integrate the intrapsychic working of the conscious and unconscious mind with ontological issues of spirituality, transcendence, wholeness, and healing.

Gender issues should also be considered when addressing the classic theories. Freudian psychology has come under fire by feminists and others for a number of reasons. From a feminist perspective, Freudian psychology is one of the best examples of how male dominance is overtly displayed in the psychological literature. This anti-female spirit is perhaps captured best in his concept of penis envy, which women are supposed to have as they progress through the psychosexual stages of development. Adler (and his colleague Dreikurs) and Jung would appear to fare much better than Freud in terms of gender considerations. Adler and Dreikurs have played an important role in promoting social equality between the sexes (Dreikurs, 1971). Jung's work also appears to have utility across the sexes in terms of his Eastern concepts, which have been integrated into the holistic health-and-wellness movement.

Brief Counseling and the Classic Theories

Although the classic theories (perhaps with the exception of Adlerian) were originally developed as a form of long-term therapy, they hold much promise for clinicians interested in brief counseling. First and foremost, the classic theories offer counselors a comprehensive means to understand the personality dynamics of the client before they develop their treatment plan and implement their interventions. Although brief-counseling approaches are not designed for personality restructuring, some comprehensive means of understanding the dynamics of behavior would seem essential in any approach to counseling.

The classic theories offer other useful concepts and procedures that could be used in brief counseling. For example, the Adlerian/Dreikursian concept of encouragement stands out as a critical counseling concept for clinicians. It can foster a positive counseling relationship and help clients begin to believe in their own inherent strengths and abilities. This strengths perspective is a focal point for brief counseling. Jung's focus on psychological health and wellness is also consistent with the brief counseling in terms of taking a positive approach with clients. Freudian psychoanalysis has also made great gains in terms of its appropriateness in brief counseling by revising its approach to fit within a time-limited format.

Summary

The theories of Freud, Adler, and Jung are considered classic theories because of their historical significance and comprehensiveness. These theories share some elements. Freud and Adler both noted the importance of early life experiences on adult personality formation. Freud and Jung both emphasized the role of unconscious forces in personality functioning.

Each theory also has its unique psychological constructs and orientation. Freud stressed the role of sexuality and developed a psychosexual model for personality development. Adler favored the importance of social interest as a major motivating force for understanding the dynamics of personality. Jung was known for his formulation of the collective unconscious, proposing that all people inherit a common set of memories from birth that are passed on from generation to generation.

The three classic schools of psychology continue to evolve in terms of theory, research, and practice. In addition, each has had a major impact on the evolution of current psychotherapies. Most contemporary counseling theories have incorporated psychological constructs from Freud, Adler, and Jung. Most noticeable is the wide recognition of the importance of early life experiences and the existence of unconscious processes. Some of the principles of Adlerian psychology have been particularly influential in the evolution of modern clinical practice (Corey, 2005). Adlerian concepts of holism and phenomenology are reflected in experiential theories. Adler's emphasis on cognition (for example, basic mistakes) has also contributed to the current cognitive behavioral approaches.

The strength of the classic schools is their foundation in personality theory. They tend to be more limited in terms of their approaches to counseling and psychotherapy. In this regard, the classic schools of psychotherapy need further development and integration with modern counseling practice to enable practitioners to develop comprehensive treatment programs.

Personal Exploration

1. What do you find interesting in terms of the classic theories of Freud, Adler, and Jung?
2. Which of the three theories do you like the best and why?
3. How could you use the theories of personality associated with the classic theories to understand behavior? Can you cite a couple of examples?
4. Why are dreams considered the "royal road to the unconscious"?

Web Sites for Chapter 7

Alfred Adler Institute of San Francisco. (unknown). *Biographical sketch of Alfred Adler.* Retrieved March 3, 2005, from http://ourworld.compuserve.com/homepages/ hstein/adler.htm
Presents a comprehensive biographical sketch of Adler.

Boeree, C. G. (1997). *Carl Jung.* Retrieved March 3, 2005, from http://www.ship.edu/ ~cgboeree/jung.html
Presents an overview of Jungian theory.

Profitt, D. (2002, May). *Adlerian theory.* Retrieved March 3, 2005, from http://www.sch-psych.net/archives/000556.html
Presents a concise outline of Adlerian theory.

Salnave, R. (1998). *Sigmund Freud and the Freud archives.* Retrieved March 3, 2005, from http://users.rcn.com/brill/freudarc.html
Provides a comprehensive overview of Freud, including excerpts of his writings as well as links.

Williams, D., Tan, E., & Clapp, M. (2005). *C. G. Jung.* Retrieved March 3, 2005, from http://www.cgjungpage.org/
Is the comprehensive and official Carl Jung Web site; updated frequently.

Experiential Theories and Approaches

CHAPTER OVERVIEW

This chapter provides an overview of experiential theories and approaches to counseling. Highlights of the chapter include

- The art and science of experiential counseling
- Person-centered theory of personality and theory of counseling
- Gestalt theory of personality and theory of counseling
- Existential theory of personality and theory of counseling
- Overview of the creative arts therapies of music, art, dance, drama, bibliotherapy, and multimodality CAT
- Research trends
- Brief experiential approaches
- Diversity issues

The Art and Science of Experiential Counseling

The art and science of counseling and psychotherapy are reflected in experiential theories and approaches. The art of counseling plays a key role in experiential counseling. Experiential counselors, like artists, attempt to bring out the hidden beauty in their clients. In this regard, experiential counselors often use creative arts modalities (such as music, art, dance, drama, and bibliotherapy) to help clients discover strengths they can use to enhance their psychological functioning.

The counseling relationship is based on humanistic psychology, which recognizes the benefits of allowing one's humanness to stimulate and enhance interpersonal relationships. Open, candid interactions are common and encourage immediacy and authenticity in the counseling process. The art of experiential counseling also allows for intense therapeutic encounters. In these instances, the counselor may utilize the process of self-transcendence to move beyond empathy and understanding to enable the counselor to directly *experience* the client's joy or suffering.

The science of experiential counseling provides objectivity as a necessary balance to the art of counseling. Experiential counseling can be emotionally exhausting and taxing for both counselors and clients. The science of experiential counseling monitors the degree of psychological intensity and, like a navigator on a ship, enables the counselor and client to chart a realistic and productive course for therapy.

The science of experiential counseling also has direct ties to research methodology. Experiential theorists such as Carl Rogers (and his person-centered approach) have played a key role in counseling research. Rogers was keenly aware of the interrelationship between theory, research, and practice (Heppner, Rogers, & Lee, 1984). Rogers developed his person-centered theory based on empirical research and extensive clinical practice. Rogers pioneered the research procedure of listening to counseling tapes to gain an understanding of the change process in counseling (Greenberg, Elliott, & Lietaer, 1994). Much of the recent interest in the change process can be traced to Rogers's early work (Greenberg et al., 1994).

Other research trends in experiential counseling are focused on analyzing the impact of specific experiential counseling strategies (such as the Gestalt empty-chair technique) on the change process. This line of research is qualitative in nature, whereby the counselor and client attempt to discover (as coinvestigators) the subtle nuances associated with the change process. Much of the research in experiential counseling is directed at this type of methodology (Greenberg et al., 1994).

As noted in Chapter 6, the art and science of counseling recommend using a multicultural perspective to conceptualize diversity issues throughout the counseling process. Experiential theories such as existentialism appear to be compatible with multicultural issues since they encourage an exploration of philosophical concepts such as the meaning of life. The art and science of the experiential theories involve making the necessary modifications to these theories by utilizing multicultural research findings and maintaining a sensitivity to the evolving needs of clients.

Experiential Counseling

This chapter presents theories and approaches to counseling that emphasize experiential processes. It begins by providing an overview of three major schools of counseling: person-centered, Gestalt, and existential. The last part of the chapter describes the major creative arts therapy (CAT) modalities of music, art, drama, and dance therapy, bibliotherapy, and multimodality CAT. The common thread among these theories is their emphasis on the importance of the *experiential* aspect of counseling.

Experiential Theories

The experiential theories focus on what the client is experiencing during the counseling process. In person-centered counseling, the client is encouraged to experience the self in an open and flexible manner (Raskin & Rogers, 2005). The focus of Gestalt counseling is to help clients become aware of what they are thinking and feeling in the here and now. Existential therapy suggests that a client can obtain personal meaning by experiencing both the joys and sorrows of life. From an existential point of view, even anxiety can be instructive.

The experiential theories maintain a humanistic orientation regarding the nature of people. These theories tend to view people as inherently positive with self-actualizing tendencies. The experiential theories can therefore be particularly attractive to counselors who share this optimistic point of view. An overview of these three theories is provided in Table 8.1.

Person-Centered Therapy

Background Information

Carl Rogers (1902–1987) was the fourth of six children. He was raised in a close-knit family with strict religious standards (Rogers, 1961). In 1931 Rogers obtained a Ph.D. degree in clinical psychology from the Teachers College of Columbia University.

Rogers then embarked on his professional career, taking a position as a psychologist with the Child Guidance Clinic of Rochester, New York. Shortly thereafter, in 1939, he

TABLE 8.1   Overview of Experiential Approaches

Theory	Founder(s)	Key Concepts	The Counseling Process	Techniques
Person-Centered	Carl Rogers	Trust in the inherent self-actualizing tendencies of people; the role of the self and the client's internal frame of reference in personality dynamics	Involves an if-then process: if certain conditions are established (such as communicating empathic understanding), then the client will move toward self-actualization.	Although no techniques are identified, the approach requires the use of listening skills to communicate empathic understanding and establish other core conditions.
Gestalt	Fritz Perls	An existential-phenomenological perspective; moving from dependence to independence; and being integrated and centered in the present	Involves a dialogue between the therapist and client whereby the client becomes aware of what is occurring in the here and now.	The therapist models authenticity and uses techniques to help the client become aware and centered in the present. Some of the techniques include the empty-chair technique and the use of personal pronouns.
Existential Therapy	Victor Frankl, James Bugental, Rollo May, and Irvin Yalom	Uniqueness of the individual; search for meaning; role of anxiety; freedom of responsibility; and being and nonbeing	Emphasizes the role of the counseling relationship over techniques. Counseling goals can include searching for personal meaning and becoming aware of choices.	Paradoxical reflection, dereflection, and existential encounter.

wrote his first book, *The Clinical Treatment of the Problem Child,* which was based on his experience at the guidance center. This led to his appointment as a full professor in psychology at Ohio State University. It was there during the 1940s that Rogers began to formulate his own approach to counseling and psychotherapy, culminating in the publication of *Counseling and Psychotherapy* in 1942.

From 1945 to 1964 Rogers held academic positions at the University of Chicago and the University of Wisconsin. During this time he was able to continue developing his personal approach and explore its implementation in education, group process, and counseling and psychotherapy. Rogers noted that he had a somewhat negative experience with his academic peers at Ohio State University and the University of Wisconsin (Heppner et al., 1984). He felt he was not liked by his colleagues, although he did not have a particularly high regard for them either. Not surprisingly, he preferred graduate students or people outside the department as friends (Heppner et al., 1984). In 1964 Rogers left academia permanently. During the last years of his career, he worked at the Institute for the Study of the Person in La Jolla, California. Today, the institute continues to provide training opportunities in person-centered counseling.

Theory of Personality

The theory of personality in person-centered counseling is humanistically oriented, focusing on phenomenology and the role of the self in psychological functioning. An overview of Rogers's theory of personality follows.

View of Human Nature. Rogers (1951) held a positive view of human nature, noting the inherent self-actualizing tendencies of people. He believed that if the right conditions existed, people would naturally proceed toward self-actualization. In addition, Rogers's theory emphasizes the phenomenological perspective by suggesting that an individual's internal frame of reference is the best vantage point to understand the person.

Key Concepts. Raskin and Rogers (2005) note that trust is the most fundamental concept in person-centered therapy. This theory contends that clients can be trusted to establish

Carl Rogers

their own goals and monitor their progress toward these goals. In addition, counselors trust that all individuals have inherent self-actualizing tendencies.

Many other key concepts can be derived from Rogers's (1951) theory of personality, which is described in 19 propositions. The key concepts emphasize the role of a person's internal frame of reference and the self in understanding the dynamics of behavior. The following are four propositions that characterize Rogers's personality theory:

1. *People react to the phenomenal field as they experience and perceive it.* A person's phenomenal field is his or her internal frame of reference for perceiving the world. This proposition suggests that what a person perceives will be influenced by past experiences.

2. *The best point to understanding behavior is the internal frame of reference of the person.* This proposition is logically related to the first proposition. Since each person's perception is unique, it can only be understood from the person's internal frame of reference. Rogers therefore advocated developing a phenomenological perspective when working with clients, which involves understanding things from the client's perspective.

3. *People tend to behave in a manner consistent with their concept of self.* The self is the center of the organism and consists of how a person sees the self in relation to others. The self attempts to foster consistency within the organism by promoting behavior that is compatible to one's view of the self.

4. *The more people perceive and accept experiences, the more they will tend to be accepting and understanding of others.* Self-acceptance and understanding are viewed as contributing factors in understanding and accepting others as unique individuals.

Theory of Counseling and Psychotherapy

Rogers's person-centered theory can be described as an "if-then" approach. If certain conditions exist in the counseling relationship, then the client will move toward self-actualization (Rogers, 1961). Rogers (1957) identified the following three core conditions as necessary and sufficient for personal growth to occur:

1. *Counselor congruence.* Counselor congruence means counselors are congruent in terms of what they are experiencing and what they communicate. For example, when counselors feel threatened by a client, it would be inappropriate for them to say they enjoy being with the client. This would communicate a confusing double message and the counselor would not be genuine or authentic.

2. *Empathic understanding.* The counselor attempts to understand the client from the client's internal frame of reference. This phenomenological perspective involves understanding what the client is thinking, feeling, and experiencing, and communicating this understanding to the client.

3. *Unconditional positive regard.* Rogers believed that it is essential for the counselor to communicate a sense of acceptance and respect to the client. There has been some misunderstanding of what Rogers meant by unconditional positive regard. He did not mean the counselor should tolerate and accept anything the client did (Martin, 1989).

He instead believed the counselor should try to "separate the deed from the doer" (Martin, 1989). The counselor should accept the client as a person worthy of respect even though the client's behavior may be inappropriate (Rogers, Gendlin, Kiesler, & Truax, 1967).

In addition to these therapist-offered core conditions, Rogers (1957) identified three other conditions that must occur for successful counseling to occur. The first two are considered preconditions for therapy: the therapist and client are in psychological contact, or aware of each other's presence, and the client is experiencing some discomfort in life to be motivated for therapy. The third condition is that the client must be able to accurately perceive and experience the core conditions set forth by the therapist.

A number of goals and therapeutic outcomes emerge from the person-centered therapy. This style of counseling is unique in that it does not attempt to resolve the client's presenting problem. It instead assists the client in the growth process to become a fully functioning individual. Rogers (1961) identified the following changes that tend to occur as the client moves toward self-actualization:

- *Open to experience.* Clients are capable of seeing reality without distorting it to fit a preconceived self-structure. Instead of operating from a rigid belief system, clients are interested in exploring new horizons.
- *Self-trust.* Initially clients tend to have self-doubts. Clients may believe that no matter what they decide, it will be wrong. As therapy progresses, clients can learn to trust their own judgment and become more self-confident.
- *Internal source of evaluation.* Person-centered therapy fosters the development of an internal locus of control. This occurs as clients are encouraged to explore their inner choices and are discouraged from looking to others for a sense of direction or locus of evaluation.
- *Willingness to continue growing.* As a result of person-centered therapy, clients will realize that self-actualization is a process and not an end goal. In this sense, no one ever becomes self-actualized. Instead, a fully functioning person is always in the state of becoming.

Techniques

Rogers (1951, 1961) minimizes the importance or use of techniques. Instead of relying on techniques, he emphasized the importance of the counseling relationship. He believed that the counseling relationship can create core conditions that are the necessary and sufficient conditions for the client's self-actualization. In addition, the person-centered therapist uses listening skills to communicate empathic understanding and help the client explore inner choices. Chapter 3 contains a vignette that provides a Rogerian-oriented example of listening skills and additional information regarding Rogers's concept of core conditions in counseling.

Summary and Evaluation

Carl Rogers made a phenomenal contribution to counseling. He was the major figure behind the humanistic movement in counseling. In addition, many principles of his person-centered therapy have been incorporated into other current psychotherapies. For example, listening skills are frequently used to help establish a positive relationship, obtain a phenomenological understanding of the client, and promote the core conditions identified by Rogers.

Several studies have provided support for Rogers's theory and its application to a wide range of counseling procedures. Watkins (1993) notes that person-centered theory can be used in the contemporary practice of psychological testing. He notes that Rogers's theory can have numerous applications in testing procedures, such as maintaining a client-centered focus to ensure that the client understands and can use test results and using facilitating conditions (such as listening skills and core conditions) to maximize the client's readiness for positive involvement throughout the assessment process. A study by Cramer (1994) examines the relationship between self-esteem and having a friend who communicates the core conditions of empathy, unconditional acceptance, and congruence. The study shows a positive relationship between self-esteem and having a friend who communicates all of these core conditions. Merrill and Andersen (1993) provide a qualitative study on Rogers's theory. They find that when Rogers's core conditions are applied to CAT, clients have gains in self-awareness, self-confidence, risk taking, and self-exploration.

One limitation associated with the person-centered approach is that counseling goals are unclear, creating ambiguity in the counseling process. Usher (1989) also notes that the person-centered approach could be prone to cross-cultural bias in terms of its emphasis on independence and individualism. In addition, research suggests that Rogers's core conditions are not necessary and sufficient but can more accurately be viewed as facilitative for personality change (Gelso & Carter, 1985; Gelso & Fretz, 1992).

Gestalt Therapy

Background Information

Frederick "Fritz" S. Perls (1893–1970) was the founder of Gestalt therapy. Born in Berlin, Perls was initially a student of psychoanalytic theory. In 1946 he moved to the United States and began to develop Gestalt therapy. Perls went on to help establish the Gestalt Institute in New York in 1952 and another one in Cleveland in 1954.

Perls is best known for the work he did at the Esalen Institute of Big Sur, California. He was a resident associate psychiatrist at Esalen from 1964 to 1969. This was Perls's most productive and creative period. In 1969, he published two of his most popular books, *Gestalt Therapy Verbatim* and *In and Out of the Garbage Pail*. Perls died a year later, after leaving the Esalen Institute to establish a Gestalt community on Vancouver Island in British Columbia.

Theory of Personality

The theory of personality in Gestalt therapy emphasizes the concepts of phenomenology, independence, and being integrated and centered in the now. An overview of Perls's theory of personality follows.

View of Human Nature.   The Gestalt view of human nature is similar to the person-centered position. According to Perls, people are self-determined, striving for self-actualization, and best understood from a phenomenological perspective. The term *Gestalt* also relates to a particular view of human nature. It draws from the principles of Gestalt psychology, which suggests that people are a whole compiled of interrelated parts of body, emotions, thoughts, sensations, and perceptions. Each of these aspects of a person can be understood only within the context of the whole person.

Key Concepts. Perls (1969) and Yontef and Jacobs (2005) describe the following key concepts associated with Gestalt therapy:

1. *An existential-phenomenological perspective.* The Gestalt therapist functions from an existential-phenomenological perspective. From this perspective, the therapist attempts to understand clients from the clients' perspective and helps clients gain personal meaning to their existence.

2. *Helping clients move from dependence to independence.* Perls referred to this concept when he said that Gestalt therapy helps clients make the transcendence from environmental support to self-support. When clients seek counseling, they tend to expect environmental support such as reassurance from the counselor. The Gestalt therapist avoids reinforcing clients' dependency needs and helps the client become an independent person. Clients will often resist moving toward self-support because change is threatening. When this occurs, the Gestalt therapist will usually frustrate and confront clients to help them work through the impasse.

3. *Being integrated and centered in the now.* Perls believed that nothing exists except the now, since the past is gone and the future is yet to come. From this perspective, self-actualization is centered in the present rather than oriented to the future. It requires that clients become centered in the now and aware of what they are experiencing. From a Gestalt perspective, being focused and centered in the here and now is referred to as *contact.*

    Anxiety can result when clients are not centered in the now but are preoccupied with the future. When this occurs, clients may develop excessive worry about what might happen and lose touch with what is happening. Unresolved difficulties from the past can also cause problems, resulting in emotional reactions such as anger, guilt, or resentment. Being unaware of this "unfinished business" can interfere with one's functioning in the now. Resentment is seen as the most frequent and worst kind of unfinished business. Perls believed that unexpressed resentment often converts to guilt. For example, a man finds out his wife has had an affair and becomes angry and resentful. Unfortunately, he doesn't express his resentment. Instead, he wonders what he could have done to prevent the affair, resulting in feelings of guilt.

4. *Experimentation.* Gestalt therapy encourages clients to try something new to achieve genuine understanding. Experimentation goes beyond the status quo and involves thought and action versus mere behavioral change. Experimentation also generates data about the client that can be used to obtain a phenomenological understanding of the client's experience.

5. *Health.* From a Gestalt perspective, health requires
    - self-regulation (i.e., meeting one's needs via awareness, prioritizing, and organization and utilization of appropriate behavior), and
    - having contact with the person-environment field (i.e., being focused and centered in the here and now in terms of oneself in relation to the environment).

6. *Relational focus.* Gestalt therapy views personality functioning in relational-contextual terms (i.e., the self in relation to others). The interpersonal perspective emphasizes the interrelationship between the individual and the environment.

Theory of Counseling and Psychotherapy

The counseling process in Gestalt therapy is experiential. It focuses on what is occurring in the here and now of the moment (Yontef & Jacobs, 2005). "Explanations and interpretations are considered less reliable than what is directly perceived and felt" (Yontef & Simkin, 1989, p. 323). Warwar and Greenberg (2000) suggest that Gestalt therapy has shifted from a focus on techniques to the counselor-client relationship as the key to the change process. Gestalt therapy involves a dialogue between the therapist and client in which the client experiences from the inside what the therapist observes from the outside (Yontef & Simkin, 1989).

The goals that emerge from Gestalt therapy are not specific to a client's concerns. The only goal is awareness, which includes knowledge of the environment, taking responsibility for choices, self-knowledge, and self-acceptance (Yontef & Jacobs, 2005).

Passons (1975) identifies common problems that can impede a client's progress in Gestalt therapy. Problems can occur with clients who are overly dependent on others and lack self-responsibility, become out of touch with the world around them, allow unresolved experiences from the past to interfere with being aware of what is occurring in the now, disown their own needs, or define themselves in absolutistic, *either-or* terms.

Techniques

Levitsky and Simkin (1972) note that authenticity symbolizes the Gestalt approach. These authors suggest that it is essential for therapists to be authentic since they cannot teach what they do not know. Gestalt institutes focus their training efforts on trainees playing the role of client. Aside from being authentic, the Gestalt therapist also utilizes several techniques: assuming responsibility, using personal pronouns, and using the "now I'm aware" and "empty-chair" techniques.

Assuming responsibility is a technique that requires the client to rephrase a statement to assume responsibility. For example, a client can be asked to end all statements with: "and I take responsibility for it." The client may also be requested to change "can't" to "won't" or "but" to "and." For example, instead of saying, "I want to get in shape *but* I don't exercise," the client says, "I want to get in shape *and* I don't exercise."

Using personal pronouns encourages clients to take responsibility by saying *I* or *me* instead of making generalizations using *we* or *us,* or *people,* for example. Clients will tend to feel they own their thoughts and feelings more by saying, "It scares *me* to think of going to college" than by saying, "It scares *people* to go to college."

Now I'm aware is a technique that can help clients get in touch with the self. One way to use this technique is to have clients close their eyes to encourage them to get in touch with their inner world and say, "Now I'm aware" before each statement. For example, "Now I'm aware of my breathing"; "Now I'm aware of some tension in my stomach"; "Now I'm aware of feeling embarrassed and self-conscious of having my eyes closed"; "Now I'm aware of feeling afraid of something, but I don't know what." The exercise can continue after clients open their eyes to help them become aware of themselves in relation to their environment.

The *empty-chair* technique can be used to help clients work through conflicting parts of their personality, such as in an approach-avoidance conflict. For example, a client wants to ask a girl out but is afraid of rejection. The empty-chair technique involves placing an empty chair in front of the client. The client is then told that sitting in the empty chair is the part of his personality that does not want to ask the girl out. The client is then encouraged to start a conversation with the empty chair by stating the reasons why he wants to ask the girl out. After the client expresses the positive side of the argument, he is asked to sit in the empty chair and respond with the reasons why he does not want to ask her out. The client continues to move back and forth until he has resolved the issue. The empty-chair technique can be useful in helping clients work through unfinished business so they can be centered in the now.

Summary and Evaluation

Gestalt therapy can be particularly appropriate for clients who lack self-awareness and feel "out of touch" with themselves. Several research studies provide some support for the efficacy of Gestalt therapy. Guinan and Foulds (1970) found clients to have increased self-actualization and self-concepts after Gestalt therapy. Clarke and Breeberg (1986) found the empty-chair technique to be more effective than problem-solving techniques in resolving decisional conflict. Paivio and Greenberg (1992) provide additional support for the efficacy of the empty-chair technique. These researchers note that empty-chair dialogue is effective in resolving "unfinished" emotional issues clients have toward others.

The main weakness of the Gestalt approach is that it lacks a strong theoretical base. It appears to emphasize techniques of therapy rather than providing an in-depth theoretical foundation for understanding human behavior or providing a comprehensive approach to psychotherapy. Additional research on Gestalt techniques and principles appears warranted.

Existential Therapy

Background Information

No single individual is responsible for the development of existential therapy. The theoretical origins of existential therapy can be traced to existentially oriented philosophy. In this regard, Nietzsche, Heidegger, Sartre, and Buber have played influential roles. For example, Buber (1970) proposes an interesting view of existence. He contends that people do not exist as isolated individuals but instead function in a state of existence that is between the I or oneself and others. In addition, several individuals have written books on existential therapy, including Victor Frankl (1963, 1967, 1971, 1978), Rollo May (1953, 1961, 1977), Irvin Yalom (1980), and James Bugental (1976). To a large degree, the basic concepts and other tenets of existential therapy identified in this section represent an integration of these major existential theorists.

Theory of Personality

The theory of personality in existential therapy sees each person as a unique individual who is struggling to derive meaning in life. Existential therapy focuses on attempting to understand the human condition. It rejects a fixed view of human nature but instead contends that each person must ultimately define his or her own personal existence. May and Yalom (2005) suggest that death, freedom, isolation, and meaninglessness represent four interrelated human concerns that characterize the existential theory of personality. Death is considered the ultimate concern. Personal meaning and authenticity are associated with confronting death. Freedom to choose to confront the realities associated with death (such as a fear of isolation and extreme separateness) is necessary to overcome meaninglessness in life.

Key Concepts.   May and Yalom (2005) identify the following key concepts associated with existential therapy:

1. *Uniqueness of the individual.* The existential position suggests that no two people are alike—each one is unique. To become aware of one's uniqueness, it is necessary to encounter oneself as a separate and distinct individual. An important part of this process is to have the experience of existential aloneness. This can be a painful experience as a person attempts to encounter the meaning of one's existence. It can also help a person discover the capability of becoming autonomous.
2. *The search for meaning.* Victor Frankl's (1963, 1967, 1971, 1978) logotherapeutic approach evolved out of his experience as a prisoner of war in a Jewish concentration camp during World War II. He described these experiences as well as the basic principles of logotherapy in his book *Man's Search for Meaning* (Frankl, 1963). Logotherapy suggests that the most prominent psychological problem facing people is a lack of meaning in life, which he called the *existential vacuum.* Frankl (1978) believed that a person can experience meaning by feeling valued or needed, which in turn can create a purposeful existence. In this regard, Frankl (1963) cited the words of Nietzsche, who said, "He who has a *why* to live can bear almost any *how*" (p. 121).
3. *The role of anxiety.* Existential therapy differentiates between two types of anxiety. One is normal or healthy anxiety, called *existential anxiety,* and the other is unhealthy anxiety, referred to as *neurotic anxiety.* Neurotic anxiety is not healthy because it is an anxiety reaction that is not in proportion to the situation and can overwhelm the person. Existential anxiety suggests that some degree of anxiety can be positive since it can motivate a person to make the necessary changes in life. Another positive aspect of anxiety is that it often occurs when a person faces a difficult situation. A person that flees from this anxiety will not be able to learn from the challenges of life. From this perspective, existentialists believe one can draw meaning from pain and suffering. Nietzsche also related to this point when he said, "That which does not kill me, makes me stronger" (Hollingdale, 1978, p. 23).
4. *Freedom and responsibility.* Existential therapy contends that freedom and responsibility are interrelated. Although people are free to choose their own destiny, they must take responsibility for their actions. Existentialists help clients become aware of their choices and the control they can exert over their own destiny.
5. *Being and nonbeing.* Being and nonbeing are also interrelated. The reality of death brings meaning to life. Being and nonbeing are also related to freedom and responsibility. People are free to be or not to be. If individuals choose to be, they must assume responsibility for their existence. Being and nonbeing have also been related to the "I-Am" experience (e.g., "I am so therefore I exist"). "I-Am" is a proclamation of a

choice of life over death, a choice of being over nonbeing. From an existential perspective, the realization that death can occur at any time motivates people to generate meaning from their existence.

6. *Three modes of existence.* According to existential therapy, there are three modes of existence (being in the world) (Nystul, 1976). All three modes of existence are necessary to have a balanced, meaningful life. These three modes of existence are the umwelt, mitwelt, and eigenwelt. *Umwelt* is the natural world around us that helps define our existence. Umwelt includes the world of biological need gratification reflected in meeting basic needs such as hunger. *Mitwelt* is the social world defined by the nature of one's interpersonal relationships. *Eigenwelt* is one's "own world" and corresponds to self-understanding. Kemp (1971) posits that eigenwelt can also be associated with an ontological at-oneness with life. For example, during meditation people can transcend to the center of their existence and achieve an ontological at-oneness with life itself.

7. *Self-transcendence.* Self-transcendence involves moving beyond the subject-object dichotomy (Nystul, 1987a). For example, a student (the subject) attempts to understand the professor (the object). The subject-object dichotomy is characterized by separateness and occurs anytime a person thinks. Meditation utilizes mantras that are non-word utterings that are said whenever people realize they are thinking. Self-transcendence results in an ontological at oneness between counselors and clients. Self-transcendence is considered the peak experience in therapy and is characterized by a very close counseling relationship and profound levels of understanding and empathy. Self-transcendence is also associated with a distortion of time and a very close feeling of connection with whatever or whoever the person feels at one with (e.g., a client, a sunset, or a musical experience at a concert).

Theory of Counseling and Psychotherapy

The goals of existential therapy relate directly to the key concepts. They can be directed at helping clients (a) discover their own uniqueness, (b) find personal meaning in life, (c) use anxiety in a positive sense, (d) become aware of their choices and the need to take responsibility for choices, and (e) not see death as a nemesis but as an eventual reality that gives meaning and significance to life.

The actual process of existential therapy emphasizes the role of the counseling relationship over the use of specific techniques. This approach is similar to the person-centered position in that both attempt to obtain a phenomenological understanding of the client and encourage the client to become aware of inner choices. The two approaches differ on the nature of the counseling relationship. Whereas Rogers focuses on the client, existentialists focus on the therapist and the client. Counseling from an existential point of view is therefore a shared responsibility, with the counselor and client taking an active role in the counseling process.

Buber's "I-thou" concept can be used to provide insight into the nature of the counseling relationship in existential therapy. Buber suggests that counseling relationships can be experienced at different levels that reflect different degrees of humanness and authenticity. For example, the "I to it" is a depersonalized relationship in which the counselor relates to the client as an object. Buber contends that the "I-thou" relationship (which is characterized by authenticity and humanness) is necessary for a genuine encounter to occur between the counselor and client. Brace (1992) goes on to note that Buber's "I-thou" concept can be used to enhance counseling relationships from various theoretical perspectives such as interpersonal psychotherapy.

Techniques

Some existential theories such as Frankl's (1963, 1967, 1971, 1978) logotherapy utilize specific techniques. Frankl (1963, 1978) described two techniques that are central to his approach. The first technique is *dereflection,* which is a procedure that involves helping clients focus on strengths rather than weaknesses. This technique seems more closely aligned to the cognitive school of counseling than to existential theory. The second technique associated with logotherapy is *paradoxical intention,* which involves asking clients to do what they fear doing, such as asking them to stutter if they fear stuttering. It is not entirely clear what makes this technique existential. Paradoxical intention is simply a technique that helps a client overcome anticipatory anxiety by redefining success and failure.

Several research studies provide support for the efficacy of paradoxical intention. It appears to be particularly effective for cases that do not respond to behavior therapy (Ascher, 1979; Ascher & Efran, 1978). One particularly well-controlled study by Turner and Ascher (1979) also shows paradoxical intention to effectively treat insomnia.

Dowd and Sanders (1994) suggest that paradoxical techniques can be useful with resistant clients who are highly reactant (have high control tendencies). Two types of paradoxical techniques can be used with these individuals: symptom prescription and restraining. *Symptom prescription* involves requiring the client to experience the symptom they are trying to overcome. This technique creates a no-lose situation for control-seeking clients. Either they experience the symptom as prescribed (and feel that they now have control over their symptom), or they choose to foster resistance toward the suggestion (and do not experience their problem). *Restraining* involves asking clients to change slowly or not to change at all. In this case, a client's need for control can manifest itself in a form of resistance that results in the client changing very quickly and overcoming his or her problem.

Frankl (1963) also referred to the process of *self-transcendence,* which means moving beyond the self. This is a uniquely existential concept that can allow the therapist to transcend the limit of the self and directly experience the client's inner world of pain or joy. When this occurs, it can be referred to as an *existential encounter.* Unfortunately, Frankl (1963) did not describe a technique that could facilitate the existential encounter.

Summary and Evaluation

Existential therapy focuses on issues such as individuality and searching for meaning in life. These issues become increasingly important especially in light of advances in cloning. Existential theory will play a key role in helping people define themselves as unique individuals in an ever-changing world.

The major weakness of this approach lies in its lack of a well-formulated theoretical foundation. Another weakness is that there are few, if any, unique existential techniques that can be utilized in the counseling process. In addition, Goldfried, Greenberg, and Mormar (1990) note a significant decline in research on experiential therapies and thus a danger of their becoming extinct or being integrated into other schools of counseling.

Creative Arts Therapy

Creative arts therapy (CAT) can be defined as promoting psychological and physiological well-being through the use of creative modalities such as art, music, dance, or drama. Two groups of individuals use CAT: members of the helping professions who use it as an adjunct to counseling and psychotherapy, such as counselors and psychologists; and CAT professionals who are certified or registered in a particular CAT modality, such as music and art therapists. CAT can be used with clients of all ages across a wide array of therapeutic modalities, such as individual, group, and marriage and family counseling (Sherwood-Hawes, 1995).

According to Fleshman and Fryrear (1981), CAT has been referred to by many names over the years. These include *expressive therapy, expression therapy,* and *creative therapy.* CAT has been shown to (a) facilitate communication of cognitively impaired and nonverbal patients with their therapists, (b) enable therapists to readily explore patients' affect, and (c) foster therapeutic bonding (Johnson, 1984a; Robbins, 1985).

CAT is not a recognized school of counseling because it lacks a clear theoretical foundation of its own. However, creative arts therapists do utilize the major psychological theories and procedures to facilitate therapeutic outcomes. Freudian, Jungian, and existential theories are three theories with special appeal and utility in CAT. For example, art therapists often utilize Freudian concepts to interpret drawings and other artwork. Jungian psychology (especially Jung's concept of the collective unconsciousness) can be useful in helping clients explore the symbolic nature of unconscious processes that emerge from creative expression (Sherwood-Hawes, 1995). Existential concepts of self-transcendence and the existential encounter can also provide opportunity for creative arts practitioners. In this regard, CAT can foster self-transcendence, enabling the counselor to feel at one with the client (Nystul, 1987a). When this occurs, the counselor directly experiences the client's inner emotional state, resulting in an existential encounter. The case of Ron, described in a *Personal Note* later in this chapter, provides an illustration of the use of CAT and the existential encounter.

Professional Issues

The profession of CAT is made up of individuals who have undertaken formal study in the therapeutic use of a particular creative arts modality such as music or drama. Professional recognition is achieved by obtaining certification or registration in a particular CAT modality. Requirements for registration or certification vary according to the CAT specialty, from a bachelor's to a master's degree and from six months to two years of supervised clinical training. Current requirements for certification or registration can be obtained by writing to the CAT professional organizations listed in Table 8.2.

Certified and registered CAT professionals work in a variety of settings, including hospitals, nursing homes, and private practice. Their role in mental health services has been primarily as "an adjunctive, secondary form of psychotherapeutic treatment" (Johnson, 1984a, p. 212). Johnson (1984a) identifies several changes that need to be made for CAT to emerge as an independent profession. These include (a) using CAT to advance the knowledge of psychology, (b) identifying the unique contribution CAT can make in the helping process, (c) overcoming CAT's dependency on other disciplines such as psychology and psychiatry by broadening the role and function of professional creative art therapists, and (d) taking a more assertive position with other professional groups and legislative agencies.

TABLE 8.2   Addresses for CAT Professional Organizations

Music Therapy
American Music Therapy Association
8455 Colesville Road, Suite 1000
Silver Spring, MD 20910
www.musictherapy.org

Music Educators National Conference
1902 Association Drive
Reston, VA 22091
www.menc.org

Art Therapy
American Art Therapy Association
1202 Allanson Road
Mundelein, IL 60060
www.arttherapy.org

National Art Education Association
1916 Association Drive
Reston, VA 20191
www.naea-reston.org

Dance Therapy
American Dance Therapy Association
2000 Century Plaza, Suite 108
10632 Little Patuxent Parkway
Columbia, MD 21044
www.adta.org

Drama Therapy
National Association for Drama Therapy
15 Post Side Lane
Pittsford, NY 14534
www.nadt.org

Bibliotherapy
Association of Hospital and Institution Libraries
Committee on Bibliotherapy
American Library Association
50 East Huron Street
Chicago, IL 60611
(Division of Health and Rehabilitative Library Services)
www.ala.org

The remaining sections of this chapter present an overview of the prominent modalities associated with CAT. Information is provided in terms of key concepts, procedures and outcomes, and special populations. These are summarized in Table 8.3.

TABLE 8.3   CAT Modalities

CAT Modality	Key Concepts	Procedures and Outcomes	Special Populations
Music Therapy	1. Music is intrinsically part of a culture. 2. Music can help clients get in touch with their thoughts and feelings. 3. Music has a basic structure in terms of rhythm, melody, and so forth, which helps clients overcome problems with thought disorders.	Music therapy consists of using a musical experience to enhance and facilitate counseling goals.	Music therapy can be used with all types of clients of all ages but can be particularly effective with young children and the elderly.
Art Therapy	1. Art offers a form of sublimation whereby clients can achieve indirect gratification of unconscious needs. 2. Visual symbols in art can be useful diagnostic tools. 3. Art allows for the expression of unconscious thoughts and feelings. 4. Art promotes a sense of internal equilibrium.	The process of art therapy varies according to theoretical orientation but typically includes color analysis and spontaneous drawings.	Art therapy can be used with clients of all ages but can be particularly useful with children and adolescents.
Drama Therapy	1. Drama therapy offers an opportunity to externalize and learn from experiences. 2. Drama therapy allows for the expression of strong feelings. 3. Drama therapy deals directly and openly with functions of the personality. 4. Emotional conflicts can be better understood by expressing them in action through drama.	Spontaneous role-play is the heart of drama therapy. A variety of procedures are used in drama therapy, such as movement, mime, and puppet plays.	Drama therapy can be used with clients of all ages, but its main use is with children who are physically, emotionally, or mentally handicapped.

(continued)

TABLE 8.3 Continued

CAT Modality	Key Concepts	Procedures and Outcomes	Special Populations
Dance Therapy	1. Dance therapy involves the integration of mind and body. 2. Dance can reflect a client's mood and indicate flexibility or rigidity. 3. Clients can channel self-expression into dance.	Dance procedures vary according to the outcomes desired. Dance therapy can involve spontaneous or structured dance experiences and can be used to improve motor skills and interpersonal relationships; facilitate expression of moods, attitudes, and ideas; and stimulate, energize, and relax the body.	Dance therapy can be used with clients of all ages.
Bibliotherapy	Bibliotherapy can be used to foster universalizing, identification, catharsis, and insight.	Books or some form of literature are read to promote particular counseling outcomes.	Any client who can read can benefit from bibliotherapy.
Multimodality CAT	Multimodality CAT involves using the full range of CAT modalities. It can broaden the client's ability to respond to creativity.	Procedures vary according to the theoretical orientation and can include counselors setting the stage for creativity, setting an example, setting themselves at ease, and developing insights from creativity after a client has finished a creative expression.	All clients can benefit from multimodality CAT.

Music Therapy

Music is the oldest form of art associated with curing the ill, according to Fleshman and Fryrear (1981), who cite instances of primitive tribes and other people using songs and chants to obtain divine assistance.

Key Concepts. Fleshman and Fryrear (1981) identify the following three key concepts associated with music therapy:

1. Music is intrinsically part of a culture.
2. Music can help clients get in touch with thoughts and feelings and communicate emotions that cannot be described by words.
3. Music has a basic structure characterized by rhythm, melody, pitch, and tempo that can be used to promote structure in clients whose thoughts are disorganized and chaotic (for example, schizophrenics).

Procedures and Outcomes. Bruscia (1987) notes that music therapy involves using musical experiences and the therapeutic relationship to enhance the client's state of well-being. According to Bruscia (1987), musical experiences can include a wide range of activities, including improvising, performing, composing, and listening to music. Bruscia (1987) contends that improvising is the fundamental approach to music therapy and involves creating and playing simultaneously.

Fleshman and Fryrear (1981) suggest that music therapy involves four basic activities: (a) recreational and entertainment-oriented experiences to foster socialization; (b) therapeutic listening groups to promote group cohesion; (c) an adjunct activity to psychotherapy to stimulate emotions, encourage discussions, promote self-understanding, and facilitate socialization; and (d) individual and group music therapy to address a client's particular problem (for example, asking clients to play a duet to foster cooperation).

Several studies have been conducted on music therapy and its implication for the counseling process. Some of this research shows that music therapy facilitates the counseling process in terms of assessment and diagnosis (Isenberg-Grzeda, 1988; Wells & Stevens, 1984). Other studies have found music therapy exerts positive influence on perceived locus of control (James, 1988) and as a stimulus to promote group cohesion (Wells & Stevens, 1984). Moreno (1988) suggests that all procedures used in music therapy should reflect a multicultural sensitivity since musical traditions vary from culture to culture.

Special Populations. Music therapy can be used with people of all ages. Gibbons (1988) suggests that music therapy can be particularly effective when working with the elderly. Gibbons (1984) notes that elderly people prefer active involvement in music and can learn new musical skills such as the guitar or piano at a level comparable to much younger people.

Music therapy has also been used successfully with children and adolescents. Eidson (1989) has utilized a behaviorally oriented music therapy program to help emotionally disturbed middle-school students improve their classroom behavior. Cripe (1986) provides guidelines for how to use music therapy with children with attention deficit disorder. Wells and Stevens (1984) find that music stimulates creative fantasy in young adolescents during group psychotherapy.

Fleshman and Fryrear (1981) identify other special populations, such as the mentally retarded and physically disabled, who can be served by music therapy. According to Fleshman and Fryrear (1981), music therapy can be useful with mentally retarded individuals to provide stimulation and teach social skills. In addition, regimental music, such as a march, can be used to help mentally retarded individuals obtain control over their impulses. Physically disabled clients can also benefit from music therapy. Fleshman and Fryrear (1981) cite examples such as using wind instruments to help clients with lung disorders and using certain instruments that require finger dexterity to help clients overcome motor control dysfunctions.

Melodic intonation therapy represents an emerging use of music therapy. According to Sparks and Deck (1994), it can be especially useful to treat aphasia (weakening or loss of language ability, which can include speech problems). Melodic intonation therapy utilizes music to stimulate portions of the brain that are associated with language functioning. The actual process of melodic intonation therapy involves teaching the person with aphasia to sing in a unique manner based on music from the Judeo-Christian period. Family members are encouraged to participate in this process (Sparks & Deck, 1994).

Art Therapy

Art therapy is one of the oldest and most established forms of CAT. Some of the earliest examples of art therapy can be traced to the prehistoric era, when people painted pictures on the walls of their caves to express their relationship with the world (Wadeson, 1980). Art therapy encompasses many of the visual art forms, including painting, sculpture, crafts, and photography (Kenny, 1987).

Key Concepts.   The following are key concepts associated with art therapy:

1. Art offers a form of sublimation whereby clients can achieve indirect gratification of unconscious needs (Kramer, 1987).
2. Art has visual symbols that can be useful diagnostic tools (Wilson, 1987).
3. Art allows for the expression of unconscious thoughts and feelings (Rubin, 1987).
4. Art promotes a sense of internal equilibrium (Fleshman & Fryrear, 1981).

Procedures and Outcomes.   The origins of art therapy can be traced to psychoanalytic theory (Rubin, 1987). More recently, however, it has been applied to most other major schools of psychology and counseling. Some examples are Gestalt (Rhyne, 1987), behavioral (Roth, 1987), and cognitive (Silver, 1987). A brief review of these applications follows.

Psychoanalytic.   Art can be analyzed for its symbolic content (Fleshman & Fryrear, 1981; Rubin, 1987).

Gestalt.   Art allows the client "to experience and express immediate perceptions and awareness" (Rhyne, 1987, p. 173).

Behavioral.   The behavioral approach to art therapy involves applying the principles of behavior modification to traditional art-therapy techniques (Roth, 1987). In this process, principles of reinforcement are used to involve the client in art therapy and other desirable behaviors (Roth, 1987).

Cognitive. Cognitive art therapy involves both the assessment and development of cognitive processes (Silver, 1987). It is based primarily on Piaget and other cognitive psychologists. Silver (1987) identifies different ways art can be used to foster cognitive and creative skills. For example, Silver (1987) describes how the concept of sequential order can be developed through painting. Several other individuals have described procedures that are common to all approaches to art therapy. For example, color analysis can be traced to the work of Jung (1959), who noted that the use of color is related to perceptions and judgment. According to Jung (1959), yellow is associated with intuition; red is related to feeling; green suggests sensation; and blue represents thinking. In addition, Kenny (1987) suggests that color selection is also associated with emotional states, with blacks and grays indicating depression and white suggesting emotional rigidity.

Stabler (1984) provides additional guidelines for analyzing art. He notes that proportion, form, detail, movement, and theme can be used to obtain an estimate of a client's psychosocial and cognitive development and level of maturity (see Chapter 11).

Stabler (1984) also identifies three types of drawings that can be useful in art therapy: self-portraits, free drawings, and family drawings. Bertoia and Allan (1988) emphasize the role that *spontaneous drawings,* which are essentially free drawings, can play in art therapy by providing a direct link to unconscious processes.

Special Populations. Art therapy can be used with clients of all ages. Fleshman and Fryrear (1981) note it can be particularly useful with disadvantaged youth, children with sexual identity problems, mentally retarded children, schizophrenics, and suicidal patients. For example, the "suicide slash," which is a slip of the pen or an inappropriate line in a picture, and powerful repetitious images can indicate suicide ideations (Fleshman & Fryrear, 1981).

The following *Personal Note* provides an example of how I used art therapy as an adjunct to my counseling approach.

Drama Therapy

Moreno (1946) was the founder of psychodrama, which was one of the first systematic uses of drama as a form of therapy. Later, drama therapy emerged as a more flexible alternative to psychodrama. Irwin (1987, p. 277) notes that drama therapy is less verbal, less structured, and less oriented toward the theater than psychodrama. Johnson (1984b, p. 105) defines drama therapy "as the intentional use of creative drama toward the psychotherapeutic goals of symptom relief, emotional and physical integration, and personal growth." Drama therapy includes any use of role-playing, but it is especially associated with the use of creative theater as a medium for self-expression (Johnson, 1984b).

Key Concepts. Although drama therapy is in its formative stage of development, the following four key concepts characterize its current status:

1. Drama offers an opportunity to externalize and learn from experiences, both real and imagined (Irwin, 1987).

A Personal Note

"Sam" was a 21-year-old self-referred client I saw at a university counseling center in Australia. He had a severe stuttering problem and also complained of loneliness and boredom. During our second session, I asked Sam to draw whatever came to his mind. Sam drew the picture shown in Figure 8.1.

After Sam finished drawing, I asked him to describe himself in terms of his picture. Soon we began to acquire information regarding Sam's motivation for therapy, possible counseling goals, and barriers to the goals. The picture seemed to provide an overview of what Sam wanted from counseling. He mentioned that he had never had a girlfriend and hadn't even kissed a girl. The catapult suggested he

was very motivated to have a girlfriend. Unfortunately, he didn't believe this was possible since there were several barriers standing in his way, as illustrated by the sharks swimming between him and the girl.

We went on to identify what these barriers were in terms of *basic mistakes,* as discussed in Chapter 7. For example, he thought he could not get a girlfriend if he was a stutterer. I then helped Sam overcome the basic mistakes as well as other self-defeating processes during the reorientation phase of counseling. (See Nystul and Musynska, 1976, for a more detailed description of this case.)

Source: Nystul, M., and Musynska, E. (November 1976). Adlerian treatment of a classical case of stuttering, *Journal of Individual Psychology, 32*(2), 194–202; by permission of the University of Texas Press.

FIGURE 8.1   Sam's Picture

2. Drama allows for the expression of strong feelings, thinking, impulses, and action (Irwin, 1987).
3. Drama deals directly and openly with different functions of the personality (Fleshman & Fryrear, 1981).
4. Emotional conflicts can be better understood by expressing them in action through drama (Irwin, 1987).

Procedures and Outcomes.   As in all CAT modalities, the procedures of drama therapy vary according to the theoretical orientation of the practitioner. Irwin (1987) notes that drama therapists draw from a variety of theoretical orientations, such as psychoanalytic, behavioral, Gestalt, Jungian, and Rogerian.

Several authors have identified what can be considered common procedures associated with drama therapy. First, spontaneous role-playing is the heart of drama therapy and can be found in all its forms (Fleshman & Fryrear, 1981). Second, the therapist uses a variety of procedures such as movement, mime, and puppet plays to involve the client in action so inner conflicts can be expressed and better understood (Irwin, 1987). Third, drama therapy contributes to assessment and diagnosis by analyzing roles that are enacted or rejected, themes and conflicts that emerge in fantasies and stories, and the process of the session in terms of emotional release (Irwin, 1987).

Special Populations.   Drama therapy can be used with people of all ages. Its main use appears to be with children, and numerous programs have been developed for children who are physically, emotionally, or mentally disabled (Fleshman & Fryrear, 1981). Drama therapy can be particularly useful in school settings to teach students how to deal with pressures relating to dating or drug and alcohol use.

Dance Therapy

The origins of dance therapy can be traced to modern dance, which began early in the 20th century (Fleshman & Fryrear, 1981).

Key Concepts.   Fleshman and Fryrear (1981) identify the following three key concepts associated with dance therapy:

1. The fundamental concept in dance therapy is the integration, or more specifically the reintegration, of mind and body.

Various moods can be expressed in drama therapy.

2. Movement can reflect a client's mood and indicate either flexibility or rigidity.
3. Dance therapy provides an opportunity for clients to express themselves in movement, channeling self-expression into dance form.

Procedures and Outcomes.   Dance therapy may involve clients dancing by themselves or with other clients. The dance method can be spontaneous or more structured in nature. Particular attention is paid to what the client communicates or discovers from the dance. Other factors worth noting are how the client interacts with others, the client's awareness of space, and how the dance may relate to a particular problem that the client is experiencing.

Fleshman and Fryrear (1981) and Lasseter, Privette, Brown, & Duer (1989) identify the following goals associated with dance therapy:

- Improving motor skills
- Enhancing the relationship between the client and therapist
- Increasing the client's movement repertoire to facilitate expression of moods, attitudes, and ideas
- Allowing for the sublimation of erotic and aggressive impulses
- Encouraging interpersonal relationships
- Stimulating, energizing, and relaxing the client's body

Special Populations.   Dance therapy can be used with people of all ages. Lasseter et al. (1989) note that dance therapy has been a primary treatment strategy for children with mental, physical, and emotional problems. In this regard, dance therapy has been used successfully with autistic children (Cole, 1982), psychotic children (Gunning & Holmes, 1973), children with cerebral palsy (Clarke & Evans, 1973), mentally retarded children (Boswell, 1983), and emotionally disturbed and learning-disabled children (Polk, 1977; Wislocki, 1981).

Bibliotherapy

The earliest uses of bibliotherapy can be traced to the Grecian times where a sign was hung over the entrance of a library proclaiming "the healing place of the soul" (Zaccaria & Moses, 1968). Riordan and Wilson (1989, p. 506) define bibliotherapy as "the guided reading of written materials in gaining understanding or resolving problems relevant to a person's therapeutic needs." There appears to be an increase in use of bibliotherapy as an adjunct to counseling (Riordan & Wilson, 1989), with 60 percent of psychologists prescribing self-help books occasionally, 24 percent often, and 12 percent regularly (Starker, 1988).

Key Concepts.   According to Fleshman and Fryrear (1981), the key concepts of bibliotherapy are derived from psychoanalytic theory and include

1. *Universalizing.* Clients minimize feelings of guilt, shame, and isolation when they discover others share similar problems in life.
2. *Identification.* Clients can identify with characters in books, which provide positive role models regarding attitudes and values.
3. *Catharsis.* Bibliotherapy group discussions provide clients with opportunities for self-disclosure and catharsis.

4. *Insight.* Clients can obtain insight by having an external frame of reference for comparison.

Procedures and Outcomes. Bibliotherapy involves asking clients to read a book or some form of literature to promote certain outcomes associated with the counseling process (for example, career awareness and exploration). The nature of the reading assignment will depend on the desired outcomes. For example, *What Color Is Your Parachute?* could be used to assist a client with making a career choice. Four of the most commonly prescribed books by psychologists are *What Color Is Your Parachute?, The Relaxation Response, Your Perfect Right,* and *Feeling Good* (Starker, 1988). Once clients have read a book or other literature, they can discuss what they learned with the counselor.

Special Populations. Bibliotherapy can be used with any client who knows how to read. Research on the efficacy of bibliotherapy has provided mixed results. For example, one study showed support for bibliotherapy in effecting behavioral change (Riordan & Wilson, 1989).

Multimodality CAT

A relatively recent addition to the CAT approaches involves the use of multiple CAT modalities instead of relying on a single modality such as dance or music. This broad-based approach to CAT has been called various names, including *creative-expressive arts, mixed-media arts,* and *multimedia approach to the expressive arts* (Fleshman & Fryrear, 1981; Talerico, 1986). The term *multimodality CAT* indicates using whatever CAT modality the therapist and client want to use.

Key Concepts. The major premise behind multimodality CAT is that it creates limitless possibilities for creative expression, whereas using one modality can be unnecessarily restrictive, discouraging creative responses from the client (Talerico, 1986).

Counselors can share their creative outlets in multimodality creative arts therapy (CAT).

Procedures and Outcomes.   A four-phase model of CAT can be used with all types of creative media, for example, art, music, or dance, with clients of all ages (Nystul, 1980a, 1987a). The following are the four phases of this model:

1. *Set the stage.* The counselor sets the stage for creative process by either having creative arts material available to use or by encouraging the client to bring a creative outlet (for example, a guitar) to the next counseling session.
2. *Set an example.* The counselor may wish to share a creative outlet with the client to set an example of risk taking and self-disclosure.
3. *Set yourself at ease.* The counselor should initially avoid analyzing a client's creative expression for psychological insights before the client is finished. This can cause a client to become self-conscious and interfere with the counselor directly experiencing the client's creative expression.
4. *Obtain a phenomenological understanding of the client.* Once the client has completed the creative expression (for example, a song or drawing), the counselor can attempt to gain a phenomenological understanding of the client. This can be accomplished by asking clients to describe what the creative expression said about them or describe themselves in terms of the creative expression.

The use of multiple CAT modalities in counseling and psychotherapy can promote the following outcomes (Nystul, 1980a, 1987a). Multimodality CAT can provide assessment and diagnostic information by having clients project their thoughts and feelings into a creative expression, promoting self-disclosure in counselors and clients as they share their creative outlets. It can also increase clients' social interest as they discover the support that can result from sharing a creative expression. Counselors can also develop a phenomenological understanding of clients as they describe themselves in terms of their creative expression, and it can promote an existential encounter as counselors directly experience their clients' emotions through the release of their creative expressions.

Special Populations.   Multimodality CAT can be used with clients of all ages. Some examples are autistic children (Nystul, 1986a), emotionally disturbed children (Nystul, 1978b, 1980a), a young adult stutterer who felt socially isolated (Nystul & Musynska, 1976), and a student in a university counseling center who had a sexual identity problem (Nystul, 1979a). In addition, the counselor is not restricted to one modality such as art therapy, so clients have more opportunities to explore and discover creative outlets.

The following *Personal Note* provides an example of how I used multimodality CAT.

Summary and Evaluation of CAT

CAT is a dynamic and powerful tool and can be viewed as an emerging profession or adjunctive strategy associated with counseling and psychotherapy. It can have many uses, such as promoting socialization, communicating thoughts and emotions, and enhancing the counseling relationship, and can be used as a projective device in assessment and diagnosis. A weakness with CAT is a lack of empirical research to determine its precise effect on psychological functioning and the counseling process.

A Personal Note

One case that was very special to me involved a first-grader named Ron. I was an elementary school counselor and Ron was referred to me for counseling services. The reason for the referral was that he spent most of his time daydreaming in class and appeared to have no friends at school.

Ron was unresponsive to my questions during our first counseling session, so I decided to see him in a play therapy setting. As described in Chapter 11, my approach to play therapy involves two parts: a self-concept program and the four-stage model associated with multimodality CAT (Nystul, 1980a).

After we finished our self-concept program, Ron was humming a song. I asked him to make up a song about how he was feeling. I attempted to accompany him on the guitar, and he responded by singing a deep, sorrowful song. These were the words to Ron's song:

My mom comes home and daddy stays home
Momma goes home, daddy stays
Momma stays in the city when she wants to
Momma stays in the city when she wants to

Momma daddy, Momma daddy
I just can't seem to go.

Daddy keep care of the baby
Daddy keep care of the baby
Daddy keep care of the baby

Please help me
I want no!
I need help!

I can't seem to stop
Daddy keep care of the baby
Good-bye, good-bye.

As Ron sang, I did not try to identify any psychological insights from the words of the song. Instead, I went with the music and allowed myself to get caught up with his creative energy. When Ron finished singing, I felt I had gone beyond attempting to understand or empathize with Ron's pain or sorrow. Instead, I had to some degree experienced these feelings as he sang.

As a result of our existential encounter, Ron and I had established a special counseling relationship. He therefore felt free to discuss his thoughts and feelings with me. Later that day, we listened to his song again, which I had tape-recorded. This time, I was interested in exploring the song for possible psychological significance. I asked Ron what the song might say about him. He responded by telling me different facets of his past.

As I listened, I began to identify basic mistakes—faulty views that may interfere with what a person wants out of life (described in Chapter 7). For example, he said his father was black, and his mother said black men are all no good. This was a basic mistake since his view of being black would have a detrimental effect on feeling good about himself and others (something he wanted out of life).

To help reorient Ron from this basic mistake, I enlisted the help of Bill, a black counselor from another school, who agreed to colead some of my play therapy groups. The students loved Bill. Soon Ron began to believe that being even part black could be beautiful. (See Nystul, 1980a, for a more complete description of this case.)

Research Trends in Experiential Counseling

Warwar and Greenberg (2000) note that one of the most significant advances in the 1990s was the empirical validation of experiential approaches. Greenberg et al. (1994) provide an overview of research trends in experiential counseling approaches. Their review includes summaries of studies directed at determining who benefits most from experiential therapies and treatment trends in experiential therapy. Studies examining the effects of client characteristics on success with experiential therapy show the following:

- Clients who rate high in social skills, affiliation, and assertiveness tend to respond well in person-centered therapy.
- Clients with high reactance (including high dominance) or resistance to influence appear to do better in person-centered therapy, whereas those low in reactance do better in Gestalt therapy.
- Internally oriented clients (open clients who are interested in inner experience) appear to do well in person-centered therapy.

Treatment trends in experiential therapies are summarized by Greenberg et al. (1994) as follows:

- Experiential therapies appear to be useful across a broad range of treatment considerations from the "worried well" to the treatment of disorders such as anxiety and depression.
- Counselors should be aware of factors in experiential therapy (such as lack of direction and intrusiveness) that can hinder therapeutic progress.
- Counselors need to move away from uniform use of an experiential theory and adapt the theory to treat specific disorders such as depression or panic attacks.
- Task interventions for counselors and clients can be developed, implemented, and processed to provide a focused means of treating specific problems and then analyzing their efficacy.

More recently, Glauser and Bozarth (2001) note that Rogers's emphasis on developing a positive counseling relationship has been singled out as one of the most important variables in counseling efficacy. For example, Duncan and Moynihan (1994) and Hubble, Duncan, and Miller (1999) estimate that the counseling relationship is responsible for 30 percent of the success variance in counseling; client resources such as family support system, problem-solving skills, and level of optimism are associated with 40 percent of success variance; techniques represent 15 percent of counseling success; and the last 15 percent is associated with the placebo effect.

Research trends are also generating support for CAT. Sherwood-Hawes (1995) notes that the various CATs are currently being used to successfully treat a wide array of clinical problems. For example, art therapy is being used successfully to treat sexual abuse. Dance therapy has proven useful in treating eating disorders. Music therapy is used in a wide array of treatments, from dementia and Alzheimer's disease to treating chronic pain and immune system disorders. And drama and poetry therapy have been found to be effective in treating posttraumatic stress disorders and substance abuse.

Brief Approaches to Experiential Counseling

Although experiential theories were not originally developed for brief counseling, they appear to offer much promise in terms of providing a useful adjunct to a time-limited format. Person-centered therapy can be of use in establishing the counseling relationship through the use of listening skills and facilitating the core conditions. Gestalt therapy has several useful concepts and techniques that could be of use in brief counseling. The key concept of awareness would seem to be a useful goal in brief counseling to maximize a client's readiness for counseling. Gestalt offers numerous useful techniques that can be used in brief counseling, such as the use of personal pronouns to help clients take responsibility for their behavior. The existential concepts of freedom, choice, and responsibility empower clients and enhance their motivation for involvement in the change process.

CAT is ideally suited for brief counseling. Any of the creative arts modalities can be used successfully in as little as one session (such as patients in a hospital listening to music) or can be used as an adjunct to brief-counseling models designed to treat specific disorders. CAT can make an instant impact because of the healing power of the CAT experience. In this regard, Hale (1990) notes that CAT often provides a superior method of healing over more traditional methods.

Diversity Issues in Experiential Counseling

Experiential theories hold both promise and concern in terms of diversity issues such as culture and gender. In terms of culture, Rogers (in his later years) provided training throughout the world in how his counseling theory could be used to foster positive interpersonal relations and overcome conflict. Rogers hoped that his theory could provide a means to alleviate interracial tension and foster world peace (Corey, 2005). Rogers was recognized for this effort by being nominated for a Nobel Peace Prize just before he died.

Glauser and Bozarth (2001) suggest that Rogers's person-centered theory provides a rich foundation for multicultural counseling. Rogerian concepts that play an important role in multicultural counseling include the importance of the counseling relationship; core conditions such as empathy, respect, and genuineness; the emphasis on the "self"; and the phenomenological perspective. These concepts can be extrapolated into multicultural counseling addressing issues of individual differences and diversity.

Corey (2005) notes that Gestalt therapy can make positive contributions in terms of cultural issues. Gestalt therapy can be useful in cross-cultural counseling by helping clients integrate the opposing forces (or polarities) that they can face, such as working through the conflicts between their culture and the dominant culture. In addition, Gestalt therapy emphasizes the importance of nonverbal communication as an authentic means of communication. Nonverbal communication can help overcome misunderstandings that result from language differences in cross-cultural counseling. The various creative arts modalities (such as art, music, and dance) also rely on nonverbal communication, which enhances their cross-cultural utility.

Corey (2005) also describes how existential therapy can play an important role in cross-cultural counseling in terms of bringing personal meaning to life and feeling a sense of control over one's destiny. For example, experiential counseling can help clients who feel oppressed and victimized by forces such as racism or sexism to realize that on some level there are choices and decisions that they are making that are influencing the direction of their lives. Awareness of choices can foster a sense of control and responsibility, which in turn can contribute to meaning in life.

Ingersoll (1995) posits that diversity issues associated with spirituality are associated with Frankl's (1963) existential theory of logotherapy. In this theory, Frankl stresses the relationship between the mind, body, and spirit, with the spirit playing the key role in one's search for meaning. Processes such as self-transcendence and ontological at-oneness with others would appear to be examples of the role of spiritual issues in logotherapy.

Experiential counseling has also been criticized in terms of diversity issues such as culture and gender (Corey, 2005; Prochaska & Norcross, 2002). These authors note that experiential theories overemphasize the intrapsychic forces as being responsible for psychological health and wellness and underestimate environmental forces. Experiential counseling techniques and procedures are reflected in this narrow intrapsychic focus, failing to incorporate current "ecological" trends such as social constructionism, systemic theory from marriage and family counseling, and environmental assessment. For example, social constructionism emphasizes the role that social forces (such as language, narratives, and culture) play in influencing how people construct reality (Gergen, 1994a).

Experiential counseling appears to be somewhat naive, with a very narrow and unrealistic focus. It fails to recognize the significant role that environmental factors such as unemployment, poverty, overcrowding, sexism, racism, and other oppressive forces can play in psychological functioning. For example, from a feminist perspective, experiential theories can be seen as men's way of controlling and blaming women for women's problems such as depression (that is, depression is due to an "intrapsychic defect" and not forces such as political and gender oppression arising from a male-dominated and male-controlled society and culture).

In the final analysis there is promise, yet work still to be done, regarding the utility of experiential counseling with issues of diversity. It is hoped that future research will focus on how experiential theories can be broadened to create a more comprehensive, inclusive explanation for human growth and development, including psychological health and wellness.

Summary

Some theories and approaches are called *experiential* because of their common view that therapeutic gains result from what the client experiences during the counseling session. The three major experiential theories—person-centered, Gestalt, and existential—reflect the spirit of humanistic psychology in conceptualizing human nature as inherently positive, self-determined, and having self-actualizing tendencies.

The strength of experiential therapies lies in their ability to help clients become aware of their thoughts and feelings, discover their inner choices, and promote personal responsibility. The weakness of experiential therapies can be their overemphasis on feelings and underemphasis on cognition and behavior. Experiential therapies may therefore lack some of the counseling strategies necessary to promote a comprehensive treatment program.

Creative arts therapy is an emerging profession with opportunities for professional certification and registration in various CAT modalities such as music, art, and drama. CAT is also an adjunctive counseling strategy that can be used to facilitate the counseling process. Multimodality CAT is a relatively new addition to the CAT field. It has the advantage of utilizing whatever CAT modality the counselor or client prefers to use.

Information on research trends, brief approaches, and diversity issues in experiential counseling shows that experiential theories and approaches can be flexible and useful in various counseling formats from long term to brief. Research trends and issues of diversity help identify some of the strengths and weaknesses of this school of counseling.

Personal Exploration

1. Do you have any favorite experiential theories, and if so, why?
2. What intrigues you about creative arts therapy?
3. How has Carl Rogers's theory influenced the field of counseling?
4. How can existential theory help a person define his or her existence?

Web Sites for Chapter 8

The Association for the Advancement of Gestalt Therapy. (unknown). *About Gestalt therapy.* Retrieved March 3, 2005, from http://www.aagt.org/html/chapter.HTM
Presents a detailed description of Gestalt therapy by current experts.

Hall, K. J. (1997). *Carl Rogers.* Retrieved March 3, 2005, from http://fates.cns.muskingum.edu/~psych/psycweb/history/rogers.htm
Includes a biography of Carl Rogers and a description of his theory.

LeBon, T. (2001). *Existential psychotherapy.* Retrieved March 3, 2005, from http://members.aol.com/timlebon/extherapy.htm
Presents an overview of existential therapy concepts and links. (Note that this is a private Web site.)

9 Cognitive-Behavioral Theories

CHAPTER OVERVIEW

This chapter provides an overview of cognitive-behavioral theories and approaches to counseling. Highlights of the chapter include

- The art and science of cognitive-behavioral counseling
- An overview of each cognitive-behavioral theory in terms of a theory of personality and a theory of counseling and psychotherapy (that is, of behavior therapy, rational-emotive behavioral therapy, cognitive therapy, transactional analysis, reality therapy, and feminist therapy)
- Trends in brief counseling
- Diversity issues
- Postmodern trends

The Art and Science of Cognitive-Behavioral Counseling

The goal of cognitive-behavioral counseling is to help clients identify how their thoughts and behaviors generate negative emotional consequences and to assist them with the necessary interventions to foster positive growth and development. The art of this theoretical approach is twofold. First, counselors can work *with* clients to help them discover dysfunctional thoughts from the perspective of the *client's* worldview and not from the *counselor's* view of what is rational or functional. Second, counselors can attempt to create a balance in terms of exploring the etiology of dysfunctional thoughts, addressing both intrapsychic forces and postmodern considerations that are reflected contextually between clients and sociocultural and political forces in their environments.

Behavioral counseling (which focuses on overt, observable, and measurable behavior) is founded on principles associated with the science of counseling. This position was articulated by B. F. Skinner (1990) in his ongoing goal of promoting the science of behavioral psychology. Cognitive-behavioral counseling continues the strong tradition in science. In this regard, the cognitive-behavioral school of counseling has the strongest research base of any school of counseling.

New trends in the science of counseling are reflected in postmodern theories such as constructivism and social constructionism. These trends are creating new perspectives for understanding concepts that are fundamental to science (for example, knowledge and reality). From a postmodern perspective, knowledge and reality are relative terms that must be understood contextually. For example, the definition of reality can vary according to culture as reflected in the culture's language and narratives. The science of cognitive-behavioral counseling can draw on qualitative research's discovery method, in which the counselor and client attempt to discover the personal meaning generated from the client's stories.

As noted in Chapter 6, the art and science of counseling recommend using a multi-cultural perspective to conceptualize diversity issues throughout the counseling process. Cognitive-behavior theories can create special concerns regarding diversity. For example, from a postmodern perspective the nature and content of cognitive and behavioral processes vary contextually according to variables such as gender. In this regard, developmental researchers such as Carol Gilligan (1982, 1990) have clearly shown that women think and behave differently with regard to processes such as moral decision making and identity development. The art and science of the cognitive-behavioral theories involve making the necessary modifications to these theories by incorporating multicultural research findings and maintaining a sensitivity to the evolving needs of clients.

Cognitive-Behavioral Theories

Cognitive-behavioral theories emphasize the role of cognition and/or behavior in psychological functioning and well-being. The recent trend toward diversifying and integrating counseling theories has altered the focus of some cognitive-behavioral theories. Theories that originally had a cognitive focus have incorporated behavioral techniques (for example, cognitive therapy and rational-emotive behavior therapy) and behaviorally oriented theories have incorporated cognitive techniques and concepts (for example, behavior therapy and reality therapy).

The integration of theories represents an attempt to develop a more comprehensive approach as opposed to highlighting what is unique about a particular school of counseling. It is hoped that this trend will continue, replacing unnecessary barriers between theories with compatible concepts and procedures.

This chapter provides a description of the following theories: behavior therapy, rational-emotive behavior therapy, cognitive therapy, transactional analysis, reality therapy, and feminist therapy. Table 9.1 provides an overview of these theories in terms of key concepts, the counseling process, and techniques.

Behavior Therapy

Background Information

The historical roots of behavior therapy can be traced to three learning theories: classical conditioning, operant conditioning, and social-learning theory. Classical conditioning evolved from Ivan Pavlov's experiments with dogs. In these experiments, Pavlov (1906)

TABLE 9.1 The Cognitive-Behavioral Theories

Theory	Founder(s)	Key Concepts	The Counseling Process	Techniques
Behavior Therapy	Ivan Pavlov, B. F. Skinner, Albert Bandura, Joseph Wolpe, and Donald Meichenbaum	Incorporation of principles from learning theories; grounding in the scientific method; focus on overt, observable behavior; view of psychopathology primarily in behavioral terms	Attempts to establish clear and precise counseling goals such as modifying maladaptive behavior, strengthening desired behavior, and helping clients learn effective decision making.	Assertive training; systematic desensitization; token economy; cognitive behavior modification; self-control.
Rational-Emotive Behavior Therapy	Albert Ellis	Basic premise that emotional disturbance results from illogical or irrational thought processes	Helps the client learn how to dispute irrational or illogical thoughts.	Cognitive restructuring emotive techniques; shame-attacking exercises; bibliotherapy; behavioral techniques.
Cognitive Therapy	Aaron Beck	The role of cognition in mental health; cognitive vulnerability; cognitive distortions; systematic bias in information processing; cognitive triad of depression; the cognitive model of anxiety	Offers a short-term treatment program for depression, anxiety, and other mental disorders. Its ultimate goal is elimination of systematic bias in thinking.	Cognitive techniques such as decatastrophizing, reattribution, redefining, decentering; behavioral techniques such as skill training, progressive relaxation, behavioral rehearsal, and exposure therapy.
Transactional Analysis (TA)	Eric Berne	The three ego states (parent, adult, child); transactional analysis; games people play; life scripts; the four life positions; strokes	Educative method to teach the client how to use TA concepts to make positive decisions regarding their lives.	Structural analysis; transactional analysis; script analysis; analysis of games.
Reality Therapy	William Glasser	Success and failure identity; emphasis on responsibility; avoidance of labels associated with mental disorders; control theory	Has primary aim to help client develop a success identity through responsible action. Teaches clients how to use control theory to fulfill basic needs and not interfere with the rights of others.	Incorporates an eight-step approach that includes creating a relationship, focusing on current behavior, having the client evaluate behavior, making an action plan, obtaining a commitment, not accepting excuses, not using punishment, and refusing to give up.
Feminist Therapy	Laura Brown, Harriet Lerner, Edna Rawlings, Carolyn Enns, and others	Marginalization; resocialization; androgyny; self-limiting horizons; social advocacy	Involves promoting equality between the sexes and overcoming oppressive forces such as the marginalization of women that can undermine self-actualization tendencies.	Feminist therapists use a wide range of techniques from the various schools of counseling as long as they do not reflect gender bias (e.g., feminist family therapy, cognitive-behavioral therapy, and behavioral therapy such as assertiveness training).

demonstrated that he could condition a dog to salivate at the sound of a bell. This was the first demonstration of what Pavlov called *classical conditioning,* the principle of conditioning people to respond to a stimulus. Pavlov's principles of classical conditioning were later applied to counseling. Joseph Wolpe (1958, 1973) played a key role in this process, integrating the principles of classical conditioning into a systematic desensitization process to treat phobias. This technique continues to be one of the most popular approaches for the treatment of phobias.

B. F. Skinner developed the second major field of learning theory, *operant conditioning.* Skinner (1938, 1953, 1961) proposed that learning cannot occur without some form of reinforcement. He contended that behaviors that are reinforced will tend to be repeated, and those that are not tend to be extinguished. Compared to classical conditioning, operant conditioning is a more active process of learning in that the person must do something to be reinforced.

Skinner developed the principles of operant conditioning in his now-famous Skinner Box experiments, which involved training a rat to press a bar for food. More recently, the principles of operant conditioning have been utilized in programmed learning, self-control, behaviorally oriented discipline procedures, and management of clients in institutions by use of token economies.

The third major learning theory that helped formulate behavior therapy is *social-learning theory.* Along with the various cognitive theories, social-learning theory represents a more recent dimension to the behavioral school. Among the individuals associated with these new trends are Beck (1991), Meichenbaum (1986), Mahoney (1991), and Bandura (1986). In particular, Albert Bandura was instrumental in the integration of cognition into behavior therapy.

Bandura's (1977) early work on social-learning theory focused on how learning occurs from observation, modeling, and imitation. The idea that learning could occur entirely as a function of cognitive control was a direct challenge to the traditional behavioral stimulus-response model (Mahoney & Lyddon, 1988). In addition, Bandura's (1974) "endorsement of an interactional reciprocity between person and environment marked a pivotal shift from exclusive environmental determinism" (Mahoney & Lyddon, 1988, p. 196).

More recently Bandura (1982, 1986, 1989) developed a theory of self-efficacy, which relates to a person's belief in the ability to successfully accomplish a particular task. Perceived self-efficacy plays a central role in mediating constructive behavior change (Bandura, 1986). Bandura's theory contends that self-efficacy can directly influence what activities people will choose to engage in, how much effort they will exert, and how long they will continue when faced with adversity (Johnson, Baker, Kapola, Kiselica, & Thompson, 1989).

Theory of Personality

The theory of personality of behavior therapy is integrated into its theory of counseling and psychotherapy. In this sense assessment and intervention are interrelated. For example, counselors and clients chart changes in behaviors to assess the relative impact of various intervention procedures.

View of Human Nature.   Historically, behaviorists viewed human nature as neutral. A person was not inherently good or bad but would become what the environment dictated. This position was in direct contrast to the humanistic stance, which suggested that people were capable of self-determination. The more recent behavioral point of view recognizes the possibility of self-determined behavior (Bandura, 1986; Meichenbaum, 1986). In this regard, individuals can take an active role in their destiny.

Key Concepts.   Behavior therapy is currently in a state of rapid change and evolution (Wilson, 2005). Rimm and Cunningham (1985) identify common elements that characterize behavior therapy. The following are five of their observations:

1. *Behavior therapy concentrates on overt, observable behavioral processes and cognitions.* Early behaviorists focused on overt behavior. More recently, the cognitive realm is also viewed as an important mediating factor in relation to behavior.
2. *Behavior therapy focuses on the here and now.* Information about past experience is considered important only as it relates to current treatment issues. The focus is on understanding and treating current problems relating to behavior and cognitions.
3. *Maladaptive behaviors are primarily the result of learning.* Models of learning (operant, classical, and social-learning theories) can be used to understand the etiology of maladaptive behavior. Learning principles can therefore be used to change maladaptive behavior.
4. *Well-defined, concrete goals are used.* Goals are stated in observable, measurable terms whenever possible.
5. *Behavior therapy is committed to the scientific method.* Behavior therapy utilizes the principles of scientific method to evaluate techniques and procedures. Assessment and treatment are viewed as part of the same process, creating a built-in mechanism for research and accountability.

Theory of Counseling and Psychotherapy

The Counseling Process.   The counselor utilizes an active and directive approach, which often incorporates problem-solving strategies (Wilson, 2005). The client is also expected to take an active role in the counseling process in terms of assessment by engaging in processes such as self-monitoring and treatment by acquiring new skills and behaviors through work and practice.

A misconception regarding behavior therapists is that they view a positive counseling relationship as unimportant to the counseling process (Wilson, 2005). Brady (1980) notes, however, that the nature of the counseling relationship can have a direct bearing on the outcome of behavior therapy. In addition, Swan and MacDonald (1978) have found that behavior therapists reported that relationship-building procedures are among the most frequently used.

Behavior therapy has concrete, specific goals that include acquiring necessary behaviors and coping skills and overcoming self-defeating cognitive processes. When possible, clients assume primary responsibility for determining treatment goals. The therapist's role and function are therefore directed at how to accomplish goals in therapy rather than focusing on which goals to work on (Wilson, 2005).

Techniques. Most behavior therapy procedures are short-term in duration, although some may extend as long as 25 to 50 sessions (Wilson, 2005). Behavior therapists use a wide variety of techniques and procedures: cognitive behavior modification, self-management and self-control, self-efficacy, participant modeling, assertiveness training, systematic desensitization, and token economy.

Cognitive Behavior Modification. Donald Meichenbaum's (1986) cognitive behavior modification has several useful strategies, such as self-instructional therapy and stress-inoculation training. Self-instructional therapy is a form of self-control therapy in which clients learn to use tools to take control of their lives. Behavior change occurs "through a sequence of mediating processes involving the interaction of inner speech, cognitive structures, and behaviors, and their resultant outcomes" (Meichenbaum, 1977, p. 218).

This theory suggests that people have a set of beliefs or cognitive structures that influence how they react to events in terms of an inner speech or self-talk. To a large degree, cognitive structures and inner speech determine how people behave. The focus of therapy is on restructuring faulty cognitive structures, altering inner speech so that it triggers coping behaviors, and if necessary using behavior therapy to teach coping responses.

Stress-inoculation training is another useful approach that utilizes a number of cognitive-behavioral techniques such as "cognitive restructuring, problem-solving, relaxation training, behavioral and imaginal rehearsal, self-monitoring, self-reinforcement, and efforts at environmental change" (Meichenbaum, 1985, p. 21). It can be used to treat different disorders but is especially useful to treat anxiety. The procedure focuses on helping clients learn coping mechanisms that they can use to "inoculate" or protect themselves against stress-related reactions. A major premise of this approach is that clients can be taught to cope with stressful situations and enhance their performance by modifying their self-statements. Stress-inoculation training is comprehensive, attempting to go beyond symptom relief and teach skills that can be useful to prevent problems in the future, including relapse. The actual process of implementing stress inoculation typically involves three stages: conceptualization, skill acquisition and rehearsal, and application and follow-through.

Self-Management and Self-Control. Kanfer and Goldstein (1986), Bandura (1986), and Meichenbaum (1986) are associated with self-management and self-control procedures, which are directed at helping clients become their own agents for behavior change (Gintner & Poret, 1987). In this process, the counselor provides support and expertise in terms of behavioral management. The client assumes responsibility for implementing and carrying out the program (Kanfer & Goldstein, 1986).

A wide range of skills can be used to promote self-management and self-control. For example, Kanfer and Goldstein (1986) identify skills in (a) self-monitoring, (b) establishing rules of conduct by contracting, (c) obtaining environmental support, (d) self-evaluating, and (e) generating reinforcing consequences for behaviors that promote the goals of self-control. Wilson (2005) describes other self-control skills such as progressive relaxation to reduce stress; biofeedback to treat psychophysiological disorders; and self-instructional training for control of anger, impulsivity, and other coping problems.

Albert Bandura

Self-Efficacy.   As noted earlier, self-efficacy is a theory developed primarily by Bandura (1982, 1986, 1989) that relates to a person's belief in his or her ability to accomplish a particular task. Self-efficacy is not a behavioral technique. It can be better viewed as a concept that should be considered when implementing a technique. Rimm and Cunningham (1985) note that treatments that foster the greatest change in self-efficacy should be the most effective. They suggest that treatment efficacy can be increased by promoting methods that foster efficacy information to clients. In this regard, Bandura, Reese, and Adams (1982) note that efficacy information can be transferred to clients by (a) actual performance, which is the most powerful information source; (b) vicarious learning or modeling; (c) verbal persuasion; and (d) psychological arousal.

Self-efficacy theory has stimulated a proliferation of research activity. It has been shown to predict many behaviors, such as depression (Davis-Berman, 1988), cessation after treatment (Gooding & Glasgow, 1985; Nicki, Remington, & MacDonald, 1984), recovery from heart attacks (Bandura, 1982), sports performance (Lee, 1982; McAuley, 1985), and success in weight-reduction programs (Weinberg, Hughes, Critelli, England, & Jackson, 1984). Based on a review of the literature on self-efficacy, Johnson et al. (1989) conclude that "across varied behavioral domains, self-efficacy has predicted differences in the degree to which people choose, present, and succeed in performing targeted behaviors" (p. 206).

Participant Modeling.   Participant modeling is based on Bandura's (1977, 1986, 1989) social-learning theory, which emphasizes the role of observation and imitation in learning. It is used primarily to treat phobias and fears (Rimm & Cunningham, 1985). Participant modeling involves two stages: observation and participation. During the observation stage, the client observes a model engaged in the feared behavior (for example, petting a dog). Research suggests that efficacy increases when the model is similar to the client in terms of age and gender (Raskin & Israel, 1981) and the manner in which the model approaches the feared task (Meichenbaum, 1972). The second stage involves the client participating or engaging in the feared behavior. During this process, the counselor guides the client through a series of exercises relating to the feared task (Rimm & Cunningham, 1985).

Assertiveness Training.   Assertiveness training can be used for clients who find it difficult to stand up for their rights or who are unable to express their feelings in a constructive manner (Wilson, 2005). Rimm and Cunningham (1985) describe the following steps involved in assertiveness training. First, the therapist and client determine whether there is a need for assertiveness training. Second, the therapist describes how increased assertiveness can be beneficial. The third step is the most important and involves a process of behavioral rehearsal. During behavioral rehearsal, the therapist models an assertive behavior, then asks the client to "rehearse" the assertive behavior, and finally provides feedback and appropriate reinforcement.

Systematic Desensitization.   Systematic desensitization is a technique developed by Wolpe (1958, 1973) to treat problems resulting from classical conditioning, such as phobias. It has also been used to treat a variety of other maladaptive behaviors, including excessive fears about issues such as death, injury, and sex (Kazdin, 1978).

The following steps can be used to implement this technique:

1. *Teach deep relaxation.* Systematic desensitization utilizes the principle of counterconditioning by introducing a relaxation response to replace the previously conditioned adverse response. It is based on the assumption that a person cannot be anxious and relaxed at the same time. The client is therefore taught to experience a state of deep relaxation when the therapist describes a relaxing scene.
2. *Develop a hierarchy.* The therapist and client develop a hierarchy of situations that elicit a fear response. The situation that elicits the lowest level of anxiety is the first item in the hierarchy, and the one that elicits the highest level of anxiety is last. It is important that the statements are specific enough that the client will be able to visualize the situation. An example is, "I walked up a flight of stairs to the fourth floor and looked out the window."
3. *Proceed through the hierarchy.* The therapist helps the client enter into a state of deep relaxation. The therapist then asks the client to imagine the first item in the hierarchy. By introducing a relaxation response to a situation that previously elicited a fear response, the therapist helps the client become desensitized by the counterconditioning process.
4. *Address the fear in vivo.* This step involves desensitizing the client to *in-vivo* or real-life situations associated with the fears. For example, if the client has a snake phobia, an item on the hierarchy may be to imagine looking at a snake. During the *in-vivo* experience, the client will be asked to look at a real snake.
5. *Follow up and evaluate.* The final step is to evaluate the client's success in dealing with the fear response in a variety of situations over an extended period of time.

Token Economy.   Ayllon and Azrin (1968) developed the technique of *token economy* to teach psychiatric patients to become more responsible. It has been used primarily in hospitals, residential settings, and schools. The technique is based on the principles of operant conditioning and involves giving tokens to reinforce a desired behavior such as cleaning one's room. After collecting enough tokens, clients can exchange them for goods or privileges such as being able to watch TV. To increase intrinsic motivation, the tokens must be gradually eliminated and replaced by social reinforcers such as encouragement. This will enable clients to maintain newly acquired behaviors after they leave the treatment setting.

Summary and Evaluation

Behavior therapy focuses on overt behavior. The counseling process emphasizes the importance of establishing clear goals stated in behavioral terms. Progress in therapy is indicated when there is a change or modification in behavior. Treatment and assessment are seen as part of the same process, creating a built-in mechanism for research and accountability.

Emmelkamp (1994) summarizes the research on behavior therapy and concludes that it has been shown to be effective to treat a number of mental disorders and client concerns such as

- Anxiety disorders such as phobias, posttraumatic stress disorder, generalized anxiety, and aggressive-compulsive disorder
- Depression (behavioral counseling is especially effective when used in conjunction with cognitive approaches such as cognitive therapy)
- Alcoholism (including treatment of controlled drinking)
- Sexual disorders (behavioral counseling is quite useful in treating sexual dysfunctions such as premature ejaculation and missed orgasm but not so effective in treating paraphilias such as exhibitionism and pedophilia)

Some weaknesses are associated with the behavioral approach. Behavior therapy tends to disregard the importance of feelings and emotions in the counseling process. It also tends to ignore historical factors that can contribute to a client's problem and minimize the use of insight in the counseling process.

Rational-Emotive Behavior Therapy (REBT)

Background Information

Albert Ellis (b. 1913) received M.A. and Ph.D. degrees in clinical psychology from Columbia University and went on to practice in the areas of marriage, family, and sex therapy. In the 1950s, Ellis initially developed his theory of counseling, which he called *rational therapy.*

In 1962, Ellis published *Reason and Emotion in Psychotherapy,* which laid the foundation for his revised theory, which he called *rational emotive therapy (RET).* Ellis changed the name of his theory in 1993 to *rational-emotive behavior therapy (REBT)* to acknowledge the interrelationship between thoughts, feelings, and behaviors in human functioning (Ellis, 1993, 2005).

Ellis is a very prolific writer, an active clinician, and the Executive Director of his institute for REBT since 1960. The following *Personal Note* provides additional information about his interests and professional activities.

A Personal Note

I had the privilege of interviewing Albert Ellis when he was 71 years old, and I found him to be very energetic (Nystul, 1985a). He noted that his typical daily schedule involves providing individual and group counseling and psychotherapy from 9:30 A.M. until 11:30 P.M. Ellis's other activities include directing his institute, supervising numerous therapists, making many presentations, conducting workshops, and writing approximately 20 articles and one or two books each year.

Although Ellis had already written more than 45 books and 500 articles, he had no intention of retiring. At the end of our interview, he said:

All this activity is infinitely more enjoyable to me than would be lying on a beach, sightseeing, or reading romantic novels. I hope that my good health continues, in spite of the diabetes that I have had for the last 30 years, and that I shall die in the saddle a few decades from now.

Many years ago, I reluctantly came to the conclusion that when I die I shall still have at least 100 books unwritten and that is a frustration I had better realistically accept. I would prefer to live forever and to keep exploring the realm of human disturbance and potential realms to happiness and self-fulfillment for eons to come, but no such luck! One of these days in the not-too-distant future, I shall run down. Too damned bad! But hardly awful and terrible. (Nystul, 1985a, p. 254)

Theory of Personality

The theory of personality for REBT emphasizes the role of cognitions (and to some degree behaviors) on emotions. REBT contends that people can be best understood in terms of the nature of their self-talk (internal cognitive dialogue).

View of Human Nature.   Ellis (1996, 2005) believes that humans have a potential to be rational or irrational—to be self-preserving or self-destructive. He contends that people perceive, think, emote, and behave simultaneously. Thus, to understand self-defeating conduct, it is necessary to understand the interrelationship between thinking, feeling, and behavior (Ellis, 1996, 2005).

Key Concepts.   The major concepts in REBT (Ellis, 1962, 1996, 2005) relate to the role of cognition and how irrational thoughts can create self-defeating, emotionally disturbing outcomes.

The Role of Cognition.   The basic premise of REBT is that emotional disturbance results primarily from cognitive processes that are fundamentally irrational or illogical in nature (Ellis, 2005). Ellis and Harper (1975) define *rational* as anything that promotes happiness and survival for the individual and *irrational* as anything that inhibits personal happiness and survival.

One way to identify illogical or irrational thought processes is to look for statements that contain the unconditional *should* or the absolutistic *must* or *ought* (Ellis, 2005; Ellis & Harper, 1975). Examples of these self-defeating statements are

- "I should get all A's, and if I don't, I'm stupid."

Albert Ellis

- "I ought to know better when it comes to choosing a boyfriend. The ones I pick are all duds."
- "I must do well at my job, and if I don't, I'm no good."

Ellis (1977, 2005) notes that not all statements of irrational beliefs contain shoulds, oughts, and musts. According to Ellis, irrational thoughts can also be in the form of other self-defeating self-statements such as

- *Self-damnation:* "I am a worthless good-for-nothing."
- *I-can't-stand-it-itis:* "I can't stand the thought of losing my girlfriend."
- *Awfulizing:* "I would never want to bring a child into this insane and awful world."

The A-B-C-D-E Acronym.   In part, REBT's popularity is due to its simplicity. The basic procedures associated with REBT can be taught to the client by using the A-B-C-D-E acronym. The letter "A" in the acronym stands for the activating event. This can be whatever the client may be reacting to, such as a recent phone conversation or a report that was received by a supervisor. "B" represents the client's belief system or cognitive reaction to the activating event. "C" is the emotional consequence that the client is experiencing, such as feeling anxious or depressed. "D" suggests that the client learn to dispute self-defeating thought processes, and "E" is the effect of the disputing process.

Ellis (1962, 2005) contends that it is not "A" that causes a serious emotional reaction ("C"). For "C" to occur, a self-defeating thought process must occur at "B." The client is therefore taught how to dispute self-defeating processes ("D") to generate a positive effect ("E").

Ellis (1962, 1996, 2005) also suggests that self-defeating cognitive reactions follow a predictable pattern. People usually start with a sane or rational reaction to the activating event. Next, they tend to engage in self-talk that is illogical or irrational. Finally, they grossly overreact to the situation, making it seem like a catastrophe.

It is important to note that for REBT to be effective, counselors must be careful to not just focus on the client's sentences and self-statements. They should also help clients explore and dispute self-defeating "meanings, evaluations, images, and other forms of cognitions" (Ellis, 1986, p. 648). From this perspective, Ellis contends that REBT has always been consistent with postmodern trends, which recognize the multiple voices reflected in social forces such as culture, language, and narratives (Ivey, 1996). The following *Personal Note* provides an illustration of REBT.

Theory of Counseling and Psychotherapy

The Counseling Process.   The primary goal of REBT is restructuring the client's self-defeating cognitions and helping the client acquire a more realistic philosophy of life (Ellis, 2005). The actual process of therapy is educational and confrontational in nature. The therapist teaches the client how to dispute irrational thoughts and also confronts and even

A Personal Note

Tim was a 30-year-old, self-referred male who came to a mental health clinic complaining of anxiety and depression and threatening suicide. Tim told me he had recently started a new job as an accountant for a firm. Two days earlier, his boss had returned a report he had written with several suggestions and one or two indications of possible errors in his statistics. His boss had asked him to look over the suggestions and revise the report accordingly. Tim told me all he could think about since then was the report and how his boss "*must* be out to get me."

I decided to use REBT, so I provided Tim with an overview of the A-B-C-D-E acronym. Together, we decided that the activating event "A" was the boss returning the report; "B" was his cognitive reaction to "A" (that is, "My boss must be out to get me"); and "C" represented his feelings of being anxious, depressed, and suicidal. Since REBT focuses on cognition, we then explored his cognitive reactions to "A." Tim's thought process followed the predictable pattern described earlier. He started with a sane reaction, "It looks like there are some mistakes here." He then began to think irrationally and said things like, "He *must* be out to get me. I know he has decided he made a mistake in hiring me and is looking for a way to let me go." Finally, his thoughts became catastrophic as he concluded, "It's just a matter of time until he fires me, and I'll never get another job. I guess there is just no hope for me."

We also explored how sociocultural forces could influence the personal meanings, evaluation,

and images associated with his story. In this regard, he mentioned that he could be overreacting to this situation, owing to repeated parental messages of "no matter what, you have to do well at work."

When I asked Tim how he felt when he said these things to himself, he replied, "Terrible." He began to realize that his thoughts could cause an intense emotional reaction at "C." Tim and I then attempted to restructure his cognitive reactions. We disrupted "D," his irrational reactions with rational reactions. For example, he changed "My boss *must* be out to get me" to "My boss seems to have some concerns about my report." We also co-constructed new narratives that were more realistic in terms of how to conceptualize work in terms of success and failure.

By the end of our first counseling session, Tim no longer had intense feelings of being anxious, depressed, or suicidal. He said he had no idea how much power thoughts could have on emotions, and he was glad he had a tool he could use to help control his emotional reactions. Tim also commented that he still felt somewhat uncomfortable about his relationship with his boss. He wanted to know how his boss thought he was doing in his job. Tim agreed to ask his boss this question as a homework assignment. At the start of our next session, Tim smiled and said, "I guess I caused myself a lot of needless worry. My boss said he thought I was doing just fine, and he really appreciated me revising my report." Counseling was terminated shortly thereafter.

attacks, if necessary, the client's self-defeating belief system. Once clients become aware of their negative self-talk, they can create a cognitive reaction that generates a more positive emotional consequence.

In terms of the counseling relationship, Ellis (2005) does not believe that a warm relationship is a necessary or sufficient condition for personality change. He believes the therapist must fully accept clients but must also point out discrepancies in their behavior when necessary (Ellis, 1996, 2005).

Techniques.   The techniques that Ellis (1962, 1996, 2005) identifies for therapists to utilize in REBT include cognitive, emotive, and behavioral techniques.

Cognitive Techniques.   To a large degree, REBT focuses on helping clients overcome self-defeating cognitions. Cognitive restructuring is the main technique used in REBT. It involves restructuring irrational and illogical cognitions through the A-B-C-D-E acronym. Other cognitive methods utilized in REBT include techniques such as *reframing,* which involves redefining (or reframing) a negative situation into a more positive perspective, and *referenting,* which involves helping clients conceptualize problems in a holistic rather than fragmented perspective (Livneh & Wright, 1999). Bibliotherapy is also used in REBT to help clients learn how to apply REBT in everyday life.

Emotive Techniques.   Emotive (or emotive-evocative) techniques focus on the client's affect or emotional domain. These techniques can play a major role in helping clients learn how to accept themselves (Corey, 2005). For example, humor can be used to help clients put their situation in perspective and stop putting themselves down. Other emotive techniques include the use of imagery to create more positive emotional patterns (for example, imagining what it would feel like to overcome fear) and shame-attacking exercises, in which clients learn to overcome shame by becoming less concerned about how they are perceived by others.

Behavioral Techniques.   REBT utilizes the full range of behavioral techniques to help clients achieve their goals. Examples of behavioral techniques include the use of operant conditioning (for example, behavior modification), assertiveness training, systematic desensitization, relaxation therapy, and self-management (including self-monitoring). Homework assignments play an integral role in the application of behavioral techniques, whereby clients try out and practice what they learn in counseling in their day-to-day activities.

Summary and Evaluation

Weinrach (1995) provides a literature review on REBT and concludes that there is some encouraging support for the efficacy of REBT. For example, Lyons and Woods (1991) conducted a meta-analysis of 70 REBT studies that showed REBT to be significantly superior to no treatment and having similar efficacy to other approaches such as cognitive behavior modification and cognitive therapy.

REBT is an educationally oriented approach that attempts to teach a client how to overcome self-defeating cognitive reactions. One of the strengths of REBT is its simplicity.

It can be taught to the client in terms as simple as the A-B-C-D-E acronym. In time, clients can learn to use the tools necessary to become their own self-therapists and gain control over their mental health.

The major weakness of REBT may be to overemphasize the role of cognition in the etiology of mental disorders and emotional disturbances. In addition, it may be an oversimplified approach in terms of what is required to effectively restructure cognition. For many clients, much more may be required than simply changing irrational statements to rational statements. REBT also avoids exploring other factors such as traumatic early-life experiences, which could represent important treatment considerations.

Cognitive Therapy

Background Information

During the mid-1950s Aaron Beck (b. 1921) developed a cognitive-oriented approach to treat mental disorders, rejecting his early training in psychoanalysis. Beck is best known for his work on depression (Beck, 1987, 1991; Beck, Rush, Shaw, & Emery, 1979) and anxiety (Beck & Emery, 1985). Beck's early work on depression resulted in the development of the Beck Depression Inventory, which is widely used as a clinical and research instrument.

Theory of Personality

The theory of personality for cognitive therapy emphasizes the role of cognitive processes on the development of mental disorders such as depression and anxiety. Cognitive therapy contends that the etiology of many mental disorders can be directly traced to cognitive dysfunctions such as misinterpreting environmental cues (for example, "My friend did not show up, so he must not like me").

View of Human Nature.   Beck contends that people are a product of the interaction of innate, biological, developmental, and environmental factors (Beck & Weishaar, 2005). He also suggests that people have the capacity for self-determination by emphasizing the role of cognition in mental health.

Key Concepts.   Beck and Weishaar (2005) describe the following key concepts associated with cognitive therapy.

The Role of Cognition in Mental Health.   Emotions and behaviors are determined primarily by how a person perceives, interprets, and assigns meanings to events.

Cognitive Vulnerability.   Personality structures have vulnerabilities that predispose them to psychological distress. These vulnerabilities are characterized by *schemata,* which are fundamental beliefs and assumptions that develop early in life and are reinforced by learning situations throughout life. They create beliefs, values, and attitudes about oneself, others, and the world. A schema can be functional or dysfunctional. Examples of statements indicating dysfunctional schemes of a borderline personality are: "There is something

Aaron Beck

fundamentally wrong with me" and "People should support me and should not criticize, abandon, disagree with, or misunderstand me and my feelings" (Beck & Weishaar, 1989, p. 294). A dysfunctional schema can contribute to cognitive distortions, systematic bias in information processing, and other problems associated with emotional distress.

Cognitive Distortions.   A cognitive distortion is a systematic distortion in reasoning that results in psychological distress. Cognitive distortions identified by Beck and Weishaar (2005) include the following:

- *Arbitrary inference,* which involves making a conclusion that has no supportive evidence or contradicts existing evidence.
- *Selective abstraction,* which occurs when taking information out of context or ignoring other information.
- *Overgeneralization,* which results when making a general rule on the basis of one or more isolated incidents and then applying it to unrelated situations.
- *Magnification and minimization,* which involves viewing something out of proportion, as either less or more significant than it actually is.
- *Personalization,* which occurs when attributing external events to oneself without evidence of a causal connection.
- *Dichotomous thinking,* which involves conceptualizing an experience in either-or terms, such as seeing it as good or bad.

Systematic Bias in Information Processing.   Mental disorders are characterized by a bias in information processing. Typically, the bias begins when a person "misreads" external events, thereby creating dysfunctional responses. For instance, someone who suffers from claustrophobia may "misread" taking an elevator as a very dangerous situation. The systematic bias then tends to shift to internal messages such as physiological responses. In this example, the person may "misread" feelings of tension and apprehension as an impending anxiety attack.

Cognitive Triad of Depression. The cognitive triad is characterized by a negative view of the self, the world, and the future. Psychological and physical symptoms of depression can evolve from the cognitive triad. Beck and Weishaar (2005) cite several examples of this phenomenon. A feeling of being unable to cope or control events can lead to a paralysis of will. Negative expectations about life can contribute to physical symptoms of depression, such as low energy, fatigue, and inertia.

Cognitive Model of Anxiety. Anxiety results when a person's information processing is faulty, resulting in perceptions of danger when no danger exists. People with this anxiety have difficulty correcting their misconception by recognizing safety cues or other evidence. The cognition of anxious individuals is characterized by themes of danger and the likelihood of harm.

Theory of Counseling and Psychotherapy

The Counseling Process. Beck sums up the major thrust of cognitive therapy in an interview by Weinrach (1988):

> Cognitive therapy is a short-term treatment that was developed primarily for the treatment of depression and anxiety. It is now being used for personality disorders, eating disorders, and some of the other types of problems that have been more refractory to psychotherapy in the past. It is based on a view of psychopathology that stipulates that people's excessive affect and dysfunctional behavior is due to excessive or inappropriate ways of interpreting their experiences. It is also based on the notion that people who are depressed or anxious have in some way a distorted image of themselves and their external situation. (p. 160)

Beck and Weishaar (2005) provide information relevant to the counseling process, which is incorporated into the following overview. The counselor initially attempts to promote a positive relationship by establishing the core conditions identified by Rogers: warmth, accurate empathy, and genuineness. The client is then encouraged to take an active role in the counseling process in setting goals, recounting cognitive and behavioral reactions to problem situations, and doing homework assignments.

The counselor functions as a guide in the counseling process by helping the client understand the role of cognition in emotions and behaviors. The counselor also acts as a catalyst by promoting corrective experiences that result in necessary cognitive restructuring and skill acquisition. In this process, counselors avoid the role of passive expert. They instead engage in a process of collaboration with the client with the ultimate goal of eliminating systematic biases in thinking. In addition, counselors do not tell the client that a particular belief is irrational or wrong. Instead, they explore with the client the meaning, function, usefulness, and consequences associated with the belief. The client then decides whether to retain, modify, or reject a belief.

Techniques. Beck and Weishaar (2005) describe the following techniques associated with cognitive therapy.

Decatastrophizing. This process is also known as the *what-if* technique and involves preparing clients for feared consequences by identifying problem-solving strategies.

Reattribution Technique. This technique encourages challenging thoughts and assumptions by exploring other possible causes of events.

Redefining. Redefining helps mobilize clients who feel they have no control over a problem by rephrasing the problem in a manner that promotes action. For instance, a student could change "I'm not a good student" to "I'm going to study more."

Decentering. This technique involves having the client make observations to obtain a more realistic understanding of other people's reactions. It can alleviate anxiety by helping clients realize that they are not the center of attention.

Behavioral Techniques. Cognitive therapy utilizes a wide range of behavioral techniques to help clients acquire necessary skills (for example, skill training), relax (for example, progressive relaxation), prepare for difficult situations (for example, behavioral rehearsal), and expose themselves to feared situations (for example, exposure therapy).

Summary and Evaluation

Cognitive therapy has become an increasingly popular form of counseling. It has primarily been a short-term treatment for depression. More recently, cognitive therapy has been used to effectively treat a variety of disorders, such as anxiety (Chambless & Gillis, 1993), eating disorders (Wilson & Fairburn, 1993), and substance abuse (Beck, Wright, Newman, & Liese, 1993).

Its popularity is due in part to the massive research efforts that have evaluated the efficacy of cognitive therapy in the treatment of depression. Beck and Weishaar (2005) conducted a literature review that showed that cognitive therapy is superior to drug therapy (Blackburn, Bishop, Glen, Whalley, & Christie, 1981; Hollon et al., 1992; Maldonado, 1982) or equal to drug therapy (Blackburn, Eunson, & Bishop, 1986; Hollon, Evans, & DeRubeis, 1983; Murphy, Simons, Wetzel, Lustman, 1983; Simons, Murphy, Levine, & Wetzel, 1986). Studies indicate that a combination of cognitive therapy and antidepressant medication is the most effective treatment for depression (Blackburn et al., 1981; Blackburn et al., 1986; Maldonado, 1982; Teasdale, Fennell, Hibbert, & Amies, 1984). Cognitive therapy also appears to have stronger long-term effects than drug therapy (Blackburn et al., 1986; Hollon et al., 1983; Kovacs, Rush, Beck, & Hollon, 1981; Maldonado, 1982).

Dobson (1989) conducted a meta-analysis of the efficacy of cognitive therapy for the treatment of depression. He analyzed 28 studies that used the Beck Depression Inventory as the outcome measure. Results of Dobson's (1989) study indicate that cognitive therapy clients do better than 98 percent of control subjects, 70 percent of drug-therapy clients, and 70 percent of other psychotherapy clients. These results were consistent with the results of an earlier meta-analysis study by Nietzel, Russell, Hemmings, and Gretter (1987).

Hollon and Beck (1994) caution that the literature that suggests that cognitive therapy is superior to drug therapy may be oversimplified and prone to methodological problems. Their extensive review of the literature cast doubts on the claims that cognitive therapy is superior to drug therapy in the treatment of depression. Methodological problems include a lack of placebo controls to allow for adequate comparisons between treatment groups. In addition, severity of symptomology may play an important role in the efficacy of cognitive therapy as a treatment of depression. In this regard, there is some indication that cognitive therapy may be less effective than drug therapy with individuals who have severe depression and more effective than drug therapy with individuals with mild or moderate depression (see the National Institute of Mental Health's Treatment of Depression Collaborative Research Program, Elkin et al., 1989).

There is some indication in the research that the effectiveness of cognitive therapy depends to some degree on the personal characteristics of the client. Prochaska and Norcross (2002) provide a review of this literature and conclude that clients who were depressed and tended to externalize did better in cognitive therapy, whereas clients who were depressed and internalized tended to do better in supportive/self-directed counseling. In addition, clients who rated low on defensiveness seemed to do better in cognitive therapy than those who rated high in defensiveness.

Transactional Analysis (TA)

Background Information

Eric Berne (1910–1970) is the originator of transactional analysis (TA). He received an M.D. degree from McGill University in Montreal in 1935 and then completed psychiatry training at Yale University.

TA is unique in its effort to avoid psychological jargon. Instead, the language of TA is easy to understand, using such terms as parent, adult, child, strokes, games, rackets, decisions, and redecisions. Its use of clear, simple language helped TA become attractive not only as a form of therapy but also as a self-help approach. As evidence of its popularity, two major books on the topic were international best sellers at various times: *Games People Play* (Berne, 1964) and *I'm OK—You're OK* (Harris, 1967).

More recently, TA has been cited as an example of an emerging school of counseling that emphasizes the role of interpersonal relationships in psychological functioning (Prochaska & Norcross, 2002). In this regard, TA can be considered one of the first major theories of counseling that focuses on interpersonal relations (Adlerian psychology also stresses the importance of the interpersonal perspective). The interpersonal orientation is depicted in the name of the theory (that is, transactional analysis, suggesting that people can learn to understand and enhance the transactions and communication patterns between people).

TA's interpersonal focus shares commonalties with another interpersonally oriented theory of counseling, interpersonal psychotherapy, which is gaining recognition as an important new counseling approach (Prochaska & Norcross, 2002). Interpersonal psychotherapy is based primarily on the work of Harry Stack Sullivan (1968) and his interpersonal school of psychoanalysis. Sullivan posited a different version of Freud's theory that emphasizes social relations over drives for sex and aggression as being primarily responsible for mental health and well-being. Adolph Meyer (1957) and individuals associated with the family therapy movement, such as John Bowlby (1973, 1988a) and his work on attachment, also contributed to the early development of interpersonal psychotherapy. Together they provide additional information on how environmental factors (such as psychosocial stressors) and family interaction patterns can influence psychological functioning.

Several other individuals have gone on to develop interpersonal psychotherapy as a short-term, present-centered approach to treat depression (e.g., Klerman & Weissman, 1993). Teyber (2000) summarizes the basic premises in interpersonal psychotherapy as follows:

1. Problems are conceptualized from an interpersonal perspective.
2. Familial interaction patterns are the best means of understanding oneself and others.
3. The counselor-client relationship can be used to work through relationship issues.

Interpersonal psychotherapy appears to offer much promise as an emerging theory of counseling. A more detailed description of this approach is beyond the scope of this text. For additional information and an excellent overview of interpersonal psychotherapy, see Teyber's *Interpersonal Process in Psychotherapy* (2000).

Theory of Personality

TA provides a rich tapestry of concepts that can be used to generate a theory of personality. TA concepts that can be used to provide an in-depth understanding of personality dynamics include *stroking, the games people play,* and *the four life positions.*

View of Human Nature.   Berne (1961, 1964) believes that people have the capacity to determine their own destiny. He contends that few people acquire the necessary self-awareness to become autonomous. Berne (1961) also stresses the importance of early-life experiences in contributing to personality development. His theory suggests that people develop scripts that are played throughout life. These scripts are derived from parental messages and other sources such as fairy tales and literature.

Key Concepts.   Berne (1961, 1964), Dusay and Dusay (1989), and Prochaska and Norcross (2002) provide an overview of the key concepts associated with TA.

The Interpersonal Perspective.   As noted earlier, TA is considered one the first major theories of counseling that emphasizes the role of interpersonal functioning in mental health. Many of the key concepts in TA (such as transactional analysis and analysis of games) are directed at understanding and enhancing interpersonal relations.

Prochaska and Norcross (2002) note that in TA, psychopathology is understood as a manifestation of intrapersonal (within the individual) and interpersonal (between people) forces. Regardless of the origins of a psychological disorder, it is always interpersonal in terms of its expression (Prochaska & Norcross, 2002). TA is therefore usually conducted in group counseling to encourage interpersonal expression. In this format, clients can gain valuable insights into their problems and learn how to use TA techniques and other counseling strategies to overcome their difficulties (Prochaska & Norcross, 2002).

Ego States.   Berne identified the three ego states of the parent, adult, and child. The *parent ego state* represents the person's morals and values and can be either critical or nurturing. The critical parent attempts to find fault, whereas the nurturing parent is supportive and promotes growth. The *adult ego state* is the rational-thinking dimension. It is devoid of feelings and acts as a mediator between the child and parent ego states. The *child ego state* is the uninhibited side of the personality, characterized by a variety of emotions such as fear, happiness, and excitement. The child ego state has two dimensions: the free child and the adapted child. The *free child* is uninhibited and playful, whereas the *adapted child* is rebellious and conforming.

An egogram can be used to assess the relative strengths and weaknesses of the various ego states. The egogram "reflects the type of person one is, one's probable types of problems, and the strengths and weaknesses of the personality" (Dusay & Dusay, 1989, p. 420). Interpreting an egogram is a complex process that requires specialized training. Clinicians are especially interested in ego states that are particularly high or low relative to the client's other ego states. For example, low critical parent (CP) suggests problems with exploitation; low nurturing parent (NP) implies loneliness; low adult (A) indicates difficulty concentrating; low free child (FC) suggests a lack of zest for life; and low adapted child (AC) indicates a person who is rigid and difficult to get along with (Dusay & Dusay, 1989). A healthy egogram is indicated when there is relative balance between the strength of the ego states, as illustrated in Figure 9.1.

Transactional Analysis.   The concept of transactional analysis involves analyzing the transactions between people. It entails assessing the three ego states of parent, adult, and child of each person to determine whether the transactions between the people are complementary, crossed, or ulterior.

Complementary transactions occur when each person receives a message from the other person's ego state that seems appropriate and expected. Figure 9.2 provides three examples of complementary transactions. In each example, both people are sending and receiving messages as expected.

Crossed transactions occur when one or more of the individuals receives a message from the other person's ego state that does not seem appropriate or expected. Figure 9.3 illustrates two examples of crossed transactions.

Ulterior transactions occur when a person's communication is complex and confusing. In these transactions, a person sends an overt message from one ego state and a covert

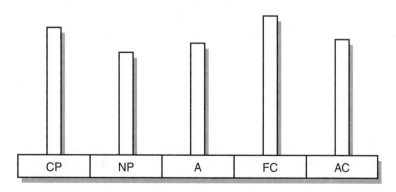

FIGURE 9.1   An Egogram with Relative Balance

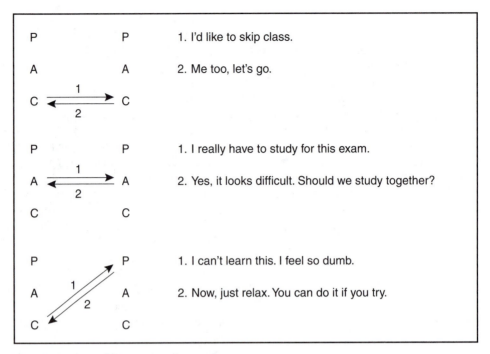

FIGURE 9.2   Complementary Transactions

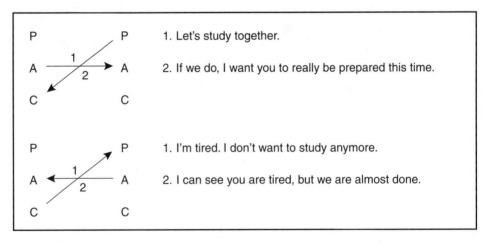

FIGURE 9.3   Crossed Transactions

ulterior message from another ego state. The ulterior message can be communicated verbally, nonverbally via body language, or by tone of voice. Figure 9.4 gives examples of each possibility.

Games People Play.   Berne (1964) defined *games* as "an ongoing series of complementary ulterior transactions progressing to a well-defined, predictable outcome" (p. 48). These

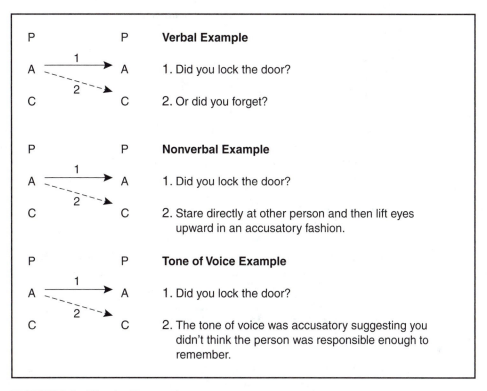

FIGURE 9.4   Ulterior Transactions

Note: Solid lines indicate overt messages; dotted lines indicate covert messages.

games are usually played at an unconscious level, with the people not aware they are playing a particular game. Some of the different games people can play are "Now I've got you, you SOB" and "Kick me."

Although game playing results in bad feelings for both players, it also offers payoffs for the participants (Dusay & Dusay, 1989). The following example illustrates what might occur during the game of "Kick me."

Mary fears dating because she believes things will never work out. She reluctantly accepts a date with John, whom she finds attractive. Within the first 10 minutes of the date, she criticizes John's hair style and then complains about the movie they are going to see. After the movie, John gets tired of Mary's insults and takes her home. As he pulls up to her house, he proceeds to tell her off ("kicks her"), saying what an ungrateful person she is.

Although Mary initially feels hurt by John's comments, she will receive a payoff from her game. As she goes into the house, she can ask herself, "Why do I always get rejected? Things never work out. I guess dating isn't for me." The game therefore provides Mary with the payoff of having an excuse to avoid dating in the future. John also receives a payoff in that her rudeness made him feel free to "kick her."

The Four Life Positions.   Berne (1961) says that in developing life scripts, people put themselves in the role of being "OK" or "not OK." They also tend to see others as basically friendly (OK) or hostile (not OK). The following four possible life positions represent combinations of how people define themselves and others:

1. "I'm OK, you're OK" represents people who are happy with themselves and others.
2. "I'm OK, you're not OK" suggests people who are suspicious of others, could have a false sense of superiority, or may be suffering from a mental disorder such as paranoia.
3. "I'm not OK, you're OK" indicates people who have a low self-concept and feel inadequate in relation to others.
4. "I'm not OK, you're not OK" implies people who have given up on themselves and life and may even be suicidal.

Life Scripts.   A major part of personality structure relates to the life scripts that are created beginning in childhood. A life script is composed of parental messages, for example, a parent saying, "You're my darling angel," and complementary messages from other sources that may include fairy tales, movies, and literature. These messages create a role that a person identifies with and acts out throughout life. For instance, a person could identify with the Superman character and play the role of the "good person who comes to the rescue" in interpersonal relations. Another possible life script is identifying with the Cinderella character, which might lead to feelings of self-pity, being taken advantage of, and never having a chance to get out and have fun.

Strokes.   TA suggests that the basic motivation for social interaction is related to the need for human recognition, or *strokes* (Dusay & Dusay, 1989). Strokes can be physical, verbal, or psychological and can be positive, negative, conditional, or unconditional. Positive strokes tend to communicate affection and appreciation and are essential to psychological development.

TA attempts to identify what types of strokes are important to clients and encourages them to take an active role in getting these strokes. For instance, after having a rough day, people could tell their partner that they need some extra strokes that evening.

Theory of Counseling and Psychotherapy

The Counseling Process.   Berne (1961) notes that the ultimate goals of TA are to help clients become autonomous, self-aware, and spontaneous, and have the capacity for intimacy. To promote these ultimate goals, some of the short-term goals of TA are that it helps clients

- Make new decisions, called *redecisions,* regarding their behavior and approach to life
- Rewrite their life script so they feel OK about themselves and can relate effectively with others
- Stop playing games that confuse communication and interfere with authentic interpersonal functioning
- Understand their three ego states of parent, adult, and child and how they can function in an effective and complementary fashion
- Avoid communicating in a manner that promotes crossed or ulterior transactions
- Learn how to obtain and give positive strokes

The counseling process in TA is educative in nature. The therapist takes on the role of teacher, providing clients information on how to use the TA concepts. TA emphasizes cognition in its approach by showing clients how they can use their intellect in applying TA principles to overcome mental disorders.

TA utilizes an active counseling process that emphasizes the importance of clients doing something outside of counseling via homework assignments. TA also relies on the use of a counseling contract, which the therapist and the client develop together. The contract is very specific in identifying the counseling goals, treatment plan, and roles and responsibilities for achieving these goals.

Techniques. The following techniques of TA relate to the key concepts described earlier:

- *Structural analysis* is a technique that helps clients become aware of their three ego states and learn to use them effectively.
- *Transactional analysis* helps clients learn to communicate with complementary transactions (for example, adult to adult).
- *Script analysis* is a process that explores the type of life script the client has developed and how it can be rewritten in a more effective manner.
- *Analysis of games* involves clients identifying what games they play and how the games interfere with interpersonal functioning.

Summary and Evaluation

TA is an educative, cognitively oriented process in which clients learn to apply TA principles so they can become self-therapists and lead autonomous, fully functioning lives. TA was one of the first theories of counseling whose goal was to focus on the role that interpersonal relations play in mental health and well-being. TA provides valuable tools such as analysis of games, which can help clients understand and enhance their interpersonal functioning as an important step in overcoming their psychological problems. The strength of TA is that the concepts are written in easily understandable words, such as parent, adult, child, strokes, and games, instead of psychological jargon. One weakness of TA is the possibility of focusing too much attention on self-analysis and intellectualization. When this occurs, clients may become self-absorbed and calculating in their relationships with others.

There is evidence to suggest that TA is becoming more popular with practitioners as they begin to integrate other schools of counseling such as Gestalt and psychodrama (Poidevant & Lewis, 1995). This wider base of application has enabled TA to be used in corporate settings such as airlines and utility companies (Poidevant & Lewis, 1995).

TA has also been shown to be useful in enhancing wellness, communication skills, family counseling, and school functioning (Poidevant & Lewis, 1995). For example, there appears to be a positive relationship between getting strokes and overall physical and psychological wellness (Allen & Allen, 1989). In addition, TA has been found useful in enhancing communication skills and productivity (Nykodym, Rund, & Liverpool, 1986; Spencer, 1977). In terms of family counseling, TA has been shown to enhance the self-esteem of parents in parent education programs (Bredehoft, 1990), and concepts and procedures such as ego states and transactional analysis were found useful in family counseling (Zerin, 1988). Miller and Capuzzi (1984) provide additional support for TA in terms of school functioning. They find that TA can be used to enhance the self-esteem of elementary school students, increase rates of attendance of high school students, and promote positive academic performance in higher education students. Poidevant and Lewis (1995) also point out that TA does not seem to be appropriate for some populations, such as people who suffer from schizophrenia and severe anxiety disorders such as phobias.

Prochaska and Norcross (2002) provide an extensive review of the TA research literature including the meta-analysis from Smith, Glass, and Miller (1980). Prochaska and Norcross find overall support for TA, suggesting "it was consistently more effective than no treatment and usually more effective than placebo treatments in adult samples" (p. 217). Prochaska and Norcross (2002) also identify limitations with TA. They suggest that a major problem with TA is that many of the concepts (such as parent, adult, and child) are difficult to evaluate empirically. In addition, these concepts (while easy to understand) may be an oversimplification of Freud's theory. This appears to have resulted in leaving major theoretical constructs "lost in the translation" (such as the id as the major driving force in the personality). From a postmodern perspective, TA may also be lacking in terms of not going far enough with its interpersonal perspective. For example, additional emphasis should be placed on sociocultural forces that can have an impact on psychological functioning.

Reality Therapy

Background Information

William Glasser (b. 1925) is the founder of reality therapy. Glasser was a consulting psychiatrist for the Ventura School for Girls in California when he attempted his first large-scale implementation of reality therapy. His program was well received, prompting an interest in the merits of reality therapy. It appeared to be a realistic approach, especially for clients who had a pattern of being irresponsible, such as delinquent children and substance abusers.

In 1961 Glasser published his first book, *Mental Health or Mental Illness?* He took an antipsychiatry position, exploring how labels such as *mental disorder* and *schizophrenia* can be harmful to a client. Glasser has since persisted with this position by not recognizing the various mental disorders described in the DSM-IV-TR.

Glasser wrote several other books that contributed to the evolution of reality therapy. In 1965, he published *Reality Therapy,* which established his approach as a major force in counseling and psychotherapy. In *Schools Without Failure,* Glasser (1969) attempts to apply the principles of reality therapy to education. His more recent publications have attempted to broaden the theoretical base of his approach. In *Positive Addiction,* he describes how positive addictions can be substituted for negative addictions (Glasser, 1976). In *Stations of the Mind,* he describes the neurological and psychological basis of reality therapy (Glasser, 1981). In the mid-1980s, Glasser's interests began to focus on the role of control in mental health. Reality therapy was therefore expanded to include control theory (Glasser, 1984, 1985). Glasser has also applied the concepts of control theory to education (1986, 1990). Glasser later replaced control theory with choice theory (Glasser, 1998; Glasser & Glasser, 1999). Choice theory recognizes the importance of helping clients learn how to make effective choices to meet their needs in a responsible manner.

More recently, Glasser (2000) published *Counseling with Choice Theory: The New Reality Therapy.* This latest volume by Glasser represents a direct integration of choice theory into reality therapy. Glasser's newest version of reality therapy suggest that 99 percent of the problems in relationships stem from external control psychology characterized by "I know what is right for you" controlling-punishing people. Glasser (2000) contends that choice theory can be used to overcome the adverse forces of external control psychology. He goes on to note that choice determines one's happiness and fulfillment, and that controlling others will not bring happiness. Glasser (2000) sums up the essence of reality therapy, saying ". . . it is what you choose to do in a relationship, not what others choose to do, that is the heart of reality therapy" (p. 1). Corey (2005) notes that "a primary goal of contemporary reality therapy is to help clients get connected or reconnected with the people they have chosen to put in their quality world" (p. 321).

Wubbolding (2000, 2003) has also played a key role in the evolution of reality therapy. He has been influential in expanding on Glasser's theory in terms of counseling procedures. His work on the four stages of reality therapy and the questions associated with these stages (for example, "What are you doing?" and "Is what you're doing working for you?") are very useful in terms of providing a structure to the process of reality therapy.

Theory of Personality

Reality therapy emphasizes the role of choice and responsibility in human functioning. Reality therapies' theory of personality proposes that enhanced awareness of choices helps clients assume responsibility for their behavior. As clients learn to make appropriate choices, they can create "quality worlds" characterized by success identities and appropriate need gratification.

View of Human Nature.   Glasser believes that the primary motivational force of people is directed at fulfilling basic physiological and psychological needs of survival, love, belonging, power, freedom, and fun. He emphasizes the choice people have over fulfilling their needs and creating their own destiny.

Key Concepts.   Glasser (1965, 1985, 1998), Glasser and Wubbolding (1995), and Wubbolding (2000, 2003) have identified several key concepts that characterize reality therapy.

Success and Failure Identity.   A *success identity* results when a person is able to fulfill the psychological needs of loving and of feeling worthwhile to the self and others in a manner that does not interfere with the rights of others. When a person is unable to meet these basic psychological needs, a *failure identity* results. Failure identities are associated with problematic approaches to life such as delinquency and mental disorders.

Emphasis on Responsibility.   Reality therapy encourages clients to evaluate their behavior in terms of whether it is helping or hurting themselves and others. When people make an honest evaluation of their behavior, they can assume responsibility for it. Glasser believes that responsibility is critical to mental health and therefore a primary goal of reality therapy.

View of Psychopathology.   As mentioned earlier, Glasser (1961) set the stage for his antipsychiatry stance regarding mental disorders with the publication of his first book,

Mental Health or Mental Illness? Since that publication, he has consistently maintained that there are no mental disorders and that the labeling process can do more harm than good.

In addition, Glasser believes that people are in control of their mental health. According to this theory, a person must behave in a manner associated with depression in order to be depressed. When clients say they are depressed, Glasser would suggest that they say instead, "I'm depressing." As a result, clients will realize the control they have over their mental health.

Positive Addiction.   Glasser's (1976) *Positive Addiction* was an innovative attempt to redefine the concept of addiction. Up to that time, the tendency was to understand addiction as something negative and to be avoided. Glasser observed that there were some positive behaviors, such as jogging and meditation, that appeared addictive since the person would become uncomfortable if these behaviors were not allowed to occur. Glasser suggested that people with a negative addiction such as alcoholism could try to discover a positive addiction that could become a substitute for it.

Control Theory.   Control theory was once a central concept in reality therapy. This theory suggests that each person has a control system that serves to exert control over the environment. It represents a direct challenge to the traditional stimulus-response notion, which suggests that people's responses are conditioned by the environment. Glasser (1986) insisted that "what goes on in the outside would never 'stimulate' us to do anything. All of our behavior, simple to complex, is our best attempt to control ourselves to satisfy our needs" (p. 17). Simply stated, people feel good when they believe they have control of their lives and feel bad when they feel their lives are out of control.

As noted, the basic tenet of control theory is that all behavior results from people attempting to satisfy basic needs. These include the psychological needs of belonging, freedom, power, and fun and the physiological need for survival.

Choice Theory.   Glasser (1998) made a major revision in reality therapy by replacing the concept of control theory with choice theory. The overall aim of choice theory is to help clients learn to make choices that can help them meet their needs in a responsible manner, and get what they want in terms of creating a "quality world." Glasser emphasizes the role of behavior in learning how to make appropriate choices and contends for the most part that behavior is intrinsically motivated.

Glasser (1998) identifies the following 10 axioms of choice theory:

- People can only control *their own* behavior.
- Information is essentially all that people exchange, and people must choose how they deal with the information they get from others.
- Long-lasting problems tend to be relationship problems.
- Problem relationships affect our *present* lives.
- Focusing on the *past* can do little to improve current significant relationships.
- People are motivated to fulfill needs of survival, love and belonging, power, freedom, and fun.
- Need satisfaction is dependent on satisfying pictures in a person's "quality world."

- People engage in behaviors relating to acting, thinking, feeling, and physiology throughout life.
- Awareness of choice associated with behavior is enhanced by the use of language such as "I am choosing to feel anxiety" or ("I'm anxieting") as opposed to "I am suffering from anxiety."
- People have direct control over their acting and thinking and indirect control over feelings and physiology.

Theory of Counseling and Psychotherapy

The Counseling Process.   The primary goal of reality therapy is to help clients choose to live their lives in a manner that is responsible and does not interfere with the rights of others.

The counseling process is educational in nature, and clients learn how to apply choice theory to effective living. Reality therapy contends that a positive counseling relationship promotes efficacy in the counseling process. In addition, reality therapy focuses on present behavior and makes no attempt to explore past events such as childhood trauma. It also does not recognize mental disorders, because they represent harmful labels.

Techniques.   The main technique in contemporary reality therapy is teaching clients how to use choice theory to meet their basic needs in a responsible manner (Glasser, 1998). Glasser (1980, 1984) set forth an eight-step approach for implementing reality therapy: create a relationship, focus on current behavior, invite clients to evaluate their behavior, make a plan of action, get a commitment, refuse to accept excuses, refuse to use punishment, and refuse to give up. Glasser (1984) suggests using a flexible approach when applying these steps and notes that the steps are interrelated and overlapping processes rather than discrete steps.

A more recent version of reality therapy emphasizes a four-stage approach that is expressed in the acronym WDEP (Glasser & Wubbolding, 1995; Wubbolding, 2000, 2003). The following is a brief overview of these four steps:

1. "W" stands for the client's wants, needs, and perceptions. In this first stage of counseling, the counselor explores what the client wants out of life by asking questions such as "What do you want?" (from your job, spouse, and so forth). Various techniques and procedures can be used in this process, such as exploring the client's inner "picture album," which reflects perceptions of his or her wants and needs.
2. "D" stands for what the client is doing and the direction he or she is taking in his or her life. In this stage, the counselor can ask "What are you doing?" or "Where are you going with your life if you continue doing what you are doing now?" This step focuses on evaluating the client's current behaviors as expressed in the here and now (rather than delving into the past).
3. "E" stands for self-evaluation, which Glasser believes is the central concept in reality therapy. Self-evaluation involves helping the client engage in a process of self-analysis to determine whether "what they are doing is working for them." Self-evaluation is a critical stage in counseling in terms of helping clients get motivated to engage in the change process.

4. "P" involves helping clients plan to make the necessary changes to meet their needs more effectively. Plans are directed related to the insights gained from the self-evaluation. Wubbolding (1986) identifies characteristics of effective planning, which are simple, attainable, measurable, immediate, involved, controlled by the client, committed to, and consistent.

Summary and Evaluation

Reality therapy is a popular short-term form of intervention that focuses on behavior that is occurring in the present. It is a particularly attractive type of treatment with people who have a pattern of acting irresponsibly, such as delinquent children, students with school-related behavioral problems, and people with substance-abuse problems.

There appear to be a limited number of recent studies that have evaluated the efficacy of reality therapy. Most of the studies cited in Glasser and Wubbolding (1995) and Wubbolding (2000, 2003) as evidence of the effectiveness of reality therapy were published before 1990. One study by Honeyman (1990) was cited as providing support for reality therapy. It suggested that reality therapy could be used in group counseling with addicts to enhance their self-esteem, help them take more responsibility for their behavior, and improve their relations with others. Additional research efforts seem warranted to provide an evaluation of the key concepts and procedures of reality therapy (for example, choice theory).

Feminist Therapy

Background Information

A number of creative individuals in the counseling profession have contributed to the evolution of feminist therapy. Some of the early pioneers were Laura Brown (1988), Harriet Lerner (1988), Edna Rawlings (1993), and Carolyn Enns (1993). Feminist therapy continues to evolve into the 21st century as a highly provocative, stimulating school of counseling. The following overview incorporates feminists' perspectives set forth by Elliott (1999), Enns (1993), Evans, Seem, and Kincade (2005), Forisha (2001), Gilbert and Scher (1999), and Kottler (2002).

Feminist therapy has evolved as an alternative to traditional schools of counseling, which, in large, have been developed by men. A few exceptions to this are Anna Freud, Karen Horney, Melanie Klein, and Virginia Satir. The roots of feminist therapy can be traced to the early 1960s and the work of Betty Friedan (1963) and others associated with feminism and the Women's Liberation Movement. Feminism became a voice for promoting equality between the sexes and for addressing oppressive forces toward women.

Different forms of feminism have contributed to this movement. Evans, Seem, and Kincade (2005) suggest that feminist perspectives (such as liberal, cultural, socialist, and radical feminism) can be differentiated in terms of how they define underlying causes of oppression. For example, socialist feminism contends that women are oppressed as a result of economic policies that exploit women as a source of cheap labor. Radical feminism suggests that oppression results from a male-dominated and male-controlled society, and that a restructuring of the society is necessary for meaningful change.

Feminist therapy reflects an integration of feminist principles into the counseling process. Numerous theoretical perspectives have emerged from this process (e.g., liberal, cultural, socialist, and radical feminist therapies; empowerment feminist therapy; feminist standpoint theory; feminist postmodernism; gender-aware therapy; and feminist family therapy).

Feminist therapy may be the most misunderstood major school of counseling, which results in an underutilization of this promising theoretical perspective. Misconceptions include that

- Feminist therapy evolved from the Women's Liberation Movement and is therefore anti-male.
- Feminist therapy has been used to address lesbian issues and is therefore a school of counseling restricted to lesbian issues.
- Feminist therapy was developed to create a voice for women and not men.

hooks (1995) addresses the relevance of feminist therapy for men and women, saying

I believe that we have to start seeing sexism and racism as practices that are profoundly anti-spirit and antilove. For me feminism is not a movement of women against men. It's a way of thinking that allows *all* of us to examine the harmful role sexism plays in our personal lives and public world and to figure out what we can do to change this. It's a movement that creates space for the spirit and for being a whole person. (p. 188)

As hooks (1995) notes, feminist therapy can have important implications for men. For example, men can benefit from androgynous socialization processes that foster the feminine side of development. In addition, male socialization can include an emphasis on emotional understanding and communication. Men can also benefit from sociopolitical action that promotes attachment and bonding with their children (e.g., paid release time from work after the birth of a child).

Theory of Personality

View of Human Nature.   Feminist therapy appears to have a postmodern-contextual perspective in terms of its view of human nature. The postmodern position conveys a healthy skepticism about universal truths such as the view of human nature (Enns, 1993). The feminist perspective recognizes the inner strength and resiliency of the human spirit and the inherent drive for freedom and equality. Feminist therapy also contends that contextual factors such as sociopolitical forces can create oppression and undermine self-actualizing tendencies.

Key Concepts

Relational Focus.   The relational focus in feminist therapy is, to a large degree, associated with Jean Baker Miller (1987) and others associated with the Stone Center for Developmental Services and Studies at Wellesley College. The Stone Center model represents an integration of principles from human development, psychodynamic theory, and feminist therapy. It also defines the "self" in relational terms (e.g., "the self in relation" or "the relational self"). Carol Gilligan's (1991, 1993) seminal work on identity development and moral decision plays a central role in this relational focus. For example, Gilligan contends that male development emphasizes autonomy and independence, whereas female development tends to revolve around relational issues such as nurturing, empathy, and connecting. Failure to recognize and value the relational qualities of women results in marginalizing (undervaluing) the role and function of women in society.

Social Constructionist Perspective.   Postmodern perspectives such as social constructionism attempt to address the interrelationship between internal and external forces (e.g., people construct their view of reality based on internalized narratives from society). Feminist therapy attempts to deconstruct problematic narratives such as socialization processes that oppress, devalue, or control women.

Diversity and Complexity of Women's Lives.   Feminist therapy recognizes the diversity and complexity of women's lives (Enns, 1993). The complexity of women's lives is reflected in the multiple roles and functions associated with being a woman (e.g., individual, friend, wife, and mother).

Theory of Counseling and Psychotherapy

The Counseling Process.   Feminist therapy is both a form of humanistic psychotherapy and a means to engage in needed social reform (Forisha, 2001). In this regard, feminist therapy promotes personal power and self-efficacy that transcends the individual (e.g., "the personal is political").

Feminist therapy can be used with a wide range of clients reflecting various forms of diversity, such as age, gender, and sexual orientation. For example, gender-aware therapy (Good, Gilbert, & Scher, 1990) provides a conceptual framework for addressing gender issues throughout the counseling process. In addition, feminist therapy is not anti-male, but is instead a positive perspective for both sexes. In this regard, feminist therapy provides a forum for freeing men and women from oppressive forces such as gender-role stereotyping. It also promotes egalitarian relationships and mutual respect between the sexes. Enns (1993) suggests that men could play a role as profeminist therapists by promoting justice and equality between the sexes. For example, men can take an active role as feminist therapists by confronting clients who undermine, control, and devalue women.

Feminist therapy can be conceptualized within several stages of the counseling process as follows.

The Counseling Relationship.   Feminist therapists promote egalitarian relationships between counselors and clients by removing power and control boundaries. In this process, counselors use self-disclosure (including sharing values and beliefs) to "bring to life" and personalize feminist ideologies and concepts. Therapists demystify the therapy process by educating clients on the theory and practice of feminist therapy. Clients are encouraged to take an active role in therapy, including having candid discussions regarding feminist principles.

Goals.　　The goals of feminist therapy are directed at relieving client distress; promoting social, economic, and political equality between the sexes; and overcoming oppressive forces such as the marginalization of women. In addition, Forisha (2001) suggests that feminist therapy fosters a number of self-actualizing tendencies such as self-awareness, self-acceptance, self-integration, self-affirmation, self-nurturance, and independence. For example, self-integration can involve integrating opposing sides of one's personality by promoting an androgynous view of the self.

Assessment and Diagnosis.　　Feminist therapy considers internal and external forces in assessment and diagnosis. In this process, emotions may serve adaptive functions (e.g., anger and rage can be coping responses to oppression). Anxiety may also serve a purpose in terms of creating motivation for necessary change, such as reassessing sex-role expectations. In addition, Forisha (2001) posits that the marginalization of women has resulted in women being overdiagnosed for mental disorders. For example, women are two times as likely as men to be perceived as having psychiatric and emotional problems. Kottler (2002) notes that diagnostic manuals contribute to overdiagnosing by portraying normative female traits as criteria for psychopathology (e.g., passive, dependent, and compliant).

Techniques.　　According to Enns (1993), feminist therapists utilize an integrative approach to counseling. They incorporate techniques and models from the various schools of counseling as long as they do not reflect gender bias. Some of these techniques are as follows.

Feminist Family Therapy.　　Feminist family therapy provides an excellent forum for exploring feminist issues such as equality between the sexes and oppression. Feminist family therapy goes beyond traditional family therapy by addressing the role of gender and sociopolitical forces on family dynamics. Feminist family therapy also promotes gender-sensitive models for socialization and identity development.

Career Counseling.　　The field of career counseling has made great strides in identifying the role of personal, family, and cultural factors that affect career choice and decision making. Feminist therapists utilize these models to help clients overcome self-limiting horizons associated with gender-role expectations.

Existential Therapy.　　Feminist therapists use existential therapy as a forum for exploring the meaning to life. Feminist therapists engage in philosophical discussions with clients on a variety of topics such as the importance of personal autonomy and what it means to live life to the fullest. Existential discussions can be useful to promote self-realization in terms of resocialization, personal identity formation, and self-concept enhancement.

Cognitive-Behavioral Therapy.　　Feminist therapists utilize cognitive-behavioral techniques such as cognitive restructuring to promote symptom relief (e.g., overcoming anxiety and depression). Cognitive restructuring is a technique that can also be used to deconstruct self-defeating narratives associated with issues such as weight and body image.

Behavioral Techniques.   Feminist therapists use behavioral techniques such as assertiveness training to promote personal autonomy and to empower clients to stand up against the tide of oppression. Assertiveness training can also be used to promote androgyny (Gilbert & Scher, 1999).

Person-Centered Therapy.   Feminist therapists use person-centered therapy to empower clients and to help them become aware of their inner choices and strengths. Person-centered techniques such as listening skills are used for a variety of counseling outcomes such as fostering self-awareness and validating emotions.

Adlerian Counseling.   Feminist therapists use Adlerian counseling techniques such as encouragement to promote self-efficacy and self-esteem. The lifestyle analysis is an Adlerian techniques that can be used to enhance self-understanding and social interest.

Bibliotherapy.   Feminist therapists use bibliotherapy to encourage clients to read books that provide information on feminist issues. Bibliotherapy also offers clients opportunities for normalizing and universalizing the experiences of women.

Gay and Lesbian Therapy.   Feminist therapists were among the first counseling professionals to normalize homosexuality (Elliott, 1999). Feminist therapy has developed models and techniques for addressing gay and lesbian issues within the counseling process (e.g., gay and lesbian identity development models). Feminist therapists also assist homosexuals with issues associated with "coming out."

Political Advocacy.   Feminist therapists contend that the "personal is political." From this perspective, problems such as oppression can only be overcome by involvement in social advocacy as by taking social and political action.

Summary and Evaluation

Feminist therapy represents an emerging theoretical perspective in the counseling literature. The overall aim of feminist therapy is to promote equality between the sexes and to overcome tendencies toward oppression. Feminist therapy has also provided a forum for addressing diversity issues such as gender and sexual orientation within the counseling process.

Elliott (1999) notes that it is difficult to find universities that offer training and supervision in feminist therapy. The lack of training opportunities is compounded by the fact that some programs appear to exclude feminist therapy from the curriculum on ideological grounds. This form of discrimination is unfortunate, to say the least. Hopefully, research efforts will provide the support necessary for feminist therapy to be fully integrated into the mainstream of counseling.

Special Issues in Cognitive-Behavioral Counseling

Cognitive-Behavioral Theories from a Brief-Counseling Perspective

Cognitive-behavioral theories have particular utility as a form of brief counseling because their techniques and procedures can easily be integrated into a brief-counseling format (for example, they are solution focused). The following highlights some of the characteristics cognitive-behavioral theories share with the brief-counseling perspective.

Behavior Therapy. Behavior therapy is well suited for brief counseling. Wilson (2005) notes that behavior therapy tends to be time-limited, with the counselor contracting with the client to resolve the concerns within a two- to three-month period (or 8 to 12 sessions). Many of the techniques and procedures used in behavior therapy fit well with the brief-counseling model in that they are solution focused (for example, they use systematic desensitization and stress inoculation to treat anxiety).

Rational-Emotive Behavior Therapy. Ellis (2005) notes that REBT is an ideal form of brief counseling. Although REBT can be used as a form of brief therapy for all clients, it is especially productive for clients who have a specific problem, such as sexual inadequacy or hostility toward a boss, but do not have a serious disturbance (Ellis, 2005). Ellis (2005) contends that REBT can help clients in just one session but typically lasts between 1 and 10 sessions. Ellis (2005) believes that the efficacy of REBT as a form of brief counseling can be enhanced when counselors have clients listen to tape-recorded sessions to process how they can apply therapy and when counselors use the REBT Self-Help Form to help clients learn how to apply REBT to a variety of problems they encounter between sessions.

Cognitive Therapy. Beck and Weishaar (2005) describe cognitive therapy as a highly structured form of short-term counseling that usually lasts from 12 to 16 sessions. It is a solution-focused approach that attempts to address problems with depression and anxiety, and to some degree other disorders, such as eating disorders and substance abuse. Cognitive therapy has received substantial research support as an effective short-term treatment approach to treating specific disorders. Managed-care organizations have therefore recognized the utility of cognitive therapy (Beck & Weishaar, 2005).

Transactional Analysis. Although TA was not initially designed as a brief-counseling approach, many of its concepts and procedures can be incorporated into a brief-counseling model. The techniques and concepts in TA can be particularly useful in brief counseling to generate a solution-focused approach to counseling. For example, concepts and strategies such as stroking, game playing, ego states, and transactional analysis (analyzing the transactions between people in terms of parent, adult, and child) can play a useful role in helping clients enhance their interpersonal functioning and foster mental health and well-being.

Reality Therapy. Reality therapy has not traditionally been considered a form of brief counseling. The recent revisions of the theory appear to have made it more attractive as a brief-counseling approach. Some of these revisions have been emphasizing choice theory and how clients can learn how to meet their needs in a manner that does not interfere with the rights of others; the concepts of success identity and failure identity and positive addictions; and Glasser's new way of conceptualizing the counseling process in terms of questions such as "What are you doing?" and "Is it working for you?" Each of these concepts and processes can be used to create a brief-time limited-solution-focused approach to counseling. In addition, Palmatier (1990) identifies common characteristics that reality therapy shares with the brief-counseling perspective. Some of these characteristics are that current behavior is the focus for change (the past is avoided), psychological jargon is minimized, clients are encouraged to take an active role in their therapy, and the counseling process is solution focused.

Feminist Therapy.   Feminist therapy is a flexible form of therapy that can be adapted to a brief-counseling format. A number of feminist therapy interventions can promote brief counseling because they can be conducted outside of formal counseling. For example, clients can be encouraged to engage in bibliotherapy by reading books about feminism and how to become an effective change agent for social reform.

Diversity Issues

Diversity issues in counseling suggest that it is important to be aware of issues such as the client's degree of acculturation, identity development, cultural background (including values and beliefs), and worldview before implementing counseling theories. For example, degree of acculturation can suggest how appropriate traditional theories may be (the higher the acculturation, the higher the probability of appropriateness).

Behavior Therapy.   Tanaka-Matsumi and Higginbotham (1994) suggest that the essence of behavior therapy is to assess the relationship between the environment and the client's behavior and to adjust counseling to address environmental conditions such as culture as necessary. Prochaska and Norcross (2002) go on to note that although behavior therapy attempts to include environmental assessment, it often falls short of this goal, especially in terms of expressing sensitivity to cultural or family systems perspectives.

Rational-Emotive Behavior Therapy and Cognitive Therapy.   REBT and cognitive therapy focus on the role of cognition in mental health and well-being. It is important to consider diversity issues such as gender, culture, and world view in applying these theories. Prochaska and Norcross (2002) note that cognitive therapies may reflect a male bias, valuing "rational thinking" over what could be considered female characteristics, such as intuition and connection, and therefore may be inappropriate and offensive to women. Cultural problems could emanate from REBT's notion that absolutistic thinking (characterized by shoulds, oughts, or musts) creates emotional distress. It is critical to ensure that a client's culture does not value absolutistic thinking as a sign of mental health before trying to dispute this type of thinking. In addition, world view recognizes that each person has a unique way of understanding and viewing the world. It is therefore important to gain a phenomenological perspective when conceptualizing a client's cognitions.

Transactional Analysis. On the positive side, TA has done a good job in moving beyond intrapsychic forces by recognizing the role of relational issues in psychological functioning. Prochaska and Norcross (2002) suggest that TA could go further in this regard by incorporating a systemic perspective and being more sensitive to cultural issues. Although TA has a number of concepts that could have wide appeal cross-culturally (for example, the need for strokes), some of the terminology may be difficult to understand from a cross-cultural perspective.

Reality Therapy. Several concepts in reality therapy may be problematic in terms of cultural issues. Three of these concepts are control, choice, and responsibility. Although these concepts may be valued in Western culture (since they promote individualism), they may not fit well with Eastern cultures (which value the group over the individual). In this sense, Eastern cultures are not as concerned with who broke something (identifying who must take responsibility) but how to fix or correct what is wrong.

Wubbolding (1990) recognizes the differences between East and West and recommends that reality therapy be adjusted to fit the needs of the client's milieu. This can include being sensitive to language differences (for example, "I'll try" in Japan may be equivalent to "I'll do it" in the United States). Some of the newer trends in reality therapy may be well suited for cross-cultural counseling. One example is structuring counseling along themes such as "What are you doing?" and "Is it working for you?" This enables clients to take an active role in personalizing counseling from the standpoint of their worldview.

Feminist Therapy. Feminist therapy has emerged as a major school of counseling and psychotherapy by addressing diversity issues such as gender and sexual orientation. Recent research initiatives have also addressed cultural issues in feminist therapy. For example, McNair (1992) suggests that non-African-American counselors should not impose their value system when counseling African-American women. In this regard, African-American women's values such as family, community, and church should be recognized and not marginalized in favor of values relating to autonomy.

Postmodern Trends

Postmodern trends such as narrative psychology, constructivism, and social constructionism are beginning to play a key role in the evolution of cognitive-behavioral counseling (Mahoney, 1995b). Central to this new perspective is a reevaluation of basic concepts such as knowledge and reality. From a postmodern perspective, knowledge and reality are relative concepts varying according to sociopolitical forces as reflected in the narrative of cultures. Gergen (1982) emphasizes the social dimension to cognition when he says that "knowledge is not something that people possess in their heads, but rather something that people do together" (p. 270).

Postmodern trends are creating a paradigm shift within cognitive-behavioral counseling, changing its focus from intrapsychic causality to a recognition of contextual forces that impact on human functioning. The process of counseling is therefore becoming more of a creative than a corrective endeavor (Lyddon, 1995). It is less concerned with overcoming internal cognitive deficits and more concerned with the counselor and client creating new narratives that no longer are of concern to the client (Lyddon, 1995).

Ellis (2005) contends that REBT embraces the major tenets of postmodernism such as considering the role of contextual (relational) issues in creating personal meaning and defining reality. In this regard, Ellis suggests that cognition, emotions, and behavior are best understood and addressed within a sociocultural and sociopolitical context.

D'Andrea (2000) questions whether Ellis's REBT qualifies as a postmodern approach. He contends that REBT does not assess clients' beliefs contextually from a multicultural perspective. On the contrary, REBT classifies beliefs as "impractical" or "irrational" if they conflict with the value system of mainstream society (D'Andrea, 2000, p. 8). Additional research appears necessary to assess the nature of postmodernism within REBT.

Summary

Several theories emphasize the role of cognition and/or behavior in the counseling process. Cognitive-behavioral approaches utilize an integration of concepts and counseling strategies. This is especially true for behavior therapy, rational-emotive behavior therapy, and cognitive therapy. These three theories have a common focus on the integral role that cognition plays in the development of mental disorders. They also incorporate behavioral techniques to teach the skills and behaviors necessary for a comprehensive treatment program. Subtle differences also exist among these three theories. Ellis's REBT focuses on confronting and disputing the client's irrational and illogical thoughts. Beck's cognitive therapy is concerned with whether a client is making a functional or dysfunctional interpretation of an event. For Meichenbaum, the central issue in behavior therapy is the nature of the client's inner speech or self-talk. He contends that a client must learn self-talk that triggers effective coping mechanisms.

Transactional analysis emphasizes the relational aspect of human behavior and how clients can use its concepts to enhance their interpersonal functioning. Reality therapy stresses the role of choice in mental health and how clients can be helped to make appropriate choices to meet their needs in a manner that does not interfere with the rights of others.

Feminist therapy utilizes interventions that are both cognitive and behavioral in nature. Cognitive interventions are directed at a number of feminist therapy concerns, such as resocialization, gender expectancies, and self-concept. For example, cognitive restructuring is used to promote symptom relief and overcome cognitive distortions associated with weight and body image. Behavioral interventions can include homework assignments associated with political advocacy.

Cognitive-behavioral counseling is particularly well suited for use in a brief-counseling format. Cognitive therapy stands out in this regard in terms of providing a time-limited approach to treat specific disorders such as depression and anxiety. Cognitive-behavioral theories have both strengths and weaknesses in terms of effectively addressing diversity issues. Postmodern trends in cognitive-behavioral counseling appear to be providing an important paradigm shift that will accommodate emerging diversity issues such as gender and culture.

Personal Exploration

1. What cognitive-behavioral theories do you like best, and why?
2. What is your opinion of feminist theory?
3. How can cognitive-behavioral theories such as Beck's and Ellis's be used to treat anxiety and depression?
4. How could you use transactional analysis to improve your interpersonal relationships?

Web Sites for Chapter 9

Bush, J. W. (2004). *Cognitive behavior therapy.* Retrieved March 3, 2005, from http://www.cognitivetherapy.com/
Presents a brief description of cognitive behavior therapy. (Note: this Web site is sponsored by New York Institute for Cognitive-Behavioral Therapy.)

Edelstein, M. R. (unknown). *REBT therapy.* Retrieved March 3, 2005, from http://www.threeminutetherapy.com/rebt.html
Provides a brief description of rational-emotive behavior therapy.

Psychnet-UK. (unknown). *Feminist therapy.* Retrieved March 3, 2005, from http://www.psychnet-uk.com/psychotherapy/psychotherapy_feminist_therapy.htm
Provides links to several articles describing feminist therapy.

Westermeyer, R. (unknown). *Cognitive therapy pages.* Retrieved March 3, 2005, from http://www.habitsmart.com/cogtitle.html
Provides a detailed description of behavior therapy.

PART THREE

Special Approaches and Settings

Part Three provides an overview of the special approaches and settings associated with the counseling profession. The following six chapters are covered in Part Three.

10. Marriage and family counseling
11. Child and adolescent counseling
12. Group counseling
13. Career counseling
14. School counseling
15. Mental health counseling

10 Marriage and Family Counseling

CHAPTER OVERVIEW

This chapter provides an overview of the field of marriage and family counseling. Highlights of the chapter include

- The art and science of marriage and family counseling
- The evolution of marriage and family counseling
- Theoretical foundations, including systems theory and the family life cycle
- Marriage counseling
- Family counseling
- Postmodern trends
- Diversity issues in marriage and family counseling
- Evaluation of marriage and family counseling

The Art and Science of Marriage and Family Counseling

Marriage and family counseling is both an art and a science. It is an art to attempt to formulate and maintain a positive counseling relationship with a couple or family and understand and work with the complex issues that emerge within the family system. This process requires patience, flexibility, creativity, and all the other dimensions associated with the art of counseling.

The spirit of the art of counseling appears to be incorporated into the recent postmodern/social constructionist trends in marriage and family counseling. This approach recommends that marriage and family counselors enter family systems not as experts but as inquisitive learners who want to discover how the family defines their strengths and weaknesses. It is a process similar to the discovery-oriented methods used in qualitative research, whereby the investigator and participant function as coinvestigators. The focus of marriage and family counseling from this perspective is on helping couples and families discover new options and opportunities for effective family living through analysis of family stories and narratives. The postmodern/social constructionist approach to marriage and family counseling may represent a bridge between art and science (that is, between counseling and qualitative research).

The science of marriage and family counseling can be found in processes such as the use of assessment and research procedures. Assessment instruments such as marital satisfaction inventories provide objective information on areas in which the couple is satisfied or dissatisfied. Research strategies such as qualitative and quantitative methodologies help provide information on the effectiveness of marriage and family counseling. Recent advances in quantitative research have done much to overcome methodological weaknesses and clearly demonstrate the efficacy of marriage and family counseling (Shadish, Ragsdale, Glaser, & Montgomery, 1995). Qualitative research also seems to offer promise to marriage and family research in that it is congruent with systems theory (Moon, Dillon, & Sprenkle, 1990). In this regard, qualitative research and systems theory emphasize "social context, multiple perspectives, complexity, individual differences, circular causality, recursion, and holism" (Moon et al., 1990, p. 364).

Evolution of Marriage and Family Counseling

The field of marriage and family counseling has evolved over the last 60 years (Everett, 1990a). Goldenberg and Goldenberg (2004) identify key events associated with this evolution, which are incorporated into the following overview.

Psychoanalysis

Nathan Ackerman's (1937) work on the family as an important psychosocial unit set the stage for the adaptation of Freudian concepts to family counseling. Prior to Ackerman's work, psychoanalysis was strictly a process of individual psychotherapy.

General Systems Theory

Ludwig Von Bertalanffy developed general systems theory in the 1940s. This theory contends that seemingly unrelated phenomena represent interrelated facets of a larger system (Von Bertalanffy, 1968). General systems theory was later applied to marriage and family counseling, providing an important theoretical foundation.

Research on Schizophrenia

Since the late 1940s numerous studies have been conducted to investigate the relationship between family dynamics and schizophrenia. Although this massive research effort has determined nothing conclusive as yet, it has drawn interest to family therapy as a potentially useful treatment modality.

Marriage Counseling and Child Guidance

Marriage counseling and child guidance represent the first counseling approaches to recognize that problems relate to both intrapersonal (within the person) and interpersonal (between people) forces. The inclusion of the interpersonal perspective prompted the necessity for counselors to work with the parent and child or husband and wife together in a counseling session.

Group Therapy

Around 1910, Morino developed what can be considered the earliest uses of group processes in counseling. Since then, many other forms of group counseling have evolved. The evolution of group counseling influenced marriage and family counseling in terms of how marriage and family counselors could use effective group-leadership skills, how the knowledge of group process could contribute to the understanding of interactions between family members, and how the concept of "the group" as a change agent could be applied to "the family" as a change agent.

Changing Family Structure

The traditional intact family characterized by a wage-earning father, a homemaker mother, and biological children is now in the minority. Current family structures in the United States represent a wide range of alternative family systems that include single parents rearing children; blended families, where the husband and wife live with children from a previous marriage; cohabiting couples, or unmarried individuals living together for an extended period of time; and gay couples living together rearing children.

Numerous problems emerge as family members attempt to adjust to changing family structures. For example, a family often experiences financial problems following a divorce (especially women with children). Marriage and family counseling has to some degree evolved as a means of assisting with these common problems of modern family life.

Marriage Counseling Versus Couples Counseling

As the concept of marriage and family continues to evolve with the changing fabric of contemporary society, there is reason to consider the terminology used in the helping process. Generally speaking, marriage counselors loosely define their services as appropriate for any couple, married or not married, who is in need of assistance. Using this definition, marriage counseling can also be referred to as *couples counseling.* Family therapists also tend to utilize a broad definition of *family* that includes two or more people cohabiting in the same household. Olson and DeFrain (1997) support this inclusive definition of family by suggesting that a "family is two or more people who are committed to each other and who share intimacy, resources, decisions, and values" (p. 9).

Although this chapter adheres to the traditional terminology of marriage and family counseling (versus couples counseling), many of the concepts described in the sections on marriage counseling may also have relevance for nonmarried couples. For example, Gottman's factors that predict divorce may also be warning signs of the impending breakup of a serious nonmarried relationship.

Professional Issues and Organizations

The field of marriage and family counseling is both a professional discipline and a specialized counseling strategy practiced by various members of the helping profession. R. L. Smith (1994) recommends that the appropriate sequence for becoming a marriage and family counselor is to first master personal and human-relation skills, then to develop general counseling skills and theory, and finally to specialize in marriage and family skills and theory.

The two main professional organizations for marriage and family counselors are the American Association for Marriage and Family Therapy (AAMFT) and the American Counseling Association (ACA)—formerly known as the American Association for Counseling and Development (AACD). The AAMFT has a much longer history; it was originally called the American Association of Marriage Counselors in 1942. As of 2005, there were approximately 23,000 members (http://www.aamft.org). The current address of AAMFT is as follows:

> American Association for Marriage and Family Therapy
> 112 South Alfred Street
> Alexandria, VA 22314
> http://www.aamft.org

In 1989, the ACA established division status to the International Association of Marriage and Family Counselors (IAMFC). As of 1999, there were approximately 5,000 IAMFC members (Gladding, Remley, & Huber, 2001). The current address of the ACA is as follows:

> American Counseling Association
> 5999 Stevenson Avenue
> Alexandria, VA 22304
> http://www.counseling.org

The AAMFT and ACA have done much to promote the professionalism of marriage and family counseling. Some of these activities have been to establish ethical codes (see Chapter 2) and promote state licensure in marriage and family counseling. By 2000, 42 states had licensure laws regarding marriage and family counseling.

Theoretical Foundations

Several important theoretical foundations have contributed to marriage and family counseling. Theories described in this section include systems theory and the family life cycle.

Systems Theory

Systems theory is the foundation and integrating force in marriage and family counseling (Smith, Carlson, Stevens-Smith, & Dennison, 1995). The systems perspective is based on the principle of circular causality (Everett, 1990a). According to this principle, actions caused by one family member influence the actions of all other family members, affecting the functioning of the family system, including the person who was responsible for the initial action (Goldenberg & Goldenberg, 2004). In addition, systems theory focuses on the function of the system rather than the individual. From this perspective, problematic individuals are understood in terms of family interaction patterns and are therefore conceptualized within the social context in which their problems occurred (Hazelrigg, Cooper, & Borduin, 1987).

Key Concepts

Goldenberg and Goldenberg (2004) and Sperry and Carlson (1991) identify key concepts associated with systems theory. The following overview of these concepts incorporates their descriptions.

Organization. The organizational structure of the family system can be understood in terms of wholeness, hierarchies, and boundaries (Gurman & Kniskern, 1981). *Wholeness* relates to the recurrent patterns reflected in the family system as opposed to individual elements of the family (Sperry & Carlson, 1991). Wholeness suggests that the family is more than the sum of its parts, with the family system having a life of its own (Everett, 1990a). *Hierarchies* involve the different levels of subsystems that make up the family system, for example, parents, siblings, and relatives. *Boundaries* represent the degree of relatedness between family members (Goldenberg & Goldenberg, 2004). Extreme separateness between family members can occur when boundaries are rigid, and extreme togetherness is associated with diffuse boundaries (Sperry & Carlson, 1991).

Communication. All behaviors, verbal and nonverbal, are considered important aspects of communication. Systems theory also attempts to identify and assess familial communication patterns.

Family Rules. Families are governed by rules that influence how family members interact and how well the family functions. For example, an alcoholic family might have an unwritten rule that no one may talk about a family member's drinking problem.

Family Homeostasis. Family homeostasis is the tendency of family systems to maintain equilibrium or restore balance if the system becomes disrupted. Family systems can resist change in an attempt to maintain homeostasis.

Information Processing. Information processing involves the exchange of information between the family and the outside world. It provides essential feedback for families to make necessary alterations in functioning. A family system is considered open if there is sufficient opportunity for information processing and closed if there is insufficient opportunity. Healthy family systems are neither too open nor too closed (Sperry & Carlson, 1991).

Change. Watzlawick, Weakland, and Fisch (1974) note that there can be first-order or second-order change. First-order changes are alterations that leave the organizational structure unchanged, whereas second-order changes result in fundamental change to the system's organization (Sperry & Carlson, 1991).

The Functional Family System. It would be presumptuous to set forth a definitive description of what constitutes a functional family, since any definition would vary from culture to culture and family to family. Therefore, findings from the following studies on this topic are presented with that caution.

Fisher and Sprenkle (1978) surveyed 310 members of AAMFT in terms of what they believe constitutes a healthy family. The results of the survey suggest that the fully functioning family is one in which the family members feel valued, supported, and safe. In addition, the researchers note, "They can express themselves without fear of judgment, knowing that opinions will be attended to carefully and emphatically. Family members are also able to negotiate when necessary" (Fisher & Sprenkle, 1978, p. 9).

Ebert (1978), Stinnet and DeFrain (1985), and Watts, Trusty, and Lim (1996) identify many additional characteristics of healthy family functioning. These characteristics are summarized as follows:

- *Sharing of feelings.* Family members feel free to openly share positive and negative feelings with each other.
- *Social interest.* Healthy families tend to have many of the characteristics associated with the Adlerian concept of social interest (for example, social relatedness and sense of connectedness to others, community feeling, and empathy).
- *Adaptability.* These families take a flexible-adaptive approach to problem solving and problem prevention as opposed to a rigid-restrictive approach to the challenges of life.
- *Boundary clarity.* These families allow for a balance between promoting a sense of community, cohesion, and belonging and encouraging family members to grow as autonomous individuals.
- *Understanding of feelings.* All members of the family sense that they are being understood by the other family members.
- *Acceptance of individual differences.* Individual differences among family members are permitted and even encouraged so all family members can develop their unique potential.
- *Highly developed sense of caring.* Family members communicate a sense of love and caring to each other. This contributes to family members feeling valued and having a sense of belonging within the family.
- *Cooperation.* Each family member is willing to work in a cooperative manner to help the family function effectively.
- *Sense of humor.* Family members are capable of laughing at themselves and joking about family events.
- *Provision for survival and safety needs.* The basic needs of food, shelter, and clothing are provided.
- *Nonadversary problem solving.* Problems are usually solved in a democratic fashion.
- *Overall philosophy.* The family has a set of values that provides a structure for family living.
- *Commitment.* Family members are committed to each other's well-being.
- *Expression of appreciation.* Family members regularly express appreciation to each other.
- *Communication.* Good communication patterns are established between family members.
- *Time spent together.* Family members spend time together to foster positive relationships and a sense of family unity.
- *Spirituality.* Family members can draw strength from their spirituality.
- *Coping skills.* The family has the coping skills necessary to meet the challenges of family life.

These characteristics collectively suggest that a functional family system creates a positive environment for individuals to grow and develop. It is characterized by love, caring, and mutual respect. Family members can effectively communicate with each other and be responsive to forces outside the family. The family has the necessary coping mechanisms to be successful in meeting the developmental tasks of family life.

Evaluation of Systems Theory

Systems theory has added an important dimension to the counseling literature. It has contributed to the understanding of how systems work and their influence on psychological functioning. The systems perspective has been particularly useful in describing the structure and process of family life and how the family system creates an entity that is greater than the sum of its individual parts (Goldenberg & Goldenberg, 2005). According to Goldenberg and Goldenberg (2005), systems thinking provides a mechanism for seeing wholes: relationships rather than isolated units and patterns of change rather than static snapshots (Senge, 1990).

Enns (1988) and Epstein and Loos (1989) also identify five weaknesses of systems theory. First, systems theory has been accused of overlooking the importance of intrapsychic issues, ignoring clients' emotions and affect, and failing to address issues of responsibility (Golann, 1987; Nichols, 1987a, 1987b). Second, feminists contend that systems theory does not take into account important familial issues such as power, equality, and sex-role function (Enns, 1988; Goldner, 1985). Third, the systems perspective does not adequately consider factors that occur outside the family system, such as at a job or in school (Elkaim, 1982). Fourth, the systems approach is not realistic in that it attempts to "heal the cracked bones of a whole number of people rather than stop the hand of those delivering the blows" (Elkaim, 1982, p. 345). Finally, systems concepts and practices are in need of empirical validation (Liddle, 1982; Shields, 1986).

Ecosystems theory (Sherrard & Amatea, 2003) and postmodern/social constructionist trends in family counseling (Anderson & Goolishian, 1992; White & Epston, 1990) represent new opportunities to overcome some of the criticisms of systems theory. Ecosystems theory emphasizes holism and is concerned with relationships between the individual, couples, the family, and the sociocultural environment (Sherrard & Amatea, 2003). Ecosystems theory appears inclusive, attempting to create a balance between intrapsychic and interpersonal forces. It recognizes the individual and expands systemic horizons beyond the family to include sociocultural forces that represent the individual's social and physical environment. Postmodern/social constructionist trends are consistent with ecosystems theory. From a postmodern/social constructionist perspective, individuals construct their own reality based on the languages and narratives passed on from culture to culture. Ecosystems and postmodern/social constructivist theories represent important trends in counseling, especially in terms of creating a more inclusive, comprehensive model for marriage and family counseling.

The Family Life Cycle

Duvall (1957) has proposed an eight-stage model for understanding family life, which provides another important theoretical foundation for marriage and family counselors. The eight stages begin with marriage and end with the death of both spouses. The model identifies developmental tasks associated with each stage as well as the approximate number of years that each stage will last. Table 10.1 provides an overview of Duvall's family life cycle model.

Duvall's family life cycle model has been integrated into theories of marriage and family counseling (Carter & McGoldrick, 1988; Haley, 1971, 1973; Kovacs, 1988;

TABLE 10.1 Duvall's Family Life Cycle Model

Stage of the Family Life Cycle	Positions in the Family	Stage-Critical Family Developmental Tasks	Approximate Number of Years in Stage
1. Married couples (without children)	Wife Husband	Establishing a mutually satisfying marriage Adjusting to pregnancy and the promise of parenthood	2 years
2. Childbearing families (oldest child birth–30 months old)	Wife-mother Husband-father Infant daughter or son or both	Giving birth to, adjusting to, and encouraging the development of infants	2–5 years
3. Families with preschool children (oldest child 30 months–6 years old)	Wife-mother Husband-father Daughter-sister Son-brother	Adapting to the critical needs and interests of preschool children Coping with energy depletion and lack of privacy as parents	3–5 years
4. Families with school children (oldest child 6–13 years old)	Wife-mother Husband-father Daughter-sister Son-brother	Fitting into the community of school-age families Encouraging children's educational achievements	7 years
5. Families with teenagers (oldest child 13–20 years old)	Wife-mother Husband-father Daughter-sister Son-brother	Balancing freedom with responsibility as teenagers mature Establishing postparental interests and careers as parents of growing children	7 years
6. Families as launching centers (first child gone to last child leaving home)	Wife-mother-grandmother Husband-father-grandfather Daughter-sister-aunt Son-brother-uncle	Releasing young adults into work, military service, college, and marriage with appropriate rituals and assistance Maintaining a supportive home base	8 years
7. Middle-aged parents (empty nest to retirement)	Wife-mother-grandmother Husband-father-grandfather	Rebuilding the marriage relationship Maintaining kin ties with older and younger generations	15± years
8. Aging family members (retirement to death of both spouses)	Widow/widower Wife-mother-grandmother Husband-father-grandfather	Coping with bereavement and living alone Closing the family home or adapting it to aging needs Adjusting to retirement	10–15± years

Source: From Marriage and Family Development (5th ed.), by E. Duvall, 1977, Philadelphia, PA: Lippincott. Copyright 1977 by Lippincott. Reprinted by permission of Addison Wesley Educational Publishers Inc.

Solomon, 1973). Carter and McGoldrick (1988) note that Duvall's model can be useful for practitioners in identifying past, present, and future developmental tasks associated with family life. Solomon (1973) suggests that failure to master the developmental tasks associated with a particular stage could have adverse effects on a family's functioning. Wilcoxon (1985) also notes that marriage and family counselors could play an important role in assisting families to develop the necessary coping skills associated with particular developmental tasks.

Haley (1973) provides additional information on the therapeutic implications of the family life cycle. He notes that the transition points between stages are the most stressful times for families and that familial problems typically occur during these periods. In addition, Haley (1973) contends that a central therapeutic task is to help families resolve developmental issues so that they can move forward in the family life cycle.

Evaluation of the Family Life Cycle

The family life cycle is a valuable model for understanding how family life proceeds through time. It has also been studied extensively in family research, including how it can be integrated with systems concepts (Kovacs, 1988). In addition, the family life cycle provides a focus for counseling by identifying developmental tasks that require assistance from the counselor.

Goldenberg and Goldenberg (2004) also identify weaknesses of the family life cycle model. They point out that it does not take into account the wide array of contemporary family structures that result from divorce and remarriage. In addition, Goldenberg and Goldenberg (2004) note that Duvall's model does not provide enough information on the transition points between stages, which can be especially problematic for families.

Marriage Counseling

Marital problems rank highest as the reason for referral to mental health services (Sperry & Carlson, 1991). Sholevar (1985) estimates that 75 percent of all clients entering counseling are seeking assistance with marital difficulties, as well as help with other problems. Goldenberg and Goldenberg (2004) note that people tend to seek marriage counseling when a family system is experiencing a state of disequilibrium owing to problems such as infidelity, sexual incompatibility, disagreements over child-rearing practices, concerns of divorce, ineffective communication, and issues relating to power and control.

Friedlander and Tuason (2000) provide evidence suggesting that marriage counseling can also be useful to treat individual problems such as depression and alcoholism. For example, depression linked to a distressed marriage is better treated in marriage counseling, whereas depression not related to marital problems responds better to individual counseling. In the treatment of alcoholism, marriage counseling is viewed as superior over individual counseling in overcoming violent tendencies, maintaining abstinence, and enhancing marital satisfaction. Marriage counseling is considered particularly useful in treating alcoholism in terms of promoting alcohol education and the motivational influences of a caring partner.

Marriage counseling can be a very challenging and rewarding experience for marriage counselors and clients. Friedlander and Tuason (2000) note that individuals requesting marriage counseling often wait "until the last minute" to seek help. By the time they enter counseling, their problems are usually well entrenched. It is therefore not so surprising that 50 percent of clients continue to be dissatisfied with their partner after completing marriage counseling. Counselors can also derive rewards from marriage counseling. It can be very gratifying for marriage counselors to successfully help clients overcome problems and build the foundations for lasting, meaningful relationships.

The Counseling Process

Marriage counseling tends to be brief, problem centered, and pragmatic (Goldenberg & Goldenberg, 2004). The most popular form of marriage counseling is *conjoint marriage counseling* (Nichols & Everett, 1986), which involves the counselor working with the couple together. Humphrey (1983) describes a slight modification of the conjoint session, suggesting that the counselor see each individual separately before the conjoint session. He contends that when the individuals are seen separately, they will more openly discuss sensitive issues such as an extramarital affair. When this approach is used, the counselor must establish a clear policy regarding confidentiality. The counselor must clarify with the client what information from individual sessions can be introduced during conjoint sessions, and how it will be conveyed.

The actual process of marriage counseling varies according to the theoretical orientation of the counselor. Marriage counselors utilize a wide variety of counseling theories, such as psychoanalytic, cognitive-behavioral, strategic, and structural (Sperry & Carlson, 1991). To a large degree these theories can be considered adaptations of those utilized in individual counseling, as discussed in Chapters 7, 8, and 9, and those associated with family counseling, as presented later in this chapter.

There also appear to be some commonalities in marriage counseling. Sperry and Carlson (1991) note that all approaches utilize a systems perspective. Goldenberg and Goldenberg (2004) suggest that marriage counselors address thoughts, feelings, and behaviors within the context of marital and family systems.

In addition, several integrative models of marriage counseling have been developed that provide a broad, flexible approach. For example, Glick, Clarkin, and Kessler (1987) and Nichols (1988) contend that marriage counseling has three stages: early, middle, and termination. Nichols's (1988) model has three tasks associated with the early stage: establishing a positive relationship, assessment and goal setting, and providing immediate assistance to the couple. The middle stage is primarily concerned with using intervention strategies to resolve counseling goals. The termination stage allows for the transition toward termination once the counseling goals have been achieved.

Skills-Based Marriage Counseling

Sperry and Carlson (1991) describe a skills-based approach to marriage counseling adapted from Dinkmeyer and Carlson's (1984) earlier work on marital enrichment. It is a practical approach that can be utilized by practitioners of different theoretical orientations. The skills-based approach to marriage counseling evolved from the following principles:

(a) healthy, productive marriages require time and commitment, (b) the skills necessary for a satisfying marriage can be learned, (c) change requires each partner to assume responsibility, (d) positive feelings such as love and caring can return with behavior change, and (e) small changes can help bring about big changes.

According to Sperry and Carlson (1991, p. 45), the 10 skills that are believed to contribute to effective marriages are that both partners do the following:

1. Individually accept responsibility for their behavior and self-esteem
2. Identify and align their personal and marital goals
3. Choose to encourage each other
4. Communicate their feelings with honesty and openness
5. Listen emphatically when feelings are expressed
6. Seek to understand the factors that influence their relationship
7. Demonstrate that they accept and value each other
8. Choose thoughts, words, and actions that support the positive goals of their marriage
9. Solve marital conflicts together
10. Commit themselves to the ongoing process of maintaining an equal marriage

The skills-based approach to marriage counseling is educative in that it provides the couple with opportunities to learn how to use the 10 skills associated with effective marriages. For example, the couple can learn how to use some of these skills in a four-step approach to conflict resolution. The four steps are (a) show mutual respect, (b) pinpoint the real issue, (c) seek areas of agreement, and (d) mutually participate in decisions. Additional guidelines for conflict resolution include being specific and oriented in the present and future, using good communication skills such as "I" messages and active listening, avoiding absolutes, and avoiding attempting to determine who was right or wrong (Sperry & Carlson, 1991).

Marital Assessment

Marital assessment is one aspect of the counseling process that deserves special attention. Comprehensive assessment is essential in marriage and family counseling (Sperry & Carlson, 1991) since 83 percent of treatment failures are associated with inadequate assessment (Coleman, 1985). Sperry (1989a) suggests that comprehensive assessment in marriage counseling involves assessing the situation, the system, each spouse, and the suitability of the couple for marriage counseling. The following is a description of these four factors:

1. *The situation.* Assessing the situation involves identifying stressors, precipitating factors to marital discord, and other factors that affect the situation.
2. *The system.* Systems theory can be used to assess the marital system to gain an understanding of its functional and dysfunctional characteristics.
3. *Each spouse.* Each spouse is evaluated to determine his or her level of physical and psychological health as well as personality style.
4. *Suitability for treatment.* It is also important to determine whether marriage counseling is appropriate for a couple. Beutler (1983) suggests that clients need to be motivated

to change and have reasonable expectations regarding outcomes to be suitable for marriage counseling.

Commonly used assessment procedures include the clinical interview in marriage counseling (Framo, 1981); the use of enactment, which involves getting clients to act out conflicts or problems during a counseling session (Nichols, 1988); and the use of standardized tests designed for marriage counseling (Boen, 1988).

Marital assessment instruments have become popular in marriage counseling. These instruments are especially useful during initial counseling sessions, but they can also be used throughout the counseling process as the need arises (Boen, 1988). Boen (1988) provides an overview of the most widely used marital assessment instruments as follows.

Stuart's Couples Precounseling Inventory (SCPI).   The SCPI was developed by Stuart (1983). It identifies 15 areas in which the couple is satisfied or dissatisfied, such as with regards to child-rearing practices or sexual practices. The SCPI also identifies the amount of commitment each member has to the relationship as well as which individual has more to gain or lose by maintaining the relationship.

Russell and Madsen's Marriage Counseling Report (MCR).   The MCR was developed by Russell and Madsen (1985). It is based on the 16 Personality Factors Questionnaire (16 PF), which was developed by Raymond Cattell, as discussed in Chapter 4. The MCR provides information on the personality of each spouse, how these personalities may be contributing to marital difficulties, and how the marriage may be exacerbating psychological problems of the spouses.

Taylor-Johnson Temperament Analysis (TJTA).   The TJTA (Taylor & Morrison, 1984) represents a revision of the Johnson Temperament Analysis developed by R. H. Johnson in 1941. It "can be used to show where a couple are similar or different to the normal population as well as where they are similar or different to each other and the degree of understanding they have for each other's personality characteristics" (Boen, 1988, p. 485).

Snyder's Marital Satisfaction Inventory (MSI).   The MSI, developed by Snyder (1981), identifies basic areas in which the couple is satisfied or dissatisfied, such as with regards to communication or problem solving. The MSI is particularly useful for couples who do not know where to begin in terms of dealing with their concerns.

Assessment of Divorce.   One intriguing method of assessing marriages is to identify factors that predict divorce. Gottman (1994) and Gottman, Coan, Carrere, and Swanson (1998) have conducted a series of studies that have identified the following variables to predict divorce:

- Criticism, contempt, defensiveness, and emotional withdrawal during conflict resolution (Gottman, 1994)
- Lack of positive affect such as humor, interest, and affection (successful marriages have higher rates of positive affect interactions, and their ratios of positive to negative

affect during conflict resolution is 5:1 as compared to unstable marriages, which have ratios of 0.8:1) (Gottman, 1994)
- Husband rejects the wife's influence during a conflict (Gottman et al., 1998)

Gottman et al. (1998) have identified the following variables to predict marital satisfaction:

- Wives soften the startup of addressing the potential conflict (for example, they take a more tentative rather than confrontational approach)
- Husbands deescalate low-intensity negative affect of wives (for example, anger, sadness, and tension)
- Wives deescalate high-intensity negative affect of husbands (for example, contempt, defensiveness, and belligerence)
- Physiological soothing for self or partner for stress management (especially important for men, who are considered to have higher levels of autonomic arousal during conflict than women)

In addition, Gottman et al. (1998) have found that listening skills may not be very useful during a conflict. They may be too direct and confrontational and require spouses to empathize with a partner when they are emotionally unable to do so (for example, after a spouse has just gotten angry at them). In this regard, listening skills may result in a celebration of the conflict. Gottman et al. (1998) note that negative emotions such as anger are not predictors of divorce. In fact, successful marriages need to have the expression of both positive and negative emotions. What appears to be important is "gentleness, soothing, and deescalation of negativity (negativity of one spouse followed by the partner's neutral affect)" (Gottman et al., 1998, p. 16).

Gottman and Notarius (2000) provide a review of a decade's research on marital interactions. The research did not focus on predicting divorce but on factors that tend to enhance or undermine marital (or couples) satisfaction. Some of these findings are as follows:

- Within one year of the birth of the first child, couples tend to revert to stereotypical gender roles, males withdraw into work, and the quality of communication and sexual relations reduces dramatically (pleasure is derived from interacting with the baby).
- Distressed couples emotionally invalidate and inhibit problem solving, whereas nondistressed couples emotionally validate, self-disclose, and facilitate problem solving.
- Engaging in a demand/withdrawal pattern (wife demands a change and husband withdraws through inaction or defensiveness) is associated with a decline in wives' marital satisfaction within two and a half years.
- The effects of humor on problem solving appear to change over the life span from negative during the middle adult years to positive during the late adult years. (Middle adults tend to use humor as an avoidance mechanism and late adults use humor as a way to express genuine positive affect.)

■ Couples who maintain change after termination of couples counseling are able to do a better job of keeping work stress out of the marriage than are couples who experience relapse relating to change.

Family Counseling

No clear definition of family counseling has emerged. Its hallmark, however, is that the process involves problems experienced by an individual that seem to indicate more fundamental problems within the family system (Horne & Ohlsen, 1982). Family counseling is superior to individual counseling in terms of the treatment of some disorders. For example, Campbell and Patterson (1995) have found that adolescents who had anorexia for three years or less had more positive treatment outcomes with family counseling than when they were treated with individual counseling. The systems perspective continues to characterize family counseling in that family counselors treat problems within a relationship context rather than working separately with individuals (Goldenberg & Goldenberg, 2004).

This section first provides an overview of six prominent theories used by family counselors, as summarized in Table 10.2. Following this overview is a discussion of the counseling process in family counseling.

Psychodynamic Family Counseling

Nathan Ackerman (1937, 1956, 1966, 1970) is credited with integrating Freud's psychoanalytic theory into family counseling. His model emphasizes the importance of both intrapersonal and interpersonal forces. Ackerman (1970) viewed the family as a system of interacting personalities, with each family member representing a subsystem. The primary aim of Ackerman's approach is to promote change and growth by altering patterns of communication, resolving pathological inner conflicts, and helping family members define their roles in a complementary manner (Goldenberg & Goldenberg, 2004).

Framo (1992) later integrated object-relations theory (see Chapter 7) into psychodynamic family counseling. The basic premise of object-relations theory is that the fundamental motivation in life is the drive to satisfy object relations (for example, satisfying relationships) (Goldenberg & Goldenberg, 2004). In addition, object-relations theory contends that intrapsychic conflicts that evolved from the family of origin play a key role in relationship difficulties. As part of the overall treatment program, psychodynamic family counselors may conduct individual counseling, couples counseling, and family counseling that includes members of the client's family of origin (Goldenberg & Goldenberg, 2004).

Experiential Family Counseling

The theoretical origins of experiential family counseling can be traced to the humanistic-existential schools of counseling, as discussed in Chapter 7. Virginia Satir (1983, 1988), Carol Whitaker (1976, 1977), and William Bumberry (Whitaker & Bumberry, 1988) are credited with incorporating the major concepts of the humanistic-existential schools into family counseling. The basic premise of this approach is that if individual family members can be freed to move toward self-actualization, the family will function effectively. The

TABLE 10.2 Theories of Family Counseling

Theory	Founder(s)	Key Concepts	Process	Goals
Psychodynamic family counseling	Nathan Ackerman, James Framo	Intrapsychic forces are believed to play a key role in family dysfunction; object relations such as meaningful relationships are the primary motivational force in life	Focuses on intrapersonal and interpersonal forces (for example, strengthening the ego, clarifying roles, helping clients obtain more satisfying relationships)	Promote change and growth by altering patterns of communication, resolving pathological inner conflicts, and defining roles of family members in complementary fashion
Experiential family counseling	Virginia Satir, Carol Whitaker, William Bumberry	Self-actualization, awareness, choice, and responsibility	Frees family members to move toward self-actualization; has an experiential focus; relates to the here and now rather than past issues	Promote clear communication; help family members become authentic, autonomous individuals; promote a positive family climate
Structural family counseling	Salvador Minuchin	Systemic concepts such as boundaries and reframing	Counselor joins the family to alter the structure of the interaction between family members	Clarify boundaries; increase flexibility of family interactions; modify dysfunctional family structure
Strategic family counseling	Jay Haley, Cloe Madanes	Communication patterns and power struggles determine the nature of relationships between family members	Attempts to directly resolve presenting problems with little attempt to gain insight from past events	Resolve symptomology of family members by redefining relationships between family members
Adlerian/Dreikursian family counseling	Alfred Adler, Rudolph Dreikurs	Family constellation, mutual respect, goals of misbehavior, use of consequences, encouragement, communication	Has an educational focus to help parents learn skills to foster positive parent-child relationships	Understand the dynamics of problems occurring within the family; promote positive parent-child relationships
Postmodern/social-constructionism	Tom Andersen, Michael White, and others	Problems are conceptualized in terms of language and narratives	Uses stories reflecting family life that are developed and rewritten, creating new opportunities for a more meaningful family life	Help families create new stories, fostering improved family functioning

goals of experiential family counseling include promoting clear communication among family members; helping family members become authentic, autonomous individuals; assisting the family in developing a positive family climate characterized by encouragement, caring, and intimacy; and promoting awareness of choice and responsibility in family members.

The counseling process in experiential family counseling focuses on the here and now instead of dealing with problems from the past. The emphasis within counseling is on experiencing rather than intellectualizing. In this regard, the counselor utilizes a variety of techniques such as sculpting, confrontation, communication skills training, and Gestalt exercises to help family members become aware of their feelings. For example, the technique of *sculpting* involves having one person physically arrange the other family members to create a "sculpture." The person creates the sculpture by using space and form to represent perceptions of family relationships, for instance, placing a child between the mother and father to symbolize interference between the marital dyad. All family members are then invited to discuss the creation. Typical themes that result from such discussions are closeness, isolation, alignment, intimacy, and power.

Structural Family Counseling

Salvador Minuchin (1974, 1984) is credited with developing structural family counseling. The role of the counselor in this approach is to join the family in a position of leadership. The goals are to clarify boundaries between family members, increase flexibility of family interactions, and modify dysfunctional family structure (Goldenberg & Goldenberg, 2004).

Minuchin (1974, 1984) has developed several innovative concepts that have played a key role in the evolution of systems theory (Goldenberg & Goldenberg, 2004). One example is the concept of *boundaries,* which are the unwritten rules that help define roles and functions of family members. Boundaries determine what will be allowed to occur between family members, and they can ensure privacy or allow for intimacy. Family dysfunctioning can result when boundaries become rigid, confused, or conflicting.

Another concept that Minuchin (1974, 1984) developed is *reframing,* a family counseling technique used to help the family see things from a more positive perspective. For example, an adolescent might complain that his mother spends too much time working. Using the technique of reframing, the counselor might help the adolescent focus on the fact that his mother enjoys her job and that it makes her a pleasant person to be with.

Strategic Family Counseling

Jay Haley (1963, 1971, 1973, 1976, 1980) and individuals such as Cloe Madanes (1981, 1984) have played key roles in the development of strategic family counseling. This approach focuses on communication patterns between family members and views intrapsychic forces as unimportant. Haley (1976, 1980) contends that the relationships between family members can be determined by the manner in which they communicate and how they position themselves in terms of power issues.

This approach is considered strategic because it focuses on resolving the presenting problem directly, with little attempt to provide insight from past events. To resolve the presenting problem, counselors use procedures oriented to concrete actions, including homework assignments, teaching new skills, and advice giving. They also use paradoxical techniques, which involve prescribing the symptom. For example, if a husband and wife have a habit of yelling at each other, the counselor might ask them to spend 10 minutes yelling at one another every day.

Strategic family counseling can be a powerful and effective form of counseling. Strategies such as advice giving and paradoxical techniques must be used carefully, however, or they may do more harm than good to the family (Nichols, 1984).

Adlerian Family Counseling

Alfred Adler's school of psychology and the later writings of Rudolph Dreikurs (see Chapter 7) have been applied to a variety of helping processes, including family counseling and parent education. Adlerian family counseling focuses on individual family members as well as the overall functioning of the family. The main goal of this approach is to improve parent-child relationships (Lowe, 1982).

The role and function of the counselor is psychoeducational—helping parents learn principles and understand the dynamics of problems occurring within the family (Lowe, 1982). The approach is therefore educative in nature. In this process, the counselor identifies basic mistakes, teaches the parents concepts that will help them understand misbehavior, helps parents deal effectively with discipline problems, and assists in establishing positive parent-child relations.

The key concepts of this approach are family constellation, goals of misbehavior, use of natural and logical consequences, encouragement, and communication. Although these Adlerian concepts are discussed in Chapter 7, they are presented here in light of the family counseling approach.

Family Constellation.   The family constellation relates to the overall structure of the family. Particular attention is paid to how birth-order characteristics can be used to understand the personality of the children (for example, first-born children tend to be bossy).

Goals of Misbehavior.   Children's misbehavior is seen as movement toward one of four goals of misbehavior: attention, power, revenge, and display of inadequacy. Additional goals of misbehavior for teenagers include excitement, peer acceptance, and superiority (Dinkmeyer, McKay, & Dinkmeyer, 1997).

Use of Natural and Logical Consequences.   Parents are taught to use natural and logical consequences as opposed to punishment to discipline children. Among the advantages of this approach over punishment are that consequences are more logically tied to misbehavior, promote choice and responsibility in the child, and minimize animosity between the parent and child.

Encouragement.   Parents are taught to use encouragement with their child. Offering encouragement focuses on effort and helps build self-esteem, confidence, and self-efficacy.

Communication Skills.   Parents learn how to use effective communication skills with their child. A philosophy of mutual respect is essential for effective communication. When parents respect the child, they will tend to communicate empathic understanding of the child's point of view. Parents may also be taught listening skills and problem-solving skills, which can be used to help their child deal with personal problems.

The concepts utilized in Adlerian family counseling have also been incorporated into parent education programs such as Dinkmeyer, McKay, and Dinkmeyer's (1997) systematic training for effective parenting (STEP) programs. Parent education programs typically involve small groups of individuals meeting to discuss parenting concepts and concerns, usually for approximately $1^1/_2$ hours each week over a 10-week period. Research efforts show that the effectiveness of parent educators is not related to whether the educators have been parents themselves (Schultz, Nystul, & Law, 1980). Research also suggests that it is important to include role-play activities to allow for the internalization and transfer from attitudes to behaviors (Schultz & Nystul, 1980).

I developed an approach to family counseling called *marathon family counseling* while working on the Navajo Indian reservation. The approach evolved out of my work with Katherine Hillis, a Navajo mental health counselor. Marathon family counseling shares the following characteristics with Mara Selvini-Palazzoli's (1980) approach. Both utilize extended family sessions lasting up to eight hours approximately once a month, and both serve clients who live in rural areas and have had to travel hundreds of miles for the session.

Marathon family counseling is based on the principles of Adlerian family counseling, which include using encouragement, establishing mutual respect, identifying basic mistakes, and providing reorientation from basic mistakes. The following *Personal Note* illustrates this approach.

Postmodern/Social Constructionist Trends in Family Counseling

Bitter and Corey (1996) note that the postmodern/social constructionist perspective is associated with recent trends in family therapy. As noted earlier, social constructivism represents a paradigm shift that recognizes the multiple realities reflected in the languages of different cultures and the stories internalized by individuals in those cultures. Social constructionism therefore parallels the postmodern position, which recognizes a subjective reality based on the context of the observational process used. The social-constructionist perspective is therefore particularly useful in infusing issues of diversity (such as gender, feminism, and culture) into family counseling.

The process of counseling (from a postmodern/social constructionist perspective) is similar to the qualitative research method of discovery. The counselor enters the relationship without preconceived ideas of what should be or should happen in therapy but instead attempts to discover with clients what is important from their phenomenological perspective. In this process, families are encouraged to engage in conversations that explore the meanings family members have given to their problems (Goldenberg & Goldenberg, 2004). In this process, "past experience is viewed as helpful not as a source of objective fact but as a source for determining and understanding the language, assumptions, and views of clients" (Giblin & Chan, 1995, p. 326). The counseling relationship is a collaborative relationship that fosters empowerment in clients. Goals and procedures vary according to the needs of clients and theoretical perspective of counselors but typically focus on helping families create new stories that enlarge their perspective and options and can bring new meaning to family life (Bitter & Corey, 1996). "Clients are invited into a reflective process,

A Personal Note

A 74-year-old grandmother arrived at the mental health center at the Navajo Indian reservation where I was working. Accompanied by her daughter, the woman appeared depressed and tearful during the initial interview. She lived with her husband 100 miles from the center and had three daughters, two sons, and twelve grandchildren.

The grandmother complained that two of her grandchildren had wrecked four of her automobiles over the years. She thought that the situation was hopeless and that it would probably happen again because "kids will be kids." While she talked, my Navajo mental health aide and I identified some basic mistakes. As discussed in Chapter 7, the Adlerian concept of a basic mistake is a self-defeating idea, such as an overgeneralization, false goal of security, misconception of life's demands, or minimization of one's worth. The client's basic mistakes were as follows.

1. Others can't survive without me.
2. The children of my family aren't responsible, so I'll have to take care of everything.
3. I'm not important. Other people are more important than I am.

At this point, my aide and I decided that the client could benefit from marathon family counseling because of the great distance she and her daughter had traveled and the depth of her distress. We then discovered that the grandchild who had most recently wrecked her car was in jail for a D.W.I. citation. Since we wanted to include that family member in the session, we decided to have the family counseling session at the local jail. We phoned several other family members, and they agreed to meet us there.

We began the session by asking the grandmother to share how she was feeling. She started to cry and said she was very sad. She didn't feel her grandchildren cared about her, but instead just wanted to use her and her cars. She said she felt that they had no respect for her or her feelings. I asked how the family members felt about what the grandmother was saying. The two grandchildren who had wrecked her cars seemed uneasy and defensive. After these feelings were explored, they were able to make some statements that seemed to express genuine concern.

I mentioned that all people make mistakes and have room for improvement. The family members agreed. My aide and I then explored ways each family member had contributed to the current problem and what they could do to help. With much encouragement, each person was able to make a specific plan for improvement.

At the end of the session, I asked the family members to express how the session affected them and what they wanted to do differently to help their family. I arranged to see them all in two weeks at the grandmother's house. We finished the session by thanking the family members and shaking their hands. Several family members also shook hands with one another and gave each other warm embraces.

We then talked with the grandmother privately and explored how she was feeling. She said she was relieved but still felt somehow responsible for her family's behavior. At this point, we discussed the basic mistakes we had identified earlier. We then used a variety of procedures to reorient the grandmother from her basic mistakes. For example, we read the section on children from *The Prophet* (Gibran, 1965). This helped her realize that she was not responsible for her grandchildren. Her job was to provide guidance and love and let them—like arrows—fly freely into the challenges of life. She began to realize that if she didn't let go, they wouldn't have the opportunity to become responsible people. She had a very positive response to the reading from *The Prophet* and wanted a copy of the book. I let her borrow mine until she could get a copy. She then left for home with her daughter.

After the initial marathon counseling session, my mental health aide and I provided counseling services for the family over an 18-month period. The grandmother was eventually able to let go of her tendency to feel responsible for her grandchildren's behavior. Her signs of depression were gone after one month. The two grandchildren who had wrecked her cars both had minor problems with the law (e.g., public intoxication) during the counseling period. On the positive side, however, they didn't wreck any more cars during that time.

Source: From "Marathon Family Counseling" by M. Nystul, 1988, *Individual Psychology: The Journal of Adlerian Theory, Research, & Practice, 44*(2), pp. 210–216, by permission of the University of Texas Press.

and the goal is to open up new meanings and possibilities for alternative behaviors" (Giblin & Chan, 1995, p. 326).

Bitter and Corey (1996) identify the following postmodern/social constructionist approaches to family counseling.

The Reflecting Team.   Tom Andersen (1991, 1992) proposes that family therapy can be enriched by the dialogues that are generated between families and professionals who are observing and processing the family counseling session. The overall process and goal of the reflecting team approach is to help families create new life stories through dialogue and reflection.

For example, a reflecting team that has observed a family session through a one-way mirror can then join the family and process the central story that characterized the session. The story can be one of concern that family members don't seem to care about each other. Together, counselors and family members can reflect on issues such as when the family does get along. The resulting dialogue can create new stories that promote hope and encouragement for the family.

The Linguistic Approach.   Harlene Anderson and Harold Goolishian (1992) are the key individuals associated with the linguistic approach to family counseling. They contend that narratives emerge from social interactions over time, and the nature of the narrative is associated with the meaning experienced in life. In this approach, the counselor enters into the session with compassion and caring and a keen interest in discovering meaning from the families' stories. The goal of counseling is to help the family create alternative stories that can enhance meaning for the family.

The linguistic approach involves helping families explore the evolution of stories that characterize family life. For example, dysfunctional stories can emerge from the narratives shared between family members, which are then passed on from generation to generation (for example, "blacks don't trust whites" or vice versa). Families can use these insights to help overcome dysfunctional elements in their stories (such as stereotyping and prejudice) and then create more meaningful and functional stories.

The Narrative Approach.   Michael White and David Epston (1990) and the earlier work of Michel Foucault (1980) are associated with the narrative approach. The narrative approach contends that narratives are a reflection of the dominant culture and therefore must be challenged to ensure that they are sensitive to diversity issues such as gender, sexual orientation, and culture. The process and goal of the narrative approach is to help families deconstruct dysfunctional narratives (from the dominant culture) and reauthor new, more functional narratives.

The narrative approach encourages families to question the assumptions on which their stories are based in terms of potential influence from the dominant society. For example, a family member who is "coming out" with his or her family in terms of sexual orientation may encounter excessive resistance from the family. In some instances, this may result in the family being torn apart and the gay or lesbian individual being psychologically abandoned. Counselors can help these families separate their values, wants, and needs from external forces that may perceive things in rigid, either-or terms. This process may contribute to more functional family narratives that are based on their cultural identities and worldviews and not the worldviews projected by the dominant society.

Solution-Oriented Therapy.   Steve de Shazer (1991) and William O'Hanlon and Michele Weiner-Davis (1989) are among some of the individuals who have promoted a solution-oriented approach to counseling. The solution-oriented approach can be used across all domains of counseling, from individual to group to marriage and family. The solution-oriented approach suggests that it is more productive to focus on solutions and strengths than on problems and weakness, and that families can be assisted in creating narratives that reflect positive change.

The solution-oriented approach focuses on family strengths and problem resolution. An example would be in Adlerian/Dreikursian family counseling. In this psychoeducational approach, parents are taught to use encouragement to foster their children's self-efficacy and to use consequences to overcome discipline problems by promoting choice and responsibility.

Feminist Psychotherapy.   Carolyn Enns (1993), Edna Rawlings (1993), Judith Avis (1986), and others have set forth the major issues associated with feminist psychotherapy. Feminist psychotherapy applied to family counseling contends that the family system is a male-dominated, patriarchal system. Male domination exists even when the father is absent from the family. From a feminist perspective, male domination and control are maintained by public patriarchy as represented by government organizations such as welfare and other family assistance programs. Male-dominated narratives are perpetuated in many ways, such as through the media, research, and even the theories that describe normal family life and human development. Carol Gilligan's (1982) seminal work on moral development of women provides an example of how male-dominated research can ignore gender difference in human growth and development.

The overall aim of feminist family therapy is to help family systems overcome oppressive forces and foster mutual respect, equality, and gender sensitivity between the sexes. Some of the goals of therapy include deconstructing patriarchy narratives and reconstructing narratives that recognize gender differences and the special needs of women in all aspects of living, empowering women within the context of egalitarian families, valuing what is considered feminine or nurturing, and promoting a positive attitude toward women.

The Counseling Process

The counseling process in family counseling varies according to the theoretical orientation of the practitioner. Many aspects, however, are common to family counseling approaches, regardless of the theoretical perspective. Friedlander and Highlen (1984), Friedlander, Highlen, and Lassiter (1985), and Friedlander and Tuason (2000) identify some commonalities associated with family counseling. Some of these are that family counselors

- View the marital subsystem as the most stressed
- Align themselves with the family's established hierarchy, interacting more with parents than children
- Focus on the nuclear family, especially the parental subsystem

- Avoid direct confrontation with family members, preferring to direct messages to other family members (such as asking the wife why she thinks her husband is afraid of her)
- Actively engage in interpretation and educational processes
- Attempt to establish a therapeutic alliance with the family by being perceived as warm, trustworthy, and having clear goals

In addition, the authors found that family counselors make few references to the future, parents emphasize current issues, and children tend to relate to here-and-now issues regarding sibling relationships.

Goldenberg and Goldenberg (2004) note there is interest in developing integrative models for family counseling that can be responsive to different populations. L'Abate (1986) has set forth the following four-stage integrative model for family counseling.

Stage One: Stress Reduction. The tasks associated with this stage are establishing a positive relationship, reducing stress and conflict, resolving an existing crisis if necessary, and reducing symptomatic behavior to a tolerable level.

Stage Two: Training and Education. This stage involves helping the family learn the skills necessary to function effectively. Counselors frequently use homework assignments during this stage for family members to practice the skills they are learning.

Stage Three: Issue of Termination. During this stage, the family is given an opportunity to deal with issues that have not been resolved, such as dealing effectively with intimacy. When all issues have been resolved, the counselor helps the family move toward termination of the counseling process.

Stage Four: Follow-Up. Follow-up involves determining the efficacy of counseling and allowing for additional counseling as needed.

Diversity Issues in Marriage and Family Counseling

Diversity issues are important in all aspects of counseling, including marriage and family counseling (Hayes, 1995; Paniagua, 1996). Marriage and family counselors must be sensitive to a wide array of diversity issues, such as gender, culture, age, sexual orientation, and socioeconomic status, to be effective in their practice. Hayes (1995) notes that Rothenberg's (1995) book on race, class, and gender may be particularly useful to marriage and family counselors. It has numerous personal narratives that depict the struggles of families with issues such as racism, oppression, and sexism. Hayes (1995) goes on to note that Linda James Myers' (1988) optimal theory offers promise to family therapists to help overcome oppression through self-knowledge and positive identity development.

As noted earlier, feminist therapy has much to offer marriage and family counseling. Giblin and Chan (1995) describe several common themes in the feminist literature that they believe have relevance for marriage and family counselors. Some of these themes are communicating respect; validating feelings; supporting social and political change to overcome oppression; promoting social equality over power, control, and dominance; understanding behavior contextually; becoming aware of the relational connectedness associated with being human; and promoting mutual empathy, mutual engagement, and mutual empowerment.

Johnson (1995) identifies 10 resiliency mechanisms in culturally diverse families. Johnson defines family resiliency as the manner in which the family renews itself each day and maintains homeostasis and a sense of collective identity as a unique living system. It also relates to the ability of family members to cope with everyday problems without compromising their moral or cultural values. These resiliency mechanisms are summarized as follows. The family serves as a "sacred ark" protecting its members from the storms of adversity and providing safety and refuge for them. These families utilize multiple support systems that include spirituality, the recognition of what the elders of the family or society can offer, and the role of the extended family in daily family life. Other resiliency characteristics include the use of native language, a high value on family socialization and communication, insulation from racism and the adverse effects of migration, and the support of individual resiliency of each family member.

Paniagua (1996) provides suggestions for incorporating a cross-cultural perspective in family counseling. First, the definition of the extended family varies considerably from culture to culture. For example, in Hispanic cultures, the extended family can include the comadre (co-mother) and the compadre (co-father) as well as folk healers. Family counselors should therefore have families define what their concept of the extended family is and how their extended family affects the overall role and function of the family.

Second, family counselors should assess the levels of acculturation in the family. Significant discrepancies in acculturation between family members (for example, between children and parents or between husband and wife) can create family dysfunction and should be identified and addressed as necessary. It is also important to recognize that although a family is from a particular ethnic minority, its members may not feel that way (they may be identifying with the majority culture) (Dana, 1993). Acculturation scales have been developed for different cultures (see Chapter 6) that can be used to determine the degree of acculturation for a family member.

Third, Paniagua (1996) notes that it is not critical for a family and a counselor to be of the same race. It is more important for the counselor to have some compatibility in terms of lifestyle and values and to be sensitive to cultural variables in the assessment and treatment of family dysfunction. It is also important that the counselor has the necessary skills to be successful in cross-cultural counseling. Paniagua (1996) provides some suggestions in terms of what counselors should communicate cross-culturally during the first and subsequent family sessions. For example, during the first session it is important for counselors to demonstrate expertise and authority with Asian families, avoid discussing the behavior of African-American parents in the presence of their children, and explore levels of acculturation and provide concrete and tangible advice to all groups. In subsequent sessions, family counselors can focus on other issues associated with a cultural group or all groups, such as being sensitive to the family's sense of powerlessness (for all families but especially African Americans) and personalizing the session through the use of first names and handshaking (Hispanic families).

Brown (1997) advocates using a cross-cultural perspective in consulting with parents. Consultation with parents frequently involves using parenting programs to help parents improve parent-child relationships and foster optimal development in children. Brown (1997) suggests that cross-cultural parenting consultants "be aware of their personal values and biases, be culturally empathic, be aware of their consulting paradigm, and be able to make culturally sensitive adaptations to their approach to consultation" (p. 29).

Evaluation of Marriage and Family Counseling

At least 20 literature reviews of marriage and family counseling were conducted between 1970 and 1990, involving the analysis of approximately 300 studies (Raffa, Sypek, & Vogel, 1990). Unfortunately, methodological flaws in many of these studies drew questions concerning the efficacy of marriage and family counseling. Some of these methodological problems included a lack of clear description of intervention strategies used in marriage and family counseling studies (Bednar, Burlingame, & Masters, 1988) and a lack of controlled studies, inadequate research design, the use of assessment instruments with questionable reliability and validity, and a lack of replication of results (Raffa, Sypek, & Vogel, 1990).

More recent research and the utilization of meta-analysis to analyze multiple studies at once have been able to adequately address these methodological problems and clearly provide evidence of the efficacy of marriage and family counseling (Dunn & Schwebel, 1995; Lebow & Gurman, 1995; Shadish et al., 1995). Shadish et al. (1995) conducted a meta-analysis of 163 marriage and family counseling studies (62 marital and 101 family). Results of their investigation provide clear support for the efficacy of marriage and family counseling, no evidence of one theoretical approach being superior over others, and no evidence that marriage and family counseling is superior over individual counseling.

Dunn and Schwebel (1995) focused on an evaluation of marriage counseling suggesting that conducting meta-analysis of marriage and family counseling could obscure the results. These researchers evaluated 15 methodologically rigorous marital outcome studies. They found that behavioral marital therapy, cognitive-behavioral marital therapy, and insight-oriented marital therapy are all successful in bringing about positive change in spouses' relationship-related behavior; insight-oriented marital therapy was the most successful in enhancing the spouses' assessment of the quality of their relationship; and cognitive-behavioral marital therapy was the best at contributing to the spouses' post-therapy relationship-related cognitions.

Lebow and Gurman (1995) provide an extensive review of research (including meta-analytic reviews) and conclude that there has been an enormous enhancement of the quality of the research on marriage and family counseling between 1985 and 1995. These individuals note that much of the research has focused on behavioral approaches, but nonbehavioral methods are beginning to receive more attention in the literature. In addition, both marriage counseling and family counseling are becoming more integrative in terms of theoretical approaches and in their recognition of the merits of designing treatment approaches that are directed at the individual, family, and larger systems, such as cultural, societal, and economic (Lebow & Gurman, 1995).

Summary

The field of marriage and family counseling is both an emerging profession and a counseling specialty practiced by various members of the helping profession. Systems theory and the family life cycle model are important theoretical foundations for marriage and family counseling.

Although theories differ with regard to key concepts, goals, and counseling approaches, commonalities in the field exist. In this regard, marriage and family counseling focus on the relationship between family members and the overall family system rather than on individual family members. There also appears to be a trend toward integration of theories in an attempt to meet the needs of different populations.

Major reviews of the research that has been conducted on marriage and family counseling note that recent studies provide strong support for the efficacy of marriage and family counseling.

Personal Exploration

1. How can Gottman's work on assessing (predicting) divorce be useful in preventing interpersonal problems in your life?
2. What do you think is important in making a marriage work, and how can you take an active role in this process?
3. What are characteristics of healthy family functioning, and how can you foster this in your family life?
4. What type of counselor would you want to see if you were having marriage or family problems?

Web Sites for Chapter 10

Franklin, D. J. (2000). *Couples therapy.* Retrieved March 3, 2005, from
http://psychologyinfo.com/treatment/couples_therapy.html
Provides a description of couples therapy.

Franklin, D. J. (2000). *Family counseling.* Retrieved March 3, 2005, from
http://psychologyinfo.com/treatment/family_therapy.html
Provides a description of family therapy.

Niolon, R. (1999). *Bowenian family therapy.* Retrieved March 3, 2005, from
http://www.psychpage.com/learning/library/counseling/bowen.html
Includes information on Bowen's theory of family therapy and other links to family therapy techniques (e.g., strategic).

Child and Adolescent Counseling

The young . . . are full of passion, which excludes fear; and of hope, which inspires confidence.

—*Aristotle, Rhetoric Book II*

CHAPTER OVERVIEW

This chapter provides an overview of child and adolescent counseling. Highlights of the chapter include

- The art and science of child and adolescent counseling
- Children and adolescents from a historical perspective
- Developmental theories
- Emerging developmental theories (optimal development, attachment theory, resiliency, and emotional intelligence)
- Special approaches to child and adolescent counseling (play therapy, conflict resolution, and guidelines for child and adolescent counseling)
- Special problems of children and adolescents (child abuse and neglect, depression, and antisocial behavior)
- Diversity and postmodern issues in child and adolescent counseling

Child and adolescent counseling is an emerging specialty within the counseling profession. Some of the most promising advances in counseling and psychology are occurring in this field. These are reflected in our understanding and treatment of common problems that children and adolescents experience, including child abuse and neglect, child/adolescent depression, and antisocial behavior. In this chapter, information is presented on these types of problems as well as other conceptual and treatment issues.

The Art and Science of Child and Adolescent Counseling

Child and adolescent counseling, like all aspects of counseling, is an art and a science. It is an art to discover the private world of children and adolescents. When working with children, the challenge is finding ways to communicate that are not restricted by language and cognitive development. Challenges when working with adolescents include keeping lines of communication open and maintaining trust. Possible venues that can be used to transcend these potential barriers include play therapy, conflict resolution, parent education, family therapy, consultation with teachers and parents, and ecological-environmental approaches directed at enhancing the world of children and adolescents.

One way of conceptualizing the art of child and adolescent counseling is "reaching in–reaching out" (Nystul, 1986). In this process, the counselor attempts to meet children or adolescents from the perspective of their internal frame of reference—the world that makes sense to them and that they feel safe in. As trust and respect are established, the child or adolescent may then feel encouraged to reach out into the world of others. This may be characterized by a movement toward success-oriented rather than failure-oriented activities in school. Throughout this process, the counselor communicates a wide range of emotions such as caring, compassion, and perhaps even anger to provide the structure and emotional support necessary for the optimal development of children and adolescents.

The science of child and adolescent counseling is grounded in developmental theory, research, and practice. It recognizes that counseling across the life span must be cognizant of the physical, cognitive, and psychosocial aspects of development and their impact on the counseling process. From a developmental perspective, children and adolescents need assistance in acquiring the coping skills necessary to master the various developmental tasks necessary to move forward in their development. Counseling strategies can be directed at helping children and adolescents achieve these coping skills by fostering resiliency, positive attachment relationships, emotional and intellectual intelligence, and other qualities that promote optimal development. Recent research in diversity issues and postmodernism must also be addressed in formulating counseling strategies with children and adolescents.

Children and Adolescents from a Historical Perspective

Children

The concept of childhood as a distinct developmental stage is relatively new (LeVine & Sallee, 1992). For many years, children were viewed as miniature adults and were forced to work alongside adults in the fields and in factories and to fight in wars. Children had no special privileges, lacking the protection of child labor laws or the advantage of formal education. They were to be "seen and not heard" and used in whatever way the their parents dictated (LeVine & Sallee, 1992).

Children were often lucky to survive long enough to become adults. Until the 19th century, parents had the right to kill a newborn child who was deformed, sickly, retarded, or even the "wrong" sex (Radbill, 1980). If children survived that possibility, there was still a very good chance they would die of illness or accident. In the 1600s, 59 percent of children in London died before they were 5 years old, and 64 percent died before they turned 10 (LeVine & Sallee, 1992). Kanner (1962) presents the following story of Emerentia to illustrate how a 7-year-old girl was viewed and treated in 1713:

This 7-year-old girl, the offspring of an aristocratic family, whose father remarried after an unhappy first matrimony, offended her "noble and god-fearing" stepmother by her peculiar behavior. Worst of all, she would not join in the prayers and was panic-stricken when taken to the black-robed preacher in the dark and gloomy chapel. She avoided contact with people by hiding in closets or running away from home. The local physician had nothing to offer beyond declaring that she might be insane. She was placed in the custody of a minister known for his rigid orthodoxy. The minister, who saw in her ways the machinations of a "baneful and infernal" power, used a number of would-be therapeutic devices. He laid her on a bench and beat her with cat-o'-nine-tails. He locked her in a dark pantry. He subjected her to a period of starvation. He clothed her with a frock of burlap. Under these circumstances, the child did not last long. She died after a few months, and everybody felt relieved. The minister was amply rewarded for his efforts by Emerentia's parents. (p. 97)

LeVine and Sallee (1992) cite the following events as forces that contributed to the recognition of children as a distinct stage of development. In 1744, Pestalozzi published the first scientific record of the development of a young child. In the late nineteenth century, two books served as models for observational and experimental approaches to analyze child development: Charles Darwin's *Biographical Sketch of an Infant* in 1877 and Wilhelm Preyer's *The Mind of a Child* in late 1892. Also during the latter part of the 19th century, G. Stanley Hall studied the physical and mental capabilities of children at Clark University. In the early 1900s, child-guidance clinics emerged to provide counseling and guidance services to children. In 1910, the Stanford-Binet IQ tests were published. In 1917, John B. Watson conducted his now-famous "Little Albert" experiments, which demonstrated that a child could be conditioned to cry at the sight of a furry object.

Although children have come a long way from the dark ages of the past, there are still signs that being a child is not easy. Wagner (1994) notes that children are faced with a wide array of sociocultural conditions that often have an adverse effect on their development. For example, 25 percent of children under 5 years of age are living in poverty, and the number of children born into a single-parent home has increased from 4 percent to 25 percent from 1950 to 1988 (Wagner, 1994). There has also been an increase in the amount of time parents are spending at work, resulting in a significant reduction in their investment in child rearing (Committee for Economic Development, 1991). Several negative forces appear to be attempting to fill the void left by a lack of parental involvement. Some of these activities include watching television, which is often laden with sex and violence (3 to 4 year olds watch an average of two or more hours a day [Sroufe & Cooper, 1996]); escaping into substance abuse; and attempting to meet basic needs such as love, belonging, and self-esteem through gang involvement.

Adolescents

Sroufe and Cooper (1996) note that it was not until the 20th century that adolescence was considered a separate stage of development. Before that time (and in some underdeveloped countries today), puberty marked the transition from childhood to adulthood. G. Stanley Hall (1904) was one of the first to recognize adolescence as a distinct stage of development. Hall's view of adolescence was characterized as a conflict-ridden period resulting from rapid and profound physical changes set off by the onset of puberty.

Contemporary views of adolescence have modified Hall's position, contending that adolescence is not normally a period of "storm and stress" but a time of relatively healthy development (Sroufe & Cooper, 1996; Wagner, 1996). Current estimates suggest that 80 percent of adolescents manage very well in terms of their overall psychological functioning, with the remaining 20 percent having significant behavioral difficulties requiring some form of clinical intervention (Weiner, 1992). More specifically, Weiner notes that 20 percent pass through adolescence with virtually no recognized mental disorders, 20 percent have mental disorders, and the remaining 60 percent have mild psychological problems that do not significantly interfere with daily functioning.

Although adolescence is typically not the stormy period professed by Hall, evidence suggests it is a time of increasingly high risk for problems that adversely affect healthy development, such as substance abuse, teenage pregnancy, depression, and violence (Takanishi, 1993; Wagner, 1996). Takanishi (1993) provides evidence that suggests that approximately 25 percent of U.S. adolescents face serious risk and 25 percent face moderate risk for health- and safety-related problems and that these problems appear to be increasing at an alarming rate. For example, more U.S. children and adolescents are experimenting with alcohol and illegal drugs than ever before and at a younger age (15 and younger); depression affects between 7 percent and 33 percent of adolescents; suicide rates tripled between 1968 and 1985 for 10- to 14-year-olds and doubled during that time period for 15- to 19-year-olds; homicide rates have escalated, especially for African American males between 15 and 19 years of age, increasing by 111 percent from 1985 to 1990; and pregnancy rates have also increased 23 percent from 1973 to 1987 for 10- to 14-year-olds (Takanishi, 1993). With all the challenges facing adolescents, it is not surprising that there has been a resurgence of interest in the counseling profession in the field of adolescent counseling [see special issues on adolescence in *The American Psychologist,* 48(2), 1993, and *The Counseling Psychologist,* 24(3), 1996].

Collins and Collins (1994) note that approximately 12 percent of individuals under the age of 18 have a serious emotional or behavioral disorder, and only a minority receive adequate mental health services. These authors suggest that the current mental health delivery system for children and adolescents is inadequate, and it is necessary to develop a community-based system of care. The community system should be ecological in nature, attempting to unite community organizations and agencies to promote family strength and optimal development.

Developmental Theories

Providing counseling services to children and adolescents differs dramatically from working with adults. Unlike adults, children and adolescents are undergoing constant change in their physical, cognitive, and psychosocial abilities. A child or adolescent may therefore express certain symptoms at one stage of development and entirely different symptoms at another stage (LeVine & Sallee, 1992). For example, a child at age 3 may resort to temper tantrums when under stress. The same child at age 13 may turn to drugs as a means of dealing with stress (LeVine & Sallee, 1992).

It is therefore important to utilize a developmental perspective when working with children. This section provides an overview of developmental theories relating to cognitive, moral, and psychosocial development as well as issues that relate to psychopathology and the classic theories of personality (summarized in Table 11.1). A more detailed description

TABLE 11.1   Developmental Theories

Developmental Theories	Founder	Key Concepts	Implications for Counseling
Cognitive theory	Jean Piaget, David Elkind	Divided cognitive development into four distinct stages: sensorimotor (birth to age 2), preoperational (age 2 to 7), concrete operations (age 7 to 11), and formal operations (begins after age 11).	Counselors should adjust the counseling approach to the child or adolescent's level of cognitive functioning.
Theory of moral development	Lawrence Kohlberg, Carol Gilligan	Identified three levels of moral development beginning with an egocentric view regarding morality (that is, a child controls behavior out of a fear of punishment).	An understanding of moral reasoning can be useful to promote self-control.
Psychosocial development theory	Erik Erikson	Identified seven psychosocial stages and their associated developmental tasks (for example, from birth to 1 year of age the central task is trust).	Counselors can help clients obtain the coping skills necessary to master developmental tasks so they can move forward in their development.
Developmental psychopathology	Alan Kazdin, Maria Kovacs, and others	Study of child and adolescent psychopathology in the context of maturational and developmental processes.	Provides a framework for understanding child and adolescent psychopathology as unique from adult psychopathology and aids in accurate assessment, diagnosis, and treatment.
The classic theories	Sigmund Freud, Alfred Adler, and Carl Jung	The theories of personality posited by the classic theorists emphasize the role of early life experiences on child and adolescent development.	Provide useful information for counselors to understand the dynamics of behavior *before* they begin to use counseling techniques to promote behavior change.

of developmental characteristics (physical, cognitive, and social-emotional) and associated counseling and consultation strategies for early childhood through the adolescence stages of development can be found in Stern and Newland (1994) and Vernon (1995).

Cognitive Theories

Many theories have attempted to explain how cognitive development occurs throughout the life span (Piaget, 1952; Brunner, 1973). Among these, Jean Piaget's theory has received significant attention in literature. Piaget (1952) divided cognitive development into four distinct stages: sensorimotor (birth to 2 years of age); preoperational (2 to 6 years of age); concrete operational (ages 7 to 11); and formal operational (age 12 through adulthood).

According to Piaget, the cognitive development of children and adolescents becomes more sophisticated as they progress from one stage to the next. For example, children are usually unable to understand cause and effect during the preoperational stage. Concepts such as divorce or death may therefore be difficult for children to understand during this stage, from 2 to 6 years old. When faced with divorce or death during this stage, they may become confused and even blame themselves. It is important for counselors to be aware of a child's and adolescent's level of cognitive development during the counseling process.

Cognitive development can also play an important role in how children respond to questions. The cognitive style of children aged 7 to 11 tends to be concrete in nature (concrete operational stage). The children therefore tend to respond well to questions that ask for specific information (probing questions), such as "Do you like school?" Open-ended statements such as "How are you doing?" can be difficult for children, often resulting in limited responses such as "Fine." Adolescents typically are functioning at the formal operational stage and have the ability to think abstractly. This enables them to be able to generate more robust responses to open-ended questions than children. Most of the other listening skills discussed in Chapter 3 can be used with children and adolescents (for example, reflection of feeling, paraphrasing, clarifying, minimal encouragers, summarizing, and so forth).

David Elkind (1984) extended Piaget's theory of cognitive development to include information on adolescent egocentrism. According to Elkind, adolescent thinking tends to be quite self-centered or egocentric in nature. This egocentricism of adolescents is characterized by several tendencies in adolescents that can impede communication processes and psychological functioning. For example, since adolescents tend to see things from their point of view, they tend to argue with opposing positions (especially with adults). Two other characteristics associated with adolescent egocentricism are the imaginary audience and personal fable. *Imaginary audience* relates to the adolescent tendency to be self-conscious. For example, when adolescents are playing tennis, they may think everyone's eyes are on them, leading to frequent bouts of giggles and other forms of embarrassment. *Personal fable* involves adolescents feeling invulnerable because they believe that what they do is so special no harm will come to them. From this perspective, adolescents may feel that it is impossible to get pregnant because they are so in love, and their love is so perfect that nothing bad can happen.

Counseling implications of the egocentricism of adolescents include being aware of this tendency and guarding against it by not overreacting (for example, getting angry at an adolescent's self-centered point of view). Counselors can also try to be patient and help adolescents discover the value of appreciating different points of view as a means of enhancing communication. Group counseling with adolescents may be particularly useful in this process. Counselors may also wish to use reality testing to help adolescents overcome the tendency to be self-conscious and feel invulnerable. This can involve objectively examining various activities (such as engaging in sex) to help them develop a realistic understanding of the consequences of their behavior.

Theories of Moral Development

Counselors are faced with an increasing number of children and adolescents who are out of control and engaging in various acts of misbehavior (McMahon & Forehand, 1988). Theories of moral development can be used to gain a better understanding of children and adolescents who misbehave in terms of their moral reasoning.

Piaget (1965) and later Lawrence Kohlberg (1963, 1973, 1981) presented theories of moral development. Kohlberg's theory is based on Piaget's work and is widely accepted in the literature. Kohlberg suggests that moral development can be conceptualized in terms of three levels, with each level containing two stages. These levels and stages are hierarchical, requiring a person to move through them one at a time without skipping any of them.

According to Kohlberg, children functioning at Level 1 have an egocentric point of view regarding morality. They control their behavior out of fear of punishment. Individuals who have reached Level 2 of moral development control their behavior and abide by laws out of a concern about how others will view them as a person, and also how they will view themselves. At Level 3, people control their behavior and abide by laws out of a rational decision to contribute to the good of society. Individuals who have reached the age of 11 or 12 are often capable of functioning at Level 3.

Carol Gilligan (1982, 1987, 1990) contends that Kohlberg's theory does not take into account gender issues associated with moral development. According to Gilligan (1982, 1987), Kohlberg's theory is based primarily on the way men perceive morality, as a set of values and moral principles that can be applied to all situations regardless of the social context and that are concerned with what is fair and equitable. Gilligan contends that female moral reasoning is more concerned with caring for the needs of others than with equity. It is also directly related to the social context in that an individual's moral reasoning is influenced by how one will be viewed by significant others.

Parr and Ostrovsky (1991) describe how theories of moral development can be used to provide directions for counseling children and adolescents. For example, a behavior modification such as a token economy may be useful with first graders since their moral decision making is strongly influenced by a fear of being punished and obeying the rules. The same approach may not be as effective with adolescents since they may be more concerned with social issues such as how their behavior conforms to shared norms and how their decisions will be perceived by their peer group. Group counseling can provide teens with a social milieu to work through their concerns and facilitate moral decision making.

Psychosocial Theories

Children's and adolescents' psychosocial development is another important issue in counseling. Erik Erikson (1963, 1968) identified seven psychosocial stages from birth to death. In his theory, each stage involves a particular task that must be accomplished before the individual can proceed effectively to the next developmental task. From birth to age 1, for example, the central task is to experience a sense of trust from the environment. Without that experience, an infant will develop a mistrustful attitude toward the environment. To accomplish each task, the individual must master various coping skills associated with that task. Counselors can help children and adolescents develop these coping skills to promote positive psychosocial development (Blocher, 1987; Stern & Newland, 1994). Chapter 14 provides a more detailed description of the role of developmental tasks in the counseling process.

Developmental Psychopathology

A recent trend in counseling is an attempt to view psychopathology from a developmental perspective (Bergman & Magnusson, 1997; Kazdin, 1993; Sroufe, 1997; Wakefield, 1997). Kazdin (1989) defines developmental psychopathology as "the study of clinical dysfunction in the context of maturational and developmental processes" (p. 180). Kovacs (1989) notes that developmental psychopathology attempts to address three issues: (a) how the developing organism mediates the development of mental disorders; (b) the impact of mental disorders on age-appropriate abilities; and (c) whether mental disorders develop continually or in stages.

According to Alan Kazdin (1989), the greatest advance in developmental psychopathology occurred with the publication of the *Diagnostic and Statistical Manual for Mental Disorders* (DSM-III) and later DSM-III-R (American Psychiatric Association, 1980, 1987). Kazdin (1989) notes, "It represented a quantum leap in the attention accorded disorders of infancy, childhood, and adolescence" (p. 183). Advances in the DSM include recognizing the variations from childhood to adulthood in the nature and course of psychopathology. For example, the DSM-IV notes that it is common for a depressed child to experience problems that are usually not found with adult depression. Some of these are somatic, or bodily, complaints; psychomotor agitation; and mood-congruent hallucinations.

Sroufe (1997) goes on to note that it is common for comorbidity (two or more diagnoses) to occur concurrently with children and adolescents. When this occurs, multiple diagnoses can obscure or mask a psychological problem, making it difficult to obtain an accurate assessment. For example, if a child has a substance-abuse problem, an oppositional-defiant disorder, and an anxiety disorder, the focus may be on the drug and oppositional problems, and the clinician could miss the anxiety problem.

Research and theory development in developmental psychopathology appear to be proliferating. Research initiatives have explored a wide range of topics such as the role of nature and nurture (Rutter et al., 1997), transition and turning points (Rutter, 1996), and emotions (Cicchetti, Ackerman, & Izard, 1995) in developmental psychopathology. For example, Cicchetti et al. (1995) investigate the role of emotional regulation in developmental psychopathology. They contend that the primary function of emotional regulation is to initiate, organize, and motivate adaptive behavior, thereby preventing abnormal conditions and responses.

One area of research that has been lacking appropriate emphasis is developmental psychopathology directed at adolescence. In this regard, Kardin (1993) notes that developmental psychopathology has tended to focus on children and overlook adolescence. Adolescence was viewed as a transitional period between childhood and adulthood that was in constant change due to biological flux, making it difficult to identify clear mental health patterns. This is changing as the unique developmental characteristics of adolescence are being recognized and accepted as an important domain for scientific investigation (Kazdin, 1993).

Developmental psychopathology holds promise in terms of refining the process of assessment and diagnosis in child and adolescent counseling. Additional research is required to determine how different developmental levels may influence symptom expression and treatment (Kazdin, 1989).

The Classic Theories

The classic theories of personality posited by Sigmund Freud, Alfred Adler, and Carl Jung (see Chapter 7) can also provide useful information on understanding children and adolescents. These theories all emphasize the role of early life experiences in child and adolescent development. Freud was one of the first to look at stages of development in children and adolescents. His psychosexual stages of development consist of the oral, anal, phallic, latency, and genital stages. Freud's theory suggests that traumatic experiences during any of these stages can fixate development at that level. Adults can spend the rest of their lives attempting to resolve unmet needs of childhood or adolescence. For example, if children do not have opportunities to meet their oral needs, they may grow up continually attempting to meet those needs. In this process, they can become an orally fixated personality. This can manifest itself in positive tendencies, such as becoming an orator, or in negative ones, such as nail biting.

Adler and his colleague Rudolf Dreikurs and others have also much to offer in terms of child and adolescent development. These individuals developed numerous psychological constructs that can be used to understand and counsel children and adolescents. Some of these constructs include birth order, the family constellation, lifestyle, goals of misbehavior, encouragement, and the use of consequences as a disciplinary technique.

Jungian psychology can provide another valuable dimension to conceptualizing the development of children and adolescents. For example, Jung's concepts of holism and balance have been integrated in Jungian forms of play therapy, described later in this chapter.

Emerging Developmental Trends

The strengths perspective has represented a major paradigm shift in counseling. The shift is characterized by a change in orientation from pathology to wellness. It represents a recognition that strength is required to overcome adversity. The strengths perspective is playing a central role in virtually all aspects of counseling from holistic health, which suggests that clients develop a wellness orientation, to brief-solution-focused counseling, which encourages clients to use what has worked before (exceptions to the problem) to overcome current difficulties. With the ongoing emphasis on strengths, it is not surprising that developmental theories and concepts are beginning to take on a strengths perspective. This section reviews four emerging developmental trends that have a strengths perspective (optimal development, resiliency, attachment theory, and emotional intelligence) (see Table 11.2). These developmental trends appear to be interrelated in that resiliency, secure attachment, and emotional intelligence facilitate optimal development.

Optimal Development. The roots of optimal development can be traced to humanistic psychologists such as Carl Rogers (1951) and Abraham Maslow (1968), who proposed a model of human growth and development based on inherent self-actualizing tendencies. In

TABLE 11.2   **Emerging Developmental Trends**

Developmental Theories and Concepts	Founder	Key Concepts	Implications for Counselors
Optimal development	No one individual: contributors include Carl Rogers, Abraham Maslow, and William Wagner	A view of human development that focuses on positive, healthy development as opposed to a pathological view of development	Optimal development can help counselors take a strengths perspective by focusing on what people can do rather than what they cannot do. This perspective promotes a positive, self-fulfilling prophecy.
Resiliency	No one individual; Emmy Werner's research stands out	A research trend that is attempting to identify coping mechanisms that provide a buffer to harmful stress and obstacles to development	Resiliency characteristics can provide useful survival responses to stress, which in turn can promote optimal development. Counselors can promote resiliency characteristics in their approach with clients.
Attachment theory	Mary Ainsworth, John Bowlby, and others	A study of the relationship between the emotional bond between a parent and child and that child's psychosocial development over the life span	An understanding of a client's present and past attachment relationships can provide useful insights into how to move toward optimal psychosocial development.
Emotional intelligence	John Mayer and Peter Salovey	A study of the role that social emotions play in psychological functioning	Counselors can promote emotional intelligence in clients by helping them gain a better understanding of how emotions foster optimal development. Counselors can also help clients enhance their emotional intelligence through such activities as social-skills training in groups.

this regard, Rogers contends that a person will move toward self-actualization (optimal development) if the right conditions are established. More recently, Wagner (1996) has presented optimal development as a developmental perspective that emphasizes health and wellness over pathology. Wagner (1996) notes that what constitutes optimal development varies to some degree contextually in terms of culture and so forth. Wagner goes on to review the literature to identify biophysical, cognitive, and psychosocial competencies that appear to characterize optimal development in adolescence. These research findings are summarized as follows:

- *Biophysical.* "Upon reaching the age of 18, an adolescent will be alive and healthy, physically mature, and engaged in health-enhancing behaviors, including proper diet and regular exercise" (Wagner, 1996, p. 364).
- *Cognitive.* "Upon reaching the age of 18, adolescents will engage in efficient and purposively idiosyncratic thinking of a more hypothetical, multidimensional, future-oriented and relative nature that is based on prior life experiences, including the completion or near completion of at least 12 years of formal education" (Wagner, 1996, p. 368).
- *Psychosocial functioning.* "Upon reaching the age of 18, adolescents will be emotionally aware, feel secure and self-confident, be determined and optimistic about the future, and possess the resilience needed to overcome adversity" (Wagner, 1996, p. 371).

Several authors have proposed a person–environmental fit model of development that can be used to understand how optimal development occurs (Chu & Powers, 1995; Eccles et al., 1993). According to this model, a person moves forward toward optimal development when there is a good fit between his or her needs and the social environment. Chu and Powers (1995) go on to note that synchrony occurs when the social environment is responsive to the individual in terms of promoting personal independence, self-determination, and decision making. In addition, synchrony plays a key role in promoting important competencies in children and adolescents, such as attachment, autonomy, and social competency.

When the fit between the social environment and the individual is strained, the person can become discouraged and lack motivation for positive involvement (Eccles et al., 1993). This can lead to disruptions in the developmental process, such as excessive rebelliousness during adolescence, dropping out of school, and drug abuse. The person–environmental fit model can be used to provide a possible explanation for why early and middle adolescence can be particularly problematic for adolescents. According to Chu and Powers (1995), once an adolescent goes to middle school, parents tend to renegotiate rules relating to autonomy and control (for example, how late the teen can stay out). At the same time, it is not uncommon for middle school teachers to also place a high premium on discipline and control. When the adolescent no longer feels a sense of empowerment, he or she can feel discouraged and lack motivation for involvement in family life or school, resulting in a variety of serious problems.

Van Slyck, Stern, and Zak-Place (1996) suggest that optimal development can be facilitated in children and adolescents by building strengths in resiliency, coping, and problem solving. These authors go on to note that preventative programs that focus on conflict resolution are effective interventions for fostering these strengths. This is especially true for adolescents since they are prone to having problems that stem from interpersonal conflicts.

Chu and Powers (1995) provide guidelines for promoting synchrony in child- or adolescent-adult relationships. For example, adolescent-adult synchrony should be flexible and open to change, sensitive, and active in terms of encouraging problem solving and decision making. These characteristics also seem to be valuable in promoting strengths associated with optimal development in children.

Resiliency.   Resiliency is a term that has been used to describe why some at-risk children and adolescents thrive, whereas others experience disruptions in their development. It can be defined as a tendency to overcome adverse conditions as a result of having growth-facilitating characteristics that promote optimal development. Research investigations have attempted to understand the dynamics of resilience. Perhaps the most significant study on resiliency was one conducted by Werner and her colleagues (Werner, 1992; Werner & Smith, 1982, 1992), which attempted to identify resiliency characteristics for 200 at-risk children in Hawaii over a 32-year period. These children had experienced at least four risk factors, such as family dysfunction, parental alcoholism, and poverty. Surprisingly, one out of three of these at-risk children grew into competent, happy, productive young adults.

Rak and Patterson (1996) provide an overview of the literature on resilience in terms of its characteristics and implications for counseling and development. Some of these resiliency characteristics are a positive self-concept, an optimistic outlook, good interpersonal skills resulting in positive social experiences, good problem-solving and decision-making skills, a well-developed sense of personal autonomy, an environmental support system (within or outside of the family), and a significant other who can provide adequate mentoring. Adams (1997) conducted a qualitative study that involved interviews with 10 individuals 85 years or older. Results of this study suggest that resiliency is related to a wide array of health factors (for example, emotional, physical, spiritual, social, and internal).

Resiliency research poses a new way of conceptualizing counseling and development. According to Rak and Patterson (1996), resiliency characteristics act as a buffer to help children and adolescents cope with stress so they can move toward optimal development. Counselors can take a strengths perspective by fostering resiliency characteristics in their clients, thereby promoting survival responses and maximizing developmental opportunities. The field of resiliency research appears to offer opportunities for counselors to utilize a strengths perspective in counseling.

Attachment Theory.   Attachment theory was originally developed by Mary Ainsworth and associates (Ainsworth, Blehar, Waters, & Wall, 1978), John Bowlby (1969/1982), and others as an investigation into the emotional bond between parents and infants and the implications that bond has on psychosocial development. Securely attached infants were believed to have a number of developmental strengths compared to insecurely attached infants. Some of these strengths are being able to form a strong emotional bond with the caregiver, maintaining meaningful ongoing relationships, being cooperative and relatively free of anger, and having superior fine and gross motor skills (Papalia & Olds, 2001).

Ainsworth (1989, 1991) and Bowlby (1988a, 1988b) also advocate what is known as a *continuity theory* regarding attachment. According to this theory, the nature of the attachment in early life influences development throughout the life span. A proliferation of research has tested this hypothesis and has also investigated the relationship between attachment styles and affect regulation and social competence in adults (Lopez, 1995). Lopez (1995) notes that there has been some evidence to support the continuity hypothesis. For example, securely attached infants and children tend to become adults who have secure attachment styles (Brennan, Shaver, & Tobey, 1991; Carnelley, Pietromonaco, & Jaffe, 1994) and also become parents who are able to establish secure attachments with their family members (Ricks, 1985). Lopez (1995) posits that the true test of the continuity hypothesis will require longitudinal studies that investigate the relationship between early attachment and development throughout the life span.

Lopez (1995) also presents a compelling body of research that suggests there is a relationship between adult attachment styles and adult affect regulation and social competence. For example, securely attached adults tend to have superior communication and problem-solving skills (Pistole, 1993; Shaver & Brennan, 1992), higher levels of marital adjustment (Kobak & Hazan, 1991), and the ability to provide more emotional support to distressed partners and solicit emotional support when they need it (Simpson, Rholes, & Nelligan, 1992).

Peluso, Peluso, White, and Kern (2004) identify several commonalities between attachment theory and Adler's individual psychology. Two key theoretical constructs in Adlerian psychology are lifestyle analysis and social interest. *Lifestyle* refers to a person's basic orientation to life. *Social interest* relates to inborn tendencies to cooperate and work with others (which is believed to enhance with mental health and wellness). Attachment and lifestyle are similar in terms of their emphasis on early family relationships. For example, being securely attached can contribute to a person being self-confident and having an active lifestyle. Attachment and social interest are also similar constructs, both of which suggest that the ability to establish meaningful social relationships is influenced by the nature of early parent-child relationships. For example, securely attached individuals are better able to establish and maintain meaningful social relationships.

One intriguing area of application of attachment theory is in career development. Blustein, Prezioso, and Schultheiss (1995) provide evidence that securely attached individuals tend to have adaptive characteristics that promote success in career exploration and decision making. Some of these characteristics are enhanced ego identity development (Rice, 1990), enhanced adult work behavior (Hazan & Shaver, 1990), and enhanced exploratory behavior (Hazan & Shaver, 1990).

Attachment theory represents a strengths perspective for counseling by providing a view of healthy personality in terms of relational issues in development (Lopez, 1995). Opportunities are beginning to emerge that offer concrete strategies for applying attachment theory in counseling practice. In this regard, several instruments have been developed that can provide an assessment of the nature and scope of a person's attachment style (for adolescent and adult attachment instruments see Lyddon, Bradford, & Nelson, 1993, and Bradford & Lyddon, 1994). Krause and Haverkamp (1996) also advocate that it may be productive to assess adults' current attachment relationships with their parents to gain insights into adult or child–older parent relationships. Clients that appear to have problematic histories or current problems with attachments may wish to address attachment issues in counseling to free the way for optimal development (Blustein et al., 1995).

Emotional Intelligence. Mayer and Salovey are credited with coining the concept of emotional intelligence (Mayer, Dipaolo, & Salovey, 1990; Mayer & Salovey, 1997; Salovey & Mayer, 1990). These scholars present a scientific description of emotional intelligence (or EI). Mayer (1999, 2001) contends that emotional intelligence is a unitary ability that can be measured reliably and is related to but independent from standard intelligence. Mayer, Salovey, and Caruso (2000) suggest that emotional intelligence is a form of alternative intelligence that can be traced to Thorndike's (1920) work on social intelligence. Social intelligence essentially explores how people make judgments regarding others and examines the accuracy of those judgments (Mayer & Geher, 1996). Emotional intelligence has evolved into a more complex process that has been defined as "an ability to recognize the meanings of emotions and their relationships, and to reason and problem-solve on the basis of them. Emotional intelligence is involved with the capacity to perceive emotions, assimilate emotion-related feelings, understand the information of those emotions, and manage them" (Mayer, Caruso, & Salovey, 1999, p. 267).

Goleman's (1997) best-selling book *Emotional Intelligence* represents a popularized version of emotional intelligence. Goleman refers to emotional intelligence as *EQ* as a contrast to the intellectual quotient (IQ). Goleman (1997) provides information on the practical applications of emotional intelligence to everyday life, suggesting that emotional intelligence may be more important in determining personal success than intellectual intelligence. According to Goleman, IQ may get you hired, but it is EQ skills that are primarily responsible for promotions and other job-related successes. Goleman notes that self-awareness may be the cornerstone of emotional intelligence since it is necessary for a wide range of prosocial behaviors such as self-control. Other key characteristics that have been linked to success are empathy and interpersonal skills (Goleman, 1997), optimism (Seligman, 1991), practical intelligence or common sense (Sternberg, Wagner, Williams, Horvath, 1995), and delay of gratification (Mischel, Shoda, & Rodriguez, 1989; Shoda, Mischel, & Peake, 1990). For example, Seligman contends that optimistic responses to setbacks have been associated with job-related success, such as increased sales in the life-insurance profession. Sternberg et al. (1995) provide additional support for the role of EQ in work success by concluding that practical intelligence or common sense is a better predictor of success in employment than intellectual intelligence.

Mischel et al.'s (1989) classic study on delay of gratification provides another example of the effects of emotional intelligence on psychological functioning. In this study, 4-year-olds were told they could have one marshmallow now or two when the researcher returned from an errand. Those who waited for two marshmallows utilized a variety of delay-of-gratification coping skills such as singing, playing games, and so forth. The researchers then conducted a longitudinal study that extended from childhood into adolescence (Mischel et al., 1989; Shoda et al., 1990). They found that the 4-year-olds who waited for two marshmallows were rated as more intelligent, better able to concentrate, and more goal-oriented than those who preferred instant gratification. In addition, children who could delay gratification went on to become adolescents who tended to have significantly higher SAT scores (Shoda et al., 1990).

Gibbs (1995) notes that much of what is being studied in the field of emotional intelligence is also being explored in the emerging field of evolutionary psychology. Evolutionary psychology is based on the work of Charles Darwin and explores all aspects of development in terms of survival of the human species (Daly & Wilson, 1983; Wright, 1994). From an evolutionary perspective, human emotions such as anger may trigger a fight-or-flight response (Goleman, 1997), empathy can act as a buffer to cruelty (Goleman, 1997), and facial beauty and attractiveness can be related to reproductive capacity

(Johnston & Oliver-Rodriguez, 1997). The research on evolutionary psychology appears to offer promise in terms of understanding human development, including the realm of emotional intelligence.

Emotional intelligence provides a strengths perspective for counselors by recognizing the vital role that social emotions play in human functioning. For example, counselors can help clients use the power of encouragement to foster self-efficacy in self and others. In addition, Goleman (1997) contends that there is a great need for preventative programs in schools that promote strengths in emotional literacy to overcome negative tendencies such as violence, loneliness, and despair. School counselors appear to be in an ideal setting to promote emotional intelligence through classroom presentations, counseling (especially group), and consultation with parents and teachers.

Treatment Issues

This section addresses treatment issues in child and adolescent counseling. It begins by describing some of the commonly used assessment procedures. The chapter then provides information on treatment in terms of research findings and a description of special counseling approaches with children and adolescents.

Assessment Procedures

Child and adolescent counseling encompasses the full range of standardized and nonstandardized assessment procedures described in Chapter 4. In addition, two child and adolescent assessment procedures warrant additional attention. The first involves the use of drawings as an assessment tool, a procedure clinicians have used for some time. The second is the use of clinical interviews with children, adolescents, and parents. Although clinical interviews have been used with adults for many years, their use with children and adolescents has begun more recently (Edelbrock & Costello, 1988), representing a major advance in the assessment of childhood and adolescent disorders (Kazdin, 1989).

Drawings.   Drawings can be used both in standardized and nonstandardized assessment procedures. One standardized procedure is the Goodenough-Harris Drawing Test (Harris, 1963). This test requires children and adolescents to make a picture of a man or woman (depending on the sex of the child) and a picture of themselves. Another commonly used standardized test is the House-Tree-Person Test (Buck, 1949), in which children and adolescents first draw a house, then a tree, and last a person. More recently, Knoff and Prout (1985) developed the Kinetic Drawing System for Family and School. Children and adolescents draw one picture of their family and another that relates to school. This test assesses important relationships at home and school.

Stabler (1984) provides information on the nonstandardized use of drawings with children and adolescents. He notes that drawings can be used to obtain an estimate of a child or adolescent's cognitive and psychosocial development and level of maturity. Stabler (1984) identifies the following five factors that are important in assessing drawings:

1. *Proportion or form.* Do figures in the drawings have appropriate proportion or form?
2. *Detail.* What is the degree of detail in the drawing (are there ears, eyes, mouth, and a nose on the face)?
3. *Movement or action.* Is there movement or action depicted in the drawing, such as having the appearance of a three-dimensional person?
4. *Theme.* Is there a theme or story conveyed in the picture, such as two people in love or Superman stopping a villain?
5. *Gender identity.* Is there evidence that the child or adolescent has a clear concept of gender identity?

Stabler (1984) also posits guidelines for assessing drawings in terms of cognitive functioning and overall maturity for children and adolescents in three age groups: aged 5 to 7, 8 to 9, and 10 to 12. For example, children from age 5 to 7 tend to be able to draw pictures that are more or less proportional; have limited detail; some evidence of gender identity emerging; rather poor movement or action; and typically no theme. Figure 11.1 provides an illustration of a typical drawing by a 6-year-old and a 12-year-old.

Stabler (1984) goes on to describe three types of drawings that are particularly useful in the assessment process: free drawings, where children are encouraged to draw whatever they like; self-portraits; and family drawings, in which children draw themselves with their family. These drawings enable the counselor to make hypotheses about what to explore with a child. For example, a free drawing may have themes that represent children's concerns, so a child who repeatedly draws a house with a child by a mother and father in the home could suggest the child is concerned with issues relating to home and family life. A self-portrait with no arms or legs could indicate a sense of lack of control over the environment. Children who draw a self-portrait without a mouth may think that others do not value their views. A family drawing that has a significant distance between the child and other family members could suggest a feeling of isolation or alienation.

Clinical Interviews.   The clinical interview has become an increasingly popular tool to assist with assessment and diagnosis (see Chapter 4 for a description of the clinical interview). The clinical interview is not designed to replace other forms of assessment but can

Drawings can provide valuable assessment information.

6-Year-Old

12-Year-Old

FIGURE 11.1   Typical Drawing by a 6-Year-Old Child and 12-Year-Old Adolescent

Source: From *Children's Drawings* (pp. 5, 8) by B. Stabler, 1984, Chapel Hill, NC: Health Sciences Consortium. Copyright 1984 by Health Sciences Consortium. Reprinted by permission.

be best viewed as an adjunct to the process of assessment and diagnosis. In this regard, the clinical interview has been shown to increase diagnostic reliability (Robins, Helzer, Croughan, & Ratcliff, 1981).

Although clinical interviews have been used with adults for some time, their development and use with children and adolescents have occurred primarily during the last 20 or so years. Interest in the utilization of clinical interviews for children and adolescents corresponds to the increased differentiation of mental disorders for children and adolescents during the past two decades.

Edelbrock and Costello (1988) identify several advantages and disadvantages of clinical interviews as compared to other child and adolescent assessment procedures, such as observation and psychological tests. Advantages of clinical interviews include the ability of the counselor to establish rapport, clarify misunderstandings, and obtain self-report data from parents, children, and adolescents. The primary disadvantages relate to questionable levels of validity and reliability owing to the newness of these instruments and the consequent lack of time to empirically evaluate them.

Many clinical interviews for children and adolescents are currently available. Edelbrock and Costello (1988) describe commonly used clinical interviews for children and adolescents. They vary in terms of structure, and the more structured interviews require less training to administer (Edelbrock & Costello, 1988). The following are three examples:

1. *The Diagnostic Interview for Children and Adolescents* (Herjanic & Reich, 1982). This is a highly structured diagnostic interview that can be used with children 6 years of age or older. It covers a broad range of childhood symptoms in terms of frequency and duration. There is also a version for parents, which solicits pertinent developmental and family history.

2. *The Interview Schedule for Children* (Kovacs, 1982). This is a semistructured interview for children ages 8 to 17. It is a symptom-oriented interview that focuses primarily on depression, although it also assesses other diagnostic criteria. A separate interview can be conducted with parents, children, and adolescents.

3. *The Diagnostic Interview Schedule for Children* (Costello, Edelbrock, Kalas, Kessler, & Klaric, 1982). This is a highly structured interview for children and adolescents ages 6 to 18. It provides information on a wide range of symptoms and behaviors in terms of onset, duration, and severity. A parallel version can be used with parents and children or adolescents.

Child and Adolescent Counseling Goals

One way to conceptualize counseling goals in child and adolescent counseling is from a developmental perspective. The developmental perspective can be applied to clients of all ages. It can be especially useful in child and adolescent counseling (such as school counseling) when developmental issues are continuously addressed. The developmental perspective differentiates between two types of counseling goals: universal-primary goals and secondary goals. Universal-primary goals address developmental issues, whereas secondary counseling goals relate to specific problems such as students procrastinating and not turning in their schoolwork on time.

Universal-primary goals promote optimal development through enhancement of developmental competencies such as self-esteem, attachment, resiliency, emotional intelligence, self-awareness, self-control, self-efficacy, intrinsic motivation, and internal locus of control. Universal-primary counseling goals are considered primary because they relate to the child's or adolescent's overall growth and development. In addition, universal-primary goals may promote developmental competencies necessary to successfully address secondary counseling goals.

Universal-primary counseling goals may be directly or indirectly related to secondary counseling goals. For example, promoting intrinsic motivation and self-control are universal-primary goals that may be directly related to overcoming problems with procrastination. Promoting self-awareness may be a developmental goal that is indirectly related to the procrastination problem but could be important to the child's or adolescent's overall growth and development.

It is important to consider both universal-primary and secondary counseling goals when assessing progress in counseling. From a developmental perspective, success should be measured both in terms of whether problems have been resolved (secondary goals) and how clients are progressing relative to their overall growth and development (primary-universal goals). Counselors and clients should be encouraged if progress is being made with either universal-primary or secondary counseling goals.

Child and Adolescent Counseling Research

Weisz, Weiss, and Donenberg (1992) and Kazdin (1993) provide an overview of a number of meta-analyses on child and adolescent counseling (for example, Hazelrigg, Cooper, & Borduin, 1987; Kazdin, Bass, Ayers, & Rodgers, 1990). Both research investigations report strong support for the efficacy of child and adolescent counseling. For example, Kazdin (1993) finds that the effects of child and adolescent counseling are superior to no treatment, the degree of positive change is comparable to adult counseling, there is little variation in efficacy of treatment modalities such as behavioral versus nonbehavioral, and treatment outcomes are similar for internalized problems such as depression and externalized problems such as aggression.

Research suggests that a developmental perspective is critical in identifying appropriate counseling interventions with children and adolescents. For example, behavioral approaches such as behavior modification have been useful in treating children (Kazdin, 1993), and adolescents (owing to their ability to think abstractly) are able to utilize cognitive-behavioral approaches better than children (Durlak, Fuhrman, & Lampman, 1991).

Kazdin (1993) also notes that there is strong support for preventative programs with children and adolescents (Goldston, Yager, Heinicke, & Pynoos, 1990; Weissberg, Caplan, & Harwood, 1991). For example, programs that provide support to a family during a child's formative years appear to prevent problems such as a child engaging in antisocial behavior later in childhood and adolescence. Research also suggests that school-based programs appear to be effective in preventing a wide array of problems such as substance use and abuse and school dropout. Kazdin (1993) posits that the success of preventative programs depends to some degree on the ability to not only change attitudes but also to change behavior. Schultz and Nystul (1980) found in an earlier study on parent education that the internalization and transfer from an attitude to a behavior requires some form of action such as role-play.

Special Counseling Approaches for Children and Adolescents

Most counseling approaches used with children and adolescents (such as behavioral and cognitive-behavioral) are adaptations of strategies used with adults (Tuma, 1989). Play therapy and conflict resolution represent two counseling approaches that have been specifically designed for working with children and adolescents. This section provides an overview of these unique methods of counseling children and adolescents as well as guidelines for child and adolescent counseling.

Play Therapy. Play represents an important developmental tool for children and adolescents. It provides a natural form of communication (Campbell, 1993) and an expression of creativity linked to learning, coping, and self-realization (Rogers & Sharapan, 1993). It is through play that children and adolescents are able to enhance cognitive, physical, and psychosocial development (Papalia & Olds, 2001). For example, playing hide and seek involves deciding where and how to hide (cognitive); mobility, such as running and squatting (physical); and cooperating with others (psychosocial). For adolescents and adults, sports such as basketball and baseball become favored forms of play and continue to provide opportunities to enhance development.

Play therapy is a counseling strategy that has been confined primarily to children. It has a number of uses, such as relationship building, assessment, promoting communication, psychological healing, and fostering growth (Orton, 1997). Play therapy involves the utilization of play media such as sand play, art, and music to learn skills and work through problems so children progress in their development. Sand play is an emerging form of play therapy (Carmichael, 1994). It involves the use of two 20-by-30-by-4-inch trays (one with wet sand and one with dry sand). Children are provided numerous objects that represent everyday life (people, fences, animals, and so forth) and are encouraged to use the objects to express themselves in fantasy play. Allan and Brown (1993) describe three stages of play therapy (including what one would expect in sand play): chaos, struggle, and resolution. During the initial stage (chaos), children tend to express negative feelings such as anger and confusion and project those feelings onto their play activities. As play therapy progresses, the therapist encourages children to utilize play as a means of working through their struggles. The last phase of play therapy is characterized by creative expressions that are more positive in nature (such as cooperation), reflecting resolution of conflicts.

The historical roots of play therapy can be traced to two major schools of counseling, Freudian and Rogerian. Anna Freud (1928), the daughter of Sigmund Freud, was perhaps the first to use play therapy with children. Melanie Klein (1960) went on to provide further development of the psychoanalytic school of play therapy. These clinicians incorporated the major principles of psychoanalysis in their approach, for example, strengthening the ego to minimize endopsychic conflicts and utilizing the transference relationship to help children overcome traumatic experiences.

The psychoanalytic counselor conceptualizes play in a manner similar to free association. From this perspective, play allows children to express themselves freely and spontaneously. The counselor's role in this process is passive and interpretive. For example, if a child painted a picture with dark objects, the counselor might ask, "Are you feeling sad or gloomy today?"

The second major school of play therapy was developed by Virginia Axline (1974). Its theoretical foundation can be traced to Carl Rogers's person-centered school of counseling, and it is therefore a humanistic-phenomenological approach. Axline's (1964, 1974) approach suggests that the counselor conveys a warm and accepting attitude toward the child and encourages the child to freely explore the different play materials. The role of the counselor is similar to that in person-centered counseling. As the child plays, the counselor attempts to convey empathic understanding by reflecting what he or she senses the child is experiencing. A more detailed description of Axline's approach can be found in *Dibs: In Search of Self* (Axline, 1964).

Contemporary forms of play therapy are based on a number of theoretical orientations such as Rogerian (Landreth, 1993), Jungian (Allan & Brown, 1993), and Adlerian (Kottman & Johnson, 1993; Nystul, 1980a). For example, current trends in Rogerian child-centered play therapy are similar to the earlier model developed by Axline and are being used to treat a wide range of problems such as regressive behavior, depression, abuse, and socially inappropriate behavior (Landreth, 1993).

Jungian play therapy involves an application of the major Jungian principles (see Chapter 7). Allan and Brown (1993) provide an overview of Jungian play therapy. It utilizes the therapeutic alliance to help the child work through unconscious struggles and conflicts reflected in play. One central goal in Jungian play therapy is to help the child create a balance between the inner world of feelings, drives, and impulses and the demands of the outer world as reflected in school, peers, and family. Another major goal in Jungian play therapy is to strengthen the child's ego so it can become an effective mediator between the child's inner and outer world. In fact, Jungians have found sand play to be particularly useful as a means of strengthening the child's ego to create a balance between the child's inner and outer world (Carmichael, 1994).

Adlerian play therapy is based on the work of Adler (1930) and Dreikurs and associates (Dreikurs & Soltz, 1964). Adlerian play therapy is used to foster a positive counseling relationship, help parents and teachers gain a better understanding of children, enable children to gain insight and self-awareness, and provide skills and experiences necessary for children to work through conflict and enhance their development (Kottman & Johnson, 1993; Nystul, 1980a).

Consultation with parents and teachers can be an important adjunct to Adlerian play therapy (Kottman & Johnson, 1993; Nystul, 1987b). In this process, counselors can use Adlerian/Dreikursian concepts to help parents and teachers develop tools they can use to better understand and work with children. Some of the more popular concepts are the goals of misbehavior, the birth-order factor in personality development, encouragement versus praise, and consequences versus punishment. Programs such as systematic training for effective parenting (STEP) by Dinkmeyer and McKay (1997) provide an excellent summary of these ideas as well as structured activities to apply them. The following *Personal Note* provides an example of how I developed my own approach to play therapy.

A Personal Note

I have developed my own approach to play therapy (Nystul, 1980a). It is grounded in Adlerian/Dreikursian psychology and also integrates the four phases of multimodality creative arts therapy described in Chapter 8: set the stage, set an example, set yourself at ease, and obtain a phenomenological understanding of the child. My approach to play therapy is based on the following seven assumptions.

1. The counselor attempts to establish a feeling of mutual respect with the child.
2. The counselor uses encouragement whenever possible.
3. The counselor attempts to understand the child by exploring the child's private logic.
4. The counselor tries to redirect the child's teleological movement to increase the child's motivation for change.
5. The session starts with 15 to 30 minutes of self-concept development and ends with 15 to 30 minutes of multimodality creative arts therapy.
6. The counselor uses logical and natural consequences to establish realistic limits.
7. The counselor recognizes the importance of parent and teacher involvement as an adjunct to play therapy.

Over the years, I have found play therapy to be a very effective way to work with children. I believe play is a natural medium to communicate with them. Play allows children an opportunity to relax and be themselves as they work through their issues of concern.

Guidelines for Play Therapy.   The following guidelines may be useful when implementing a play-therapy program.

Play therapy can be conducted individually or in small groups of two or three children. The play-therapy room should be approximately 15 by 15 feet. It should be big enough for two adults and four children, but small enough to promote a sense of closeness between the counselor and the child. If the room is too large, for example, the child may wander off. The counselor should ensure privacy. No one should be permitted to come into the play-therapy room while a session is in progress. Interruptions can be a major distraction from the counseling process.

The counselor should obtain different play materials, such as play houses, puppets, babies, and other family members. It is also useful to have art supplies such as molding clay and watercolors and musical instruments such as bongo drums and a tambourine.

The counselor should establish limits with the child during the first session regarding time and behavior. In terms of time, the session length can vary according to the time available but should not exceed one hour. The length of time should be determined before the first session and adhered to as much as possible. Regarding behavior, the counselor should restrain a child who acts in an aggressive, hostile manner. It may even be necessary to discontinue the play-therapy session if the child persists in being hostile. When a child abuses a toy, the counselor can use a logical consequence. For example, a counselor might say, "It looks like you're not ready to use the drum today. I'll put it up for now. Some other time, you can try to use it the way it is supposed to be used."

In communicating, counselors should use a friendly, kind voice, especially if they sense a child feels insecure; not talk down to a child in terms of tone of voice; and use an appropriate vocabulary level so that the child will understand their words. While it may be necessary to be firm with a child, it is probably counterproductive to be stern. Counselors should let themselves laugh and have fun with the child, and they should talk from a positive perspective, using encouragement whenever possible.

Play therapy offers a means to reach into the world of the child and help the child reach out to the world of others. It can be used to treat a wide range of problems and concerns. For example, play therapy can be used to help autistic children learn language and

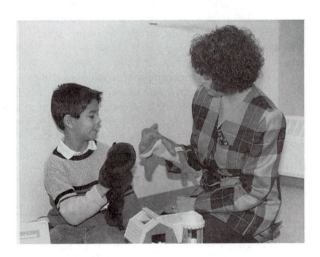

Puppets can help children express themselves in play therapy.

other skills necessary to overcome some autistic tendencies (Nystul, 1986a). Campbell (1993) suggests that play therapy can provide an important dimension to comprehensive developmental counseling programs by helping children overcome tendencies toward reluctance and resistance, fostering problem solving and so forth. Cochran (1996) goes on to note that play therapy has cross-cultural potential by creating a universal language through play and involvement in the creative arts. Play therapy can help overcome language barriers and other sources of resistance to foster school success in children and adolescents (Cochran, 1996). Reams and Friedrich (1983) conducted a meta-analysis of 15 research reports on play therapy. Results of their investigation show that play therapy is superior to nontreatment and promotes general adaptation and intellectual skills. Additional research seems warranted to provide a clearer understanding of how play therapy can be used with children.

Conflict Resolution. Youth-oriented conflict-resolution procedures can be used with children (Stern & Newland, 1994) and adolescents (Van Slyck et al., 1996). As noted in Chapter 14, conflict resolution is particularly useful in middle school counseling, where problems tend to be related to interpersonal conflict.

Youth-oriented conflict resolution has its own unique theories, techniques, and training requirements and is utilized in school and mental health counseling (Van Slyck et al., 1996). Van Slyck et al. (1996) provide an overview of this field that is summarized as follows. Youth-oriented conflict resolution is considered distinct from adult conflict resolution in that the youth takes an active role in the process by learning how to manage his or her own conflicts, and adults tend to take a more passive role by bringing in a mediator to resolve the conflict (such as in divorce mediation). The overall goal of youth-oriented conflict resolution is to foster problem-solving skills, coping skills, and resiliency characteristics that can be used to overcome conflict and foster optimal development.

Youth-oriented conflict-resolution programs can be both preventative and remedial in nature. Preventative programs are directed at helping young people learn how to apply conflict-resolution theory and skills to foster a life with minimal adverse conflicts and stress. Large and small group guidance activities on conflict resolution as well as adaptations in the school curriculum can play a major role in implementing preventative programs. Remedial conflict resolution relates to overcoming currently existing conflicts. This can involve the use of peer counseling (for example, peer mediation) or direct intervention by teachers, staff, and counselors. Regardless of the level of intervention (prevention or remedial), the focus is on helping young people use problem-solving skills to successfully mediate and negotiate problems of living.

Dysinger (1993) describes a conflict-resolution model that can be used with young people. It has several steps that have been incorporated into the following framework for conflict-resolution problem solving:

1. "Take a positive approach." It begins by encouraging young people to approach conflict resolution from a win-win perspective. Ground rules are established that promote a positive, strengths perspective rather than an adversarial approach (for example, no name calling or threatening).
2. "Listen and respond appropriately." It involves helping the conflicting parties learn to use listening skills to understand opposing points of view and to respond constructively.

Ground rules include no interrupting while others are talking (so they can be in the role of listener and learner) and respond from a position of caring.

3. "Become aware of choices and responsibility." Youths are encouraged to become aware of the choices they have made and the responsibility they must assume in relation to the conflict. Ground rules include no blaming or whining. Use of personal pronouns can be encouraged to help young people take responsibility for their behavior.

4. "Create solutions that promote friendship." This step identifies a new approach, which can be used to overcome the conflict. The nature of the new approach will vary with the situation and people involved. For some, assurance that the other person will not engage in a certain behavior will be enough, for others, simply understanding the other person's point of view can resolve the conflict.

5. "Follow up." Follow-up involves checking to see whether the conflict has been resolved and encouraging the youths to engage in conflict-resolution problem solving if there continues to be a problem. Through cooperation and caring, friendships can be enhanced and conflicts and stress can be minimized.

Guidelines for Child and Adolescent Counseling

The following guidelines can be integrated into one's personal approach to counseling children and adolescents.

Maintain a Line of Communication.   Parents, teachers, and counselors can get discouraged when counseling children and adolescents. Parents can contribute to communication problems by utilizing a rigid parenting style such as presenting children and adolescents with ultimatums such as "While under my roof, you do as I say, or else." Children and adolescents may create special challenges for adults as they act out rebellious stages, say and do hurtful things, and find ways to annoy others. When this occurs, it is important for concerned adults to maintain a line of communication with the child or adolescent.

The following *Personal Note* provides examples of clinical issues associated with maintaining a line of communication.

A Personal Note

I will always remember what a woman who specialized in working with adolescents told me. She said the most important thing in counseling adolescents is to always maintain a line of communication. It is very easy to lose that connection with adolescents due to their rebelliousness, parental rigidity, and so forth. Without communication, problems cannot be resolved and bad situations only get worse.

I have found that several theoretical perspectives can be used to maintain a line of communication with children and adolescents. For example,

Glasser (1980) suggests that counselors convey to their clients that they will never give up on them regardless of what they do. Children and adolescents often test their counselors by escalating their misbehavior to see if their counselors really mean it. My theory of emotional balancing (described in Chapter 3, Nystul, 2002a, b) provides another tool for maintaining a line of communication. According to this theory, a person can maintain meaningful communication and emotional balance by avoiding emotional disengagement and emotional enmeshment.

Use Interventions Grounded in Theory. Theory provides a conceptual framework for understanding and addressing clinical issues. The following *Personal Note* describes why I have found theory to play a key role in child and adolescent counseling.

A Personal Note

I recently went to an Adlerian conference and attended a presentation by Professor James Croake. During the presentation, he said that having a solid grounding in theory could be very beneficial in helping relationships, and it should be emphasized over technique. I could not agree with him more. I have found that theories (such as theories of personality and theories of child development) promote understanding of *why* the child is misbehaving and so on, and understanding tends to promote interest and compassion, which in turn can foster positive outcomes such as problem resolution.

Interventions grounded in theory are also useful to those in the role of consultant. As a school psychologist, I am often asked by teachers what they should do about a student's misbehavior. My consultation usually focuses on helping them understand the dynamics of the child's or adolescent's misbehavior. In this process, we explore the application of simple, practical theories such as Glasser's (1969) concept of success versus failure identity and Dreikurs's concepts of goals of misbehavior and encouragement versus praise (Dreikurs & Soltz, 1964). These theories are great because they have stood the test of time.

Incorporate Parenting Concepts in One's Approach. Parenting programs such as Dinkmeyer and McKay's (1997) systematic training for effective parenting (STEP) can be important adjuncts to child and adolescent counseling. Parenting concepts and ideas can be used to address child/adolescent problems and enhance family relationships (Nystul, 1980b, 1982b, 1984, 1987b). Parenting programs such as STEP do not require licensed professionals and are often led by interested parents.

In some instances, more in-depth parenting interventions are required. In these cases, counselors can utilize parenting programs as an adjunct to child and adolescent counseling. Parent management training (PMT) is the most popular parenting program used by counselors to assist parents (Friedlander & Tuason, 2000). PMT is a psychoeducational intervention that involves helping parents learn parenting procedures to address child and adolescent problems. PMT has been used to successfully treat a number of child and adolescent problems, such as oppositional and conduct disorders, attention-deficit hyperactivity disorder, and delinquency (Estrada & Pinsoff, 1995). PMT has also been used to enhance overall family functioning by reducing family conflict and increasing family cohesion and expression (Sayger, Horne, & Glaser, 1993). Positive gains associated with PMT can be significantly reduced when parents are depressed or experiencing high levels of stress (Webster-Stratton, 1990) or families are disadvantaged or isolated (Estrada & Pinsof, 1995).

Emphasize Choice and Responsibility. Glasser (1998) emphasizes the role of choice and responsibility in promoting mental health. Choice and responsibility can be especially useful in child and adolescent counseling strategies to promote optimal development. Parents, teachers, and others can help children and adolescents become aware of their choices and assume responsibility for those choices. Personal and relational benefits can occur when the choice-responsibility approach is used. Personal growth resulting from choice-responsibility can include self-efficacy, self-control, self-esteem, and internal locus of control. Relational benefits can include minimizing conflict between the adult and child or adolescent (because the parent is focusing on the child's or adolescent's choices rather than getting sidetracked into issues such as power and control).

Utilize the Reaching In–Reaching Out Model.   Reaching in–reaching out is a counseling approach that can be useful in child and adolescent counseling (Nystul, 1986). Reaching in–reaching out involves counselors finding a way into the world of the client and then helping the client reach out to the world of others. The more rigid and ritualistic clients are, the more resistant they can be, and therefore the more important it is to meet them on their terms. When clients are met on their terms, they tend to feel safe, thereby lowering their resistance to being with their counselor. As clients let counselors into their world, the resultant existential encounter can be enhanced by enjoyable experiences such as "having fun" with puppets, music, or other creative play modalities.

"Having fun" can set the stage for the "reaching out" phase of counseling by increasing the client's motivation for working with the counselor. The "reaching-out" phase involves a "transformation of the self" reflected in a shift in the client's private logic to increased social interest and willingness to cooperate with the counselor (e.g., "I want to listen and cooperate with my counselor because he can be fun."). Once the "transformation of the self" has occurred, counselors can help clients reach out to the world of others by directly addressing their problems (such as helping an autistic child learn language skills). Counselors can then work with other concerned adults such as parents and teachers to help them effectively relate to children and adolescents by applying the reaching in–reaching out approach.

The following *Personal Note* provides an illustration of how to reach into a child's world. A description of this case was provided in Chapter 1 in a *Personal Note* relating to the art of counseling. The case involved a first-grade girl who had been placed in a class for the mentally retarded. As it turned out, she was misdiagnosed and was not retarded but was autistic.

A Personal Note

When I first saw her I was not aware that she was autistic. I had brought puppets that I was going to use to present self-concept material and other activities. Her idea of using the puppets was to throw them all in a pile and redo a throw if it didn't land right on the other puppets (that type of ritualistic behavior is common with autistic children). As I attempted to reach into her world (a world she felt safe with and understood), I became a "puppet basketball net." I circled my arms around her pile of puppets and yelled "two points" when she threw one in my circle. Over time, she felt safe with me and began to welcome my company. I used this interest to encourage her to reach out to the world of others by fostering her language development

and eventually finding ways to help her break out of some of the rigidity of her autistic world.

Over the years I have reflected on this case and have come to believe that, to some degree, all counseling is a reaching in–reaching out process. Initially in counseling, I find ways to reach into my client's world. With children it can be through play therapy; with adults perhaps creative arts therapy or listening skills to discover the personal meaning of their stories. After a while, we establish a positive counseling relationship that provides the basis for encouraging my clients to reach out in new directions, expand their horizons, and foster their optimal development.

Special Problems of Children and Adolescents

This section provides an overview of some of the special problems experienced by children and adolescents: child abuse and neglect, depression, and antisocial behavior. For each type of problem, information is presented on incidence, assessment, causes, effects, and treatment.

Child Abuse and Neglect

Children have been abused and neglected throughout history, but it was not until the early 1960s that child abuse and neglect became recognized as social problems that require comprehensive treatment (Wolfe, 1988). This section reviews some of the issues associated with child abuse and neglect.

Incidence. The incidence of child abuse and neglect continues to increase at an alarming rate in the United States, with current estimates to be as high as two million children a year (Papalia & Olds, 2001). Many of these abused children have been sexually abused (Papalia & Olds, 2001). The incidence of sexual abuse in the United States is also staggering. Current estimates suggest that one in every four girls and one in every seven to ten boys will have a sexual experience with an adult before reaching 18 years of age (England & Thompson, 1988). In addition, psychological abuse may be the most prevalent and destructive form of child abuse (Dworetzky, 1996).

Assessment. Early identification and treatment of child abuse and neglect are critical to minimize negative effects on the child. Salkind (1994) identifies the following warning signs of the various forms of child abuse and neglect:

- *Physical abuse.* Signs of bruises, burns, and broken bones.
- *Child neglect.* Poor health and hygiene and excessive school absenteeism.
- *Sexual abuse.* Use of sexually explicit terminology, nightmares, genital injury, and sexually transmitted disease.
- *Psychological (emotional) abuse.* Depression, self-deprecation, somatic (bodily) complaints such as headaches or stomachaches, and fear of adults.

The assessment of child abuse and neglect is a multistage process (Wolfe, 1988). The process usually begins with impressionistic data from the reporting and referral source. That stage is followed by a refinement of information during interviews with parents and the child (Wolfe, 1988). Much of the initial information regarding the functioning of the parent and child can be obtained in a semistructured interview with the parent (Wolfe, 1988). The Parent Interview and Assessment Guide can be used to structure the interview and provide information on family background, marital relationship, areas of stress and support, and symptomatology (Wolfe, 1988). Several instruments have been developed that can be used to survey the attitudes of parents on topics relating to marriage and the family. The Child Abuse Potential Inventory (Milner, 1986) identifies familial patterns associated with child abuse. The Childhood Level of Living Scale (Polansky, Chalmers, Buttenwieser, & Williams, 1981) measures the degree of positive and negative influences in the home and is particularly useful for assessing neglect (Wolfe, 1988).

Causes.   Current research shows that child abuse results from a complex interaction of events. Wolfe (1988) summarizes the research by noting that child abuse is a special type of aggression resulting from proximal and distal events.

Proximal events are those that precipitate abuse. A proximal event can involve a child's behavior or an adult conflict that triggers the abuse. Common child behaviors that can trigger child abuse are aggression, unspecified misbehavior, lying, and stealing (Kadushin & Martin, 1981). Straus, Gelles, and Steinmetz (1980) suggest that marital problems and violence are also associated with child abuse.

Distal events are those that are indirectly associated with child abuse. Indirect factors that have been shown to contribute to child abuse include low socioeconomic status and poverty, restricted educational and occupational opportunities, unstable family environment, excessive heat, overcrowding, ambient noise level, and unemployment (Wolfe, 1988).

Other research efforts have attempted to identify characteristics of abusive parents as a means of understanding the causes of child abuse. Talbutt (1986) summarizes this research by noting that abusive parents tend to be abused as children, have difficulty coping with stress, suffer from substance-abuse problems, be immature and hold unrealistic expectations of children, and have children with special needs that require extra time and energy.

Sroufe and Cooper (1996) describe a typical profile of parents at high risk for child abuse. They tend to be young, poorly educated, single, living in poverty, and socially isolated, and feel little support from a significant other. The authors also note that abusive mothers tend to have a negative attitude toward their pregnancy. Compared to nonabusive parents, they tend to have less understanding of what is involved in caring for an infant, are less prone to plan for pregnancy, do not attend childbirth classes, do not have special living quarters for the baby to sleep, and have unrealistic expectations about raising an infant.

Effects.   Sroufe and Cooper (1996) describe the effects of child abuse and neglect on the child. Physical neglect that results from not meeting a child's basic needs such as food and shelter tends to produce a lack of competency in dealing with the tasks of daily living, such as personal hygiene. Physical abuse and emotional unavailability often result in behavioral and emotional problems, such as avoidance of intimacy in relationships, aggressiveness with peers, and blunted emotions. Psychologically abused children can develop neurotic traits, conduct disorders, negative self-image, and distorted relations with others (Craig, 2002; Hart & Brassard, 1987).

Sexual abuse can have traumatic and enduring effects. Feinauer (1990) notes that children who have been sexually abused can develop symptoms associated with posttraumatic stress disorder, such as flashbacks of the trauma and nightmares. These symptoms also tend to persist into adulthood (Feinauer, 1990). In addition, sexually abused individuals have a high risk of developing psychiatric problems as adults (Herman, 1986).

O'Brien (1983) identifies several ways in which sexual abuse can damage a child:

- *Psychological effects.* Sexual experiences can be confusing for children because they are unable to understand the strong emotional feelings associated with sex.
- *Low self-esteem.* Children may blame themselves for permitting the sexual contact or may feel dirty or ashamed as a result of the experience.

- *Exploitation.* Sexually abused children may feel used and develop a hostile, suspicious attitude toward others.
- *Vulnerability.* Because children are dependent on adults, they are vulnerable to and trusting of adults. When that trust is broken, children may develop a negative attitude toward vulnerability, making it difficult for them to develop trust and intimacy in their relationships.
- *Distorted view of sexuality.* It is common for sexually abused children to develop a very negative or perverted attitude toward sex. As they grow up, they may avoid sex or become sexually promiscuous.
- *Violation of the child's privacy.* After an incestuous relationship is discovered, the abused child must cooperate with the authorities. This violation of the child's privacy can be very traumatic and anxiety-provoking.
- *Distorted moral development.* Sexual abuse often occurs between the ages of 9 and 11 when a child's moral development is being formulated. Children can become quite confused about what is right and wrong when an adult is allowed to violate them sexually.

The following *Personal Note* illustrates how difficult it can be for a child to deal consciously with the trauma of sexual abuse.

A Personal Note

When I was a psychologist at a hospital, I worked with several girls who had babies as a result of incestuous relationships with their fathers. These girls tended to use denial as a means of coping with what had happened.

For example, I met a 14-year-old girl the day before she had her baby. She insisted that she was not even pregnant. After she had the baby, she said that the baby was not hers. This patient required extensive counseling and psychotherapy to develop a realistic approach to her situation.

Treatment. Brockman (1987) has suggested that the most hopeful treatment for abusive parents involves "resocialization" tasks, which help parents overcome isolation and foster interpersonal relations and support. These efforts can include encouraging parents to join Parents Anonymous or other self-help groups. Brockman (1987) also identifies several preventive programs that could be promoted in schools. These programs include adult education, interpersonal training for students, courses on sexuality and parenting in high school, and guest speakers for students from organizations such as Parents Anonymous.

Thompson and Wilcox (1995) go on to note that there is little empirical evidence to support the social-isolation theory of child abuse, citing numerous examples of parents who are provided social support and who continue to engage in child abuse because of many other stressors (such as substance-abuse problems). They contend that child abuse and neglect is a cross-disciplinary problem that should be addressed by research and intervention teams composed of people from disciplines such as psychology, social work, and sociology. Together they can gain a more comprehensive understanding of the causes and treatment strategies associated with child mistreatment.

Treatment efforts can also be directed at the abused child. Group counseling can be especially effective in working with abused and neglected children (Damon & Waterman, 1986) and adolescents (Hazzard, King, & Webb, 1986). Kitchur and Bell (1989) note that group counseling can be useful with this population to foster self-esteem, overcome problems with trust, correct distorted cognitions, and enhance self-control skills.

White and Allers (1994) also note that play therapy has been used extensively with abused children. A review of this literature shows a pattern of unique behaviors that emerged in conducting play therapy with abused children. Some of these behaviors include developmental immaturity; repetitive and compulsive behavior; opposition and aggression; withdrawal and passivity; self-depreciation and self-destructive behavior; hypervigilance; sexual behavior; and dissociation (an unconscious denial of abuse). The nature of play is also unique. Abused children are not very imaginative in their play, and their play does not seem to elevate their anxiety.

Orenchuk-Tomiuk, Matthey, and Christensen (1990) identify special treatment considerations relating to sexual abuse. The authors propose a three-stage model for treating sexual abuse called the *resolution model*. The three stages are (a) the noncommittal or oppositional stage, (b) the middle stage, and (c) the resolution stage. The model differentiates treatment issues for the child, the nonoffending parent, and the offending parent at each stage, as follows.

The child feels responsible for the abuse during the noncommittal or oppositional stage, feels angry and experiences symptoms associated with posttraumatic stress disorder during the middle stage, and no longer feels responsible for the sexual abuse nor experiences problematic symptoms during the resolution stage.

The nonoffending parent denies occurrence of sexual abuse, blames the child for disclosure, and defends the offender during the noncommittal or oppositional stage, believes the abuse has taken place and begins to become an ally for the child during the middle stage, and becomes a positive ally for the child and works through guilt associated with not protecting the child during the resolution stage.

The offender refuses to accept responsibility for abuse and/or denies its occurrence during the noncommittal or oppositional stage, is able to admit to the abuse but may blame the child during the middle stage, and assumes responsibility for the abuse and establishes a more positive parental role during the resolution stage.

The resolution model recommends that individual and group counseling can be useful during the noncommittal or oppositional stage. Couples and family counseling should not be used until the middle or resolution stages and should involve the child only if the child is ready.

England and Thompson (1988) provide additional guidelines that counselors can use with children who have been sexually abused. Counselors should take on the role of advocate for sexually abused children; help them overcome feelings of guilt and shame, emphasizing that the abuse was not their fault and that it will stop; use open-ended questions when assessing for sexual abuse and thus avoid leading questions; and take their accusations seriously since children tend not to lie about sexual abuse, and psychological harm can occur if they are not taken seriously.

Depression

The recognition of childhood and adolescent depression is a relatively recent occurrence (Petersen et al., 1993; Wagner, 1994, 1996). This section reviews some of the major issues associated with depression in children and adolescents.

Incidence.   Research investigations suggest that children are as capable of experiencing clinical depression as adults (Alper, 1986; Kovacs, 1989). Serious depression has been found in infants (Field et al., 1988; Spitz, 1946), preschool and school-age children (Digdon & Gotlib, 1985; Kazdin, 1988; Kovacs, 1989), and adolescents (Petersen et al., 1993; Rice & Meyer, 1994; Wagner, 1996). The average duration of a major depression in children and adolescents is seven to nine months, and a dysthymic depression lasts an average of three or more years (Kovacs, 1989).

Manic disorders in their classic form are rare and hard to diagnose accurately in children and adolescents (Strober et al., 1989). Hammen and Rudolph (2003) provide an overview of bipolar disorder in children, noting that children experience much higher rates of bipolar disorder than previously believed. The disorder was apparently underdiagnosed because children do not present with the traditional symptoms of bipolar disorder experienced in adults. For example, children can cycle from their manic-depressive states in one day (versus days in each state as in adults). In addition, children do not experience the euphoria and grandiosity states common in adults with bipolar disorder.

Hammen and Rudolph (2003) note that difficulty with diagnosis of bipolar disorder in children is associated with a wide array of psychological symptoms, including rapid mood shifts often characterized by intense irritability, aggression, and rage; destructive, social, and academic problems; and psychosis, delusions, and suicidal thoughts and behaviors. Bipolar disorder in children typically is comorbid with other mental disorders such as attention deficit hyperactivity disorder (ADHD), anxiety disorders, oppositional-defiant disorder, and substance abuse.

Assessment.   As noted earlier in this chapter, developmental psychopathology provides a framework for understanding how mental disorders such as depression vary over the life span (including during childhood and adolescence). Sakolske and Janzen (1987) identify some major symptoms associated with childhood depression. Changes in mood and affect are the most obvious indications. Examples include children who were relatively happy and had positive self-images suddenly saying they are sad, miserable, and no good. Another indication is that depressed children tend to lack interest in activities that were previously enjoyable, such as hobbies and sports. They may also lose interest in friends and family members. Other symptoms include physical complaints such as headaches and abdominal discomfort; sleep disturbances including nightmares; changes in appetite; impaired cognitive processes such as difficulty concentrating; and problems in school, work, and interpersonal relationships.

Petersen et al. (1993) provide a description of adolescent depression. They suggest that depressed adolescents typically show signs of unhappiness and have a number of fears and worries such as a fear of not being loved, not having friends, and worry about their appearance and relationships. In addition, it is estimated that adolescents experience major depression at a much higher rate than children (Petersen et al., 1993).

To obtain a diagnosis for a major depression, a person (regardless of age) must meet the established criteria. For example, the DSM-IV-TR (American Psychiatric Association, 2000) includes such things as depressed mood, decreased ability to experience pleasure, weight loss (or failure to thrive in children), loss of energy, thoughts of death, and so forth. The DSM also notes that "certain symptoms such as somatic complaints, irritability, and social withdrawal are particularly common in children, whereas psychomotor retardation, hypersomnia, and delusions are less common in prepuberty than in adolescence and adulthood" (American Psychiatric Association, 2000, p. 354).

Multiple diagnoses (comorbidity) are common with depressed children and adolescents. When this occurs, it is sometimes referred to by clinicians as a "masked depression" since the symptoms of depression are obscured by the additional diagnosis (Kovacs, 1989). The DSM-IV-TR notes that major depression in children normally does occur with other mental disorders such as anxiety disorders, disruptive behavioral disorders, and attention deficit disorders. Comorbidity in adolescents is often associated with mental disorders such as eating disorders, substance-abuse disorders, and disruptive behavioral disorders (American Psychiatric Association, 2000).

Hammen and Rudolph (2003) note that bipolar disorder is particularly difficult to diagnose in children because it typically occurs in conjunction with severe symptoms such as psychosis and mental disorders such as ADHD and anxiety disorders. ADHD poses a significant challenge to the diagnostic process as it potentially masks bipolar disorder.

Several instruments have been designed specifically to assess childhood and adolescent depression. For example, diagnostic interviews have been developed to assess child and adolescent mental disorders (Edelbrock & Costello, 1988). Most other instruments are directed at children. The most widely used instrument for children is the Children's Depression Inventory (Kovacs, 1981), which was developed from the Beck Depression Inventory. It assesses the cognitive, affective, and behavioral signs of depression. Other instruments include the Short Children's Depression Inventory (Carlson & Cantwell, 1979); the Children's Depression Scale (Lang & Tisher, 1978); and the Schedule for Affective Disorders and Schizophrenia for School-Age Children (Chambers, Puig-Antich, & Tabrizi, 1978). Kazdin (1988) provides a description of each of these instruments.

Causes.   Several factors have been associated with childhood depression. These include parents who have high standards and do not express positive affect to their child (Cole & Rehm, 1986); children who have negative cognitive schemata characterized by self-deprecation, hopelessness, and despair (Hammer & Zupan, 1984); and social-skill and problem-solving deficits (Altmann & Gotlib, 1988). Hammen and Rudolph (2003) note that the underlying etiology of bipolar disorder in children is primarily associated with genetics.

Wagner (1994) goes on to provide an ecological perspective for conceptualizing mental health problems of children. He describes the "povertization of childhood" by noting that 25 percent of children aged 5 or younger are living in poverty, and a great number of these children are born to single mothers. This "povertization" has been associated with impeding the development of children and having a devastating effect on their well-being (Wagner, 1994).

Petersen et al. (1993) identify causes associated with adolescent depression (many of which also seem relevant to childhood depression). Major causes of adolescent depression include pessimistic-negative cognitions; genetic predisposition (a parent with a history of depression); and social-systemic factors such as excessive environmental stress, problems with home (including family and marital discord), school, and peer group. It is interesting to note that one of the best predictors of adult depression is impaired peer-group relations during adolescence.

Blair (2004) addresses adolescent depression from an existential perspective. He suggests that Frankl's (1963) logotherapy is ideally suited to address adolescent depression, noting that adolescence can be a challenging period of development as youth struggle with issues of self-awareness, personal identity, peer pressure, and experimentation with alcohol, drugs, and sexuality. As adolescents attempt to define their existence, they can be left with an existential vacuum or lack of meaning in life associated with not living up to one's potential.

Effects. Depression in childhood and adolescents can have serious consequences. Some problems with childhood and adolescent depression are impaired cognition (Kovacs, Gatsonis, Marsh, & Richards, 1988; Petersen et al., 1993); problems with social and educational progress (Kovacs et al., 1988; Petersen et al., 1993); and suicidal tendencies (Garland & Zigler, 1993; Kovacs, 1989). Bipolar disorder in children is associated with suicidal tendencies and impairment in social relationships, academic achievement, self-control, and ability to maintain contact with reality (Hammen & Rudolph, 2003).

Even if a person does not become depressed as a child, childhood experiences can make an individual prone to depression as an adult. Brown and Harris (1978) found that children who experience the death of their mother before they are 11 years of age are more prone than other children to develop depression as adults.

Blair (2004) notes that adolescents struggle with identity issues as they attempt to define themselves and give their life meaning. For example, problems regarding the emergence of the "self" can result from the conflicting demands from the adolescents' peer group and the expectations of their parents. In this process, adolescents can experience symptoms of depression such as sadness and despair.

Treatment. Several counseling approaches are available to treat childhood depression. Cognitive approaches have been shown to be particularly effective (Reynolds & Coats, 1986). Another approach is parent education, which can be used to help parents learn skills to promote a positive environment for the family. Play therapy is another option, which enables children to work through traumatic experiences and enhance their social skills and self-image. Antidepressant medication can also be considered in the treatment of depression, although there are mixed reports regarding its efficacy for children (Puig-Antich et al., 1987).

The most important treatment issue relating to bipolar disorder in children is an accurate diagnosis. In fact, some clinicians contend that early detection and treatment of bipolar disorder in children can make the effects of the disorder more benign and that misdiagnosis can make the course of the disorder worse (Hammen & Rudolph, 2003). However, accurate diagnosis of bipolar disorder in children can be a daunting task since, as noted earlier, it is often comorbid with other disorders such as ADHD and a wide range of psychological features such as extreme mood changes and rage. Medication plays a major role in the treatment of bipolar disorder. Establishing an effective treatment regime can be challenging, however, since medications used to treat one disorder can undermine the treatment of a coexisting disorder. For example, antidepressant medications may trigger hypomania and the rapid cycling associated with bipolar disorder, while psychostimulants used to treat ADHD can have an adverse effect on both depression and mania (Hammen & Rudolph, 2003).

Petersen et al. (1993) provide an overview of the major treatment modalities for adolescent depression. They note that antidepressant medication has not been shown to be effective with adolescents, perhaps due to the dramatic physiological changes associated with adolescents or the comorbid conditions that may complicate treatment responses. A number of counseling and psychotherapeutic approaches have been used to successfully treat adolescent depression. Some of these approaches include cognitive-behavioral, psychodynamic, family therapy, social skills training, and group counseling. Preventative programs show promise as a means of treating adolescent depression (Rice & Meyer, 1994). For example, Rice and Meyer (1994) have developed a psychoeducational intervention program that can be used in schools to enhance coping responses to stress.

Blair (2004) provides an overview of existential strategies, based on Frankl's (1963) logotherapy, that can be used to treat adolescent depression. These strategies are summarized as follows:

- Counselors should build a relationship of respect and trust by emotionally connecting with clients and maintaining a nonjudgmental position.
- Counselors should help clients understand the purpose behind the depression (e.g., it can create motivation for self-exploration and change).
- Counselors should assist clients in identifying what is missing in their lives (i.e., what is necessary to reach their full potential).
- Counselors should address the clients' strengths, talents, and interests that they can use to achieve necessary change.
- Counselors should facilitate clients' search for meaning by emphasizing that they have choices, are free to make choices, and must ultimately take responsibility for their choices.

Suicide

Suicide represents a special problem for children and adolescents that has far-reaching consequences extending beyond the victim to the family, community, and society. Suicide among children and adolescents is considered a complex phenomenon that has been linked to factors such as depression. This section reviews some of the trends in suicide among children and adolescents discussed by Capuzzi and Nystul (1986) and Goldman and Beardslee (1999).

Incidence.   Suicide rates for children and adolescents have increased dramatically since 1950. For example, adolescents made 2.7 suicides per 100,000 in 1950; 5.2 per 100,000 in 1960; and 13.8 per 100,000 in 1994. Suicide rates of children are approximately one-tenth of that for adolescents. For children, suicide is the fifth leading cause of death as compared to the third leading cause of death for adolescents. Of particular concern is the fact that suicide rates have recently doubled for children.

The disparity between suicide rates of children and adolescents has been attributed to a number of factors. Children have less ability to plan and carry out a successful suicide than adolescents. This is in part due to the lower level of cognitive functioning of children and the fact that they have less access to lethal weapons. Children also have fewer problems with feelings such as hopelessness and helplessness that are often associated with suicide. In this regard, children tend to live in the present and, therefore, do not believe that feelings of hopelessness and helplessness will be ongoing. In addition, children tend to be more comfortable with feelings of helplessness because childhood is characterized by high levels of dependence for survival. Lower suicide rates of children can also be attributed to parents more closely monitoring children than adolescents.

Incidences of suicide vary according to gender, sexual orientation, and culture. In terms of gender, females think about and attempt suicide at significantly higher rates than males (4:1 and 3:1, respectively). Surprisingly, males commit five times as many successful suicides as females. This can be due in part to males using more violent suicidal methods such as lethal weapons and females tending to use pills, which may allow for successful medical interventions. Sexual orientation has been associated with increased risk of suicide. The rates of successful suicides are much higher for gay and lesbian adolescents than the general population. In these instances, identity formation during adolescence can be undermined when there is a lack of acceptance of sexual orientation by friends, family, and society. Culture has also been associated with different rates of childhood and adolescent suicide. Native Americans have the highest rates of adolescent suicide, followed by Anglos, and then African Americans. Native-American youth suicide rates appear higher in tribes that place a lower emphasis on traditional values.

Assessment. The pathway to child and adolescent suicide represents a complex set of factors. Increased vulnerability to suicide is associated with psychopathology, such as depression and substance abuse; stress from problems of living, e.g., teen pregnancy; family factors, such as family dysfunction, violence, and abuse; a lack of coping and problem-solving skills; and an insufficient social-emotional support system. The MMPI (means, motive, plan, and intent) acronym can also be used to assess for suicide. For example, an adolescent who insists he wants to kill himself because of a recent breakup would have high intent and motive. If he had a loaded gun in his car, he would also have the means and plan and would be considered a high risk for suicide.

Causes. Suicide can be understood from a number of perspectives. The biochemical model relates to the chemical imbalance associated with depression and resultant increased risk for suicide. The psychological perspective focuses on feelings such as hopelessness and despair and how a child or adolescent can view suicide as a way out of his or her problems. Developmental theory provides another explanation for suicide, suggesting that a child or adolescent can commit suicide as a response to conflict over identity formation.

Effects. The effects of suicide transcend the victim, affecting the victim's family, school, community, and society. Loved ones are left to contend with a wide array of feelings, such as anger and guilt. It is also common for friends and family members to spend considerable time and energy wondering why the act was committed and whether there was anything they could have done to prevent the suicide.

Treatment. Suicide prevention plays a central role in treatment. Children and adolescents must be assessed and monitored for suicidal ideations and actions. Parents and school officials can play an important role in this process. For example, any child who appears sad or depressed should be referred to the school counselor for possible suicide assessment. Other preventive efforts can be made in schools, such as promoting resiliency characteristics to enhance coping mechanisms to stress. Suicide contracts can be used once a child or adolescent is identified as suicidal. These contracts require that a parent and/or child/adolescent notify a mental health worker if the child/adolescent becomes actively suicidal. Hospitalization and treatment should be considered when a child/adolescent becomes a high risk for suicide. Once children/adolescents are stabilized in terms of their suicidal ideations, counseling can focus on identifying underlying causal factors associated with their suicidal tendencies. Treatment can then be directed at resolving these issues to enhance overall psychological functioning.

Antisocial Behavior

Antisocial behavior in children and adolescents includes acts that violate major social rules, including violence and aggression, bullying, lying, stealing, and truancy (Kazdin, Bass, Siegel, & Thomas, 1989). This section reviews some of the major issues associated with antisocial behavior in children and adolescents.

Incidence.   The incidence of children engaging in antisocial behavior is high and involves one-third to one-half of all mental health clinical referrals (Kazdin et al., 1989). Rates of antisocial behavior in the form of delinquency are also staggering, with 6 percent of serious crimes in the United States (such as rape and murder, assault, and robbery) being committed by youth under 15 and 16 percent committed by adolescents 15 to 18 years of age (Berger & Thompson, 2000). In addition, worldwide, a person is more likely to be arrested during adolescence and young adulthood than at any other time.

Incidents of school shootings are on the increase. Although there can be multiple factors associated with violence, bullying is receiving attention as a contributing factor in school violence. Bullying has been defined as unprovoked and repeated aggressive behavior that causes distress to its victim and verbal or physical behavior that disturbs someone who is less powerful (Goldstein, 1999; Nansel et al., 2001). Bullying incidences vary with age and setting and appear to peak in middle school and junior high (Goldstein, 1999). Incidences of bullying appear to be widespread, affecting one in three students between sixth and tenth grade (Nansel et al., 2001). Wartik (2001) notes that children and adolescents who were bullied may later retaliate with violence. For example, two of the Columbine High School shooters and the Santee, California, shooter were believed to have been victims of bullying.

Assessment.   Children or adolescents who engage in a well-established pattern of antisocial behavior for at least six months tend to receive a DSM-IV-TR diagnosis of either conduct disorder or oppositional-defiant disorder. Conduct disorder is the more serious mental disorder and requires that the individual has violated the rights of others and age-appropriate norms or rules of society. McMahon and Forehand (1988) note that most behaviors associated with conduct disorder involve "direct confrontation or disruption of the environment" and "are basically the same type of behavior that Patterson (1982) and Loeber and Schmaling (1985) have labeled 'overt antisocial behavior'" (p. 107). The major feature of oppositional defiant disorder "is a recurrent pattern of negativistic, defiant, disobedient, and hostile behavior toward authority figures that persists for at least 6 months" and is characterized by the frequent occurrence of at least four of the following behaviors: losing temper, arguing with adults, actively defying or refusing to comply with the requests or rules of adults, deliberately doing things that will annoy other people, blaming others for his or her own mistakes or misbehavior, being touchy or easily annoyed by others, being angry and resentful, or being spiteful or vindictive (American Psychiatric Association, 2000, p. 100).

McMahon and Forehand (1988) identify instruments that can be used to assess antisocial behavior. Several structured interviews have been developed for children. For example, the Diagnostic Interview Schedule for Children is a highly structured interview that can be used with children ages 6 to 18 and their parents (Costello, Edelbrock, Dulcan, & Kalas, 1984). It provides scores that correspond to DSM-IV-TR diagnosis of conduct disorder and oppositional-defiant disorder.

Several behavioral rating scales are also available for assessing antisocial behavior in children and adolescents. The Child Behavior Checklist (Achenback & Edelbrock, 1983) is one of the most popular rating scales in use. It can be used with children ages 2 to 16 and provides a comprehensive assessment of behaviorally disordered children (McMahon & Forehand, 1988). An advantage of this scale is that it has parallel forms for the child, parent, teacher, and observer. The Revised Behavior Problem Checklist (Quay & Petersen, 1983) is a rating scale that can be used to detect tendencies toward conduct problems, personality problems, inadequacy and immaturity, and socialized delinquency. This scale is completed by parents or teachers.

Assessment of aggression can involve identifying types of aggression. Strassberg, Dodge, Pettit, and Bates (1994) suggest that there are three types of aggression: instrumental, reactive, and bullying. *Instrumental aggression* involves the use of aggression to retaliate against someone who is caught doing something wrong (e.g., someone who has stolen or is trying to steal something). *Reactive aggression* is impulsive violence in response to a perceived wrongdoing and involves attributing blame without understanding whether the act was intentional or accidental. *Bullying aggression* is a hostile response to others for no apparent reason. Brown and Parsons (1998) provide a different perspective of bullying aggression. They refer to bullying aggression as *proactive aggression*. Proactive aggression is a socially learned response such as believing that problems can be solved by aggression. Proactive aggression tends to be well planned and goal directed and includes bullying or other acts of aggression to achieve a desired goal.

Causes. Patterson, DeBaryshe, and Ramsey (1989) suggest that antisocial behavior is a developmental trait that begins in childhood and often continues into adolescence and adulthood. These authors utilize a social-interactional perspective, which suggests that family members train children to engage in antisocial behaviors (Patterson, 1982; Snyder, 1977; Wahler & Dumas, 1987). According to this theory, parents do not adequately reinforce prosocial behavior or effectively punish deviant behavior. On the contrary, these children learn to use antisocial behaviors to stop aversive intrusions from other family members. From this perspective, antisocial behavior can be viewed as the manifestation of survival skills necessary to cope with a dysfunctional family.

Causes of aggression have been linked to the use of spanking as a disciplinary measure by parents (Strassberg et al., 1994). Spanking does not appear to be related to instrumental aggression (i.e., children will retaliate to a known threat regardless of whether they were spanked). Spanking is related to reactive aggression. Children who are spanked were twice as likely as children who were not spanked to use an aggressive response to an accidental or intentional provocation. Bullying aggression was related to children who have been severely punished.

McMahon and Forehand (1988) provide an overview of studies that identify factors associated with conduct disorders and antisocial behaviors. These studies suggest that children with conduct disorders also tend to exhibit impaired peer relationships (Achenback & Edelbrock, 1983), misattribute hostile intentions to others (Milich & Dodge, 1984), have deficits in social problem-solving skills (Asarnow & Calan, 1985), lack empathy (Ellis, 1982), are prone to hyperactivity (Loeber & Schmaling, 1985) and depression (Chiles, Miller, & Cox, 1980), have low levels of academic achievement, and have a genetic predisposition to develop antisocial tendencies (Kazdin, 1985). Kazdin et al. (1989) also note that antisocial children have deficits in interpersonal cognitive problem-solving skills (such as formulating solutions to problems), impaired cognitive development (such as moral reasoning), and maladaptive cognitive strategies (such as impulsiveness). Another series of studies has found a link between the influence of the peer group and acts of delinquency and substance abuse (Elliott, Huizinga, & Ageton, 1985; Huba & Bentler, 1983; Kandel, 1973).

Effects. Kazdin et al. (1989) suggest that the effects of antisocial behavior tend to prevail from childhood to adulthood. In addition, individuals diagnosed with antisocial behavior disorders tend to experience disproportional problems as adults, including criminal behavior, alcoholism, and antisocial personality disorders.

Patterson et al. (1989) note that children who engage in antisocial behavior are also prone to become delinquents. Approximately one-half of antisocial children become delinquent adolescents, and one-half to three-fourths of delinquent adolescents become adult offenders. The cost of delinquency transcends the offender, with $500 million spent annually on school vandalism alone (Feldman, Caplinger, & Wodarski, 1981).

Patterson et al. (1989) also suggest that many factors that are typically seen as causes of antisocial behavior, such as academic failure and peer rejection, can more accurately be understood as effects. For example, research has shown that childhood aggression leads to rejection by the peer group, not the reverse (Cole & Kupersmidt, 1983; Dodge, 1983).

Childhood/adolescent aggression can evolve into bullying if the bullying is rewarded (i.e., if the child/adolescent gets away with being a bully). Victims of bullying are believed to have increased risks for suicide and for engaging in retaliatory violence against others (Wartik, 2001).

Treatment. Providing counseling to antisocial individuals can be a very difficult endeavor. It can involve trying to stop a pattern of behavior that has begun during childhood and has evolved into a lifestyle. By the time these individuals are adolescents, many are active in gangs and find the possibility of getting out of a gang either undesirable or impossible. It is therefore not surprising that there has been limited success in attempting to overcome different forms of antisocial behavior (Kazdin, 1987; Wilson & Herrnstein, 1985).

One treatment modality that has been successfully used with antisocial youth is special education programs, which provide services to seriously emotionally disturbed/behaviorally disordered students (Thompson & Rudolph, 2004). In the United States, public schools provide closely supervised educational experiences for students with serious emotional disturbance and behavioral disorders (many have a history of antisocial behavior). These classes utilize a number of procedures such as behavioral contracting, token economy, individual and group counseling, parent consultation, and individualized instruction. Several studies provide evidence that teachers can make a difference in overcoming antisocial tendencies (Kupersmidt & Patterson, 1991; Tremblay, LeBlanc, & Schwartzman, 1988). The following *Personal Note* provides an example of my involvement in these programs.

Cashwell and Vacc (1996) provide some directions for preventing and overcoming delinquency problems with adolescents. Their research has found that two of the strongest predictors of adolescent delinquency are being involved with delinquent peers and a lack of family cohesion. They suggest that preventative programs should be started during elementary school to promote social-skills training and an awareness of the dangers of involvement in antisocial groups such as gangs. In addition, counseling could be directed at enhancing family cohesion through such efforts as parenting training and family counseling.

Treatment of aggression can involve a number of interventions. Brown and Parsons (1998) emphasize the importance of developing different strategies for different types of

A Personal Note

Over the past eight years I have been involved in working with special education students in elementary schools who have been placed in a classroom for students with serious emotional disturbance and behavioral disorders. During this time, I have been amazed by the "miracle" that special education programs can achieve with students. The miracle is that the students go from what Glasser (1969) would refer to as a *failure identity* to a *success identity.* When they come into the program, they have a failure identity. They hate school because they have never been successful at it. Many are a step away from dropping out. They are some of the best blamers and whiners I have ever encountered. Their problems are always someone else's fault. In addition, they are usually so busy trying to avoid doing school work and having fun that they are constantly running into problems with their teachers and are experiencing adverse consequences, such as not having the privileges that others are getting.

With these programs, in time these students begin to gain a success identity. They learn to follow the rules and get their work done. Gradually, they begin to feel pride in accomplishment, which plants the seed for intrinsic motivation. In addition, they become aware of choices regarding their

behavior and learn to assume responsibility for what they have done. An example of this is when I walked into a class and was talking with a student. I asked him how he was. He told me, "I got caught hitting some guy on the bus and got a level drop." That was it, no whining or blaming. Becoming responsible leads to self-respect, which in turn earns the respect of others.

Perhaps the best example that illustrates the success of these programs was what I experienced at a Christmas party. I was observing a new boy who had only been in the program for about 10 weeks. When he came into the program he hated everything, and his parents had to "drag him to school." Now he was doing really well in the program and felt pride in his achievements (instead of frowning, he was usually beaming). When the Christmas show finished, it was about 2:00 P.M. and school got out at 3:00 P.M. As his mom was about to leave, the teacher asked the boy if he wanted to go home with his mom. To my surprise, he said, "No, I want to stay until school gets out." Now that indeed is a miracle, to see a boy go from hating school and wanting no part of it to taking pride in school and enjoying it!

aggression. Proactive aggression (including bullying aggression) conceptualizes aggression as a learned response. Treatment approaches should, therefore, be directed at helping children/adolescents learn alternative responses to problem solving that do not entail aggression. For example, parents can avoid using severe punishment to prevent bullying aggression in their children/adolescents. Therapists can also use behavior approaches such as shaping and reinforcement to promote prosocial and appropriate goal-attainment behaviors.

Reactive aggression involves impulsive, nonmediated aggression. Children/adolescents engaging in reactive aggression can benefit from interventions that help with impulse control. Behavioral interventions can be used to target the antecedents to aggressive responses (e.g., moving a student away from other students to prevent potential conflict situations). Cognitive approaches can also be used to help children/adolescents reframe an intrusion as a potentially nonthreatening accident.

Additional research and development appear warranted in the area of providing counseling and mental health services for children and adolescents with antisocial behavior problems. The casualties extend beyond the victim, infusing fear and negativity into society itself. Much needs to be done to develop realistic and effective means to defeat needless violence, aggression, and hostility.

Diversity and Postmodern Issues in Child and Adolescent Counseling

Diversity and postmodern issues are playing a major role in the evolution of child and adolescent counseling. Diversity and postmodernism are redefining the foundation and evolution of child and adolescent counseling in terms of theory, research, and practice. From a theoretical perspective, the foundation of child and adolescent counseling is grounded in developmental theory. Carol Gilligan's (1982) seminal work on female moral development is credited with generating an awareness of the male bias in development theory.

Gilligan's (1982, 1991) research has contributed to a wave of interest in reassessing gender issues in developmental theory. Gilligan and, more recently, Allen and Stoltenberg (1995), Horst (1995), and Wastell (1996) have begun to reassess other developmental theories. For example, they contend that Erikson's (1968) theory of psychosocial development is in need of modification to overcome gender bias favoring males. From a feminist perspective, two of Erikson's stages stand out in need of revision (identity formation during adolescence and intimacy during young adulthood). For example, during identity formation, Erikson appears to recognize male values of autonomy and individualism over relational values favored by females. A more accurate conceptualization of female identity development would describe the self as being organized around the goal of establishing and maintaining meaningful relationships.

Sexual orientation can be another important diversity issue in counseling across the life span. This is especially true as adolescents and young adults strive for identity formation and intimacy. According to Kottman, Lingg, and Tisdell (1995), gay and lesbian adolescents face a wide array of obstacles to development, such as homophobia, discrimination, negative stereotyping, and even violence. The grip of homophobia often extends into the adolescents' support system, with friends and family often unable to recognize and accept a homosexual orientation. This often leaves the homosexual adolescent feeling alienated and isolated, with self-esteem and self-acceptance problems (fundamental building blocks for identity development and intimacy).

Kottman et al. (1995) note that with so much negativity to contend with, it is not surprising that homosexual adolescents are at risk for mental health problems. For example, Remafedi (1987) reports that approximately one-third of gay teens in a study had attempted suicide and/or been hospitalized for mental health problems, 48 percent had run away from home, and 58 percent regularly abused substances. In addition, O'Connor (1992) notes that approximately one-third of all successful adolescent suicides are individuals with homosexual orientations.

Hammond and Yung (1993) address ethnic minority issues that have an impact on violence and death of adolescent youth. They suggest that African-American male adolescents experience a disproportionate risk of death or injury due to violence. Perhaps the most telling statistic regarding this problem is that the number one reason for the death of an African-American male adolescent in the United States is assaultive gunshot by a friend or acquaintance. These authors go on to provide an overview of causes of violence among African-American adolescent males. Some of the contributing forces identified are psychosocial, cognitive-behavioral, and environmental. Environmental-ecological forces appear to play a major role in promoting violence in the lives of these adolescents. For example, many of these individuals live in the inner city, where violence and crime are a part of everyday life. Hammond and Yung (1993) go on to suggest that preventative programs need to be directed at overcoming the legacy of violence that perpetuates this ethnic minority group. They describe a multifaceted program directed at challenging beliefs and assumptions regarding violence, overcoming sociopolitical and ecological barriers to optimal development (for example, family and community instability), and fostering cultural awareness and sensitivity.

Gender issues should also be considered when conceptualizing mental health issues such as depression in children and adolescents. For example, Petersen et al. (1993) note that female adolescents are more prone to depression than male adolescents. Female adolescents also engage in different responses to depression because they tend to internalize (ruminate), whereas males tend to externalize (distract themselves with activities). Comorbitity in depression also tends to vary between male and female adolescents, with female depression often occurring with eating disorders and males having disruptive disorders co-occurring with depression (Petersen et al., 1993).

Postmodern considerations such as culture and environmental-ecological forces also affect the assessment and treatment of mental disorders of children and adolescents. The prevalence of mental disorders varies from culture to culture. Some cultures (such as Native American) have significantly high rates of depression and suicide, owing in part to environmental forces such as extreme levels of unemployment (Harrar, 1984). Community psychology that utilizes an ecological perspective can provide a useful dimension to mental health services with Native Americans (Harrar, 1984). In addition, the experience of mental disorders may vary widely from culture to culture in terms of the language and knowledge bases associated with mental health and mental illness. For example, some cultures (such as Latino) experience depression in mainly somatic terms such as complaints of nerves or headaches, whereas other cultures (such as Asian) may relate to feelings of being tired or being off-balance (American Psychiatric Association, 2000). It is therefore important to consider cultural forces reflected in the language and narratives used by children and adolescents as a means of assessing and treating problems such as depression.

Summary

Child and adolescent counseling is an emerging counseling specialty. The concept of child-hood and adolescence as distinct developmental stages is relatively new, as previously the special needs of children and adolescents were generally ignored. More recently, theories of child and adolescent development have been formulated, providing information on the cognitive, moral, psychosocial, and mental health development of children and adoles-cents. These theories provide an important conceptual framework for understanding and treating children and adolescents.

Assessment procedures unique to this field of counseling include the use of drawings and clinical interviews. Other treatment issues are play therapy, conflict resolution, cognitive-behavioral therapy, and the use of psychotropic medications.

Information on child abuse and neglect, childhood and adolescent depression, and antisocial behavior is provided in terms of incidence, assessment, causes, effects, and treat-ment to illustrate some of the current trends in child and adolescent counseling.

Personal Exploration

1. How can parent education be useful in enhancing your parenting skills?
2. What intrigues you about play therapy?
3. What do you think is behind the increase in school shootings, and what should be done about it?
4. What do you think about emotional intelligence and resiliency, and how do you think it can be fostered in children and adolescents?

Web Sites for Chapter 11

Atherton, J. S. (2003). *Learning and teaching: Piaget's developmental psychology.* Retrieved March 3, 2005, from http://www.dmu.ac.uk/~jamesa/ learning/piaget.htm#Stages
   Covers Piaget's cognitive stages of development and key concepts.

Barger, R. N. (2000). *A Summary of Lawrence Kohlberg's stages of moral development.* Retrieved March 3, 2005, from http://www.nd.edu/~rbarger/kohlberg.html
   Presents a summary of Kohlberg's stages of moral development.

Cramer, C., Flynn, B., & LaFave, A. (1997). *Introduction to Erikson's 8 stages.* Retrieved March 3, 2005, from http://web.cortland.edu/andersmd/ERIK/stageint.HTML
   Presents an introduction to Erikson's stages of development.

Henderson, N. (2002). *The resiliency quiz.* Retrieved March 3, 2005, from http://www.resiliency.com/htm/resiliencyquiz.htm
   Provides a resiliency quiz to help make the concept of resiliency more concrete.

Kid Power. (unknown). *What is play therapy?* Retrieved March 3, 2005, from http://users.snowcrest.net/kidpower/play.html
   Provides basic information about play therapy and a sample of how play therapy might progress.

CHAPTER OVERVIEW

This chapter provides an overview of group counseling. Highlights of the chapter include

- The art and science of group counseling
- Group counseling from a historical perspective
- Comparison to individual and family counseling
- Types of groups and goals
- Problem solving and group process
- Group size, composition, and duration
- Use of coleaders
- Pregroup screening and orientation
- Stages in group counseling
- Brief-solution-focused group counseling
- Dealing with disruptive group members
- Common mistakes of group leaders
- Qualities of effective group leaders
- Diversity issues

The Art and Science of Group Counseling

Group counseling is both an art and a science. It is an art in the sense that the group facilitator must be flexible and creative in adapting to the ongoing movement within the group process. Groups are dynamic entities and in that regard have a life and purpose of their own. Facilitators need to let go of preconceived ideas of what will occur within a group and allow the group to move toward the realization of its own unique potential. In addition, facilitators must be sensitive to issues of diversity that present themselves in the group. In doing so, facilitators, like artists, can help members create opportunities for sharing and learning.

The science of group counseling is directed at a number of important issues relating to group work. Contemporary group work emphasizes the importance of structure in the group to give individuals and the group a focus to enhance motivation and productivity within the group. Structure can include ensuring that prospective members are appropriate for the group, establishing rules or guidelines for the functioning of the group, encouraging members to formulate personal counseling goals, and using a conceptual frame of reference for facilitating the group (such as a solution-focused brief-counseling perspective). The science of group counseling can also involve research and evaluation to determine the efficacy of group theory and practice. In 1997, an effort was made to create a balance between the art and science of group counseling through a special issue of the *Journal for Specialists in Group Work* (November 1997). The issue provides numerous articles that encourage collaboration between science and practice in group work.

Group Counseling

Group counseling is an important specialty within the counseling profession. The practice of group counseling is found in most counseling programs and is therefore an integral part of the counselor's identity (Fuhriman & Burlingame, 1990). Several organizations have done much to advance the professionalization of group counseling. The American Counseling Association (ACA) charted a special division for group counseling in 1973 called the Association for Specialists in Group Work (ASGW). Ethical guidelines were established in 1980 and revised in 1989. In 1998, the ASGW replaced their ethical code with the *Best Practices Guidelines* for group work (Rapin & Keel, 1998). These guidelines identify ethical issues in group work and responsibilities for planning, performing, and processing groups. The ASGW also set forth professional standards for the training of group workers (Wilson, Rapin, & Haley-Banez, 2000) and standards for multicultural counseling (Haley-Banez, Brown, & Molina, 1998). Several other professional organizations have furthered the cause of group counseling, including the American Group Psychotherapy Association, the International Group Psychotherapy Association, and the American Association of Group Psychotherapy, Psychodrama, and Sociometry.

This chapter provides an overview of group counseling. It begins by describing group counseling from a historical perspective. Group counseling is then differentiated from individual and family counseling. Information on the practice of group counseling and a description of the stages of group counseling are also provided.

Group Counseling from a Historical Perspective

Group counseling has a rich and fascinating history. The group movement can be traced to the pioneering work of J. L. Morreno and Kurt Lewin in the 1920s and 1930s (Bonner, 1959). Lewin's field theory provided an important theoretical foundation for group work, and Morreno developed a unique approach to group counseling called *psychodrama.*

Initially, group counseling was met with skepticism in the professional community. Some perceived this new technique as a radical, unorthodox procedure that would undermine confidentiality. In addition, it conflicted with the basic definition of counseling, that of counselors working with individual clients. Gradually, however, group counseling gained respectability. In 1946, the National Training Laboratory (NTL) was founded in

Bethel, Maine (Baruth & Robinson, 1987), and soon became a major training institute for group work. The institute focused on how to use group dynamics to promote personal growth and interpersonal functioning.

During the 1960s, encounter and sensitivity groups became popular in general and the "in" thing on many college campuses. The spirit of the group movement seemed to blend with the cultural revolution also taking place in the 1960s. Both encouraged self-exploration, mind expansion, spontaneity, openness, honesty, and confrontation when necessary.

Perhaps in part due to its association with the hippies of the 1960s, the group movement came under criticism. Because of a few unusual encounter groups that were conducted in Northern California with nude participants, implications were made that all group counseling evolved into sex orgies. In addition, charges were made that the group movement was a contributing factor to social unrest among youth. As a result, an antigroup movement began in California in the late 1960s. Some of its leaders even suggested that group counseling was part of a communist conspiracy to undermine the minds of youth. Patterson contended that there were legitimate criticisms of many of the groups run in the 1960s (Vacc, 1989). He believed that problems resulted from inadequate training of group leaders, too much emphasis on uncovering people's problems and doing whatever "feels right" without concern for one's effect on other group members, and the use of gimmicky, manipulative techniques and games.

During the 1970s and 1980s, several factors contributed to group counseling's return to respectability. The major factor was a shift away from the lack of structure associated with sensitivity and encounter groups, which was seen as a contributing factor not only to negative perceptions about the specialty but also to "casualties" in counseling. Professionals believed that groups based on clear goals and objectives could generate more productive outcomes.

Commenting on group counseling in the 1990s, Gazda (Elliot, 1989) said there was a continuing emphasis on family group work, social-skills training, and life-skills training groups. In addition, he believed that the popularity of self-help groups would grow faster than that of any other type.

Horne (1996) related to trends in group counseling by noting that group practices are accommodating increasingly diverse populations in various types of settings. In addition, group counseling is incorporating current paradigm shifts such as the solution-focused brief-counseling perspective.

Comparison to Individual and Family Counseling

Group counseling is a specialty that has unique features in terms of theory and practice. At the same time, it has common elements with other forms of counseling, such as individual and family counseling. This section describes the similarities and differences between group counseling and individual or family counseling. It also identifies advantages and disadvantages of group counseling.

Group Counseling Versus Individual Counseling

Fuhriman and Burlingame (1990) suggest that there are few differences between group counseling and individual counseling. This is not surprising since theories and techniques tend to be transferred from individual counseling to group counseling.

Although the techniques used in group counseling and individual counseling are similar, the counseling process varies in group counseling to accommodate the increased complexities that result from multiple clients. Drawing primarily from Yalom's (1995) 11 therapeutic factors for group work, Fuhriman and Burlingame (1990) identify the following six factors that differentiate group counseling from individual counseling:

1. *Vicarious learning.* Group counseling offers opportunities for members to learn from observing other group members as they explore their concerns.
2. *Role flexibility.* Clients in group counseling can function both as helpers and helpees. Clients in individual counseling can only maintain the role of helpee.
3. *Universality.* Group counseling creates opportunities for clients to discover that other group members have similar concerns, fears, and problems. This experience of universality can help clients put their problems in perspective and not overreact to them.
4. *Altruism.* During group counseling, members are encouraged to offer help to other group members. Clients who engage in altruistic behavior can provide support for other group members and enhance their self-image.
5. *Interpersonal learning.* Interaction between group members creates opportunities to enhance interpersonal skills.
6. *Family reenactment.* The therapeutic climate created in a group can be similar to what was experienced in a client's family of origin. Group counseling can therefore be particularly useful in working through early familial conflicts.

The following *Personal Note* is an illustration of how I helped a client work through an early familial conflict in group counseling.

A Personal Note

I was a counseling psychologist at a university counseling center, and a client in the group was a young man in his early twenties. Tom was having problems, feeling a lack of confidence and courage.

During one session, Tom told the group about an experience he had as a teenager. He said his father was an alcoholic who verbally and physically abused Tom's mother. Tom described one instance that he often thought about. He and his mother were sitting in the living room when his father started yelling terrible things at his mother, then went over and slapped her on the face. Tom

just sat and watched. He felt angry at his father but also at himself because he couldn't help his mother. As he reflected on the incident, he said he just wished he would have had the courage to "stand up like a man" and come to the aid of his mother.

I suggested that we reenact the situation. I arranged to have a group member play the role of mother; Tom would be himself; I would play the role of father; and the rest of the group members would be the audience and provide feedback.

When we started the scene, Tom initially had a difficult time taking his role seriously. He started

(continued)

to laugh and said, "You don't look like my father." I intensified my yelling and abusive language toward his "mother." I then went over and started to shake her. The next thing I realized was that Tom was standing in front of me. He grabbed my shoulders and told me to leave his mother alone. His face was bright red with anger. He was breathing hard and then started to cry.

At this point, I stopped the reenactment and held the client for a few moments and encouraged him to cry and get his feelings out. We then discussed the experience with the group members. Tom said something seemed to snap in him when I

began to yell at his "mother." He really felt he was there with his mother and father. Tom said it made him feel better to be able to tell his father how he felt and to stand up for his mother. He went on to say that his tears were tears of relief that he was finally able to let go of his feelings of helplessness and shame.

This case provides an illustration of the intense emotions that can result from group-counseling procedures. The procedures should therefore be used carefully. It is especially important not to push clients to the point where they are forced to deal with emotions that they are not ready to handle.

A number of research studies have been undertaken to compare the efficacy of individual counseling versus group counseling. McRoberts, Burlingame, and Hoag (1998) conducted a meta-analysis of 23 outcome studies that compared individual counseling to group counseling. The results of their study show no difference in overall efficacy of individual counseling versus group counseling, and both forms of counseling are more effective than no counseling. They note that efficacy rates vary to some degree according to clients' problems. Group counseling appears superior to individual counseling for treatment of chemical dependencies, vocational choice, stress syndromes, and V-codes (problems of living such as parent-child relational difficulties). Individual counseling appears particularly well suited for the treatment of depression, especially when the treatment program utilizes a cognitive-behavioral theoretical orientation. These researchers conclude that under most conditions, group counseling is an effective, cost-efficient alternative to individual counseling.

Barlow, Burlingame, and Fuhriman (2000) reviewed research on therapeutic applications of groups. One of their most robust findings was that research conducted over the past four decades shows clients are better off utilizing both individual counseling and group counseling versus having only individual counseling or group counseling alone.

Group Counseling Versus Family Counseling

Group counseling and family counseling also have similarities and differences. In terms of similarities, both "bring people together to resolve problems by emphasizing interpersonal relationships" (Hines, 1988, p. 174). The processes of group counseling and family counseling are also similar. The focus of the initial sessions in both is for the counselor to define the presenting problem from an interpersonal perspective (Hines, 1988; Whitaker & Keith, 1981; Yalom, 1995). In addition, the working stage in both is an interactive process in which the client and counselor are actively engaged (Hines, 1988; Whitaker & Keith, 1981; Yalom, 1995).

Hines (1988) identifies differences between group counseling and family counseling in terms of inclusion, structure, and interrelatedness. According to Hines (1988), inclusion must be gained by participation in a group, whereas it is a biological given in a family. Structurally, group members have equal power, whereas family members have hierarchical power (Couch & Childers, 1989; Hines, 1988). Group members have a lesser degree of interrelatedness than family members, who have spent years living together (Hines, 1988). As a result, family members have well-established interpersonal processes, whereas group members are strangers to one another when they form the group (Couch & Childers, 1989).

Another difference between group counseling and family counseling is the role of the counselor. During the initial stage of group counseling, the leader attempts to assist group members with the process of inclusion (Hines, 1988; Schultz, 1977). The reverse is true in family counseling, since the counselor initially feels like an outsider and attempts to be included in the family (Hines, 1988). The counselor's role also varies between group counseling and family counseling in terms of establishing norms (Couch & Childers, 1989; Hines, 1988). During the initial phase of group counseling, the leader plays an active role establishing group norms (Couch & Childers, 1989; Hines, 1988). This is not the case in family counseling because the family already has a well-established norm system (Couch & Childers, 1989; Hines, 1988).

Perhaps the biggest difference between group counseling and family counseling lies in the goals of each process. Couch and Childers (1989) note that group counseling has goals for the group, such as creating a climate of trust and acceptance, as well as specific goals for each individual member. In contrast, the goal of family counseling is to improve the overall functioning of the family unit.

Although there are differences between group counseling and family counseling, there are also opportunities for integration (Vinson, 1995). A systemic perspective can be used in both forms of counseling to enhance awareness of the interactional processes between clients and the system as a whole (Horne, 1993). Vinson (1995) identifies numerous examples of how family therapy can be integrated into group counseling such as psychoeducational support groups (Gregg, 1994) and separation divorce/adjustment groups (Addington, 1992). Vinson (1995) also suggests that there are numerous techniques from family counseling that can be used in group counseling, such as the use of the genogram to explore family-of-origin issues.

Advantages and Disadvantages of Group Counseling

As with any counseling strategy, group counseling has potential advantages and disadvantages. The main advantage of group counseling is that it provides a safe environment for clients to try out and experience new behaviors with other group members. Other advantages include

- Clients can learn from other group members as they explore their personal concerns.
- The process is more economical in terms of time, since several clients can be seen during a session.
- Clients can have an opportunity to help others during the session, thereby minimizing tendencies to be overly concerned with their own problems.
- Problem solving for a client can be enhanced by the ideas generated by other group members.
- The group can foster energy and enthusiasm, which can help motivate a client to pursue personal goals.

The main disadvantage of group counseling is that it may be inappropriate for some clients. This is especially true for clients with serious mental disorders or a low self-concept. It may even be dangerous for these clients to participate in a group because they may feel threatened or personally attacked by the feedback they receive from other group members. In these cases, the client may first need to participate in individual counseling to be able to utilize group counseling successfully. Corey and Corey (2002) also identify risks associated with group counseling, including problems with confidentiality that can arise in groups; inappropriate self-disclosing owing to group pressure; participants feeling attacked as a result of confrontation; and negative emotional consequences that can occur from scapegoating.

Group Goals and Processes

The science of counseling recognizes the structure that goals can bring to the counseling process. Goals create a focus for individuals and the group itself, enhancing motivation and constructive action. There are both group goals and individual goals in group counseling. Group goals vary to a large extent according to the type of group. Some groups focus on providing guidance information on such topics as parent education whereas others have the goal of overcoming mental problems such as depression.

Group goals can also relate to the counseling process and can include fostering trust and acceptance, and promoting self-disclosure, feedback, and risk taking (Corey & Corey, 2002). Most approaches to group counseling also encourage group members to formulate individualized goals (Couch & Childers, 1989). Members are then assisted in learning problem-solving strategies they can utilize outside the group setting (Couch & Childers, 1989).

Waldo and Bauman (1998) suggest that it is critical to describe groups in terms of the interrelationship between group goals and processes. These scholars suggest that a new method of categorizing groups, the Goals and Process Matrix (GAP), be used as a classification system for group work. This model attempts to define (or classify) groups by answering the question, "Which group process is best for pursuing which group goal?" (Waldo & Bauman, 1998).

The GAP appears to promote individualized description of groups, which allows for integration of group formats (for example, task groups and guidance groups) in terms of their goals and processes. At the very least, the GAP model seems to offer opportunities to enhance existing models for categorizing group counseling by recognizing the overlapping function of groups in terms of their goals and processes. Additional research on the GAP seems warranted to obtain a clearer understanding of how it can be used to describe the types of groups used in group counseling.

Types of Groups

The ASGW revised its *Professional Standards for Training of Group Workers* in 2000. This publication broadly conceptualizes group counseling within the context of group work. Group work is defined as processes that involve giving help and accomplishing tasks in a group setting. The major types of group work utilized by people in the helping profession are summarized as follows.

Task/work groups encompass all the different types of groups utilized in contemporary society to accomplish various tasks. Examples of task/work groups include committees, study groups, and discussion groups.

Guidance/psychoeducation groups focus on providing information that can be used to facilitate human growth and development and prevent problems from occurring. These groups are widely used in schools and other settings. They provide an opportunity to explore a variety of topics such as how to avoid involvement in gangs and how to be an effective parent.

Counseling/interpersonal problem-solving groups use interpersonal support and problem-solving methods to help individuals with problems of living. These groups also attempt to help group members learn how to use various counseling strategies so they can work through or prevent future problems.

Psychotherapy/personality reconstruction groups are designed to help individuals overcome in-depth personal or mental health problems such as anxiety or depression. These groups attempt to remediate or overcome significant psychological difficulties by a variety of processes, which can include personality restructuring.

Nelson-Jones (1992) and Jacobs, Harvill, and Masson (2002) have identified additional types of groups, which are summarized as follows.

Life-skills training groups, also called *education groups,* are defined as "time-limited, structured groups in which one or more leaders use a repertoire of didactic and facilitative skills to help participants develop and maintain one or more specific life skills" (Nelson-Jones, 1992, p. 6). These groups are characterized by an emphasis on wellness versus sickness, systematic instruction, an experiential focus, and participant involvement. Life-skills training groups promote skills relating to all aspects of life, such as parenting, intellectual development, self-management, and physical development.

Mutual-sharing groups, also called *support* or *self-help groups,* are composed of people with similar concerns providing support to one another. The fundamental goal of mutual-sharing groups is to provide support to members. Examples of these groups are children of divorced parents, adult children of alcoholics, and adults who are prone to engage in child abuse.

Growth groups are designed to help group members increase their self-awareness. Their goal is to assist members in improving their lives by clarifying their values, personal concerns, and interpersonal relationships.

Family groups involve inviting different families to a group setting to discuss issues of concern. The primary goal is to enhance the functioning of the family system. Multiple-family group work can be used when a counselor wants to work with several families at a time. Family network groups can be established with the goal of providing information and support to families.

Discussion groups provide an opportunity to discuss a topic of interest rather than the personal concerns of group members. Examples of discussion group topics are the pros and cons of having children, the effects of drug abuse, and attitudes toward marriage. The goal of discussion groups is to have members share ideas and knowledge regarding a particular topic.

Online group counseling represents an emerging trend in group work. The Internet offers a unique opportunity for computer-based group counseling. Mutual sharing (support groups) is particularly well suited for online group work, with approximately 900,000 listings of support groups such as recovery from addictions as of 1999. Guidelines for setting up online support groups have recently been established (Page et al., 2000). There appears to be much promise regarding the future of technology in group counseling. Innovative applications of technology in group work were reviewed by McGlothlin (2003). For example, PalTalk provides software for online audio group conferencing (Page et al., 2003). Page et al. (2003) described how PalTalk can be used in nonconfidential discussions relating to counseling supervision. Students had an overall positive response to PalTalk. They noted that the audio dimension to online discussions provided group members with a chance to participate, facilitated meaningful connections between students, and promoted learning. Problems with PalTalk were associated with difficulty obtaining clear audio signals in rural areas. This created frustration for group members and delayed the start of some groups.

Page et al. (2000) and McGlothin (2003) identify advantages and disadvantages of online support groups and online counseling. Advantages include enhanced opportunity to reach large numbers of interested persons. Online group counseling is not restricted by time or facilities. Thus, individuals who do not ordinarily have access to groups due to geographic isolation or personal disabilities can be served through online group work. In addition, some group members find it easier to participate online than face to face. Supplemental materials can also be easily accessed and downloaded from Internet sites. Potential disadvantages include dehumanization due to a lack of human contact and communication problems resulting from a lack of visual or auditory cues. In addition, there can be problems relating to a lack of training in technology, technological breakdown, and access to technology. There can also be a number of hard-to-deal-with group process issues such as screening members to ensure suitability for the group, and ethical issues such as informed consent and confidentiality.

Problem Solving and Group Process

Group counseling is characterized by two dimensions that are critical to the success of the group: problem solving and group process. These dimensions are interrelated, and success in one dimension fosters success in the other.

The problem-solving strategies of individual counseling discussed in Chapter 3 can also be used in group counseling. These strategies typically involve the group leader and members first listening to a particular concern of a group member and then helping that member resolve the concern. Members taking action and assuming responsibility is an important part of the problem-solving process (Burlingame & Fuhriman, 1990).

Burlingame and Fuhriman (1990) identify the following four factors associated with group process:

1. *Engagement.* Engagement entails members sharing their feelings with one another. This practice is believed to foster cohesion (Aiello, 1979) and universality (Brabender, 1985).
2. *Group versus individual focus.* Opinions vary as to whether the process in group counseling should focus on the group, the individual, or alternately on the group and the individual (Burlingame & Fuhriman, 1990). A more equitable position might be to focus simultaneously on the individual and the group. Having coleaders is a useful

format, with one leader focusing on the concerns of an individual client and the other on issues that relate to the group process.

3. *Here-and-now focus.* Most approaches to group counseling emphasize the importance of maintaining a focus on the here and now in terms of group process (Burlingame & Fuhriman, 1990). Yalom (1995) suggests that a primary task of the group leader is to encourage group members to relate in the here and now, and then to have the group reflect on the here-and-now behavior that has just transpired. The here-and-now focus is believed to help group members learn about themselves through self-disclosure and feedback as they interact with each other (Sklare, Keener, & Mas, 1990).

4. *Goals of the group.* To some degree, a group's goals determine the nature of the group. For example, a group designed to discuss parenting may have a didactic emphasis, whereas groups designed to improve interpersonal relationships tend to be experiential in nature.

Group Size, Composition, and Duration

Appropriate group size varies according to the type of group and the ages of its members. For example, a play-therapy group should not exceed four children for the counselor to be effective. In contrast, a school counselor may work with a classroom full of students effectively. For group counseling and psychotherapy, the average group size ranges from four to ten members (Burlingame & Fuhriman, 1990). This range is large enough to create a diversity of ideas, yet small enough to provide an opportunity for each member to participate.

Group composition is another important issue to consider in formulating a group. Groups can be either heterogeneous or homogeneous. Heterogeneous groups are composed of a diversity of individuals of different ages, gender, cultures, socioeconomic status, and so forth. These groups can help promote a diversity of ideas for group members to consider. Heterogeneous groups are also believed to foster greater individualization because of the wide range of issues they can address (Unger, 1989). Heterogeneous groups are commonly used in schools, where a counselor might conduct a session on alcohol and drug use with an entire classroom, or in community mental health centers, where a counselor might have several clients participate in group counseling to resolve personal problems. Homogeneous groups are composed of individuals who have something in common, such as parents who want to learn about parenting or clients who suffer from eating disorders. An advantage of homogeneous groups is that they enhance universality by bringing together individuals with similar problems or concerns. Homogeneous groups are also believed to promote more cohesion and identification than are heterogeneous groups (Unger, 1989).

Duration relates to three issues: whether the group is open or closed, the length of each session, and the number of sessions. *Open groups* are ongoing, with no termination date, and they allow new members to join at any time. Alcoholics Anonymous uses an open-group format, encouraging new members to start attending sessions whenever they can. *Closed groups* have a specific starting date, and they do not allow new members to join after the first session. Closed groups are often utilized when the members want to learn certain principles and do not want to have to keep reviewing what was covered in an earlier session. A parent education group designed to help members learn about parenting might be an example of a closed group. Burlingame and Fuhriman (1990) have found that hospital outpatient groups tend to be about half open and half closed, whereas inpatient groups tend to be open to accommodate new patients as they are admitted to the hospital.

For most groups, each session lasts approximately 90 minutes (Burlingame & Fuhriman, 1990). The group leader and members should determine the length of the session in advance and adhere to it as much as possible so group members can plan accordingly.

The number of sessions associated with group work varies according to the type of group, the needs of the group members, and the theoretical orientation of the group leader. Education groups might require from six to ten sessions or extend over an entire school year. For counseling and psychotherapy groups, the number of sessions varies according to the setting. Groups for inpatient psychiatric patients usually meet at least once each day while the patients are in the hospital. Ideally, group counseling and psychotherapy in outpatient mental health settings such as private practice occur once a week for several months. Managed care's emphasis on short-term, symptom-focused treatment is making it increasingly difficult to obtain approval for these types of treatment programs.

Use of Coleaders

Several advantages are associated with having a leader and coleader in group counseling. First, group members can benefit from the expertise of two counselors. Second, there may be an advantage in having male and female counselors to create a more balanced perspective. Third, at the end of a session, the leader and coleader can spend time debriefing, or sharing ideas about the session. As a result, they can gain a more comprehensive understanding of what occurred. A fourth advantage is that the leader can focus on helping a client work through a personal problem while the coleader focuses on the group process. Facilitating the group process can involve creating a positive, trusting climate; keeping the group on task; helping each member feel valued; assisting reluctant clients in becoming involved in the group; and dealing with difficult members who may want to monopolize or sabotage the group.

Corey and Corey (2002) identify additional advantages of using coleaders in groups. These include avoiding burnout, allowing for coverage if a group leader is ill, processing strong emotional reactions of group leaders, and working through countertransference if it occurs. Corey and Corey (2002) also note that there can be potential disadvantages to using coleaders. Many of the problems can deal with a lack of trust and cooperation between the leaders. When this occurs, a leader can compete with the other leader for the support and admiration of the group members. Problems between group leaders can take up group time as the leaders deal with their unresolved issues.

Pregroup Screening and Orientation

There appears to be a positive correlation between the amount of time spent in preparation for a group and positive outcomes occurring from the group (Lynn & Frauman, 1985). A pregroup interview is typically used to help screen and orient prospective group members. Couch (1995) identifies four steps in conducting a pregroup screening interview. These steps are identifying needs, expectation, and commitment; challenging myths and misconceptions;

conveying information; and screening. In this process, the counselor can attempt to ensure that client expectations are consistent with group goals. Group counselors can also screen out potential members who may lack the necessary ego strength to handle the open feedback that commonly occurs within group counseling.

Pregroup orientation is designed to help members prepare for entry into the group. Corey and Corey (2002) provide the following list of issues that should be discussed with prospective group members before they join the group:

- Describe the purpose of the group.
- Provide information on the group format, procedures, and ground rules.
- Determine whether the group is appropriate for the client.
- Explore client concerns.
- Provide information regarding the leader's education, training, and qualifications.
- Discuss possible psychological risks that could result from the group.
- Provide information on fees and expenses.
- Discuss limits of confidentiality.
- Clarify what services can be provided by the group.

Pregroup screening issues can vary according to setting. For example, Hines and Fields (2002) suggest that pregroup screening can be used to promote appropriate group composition in school counseling. School counselors should consider diversity issues such as age, level of maturity, gender, and culture to create a balance in terms of group composition. Other factors deemed important in formulating a group include ensuring a good fit between the type of group and the needs of the student and ensuring that the students will work well together.

Stages in Group Counseling

Several authors have attempted to delineate stages in group counseling (Corey, 2001; Gazda, 1989). These authors contend that a model of the stages in group counseling provides a structure to the process that helps us better understand it.

Corey and Corey (2002) have developed the following model, which consists of four stages: the initial, transition, working, and final stages.

Stage 1: The Initial Stage

The initial stage of group counseling involves screening, orientation, and determining the structure of the group. The major functions of the group leader during this stage are establishing ground rules and norms for the group, helping members express their fears and expectations, being open and psychologically present, assisting group members in identifying concrete personal goals, and sharing expectations and hopes for the group. During the initial stage, members attempt to create trust; learn to express their feelings and thoughts, including fears or reservations about the group; become involved in establishing group norms; establish personal goals; and learn about the dynamics of the group process.

Stage 2: The Transition Stage

The transition stage is characterized as a time when group members experience anxiety and defensiveness as they begin to question the value of the group. The major functions of the group leader during this stage are encouraging members to express their anxiety, dealing openly with conflicts that occur in the group, and helping group members become autonomous and independent. During this stage, it is common for group members to become concerned about being accepted by the group. A central task for members is to recognize and express feelings of resistance toward the group process.

Stage 3: The Working Stage

The working stage occurs when group members feel free to explore their thoughts and feelings and work on their concerns. The major functions of the group leader during this stage are encouraging members to translate insight into action and helping them make the necessary changes to achieve their goals. The working stage is characterized by group members introducing personal issues that they are willing to work on, providing and receiving feedback, applying what they learn in the group to their daily lives, and offering support and encouragement to other group members.

Stage 4: The Final Stage

The final stage should offer group members a smooth transition toward termination of the group. The major functions of the group leader during the final stage are assisting clients in working toward termination, providing opportunities for them to receive additional counseling if necessary, and helping them gain a useful understanding of what they have learned. This stage is often characterized by sadness and anxiety regarding the termination of the group. Members may begin to decrease their intensity of participation to prepare for termination, and they may also evaluate how they experienced the group.

Some authors have questioned whether group counseling actually has stages. Yalom (Forester-Miller, 1989) claims that stages are merely a way of imposing a type of structure that does not exist in groups. Patterson (Vacc, 1989) also expresses a negative view of the stage model of group counseling. He contends that group counseling is a continuous process that does not have discrete stages (Vacc, 1989). In addition, Patterson believes that the stage model creates expectations for group members that can interfere with the normal development process of the group (Vacc, 1989). Additional research on this topic appears warranted.

Brief-Solution-Focused Group Counseling

The trend in counseling is for brief-solution-focused approaches. Group counseling has therefore been conceptualized within this framework. Coe and Zimpfer (1996) apply the basic principles of brief counseling (described by de Shazer, 1985, 1988, and Walter & Peller, 1992) to group counseling. Coe and Zimpfer contend that group counseling is particularly well suited to incorporate the major tenets of the brief model, which are solution focused and have a strengths perspective. For example, group members can help identify when a person does not have a problem such as controlling anger. These "exceptions" to the problem can then be explored by group members to help the individual learn how to use what works in isolated situations to problem situations.

Solution-focused brief models of group counseling are being applied to specialty groups such as small-group debriefing for victims of violence or disaster (Juhnke & Osborne, 1997; Mitchell & Everly, 1993; Thompson, 1993). Critical incident stress debriefing is an intensive (1- to 3-hour) session that helps victims of violence and disaster process and debrief issues associated with their traumatic experience (Thompson, 1993). These groups have both experiential and didactic components, enabling participants to work through issues as well as obtain useful information regarding pertinent topics such as posttraumatic stress disorder.

Juhnke and Osborne (1997) integrate critical incident stress debriefing with solution-focused counseling techniques as an alternative method of counseling victims of violence. Their model is a structured program that extends over a three-week period. This approach utilizes solution-focused techniques to promote positive change and recovery as quickly as possible. Some of these strategies are identifying behaviors that promote change and using scaling questions to identify the degree of positive change between sessions.

Brief group counseling may not be appropriate for all clients. Couch (1994) suggests that individuals who need long-term supportive care would not be suited for the brief group counseling model. Certain aspects of the brief model, such as its focus on a strengths perspective, appear to hold promise for all models of group counseling.

Dealing with Disruptive Group Members

Kottler (1994) notes that there is at least one difficult member in every group. He suggests that regardless of the screening procedures, difficult members end up in groups, creating challenges. The most difficult types of group members that Kottler has encountered are those who feel entitled, are manipulative, or have character disorders. Kottler contends that difficult members can benefit from honest and caring feedback from other group members and compassionate and firm interventions from group leaders. Group leaders also need to

Group members can obstruct group progress by acting as if they are not interested.

be open to possible contributions they are making to the difficulties group members are experiencing. The following *Personal Note* provides an example of how I have worked with problematic group members.

Common Mistakes of Group Leaders

Jacobs et al. (2002) identify the following common mistakes group leaders make in therapy groups:

- *Attempting to conduct therapy without a contract.* It is important to ensure that a member wants help with a particular problem by directly inquiring whether the member would like assistance. Assuming a member wants help may waste the group's

A Personal Note

I have also been challenged by difficult group members. When this occurs, I try and understand each group member as a unique individual. At the same time, I have found there are several typical problematic behaviors that present themselves. Individuals who engage in these behaviors are referred to as aggressors, obstructors, storytellers, and attention seekers.

Aggressors may be overt or covert in their aggressive behavior toward other group members or the leader. When this occurs, the leader should try not to become angry or threatened. The aggressor is often trying to create a conflict, so an angry reaction may only reinforce that behavior. An approach that may be more productive is to inform the aggressor firmly but kindly that group process is based on a philosophy of encouragement and support. It may also be productive to explore and work through the aggressor's feelings.

Obstructors tend to be negative and obstruct the group process. They often find ways to sidetrack the issues being discussed and prevent the group from staying on task. This may involve a variety of disruptive behaviors, such as constantly trying to change the topic or complaining that nothing seems to be happening in the group. Obstructors often engage in their disruptive behavior as a means of gaining power and control. It is therefore important for the leader to avoid reacting with anger since that reaction may only create a power struggle. When

the obstructor tries to change the topic, the leader might say, "No, let's not change the focus of our work. We need to spend more time with this so we can reach a meaningful conclusion."

Storytellers often like to monopolize the group by telling drawn-out stories about things that have happened months ago. What they say usually holds little interest for the group because they typically have already resolved the issue or have no desire to do anything about it. When this occurs, the leader can ask what the storyteller is thinking and feeling at the moment. The leader can emphasize that it is important to try to stay in the here and now so the group can have something concrete to work on.

Attention seekers find different ways to draw attention to themselves. Since their goal is typically gaining attention, the leader must be careful not to reinforce the behavior. Two strategies can be used in working with attention seekers. The leader should first attempt to channel the attention seeker's need for attention in a positive direction by asking for assistance when possible. When that fails, the leader should ask the attention seeker to refrain from the behaviors that are creating a problem. For example, if the behavior is making frequent, inappropriate jokes, the leader might say, "Turning a serious issue into a joke does not allow the group to work on issues realistically."

valuable time on someone who is not ready to make a commitment to work on his or her problem.

■ *Spending too much time on one person.* Group time can be dominated by difficult group members or by members who are interesting and attractive and are eager for assistance during *each* session. Group leaders have an ethical responsibility to ensure that all members have an opportunity to participate.

■ *Spending too little time with one person.* Group leaders can spend too little time with a member during the problem-solving process in an attempt to give everyone a chance to talk. While it is important to ensure that all members are encouraged to participate, this does not mean they all need to talk. Problem solving requires that one member be the focus of attention for a sufficient period of time.

■ *Letting members rescue each other.* There can be a tendency for group members to rescue other members when they sense pain or sorrow. Emotional rescuing is not productive in any form of counseling because it communicates sympathy. Group leaders should instead encourage members to convey support, concern, and empathy.

■ *Letting the session turn into advice giving.* Premature advice giving can be particularly prevalent when group members attempt to offer help to other members during problem solving. Premature advice giving is not productive in any counseling, including group counseling. When this occurs, the leader could suggest that members take more time using listening skills to gain a better understanding of the problem before attempting to solve it.

Qualities of Effective Group Leaders

Perhaps the most important factor in effective group counseling is the personal qualities of the group leader. DeLucia-Waack (1999) addresses both the art and science of effective group leadership. The art of group leadership involves moving out of one's comfort zones and experiencing new and varied types of group experiences. Personal growth and renewal can be generated by ongoing self-reflection in terms of identifying strengths and weaknesses in group facilitation. DeLucia-Waack (1999) also speaks to the science of group leadership by suggesting that group counselors should function as "N of 1" researchers engaged in ongoing evaluation and development of group skills, techniques, and competencies.

Several others have attempted to describe effective qualities of group leaders. Ohlsen (1970) notes that effective group counselors are in tune with the group process. They can then make the necessary changes to ensure positive therapeutic movement. Corey (2001) identifies personal qualities associated with effective group leadership, which include presence, personal power, courage, willingness to confront oneself, self-awareness, sincerity, authenticity, a sense of identity, belief in the group process, enthusiasm, inventiveness, and creativity. Yalom and Lieberman (1971) suggest that the group leader sets the emotional climate for the group. When the leader acts in an autocratic, confrontational, or emotionally distant fashion, the group experience may actually do more harm than good to members. These authors point out that a leader with moderate amounts of executive function and emotional stimulation and high amounts of caring and meaning attribution contributes to improvements in group members. Taken collectively, the literature suggests that the qualities of effective group leaders are having a positive presence, which can instill trust and enthusiasm; being sensitive to the group process and capable of making adjustments as necessary; setting a positive and encouraging therapeutic climate; and seeking out new group experiences as opportunities to grow and develop.

Diversity Issues

Horne (1996) notes that populations being served in group counseling are becoming more diverse. Group-counseling paradigms are expanding to accommodate these diverse populations and settings. McRae (1994) suggest that counselors need to be aware of how cultural diversity can affect group dynamics. For example, individuals with similar world views can formulate coalitions or alliances within the group. These alliances can evolve between or within races. McRae (1994) recommends that counselors avoid stereotyping group members along racial lines and attempt to understand members as individuals functioning within a group environment.

Johnson, Torres, Coleman, and Smith (1995) suggest there are both challenges and opportunities in multicultural group counseling. Challenges can evolve from prejudice, difficulty communicating, misunderstandings, and fear between group members. These types of challenges can impede or enhance group growth. The authors suggest that when problems present themselves, they should be directly dealt with in the group. Within this context, the group process can be used to help members develop new levels of communication, understanding, trust, and sensitivity with other cultural groups (Johnson et al., 1995). Opportunities also present themselves in terms of how diverse individuals in groups can broaden the perspective for problem solving and decision making.

Feminist group therapy is one example of infusing diversity issues into group work. Rittenhouse (1997) notes that the feminist perspective could be useful in survivor groups to help women recover from sexual trauma or other adverse life experiences. Rittenhouse (1997) contends that the key to achieving success in feminist group counseling is to create an egalitarian relationship between the group members themselves and between the members and the leader. In addition, fostering equality and empowerment can play important roles in encouraging members to take an active role in their recovery and in overcoming oppressive forces that have impeded their development.

A second major principle is to help members look beyond intrapsychic causality and explore problems from an ecological perspective. This process can help members shift from internalizing and self-blaming to exploring sociocultural and political forces such as oppression in family roles and the workplace. It does not imply a shift in blame from self to others but an attempt to identify how members can "reinvent their world" in a more gender sensitive and meaningful manner. This process of discovery can involve activities such as understanding the self in more gender-accurate terms, such as those found in Carol Gilligan's (1982) seminal work on female moral development. The group format is ideal for the discussion of such material since it allows for experiential processing of ideas and concepts.

DeLucia-Waack (2000) notes that group counseling must reflect a life-span perspective with different models and procedures depending on clients' age and developmental status. For instance, children tend to need extensive structure to maintain attention and concentration. Group-counseling interventions must also be appropriate in terms of cognitive and psychosocial development. Group-counseling models have been developed to specifically address concerns of children and adolescents, such as depression (Sommers-Flanagan, Barrett-Hakanson, Clarke, & Sommers-Flanagan, 2000), eating disorders (Daigneault, 2000), and psychosocial development through empathic skill enhancement (Akos, 2000).

Diversity is not restricted to gender or culture but can include other attributes such as individuals with disabilities. In 1995, there were 43 million disabled Americans, making them the largest minority group in the United States (Patterson, McKenzie, & Jenkins, 1995). Unfortunately, this large group of individuals has historically been systematically excluded from many opportunities, including group counseling, because of attitudinal and environmental barriers (Patterson et al., 1995). The Americans with Disabilities Act of 1990 provides rights for the disabled in terms of inclusion in the mainstream of society (Brown, 1995).

Specialists in group work are beginning to make strides in breaking down the barriers that the disabled face in participating in group work (Horne, 1995). Patterson et al. (1995) note that group counselors must sensitize themselves to the needs of the disabled. They must practice disability etiquette by treating all people of diversity as people first and foremost and adjusting the group process, such as ensuring that a person with a hearing impairment can see the speaker's lips. It is also the responsibility of the leader to address attitudinal and environmental barriers that could impede the growth of the disabled member and have an adverse effect on the group process.

In the final analysis, diversity in all its forms creates unique opportunities and challenges. In 1998, the ASGW responded to these challenges by identifying principles for diversity-competent group workers (Haley-Banez et al., 1998). These principles address a wide array of issues, such as having knowledge of various cultures and having the skills necessary to address the unique and emerging needs of clients in a multicultural society.

Summary

The art and science of group counseling is a dynamic and interesting dimension of the counseling process. As artists, counselors can adjust counseling approaches to the unique and emerging needs of diverse clients in a group setting. As scientists, counselors can engage in pregroup screening to ensure that prospective group members are appropriate for group work and can incorporate appropriate structure to the group process, such as ensuring that group members have personal counseling goals and that the group functions from a clear theoretical perspective.

Professional helpers routinely utilize group work in their counseling practice in all types of settings, including in schools, hospitals, agencies, and private practice. It can be used as the only form of counseling intervention, such as in parent education or in groups like Alcoholics Anonymous. Groups can also provide an important adjunct to other counseling processes, especially individual counseling. In this regard, clients can try out what they have learned in individual counseling within the context of a group.

Personal Exploration

1. What issues do you feel are important in terms of group dynamics, and how do you address these issues?
2. How would you assess your group leadership skills, and how can you work toward improving them?
3. What aspects of group work make you uncomfortable, and how might you address these issues?
4. How could group counseling be useful to you?

Web Sites for Chapter 12

Franklin, D. J. (2000). Group therapy. Retrieved March 3, 2005, from
http://psychologyinfo.com/treatment/group_therapy.html
Presents a description of group therapy.

Get Mental Help, Inc. (2003). *Group therapy for adolescents: Clinical paper.* Retrieved
March 3, 2005, from http://www.mental-health-matters.com/articles/
article.php?artID=251
Presents a clinical article on adolescent group counseling strategies with information on Gartner's group process theory.

Weinberg, H. (2000). *Group psychotherapy: An introduction.* Retrieved March 3, 2005,
from http://www.group-psychotherapy.com/intro.htm
Presents an elementary introduction to group psychotherapy.

Career Counseling

CHAPTER OVERVIEW

This chapter provides an overview of career counseling, a challenging and evolving specialty that helps individuals with career planning and decision making throughout the life span. Highlights of the chapter include

- The art and science of career counseling
- The evolution of career counseling
- Theoretical foundations in terms of career development and decision making
- Treatment issues, including personal counseling versus career counseling, assessment instruments, intervention strategies, and the process of career counseling
- Special issues, including career counseling for women and computer-assisted career counseling
- Diversity issues in career counseling

The Art and Science of Career Counseling

A fairly recent trend in career counseling is to integrate career theory and practice. These two dimensions of career counseling parallel the art and science dimensions of counseling with career theory representing the science and practice reflecting the art. Krumboltz (1996) provides a rationale for the movement toward integration of career theory and practice when he notes that the reason that career theories have been largely ignored by practitioners is that they have focused on career development and not on intervention strategies. They therefore have provided little practical information on what career counselors can *do* during the counseling process.

Herr (1996) points out that theorists such as Holland, Super, and Krumboltz have made progress toward this integration. One obvious example is the assessment instruments developed by Holland (Vocational Preference Inventory), Super (Career Development Inventory), and Krumboltz (Career Beliefs Inventory). Several other individuals have attempted to bridge the gap between career theory and practice (for example, Chartrand, 1996; Harmon, 1996; Holland, 1996; and Savickas, 1996). For example, Savickas (1996) provides a framework that can be used to link career theories to practice. His model is an adaptation of "Wagner's (1971) theory of structural analysis of personality to the domain of vocational psychology" (Savickas, 1996, p. 196). It is a comprehensive model that includes six types of career services: occupational placement, vocational guidance, career counseling, career education, career therapy, and position coaching (Savickas, 1996). Although progress is being made toward integration, Savickas and Walsh (1996) contend that more work needs to be done to bridge the gap between theory and practice.

Another dimension of the art and science of career counseling is the trend toward integrating traditional career counseling with personal counseling. Traditional career counseling has relied to a large extent on the use of assessment instruments such as interest inventories, which can be used with or without computer assistance. Career assessment instruments represent an important dimension of the science of career counseling, providing objective information that can enhance the counseling process. The art of career counseling is to attempt to interface objective information with the subjective, ever-changing world of the client. Central to this process is the art of addressing personal issues and problems that may arise during the counseling process. From this perspective, career issues are not viewed as separate, isolated entities but interrelated to the person's overall psychosocial functioning.

Evolution of Career Counseling

The world of work has changed dramatically over the centuries along with the evolution of the human species. Our early ancestors had limited opportunities and choices regarding work (Axelson, 1999). What people did was primarily restricted to preserving the survival of the species. Today, people work for many reasons that go beyond obtaining money for food and shelter. Some work to enhance their self-esteem, others have a goal of independence, some want to help people, and others work to experience power and control. As people's needs change over the life span, so too does the type of work they find rewarding. This in turn can account for the career changes that can take place throughout one's life.

Career counseling has evolved as a means of assisting individuals in developing career-planning and decision-making skills to facilitate career choice. It has been referred to by several different names over the years, including *occupational counseling, vocational guidance,* and *vocational counseling.* These names tend to have a narrower focus than career counseling since they emphasize the importance of obtaining occupational information in selecting a particular career. Career counseling is a more comprehensive concept, incorporating the various career-development theories to formulate a strong theoretical foundation.

Career counseling can be defined as "a series of general and specific interventions throughout the life span, dealing with such concerns as self-understanding; broadening one's horizons; work selection, challenge, satisfaction, and other interpersonal phenomena; and lifestyle issues, such as balancing work, family, and leisure" (Engels, Minor, Sampson, & Splete, 1995, p. 134).

Career counseling, as with all counseling specialties, must begin with general counseling competencies to ensure the necessary foundations for specialization (Engels et al., 1995). Career counseling is practiced by professional counselors in schools and agencies. Some counselors incorporate career counseling into their repertoire of helping skills to assist clients in exploring career issues and personal problems. Counselors can also specialize in this field and identify themselves as career counselors or career development professionals. In 1952, the American Counseling Association recognized the special skills and professional interests associated with career counseling by creating a special division for career counselors called the National Career Development Association (NCDA).

The NCDA took an active role in establishing credentials for career counseling. These efforts resulted in career counseling becoming the first specialty designation offered by the National Board of Certified Counselors. Requirements for certification include

- Becoming certified by the National Board of Certified Counselors (see requirements in Chapter 2)
- Earning a graduate degree in counseling or a related profession
- Working at least part-time in career counseling for three years following graduate study
- Passing the National Career Counselor Examination

As we approach the 21st century, the world of work is evolving into a constant state of flux, creating opportunities and challenges. Stoltz-Loike (1996) identifies some of the defining features of the present work environment as well as some recommendations to be successful in the new millennium. Current work environments are characterized by downsizing and a lack of job security, reduced opportunities for lifetime employment within the same industry, and increased global competition and expanding global marketplaces. According to Feller (1995), the modern workplace is a "joint venture between the employer with problems to be solved and tasks to be done, and the employees who have the skills to sell and needs to be met" (p. 158). Individuals who develop these skills will be successful. Factors critical to this skill development are broad-based flexible skills, educational credentials that promote lifelong learning, adaptability, and problem-solving skills (Stoltz-Loike, 1996).

Theoretical Foundations

Several individuals have provided theories of career development and career decision making. These theories provide a description of how career development occurs over the life span and what is entailed in the process of career choice and decision making.

Career Development Theories

Career development theories relate to how career issues develop over the life span. This section provides an overview of three prominent career development theories, those of Donald Super, John Holland, and Ann Roe. In addition, this section reviews the influences of family of origin on career development.

Super's Theory. Super (1990, p. 199) describes his theory as "a loosely unified set of theories dealing with specific aspects of career development, taken from developmental, differential, social, personality, and phenomenological psychology." Super's (1957, 1980, 2002) theory emphasizes the role of self-concept in career development. He contends that how individuals define themselves has a major effect on their career choices. For example, a person with a self-image of a strong, hard worker but not particularly intellectual may be attracted to a physical job such as an auto mechanic.

Super's (1957) theory can be considered developmental because he suggests that there are five stages of career development, each with corresponding developmental tasks: growth, exploration, establishment, maintenance, and decline. An overview of these stages follows.

The *growth stage* spans from birth to 14 years of age. The self-concept develops as the individual identifies with significant others. Developmental tasks during the growth stage include gaining self-understanding and obtaining an overall understanding of the world of work.

The growth stage has three substages. The *fantasy* substage occurs from age 4 to 10 and involves the child role-playing various fantasies regarding the world of work (for example, playing doctor or nurse). The *interest* substage extends from age 11 to 12. During this period, a child's likes and dislikes have a major impact on career aspirations. The third substage is *capacity,* which takes place from age 13 to 14. The capacity substage is characterized by a more realistic view of the world of work as individuals consider their abilities and job requirements.

Super's second stage is the *exploration stage,* which spans from 14 to 24 years of age. This is a period of self-examination in relation to the world of work. During this time, the individual also begins to directly experience work by involvement in part-time jobs. Developmental tasks associated with the exploration stage include crystallizing, specifying, and implementing a career preference.

The exploration stage has three substages. The *tentative* substage extends from age 15 to 17 and involves identifying appropriate fields of work. The *transition* substage begins at age 18 and continues to age 21. During this substage, the individual may pursue special educational or vocational training related to a field of work or enter directly into the job market. The third substage is referred to as *trial–little commitment* and ranges from age 22 to 24. During this period, the individual usually begins a first job. The commitment is usually tentative as the person decides whether the career choice was appropriate.

The third major stage is the *establishment stage,* spanning from 24 to 44 years of age. During this stage, individuals have identified an appropriate field of work that they want to make a long-term commitment. The key developmental task involves consolidation and advancement.

Two substages are associated with the establishment stage. First is *trial-commitment and stabilization,* which occurs from age 25 to 30. During this substage, the individual either settles down with a particular occupation or becomes dissatisfied and begins to explore other occupational possibilities. *Advancement* is the second substage and extends from age 31 to 44. This is typically a time for stabilization, during which seniority is required. It also tends to be a very creative, productive period.

Super's fourth stage is the *maintenance stage,* which spans from 44 to 64 years of age. This is a time for the individual to enjoy the security of seniority while attempting to maintain status as a current and productive professional. The major developmental task is preservation of achieved status.

The final stage in Super's model is the *decline stage,* which begins at age 64. During this stage, the individual adjusts to retirement as well as declining mental and physical skills and abilities. The key developmental tasks are deceleration, disengagement, and retirement.

The decline stage is composed of two substages. First is *deceleration,* which occurs between 60 and 65 years of age. This is a time when the individual begins to adjust to impending retirement, perhaps pursuing part-time jobs as a transition from full-time work. *Retirement* is the second substage and usually begins at age 61 or later. During this time, the individual may continue some part-time work or discontinue work and devote time to leisure activities.

Super (1980, 2002) refers to his theory as a life-span, life-space approach to career development. Its purpose is to add role theory into the five-stage model to create a model composed of multiple-role careers (Super, 2002). According to this theory, "career is defined as the combination and sequence of roles played by a person during the course of a lifetime" (Super, 1980, p. 282). These roles vary as a person proceeds through the life span and include such possibilities as student, worker, husband, wife, and parent (Super, 1980).

Many research studies have tested various aspects of Super's theory. Osipow (1996) concludes that most of the literature has provided support for Super's model. Savickas (1994) recognizes Super's impact on career counseling in a special issue of *The Career Development Quarterly* that highlights his contributions to career theory and practice. For example, Savickas (1994) notes that Super helped shift the field from a focus on occupational choice to career development and extended vocational guidance into career counseling. It is therefore not surprising that Super's work has generated a wide range of research activity on topics such as the role of the self-concept in career development (Betz, 1994), work values (Zytowski, 1994), and career adaptability (Goodman, 1994).

Super's theory appears to share some commonalties with current trends, such as recognizing the contextual nature of career decision making (Phillips & Blustein, 1994). In this regard, Super notes that career decision making takes place within the context of a broad landscape of issues, such as economic, cultural, family, peer, and historic (Phillips & Blustein, 1994). Jepsen (1996) observes that Super's description of the role of the self-concept in decision making provides valuable information on the subjective-phenomenological dimension of career counseling.

Swanson and Gore (2000) note that although Super has died, his theory continues to evolve and be redefined in terms of the ever-changing career landscape. For example, Savickas (1997) suggests that Super's concept of career maturity be replaced with the concept of career adaptability to reflect an individual's need to adjust to the changing forces in the work world, such as increasing diversity, global marketing, downsizing, and the influence of technology.

Holland's Theory.   Holland's (1973, 1985a, 1996, 1997) theory suggests that career choice results in an attempt to obtain a satisfactory fit of the person with the environment. Job satisfaction results when there is a congruence of personality type and work environment (Holland, 1996). In addition, Weinrach and Srebalus (2002) note several practical applications of Holland's theory in terms of career-counseling instruments, such as Holland's (1985b) Vocational Preference Inventory and Holland's (1994) Self-Directed Search.

Holland's (1973, 1985a, 1996, 1997) theory is based on the following four assumptions:

1. *People tend to be characterized by one of six personality types.* Holland (1973) originally believed that people could be characterized by six personality types. Holland (1985a) expanded this conception of personality types to include the possibility of subtypes or patterns that would provide further differentiation of a person's personality characteristic. The original six personality types with brief descriptions are as follows:

   - *Realistic* individuals take a logical, matter-of-fact approach to life.
   - *Investigative* people use an investigative, analytic approach to problem solving.
   - *Social* individuals tend to be social, cooperative, and people-oriented.
   - *Artistic* people tend to be sensitive, creative, spontaneous, and nonconforming.
   - *Conventional* individuals are conforming, inhibited, and have a preference for structured situations.
   - *Enterprising* individuals tend to take an extroverted, aggressive approach to problem solving.

2. *There are six kinds of environments that correspond with the six personality types (realistic, investigative, artistic, social, enterprising, and conventional).* Most environments attract workers with corresponding personality types. For example, artistic people work in places such as the theater. A congruent person-environment fit tends to promote job satisfaction.

3. *People seek out work environments that enable them to use their skills, express their values, and enter into agreeable roles.* People are motivated to work in settings that have complementary personality structures.

4. *The interaction of the environment and personality determines behavior.* An individual's behavior, such as his or her career choice and achievement, is determined by the nature of the person-environment fit.

Walsh and Srsic (1995) report that Holland's theory continues to generate a substantial amount of research into investigating constructs such as personality types (Holland, Johnston, & Asama, 1994) and person-environment fit (Thompson, Flynn, & Griffith, 1994). Holland (1996) notes that studies support the theory that people do well in their careers when there is a good fit between their personality type and the environment. In addition, evidence suggests that people experience dissatisfaction, poor job performance, and disruption in their career path when there is incongruence between their personality type and environmental fit (Holland, 1996).

Swanson and Gore (2000) report that Holland's theory has generated more research activity than any other career-development theory. Fitzgerald and Rounds (1989) provide a literature review of some of these studies and conclude that Holland's congruence hypothesis relating to the person-environment fit has received the most empirical support. Swanson and Gore (2000) posit that Holland's theory is well defined and has a substantial amount of research interest. These scholars go on to note that Holland's most recent revision of his theory (Holland, 1997) should generate another extended period of research investigation.

Roe's Theory.   The major principles of Roe's theory evolved from Maslowian and psychoanalytic theory (Roe, 1956; Roe & Lunneborg, 2002). Simply stated, Roe contends that unmet needs in childhood can have a major influence on career choice as an adult. In addition, her theory suggests that people can fulfill all basic and higher-order needs associated with Maslow's hierarchy in their careers. These include needs related to physiology, safety, love and belonging, self-esteem, and self-actualization.

Roe (1956) identifies three types of parent-child relationships that could foster need satisfaction in particular careers. Osipow (1996) provides an overview of these relationships as follows:

1. *Overprotective or excessively demanding parents.* Parents who are overly protective or make excessive demands tend to satisfy physiological needs, but they may be less prone to gratify psychological needs such as love and self-esteem. These parents foster dependency within their children since gratification of psychological needs is contingent on children engaging in socially desirable or high-achieving behaviors. Their children grow into adults with an excessive need for recognition and approval. As a result, they may choose highly visible occupations, such as politics or a branch of the performing arts such as acting.
2. *Rejecting parents.* These parents either neglect or reject their children. Their children tend to have many unfulfilled needs and may become suspicious or untrusting of others. They may therefore select careers where their needs can be met in activities that involve working with things (such as computers) rather than people.
3. *Accepting parents.* These parents tend to be very accepting and loving toward their children. They engage in unconditional love rather than conditional love. Their children's basic and higher-order needs are therefore met, promoting a sense of autonomy and independence in the children as they grow into adulthood. Since these individuals tend to feel secure with themselves, they may choose a profession such as teaching or medicine in which they can assist others in moving toward their own self-realization.

Osipow (1990) notes that Roe's theory is almost impossible to test empirically because of the subjective nature of the constructs on which the theory is based. Additional refinement of the theory and empirical investigation of its principles appear warranted.

Family of Origin and Career Development.   As noted earlier, Roe (1956) was perhaps the first to investigate the relationship between family-of-origin issues and career development. She contends that the nature of the parent-child relationship can play an important role in career development. Vondracek, Lerner, and Schulenberg (1986) go on to suggest that career development is a dynamic process influenced by relational, developmental, and contextual forces. Vondracek et al. (1986) set forth a systemic model that recognizes the role that family dynamics play in career development. In this regard, Vondracek et al. (1986) note that "perhaps the most important way in which roles and role expectations link the family microsystem and children's career development entails the roles children learn in the context of the family setting" (p. 53). Vondracek et al. (1986) have stimulated a wide body of research activity. Whiston & Keller (2004) summarize this literature as follows:

Across the lifespan, both family structure variables (e.g., parent's occupations) and family process variables (e.g., warmth, support, attachment, autonomy) were found to influence a host of career constructs; however, the process by which families influence career development is complex and is affected by many contextual factors such as race, gender, and age. (p. 493)

Career Decision-Making Theories

Career decision-making theories provide another theoretical foundation for assisting with career counseling. These theories provide "guidelines for collection, processing, and utilization of information in order to improve decision making" (Gati, 1990a, p. 508). Several theories have been developed on career decision making. This section provides an overview of decision-making theories based on cognitive-dissonance theory, social-learning theory, and a multiple-career decision-making theory.

Cognitive-Dissonance Theory. Hilton (1962) was one of the first to suggest that career decision making is based on the theory of cognitive dissonance. According to Festinger (1957), cognitive dissonance occurs when an individual has two incompatible cognitions. For example, an individual may contend, "I don't like my job, and it has low pay." The person may then attempt to remove the dissonance by changing one of the cognitions or by aiding dissonance-reducing cognitions, saying, "I like my job even though it does not pay well."

Osipow (1996) identifies the following implications of cognitive-dissonance theory on career decision making:

- *It is important for counselors to identify factors that can increase occupational dissonance.* One example is a person with an interest in an occupation that has limited opportunities, such as a person wanting to be a professor in a field that has few academic positions available. If the dissonance cannot be resolved, the counselor might advise the client to avoid that occupation.
- *Counselors should develop strategies to deal with dissonance.* This can involve a career counselor introducing "counter-dissonance agents." For example, the counselor might tell a premedical student who lacks the aptitude for medical study that being a physician involves working long hours, resulting in little time for family life.
- *Counselors can help clients avoid making a premature choice.* One way to accomplish this is by noting that modifying a choice in the future may cause excessive dissonance. This in turn can interfere with making a more appropriate choice in the future. For example, a person with a strong need to be perceived as having clear goals and objectives may decide to pursue a career as a computer analyst. After several courses on the topic, the person might discover an aversion to computers and want to consider other occupations. This would create dissonance with the need to be perceived as "having clear goals and objectives." To avoid such perceptions and reduce dissonance, this individual may then decide to continue working in an undesirable career.

The following *Personal Note* provides an example of how I overcame cognitive dissonance in my career choice and decision making.

A Personal Note

I entered college as a predental major. I had wanted to be a dentist because my father was a dentist. As part of my predental studies I had to take a lot of chemistry and biology courses, which I hated and in which I had limited ability. This created dissonance, since I thought I wanted to be a dentist but discovered I did not have the aptitude to do so.

I soon found myself changing my attitude toward becoming a dentist. Before I knew it, I began to think, "I don't want to be a dentist." I soon began to think of a lot of good reasons for not want-

ing to be a dentist, including not wanting to bend over all day and stick my hands in people's mouths. At this point, I had begun to resolve my dissonance by creating a new attitude. I was able to conclude, "I don't want to be a dentist, and I don't have the ability to become one." During my next semester at the university I was attending, I took a psychology course and quickly became interested in the subject. I also discovered that I had the aptitude to become a psychologist.

Social-Learning Theory.   Krumboltz (1979, 1996) and Mitchell and Krumboltz (2002) have developed a career decision-making model based on social-learning theory. The social-learning model contends that learning experiences play a key role in occupational selection. Krumboltz (1979) suggests that career choice is influenced by the following factors:

- Genetic endowment creates limits to career choice.
- Environmental factors, such as the economy and educational requirements, determine occupational choice to some degree.
- Learning experiences (for example, being reinforced for pursuing intellectual endeavors) influence one's interest and aspirations.
- Task-approach skills, such as work habits and interpersonal skills, affect one's ability to be successful in a particular occupation.

Mitchell and Krumboltz (2002) have expanded their model to include cognitive behavioral theory. From this perspective, career decision making is also influenced by cognitions and behaviors of clients. Mitchell and Krumboltz (1987) provide empirical support for the importance of cognitive-behavioral strategies in career counseling. They have found that cognitive-behavioral approaches contributed to appropriate career decisions and also reduced anxiety regarding career decisions.

More recently, Krumboltz (1996) has attempted to integrate his theory of career decision making into a theory of career counseling. The overall goal of his model "is to facilitate the learning of skills, interests, beliefs, values, work habits, and personal qualities that enable each client to create a satisfying life within a constantly changing work environment" (Krumboltz, 1996, p. 61). In this regard, Krumboltz (1994) developed the Career Beliefs Inventory (CBI) as a tool that counselors can use to help clients identify beliefs and assumptions that can impede career decision making. It can be used during the early phases of counseling to help clients develop cognitions and behaviors that enhance career progress (Krumboltz, 1994). Swanson and Gore (2000) note that Krumboltz has made great strides in developing a theory of career counseling that integrates career theory and career practice. These scholars go on to stress the need for empirical validation of Krumboltz's social-learning theory of career decision making.

Multiple Career Decision-Making Theory. Gati (1986) and Gati and Tikotzki (1989) have developed a multiple career decision-making theory. They contend that all career decision-making theories can be described in terms of three major models. These models are prescriptive in nature, using logic and rational approaches to identify the best way to make career decisions (Sharf, 2001). A detailed description and analysis of these models is provided by Gati and Tikotzki (1989), Carson and Mowsesian (1990), Gati (1990a, 1990b), and Gati, Fassa, and Houminer (1995). Reduced to their most basic elements, these three models can be summarized as follows:

- *Expected Utility Model.* This model suggests making separate evaluations of the advantages and disadvantages of various occupations and comparing them to other occupational alternatives. The individual then chooses the occupation with the highest overall value.
- *Sequential Elimination Model.* This model involves identifying attributes of an ideal occupation (for example, working outdoors) and ranking the attributes in terms of importance. Minimal levels of acceptability regarding these criteria are established. Occupations are evaluated on the basis of this criterion and sequentially eliminated if they do not meet the established criterion.
- *Conjunctive Model.* In this model, occupational alternatives are given consideration only when they meet basic occupational requirements, such as a minimal salary level.

Gati (1986) suggests that no single model of career development is superior to another. Instead, the models should be empirically investigated to determine the conditions that would be most appropriate for their use.

Treatment Issues

This section provides an overview of several important treatment issues that relate to career counseling. Information is provided on personal counseling versus career counseling, assessment instruments, intervention strategies, and the process of career counseling.

Personal Counseling Versus Career Counseling

There appears to be a shift in interest from career counseling to personal counseling (Birk & Brooks, 1986; Spengler, Blustein, & Strohmer, 1990; Watkins, Lopez, Campbell, & Himmell, 1986; Watkins, Schneider, Cox, & Reinberg, 1987). For example, Birk and Brooks (1986) surveyed 300 members of the Division of Counseling Psychology of the APA on their attitudes toward various counseling activities. Personal counseling was ranked as the most important activity, whereas career counseling was ranked tenth. Watkins et al. (1986) also surveyed members of the Division of Counseling Psychology of the APA regarding their attitudes relating to career counseling. Results of this study showed that members in private practice spend 59.2 percent of their time conducting psychotherapy and only 3.5 percent of their time conducting career counseling. The study also suggested that counseling psychologists are minimally engaged in career counseling and view it as an uninteresting and unattractive alternative to personal counseling.

With career counseling receiving less interest than personal counseling, an apparent treatment bias in favor of personal counseling is not surprising. Spengler et al. (1990) find that counselors who prefer personal counseling over career counseling engage in diagnostic and treatment overshadowing. In this process, issues relating to personal counseling overshadow the importance of diagnostic and treatment issues relating to career counseling. Other studies have shown that vocational problems receive poorer prognosis and less counselor empathy than personal problems (Hill, Tanney, & Leonard, 1977) and less of the core conditions and affective and exploratory responses (Melnick, 1975).

A trend in the literature suggests it is not necessary to conceptualize career counseling and personal counseling in dichotomous terms. Several authors have contended that career counseling should be integrated into nonvocational treatment approaches (Blustein, 1987; Blustein & Spengler, 1995; and Richardson, 1996). Blustein (1987, p. 794) provides a rationale for integration by noting that "separating work issues from other psychosocial concerns creates an artificial distinction between aspects of life that are clearly interrelated." In addition, the manner in which a person relates to career issues involves coping strategies similar to those utilized in other life concerns (Blustein, 1987).

Blustein and Spengler (1995) describe a comprehensive model that can be used to integrate personal counseling with career counseling. It is a model that incorporates a number of the recent trends in counseling, such as social constructivism and problem-oriented brief psychotherapy. Richardson (1996) suggests that an important first step in overcoming the personal counseling–career counseling split is to change the name of career counseling to counseling/psychotherapy and work, jobs, and careers. By placing counseling and psychotherapy first, it acknowledges the role that counseling and psychotherapy theories can play in career development, and it may also encourage more counselors and psychotherapists to address career issues (Richardson, 1996).

Blustein (1987) identifies guidelines for integrating career counseling with psychotherapy. He recommends that counselors take a first step of incorporating a detailed work history during the intake process to obtain important diagnostic considerations. The next step is to gain a comprehensive understanding of career development and career decision-making theories to broaden one's understanding of human behavior. In this process, counselors can select career theories that are compatible with their theories relating to personal counseling. For example, Super's theory of career development with his emphasis on the self could supplement Rogers's person-centered approach. As another example, Krumboltz's social-learning theory might be used in conjunction with the cognitive-behavioral school of counseling. Blustein (1987) also notes that it is important to integrate career counseling with personal counseling in cases that involve substance-abuse problems since clients with these problems often have trouble with work and personal issues.

Other individuals have attempted to integrate career counseling with personal counseling. Raskin (1987) integrates career counseling with interpersonally oriented schools of counseling; Yost and Corbishley (1987) conceptualize career counseling from a cognitive-behavioral perspective; and Gysbers and Moore (1987) describe career counseling within a broad framework that includes marriage and family counseling and cognitive psychology. It is hoped that this trend toward integration will promote more interest in career counseling so that these vital issues and concerns of clients will receive the attention they deserve.

Some individuals may have difficulty with career decision making even though they have been provided ample opportunity to obtain information regarding their interests, aptitude, the world of work, and so forth (Larson, Busby, Wilson, Medora, & Allgood, 1994). In these instances, Larson et al. (1994) suggest that these individuals may have psychological blocks associated with problematic behaviors, cognitions, or feelings (for example, fear of success or failure and fear of change). These psychological blocks can in turn contribute to problems within the personality structure, such as low self-esteem, lack of self-awareness, external locus of control, and anxiety, which can undermine the career decision-making process (Larson et al., 1994). Larson et al. (1994) note that the Career Decision Diagnostic Assessment (CDDA) (Bansberg & Sklare, 1986) instrument can identify potential psychological blocks that can interfere with career decision making. The CDDA can be used as a screening device to alert counselors that more intense personal counseling may be required to help these clients overcome impasses to the career counseling process. Kjos (1995) goes on to provide suggestions for career-focused interventions and treatment planning for individuals who are in need of personality restructuring.

Assessment Instruments

Career counseling has historically placed a major emphasis on assessing interests, abilities, and personality traits (Phillips, Cairo, Blustein, & Meyers, 1988). These assessment procedures play a vital role in career planning and decision making by increasing self-understanding and providing information on careers and educational programs.

Zunker (2002) and Drummond (2000) provide an overview of standardized assessment instruments used in career counseling to assess aptitude, achievement, personality, values, and career maturity. These instruments are summarized as follows:

- *Aptitude.* Aptitude tests provide a measure of a particular skill or the ability to acquire a skill. Aptitude tests can be used by career counselors to predict a person's success in career/education training. Examples of aptitude tests are the General Aptitude Test Battery (GATB), the Differential Aptitude Test (DAT), the Flanagan Aptitude Classification Tests (FACT), and the Armed Services Vocational Aptitude Battery (ASVAB) (see Zunker, 2002, for information and addresses regarding these instruments).

- *Achievement.* Achievement tests assess current level of functioning regarding abilities such as reading, arithmetic, and language usage. Career counselors use achievement tests to determine academic areas of strengths and weaknesses to assist with educational and career planning and placement. The three major types of achievement tests are diagnostic, broad survey, and subject area tests. Diagnostic tests can be used to assess strengths and weaknesses to determine whether the individual has the essential skills and competencies to be successful in an educational program. Survey tests can provide a general assessment of fundamental skills and competencies with little information on skills in a particular subject. Subject area tests are designed to assess functioning in specified subject areas such as chemistry and biology. Examples of achievement tests are the Wide Range Achievement Tests (an example of a diagnostic test), the National Assessment of Education Progress (NAEP) (an example of a survey test), and the College Board Achievement Tests (an example of a subject area test).

■ *Interests.* Interest inventories, perhaps more than any other assessment instruments, have been associated with career counseling. Interest inventories are used to assess personal and career interests to facilitate education/career planning and placement. Many of these interest inventories can provide useful information regarding the person-environmental fit discussed by Holland. Examples of interest inventories are the Self-Directed Search (Holland, 1994), the Strong Interest Inventory (Harmon et al., 1994), and the series of Kuder interest inventories based on the Kuder General Interest Survey (Kuder, 1964) (for example, the Kuder Occupational Interest Survey [Zytowski, 1985]).

■ *Values.* Values inventories have emerged in the past 25 years to assess the interface between personal values and the world of work. Mid-life career changes that correspond to radical lifestyle changes are examples of the potent force that values can have on career choice. Congruence between values and career choice is considered an important component in career success and satisfaction. Examples of values inventories are the Work Values Inventory (WVI) (Super, 1970), the Study of Values, the Survey of Interpersonal Values, the Survey of Personal Values, and the Values Scale (see Zunker, 2002, for the address and current information regarding these instruments).

■ *Personality.* Career development theorists such as Roe and Super recognized the importance of considering personality in career counseling. Roe's (1956) theory suggests that early personality development within the context of the family influences career direction. Super (2002) formulated a theory based on the relationship between self-concept and career development. Although the relationship between personality and career choice has been established, there has been limited use of personality inventories in career counseling. The movement toward integrating personal counseling with career counseling could provide a venue for more meaningful use of personality inventories in career counseling. Some of the personality instruments that are used in career counseling are the California Test of Personality, the Edwards Personal Preference Schedule (EPPS), the Guilford-Zimmerman Temperament Survey, the Minnesota Counseling Inventory, the Sixteen Personality Factor (16 PF), Temperament and Values Inventory, and the Myers-Briggs Type Indicator.

Diversity issues such as culture and clients with disabilities should be considered in career assessment. In terms of culture, several interest inventories have been evaluated to determine whether they are valid for ethnic minorities. Carter and Swanson (1990) conducted a literature review of studies that investigated the validity of the Strong Interest Inventory (Hansen & Campbell, 1985) for African-American clients. This review found little evidence of the validity of the Strong Interest Inventory for these clients. These findings are particularly significant because this instrument is the most frequently used interest inventory in college counseling centers (Zytowski & Warman, 1982). On a more positive note, Haviland and Hansen (1987) found that the Strong Campbell Interest Inventory (Hansen & Campbell, 1985) has adequate criterion validity for Native-American college students. Additional research on the cross-cultural use of interest inventories appears warranted.

Levinson (1994) addresses career assessment issues for students with disabilities. A number of programs and initiatives have been implemented in an effort to meet the special needs of students with disabilities. Transition planning is one example of the need for career assessment with these individuals. According to the 1990 Public Law 94–142, schools are required to formulate transition plans for students with disabilities by the time the students reach the age of 16. The overall goal of transition planning is to assist students in making a successful adjustment from school to work and to facilitate effective community living.

Contemporary career assessment for students with disabilities is typically structured in terms of three levels. Level 1 begins in elementary school and is focused on building self-awareness. During this time, students explore needs, interests, values, and careers, and receive assistance in developing decision-making skills. Level 2 starts in middle or junior high school. Its aim is to assist students in making tentative career choices based on assessment of interests, aptitudes, career maturity, and work habits. Level 3 begins when students reach high school. During this time, assessment can involve a wide range of activities relating to career planning and decision making such as refinement of issues associated with career choice and assistance with post-secondary education, training, employment, and community living.

Central to the task of counseling students with disabilities is to first and foremost treat them as people who have more in common with others than they have differences. It is also important to be aware of the special needs and requirements associated with their disabilities to facilitate the self-realization of their full career potential.

The Process of Career Counseling

Frank Parsons was one of the first individuals to identify stages of career counseling. Parsons (1909) described his three-stage approach as follows. To make an appropriate career decision, the person needs "(1) a clear understanding of aptitudes, abilities, interests, ambitions, resources, limitations, and their causes; (2) a knowledge of the requirements and conditions of success, advantages and disadvantages, compensations, opportunities, and prospects in different lines of work; and (3) true reasoning on the relations of these two groups of facts" (Parsons, 1909, p. 5).

Salomone (1988) has added two stages to Parsons' (1909) three-stage model. These additional stages focus on interventions that counselors can use after a client makes a career decision. The first stage involves helping the client implement educational and career decisions. This stage might involve helping the client with job-seeking skills and assisting with job placement. The second stage involves helping the newly employed individual adjust to the new job. This process might involve helping the client deal effectively with job stress, fear of failure, or other barriers to a successful job placement.

Salomone (1988) provides additional information on how to conceptualize these stages. He suggests that counselors do not necessarily have to proceed through these stages sequentially, but can instead work in several stages simultaneously. Salomone (1988) also notes that many counseling strategies are available for counselors to use in helping clients move through these stages. Some of these strategies are establishing a positive counseling relationship; helping clients assess their abilities and aptitudes regarding work, including promoting self-assessment; providing information about careers and the world of work; and offering assistance with career placement.

Gysbers, Heppner, and Johnson (1998) provide another model of the process of career counseling. It is similar to the six-stage model of counseling described in Chapter 3. These scholars put the working alliance at the center of the career-counseling process, emphasizing the importance of maintaining a positive counseling relationship throughout the career-counseling process. The first stage is referred to as the *opening stage.* It provides an opportunity to establish a working alliance and to work through possible obstacles to career counseling such as client resistance. Career and personal issues may be addressed at any time throughout the career-counseling process. Other stages of this model include gathering client information, understanding and hypothesizing client behavior, developing career goals and plans of action, evaluating results, and closing the relationship. The number and order of stages utilized in career counseling vary according to the unique and emerging needs of clients.

Intervention Strategies

A wide range of intervention strategies can be used in career counseling. These include strategies associated with career planning and decision making, assisting with vocational adjustment, and helping clients overcome personal problems. Career counseling can also take place in a variety of formats, including individual, group, self-help, and computer-assisted programs.

A large body of research has evaluated the various forms of career interventions. These studies have been summarized in several reviews (Brown & Ryan Krane, 2000; Morrow, Mullen, & McElvoy, 1990). For example, a study by Kivlighan and Shapiro (1987) shows that it is important to consider client characteristics when formulating treatment strategies in career counseling. This study finds that the clients most likely to benefit from self-help career counseling are rated as realistic, conventional, and investigative on the Vocational Identity Scale of Holland's Vocation Situation (Holland, Daieger, & Power, 1980).

Several meta-analyses of career counseling have been conducted that have provided support for the efficacy of career counseling. Oliver and Spokane (1983, 1988) conducted two meta-analyses of career counseling that have received considerable attention in the literature. Both studies provide support for the efficacy of career counseling. Their 1988 review involves an analysis of 58 studies on career counseling published from 1950 to 1982. It attempts to gain a more precise understanding of the variables associated with efficacy in terms of types of intervention, client characteristics, and outcome measures. Results of the study show differences in type and intensity of intervention. In terms of type of intervention, individual career counseling produced the most gain per hour of any intervention strategy. Group career counseling and workshops were the least effective intervention per hour of treatment. The study also shows intensity of intervention to be important. Efficacy improved with increased length of sessions and number of sessions.

More recently, Whiston, Sexton, and Lasoff (1998) and Ryan (1999) conducted meta-analyses of career-counseling outcomes that provide additional support of the overall efficacy of career counseling. The Whiston et al. (1998) analysis was based on 47 studies published between 1983 and 1995. Results show that career interventions are effective "but how and why they work and for whom they are most (and least) effective is unknown" (Brown & Ryan Krane, 2000, p. 743). Ryan's (1999) meta-analysis was based on 62 studies. Her results not only provide support for the overall efficacy of career counseling, they also have implications for enhancing the process of career counseling.

Ryan (1999) identifies five critical components associated with brief (four- to five-session) group career interventions. These components are summarized by Brown and Ryan Krane (2000) as follows:

1. *Have clients write down information* on their career goals and their plans for implementation. Also engage them in written exercises designed to gain accurate information on careers.
2. *Information on the world of work* emphasizes the importance of ensuring that clients have up-to-date, accurate information on careers, including educational requirements, rewards, and potential challenges associated with different career paths.
3. *Modeling* involves exposing clients to individuals who have been successful in a career to demonstrate how to proceed with career planning and decision making.
4. *Attention to building support* suggests that clients can benefit from a culturally similar support system that can teach the necessary skills to successfully overcome environmental barriers such as racism.
5. *Individualized interpretation and feedback* ensures that clients receive accurate and relevant information regarding self-appraisal, career choice, and decision making.

Brown and Ryan Krane (2000) identify three areas for future research on career counseling. First, the five critical components for career counseling identified by Ryan (1999) require further scientific investigation. Second, career interventions must be developed to determine how to work with clients facing difficulty with career choice. Third, research should attempt to determine how career-counseling interventions can be modified to address diversity issues such as culture, gender, and sexual orientation.

Special Issues

This section covers two special issues in career counseling: career counseling for women and computer-assisted career counseling.

Career Counseling for Women

A major criticism of career counseling is that the majority of its theories and approaches have been based on men and are therefore not sensitive to the special issues of women (Brooks, 2002). Several theories have therefore attempted to make career counseling more responsive to the special needs of women. This section provides an overview of two theories and identifies their implications for career counseling for women.

Self-Efficacy Theory. Self-efficacy, as described in Chapter 9, is the belief in one's ability to successfully perform a particular behavior (Bandura, 1986, 1989). Self-efficacy has been related to which behaviors will be initiated, the amount of effort that will be exerted, and how long the behavior will continue in the face of difficult circumstances (Luzzo, 1996). The origins of career self-efficacy can be traced to the work of Hackett and Betz (1981) and Betz and Hackett (1986). It can be broadly defined as the relationship between self-efficacy and various behaviors associated with career choice and adjustment (Lent & Hackett, 1987).

Hackett and Betz (1981) contend that self-efficacy theory has particular relevance to career counseling for women. A central factor to this position is that women and men acquire different efficacy expectations owing to differential gender-role experiences and limited access to efficacy information (Lent & Hackett, 1987). This in turn can contribute to the limited positions women hold in the labor force (Brooks, 2002). In addition, Bonett (1994) notes that the career aspirations of women may be restricted by the perception that they lack the necessary job-related skills associated with male-dominated professions and that pursuing those professions may be in conflict with home and family responsibilities.

Morrow et al. (1990) describe two studies that identify gender differences in self-efficacy and career behavior. Matsui, Ikeda, and Ohnishi (1989) found that men report equal levels of self-efficacy in male- and female-dominated occupations, whereas women have higher self-efficacy perceptions in female-dominated fields than in male-dominated ones. A second study shows that women have lower self-efficacy perceptions than men in mathematical activities, although mathematical accomplishments are equivalent for men and women with similar preparatory backgrounds (Lapan, Boggs, & Morrill, 1989).

Brooks (2002) describes implications of self-efficacy theory for career counseling for women. She suggests that its primary use could be to broaden career options for women and facilitate the pursuit of those options. Brooks (2002) also identifies several counseling strategies that can be used to promote these outcomes. These include cognitive strategies to help clients view their abilities more realistically; reattribution training to enable clients to attribute success to internal rather than external causes (Fosterling, 1980); the use of incremental graded success experiences (Lent & Hackett, 1987); vicarious learning, which can be promoted by arranging experiences for clients to "shadow" successful career women; and desensitization procedures to reduce anxiety that relates to career choice and performance.

Watkins and Subich (1995) identify current trends in career self-efficacy research such as integrating career self-efficacy with social-cognitive career models (for example, Lent, Brown, & Hackett, 1994) and the role of self-efficacy in work and nonwork settings as a coping mechanism (Matsui & Onglatco, 1992). Watkins and Subich (1995) conclude that career self-efficacy is a robust theoretical construct that has only begun to be realized.

Social-cognitive career theory has attracted considerable attention in the literature. This theory suggests that people will pursue career aspirations associated with perceived self-efficacy, environmental support, minimal environmental obstacles, and desirable outcome expectations (Lent et al., 1994). Swanson and Gore (2000) note that research on the efficacy of career self-efficacy theories has received much support from the literature. These scholars provide a review of this literature and conclude that there is substantial support for the interrelationship between career interests, self-efficacy, and desirable outcomes.

Gottfredson's Theory.   Gottfredson's (1981, 1996) theory of occupational operations was one of the major vocational theories to emerge in the 1980s (Hesketh, Elmslie, & Kaldor, 1990) and applies to both men and women (Brooks, 2002). Hesketh et al. (1990) note that this theory is important to career counseling for women because it explains how compromise takes place in vocational decision making, identifies factors associated with social identity, and explores the difficulties that women face entering nontraditional careers.

Brooks (2002) identifies the following major principles associated with Gottfredson's model:

- People differentiate occupations in terms of sex type (job preferences relating to gender), work level, and field of work.
- People determine the appropriations of an occupation in terms of their self-concept.
- Self-concept factors that have vocational reliance include gender, social class, intelligence, values, interest, and abilities.
- Vocationally relevant self-concept factors emerge in the following developmental sequence. From age 3 to 5, individuals understand the concept of being an adult; from age 6 to 8, they develop the concept of gender; from age 9 to 13, they understand the abstract concepts of social class and intelligence; and beginning at age 14, they refine their attitudes, values, traits, and interests.
- People reject occupations on the basis of self-concept as they proceed through the developmental stages.
- The reasons for rejecting occupations have the following hierarchy: individuals reject occupations when they are not suitable, first, in terms of gender; second, for social class and ability reasons; and third, on the basis of interests and values.
- Occupational preferences result from compatibility between job and self-concept and from judgments about job accessibility.
- Compromise in job choice follows a predictable pattern. People will first sacrifice their interests, then prestige, and finally sex type, or job preferences related to gender.

Gottfredson's (1981, 1996) theory has stimulated a wide range of research activity. Brooks (2002) has identified several studies that provide general support for Gottfredson's (1981) model (Henderson, Hesketh, & Tuffin, 1988; Holt, 1989; Taylor & Pryor, 1985). Two more recent studies do not support Gottfredson's theory regarding the predictable nature of compromise in job choice. Leung and Plake (1990) found that prestige and not sex type is the most important factor in job choice. Hesketh et al. (1990) further challenge Gottfredson's (1981) position regarding the process of compromise. Results of their study suggest that interests incorporate attributes of prestige and sex type and are therefore the most important factor in job choice and compromise. Swanson (1992) and Watkins and Subich (1995) have reviewed the literature on Gottfredson's theory and suggest that it is in need of modification in terms of the role of compromise in career decision making. They conclude that compromise appears to be a complex factor in career decision making, varying according to gender, sex-role attitudes, and interests. Swanson and Gore (2000) posit that Gottfredson's theory appears useful in understanding vocational behavior regarding the role of compromise in career choice and decision making. They go on to note that Gottfredson's theoretical constructs are difficult to test and lack empirical validation.

Brooks (2002) identifies several implications of Gottfredson's theory for career counseling for women. First, Gottfredson's model suggests that clients may experience problems with indecision when they do not have an awareness of the effects of sex type, prestige, and interests on career choice and compromise. Counselors can assist these clients by helping them clarify their vocational priorities regarding these factors. Second, clients may need assistance in identifying occupations that are acceptable in terms of their self-concept. Third, clients may have aspirations that are incongruent with their abilities or interests. In these instances, counselors can evaluate the client's aspirations to determine whether the aspirations are associated with self-defeating processes, such as trying to live up to other people's standards.

Computer-Assisted Career Counseling

Computer-assisted career counseling (CACC) has become an important dimension to the delivery of career counseling in North America (Sampson, 1994). Although most clients can benefit from CACC, Kivlighan, Johnston, Hogan, & Mauer (1994) have found that clients with stable goals make the most gain in vocational identity as the result of using CACC. Sampson (1994) identifies several factors that have contributed to the increased use of CACC. Some of these are reduced hardware costs, improved hardware and software capabilities such as color graphics and more comprehensive and diversified programs, and increased expertise by counselors and other professional helpers in using CACC.

Several authors have commented on the importance of including direct counseling services when utilizing computerized career counseling. Sampson, Shahnasarian, and Reardon (1987) identify the following problems that could occur when computerized career counseling is used without direct counselor contact: inappropriate clients can use the system, clients may not understand the purpose or operation of the system, and clients may not be able to integrate their computerized counseling experience into their decision-making process.

In addition, Johnston, Buescher, and Heppner (1988) note that ethical standards require orientation of information prior to and following administration of tests, including those utilized in computer-assisted career counseling programs. Dungy (1984) provides further support for the importance of direct counseling by noting that it enhances the effectiveness of subsequent computer-assisted program use.

CACC can be viewed as an adjunct to direct career counseling. It provides a useful starting point from which clients can gain information to narrow down their career choice (Sampson, 1994). Gati (1994) goes on to note that counselors must monitor the client's use of CACC by engaging in an ongoing dialogue with the client and assisting with the integration and interpretation of information to foster appropriate decision making.

Numerous computerized career programs are currently available. Heppner and Johnston (1985), Maze (1984), and Zunker (2002) provide a description and comparative analysis of the major programs. Table 13.1 incorporates computer-assisted career programs described by Zunker (2002) and some of the most current programs available.

The wide variety of computer-assisted career programs can overwhelm counselors, making it difficult to select one for use. Maze (1984) provides the following guidelines for selecting the most appropriate program:

- *Obtain staff input.* Perform a needs assessment with the staff, identifying areas that could be improved by computerized programs.
- *Obtain relevant information about the programs under consideration.* Evaluate each program in terms of cost, software packages, hardware requirements, and user population.
- *Arrange for demonstrations of software programs.* If possible, preview all software before purchasing a program.
- *Evaluate samples of the system's output.* Review sample printouts produced from each module or component of the system before deciding on a program.
- *Determine the total cost of the system.* Calculate the total cost of each software and hardware system under consideration.

TABLE 13.1 Computerized Career Programs

Program Name	Publisher and Year	Program Overview	Special Features	Role of Counselor Client
Computerized Career Assessment and Planning Program (CCAPP)	Cambridge Career, 1989 (updated every two years)	Assists with career assessment, selecting alternatives, career planning, and career exploration	Provides information on over 1200 occupations; a list of college majors or vocational courses relating to career interest; and an individual career plan and a job-hunting plan	Some aspects can be used independently by client, but counselors explain how a counselor can use the program to assist the client
C-LECT	Chronicle Guidance, 1991 (updated annually)	Assists with career awareness, exploration, decision making, and educational planning	Connects 14 school subjects with over 700 occupations; describes 717 occupations; has five self-assessment options; provides information on financial aid; and answers questions on specific colleges and universities	Can be used with minimal counselor assistance
Choices	Human Resources Development-Canada, 1997	Assists with self-knowledge and assessment, career exploration, planning, and decision making	Matches interest with careers; indentifies schools that have programs and majors associated with career choice; and provides information on schools	Can be used with minimal counselor assistance
DISCOVER	The American College Testing Program, Version 4.3, 1990	Assists with career choice and decision-making skills; enhances the general adjustment of the client	Provides opportunities to take interest, ability, and value inventories, producing scores that are used to conduct job searches and search for college majors or programs of study; provides information regarding various occupational fields and educational institutions	Can be used in conjunction with career planning, curriculums, or workshops
The Guidance and Information System (GIS)	Riverside, Houghton Mifflin, 1991	Provides information on 1200 primary occupations and 3000 related occupations; grouped according to the U.S. Office of Educational Occupational Clusters and the Dictionary of Occupational Titles (DOT)	Provides accessibility through a telephone and teletypewriter or display terminal that receives signals and prints or displays copy, thus does not require an institution to have its own computer	Not designed to be the sole source of career and educational information but can be a meaningful tool for the career counselor

■ *Determine the cost per user.* Calculate the maximum, minimum, and average estimates for potential users to determine the cost-effectiveness of the system.

■ *Determine one-time charges and ongoing charges.* Examples of one-time charges are the cost of a printer and a telephone adapter. Ongoing charges include the costs of renewing software packages and maintaining equipment. There may also be ongoing expenses associated with mainframe or centralized systems that should be determined.

Diversity Issues in Career Counseling

Diversity issues such as culture, socioeconomic status, education, gender, age, and sexual preference are becoming increasingly important in career counseling. Hackett and Byars (1996) note that there are no comprehensive models of career development for ethnic and racial minorities. Practitioners must therefore take care when extrapolating from theory to practice and infuse culturally sensitive issues when appropriate. Arbona (1996) believes that education and socioeconomic status are critical variables in the utility of career-counseling theories with ethnic minorities. Arbona (1996) suggests that career-counseling theories can be useful cross-culturally with individuals who are progressing educationally or with those who are middle or upper class. On the other hand, career-counseling theories that emphasize career choice appear to have less utility for individuals who live in poverty and/or are school dropouts. In these instances, a more appropriate approach may be to foster cognitive, academic, and socioemotional development (Arbona, 1996).

Leong and Chou (1994) have identified additional cultural considerations in career counseling that relate to Asian Americans and other ethnic minorities. They contend that identity development, acculturation, and assimilation are key variables in career counseling that can affect perceived prejudice, stress, and educational and career aspirations and expectations. For example, Asian Americans who rate low on acculturation and assimilation tend to score high on perceived prejudice and stress. Issues of prejudice and stress should therefore be monitored and addressed with these individuals as potential barriers to career counseling.

Asian Americans also tend to suffer the highest degree of career stereotyping and segregation of all minorities. Asians tend to be perceived as having skills in the fields of science and mathematics but not in careers that emphasize language and interpersonal relations. It is therefore not surprising that they are underrepresented in careers such as law and overrepresented in science and engineering. Acculturation and assimilation levels may be important intervening variables in this process. Individuals who have low levels of acculturation appear to be more vulnerable to the adverse effects of stereotyping and segregation than people who have assimilated more into mainstream society. In this regard, movement toward assimilation and acculturation may promote a corresponding stage of identity development that rejects stereotypical views of career choice and decision making.

Asian Americans, African Americans, and Hispanics experience a potential career barrier that relates to educational and career aspirations and expectations. These individuals tend to experience a higher discrepancy between their educational and career aspirations (for example, goals) and the degree to which they expect to achieve these goals. This discrepancy is owing in part to perceived education and career barriers associated with discrimination against minorities. Career counselors must therefore be cognizant of these perceptions and associated issues such as problems with motivation and discouragement. In addition, counselors can take a proactive role in helping clients overcome discriminatory practices that are having adverse effects on clients.

Swanson and Gore (2000) posit that women's career development has received the most attention in the career-counseling literature and continues to be at the forefront of scholarly investigation. These scholars suggest that issues of gender permeate all aspects of career development, including the complex interaction of personal/family life and the world of work. Gender issues are perhaps more important in career counseling than in other specialty areas of counseling. This is in part owing to a long history of sexual discrimination in the workforce and practices of sex-role stereotyping with its adverse consequences on career choice and decision making. Self-efficacy theory and Gottfredson's theory are described earlier in this chapter as theories that can be useful in addressing career issues in women. For example, Hackett and Byars (1996) have found that one of the most important issues that career counselors should address when working with African-American women is how experiences of racism have an impact on their self-efficacy expectations.

Age is another important consideration in career counseling. Career counseling has historically focused on helping high-school-age students with the process of career choice and decision making. In a rapidly changing technological world and in an era when people are living longer, it is becoming increasingly common for individuals to change careers numerous times throughout their life span. Career counseling is therefore broadening its base to include a life-span perspective. Watts (1996) suggests that the concept of *career* needs to be redefined in order to facilitate the developmental perspective in career counseling.

According to Watts (1996) the old concept of *career* as a progression up a hierarchical ladder within a profession or organization is obsolete. Watts (1996) suggests that a more realistic concept of *career* is that it is a subjective experience that is a lifelong progression in learning and work. This definition recognizes that people are ultimately responsible for defining their existence in terms of the world of work, and the focus of their experience is on what they have learned and what they have contributed in their work. Seligman (1994) provides additional information regarding the theory, research, and practice of career counseling across the life span (childhood, adolescence, early adulthood, middle adulthood, and late adulthood). For example, self-esteem enhancement and career education can be important components of career counseling with children, and postretirement issues of work and leisure can become a focus in career counseling during late adulthood.

Issues of sexual orientation represent another example of diversity in career counseling. It is especially important for career counselors to be aware of the special career issues that relate to lesbian, gay, and bisexual individuals. Sexual orientation and degree of openness relating to sexuality (for example, being open about one's homosexuality) can influence the type of job and work environment one chooses (Chung, 1995). Unfortunately, there has been a lack of theoretical development regarding the career development of lesbian, gay, and bisexual individuals (Chung, 1995). Several researchers have attempted to fill this void, such as Fassinger's (1995) study on lesbian identity in the workplace and Prince's study of career development of gay men. For example, Fassinger's research describes how lesbian identity development and theoretical constructs of vocational psychology of women can be integrated with vocational issues of lesbians. Fassinger goes on to provide useful information regarding career counseling with lesbians that can help sensitize counselors to lesbian issues. For example, lesbians do not tend to rely on men for financial support and therefore tend to seek employment where they can be more financially independent than their heterosexual female counterparts.

Summary

Career counseling is represented by several emerging issues such as the use of computer technology in career counseling. Popular career programs are described along with information that can aid in selection of computer software. Diversity issues such as gender, age, culture, and sexual orientation must also be carefully considered in career counseling. This chapter provides an overview of diversity issues with considerable attention directed at women's issues in career counseling.

Personal Exploration

1. How do you view the concept of career across your life span?
2. What do you believe are potential obstacles to career growth for you?
3. How important is your career relative to other parts of your life, such as your personal relationships, social life, and family life?
4. Could you relate any of the career theories to your own career development, and if so, how?

Web Sites for Chapter 13

Brown, K. M. (1999). *Cognitive consistency theory.* Retrieved March 3, 2005, from
http://hsc.usf.edu/~kmbrown/Cognitive_Consistency_Overview.htm
Provides background information on cognitive dissonance theory (referred to as cognitive consistency theory on this site).

Maryland's Career Net. (unknown). *Career development theory.* Retrieved March 3, 2005, from http://www.careernet.state.md.us/careertheory.htm
Presents various career development theories, including those of Super and Holland.

SimilarMinds.com (unknown). *Personality tests.* Retrieved March 3, 2005, from
http://similarminds.com/personality_tests.html
Provides free online personality tests and assessment tools used by some career counselors.

CHAPTER OVERVIEW

This chapter provides an overview of the issues relating to school counseling. Highlights of the chapter include

- The art and science of school counseling
- A comprehensive developmental model for guidance and counseling
- The role and function of school counselors
- Special skills and problems, including counseling exceptional students
- Trends in school counseling

The Art and Science of School Counseling

School counseling is an art and science. It is an art to try to reach a reluctant or resistant student who has problems with drugs, gang involvement, and family. School counselors work closely with community agencies and organizations and consult with parents, teachers, and staff to provide services for these and other problems that students face. The art of counseling suggests that school counselors be sensitive to individual differences and embrace diversity as an opportunity to expand educational horizons. Flexibility and creativity are other dimensions of the art of school counseling. In this regard, counselors can adjust their counseling approach by using innovative strategies such as play therapy (Campbell, 1993), music therapy (Newcomb, 1994), and sand play (Carmichael, 1994).

The science of school counseling complements the art of counseling by offering the objective-scientific dimension to the counseling process. One research study provides empirical support for the science of school counseling. A meta-analysis of school counseling research suggests that school counseling activities (such as individual counseling and group counseling) play an important role in enhancing students' academic and personal development (Borders & Drury, 1992). Baker (1995) notes that qualitative research such as the use of semistructured interviews is an emerging trend in school counseling research. These more naturalistic forms of research offer a practical alternative to the more traditional statistical hypothesis testing associated with quantitative research. Capuzzi (1988) emphasizes that research has an essential role in the future of school counseling. He identifies nine problem areas that students commonly face: self-esteem, eating disorders, child and adolescent suicide, depression, teenage pregnancy, drug abuse, physical and sexual abuse, stress, and divorced parents. The author notes that a school counselor's expertise on these issues is critical because the problems present roadblocks to children's psychosocial development. He suggests that additional research is required for school counselors to deal effectively with these problems.

A Comprehensive Developmental Model for School Counseling

School counseling has been conceptualized in terms of a comprehensive developmental model (Paisley & Benshoff, 1996; Paisley & Borders, 1995; and Paisley & DeAngelis-Peace, 1995). The term *comprehensive* refers to the notion that school counseling programs should function as an integrated part of a K–12 program, not as separate entities. The *developmental* focus suggests that school-counseling programs should be organized from a life-span perspective. Developmental school counseling represents a shift from remediation and crisis intervention to learning and development (Paisley & DeAngelis-Peace, 1995). "The developmental program is proactive and preventive, helping students acquire the knowledge, skills, self-awareness, and attitudes necessary for successful mastery of normal developmental tasks" (Paisley & DeAngelis-Peace, 1995, p. 87).

Robert Myrick and Norman Gysbers are two individuals who have played key roles in formulating comprehensive developmental school counseling. In his model, Myrick (1987) identifies a number of goals and objectives that show counselors to be focused on personal and social development, decision making and problem solving, career education, and educational planning.

Gysbers (2004) suggests that a comprehensive guidance and counseling program should be K–12 and provide school counselors with an opportunity to communicate accountability. Gysbers's comprehensive guidance and counseling program has three elements: content, an organizational framework, and resources (Gysbers, 2004; Gysbers & Henderson, 2000). The first element, *content,* relates to the mission statement and provides a rationale for school counseling and assumptions on which the program is based. The second element, *an organizational framework,* consists of the following four program components:

- *Individual planning.* This consists of assisting students (in conjunction with parents) in carrying out their academic, career, and personal plans.
- *Guidance curriculum.* This consists of structured activities such as classroom presentations on time management.
- *Responsive services.* This consists of individual and small-group counseling, consultation, and referral.
- *System support.* This consists of utilization of system support to organize and administer the program.

The third element, *accountability*, relates to resources associated with finances, personnel, and politics. According to Gysbers, a comprehensive guidance and counseling program requires adequate finances, personnel, and political support.

Gysbers spent considerable time developing his program in 75 schools in Missouri between 1984 and 1988, resulting in his model being referred to as the *Missouri model* (Good, Fischer, Johnston, & Heppner, 1994). Gysbers estimates that the Missouri model is being used in some form in approximately 30 states in the United States. Gysbers also played an influential role in the recent National Model of School Counseling (ASCA, 2003), which incorporated an organizational framework of individual planning, guidance curriculum, responses services, and systems support and also included his emphasis on program accountability.

Neukrug, Barr, Hoffman, and Kaplan (1993) set forth a developmental school counseling and guidance model that has been supported by the American School Counseling Association (ASCA). It was designed as a simple yet flexible model that school counselors could use to address the special needs of the students they serve. The model is grounded in developmental theory, encouraging counselors to implement interventions consistent with students' developmental tasks. It is a proactive model "whose primary emphasis is fostering the learning and growth of all students, with a secondary emphasis on assisting individual students with the resolution of special problems and concerns" (Neukrug et al., 1993, p. 358).

Bergin, Miller, Bergin, and Koch (1990) identified some of the states that have comprehensive K–12 developmental guidance programs: Arkansas, Illinois, Iowa, Missouri, New Hampshire, North Carolina, Ohio, Oklahoma, and Wisconsin. A limited amount of research has been conducted to evaluate these programs. A study by Bergin et al. (1990) evaluated a developmental guidance model called *Building Skills for Tomorrow* (Oklahoma State Department of Education, 1988) that was being implemented in a rural school district. The study found that the program elicited positive responses from parents, teachers, and community leaders.

Hughey, Gysbers, and Starr (1993) provide additional support for the comprehensive developmental model for school counseling. These scholars surveyed the attitudes of students, teachers, and parents regarding the Missouri Comprehensive Guidance Program. Results of the survey indicate that school counselors were perceived as caring individuals who students could freely go to for assistance for career and college planning and individual and group counseling. In addition, students, parents, and teachers believed that schools should hire additional school counselors.

Paisley and Borders (1995) contend that school counselors have had difficulty implementing comprehensive developmental school-counseling programs because they do not clearly understand the concept and have difficulty translating these ideas into practice. Paisley and Benshoff (1996) identify the knowledge and skills necessary to implement a comprehensive developmental school-counseling program. Knowledge necessary for program implementation includes being well grounded in developmental theory (including understanding how change occurs); being familiar with programs such as peer helping programs, which have successfully fostered development; and being aware of emerging strategies such as person-to-environment fit (Paisley & DeAngelis-Peace, 1995). Skills to promote program implementation include using developmental theory in assessment to determine appropriate interventions and skills in consultation with parents and teachers. Other strategies include dilemma discussions to help students explore difficult situations and the reasoning they use relative to their choices (Paisley & Benshoff, 1996).

Casey (1995) suggests that technology could play a key role in the implementation of developmental school counseling. Casey contends that modern technology must be integrated into all aspects of the school-counseling program (for example, individual counseling, small- and large-group counseling, and consultation). Casey provides examples of how technologies such as interactive CD-ROMs and the Internet can be used with students of different ages. For example, a possible technology strategy with 10-year-olds is to develop a technology club, since fostering friendships is an important priority of students at this age.

A Developmental Perspective

The developmental perspective is central to the comprehensive developmental school-counseling model. This perspective represents a shift from an orientation of counselors as clinicians to a role of counselors promoting prevention (Gysbers & Henderson, 1988). In this role, counselors work closely with teachers to promote developmental guidance and counseling as an integral aspect of the overall school program. Myrick (1987) notes that the goals of developmental school counseling can never be fully realized unless teachers take an active role in offering guidance activities in the classroom.

Several individuals have applied the developmental perspective to counseling theories, such as Blocher's (1974, 1987) developmental counseling and Ivey's (1986) developmental therapy. These theories suggest that counselors should first identify a client's developmental level and then implement an approach that addresses the needs for that level. Developmental counseling approaches incorporate various theories of development. Ivey (1986) emphasizes Piaget's (1955) theory of cognitive development, whereas Blocher (1974, 1987) focuses on Havighurst's (1972) concept of developmental tasks and Erikson's (1963) psychosocial theory. Developmental theories are becoming increasingly sensitive to diversity issues such as Carol Gilligan's (1982) seminal work on gender issues in moral development.

Blocher's (1974) model suggests that there are certain developmental tasks associated with each stage of development. In addition, clients must master coping skills to meet the challenges of these tasks to successfully move forward to the next developmental task. Blocher (1974) contends that counseling goals and strategies can be developed to help individuals master the necessary coping skills as they proceed through the life span.

According to Blocher (1974, 1987), elementary school students face the developmental tasks of industry and initiative. These tasks can be facilitated by counseling goals that help students implement activities on their own and feel competent when competing with peers. Counselors can promote industry and initiative in students by helping them value themselves and feel a sense of control over their environment. Counseling strategies (such as consultation, individual counseling, and group counseling) that foster self-concept development and encouragement can be used to facilitate these counseling goals.

Blocher's (1974, 1987) theory can also be applied to middle school students. The main developmental task during these years is identity formation. Counseling goals can be developed to assist with this task, such as helping students enhance their self-awareness and clarify their values. Consultation, individual counseling, and group counseling can be used to address these issues as well as other problems that require attention.

The primary developmental task for high school students is intimacy. This task requires developing the skills necessary to establish close, trusting relationships with siblings, peers, parents, and others. The counseling goals associated with this task include promoting students' concern and interest in others and enhancing interpersonal relationship skills. Consultation, individual counseling, and group counseling that focus on social-skills training can be particularly useful as strategies to promote interpersonal effectiveness.

An overview of these developmental tasks, counseling goals, and associated counseling strategies according to Blocher's model is provided in Table 14.1.

The developmental tasks and their associated counseling goals and strategies shown in Table 14.1 can be useful in providing a focus for counseling services. At the same time, counselors should not limit their programs to these tasks and related counseling strategies. A comprehensive developmental school-counseling program should address the wide array of issues that concern school-age children, such as divorced parents, drug and alcohol abuse, and teenage pregnancy.

Role and Function of School Counselors

One of the most controversial issues in school counseling has been the role and function of school counselors. The controversy has centered on the difficulties that school counselors have faced in trying to establish a clear professional identity (Paisley & Borders, 1995) and what steps should be taken to overcome these problems. One way to make a clear statement about the role and function of school counselors is to describe the main mission of school counseling in terms of enhancement of learning. Ultimately, all school-counseling activities maximize learning potential in students. For example, self-concept and school achievement have been shown to have a positive correlation (Hamachek, 1995). Therefore, a

TABLE 14.1 Developmental Tasks, Goals, and Counseling Strategies

Age Level	Developmental Tasks	Counseling Goals	Counseling Strategy
Elementary school	Industry and initiative	Foster independence and self-autonomy	Consultation and individual and group counseling to promote self-concept development; encouragement strategies to help students believe in their capabilities and implement activities on their own; self-control interventions for students whose impulse control interferes with their ability to complete tasks
Middle school	Identity formation	Help students gain a clear understanding of who they are as individuals	Consultation and individual and group counseling to promote self-awareness and value clarification
High school	Intimacy	Promote social interest and interpersonal effectiveness	Consultation and individual, group, and family counseling to promote social interest and compassion for others; group counseling to foster interpersonal effectiveness; career counseling to relate to the world of work

counselor that enhances a student's self-concept will contribute to the student's learning potential.

This section addresses the central issues associated with the school counselor's role and function, such as counseling from a historical perspective, the current ASCA role statement, and the role and function of school counselors working in elementary, middle, and high schools and in rural schools.

A Historical Perspective

A historical perspective can be useful for understanding how the school counselor's role and function have evolved. Gysbers (1988) provides a description of the history of school counseling, and his observations have been incorporated into the following overview.

The period from 1909 to 1920 represents the beginning of school counseling as a specialty. Its origins can be traced to the pioneering work of Frank Parsons (1909), who provided vocational guidance services in schools.

During the 1920s, the emphasis shifted from vocational guidance to assistance with personal adjustment.

The 1930s was an era in which there was an attempt to differentiate guidance from vocational guidance. The term *guidance* was broadly defined as assisting individuals with problems of adjusting to any aspect of life, including health or family and friends as well as work. *Vocational guidance* was more narrowly defined as helping people with choice, preparation, placement, and advancement in a vocation. During this period, school counselors also began to use more formal terms, such as *counseling, assessment, information, placement,* and *follow-up,* to describe what occurred in the helping process.

The counseling profession experienced the initial impact of Carl Rogers's views of counseling in the 1940s. Rogers's (1942) *Counseling and Psychotherapy* had a dramatic effect on the role and function of the school counselor. His person-centered approach provided a theoretical framework for individual counseling and resulted in school counselors utilizing a clinical emphasis in their overall role and function. Rogers's work continues to have a major impact on contemporary school counselors as they attempt to assist students with an ever-increasing array of personal problems.

During the 1950s, support for school counselors increased with the passage of Public Law 85-864, the National Defense Education Act. This act allocated funds for colleges and universities to train students to become secondary school counselors.

In the 1960s, the focus shifted from guidance as adjustment to developmental guidance. Developmental guidance stresses the importance of understanding and working with students from a developmental perspective. It also places greater emphasis on preventing the occurrence of problems rather than merely helping students adjust to their existing problems. School counselors continue to utilize the developmental perspective.

The 1970s involved an expansion of the developmental perspective to include a K–12 comprehensive developmental guidance model. During this period, there was also a national effort to integrate career education into the overall school program. This effort was met with resistance from some teachers and administrators because they believed it took valuable time away from necessary academic endeavors. Career education therefore had limited success in terms of being integrated into the public schools. The passage of Public Law 94-142, the Education for All Handicapped Children Act, in 1975 (Public Law 94-142,

1975) also affected the role of the school counselor. As a result of this act, school counselors expanded their role to include coordinating the testing and placement of exceptional students and assisting with the development and implementation of individual education programs for each student. Another force that had an impact on the role and function of the school counselor during this period was the use of personal computers in scoring tests, scheduling, and career counseling. In addition, school counselors began to incorporate group counseling in their guidance and counseling programs in the early 1970s.

During the 1980s, career guidance received renewed federal support. The Carl D. Perkins Vocational Education Act was passed in 1984 in response to the belief that public schools were not providing adequate preparation for students to obtain employment or continue post-secondary education. Several states have utilized funds from the Perkins bill to develop K–12 counseling and guidance programs. To qualify for these funds, states must provide opportunities for students to acquire employability skills. Another force that occurred in the 1980s was an awareness of the importance of multicultural issues in counseling. School counselors therefore began to modify their counseling approaches to include a multicultural perspective.

The decade of the 1980s was also a time of changes in the fabric of society that dramatically affected school-age children. During this period, school counselors witnessed substantial increases in divorce, suicides, drug and alcohol abuse, teenage pregnancies, and eating disorders. School counselors invested increasing amounts of energy in implementing prevention and treatment programs addressing these complex issues. Examples include drug prevention and awareness programs, group counseling for children of alcoholics and children of divorce, parent education, and family counseling. Also during this time, financially conscious educational systems began to scrutinize the effectiveness of school counseling. As a result, schools placed greater emphasis on counselor accountability.

School counseling in the 1990s faced many opportunities and challenges. Counselors continued to deal with an ongoing array of social problems that students faced, such as drug use, violence in the schools, teenage pregnancy, and school dropout. Diversity issues were also emphasized as counselors conceptualized their role and function.

Numerous challenges and opportunities face school counselors in the 21st century. One central challenge relates to job security for school counselors. Paisley and Borders (1995) note that one threat to school counselors is the trend toward downsizing and the movement to hire part-time employees to provide school counseling. The school-based mental-health movement is one example of how external funding is being used to bring in people from different disciplines in the helping profession to provide counseling services in schools.

The school-counseling reform movement associated with the Transforming School Counseling Initiative (Erford, House, & Martin, 2003) and the Education Trust (The Education Trust, 1999) are also beginning to reshape the school-counseling profession. For example, school counselors are being encouraged to establish school-community partnerships in the delivery of counseling services.

Romano and Kachgal (2004) suggest that school counseling and counseling psychology represent an underutilized partnership. These researchers suggest that these counseling specialties appear to be good candidates for collaboration since they both have roots in career counseling and human development and promote client strengths over deficits. Counseling psychologists have much to offer school counselors, such as supervision and research skills with regards to school community teamwork and collaboration. Counseling psychologists in turn can be enriched by their association with school counselors in terms of realigning their professional identity. For example, school counseling's developmental/ preventative perspective can be a welcomed alternative for counseling psychologists in terms of their recent emphasis on remediation in clinical work (Kenny, Waldo, Warter, & Barton, 2002). School counseling and counseling psychology therefore appear to represent an underutilized partnership that warrants further investigation (Romano & Kachgal, 2004).

The American School Counselor Association (ASCA) is also taking a role in redefining school counseling. The ASCA National Standards for School Counseling Programs (Campbell & Dahir, 1997) and the ASCA National Model (ASCA, 2003) provide a framework for developing and implementing school-counseling programs. The ASCA (1998) also has an ethical code that provides guidelines for professional practice.

Increased federal legislation (especially regarding students with exceptionalities) and other legal considerations are also having a major impact on education and the role and function of school counselors in the 21st century. For example, school counselors must be aware of the impact of legislative acts such as Section 504 of the Rehabilitation Act and the Individuals with Disabilities Education Act (IDEA) to ensure that issues of disability are considered in the educational process, including the manner by which students are disciplined. In addition, the Health Insurance Portability and Accountability Act (HIPPA) Privacy Rule provides safeguards regarding the security and privacy of individually identifiable health information.

The Current ASCA Role Statement, Definition, Standards, and National Model

In 1990 the ASCA revised its role statement of 1981. A significant change in the revised statement was the absence of the earlier differentiation in the role and function of counselors working in elementary, middle, and high schools. Instead, the statement identified five interventions that apply to all school counselors. The motivation for this change was to promote a clearer and more concise understanding of the overall role and function of school counselors.

In the statement, the ASCA recognized and supported the comprehensive developmental guidance and counseling model. In this regard, school counselors should adjust the counseling approach to the developmental levels of students as they progress through the educational system. The aim of school counseling is to promote educational, social, career, and personal development so that students can become responsible, productive citizens.

The statement also identified five basic interventions common to all school counselors. These are individual counseling; small-group counseling, which involves five to eight students; large-group guidance, which includes nine or more students such as in a classroom; consultation; and coordination of the counseling program. In addition, the ASCA recommends that the ratio between counselors and students should be 1:250 and school counselors should spend 70 percent of their time providing direct services to students (Lum, 1999).

In 1997 the ASCA adopted a new definition of school counseling:

> Counseling is a process of helping people by assisting them in making decisions and changing behavior. School counselors work with all students, school staff, families, and members of the community as an integral part of the education program. School counseling programs promote school success through a focus on academic achievement, prevention and intervention activities, advocacy and social/emotional and career development.

This definition of school counseling is consistent with the comprehensive developmental school-counseling movement, which is focused on prevention and maximizing the learning potential of all students.

Campbell and Dahir (1997) assisted the ASCA in establishing national standards that could be incorporated in a K–12 comprehensive school-counseling program. The national standards identified student competencies in three general areas: academic, career, and personal/social development. An example of a personal/social standard would be, "Students will acquire the attitudes, knowledge, and interpersonal skills to help them understand and respect self and others" (Campbell and Dahir, 1997, p. 17). The ASCA (2003) suggests that these national standards be conceptualized as content standards for students (i.e., things they should know and be able to do in school).

More recently the ASCA (2003) established the ASCA National Model, which provides a framework for developing and implementing a comprehensive K–12 school-counseling program. The ASCA National Model is based on a number of principles consistent with the evolution of school counseling. Some of these principles include the following:

- It is preventative/developmental in nature.
- It is a comprehensive K–12 program.
- It is an integral part of the mission of the school.

Romano and Kachgal (2004) note that the ASCA National Model incorporates principles and recommendations from the ASCA national standards (Campbell and Dahir, 1997), the Education Trust (The Education Trust, 1999), and the Transforming School Counseling Initiative (Erford et al., 2003). Four themes emerged from the ASCA National Model: leadership, advocacy, collaboration and teaming, and systemic change. Implementation of these themes promotes a shift in the role of the school counselor from an emphasis on direct services to a limited number of students with serious problems to systemic change that promotes positive outcomes for all students (e.g., enhanced school climate and school/community relationships). In addition, school counselors are encouraged to engage in leadership, advocacy, and teaming/collaboration to address barriers to learning so that all students can be successful and benefit from the program. For example, school counselors are encouraged to collaborate with counseling psychologists to create prevention programs.

The ASCA National Model also recommends that school-counseling programs be based on four central elements: a foundation, a delivery system, a management system, and accountability:

- *Foundation.* "Identifies *what* every student will be able to know and do" (ASCA, 2003, p. 22). It is based on the national standards for school counseling and describes the basic competencies that are addressed in the program.

- *Delivery system.* "Addresses *how* the program is implemented" (ASCA, 2003, p. 22). The delivery system utilizes four modes of delivery: guidance curriculum (developmental lessons presented in classroom and group activities); individual student planning (coordinating activities to assist students in establishing goals and plans); responsive services (addressing students' immediate needs through activities such as counseling, consultation, and referral); and systems support (activities that enhance the overall school-counseling program, such as professional development, collaboration, teaming, and program management).
- *Management system.* "Addresses the *when* (calendar and action plan), *why* (use of data) and *on what authority* (management agreement and advisory council) the program will be implemented" (ASCA, 2003, p. 22).
- *Accountability.* "The accountability system answers the question: 'How are students different as a result of the program?'" (ASCA, 2003, p. 23).

The ASCA National Model for school counseling appears to offer much promise to the field of school counseling and can be considered a zeitgeist in the evolution of the counseling field. The model provides a framework that can be used by school districts to develop and implement a comprehensive K–12 school-counseling program. Additional research and evaluation of the ASCA National Model will be necessary to evaluate its effect on promoting student competencies and educational success.

Role and Function by Grade Level and Setting

The literature provides extensive information about the specific goals and strategies for school counselors working with students at various levels and in various settings. For example, Hardesty and Dillard (1994) surveyed 369 school counselors in terms of the activities they perform at elementary, middle, and high schools. Results of the survey showed that elementary school counselors focus on consulting with teachers, staff, and parents and engage in small- and large-group guidance programs that have a preventative focus (for example, drug prevention). Middle school counselors direct their efforts primarily on relationships counseling (such on conflict resolution between students). Scheduling and other administrative tasks also rated high on the middle school counselors' activity list. High school counselors' top priorities include assisting with college or trade school admission (including help with scholarships and financial aid), career counseling, and scheduling and other administrative tasks. More specific information regarding the role and function of elementary, middle, and high school counselors follows.

Elementary School Counseling.   Elementary school includes students from kindergarten through the fifth grade. The emphasis of elementary school counseling is on prevention (Muro, 1981). In this regard, counselors spend a large percentage of their time consulting with teachers and parents to promote the child's mental health and in group guidance activities (such as self-concept development).

Several authors have attempted to describe the role and function of elementary school counselors. Morse and Russell (1988) surveyed 130 elementary school counselors in terms of how they perceive their current role and their ideal role. Their findings are summarized in Table 14.2, with actual and ideal roles each shown in rank order of importance to counselors.

TABLE 14.2   Actual Versus Ideal Roles of Elementary School Counselors

Rank Order of Actual Role	Rank Order of Ideal Role
Assist students with special needs by making appropriate educational referrals	Assist the teacher to better understand the needs of individual students
Work with school psychologist and educational specialist to meet the special needs of individual students	Provide group counseling to help students learn effective social skills
Provide individual counseling for students to help them understand their feelings	Work with students in groups to promote a positive self-concept
Help teachers better understand the needs of individual students	Counsel students in groups to help them become aware of their feelings
Work with students individually to promote a positive self-concept	Conduct groups to help students learn problem-solving skills

Source: Reprinted from Morse, C. L. and Russell, T., "How Elementary Counselors See Their Role: An Empirical Study," 1988, *Elementary School Guidance & Counseling, 23*(1), pp. 44–62. © ACA. Reprinted with permission. No further reproduction authorized without permission of the American Counseling Association.

Three interesting observations can be made from the survey results shown in Table 14.2. First, three of the top five functions listed as actual roles involve consultation. Second, these counselors ranked the function of helping teachers understand students' needs first as an ideal role, but only fourth as a function they currently perform. Third, four of the top five ideal roles indicate that counselors want to engage in more group counseling involving activities such as social-skills training. Results of this study emphasize the importance of elementary school counselors obtaining skills in consultation and group counseling.

Ginter, Scalise, and Presse (1990) conducted a study that surveyed 313 teachers in terms of their perceptions of elementary school counselors' role and function. Results of this study show that teachers view elementary school counselors as functioning primarily with the dual role of helper and consultant. The helper role entails activities such as individual and group counseling, assessment, interpreting tests, and conducting guidance activities. The consultant role involves providing technical advice and expertise to school staff and parents. The authors conclude that there appears to be congruence between how teachers and elementary school counselors view their role and function.

In another study, Miller (1989) surveyed teachers, principals, and parents to determine their views regarding the role and function of elementary school counselors. The survey identifies 28 functions that elementary school counselors were believed to fulfill. These functions related to six tasks: developmental or career guidance, consulting, counseling, evaluation and assessment, guidance program development, and coordination and management. Results of the survey show that teachers, principals, and parents strongly endorse these six tasks as being relevant functions for elementary school counselors. Miller (1989) believes the study provided grass-roots support for a developmental model of elementary school guidance and counseling. These studies collectively show recognition of the importance of the developmental model of counseling and the necessity for elementary school counselors to develop skills in direct services such as group counseling.

The following *Personal Note* relates to why I have found elementary school counseling very rewarding.

A Personal Note

I enjoyed working as an elementary school counselor. I liked the diversity of activities, which included play therapy, counseling, consulting, and working with parents. I also found children fun and exciting to work with because they are so open, spontaneous, and interested in exploring the world around them.

When I work with children, I feel a sense of optimism that real and lasting changes can be made. Their problems have usually not yet become well-established facets of their personality. I firmly believe that early intervention can prevent children's problems from blossoming into major mental disorders and can prevent them from becoming school dropouts. I often think that more of the educational and mental health budget should be invested in elementary school counseling. In the long run, I think it would be the most effective approach.

Middle School Counseling.   The middle school phenomenon is a relatively recent occurrence. This level of schooling provides educational opportunities for students from grades 6 through 8. This concept evolved from the junior high educational system, which encompassed grades 7 through 9. The middle school concept represents an attempt to group students together as they make their transition from childhood to adolescence.

The literature shows that the role and function of the middle school counselor are just beginning to be formulated. Bonebrake and Borgers (1984) conducted a study in which they compared the ideal role of middle school counselors as perceived by counselors and principals. Their results show essential agreement between the perceptions of counselors and principals. Both groups ranked individual counseling first in importance. Other tasks ranked high by both groups include consultation, coordination of student assessment, interpretation of tests, and evaluation of guidance programs. This study suggests that middle school counseling is similar to elementary school counseling in terms of the emphasis on consultation and direct services. One difference is that middle school counseling appears to place emphasis on individual counseling, whereas elementary school counseling stresses the importance of group counseling.

Conflict-resolution skills are important for all students. Middle school students seem to be particularly prone to problems with interpersonal conflict such as jealous reactions within peer groups. Conflict-resolution strategies can be used with couples, small groups, or a classroom. Dysinger (1993) provides some goals and objectives for conflict resolution for middle school students. These are summarized as follows. The overall goal is for the participants to attempt to create a win-win experience based on understanding, accepting disagreements, and working toward resolution, not establishing who is right and wrong. The actual process of conflict management can involve tasks such as helping students to (a) separate the problem from the person, (b) enhance their tolerance for individual differences, (c) create insight into how relationships deteriorate, (d) learn how to sensitively respond to conflict rather than abrasively react, and (e) become aware of choices and options.

One method of conflict resolution that can be used in a classroom is the inside-outside fishbowl approach (Nelson, Thomas, & Pierce, 1995). This is an Adlerian-based approach that attempts to foster encouragement and mutual respect among students. The process involves a facilitator working with a small group of students in a time-limited, focused discussion on a topic of concern while the rest of the class listens and provides feedback at the end of the discussion. The fishbowl approach can create opportunities to gain a broad perspective for understanding and resolving conflicts. As in all group work, issues regarding confidentiality and informed consent must be addressed.

Secondary School Counseling. The origins of secondary school counseling can be traced to the vocational guidance movement that began in the early 1900s. Since that time, secondary school counseling has maintained a close identity with vocational and career guidance and counseling. The role and function of secondary school counselors have centered on assisting students in making the transition from public school to post-secondary education, acquiring vocational training, and entering the world of work.

Secondary school counselors tend to be assigned numerous clerical tasks, including scheduling and administrative functions such as assistance with disciplinary programs. The result has been a loss of clear mission (Aubrey, 1982) and a "role mutation" that has seriously damaged the professional image of school counselors (Peer, 1985). Hutchinson, Barrick, and Groves (1986) provide evidence of the role mutation phenomenon cited by Peer (1985) in a study that compared actual and ideal functions of secondary school counselors. According to the study, counselors believe they should ideally provide the traditional counseling activities of personal, academic, and group counseling. In actual practice, however, scheduling requires more time than any activity except personal counseling. The authors conclude that counselors are performing noncounseling activities at the expense of more important functions such as group counseling, career and life planning, and classroom guidance. Tennyson, Miller, Skovholt, and Williams (1989) provide support for this observation by noting that scheduling of students appears to take a higher priority over the critical functions of promoting developmental guidance and counseling.

When high school counselors do engage in direct counseling services, they are often unable to invest the necessary time and energy because of the large numbers of students and conflicting role demands. Rowe (1989) surveyed the type and extent of involvement that high school counselors have with high school students. He found that counselors had sessions with 80 percent of the students who went to college. The primary purpose of their contact was to assist with college plans. Unfortunately, counselors averaged only two sessions with each student, for a total of 15 minutes. These students received the largest number of contacts—approximately five—regarding college planning from parents and friends. Results of this study suggest that high school counselors are not providing sufficient information about college planning, even though it is the main topic they are addressing with high school students (Rowe, 1989).

Rural School Counseling. The role and function of school counseling vary not only according to educational level but also in terms of rural versus urban settings. Sutton and Southworth (1990) report that rural counselors have fewer referral sources and must therefore rely on their own resources and become jacks-of-all-trades. This can contribute to rural counselors experiencing more job-related stress than do urban school counselors (Sutton & Southworth, 1990). At the same time, they feel more freedom, strength, optimism, and happiness than urban counselors (Sutton & Southworth, 1990). In addition, rural school counselors tend to have more positive relationships with their principals than do urban counselors (Sutton & Southworth, 1990). These relationships may result from rural counselors having more contact and involvement with their principals than do urban counselors (McIntire, Marion, & Quaglia, 1990).

McIntire et al. (1990) note that 40 percent of rural counselors do not work with other counselors and must therefore develop their own support systems. They also suggest that for counselors to be successful in rural settings, they must be aware of the special needs and circumstances of the community and become actively involved in the community.

More recently, Morrissette (2000) conducted research on rural school counseling that supports earlier research by McIntire et al. (1990) and Sutton and Southworth (1990). Morrissette found that rural school counseling is characterized by

- Lack of personal privacy and anonymity, thus minimizing personal space and freedom
- Feelings of isolation (e.g., having other school counselors with which to formulate a distinct professional identity)
- A lack of community resources, requiring school counselors to be generalists and handle a wide range of problems
- Continuity of relationships with students that enable school counselors to get to know their students and their families over a long period of time

Rubisch (1995) notes that students in rural schools face special challenges in terms of promoting post-secondary education. Three interrelated problems are academic runoff, low self-esteem, and low career expectations. *Academic runoff* involves the brightest students leaving the rural community and not returning, which reduces the amount of role models and mentors available for students. This in turn can have an adverse effect on students' self-esteem and career expectations. Rubisch contends that rural school counselors can play a pivotal role in enhancing student's career aspirations by exposing them to post-secondary educational alternatives in junior and middle school, including field trips to college campuses.

Special Skills and Problems

This section discusses the special skills and problems associated with school counseling. These include consultation, counseling exceptional students, and some of the special problems that students face: drug abuse, teenage pregnancy, divorced or single parents, and dropping out of school.

Consultation

Dougherty (1995) defines consultation as "a process in which a human service professional assists a consultee with a work-related (or caretaking-related) problem with a client system, with the goal of helping both the consultee and the client system in some specified way" (p. 9). The individual who functions as a consultee varies according to the situation and may be a parent or teacher requesting assistance on how to provide effective discipline for a child so the child can function better at home or school.

Consultation with teachers is an integral aspect of school counseling.

Dougherty's (1995) four stages of consultation are summarized as follows.

Stage One: Entry.   Consultation begins with the consultant formulating a relationship with the consultee, determining the nature of the problem, and formulating a contract regarding the nature and scope of the consultation activities.

Stage Two: Diagnosis.   Diagnosis involves making an assessment of the problem and determining possible goals and objectives.

Stage Three: Implementation.   Once a diagnosis is made, an action plan can be formulated, implemented, and evaluated.

Stage Four: Disengagement.   When the goals and objectives have been met, consultation processes can allow for a natural process of disengagement or "winding down" of services.
Dougherty (1995) also identifies the following three models of consultation.

1. *Organizational consultation* conceptualizes the problem and directs interventions from a systems or organizational perspective.
2. *Mental health consultation* conceptualizes the problem and directs interventions with the goal of enhancing the mental health of individuals within the organizational structure.
3. *Behavioral consultation* takes a behavioral perspective (such as social-learning theory) in terms of conceptualizing problems and implementing interventions.

Dougherty (1995) notes that these three models are interrelated and that all consultation to some degree utilizes all three perspectives (that is, it focuses on behaviors and the overall system to enhance mental health).

School Consultation.   Hall and Lin (1994) note that consultation is one of the primary functions of school counselors and involves providing assistance to teachers, parents, and administrators. Hall and Lin developed an integrative model of school consultation based on Dougherty's (1995) four-stage model of consultation (entry, diagnosis, implementation, and disengagement). These authors address some special considerations in school consultation, such as potential confusion in terms of role expectations since the consultant and consultee will typically know each other and work in the same building (for example, counselor-teacher or counselor-administrator). In these instances, they recommend that expectations be made clear during the entry phase of consultation and that the use of empathy, genuineness, respect, and concreteness be used to facilitate this process.

The following *Personal Note* provides an example of how a school counselor conceptualized consultation in her problem-solving model.

Hall and Lin (1994) suggest that consultation is especially important to the role and function of elementary school counselors. To a large degree, the success of consultation in elementary school can be traced to the pioneering work of Don Dinkmeyer and Jon Carlson, who were able to demonstrate how Adlerian principles can be used effectively in consulting with teachers, administrators, and parents (Dinkmeyer & Carlson, 1973). Dinkmeyer (1971, 1973) developed a collaborative model of consultation called the "C" group model, which can be used with groups of parents and teachers. The "C" group model was designed to create a channel for communication regarding issues pertaining to children, such as how to deal with children's misbehavior. It was so-called because the forces that operate in the group begin with the letter C: collaboration, consultation, clarification, confrontation, communication, concern, caring, confidentiality, change, and cohesion.

Opportunities exist for school counselors to provide consultation services at all levels of public schools. Griggs (1988) suggests that school counselors should expand their consultation role to become facilitators of learning. Ferris (1988) also notes that consultation is needed to provide safe, secure, and positive learning environments.

A Personal Note

While I was teaching a school counseling course, I asked my wife, Laura (an elementary school counselor), if she had any material that would illustrate what school counselors do. She smiled and showed me a flowchart she recently developed that describes what happens when a child is referred for counseling services. The flowchart (shown in Figure 14.1) provides a description of how she addresses problems that are presented by students in her school. The flowchart also communicates to staff, teachers, and parents what procedures she utilizes in the referral process. In addition, the flowchart is a required part of the Baldridge accountability program utilized in her school (all staff/teachers are required to develop flowcharts to depict tasks they perform).

Laura posited that her flowchart was not meant to be a blueprint for how school counselors

should address problems. She also noted that she did not apply the flowchart in a rigid fashion but would modify it to address special issues as necessary.

In addition, the flowchart provides an illustration of the role of consultation in the school-counseling process. Consultation in school counseling encourages ongoing communication and input from stakeholders. Consultation may be unique in school counseling because it occurs so often, interfacing with many aspects of the counseling process. Many consults are informal interactions, such as a teacher "running a problem by" the school counselor for informal input. The flowchart also provides an illustration of other aspects of the school-counseling process, such as obtaining informed consent from parents/guardians and how referral to a specialist may be required as part of the problem-solving process.

(continued)

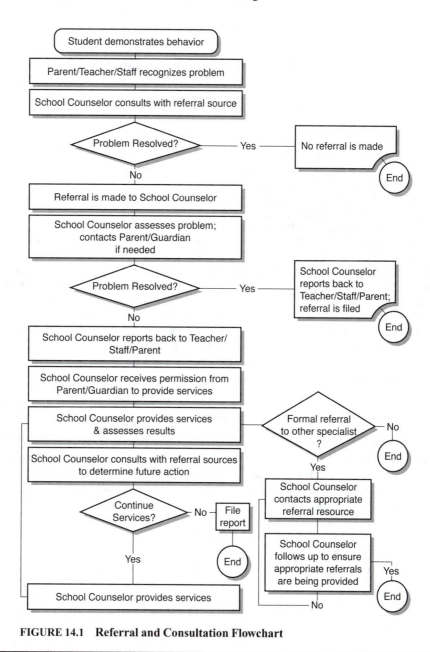

FIGURE 14.1 Referral and Consultation Flowchart

Ritchie and Partin (1994) have conducted a survey of school counselors on the merits of parent education as a consultative service. Results of the survey show wide support for parent education among school counselors. Although 84 percent of the school counselors surveyed recognized the need for parenting consultation, only half have offered training and have an interest in providing this service. There appears to be a gender and grade-level bias in parent education, with more female counselors expressing interest and higher levels of involvement associated with elementary school counseling. Perhaps counselor educators need to focus more on this form of school consultation to enhance involvement in this area.

The following *Personal Note* describes some of the rewards I have experienced in consultation in schools.

A Personal Note

Some of my most rewarding experiences over the years have involved consultation with teachers, parents, and staff. It is really exciting to see these individuals gain skills and confidence that they can use to overcome problems and enhance their life experiences. I see consultation as having the goal of educating for empowerment. In this process I attempt to share information and strategies in a manner that can be easily understood and applied. I begin with sharing tools for understanding problems (such as why children misbehave) because I believe that understanding should always be a prerequisite to change. In addition, I contend that understanding can foster connecting, which in turn can lead to caring and compassion between people. And the caring and empathy between people can often be an important first step toward overcoming problems.

Tools for change can then be explored in relation to the client's concerns. This, as in all phases of consultation, must be a highly individualized process that takes into consideration issues of diversity and the client's phenomenological perspective. In this regard, I believe that for consultation to be successful, it must be something that has meaning in terms of the client's worldview and can be integrated into the client's internal frame of reference. The outcome of consultation is therefore for clients to achieve a heightened state of self-efficacy regarding the development of skills to understand and solve problems.

Counseling Exceptional Students

Glenn (1998) estimates that between 10 and 12 percent of (40 to 50 million) school-age children in the United States have some recognized exceptionality. Issues that relate to counseling exceptional students have had a major impact on school counseling. An exceptional student can be defined as an individual whose physical or behavioral condition deviates from the norm in a manner that requires special services to meet the individual's needs (Hardman, Drew, Egan, & Wolf, 2002). The following provides an overview of legislative acts and guidelines for counseling exceptional students.

Legislative Acts.   Several federal laws have been passed that have had a direct impact on exceptional students in terms of identifying and educating them. Key legislative efforts have included Public Law 94-142, the Americans with Disabilities Act, Section 504 of the Rehabilitation Act, and IDEA legislation. A brief overview of these legislative acts follows.

The passage of the Education for All Handicapped Children Act (Public Law 94-142) in 1975 and the Americans with Disabilities Act (Public Law 101-306) in 1990 had a major impact on education and school counseling. Public Law 94-142 provided for public education within the least restrictive environment for all students with disabilities. Cole (1988) observes that this law has had a dramatic effect on the role of the school counselor. She observes that in many schools, the counselor has become the case manager for exceptional students. This role requires counselors to devote enormous amounts of time to coordination activities such as handling paperwork, attending meetings, and placing students. In addition, counselors have become more involved in providing counseling services to disabled students and their families.

The Americans with Disabilities Act's goal is to ensure civil rights protection to people who have disabilities (Helwig & Holicky, 1994). This landmark legislation prohibits discrimination in employment, public services (including education), transportation, and telecommunication (Parette & Hourcade, 1995). Parette and Hourcade (1995) go on to note that there can be physical, policy, and procedural barriers that can contribute to discrimination against individuals with disabilities. This includes equal access to all public places, such as wheelchair ramps providing access to schools and libraries.

Two more recent trends in education relate to Section 504 and IDEA. These two forms of federal legislation are playing key roles in educational reform in terms of individualizing education according to disabilities. These laws are redefining educational policies and procedures, creating enormous opportunities and challenges for educators.

In 1990, PL 94-142 was renamed the Individuals with Disabilities Education Act (IDEA). IDEA legislation is updated every three to five years and covers the policies and procedures regarding the assessment, placement, education, and discipline of students with disabilities. IDEA guidelines are used to qualify students for special education services relating to a number of disabilities, such as physical, intellectual, and emotional disabilities. Once students have been placed in special education services, individual education programs (IEPs) are developed according to their special needs. IDEA legislation also ensures that disciplinary procedures take into consideration students' disabilities and avoid penalizing students for misbehavior that was the result of a disability. When possible, schools must first attempt to adjust students IEPs to remediate problems associated with misbehavior.

Section 504 of the Rehabilitation Act of 1973 provides additional assistance to disabled students. Students who do not meet the full criteria as disabled according to IDEA may still be considered disabled if they have physical or mental impairments that substantially limit their ability to learn and function at school. These students are not classified as special education students.

Examples of 504 disabilities are medical conditions such as a broken arm or being HIV positive, substance-abuse problems, or students who have attention-deficit hyperactivity disorder but who do not qualify for special education. Students who are identified as fulfilling the criteria of 504 are entitled to receive special accommodations regarding their disabilities. For example, if a student has a broken leg, the student can be given extra time to get to class. Other modifications and special considerations can also be required for 504 students, such as enhanced physical access to school facilities, individualization of the educational program, and ongoing assessment and reevaluation as a prerequisite to educational placement. As was the case with IDEA, 504 requires disciplinary action to take into consideration students' disabilities. For example, common disciplinary actions such as suspension will probably not be appropriate if the students' misbehavior was due to their disability.

IDEA and 504 legislation offer opportunities and challenges for school counselors. Opportunities are associated with the establishment of policies and procedures that encourage consideration of diversity issues associated with students' disabilities. Individualizing education helps identify special needs and conditions that may undermine the learning process. Individualization of rules and policies can also be a very taxing process for educators. Special challenges that present themselves can include legislative restrictions in discipline, which may impede attempts to keep schools safe from student violence and aggression. School counselors can play an important role in educational reform by ensuring that federal guidelines are applied in a manner that maximizes the learning potential for all disabled students.

School counselors may wish to take a leadership role in terms of emerging legislative acts such as Section 504 and IDEA. Appropriate implementation of these laws is considered a high priority in school districts to ensure dissemination of available federal and state funding, to avoid lawsuits and time-consuming legal action, and to promote safeguards and educational opportunities for students.

The Health Insurance Portability and Accountability Act (HIPAA) of 1996 and the HIPAA Privacy Rule of 2003 (Code of Federal Regulations, Title 45, Part 164) have wide implications for how health care information is communicated. HIPPA required the U.S. Department of Health and Human Services to create a series of rules to safeguard health-related information. HIPPA legislation relates to medical and mental health issues and can therefore affect school health care workers, such as nurses, psychologists, and physiotherapists. Particular concern relates to issues of confidentiality and the release of health-related information (e.g., under what conditions information can be released to a third party).

Implementation of the various federal mandates described above is an extremely complex process requiring various legal-ethical decision-making skills. School counselors can play a role in facilitating programs such as Section 504 to ensure that all students (regardless of their disability) have access to equal educational opportunities. Involvement in these legislative acts creates opportunities for school counselors to perform highly specialized and essential services. This can go a long way in disbanding the perception that school counselors lack specialized, essential skills and are therefore in danger of becoming obsolete.

Guidelines for Counseling Exceptional Students. Helwig and Holicky (1994) suggest that school counselors should be familiar with the special needs and services associated with different types of disabilities. It has therefore become important for school counselors to be aware of the special issues associated with counseling exceptional students.

Perhaps the most basic guideline for counseling exceptional students is to consider that these individuals are more similar to those without disabilities than they are different (McDowell, Coven, & Eash, 1979). Exceptional students should therefore be treated as unique individuals first and people with special needs second. This focus can help counselors become sensitive to individual differences and avoid stereotyping clients.

A second guideline for counselors is to be aware of the common problems that exceptional students face. Ciechalski and Schmidt (1995) note that students with exceptionalities often lack social skills and have problems with interpersonal relationships. These authors found that social-skills training has a positive effect on the social relationships of exceptional students and that the benefits can be enhanced by involvement with non-special-education students. Rotatori, Banbury, and Sisterhen (1986) also note that students with exceptionalities also tend to have problems with self-concept, body image, frustration, and dependency.

Bello (1989) suggests that students with disabilities tend to suffer self-concept problems as a result of a history of frustration and failure. These failure-oriented experiences can contribute to irrational beliefs such as "I am not able to do school work"; "People think I'm dumb"; and "In order to be successful, I must be able to do as well as nondisabled people" (Bello, 1989). Bello (1989) therefore recommends that cognitive approaches can play a key role in helping students overcome a failure orientation and improve their self-concept.

Exceptional students whose bodies have physical abnormalities may be particularly prone to interpersonal difficulties (Goldberg, 1974). In addition, parents tend to discourage these students from exploring their bodies, contributing to a sense of denial (McDowell et al., 1979). Rotatori, Banbury, and Sisterhen (1986) therefore recommend that these students be encouraged to explore their bodies and accept their particular disabling condition.

Rotatori, Banbury, and Sisterhen (1986) suggest that exceptional students can become frustrated when they do not feel they can measure up to expectations. In addition, they note that a disabling condition limits opportunities for participation, that exceptional students' confidence or competence are threatened, and that they do not feel support. Frustration can lead to behavioral problems such as aggression (Talkington & Riley, 1971), sarcasm and cynicism (McDowell et al., 1979), and stubbornness (Clarizio & McCoy, 1983). Counseling strategies can be directed at resolving frustration by providing a means for venting the negative emotions and fostering competency skills that prevent frustration (Rotatori, Banbury, & Sisterhen, 1986).

It is not uncommon for parents and teachers to foster dependency in an exceptional student because they believe the individual is incapable of functioning independently. Overdependent students can lack motivation and experience academic difficulties. They can also be easily influenced by peer pressure, resulting in inappropriate behavior (Rotatori, Banbury, & Sisterhen, 1986). Counseling strategies should be directed at helping these students feel capable, maximizing their self-confidence, and promoting self-reliance.

A third guideline for counseling exceptional students is to be aware of the special needs and counseling strategies associated with the various types of exceptionality. For example, mentally retarded students tend to experience social and emotional problems due to rigid behavior. Behavior therapy has been proven effective with this population to teach self-help skills, enhance social skills, and eliminate inappropriate behavior. Table 14.3 incorporates information from Rotatori, Gerber, Litton, and Fox (1986) and Parette and Hourcade (1995) to provide a description of the special needs, counseling goals, and associated counseling strategies for nine categories of exceptionality.

The following *Personal Note* provides information on how pet therapy can be used on students with exceptionalities.

A Personal Note

I have found that pet therapy is an excellent tool for working with clients of all ages, especially with students with exceptionalities. Pet therapy involves using animals such as dogs, cats, birds, fish, and horses to help individuals overcome various kinds of physical and emotional problems. I first learned of pet therapy from Dr. Herman Salk, the brother of Dr. Jonas Salk, the person who developed the polio vaccine. I met Herman when I worked on the Navajo Indian reservation. He was a veterinarian and had used pet therapy in a wide variety of settings. I was inspired by the passion he had for animals and his method of using pet therapy to overcome communication barriers, foster positive relationships, and enhance social interest.

Over the years, I have used pet therapy in a wide variety of settings, in nursing homes, schools, mental health clinics, and hospitals. My research on pet therapy has shown that it can help promote physical and mental health (Nystul, Emmons, & Cockrell, 1992). For example, hospitalized patients tend to have a higher survival rate and faster recovery if they have a pet to go home to. Pet therapy has also been used to help individuals overcome shyness, aid in self-confidence, and provide a means of working through emotional disorders.

(continued)

Pet therapy appears to be particularly useful in counseling exceptional students. Pets, such as seeing-eye dogs for the visually impaired, can provide meaningful stimulation and facilitation of sensory modalities. Pets can also be useful with seriously emotionally disturbed students. For example, caring for a pet can help a student overcome problems with anger management. Counselors may also bring a pet to a counseling session to overcome problems with resistance and to enhance the counseling relationship. A friend of mine used to bring her parrot to work with her. The parrot was very friendly and would talk to her clients. As you can imagine, she was very popular and always had an abundant supply of students who wanted to see her. Naturally, some schools may have a policy against bringing pets to school.

I once was treating a suicidal student. With the approval of her parents, I was able to have her pick a pet out of the local animal shelter and adopt it as her own. I explained to the student that she would be saving a life instead of taking a life. This seemed to bring meaning to her life and the suicidal ideations soon subsided. I have been amazed by the profound effects that pets have on people. I encourage you to explore this exciting dimension to the counseling process.

TABLE 14.3 Counseling Exceptional Children

Disorder	Special Needs or Problems	Counseling Goals	Counseling Strategies
Mentally retarded students (Litton, 1986; Parette & Hourcade, 1995)	High incidence of social-emotional problems due to rigid behavior; restricted life experience; problems perceiving personal and social situations	Improve social adaptation; enhance self-help skills; increase awareness of self and others; assist with development of interpersonal relations skills; promote a positive self-image	Behavior therapy to teach self-help skills, enhance social skills, and eliminate inappropriate behavior. Be clear and concise when communicating; limit the number of directions; communicate respect; provide positive feedback when possible.
Learning-disabled students (Gerber, 1986)	Poor self-concept and self-esteem; tendency to be rejected by peers; lack of self-appraisal skills; fear of failure; test anxiety; lack of motivation	Enhance self-esteem and self-concept; promote effective social skills; help overcome fear of failure; promote a positive attitude toward the learning process	Self-concept programs, interpersonal relations training, and cognitive-behavioral approaches to overcome a fear of failure.
Mildly behaviorally disordered students (Raiche, Fox, & Rotatori, 1986; Parette & Hourcade, 1995)	Problems with impulse control, aggression, and defiance; emotional problems; hyperactivity; academic problems	Increase frustration tolerance and self-restraint; help overcome academic difficulties; improve interpersonal relations skills	Cognitive-behavioral techniques to teach anger control, play therapy and group counseling to assist with social-emotional problems, interpersonal relations training to enhance social skills. When a student misbehaves, don't overreact. Also, ask concrete, direct questions.

TABLE 14.3 Continued

Disorder	Special Needs or Problems	Counseling Goals	Counseling Strategies
Speech- or language-disordered students (Kelley & Rotatori, 1986)	Interpersonal problems resulting from exclusion, overprotection, and ridicule; educational difficulties; self-esteem problems; anxiety	Help develop coping mechanisms to deal effectively with negative remarks of peers; help broaden and adapt communication skills to various settings; improve interpersonal relations skills; enhance self-concept and self-esteem; overcome educational difficulties	Cognitive-behavioral approaches to deal effectively with negative remarks, self-concept programs and communication development in small groups.
Hearing impaired students (Sisterhen & Rotatori, 1986; Parette & Hourcade, 1995)	Language difficulties, including problems with articulation and voice quality, vocabulary, syntax, and grammar; social-emotional problems such as social isolation, emotional immaturity, behavioral problems, difficulty with interpersonal relations, identity problems	Assist with identity formation; encourage independence; help develop appropriate social skills (for example, reduce tendencies to appear physically aggressive)	Behavioral counseling strategies that incorporate social modeling (particularly effective since deaf children tend to follow examples set by significant others); guidance programs that focus on self-concept development to promote identity formation. Speak directly to the student and look toward the student (not at an interpreter) to make it clear that your communication is directed at the student. Also, speak slowly and clearly and emphasize nonverbal communication such as facial expressions and gestures.

(continued)

TABLE 14.3   Continued

Disorder	Special Needs or Problems	Counseling Goals	Counseling Strategies
Visually impaired students (Heinze & Rotatori, 1986)	Low self-confidence; low self-concept; self-criticism; social isolation	Increase self-confidence; improve self image; reduce tendencies toward self-criticism and social isolation	Assertiveness training to help increase self-confidence; cognitive-behavioral approaches to reduce tendencies toward self-criticism; inter-personal relations train-ing to increase social interest. Introduce your-self before you begin talk-ing and cue the student when a discussion is about to end and you are going to leave. Offer assistance if the student looks con-fused. If necessary, pro-vide assistance that meets the student's needs.
Physically disabled students (Griffin, Sexton, Gerber, & Rotatori, 1986; Parette & Hourcade, 1995)	Problems vary according to disability type: some need assistance with basic functioning such as eating, personal hygiene, and locomotion; others need assistance in establishing intimate relationships (including sexuality) or dealing with ridicule	Help identify personal strengths to overcome physical disabilities; encourage students to become involved in self-advocacy to foster a sense of self-control over their life	Adlerian counseling to help identify strengths to overcome weaknesses; existential approaches to help discover personal meaning in life; sex education and sex therapy to help deal with sexuality issues. Sit when talking with someone in a wheelchair to maintain appropriate eye contact (that is, avoid talking down to the student).
Health-impaired students (Griffin, Gerber, & Rotatori, 1986)	Health problems such as leukemia, diabetes, asthma, or a seizure disorder that can interfere with academic functioning or psychosocial development	Alleviate anxiety, depression, and bodily discomfort; maximize bodily functioning; assist with academic difficulties	Cognitive-behavioral strategies for anxiety and depression; stress-management techniques and an exercise program to maximize bodily functioning; family ther-apy to help with familial factors associated with a seriously ill individual.

TABLE 14.3   Continued

Disorder	Special Needs or Problems	Counseling Goals	Counseling Strategies
Gifted students (Kaufmann, Castellanos, & Rotatori, 1986)	Difficulties with peer relations due to being singled out as the "brain of the class"; lack of motivation and under-achievement when not challenged	Increase awareness of self and others; enhance problem-solving and decision-making skills; clarify values and personal aspirations; maximize intellectual potential	Appropriate classroom placement to ensure adequate academic challenge; career counseling (including the use of a mentor) to encourage pursuing personal goals and aspirations; personal counseling to increase awareness of self in relation to others.
Abused students (Kennell & Rotatori, 1986)	Multitude of problems such as dependency, anger, depression, anxiety, self-blame, withdrawal, low self-esteem, interpersonal relations, educational problems	Improve self-image; promote positive inter-personal relations skills; assist with anger control; alleviate anxiety and depression; help overcome educational difficulties	Counseling strategies that focus on helping students realize that they were not responsible for what happened, that the abuse was wrong, and that it will stop; self-concept development programs; cognitive-behavioral approaches to promote anger control and alleviate depression.

Source: From *Counseling Exceptional Students* by A. F. Rotatori, P. J. Gerber, F. W. Litton, & R. A. Fox (Eds.), 1986, New York: Human Sciences Press. Copyright 1986 by Human Sciences Press. Reprinted by permission.

Special Problems

Students do not have to be exceptional to encounter problems in school. They face an increasingly diverse array of problems and challenges as they progress through the school years. McWhirter, McWhirter, McWhirter, and McWhirter (1994) have identified the "five Cs of Competency" that are associated with students doing well in life. These qualities are critical school competencies (including basic academic skills), the concept of self and self-esteem, communication skills, coping skills, and a sense of control. Students who lack these qualities are at a high risk for self-destructive behaviors such as school violence, substance abuse, teenage pregnancy, and school dropout (McWhirter et al., 1994). An overview of these and other problems and challenges follows.

School Violence.   School violence involving fighting, bullying, and fatal shootings is on the increase. A nationwide survey of 15,000 students in 2000 shows that 37 percent of middle school boys and 43 percent of high school boys believe that it is OK "to hit or threaten a person that makes me angry" (Josephson Institute of Ethics, 2001). In addition, the survey shows that 75 percent of male students and 68 percent of female students had hit someone who made them angry in the past year. Perhaps more concerning is the fact that 11 percent of middle school students and 14 percent of high school students had taken a weapon to school in the past year, and 31 percent of middle school boys and 60 percent of high school boys said they can get a gun if they want to. With the high incidences of aggression and violence in schools, it is not surprising that 39 percent of middle schools students and 36 percent of high school students report that they did not feel safe in school.

A number of factors are believed to contribute to school violence. For example, Popkin (2000) emphasizes the role of the media (television, music, video games, the Internet) in promoting youth violence. Popkin suggests that up to 15 percent of violence can be directly related to violence in the media. Other factors associated with youth violence cited by Popkin include family dysfunction and societal values that promote getting even over social interest. Popkin goes on to suggest that positive parenting programs and spirituality that promotes forgiveness over revenge can play an important role in overcoming youth violence.

Bullying has been receiving considerable attention as a possible factor associated with school violence. Bullying can be defined as teasing, harassing, or taking advantage of someone less powerful. Bullying is widespread, with 41 percent of respondents claiming they have been picked on in school (Labi, 2001). Bullying has been linked to fostering a negative school climate and to school violence, including suicide and homicide. For example, the U.S. Secret Service found that 37 percent of school shootings involved a shooter who at one time had felt bullied, threatened, or had been the victim of violence (Labi, 2001). In addition, individuals who engage in bullying have a fourfold increased risk of engaging in criminal behavior by the time they reach early childhood (Spivak & Prothrow-Stith, 2001).

A number of schools have implemented programs to address the problem of bullying. Labi (2001)and Lazar (2001) summarize these programs as follows:

- School climates need to be changed so that students do not feel it is appropriate to bully. For example, parents and students can sign a contract at the beginning of the school year agreeing that students should not be teased or harassed because of their appearance, gender, race, performance, and so forth.
- Skill improvement in areas such as problem solving, conflict resolution, moral-ethical decision making, character building, as well as assertiveness training can help prevent aggression and bullying before it starts.
- Students, teachers, administrators, staff, and parents need to agree not to tolerate bullying and to report it when it occurs.
- Training on bullying intervention is necessary.

School counselors can play a vital role in implementing anti-bullying programs, thereby promoting positive school climates and safer schools. Beale and Scott (2001) describe how school counselors can use psychoeducational drama with the victims of bullying (to empower) and bullies themselves (to overcome bullying tendencies).

School counselors can also promote safe schools by working with school personnel such as school psychologists to identify students who are at a high risk for engaging in violent acts. Hawkins et al. (2000) identify an extensive list of potential risk factors associated with youth violence. Potential risk factors associated with violence can be especially useful in assessing students' threats to harm other students. Examples of risk factors are as follows:

- Having a mental disorder (especially substance abuse), participating in antisocial behavior, and having deviant beliefs
- Being in a victim role (such as having been abused or bullied)
- Being socially isolated and lacking social ties
- Having low levels of parental involvement
- Having a history of violence and aggression (especially early onset)
- Experiencing high levels of exposure to crime and delinquency at school, at home, or in one's neighborhood
- Experiencing academic failure, truancy, and lack of bonding to school
- Having easy access to firearms

Several violence-prevention programs have emerged that address school violence. D'Andrea (2004) has developed a comprehensive school-based violence prevention training model that focuses on providing training on violence prevention to administrators, counselors, and teachers. Topics covered in this model include such issues as identifying early warning signs of violence and developing and implementing intervention strategies associated with violence prevention. Smith and Sandhu (2004) recommend taking a positive approach to violence prevention that focuses on building connections. The overall goal of this approach is to enhance the well-being and optimal development of students. These authors contend that violence prevention is directly related to the students' ability to connect with their school and peer group. Developmental tasks associated with violence prevention include

- Secure attachment with family
- Awareness of self and others
- Emotional literacy (e.g., understanding and expressing emotions)
- Self-regulation (e.g., anger management and impulse control)
- Resiliency (e.g., ability to handle stress)

As schools continue to investigate ways to make their environment safe, school counselors can play an important role in preventing violence and promoting a positive school climate. This can involve promoting anti-bullying programs, identifying students at high risk for violence, training staff and others on violence prevention, helping students make meaningful connections, and initiating other innovative programs and activities.

The following *Personal Note* relates to my experience with violence prevention in schools.

Substance Use and Abuse. In this discussion, the term *substance use* refers to alcohol, cigarettes, and illicit drugs such as cocaine, marijuana, or heroin. Substance use among students in the United States continues to rise, with an estimated 5.5 million Americans in need of treatment for substance abuse (Mason, 1996). The cost of substance abuse to society has been estimated in the billions of dollars, and the psychological cost in terms of human suffering is incalculable (Mason, 1996).

A Personal Note

I have been providing services as a school psychologist one day a week for over 12 years. Recently, I developed a school-wide violence-prevention program aimed at identifying students who pose a serious risk of harm to others. My initial efforts focused on assessing students who made verbal threats to harm others. Several scholars have provided recommendations from the U.S. Secret Service regarding violence prediction (Reddy et al., 2001; Vossekuil, Reddy, & Fein, 2001). The U.S. Secret Service notes that school officials often do not hear about threats that result in shootings. Shooters often tell students before a shooting, but do not tell adults. The U.S. Secret Service contends that focusing on identifying students who appear to be on psychological and behavioral pathways associated with violence (e.g., students who are obsessing about guns and getting even) is often more productive than simply assessing verbal threats.

I developed a three-level threat-assessment system based on an extensive literature review of existing programs. Level 1 can be used by individuals who have little formal background in threat assessment or by individuals who want to perform a quick threat assessment. Level 2 can be used by individuals with some formal training in threat assessment, such as a school counselor. Level 2 provides a comprehensive assessment of threats. Level 3 can be used by individuals with in-depth training in threat assessment, such as licensed psychologists. Level 3 is the most in-depth assessment and provides a comprehensive clinical assessment of threats.

Level 1 threat assessment includes

- Assessment of the threat in terms of a description of the threat; whether there is a means, motive, plan, and intent (MMPI); and according to FBI guidelines identified by O'Tolle (1999) for assessing a threat
- Exploration of psychological and behavioral pathways associated with violence
- Summary and recommendations

Level 2 comprehensive threat assessment includes the same sections as Level 1 plus the following:

- Assessment of risk factors, including history of mental disorders; traumatic brain injury;

violence, aggression, and belligerence; being in the victim role (including child abuse or involvement in bullying); and being exposed to domestic violence
- Assessment of FBI guidelines addressing personality, social, family, and school dynamics

Level 3 comprehensive clinical threat assessment includes the same sections as Levels 1 and 2 plus the following:

- A clinical interview including academic, medical, and developmental history and a mental-status exam

Once I had my three-level assessment program in place, I worked with central administration to develop a district-wide threat-assessment policy. The policy required a number of procedures, such as school principals ensuring that a threat assessment would take place if a student brought a weapon to school, made what appeared to be a serious threat, or was perceived to be on a psychological or behavioral pathway associated with violence. Staff throughout the school (including school counselors, social workers, school psychologists, principals, and assistant principals) were required to attend training on threat assessment.

Initially, principals were reluctant to participate in the inservice training. I was able to get their full cooperation when I informed them that if they could document that they had training in threat assessment and could show they were following school policy regarding threat assessment, they would be in a much better position to garner school-district support if something went wrong (e.g., if a student shot another student).

It has been one year since I began my inservice training program. Follow-up research conducted at the end of last year provided evidence that participants were using skills they learned at the workshop to assess threats and that they felt the training did promote safer schools. The superintendent's office has informed me that they want continued inservice training on violence provocation strategies.

A survey conducted in 2000 (Josephson Institute of Ethics, 2001) provides information on drug and alcohol use for middle and high school students. This survey reports that 24 percent of middle school students and 66 percent of high school students believe they can get drugs if they want to; 14 percent of middle school students and 37 percent of high school students had used illegal drugs during the previous year; and 7 percent of middle school students and 16 percent of high school students had been drunk at school within the previous year. In addition, Hubbard, Brownlee, and Anderson (1988) report that many students initiate substance use during the middle school years. Kluger (2001) cites recent research showing that students who begin drinking before the age of 15 have significantly higher risk for problems than those who start drinking after age 15. Early drinkers, as compared to those who start drinking after age 15, have five times the risk of developing alcohol dependence, ten times the risk of being involved in a fight while drinking, seven times the risk of being in a car accident, and twelve times the risk of being seriously injured. There are clearly more reasons than ever for school counselors to develop interventions that prevent the early experimentation with alcohol and other substances at the elementary and middle school levels.

Newcomb and Bentler (1988) have identified factors associated with substance use and abuse. High levels of drug use are related to limited educational pursuits and early marriages. Polydrug use, or the use of many drugs, among teenagers is associated with their later difficulty as young adults in role acquisition (for example, as a spouse or an employer). Heavy use of so-called hard drugs is associated with loneliness, drop in social support, psychoticism, and suicidal tendencies.

Newcomb and Bentler (1989) provide information on the etiology, or cause, of substance use and abuse. These authors note that *use* is prompted most by peer influence, whereas *abuse* stems from internal psychological distress. They also identify risk factors associated with substance use and abuse, including a personal history of drug use, use by peers, a lower socioeconomic level, family dysfunction, a family history of abuse, poor school performance, low self-esteem, lack of abidance with the law, need for excitement, stressful life events, and anxiety and depression.

Children of alcoholics (COA) are a particularly high risk group for developing drug and alcohol problems (Vail-Smith, Knight & White, 1995). Vail-Smith et al. (1995) find that a substantial number of elementary school students are COA and require special help. Some of the special problems associated with COA include negative emotions such as anger (Clair & Genest, 1987), low self-esteem (Werner, 1986), and an external locus of control (Werner, 1986). Vail-Smith et al. (1995) note that elementary school counselors are in a particularly good position to provide services to COA. These services include fostering resiliency skills to help these students cope with family dysfunction (Vail-Smith et al., 1995). In addition, Brake (1988) suggests that group counseling that focuses on the special problems of COA can be beneficial for this population.

Preventive programs for substance abuse have received much attention in the literature. Two studies conducted meta-analyses of the literature. Bangert-Drowns (1988) found that none of the existing preventive programs had any appreciable effect on reducing substance use or abuse. Tobler's (1986) review of the research suggests that programs focusing on increased knowledge about drugs and alcohol are not effective in reducing use or abuse. On the positive side, Tobler (1986) found that peer programs that included assertiveness, especially refusal skills, and social-skills training prove the most effective in preventing abuse.

Several programs are available to promote assertiveness and social skills. A program called *Children Are People* (Lerner & Naiditch, 1985) can be used at the elementary school level, and the SMART program (Pearson, Lunday, Rohrbach, & Whitney, 1985) applies to the middle school level. For teens who have substance-abuse problems, the most effective programs are those that promote alternative activities, such as camping and sports; enhance confidence and social competence; and provide broadening experiences (Tobler, 1986).

Teenage Pregnancy.   Teenage pregnancies in the United States continue at an alarming rate. Maynard (1996) notes that one million teenagers in the United States become pregnant each year, which is approximately 10 percent of 15- to 19-year-olds. The United States has by far the highest teenage pregnancy rate for an industrialized nation, with it being twice as high as the United Kingdom and 15 times the rate in Japan (Maynard, 1996). The cost of teenage pregnancy to the individual and society can be staggering. Maynard (1996) estimates that the cost to society from such forces as lost wages and social services is between 13 billion and 19 billion dollars a year. There are other costs to teenage mothers and their children, such as their having a tendency to have low-birth weight and premature babies, having higher rates of school dropouts and lower high-school graduation rates for teenage mothers and their children, having higher rates of abuse and neglect, and having lower lifelong earning for teenage mothers and their children (Maynard, 1996).

Preventive programs can address the special problems associated with teenage pregnancy. Furstenberg, Brooks-Gunn, and Chase-Lansdale (1989) note that the most promising forms of prevention of teenage pregnancy are contraceptive and family-planning services. These authors conclude that other preventive programs that focus on sex education or attempting to change attitudes toward early sexual involvement have had limited success.

Several preventive programs that are implemented after a teenager becomes pregnant have been found to be successful. Prenatal programs have been shown to promote healthy babies for teens (Brooks-Gunn, McCormick, & Heagerty, 1988; Brooks-Gunn et al., 1989). Parent-education programs have been used to enhance parenting skills as well as the development of the child (Clewell, Brooks-Gunn, & Benasich, 1989). Emmons and Nystul's (1994) research on the effects of parent education utilizes the PREP for Effective Family Living program (Dinkmeyer, McKay, Dinkmeyer, Dinkmeyer, & Carlson, 1985) in small groups with pregnant teenagers. They found that the PREP program increases the teenagers' self-concept and fosters democratic parenting attitudes.

MacGregor and Newlon (1987) suggest that the most useful approaches for working with pregnant teenagers include group counseling to provide necessary peer support; parent education after delivery of the baby, but not before; and creative, imaginative prenatal class presentations that encourage active involvement of participants. Berger and Thompson (2000) describe a social inoculation program that involves group work with female adolescents. The groups utilize role-play and discussion and focus on helping these individuals learn how to resist pressures to have sex. Social inoculation is shown to be useful, especially for individuals who are not already sexually active.

Divorced or Single Parents.   Berger and Thompson (2000) contend that high divorce rates are expected to continue into the 21st century, with only 40 percent of children being reared by both biological parents until they reach 18 years of age. Frieman (1993) suggests

The incidence of teenage pregnancy is increasing.

that school counselors can play key roles in helping students overcome some of the adverse outcomes associated with divorce and single-parent homes. Active positive involvement in child-rearing by both biological parents can minimize adverse consequences of divorce. Frieman (1993) notes that a special challenge can be to involve the father, since fathers tend to have lower levels of parental involvement (than mothers) before the divorce. Frieman posits that group work with divorced men can be useful to help them become more involved in their children's lives. Topics that may be especially relevant in these groups are common problems of fathers, parenting skills, developmental issues, dealing with negative emotions of anger and jealousy, and information on child care.

Robson (2002) describes variations in the effects of divorce according to the age of the child. Children up to 5 years of age tend to regress by developing feeding and toileting problems. Children from age 6 to 8 initially use denial to cope and later remain hopeful that their parents will get back together. From age 9 to 11, children typically react with shock, surprise, denial, and disbelief. In addition, these children can experience conflicts in loyalty to their parents, often viewing one parent as good and the other as bad. Adolescents from 13 to 18 years of age appear to have increased risk of mental health problems and a negative view of their future, their parents, and their environment. Adolescent females also tend to engage in early heterosexual behavior.

Group counseling has been found effective for dealing with the special issues associated with divorce, such as alleviating guilt and dealing with anger and feelings of abandonment. Many different kinds of divorce groups have emerged (Bowker, 1982; Hammond, 1981). These groups tend to focus on easing children's level of stress and enhancing their self-esteem. Hammond's (1981) program is typical of these group approaches. It utilizes a structured format that includes a multimedia presentation and exercises providing information on divorce as well as opportunities to process feelings. Burke and DeStreek (1989) have found empirical support for Hammond's approach in terms of enhanced self-concept. Additional research on these groups appears warranted.

Dropping Out of School. Eggen and Kauchak (1994) estimated that 25 percent or more of the high school class of 2001 would not finish high school. The percentage of school dropouts is even higher for some minority groups (for example, Native-American students have the highest rate at 35.5 percent; Garrett, 1995). Students who are at a high risk for dropping out of school are referred to as *at-risk students*. Eggen and Kauchak (1994) identify common characteristics of at risk students, which include low socioeconomic status, transience, being minority, being male, having English as a second language, and being from divorced families. Students who are at risk not only have a higher tendency to drop out of school, but they also have a tendency to have other problems such as substance abuse, delinquency, low self-esteem, and low motivation and underachievement in school (Eggen & Kauchak, 1994).

An increasing amount of research is focusing on identifying resiliency characteristics that can help students become less vulnerable to academic failure (for example, Alva, 1991; Arellano & Padilla, 1996; and Zimmerman & Arunkumar, 1994). Arellano and Padilla (1996) identify personal and environmental factors that promote academic success in Latino students. These characteristics include parental support and encouragement; role models and mentors; ethnicity as a source of support, pride, and strength; the drive to succeed; and an optimistic outlook. School counselors can attempt to foster resiliency characteristics to maximize academic achievement in students.

Several counseling strategies can address the school dropout phenomenon. Preventive programs can provide special counseling services for students who are at risk for dropping out of school. Bearden, Spencer, and Moracco (1989) have found that males have a higher risk of dropping out of school than females. The authors identify other at-risk characteristics, including low socioeconomic status, a history of previous failures, drug abuse, academic and behavioral problems, poor school attendance, and boredom. Gibson (1989) describes several programs that have been used to work with at-risk students. For example, Florida's Dade County Public Schools uses peer counseling, academic support, and help with educational deficiencies (Dade County Public Schools, 1985). The Los Angeles Unified School District (1985) employs counseling, special tutoring, and vocational assistance. More recently, Ruben (1989) has recommended that preventive efforts should be geared to the elementary level by providing classroom guidance programs like Gerler and Anderson's (1986) program called *Success in Schools*.

Trends in School Counseling

School counseling appears to be at a crossroads. School counselors are needed more than ever as students experience a complex array of personal and social problems. Yet concerns persist that school counseling cannot deal effectively with these challenges.

Sandhu and Portes (1995) contend that school counseling is in deep trouble as a profession and is in danger of becoming obsolete. These scholars suggest that the fundamental problem facing school counseling is that it tends to be perceived as a nonessential ancillary service that does not require specific expertise to perform. Sandhu and Portes (1995) suggest that it is essential for school counselors to become proactive rather than reactive in their roles, priorities, and activities. These individuals describe a proactive model of school counseling that can help move school counseling from the peripheral to the central position in educational reform. Welch and McCarroll (1993) provide additional suggestions on how school counselors can be perceived as vital to their school and community. They recommend that school counselors become more involved in the family and community by providing family counseling and becoming community resource specialists to help link students with appropriate services to meet their needs. They also recommend a shift in emphasis from individual counseling to group work and suggest that counselors utilize a systems perspective in conceptualizing the overall functioning of the school.

As noted earlier, school counselors may attempt to receive additional training in areas such as school law and administration to take a leadership role in emerging legislative acts such as Section 504 and IDEA. This would enable school counselors to expand their role in an area that is associated with specialized and essential services (for example, interface between discipline and legal mandates and development of behavior management plans).

The College Entrance Examination Board (1987) also concluded that the school-counseling profession was in trouble and in need of change. Based on an examination of school counseling, its report recommended (a) making better use of the school counselor's special skills rather than imposing clerical tasks such as scheduling, (b) increasing support for federal programs that assist disadvantaged students, (c) placing more emphasis on counseling programs at the elementary and middle school level to prevent problems from becoming more serious, and (d) promoting greater involvement of parents in the school-counseling program.

Russo and Kassera (1989) note that school counselors have been unsuccessful in clearly communicating the importance of their services. These authors suggest that school counselors should establish a comprehensive ongoing accountability program to overcome these difficulties. They recommend that school counselors use Wiggins's (1985) accountability program, which includes setting goals, assessing needs, setting priorities, evaluating outcomes, and reporting results.

Green (1988) suggests that image-building activities play a key role in school counseling. He suggests that school counselors must be accepted as practitioners with specialized knowledge before they can establish professional autonomy. Green (1988) identifies the following activities that could be used to promote a sense of professionalism for school counselors:

- Conduct a survey among colleagues to determine how they perceive the role of the school counselor. This type of peer review is a necessary component of professional behavior.
- Compile a list of professional activities during the previous three years. Determine whether these activities have promoted a professional image, required the special skills of a counselor or simply duplicated services offered by other professionals, and educated others on the complexity of the counselor's role in these activities.
- Provide programs for parents on topics such as parent education, drug abuse, and student achievement.
- Publish a newsletter describing activities of the school-counseling program as well as issues that interest students, teachers, and parents.
- Become active in conducting research and writing articles for publication in professional journals.

- Become involved in professional organizations.
- Schedule special consultation days for parents and staff to assist with special needs.
- Provide inservice training to teachers.
- Sponsor a community seminar on a topical issue (for example, teenage pregnancy).

Several authors have commented that school counselors should take a more active role in educational reforms (Kaplan & Geoffroy, 1990; Thomas, 1989). These authors suggest that school counselors can play an important role by promoting a positive school climate. The activities they recommend include encouraging success orientation in the school, fostering self-esteem of teachers and students, and helping integrate cognitive and affective dimensions in the educational process.

Counselor educators can also play an integral role in helping school counseling successfully move forward. Sweeney (1988) notes that school counseling has been deemphasized in most counselor-education programs. The current focus appears to be on providing coursework and skills for agency counselors and not school counseling. According to Sweeney (1988), counselor educators have also neglected research on school counseling. For example, the number of articles published in *Counselor Education and Supervision* on the role and function of school counseling has steadily declined. For example, 39 articles appeared on this topic from 1961 to 1968, but none from 1980 to 1988. Besides helping school counselors formulate a professional identity, counselor educators can provide more emphasis on the educational needs of students interested in school counseling.

These studies collectively suggest that school counseling is a profession at risk and in need of dramatic changes. Briefly, school counselors should

- Become proactive in their roles, priorities, and activities
- Use a family-systemic perspective to become more involved in the family and community
- Assume leadership responsibilities for coordinating and acting as a liaison for legislative programs such as Section 504 and IDEA
- Clarify their role and function by encouraging others to focus on their special skills and not on clerical tasks such as scheduling
- Incorporate image-building activities and an ongoing accountability program
- Encourage parents to involve themselves more in their children's counseling programs
- Advocate greater emphasis on elementary and middle school counseling
- Become more actively involved in the school-reform movement
- Promote research efforts on special problems such as suicide and depression
- Convince counselor educators to place more emphasis on school counseling

Three trends in the school counseling literature that are receiving an increasing amount of attention are diversity issues, solution-focused counseling, and technology. An overview of these topics follows.

Diversity Issues

School counselors must consider diversity issues in all aspects of counseling. Three examples of diversity issues are culture, religion, and sexual orientation. All facets of society are becoming increasingly multicultural. It is therefore imperative for school counselors to develop the necessary knowledge, skill, and understanding to work with students in a multicultural society. Hobson and Kanitz (1996) note that the recently revised American Counseling Association (1997) Code of Ethics and Standards of Practice advocates that counselors acquire and maintain the necessary multicultural competencies to practice, and that school counselors generally are in need of additional training in this area. Whitledge (1994) goes on to suggest that sensitivity to multicultural issues in schools is necessary to maximize learning in students. School counselors should therefore engage in activities to enhance the school climate by overcoming adverse stereotyping and promoting an acceptance and integration of the student's culture in the overall school curriculum (Whitledge, 1994).

Spiritual and religious issues represent an emerging dimension to school counseling. For example, Miller (1995) identifies special considerations for providing school counseling services to Christian fundamentalist families. He notes that these families tend to respond to a school counselor's referrals with fear and apprehension because they do not believe their religious beliefs will be considered in the counseling process.

School counselors can overcome reluctant tendencies by giving voice to the clients' manner of conceptualizing problems and solutions. For example, it is common for Christian fundamentalists to attribute problems of misbehavior to problems with religion (for example, not spending enough time studying the Bible) (Miller, 1995). When this occurs, school counselors should recognize the role that the church may play in overcoming students' problems. In this process, school counselors must make every effort to listen to their clients' stories in an accepting and nonjudgmental manner. As trust develops, counselors can be in a better position to facilitate the construction of new stories that reflect a movement toward problem resolution and enhanced meaning.

Ribak-Rosenthal and Russell (1994) address another important religious issue in school counseling. Their study found that non-Christian fourth to sixth graders experienced more negative perceptions of themselves and their classroom's social environment than Christian students during the month of December. The study suggests that 20 to 30 percent of the non-Christian students may experience negative emotions during December because it is focused on the celebration of Christmas in terms of classroom parties and holiday breaks.

These authors suggest that school counselors could strive to create a positive school climate that recognizes diversity in religion in the schools. In this process, counselors could refer to the school break in December as a holiday vacation and not Christmas vacation. In addition, counselors could create opportunities to recognize other religious holidays and festivities in small- and large-group guidance and counseling activities.

Sexual orientation represents another important diversity issue, with approximately 10 percent of students having gay or lesbian sexual preferences. Unfortunately, sexual orientation has received so little attention in schools that it can be considered "a blind spot in the school mirror" (Marinoble, 1998). In fact, sexual orientation tends to be a subject that is often avoided altogether in all aspects of school functioning from the curriculum to school policies, and even to the invitation of guest speakers (Marinoble, 1998). It is not surprising that exclusionary forces such as these contribute to gays and lesbians often feeling like "invisible people" (Ritter & O'Neill, 1995).

Marinoble (1998) identifies some of the special challenges and opportunities that gay and lesbian students pose to school counselors. Challenges include helping these students overcome difficulties associated with being gay or lesbian in a heterosexual/homophobic world. Some of the common problems experienced are identity conflict, feelings of isolation and stigmatization, peer-relation problems, and family disruptions. Identity conflicts can in part be due to schools' fundamental orientation to recognizing the world in heterosexual terms (Marinoble, 1998). Although the existence of homosexuality is generally ignored, when it is recognized, it tends to have a negative, derogatory connotation. This can contribute to gays and lesbians struggling to define themselves as unique and positive individuals in a tide of negativity.

As noted, gay and lesbian students experience problems such as isolation and stigmatization, peer-relation problems, and family conflicts that can contribute to serious mental health problems. For example, Marinoble (1998) notes that suicide accounts for most of the deaths of gay and lesbian adolescents, occurring at a rate two to three times that of heterosexual teens. Ritter and O'Neill (1995) also note that gay and lesbian individuals also tend to have problems with spirituality owing to limited access to organized religion. This can compound mental health problems because people tend to turn to spirituality for strength and support during times of need (Miranti & Burke, 1995).

School counselors are in an ideal position to take a proactive role in assisting gay and lesbian students with their special problems and fostering their optimal development. Some of the possible interventions suggested by Cooley (1998), Fontaine (1998), Marinoble (1998), Muller and Hartman (1998), and Ritter and O'Neill (1995) are as follows:

- Promote a school climate (in terms of the curriculum and school policy) that is sensitive and values diversity in sexual orientation.
- Ensure that *all* students have an opportunity to develop a positive self-image, self-acceptance, and personal identity.
- When appropriate, assist students in the process of "coming out" (sharing their sexual orientation with friends and family).
- Utilize individual and group counseling to help gay and lesbian students overcome negative feelings such as isolation and despair.
- Monitor students who are at a high risk for suicide and ensure treatment as necessary.
- Assist students with spiritual needs to promote inner strength and support necessary for problem resolution and movement toward optimal development.

Implementation of these interventions may create serious challenges for school counselors. Schools tend to be a reflection of the culture in which they are created. Successful implementation may therefore require strength and courage to fight against negative forces such as homophobia, racism, stereotyping, discrimination, and prejudice. If schools exist to truly educate *all* students (regardless of race, color, and creed), then school counselors have an opportunity to advocate for school reform necessary to address these important issues.

Brief-Solution-Focused Counseling

Brief-solution-focused models of counseling continue to receive attention from the literature as an innovative alternative to standard approaches to school counseling (Bonnington, 1993; Bruce, 1995; LaFountain, Garner, & Eliason, 1996; and Murphy, 1994). Murphy (1994) summarizes advantages that brief-solution-focused counseling has for school counselors over more traditional counseling methods:

1. It is a strengths approach that focuses on what works and exceptions to problems and therefore promotes collaborative relationships with students, parents, teachers, and staff.
2. It is time-limited, focusing on the present and future rather than lengthy excursions into past history.
3. Its goal of small, concrete changes (such as increased class attendance and conflict resolution) is more realistic than more ambitious goals such as personality change.
4. It recognizes the importance of students being aware of the need for change as a prerequisite for change.

Bruce (1995) and Murphy (1994) describe tasks associated with brief-solution-focused counseling in school counseling. Collectively they suggest that school counselors should first establish a positive counseling relationship. This of course is important regardless of the approach that is being used. Second, school counselors must assess the problem in concrete behavioral terms and identify exceptions to the problem (that is, examples of when the problem does not occur). Third, school counselors must identify a short-term goal that the student can successfully achieve. Fourth, they must elaborate on what worked in the past (the exceptions to the problem identified in step 2) and use this information to develop a new approach for the student. Fifth, they must evaluate the new approach with methods such as the scaling technique (on a 1:10 scale with 1 being the worst and 10 being the best, how would you rate the situation now?) and make changes to the new approach as necessary. And sixth, they must empower students to use the brief-solution-focused method to deal with future problems.

Only a limited amount of research has evaluated the efficacy of brief-solution-focused counseling. Littrell, Malia, and Vanderwood (1995) found brief-solution-focused counseling (one session with high school students) to be as effective as brief-problem-focused counseling in terms of decreasing the degree of undesired feelings, but brief-solution-focused counseling took less time. Brief-solution-focused and other forms of brief counseling appear to offer much to school counselors who are continually faced with large numbers of students to whom they must provide counseling services.

The following *Personal Note* describes a brief-solution-focused model of counseling I developed.

A Personal Note

I have developed a simple three-phase model of brief-solution-focused counseling based on the Adlerian principle of encouragement. Each phase has two steps. Although the model is particularly well suited for school counseling, it can also be used in other settings. An overview of these three phases follows.

Phase One: Celebrating Success. Celebrating success involves the counselor identifying what is working, exceptions to the problem, strengths, good news, and so forth. I associate "celebrating success" with taking a mental picture of something a student has said or done. Together (with the student's permission), the student and counselor share the success with a significant other such as a parent, teacher, or school principal.

Phase Two: Application of Strengths. In this phase, the counselor and student explore how a student's strengths can be used to address counseling goals (successes celebrated in Phase One can be important strengths). For instance, a student who has had trouble finishing his schoolwork may realize that it is important to listen to his teacher.

Phase Three: Creating Hope and Encouragement. In the final phase, the counselor promotes hope and encouragement by creating a connection between effort and success: "When you work hard, good things will happen." The "incomplete sentence" technique can be used to foster student ownership of the encouragement message (i.e., let the student say the last half of the sentence: "Good things will happen _____"). Encouragement fosters self-efficacy (a "can do" spirit) and promotes a self-fulfilling prophecy of success.

Use of Technology

Technological advances offer numerous opportunities and challenges to school counselors. Challenges relate to the inherent difficulties of trying to keep up with the escalating changes in technology (for example, the computer you just purchased is already out of date). Opportunities include being able to do the job of school counseling better and more efficiently. Technologies such as multimedia authoring (the use of at least two media simultaneously, such as image processing, graphics production, sound editing, and three-dimensional modeling) are the wave of the future for state-of-the-art delivery of counseling programs to students (Gerler, 1995). There are limitless other possibilities for the use of technologies in school counseling. Some of these are to enable students to use CD-ROMs, the Internet, and other technologies to take an active role in their counseling by exploring such topics as career exploration, drug and alcohol abuse, and prejudice (Casey, 1995).

A growing number of school counselors are also finding that the Internet can be an excellent tool to communicate with other school counselors regarding issues from counseling theory to crucial matters that they face daily (Gerler, 1995). Counselor educators are also expanding their use of technologies in the schools. Myrick and Sabella (1995) note that e-mail can be a useful tool in supervision of student interns in school counseling. It can provide a means to send information immediately and directly to one's supervisor without having to wait for a weekly supervision meeting or playing "telephone tag." E-mail supervision also helps students become more succinct in describing what is going on with a particular case and contributes to an enhanced focus in counselor supervision (Myrick & Sabella, 1995).

Summary

School counseling is a dynamic and challenging field in the counseling profession. It can best be understood within the context of a comprehensive K–12 developmental model. In 1990, the ASCA supported this model in a revised role statement, suggesting that school counselors engage in individual counseling, small-group counseling, large-group guidance, consultation, and coordination activities. More recently, ASCA has set forth national standards and a national model for school counseling. These new initiatives could be the zeitgeist for the school-counseling profession, setting national standards and a framework for developing and implementing a comprehensive K–12 school-counseling program.

The role of consultation is receiving increasing attention in school counseling. Guidelines for counseling exceptional students and students with the special problems of drug abuse, teenage pregnancy, divorced or single parents, and dropping out of school are also important.

School counseling appears to be at a crossroads. Several studies have suggested that changes are needed for school counseling to successfully move forward as a profession. Some of these are becoming more proactive and enhancing family-community involvement; taking leadership responsibility for legislative programs such as Section 504, IDEA, and HIPPA; increasing direct services and reducing clerical activities; putting more emphasis on elementary and middle school counseling to maximize preventive effort; and engaging in image-building activities. In addition, school counselors need to be cognizant of emerging trends, such as incorporating a multicultural perspective, using brief-solution-focused counseling, and making effective use of technology. More recently, the ASCA National Model suggests that school counselors should engage in a broader base that includes leadership, advocacy, teaming/collaboration, and systemic change to ensure that all students have opportunities for success in school.

Personal Exploration

1. What do you believe are the challenges and opportunities in the field of school counseling?
2. What do you think are the major challenges facing children/adolescents today, and how might you address them if you were a school counselor?
3. If you were a school counselor, what level would you want to be (elementary, middle, or high school), and why would that level appeal to you?
4. How do you think public school education can be improved, and what should the school counselor's role be in this process?

Web Sites for Chapter 14

American School Counselor Association. (2004). *One vision one voice.* Retrieved March 3, 2005, from http://www.schoolcounselor.org/
Is the official national site for the American School Counselor Association.
University of Massachusetts. (2000). *Center for school counseling outcome research.* Retrieved March 3, 2005, from http://www.umass.edu/schoolcounseling/

CHAPTER OVERVIEW

This chapter provides an overview of mental health counseling. Highlights of the chapter include

- The art and science of mental health counseling
- Professional issues for mental health counselors, including professional organizations and certification
- The role and function of the mental health counselor, including direct and indirect intervention strategies
- Categories of mental health services: "problems of living" and mental disorders
- Strategies for suicidal clients
- Strategies for clients with substance-abuse problems
- Postmodern trends, diversity issues, and managed care

The Art and Science of Mental Health Counseling

Mental health counseling is both an art and science. It is an art for mental health counselors to attempt to walk the tightrope between adjusting to the demands of health-care reform (such as managed care) and maintaining a high-quality mental health service. One of the challenges associated with this process is maintaining the philosophical core of mental health counseling (the developmental/preventative perspective) while continuing to be perceived as a viable provider for managed-care organizations, which tend to focus on symptom relief. In addition, it is an art for mental health counseling to make appropriate changes in its philosophical and theoretical orientation to interface effectively with current trends such as postmodernism and issues relating to diversity.

The art of mental health counseling is reflected in the challenging population that this discipline serves (for example, clients with mental disorders such as serious depression, schizophrenia, and substance abuse). Mental health counselors must strive to develop innovative, creative methods to address these challenges. The art of mental health counseling is expressed in the personal characteristics of patience, humbleness, kindness, and compassion.

Clearly, for mental health counselors to be effective, they must be affected by their clients and the counseling process.

The science of mental health counseling can be an effective balance to the emotionally charged art of counseling. Without a balance, the art of counseling will not be as effective. In this regard, counselors can become overly enmeshed in their clients' lives, obscuring boundaries and undermining essential professional objectivity.

Numerous objective practices can contribute to this balance. Some of these are the use of assessment instruments and procedures such as psychological tests and the clinical interview. Research strategies such as qualitative and quantitative methods can also be useful in establishing the science of counseling in mental health counseling. Assessment and research methodologies can help the mental health counselor stand back and evaluate what is going on in the counseling process, provide new direction for innovations in theory and practice, and determine the efficacy of the mental health services being offered.

Professional Issues

Mental health counseling is both an emerging counseling profession represented by mental health counselors and an amorphous job role performed by various members of the helping professions such as counselors, psychologists, psychiatrists, psychiatric nurses, and social workers. Mental health counselors can be defined as individuals whose "primary affiliation and theoretical basis is counseling and not psychiatry, psychology, or social work" (Palmo, 1986, p. 41). Mental health counselors represent the fastest-growing segment of the mental health field (Dingman, 1988). Burtnett (1986) reported that 57 percent of mental health agencies have a mental health counselor. These counselors handle some of the most difficult cases, including crisis intervention (Ivey, 1989), and have therefore become an integral aspect of the mental health delivery system.

Until relatively recently, mental health counselors did not have a professional organization. In 1976, the American Association for Counseling and Development (AACD)— now called the American Counseling Association (ACA)—addressed this need by creating a special division called the American Mental Health Counselors Association (AMHCA). By 1985, the AMHCA had become the largest division of the AACD. Since its inception, the AMHCA has embarked on numerous activities that have contributed to the professional identity of the mental health counselor. Its most important contributions include creating a code of ethics for mental health counselors, which was revised in 2000; publishing the *Journal of Mental Health Counseling,* which provides information regarding the theory, research, and practice of mental health counseling; spearheading a movement for counselor licensure in all states; and setting up national standards for certification of mental health counselors.

Smith and Robinson (1995) note that in 1988, national preparation standards were established for mental health counselors to ensure adequate professional training and recognition in the health-care delivery system (for example, that mental health counseling be eligible for third-party insurance reimbursement and participation in managed care). Smith and Robinson delineate the national clinical standards for mental health counselors as follows. Individuals must graduate from a program that is accredited by the Council for Accreditation of Counseling and Related Educational Programs (CACREP) or has CACREP equivalency; have 3000 hours of experience in the mental health field; have 100 hours of face-to-face supervision; adhere to the AMHCA standards of clinical practice and code of ethics; pass a national clinical exam; successfully have work samples of counseling reviewed (for example, videotapes); and fulfill state licensure requirements.

More than 1400 individuals have been endorsed as Certified Clinical Mental Health Counselors (CCMHC) by the National Academy of Clinical Mental Health Counselors since 1979 (Brooks & Gerstein, 1990). The academy bases its standards on criteria deemed essential for independent practice as a mental health provider and also what would be acceptable standards to third-party insurance programs (Brooks & Gerstein, 1990). CCMHC providers have been recognized by the Civilian Health and Medical Program of the Uniformed Services (CHAMPUS) for third-party insurance reimbursement when clients are referred by a physician (Brooks & Gerstein, 1990).

Mental health counselors work in a variety of settings, including private practice, community mental health centers, hospitals, alcohol and drug centers, social-service agencies, and in business and industry (Brooks & Gerstein, 1990). Hershenson and Power (1987) note an apparent shift in work settings for mental health counselors during the 1980s. For example, Weikel and Taylor (1979) reported that in 1978, the highest percentage (39 percent) of AMHCA members worked in community mental health centers, 18 percent in private practice, and the remainder in a variety of other settings, including college counseling centers and as college teachers. Weikel (1985) noted that in 1985, 22 percent of AMHCA members worked in private practice, 13 percent in private counseling centers, 13 percent in colleges and universities, only 11 percent in community mental health centers, and the rest in other settings, such as rehabilitation agencies and state and local government. The trend of private practice becoming the dominant work setting for AMHCA members continued in the 1990s (Brooks & Gerstein, 1990).

Several other studies have shown that a high percentage of mental health counselors work in substance-abuse centers (Hosie, West, & MacKey, 1988; Richardson & Bradley, 1985). Hosie et al. (1988) report that the largest percentage of professionals working in substance-abuse centers hold a master's degree in counseling or a Master of Social Work (MSW) degree. In addition, Hosie et al. (1988) note that mental health counselors are more likely to hold a position as program director than are individuals from other disciplines.

Smith and Robinson (1995) suggest that mental health counselors must continue to receive training in the diagnosis and treatment of mental disorders and that this training should emphasize a developmental/preventative perspective. They also suggest that specialty skills (such as marriage and family counseling) can enhance the standing of mental health counselors within the health-care community.

In an era of rapid change within the health-care system, mental health counseling appears to be posed to have greater inclusion and recognition as a mental health provider. In this regard, mental health counseling appears to represent a cost-effective alternative to mental health delivery, which would be very attractive to managed-care organizations. It is imperative that mental health counseling continues to evolve in a manner that corresponds appropriately to the changing needs and challenges of society.

The Role and Function of Mental Health Counselors

Nicholas, Gerstein, and Keller (1988) note that mental health counselors perform most of the same tasks as other mental health practitioners, such as marriage and family counselors, social workers, and psychologists. These tasks include psychoeducational services, clinical or direct services, supervision, administration, program development, and consultation. Two tasks that mental health counselors do not tend to engage in are program evaluation and research. These tasks are often performed by doctoral-level counselors and psychologists (Nicholas et al., 1988).

Brooks and Gerstein (1990) note that while mental health practitioners serve similar functions, they vary in terms of treatment philosophies. These authors found that mental health counselors typically utilize a psychoeducational, developmental, and psychopathological point of view; marriage and family therapists use a systemic orientation; psychologists rely on a psychopathological frame of reference; and social workers adhere to a sociological perspective (Brooks & Gerstein, 1990). Ivey (1989) also differentiates mental health disciplines according to philosophical orientation, noting that mental health counselors define themselves primarily within a developmental perspective, whereas psychologists adhere to a medical/therapeutic model and social workers focus on the environment. Ginter (1996) provides additional information on the philosophical orientation of mental health counselors. He identifies three pillars of counseling that provide a framework for mental health counseling. These pillars are that counseling is contextually an interpersonal medium, it recognizes the importance of both prevention and remediation, and it has a developmental perspective.

Messina (1999) states that there is a debate raging within the mental health profession regarding the validity of the developmental-preventative model versus the medical model, which emphasizes diagnoses and treatment. The developmental-preventative model can be traced to graduate training programs in mental health counseling. Messina (1999) suggests that the developmental-preventative legacy may be an inhibiting factor for the mental health profession. Clearly, managed care rewards clinicians who embrace the medical model. Mental health counselors who do not adhere to the medical model may undermine their ability to compete with psychologists and social workers who promote their ability to diagnose and treat mental disorders.

It would seem to be in the best interest of managed care and mental health counselors to strike a balance between prevention and treatment. For example, managed care has emphasized symptom relief over comprehensive treatment of disorders. Tertiary prevention involves providing comprehensive treatment programs for disorders such as depression, thereby preventing future problems. Ongoing research and evaluation will be necessary to shape the identity of mental health counselors in the ever-changing landscape of mental health services.

Kelly (1996) looks to the future in terms of the role and function of mental health counselors. He suggests that mental health counselors are attempting to address three broad, interrelated challenges. First, mental health counselors must continue to assert their right to be mental health service providers in a health-care venue that reflects shrinking resources. This challenge can only be met with continued support for mental health counseling licensure and recognition and utilization by managed-care providers. A second challenge facing mental health counselors is to communicate accountability by documented improvement in clients. Research and evaluation will play a key role in this process. And third, mental health counselors must effectively adjust to the changing landscape of the mental health field in terms of technology, diversity, and health-care reform. The evolution and refinement of mental health counseling will enable this profession to continue to be a viable counseling service in the mental health delivery system.

Central to the role and function of mental health counseling is providing direct and indirect intervention strategies.

Direct Intervention Strategies

Mental health counselors provide direct counseling services to clients with a wide range of mental disorders (West, Hosie, & MacKey, 1988). This section addresses two commonly used direct intervention strategies: counseling and crisis intervention.

Counseling.   Mental health counselors utilize a wide range of direct counseling strategies, such as individual counseling, group counseling, marriage and family counseling, and substance-abuse counseling (NeJedlo, Arredondo, & Benjamin, 1985; Spruill & Fong, 1990; West et al., 1988). In addition, Spruill and Fong (1990) suggest that there appears to be a shift in emphasis in mental health counseling from preventive approaches to direct counseling services such as individual, group, and family counseling.

Crisis Intervention.   Mental health counselors also provide crisis-intervention services (Ivey, 1989; West et al., 1988). George and Cristiani (1995) suggest that crisis intervention is not the same as counseling, even though it is a helping strategy. Its focus is more narrow and superficial, its goals are more modest, and it has a briefer duration than counseling. The following is a four-step model for crisis intervention.

The first step is to determine whether the client is in crisis. To determine whether crisis intervention is necessary, the counselor must first decide whether the client is experiencing a personal crisis. Gilliland and James (1997, p. 3) define a *crisis* as "a perception of an event or situation as an intolerable difficulty that exceeds the person's resources and coping mechanisms." Puryear (1979) identifies five factors associated with a crisis:

1. The symptoms of stress result in psychological and physiological discomfort.
2. The client feels intense emotions such as feelings of inadequacy, helplessness, panic, or agitation.
3. The client is more concerned with gaining relief from the symptom than with the problem that precipitated the symptom.
4. The client has a reduced ability to function efficiently.
5. The crisis occurs during a short period of time.

Gilliland and James (1997) recommended that the counselor use listening skills during the initial phase of crisis intervention to gain a phenomenological understanding of the client. This practice can also help the counselor determine whether the client is experiencing a crisis. At the same time, it will enable the counselor to establish rapport and communicate support to the client.

The second step in crisis intervention involves assessment, using two separate procedures. First, the counselor must assess the severity of the crisis in terms of the potential for serious harm to the client or others. Gilliland and James (1997) emphasize that the primary goal of crisis intervention is to avoid a catastrophe in which someone would be seriously injured. The second assessment procedure involves determining whether the client is mentally able to take an active role in resolving the crisis situation. A useful tool in this process is a mental status exam (Othmer & Othmer, 1989), which can help determine whether the client is oriented to person, place, and time; free of hallucinations; and capable of coherent thinking. When a client does not appear to be capable of realistic decision making, the counselor may need to take a more active role in the crisis-intervention process.

The third step in the crisis-intervention model involves action. During a crisis, some form of action will usually be required to restore equilibrium to the client. Providing the client with rest can be an important part of this process. For example, if the client is acutely suicidal, the counselor may work with family members to arrange for the client to be hospitalized. Once the client receives rest and equilibrium has been restored, counseling strategies can be implemented. The counselor can attempt to identify the precipitating factors associated with the crisis and help the client overcome these problems in the future.

The fourth and final step entails follow-up. Cavanaugh (1982) notes that clients can have delayed reactions to a crisis, which may occur weeks or even months after the precipitating event. It is therefore important to arrange for appropriate follow-up counseling services.

The following *Personal Note* provides an illustration of crisis intervention.

A Personal Note

Mary arrived at an outpatient mental health clinic where I was a counselor and said that she was having trouble sleeping and wanted sleeping pills. She appeared agitated and tearful, and she spoke in monotone. It soon became clear that there was much more on her mind than her trouble with sleeping. She began to talk about an affair that her husband was having. She went on to say that because of her "religious beliefs," it was necessary for her to kill her three children and herself. Mary reasoned that since her husband had an affair, he had lost his right to have any more contact with his family.

I asked Mary what religion would want her to kill herself and her children. At this point, she seemed to ramble on incoherently. A brief mental status examination showed her to be oriented to person and place—she knew who and where she was—but not to time—she didn't know the day, month, or year. There was no evidence of hallucinations but some possibility of a delusion since she described herself as the "savior" of the family. She intended to kill herself and her children to "save" them all from the sins of her husband.

I then explored the seriousness of her suicidal and homicidal threat. I discovered that she had a gun and planned to use it. Since Mary had a plan and a method of carrying it through, I saw this as a crisis that required immediate action. I became very concerned about the safety of Mary and her children. I decided that it would be best if Mary were hospitalized so that she could receive mental health treatment and be protected from hurting herself or her children.

I emphasized to Mary that I wanted her to be hospitalized for her safety and the safety of her children. Since there was not a mental health code on the Indian reservation where I was working, I could not insist that she be hospitalized. Fortunately, Mary agreed to be admitted to the hospital for a couple of days. For the first two days, Mary slept around the clock, only getting up occasionally for water. After she rested, she said she felt much better. Although Mary was still very angry with her husband, she realized that killing herself and her children would accomplish nothing. Before Mary was discharged from the hospital, she made an appointment with me for individual and marriage counseling.

Indirect Intervention Strategies

Hershenson and Power (1987) identify six indirect activities associated with the mental health counselor's role and function. They can be considered indirect intervention strategies in that they provide an indirect form of treatment. An overview of these activities follows.

Prevention.   Prevention represents the inverse of coping with a crisis (Barclay, 1984). Prevention of mental disorders and the promotion of mental health have been an integral part of the community mental health movement (Matus & Neuhring, 1979). An example of a preventive focus is the holistic health movement, which promotes healthy lifestyles to prevent the development of illness.

Hershenson and Power (1987) identify three types of prevention: primary, secondary, and tertiary.

1. *Primary prevention* evolved from the public-health model. It refers to strengthening the resistance of a particular population and offsetting harmful influences before they can make an impact (Caplan, 1964). Primary prevention takes place before a problem has manifested itself or when its symptoms are barely noticeable (Gilbert, 1982). Shaw and Goodyear (1984) note that primary prevention reduces the number of individuals requiring mental health services and is therefore an important aspect of any comprehensive human services program. Unfortunately, primary prevention has historically taken a backseat to other strategies because resources are instead applied to people with existing problems.
2. *Secondary prevention* involves programs that attempt to identify individuals who are at risk for developing certain problems and then prescribing remedial activities to prevent those problems from occurring (McMurty, 1985). For example, there has been some interest in working with children of alcoholics to prevent them from becoming alcoholics.
3. *Tertiary prevention* attempts to avert further consequences of a problem that has already manifested itself (Hershenson & Power, 1987). The present mental health system puts most of its efforts in tertiary prevention, focusing on alleviating existing mental health problems.

Although prevention is clearly a recognized intervention in mental health counseling, it has not been adequately integrated into the training process or practice of mental health counselors (Kiselica & Look, 1993). The disparity between philosophy and practice may be due in part to a lack of insight into the "what and how" of prevention. Apparently, mental health educators and providers lack a clear understanding of what prevention is and how a clinician can engage in this endeavor. In addition, mental health trainees appear to be more interested in remedial interventions such as psychotherapy than prevention. Kiselica and Look (1993) suggest that counselor-educators should make a renewed effort to provide adequate training and emphasis on prevention. In this regard, mental health counselors must work together to make primary prevention the principal mode of intervention for mental health counseling. In addition, these authors recommend that increased efforts need to be directed at pursuing grant money for prevention, and journals such as the *Journal of Mental Health Counseling* should make articles on prevention a higher priority.

Advocacy. Advocacy is another indirect intervention strategy used by mental health counselors. *Advocacy* means to plead the cause of another person and follow through with action in support of that cause (Myers, Sweeney, & White, 2002). Hershenson and Power (1987) further explain that "a mental health counselor-advocate is one who is the client's supporter, the advisor, the champion, and if need be, the client's representative in dealing with the court, the police, the social agency, and other organizations that affect one's well-being" (p. 246). Myers et al. (2002) also suggest that counselors should advocate for the profession of counseling and for counselors. In this role, advocacy can advance the cause of counseling so more individuals can benefit from counseling services.

Advocacy is an action-oriented form of intervention in which the counselor does something for the client. This can have a positive impact on the counseling relationship in that the client may perceive the counselor as someone who can get things done. Mental health counselors can function as advocates in many ways, such as working with a human services department to ensure that clients receive benefits to which they are entitled.

Hershenson and Power (1987) identify the following advocacy skills as being important to mental health counselors:

- *Timing.* Counselors must decide when to be an advocate and when to let the client take the initiative. As a basic rule, counselors should intervene when it becomes clear that the system is not working for the client or even appears to be working against the client.
- *Support.* Counselors must have the support of the system to be capable of working effectively with that system. In this vein, it is important for counselors not to alienate themselves from co-workers. Counselors are more successful when they work in a cooperative manner and avoid being perceived as blindly fighting for another cause.
- *Compromise.* To maintain support from the system, counselors should be flexible and willing to compromise. A give-and-take approach can also yield creative solutions to complex problems.
- *Communication.* Several communication skills can be useful in the role of advocate. It is important to be able to listen and communicate an understanding of different points of view regarding the client. This can promote a cooperative approach. Another communication skill that may be necessary is assertiveness. Occasionally, mental health counselors need to take an assertive position to obtain the desired results. Naturally, this must be done in a tactful, caring fashion to be effective.

Consulting. Since the passage of the Community Mental Health Act in 1963, consultation has been an important aspect of the mental health worker's role and function (Kurpius, 1978). The act noted that consultation services were to become an essential part of community mental health programs of the future (Hershenson & Power, 1987). This legislation was viewed as an attempt to broaden mental health services to include more developmental and preventive approaches (Kurpius, 1978).

Caplan (1970) provides the following definition of mental health consultation:

> A process of interaction between two professional persons—the consultant, who is a specialist, and the consultee, who invokes the consultant's help in regard to a current work problem with which he is having some difficulty and which he has decided is within the other's area of specialized competence. (p. 19)

Hansen, Himes, and Meier (1990) note that Caplan's definition of mental health consultation has been broadened to include professional consulting with a layperson, such as a counselor consulting with a parent. In addition, Brown (1993) notes that consultation can involve working with individuals, couples, groups, families, organizations, and larger systems such as communities.

Brown (1993) posits that although consultation holds an important role in the overall philosophy of counseling, it does not appear to be a high priority for counselor-educators or counselors. Brown makes several recommendations that could increase the role that consultation plays in all aspects of the counseling profession, including mental health counseling. First, more effort needs to be made to integrate consultation into the counselor education curriculum in terms of coursework and fieldwork experiences (for example, counseling and consultation should both be considered during treatment planning). Second, licensing and accreditation boards should ensure that individuals and programs show evidence of appropriate consultation skills and activities.

The lack of attention to consultation appears to parallel the underutilization of preventative services by mental health counselors (Albee & Ryan-Finn, 1993). It therefore seems imperative that prevention and consultation be linked together so that counselors can gain a better understanding of how to promote prevention through consultation. Clearly the interrelationship between theory, research, and practice regarding these concepts requires further development.

Mediation.   Mediation is one of the newest roles of mental health counselors. Many states now offer mediation services to assist individuals who are going through a divorce (Hershenson & Power, 1987).

Witty (1980) defines *mediation* as the "facilitation of an agreement between two or more disputing parties by an agreed-upon third party" (p. 4). Kessler (1979) and Koopman (1985) note the following components of mediation: each party agrees to utilize the services of a mediator, the outcome is an agreement made by the disputants themselves, conflict resolution is cooperative instead of competitive, the focus is on "where we go from here" as opposed to fault-finding, self-disclosure and empathy are promoted in place of deception and intimidation, decisions are self-imposed instead of imposed by others, and creative alternatives are promoted rather than win-or-lose positions.

Kessler (1979) describes the actual process of mediation as a structured decision-making process that usually lasts one to three sessions. Hershenson and Power (1987) identify the following three steps that a mental health counselor could use to provide structure to the mediation process:

1. The counselor initially provides the necessary structure by establishing a cooperative tone, setting the rules, obtaining a commitment to the process, and providing an overview of what is to come (Kessler, 1979).
2. In this strategic and planning phase, the mediator obtains an overview of the conflict by reviewing all pertinent information. Toward the end of this step, the mediator can begin to develop a specific plan of action with the disputants.
3. The third step is the problem-solving phase, in which the mediator works with the disputants to help them reach a specific agreement. The mediator may use a variety of tactics during this process, including negotiation, creative problem solving, joining

meetings, and private caucuses. The final agreement is usually written out by the disputants so they will have a permanent record of the mediation process.

Mentoring. Mentoring is another relatively new role for mental health counselors. Krupp (1982) defines *mentoring* as a process in which a trusted and experienced individual takes a direct interest in the development and education of a younger, less experienced individual. Numerous studies have shown that mentoring has a positive impact on the mentor, the less-experienced individual, and the organization involved (Lynch, 1980; Valliant, 1977).

Farren, Gray, and Kaye (1984) identify several guidelines for establishing a mentoring relationship: participation should be voluntary, there should be minimal rules and maximum freedom, the mentor and the less-experienced individual should share and negotiate expectations, and mentors should be rewarded for their efforts.

Education. The mental health counselor can also function as an educator, a role that may involve indirect and direct intervention strategies. Education is often an important facet of both types of strategies described in this section, as shown in the following examples:

- Counseling can help a client learn how to become more autonomous.
- Crisis intervention may teach a client how to avoid future crises.
- Prevention often occurs through programs that emphasize an educational component such as parent education.
- Advocacy can teach a client how to be assertive without alienating others.
- Consultation may involve inservice training programs that teach special skills, such as how to avoid burnout.
- Mediation can help a client learn how to resolve conflicts in a cooperative fashion.
- Mentoring provides opportunities for a less-experienced individual to learn from a more experienced person.

Categories of Mental Health Services

The majority of mental health services are directed at helping clients who are dealing with problems of living or who have mental disorders. This section provides an overview of the clinical issues associated with these two categories of problems clients typically face.

Problems of Living

Hershenson and Power (1987) define *problems of living* as "aberrations and/or natural rough spots as one moves through the course of the life-span development" (p. 87). Typical problems of living that clients face include relationship difficulties, such as marital problems; lack of meaning in life, such as not feeling valued at work; and problems associated with stress, such as psychosomatic illness. Although mental disorders may contribute to problems of living, a client can have these problems without a recognized mental disorder.

Counseling is the primary treatment strategy used to help clients deal with problems of living. Counseling can help clients deal with specific problems, prevent future problems, and cope with stress. Since problems of living typically do not involve mental disorders, the use of psychoactive drugs is usually not part of the treatment program.

Mental Disorders

A *mental disorder* can be broadly defined as a dysfunctional behavioral or psychological pattern associated with distress or disability (American Psychiatric Association, 2000). In 1984, the National Institute of Mental Health conducted a survey of mental health problems in the United States ("Mental Disorders," 1984). It was an in-depth study costing $15 million. The study estimated that 40 million people in the United States experience mental health problems at any given time. More specifically it found that

- One in five adults suffered from a recognized mental disorder.
- The three most common disorders in order of incidence were anxiety, substance abuse, and depression.
- Only one out of five people with a mental disorder sought professional help. Those who did tended to seek help from someone at their church or from a family physician.
- Women tended to suffer from phobias and depression, whereas men tended to have problems with alcohol and drugs and antisocial behavior.
- The rates for mental problems were higher for those under 45.
- College graduates tend to be less prone to mental disorders than those who did not graduate from college.

The results of this survey suggest that a large percentage of Americans suffer from mental disorders. Another important implication is that when people experience mental problems, they tend not to utilize mental health services. Instead, they often turn to other professionals, such as physicians or members of the clergy. A challenge for mental health counselors has been to overcome the stigma often associated with mental health services so that individuals will seek help when they need it.

Treating Mental Disorders. Treatment approaches for mental disorders include the use of psychoactive drugs and counseling. Psychoactive drugs are used by psychiatrists primarily to treat psychosis, depression, and acute anxiety reactions. It is important to note that these medications do not cure a person of a mental disorder. They are used primarily to treat underlying brain chemistry dysfunctions and provide symptom relief, such as alleviating depression or anxiety. There are potential dangers, such as the possibility of clients becoming dependent on these medications, especially in the case of tranquilizers to treat anxiety. There can also be serious side-effects, such as tardive dyskinesia, an irreversible neurological disorder that can result from the prolonged use of antipsychotic medications.

Although psychoactive medications can have drawbacks and inherent dangers, their benefits usually outweigh the risks. For example, a schizophrenic client who does not receive medication may be overwhelmed by threatening hallucinations, dangerous delusions, or a disruptive thought disorder. Although medication cannot remove these symptoms entirely, it can usually control them to the degree that the client can function in society. Antidepressant medications can also be an important aspect of a treatment program for severely depressed clients, who may require medication to be able to work and engage in daily activities. Medication can also be very useful in treating a severe anxiety reaction since it can reduce anxiety to a point where the client can cope.

Counseling can also play a vital role in the overall treatment program for mental disorders (see the section on cognitive-behavioral approaches in Chapter 9). Counseling may not be indicated until a client has been medically stabilized by the psychoactive medication. A client can be considered *medically stable* when the symptoms associated with the mental disorder have been reduced to the extent that the client is capable of actively engaging in the counseling process.

Counseling can also be used, of course, to treat mental disorders that do not require medication. The actual counseling strategies will vary according to the unique needs of the client and the clinical indicators associated with the particular mental disorder. The following *Personal Note* describes some of the things I have learned about the treatment of mental disorders.

A Personal Note

Over the years, I have learned many important lessons from clients who had mental disorders. Several clients have said something in particular that I have never forgotten. As I reflect on these cases, their comments symbolize lessons that I learned from them. I will describe five cases, giving the client's statement, a brief description of the situation, and the lesson I learned from each person.

Client's Statement: "Someone said pull my eyes out and I did."

Description of Client's Situation: The client who made this statement was a 25-year-old male who was in jail for theft. A psychiatrist had been asked to make an evaluation because the client was acting strangely. The psychiatrist made a provisional diagnosis of schizophrenia and arranged to have the client admitted to a psychiatric hospital.

The client was not given any antipsychotic medication and was to be transferred to the hospital the next day. That night, he began to hallucinate that he was hearing voices. A "voice" told him to take his eye out, and he did. Then a "voice" said to take the other eye out, and he took it out as well. He was standing and holding his two eyes when a jailer walked by and saw with horror what had happened. The client was immediately taken to a hospital and provided treatment. At the hospital, the client was diagnosed as schizophrenic. I met this man while I was at the hospital checking on several clients. He told me about the voices he had heard, asking him to take his eyes out when he was in jail.

What I Learned: I learned that clients who are actively hallucinating can do serious harm to themselves. Antipsychotic medications must therefore be considered to help control the hallucinations and other psychotic symptoms.

Client's Statement: "Would you like to see the picture I painted?"

Description of Client's Situation: The client was a 23-year-old woman who had a long history of severe depression. I had been providing counseling for the client for about one year. Although she had weekly appointments, she often missed them. I was actually surprised when she did make an appointment because she always seemed so disoriented.

One day, the client walked into the counseling center and said she wanted to see me. She told me she had painted a self-portrait and asked if I would like to see it. I could not believe my eyes. She painted the most beautiful painting I had ever seen!

What I Learned: This client made me realize never to "write off" a client. Regardless of how incapacitated I may think some clients are, I will always remember that they are still capable of doing fantastic things with their lives.

(continued)

Client's Statement: "There were spiders crawling all over my face and voices telling me I was going to die. I was terrified!"

Description of Client's Situation: This was a 54-year-old female who had been an alcoholic for 26 years. The client was on a drinking binge for two weeks and then experienced alcohol hallucinosis, which involved spiders crawling on her face and her hearing terrifying voices. The client came to the counseling center the next day and said she would never drink again. I provided weekly counseling services for her over the next year. During that time, the client did not drink. She later moved to another city.

What I Learned: I discovered that the prognosis for overcoming alcoholism is good when the client decides that the costs outweigh the rewards of use. During the first few sessions, it became clear to me that this client had decided that drinking was just not worth it anymore.

Client's Statement: "We just caught on fire."

Description of Client's Situation: The client who made this statement was one of two brothers who caught on fire when they were sniffing gasoline. Both had a long history of inhalant abuse, spanning a five-year period. I had been seeing them in counseling for two years prior to their accident with gasoline. During the years I worked with them, they were hospitalized on numerous occasions for treatment of acute lead poisoning. On one occasion, one of the brothers became psychotic, jumping out of a moving car and running down the street pounding on cars during 8:00 A.M. rush-hour traffic.

What I Learned: I learned several things from this case and similar cases involving inhalant dependency. First, I found these individuals have a very difficult time attempting to overcome inhalant dependency. My success rate has been very low with this population: only one out of five stopped using inhalants while I worked with them.

I soon discovered that lead poisoning can produce serious side-effects. For example, both of the brothers I worked with showed significant intel-lectual impairment. Their overall IQ scores on the Wechsler Adult Intelligence Scale dropped 15 and 20 points over a 12-month interval while they were using inhalants. I also discovered that gasoline sniffing can make a person psychotic. In addition, I learned that lead poisoning was very difficult to treat. I found out that when an individual inhales lead, the lead is absorbed into the bone structure as well as other parts of the body. Unfortunately, the lead tends to remain in the bone structure, gradually releasing lead into the body.

Client's Statement: "I got my meat, my flour, and my Jesus."

Description of Client's Situation: This was a 45-year-old woman who had been suffering from chronic schizophrenia for 20 years. A residential program had just opened for people who were chronically mentally ill and who had no relatives to assist them. I asked the client whether she would like to be admitted into the program, and she said, "Yes."

Getting the client admitted into the program was a very long and drawn-out process. It involved filling out numerous forms and dealing with other seemingly endless aspects of the bureaucracy. I was finally told that my client could get into the program. I couldn't wait to tell her the good news.

When I told her she was accepted into the program, she looked puzzled. She then smiled and told me that she didn't want to go. She said, "I got my meat, my flour, and my Jesus." When I asked her what she meant, she said she had plenty of meat to eat and flour to make bread. Then she turned on her portable radio and played a religious station featuring a preacher giving a high-powered sermon. She pointed to the radio, smiled, and said, "That's my Jesus."

What I Learned: I learned that freedom is essential to human dignity. Whenever possible, people need to have freedom of choice and be able to act on those choices. My job as a counselor was simply to help create choices. When I did create choices for this client, it seemed to bring more meaning to her existence—an existence that she already had.

Strategies for Suicidal Clients

Mental health services must continually adapt to the changes in society. Two mental health problems requiring increasing efforts from mental health counselors and other members of the helping profession are suicidal clients and clients with substance-abuse problems. To illustrate the contemporary issues and skills associated with mental health counseling, this section provides an overview of suicide, and the next will cover substance abuse.

The rate of suicides per 100,000 people increased over the past 40 years and now has leveled off. In 1950 there were 4.2 suicides per 100,000; in 1974, 10.9; in 1984, 12.8; and in 1996, 11.65 (NIMH, 1999; Shneidman, 1984). Suicide rates are high across all levels of society. Among girls, the gifted have the highest rate of suicide nationally and are therefore considered to have an especially high risk (Taylor, 1979).

Capuzzi and Nystul (1986) provide a comprehensive overview of suicide—causes, myths, and treatment strategies. The remainder of this section is adapted from that work.

Causes

Shneidman (1984) identifies four theoretical perspectives for understanding the motivation for attempting suicide.

Sociological. Durkheim (1897) described sociological reasons for suicide that seem to have withstood the test of time. These reasons can be categorized as *egoistic,* when a person lacks a sense of belonging and therefore lacks a sense of purpose; *altruistic,* when a person is willing to die for a particular cause (for example, Japanese kamikaze pilots); *anomic,* when a person believes his or her relationship with society has been shattered (for example, after being fired from a job); and *fatalistic,* when a person feels society does not offer any hope for a better future (for example, someone who feels trapped in poverty).

Psychodynamic. Freud (1933) emphasized the role of unconscious forces in personality dynamics. In this regard, he believed that all people have an unconscious death wish that could contribute to suicidal behavior.

Psychological. Shneidman (1976) provides a psychological perspective of suicide, suggesting that suicide is associated with the following psychological conditions: *acute perturbation,* when a person is in a heightened state of unhappiness; *heightened inimicality,* when a person has negative thoughts and feelings toward the self, such as self-hate and guilt; *constriction of intellectual focus,* when a person experiences a tunneling of thought processes, resulting in an inability to see viable options; and *cessation,* when a person believes that suicide will make his or her suffering stop.

Constitutional or Biochemical. The medical model suggests a link between depression and suicide and views depression as having an organic basis. In this model, therefore, suicide can be prevented by using psychoactive medication to restore an individual's biochemical balance.

Myths About Suicide

Numerous myths are associated with suicide. The following are some of the myths and the facts that counteract them, as provided by Capuzzi and Nystul (1986) and Gilliland and James (1997):

- *Suicide is only committed by people with severe psychological problems.* Studies have shown that most individuals who commit suicide had not been diagnosed as having a psychological disorder (Shneidman, Farberow, & Litman, 1976).
- *Suicide usually occurs without warning.* In fact, most suicides are preceded by warning signs. The nature of the warning signs may be a sudden change of behavior, self-destructive behavior, verbal threats of suicide, talk of hopelessness and despair, and depression.
- *People who are suicidal will always be prone to suicide.* In truth, most people who become suicidal do not remain in that state forever. They may be struggling through a temporary personal crisis. Once they work through the crisis, they may never be suicidal again.
- *Discussing suicide may cause the client to want to carry out the act.* The opposite is actually true. Talking with a caring person can often prevent suicide.
- *When a person has attempted suicide and pulls back from it, the danger is over.* Actually, the greatest period of danger is usually during the upswing period, when the person becomes energized following a severe depression and has the energy to commit suicide.

Treatment Strategies

Capuzzi and Nystul (1986) and Westefeld et al. (2000) provide an overview of treatment issues relating to suicide, such as prevention, assessment, suicide risk factors, crisis intervention, post-crisis counseling, post-intervention, and rational suicide.

Prevention. Three types of prevention were described earlier in this chapter (primary, secondary, and tertiary). All three can be related to suicide. Primary prevention focuses on individuals before they become suicidal, such as an elementary school counselor making classroom presentations on dealing with stress. Secondary prevention attempts to recognize people who are at risk for suicide and provide the necessary assistance before their problems exacerbate. Tertiary prevention involves assisting people who are currently suicidal. For example, crisis-intervention services such as telephone hotlines have been used to prevent individuals from committing suicide (Lester, 1993).

Assessment. Assessment of suicide should be a comprehensive process involving standardized and nonstandardized assessment procedures and the clinical interview discussed in Chapter 4. Westefeld et al. (2000) identifies assessment tools that have been developed to specifically assess suicide. Some of these assessment tools are the Suicide Ideation Scale (Rudd, 1989), designed primarily for college students; the Reasons for Living Inventory (Linehan, Goodstein, Nielsen, & Chiles, 1983), based on Victor Frankl's (1959) existential theory; and the Fairy Tales Test (Orbach, Feshbach, Carlson, Glaubman, & Gross, 1983), which can be used with children.

Suicide Risk Factors. Gilliland and James (1997) and Westefeld et al. (2000) identify a number of empirically identified risk factors associated with suicide.

Mental Disorders. A number of mental disorders have been associated with suicide. These include depression, substance abuse, psychotic disorders, and personality disorders (especially borderline). For example, suicide can be a response to escape the sadness of depression.

Loss. Loss can be a factor in any suicide. For example, the breakup of a relationship or a divorce can trigger a suicide attempt. Multiple issues of loss can characterize the late adult stage. Challenges associated with loss during the late adult stage include unwanted retirement, chronic illnesses and pain, and death of loved ones. Loss for seniors can, therefore, result in suicidal tendencies associated with lack of purpose and meaning, pain and suffering, and social-emotional isolation.

History. A history of past suicide attempts creates a high risk for suicide. Suicide risk also increases if there is past family history of suicide. In this regard, suicide can be perceived by family members as a way of coping with mental problems such as depression. Another historical factor that may be associated with suicide is the contagion factor (that is, being exposed to suicide may cause a person to be more prone to engaging in suicide).

Diversity Issues. Diversity factors such as age, gender, culture, and sexual orientation can be associated with increased risk of suicide. In terms of age, adolescents and adults over age 65 are at a higher risk of suicide than the general population. Gender statistics in suicide indicate that women *attempt* suicide at a much higher rate than men. Surprisingly, men actually commit suicide 4.5 times as often as women. It is not clear what accounts for this discrepancy. Some have hypothesized that fatal suicides for women are often incorrectly reported as accidental deaths (Westefeld et al., 2000). Culture also plays a role in suicide. Native Americans have the highest suicide rates in the United States. They are estimated at 1.6 to 4.2 times higher than the national average. The increased risk for suicide for Native Americans can be related to high rates of alcoholism and difficulty with acculturation and identity development. Sexual orientation has also been related to increased risk for suicide. This is especially true during adolescence, when gays and lesbians are 2 to 3 times more likely to die from suicide than are their heterosexual counterparts. A lack of public acceptance or tolerance of homosexual orientations can undermine identity development when adolescents need understanding and acceptance the most.

MMPI. MMPI does not stand for the commonly used personality inventory described in Chapter 4. Rather, MMPI is an acronym for means, motive, plan, and intent and can be used to identify risk factors associated with suicide. The following *Personal Note* provides an example of how I used the MMPI to assess for suicide.

Crisis Intervention. The section on crisis intervention discussed earlier in this chapter provides guidelines for crisis intervention. As was noted, the aim of crisis intervention is taking the necessary steps to avoid a catastrophe whereby the client is seriously hurt.

Crisis-intervention strategies used with suicidal clients include contracts, assistance from relatives, medication, counseling, and hospitalization. Suicide contracts are commonly

A Personal Note

Anne was a 32-year-old teacher who sought mental health services for depression and insomnia. Anne told me that she wanted to kill herself because her mom had recently died, and she could no longer go on living. As I assessed her suicidal tendencies, Anne reported she had a bottle of sleeping pills she planned to take (means and plan). The intensity and sincerity of her tone of voice suggested she really did plan to do this (intent). Anne went on to justify killing herself by noting that her mom was her best friend and she felt she had nothing to live for (motive). On the basis of the MMPI, clinical interview, and other input, I determined that Anne was a very high risk for suicide and arranged to have her hospitalized.

used to prevent suicide. They involve having clients sign a contract promising not to kill themselves and to let the counselor know if they become suicidal. Family members can play an integral role in suicide intervention by providing social-emotional support to clients, monitoring clients for suicidal ideations, and helping clients obtain professional help as needed. Other suicide interventions include use of medication to treat mental disorders such as depression. Counseling involves encouraging ventilation to defuse the crisis and to promote psychological equilibrium. Hospitalization provides the safest means to prevent suicide and should be considered for acutely suicidal individuals.

Post-Crisis Counseling.   Post-crisis counseling can be conducted when individuals are no longer at a high risk for suicide. It can help determine underlying reasons why clients were suicidal and foster coping mechanisms to prevent future psychological problems. Dialectic behavior therapy (Linehan, Armstrong, Suarez, Allmon, & Heard, 1991) was specifically designed to treat clients who have a history of suicidal ideations. This approach is directed at teaching skills associated with suicide prevention, such as emotional regulation, interpersonal effectiveness, and distress tolerance. Beck's (1986) cognitive therapy can also be a valuable approach to help clients who have had a history of suicidal ideations (Tyrer et al., 1999).

Post-Intervention.   Post-intervention involves providing mental health assistance to bereaved individuals, families, and communities. The American Association of Suicidology (1990) identifies the following post-intervention strategies for suicide:

- Planning how schools and community agencies respond to suicide
- Providing opportunities to work through emotions such as grief, anger, and guilt associated with survivors of suicide
- Taking necessary steps to prevent contagion suicide (such as avoidance of glamorizing the suicide)
- Providing debriefing counseling for mental health staff involved

The following *Personal Note* provides additional insight into the suicidal phenomenon.

Rational Suicide.   *Rational suicide,* also referred to as *hastened death* and *assisted suicide,* may be the most controversial issue in suicidology. Rational suicide relates to a

A Personal Note

When I was the psychologist for an Indian reservation, I provided mental health counseling to more than 100 clients who attempted suicide. Most of these clients were female adolescents who tried to kill themselves by taking large amounts of pills they found in a medicine cabinet.

The thing that surprised me about these clients was that nearly all of them truly seemed to want to die. They did not appear simply to be making a cry for help. Several nearly died when their hearts stopped. Each time, fortunately, the medical team was able to bring the client back from the grips of death. When these young women regained consciousness, however, almost all of them immediately said something that expressed their disappointment that they had not died.

As I explored their reasons for wanting to die, the majority seemed to believe that life had nothing to offer them. They had reached a dead end, with nowhere to go. They felt that if they did try to continue living, things would probably just get worse. There were feelings of futility and sorrow in their words and tone of voice. Their desire for life seemed to be gone and in its place grew a sense of apathy. I would often use nontraditional approaches to counseling to help these clients overcome their preoccupation with suicide, death, and dying. For example, I might meet with clients under a tree to awaken them to the beauty and innocence of life. During a session, we might stop and take time to hear a bird sing. Focusing on the wonder of nature helped clients shift from the negative associated with their suicidal ideation and open their eyes to the simple, basic splendor of life that only nature can portray. The focus of counseling with these clients was to help them discover some personal meaning in life. Together, we worked to cultivate dreams and develop the means to turn those dreams into reality. This process required intensive individual counseling and psychotherapy. In addition, I often utilized couples counseling and family therapy as an important facet of the overall treatment program.

rational choice to hasten the end of one's life. Hastened death can be requested in instances of terminal illnesses or insufferable pain.

Oregon's Death with Dignity Act of 1999 (Oregon Act), as amended from the 1994 Oregon Act, has played a major role in the evolution of rational suicide. The Oregon Act legalizes physician-assisted suicide in Oregon. The Oregon Act includes conditions that must be met for physicians to participate in assisted suicide. For example, physicians must refer patients to state-licensed psychologists or psychiatrists if the patient appears to have a psychological or psychiatric condition such as depression that impairs judgment (Cohen, 2001). Lee and Tolle (1996) note that care of the dying in Oregon appears to have improved since the Death with Dignity Act and suggest that the Oregon Act represents a "wake-up call" for physicians to do a better job in assisting individuals to prepare and move toward the end of their lives.

Rational suicide encompasses health-care workers such as a psychologists in promoting the psychological means to achieve a death with dignity and meaning. The American Psychological Association (1997) position on rational suicide is as follows:

> The American Psychological Association does not advocate for or against assisted suicide. What psychologists do support is high quality end-of-life care and informed end-of-life decisions based on the correct assessment of the patient's mental capacity, social support systems, and degree of self-determination. (p. 1)

In addition, the APA provides guidelines regarding the role of mental health workers in rational suicide. These activities include providing support to the patient and family, ensuring that patients receive proper diagnosis and treatment for mental disorders, and assisting in determining whether patients' decisions regarding hastened death are rational.

Although rational suicide appears to offer promise in terms of promoting a death with dignity and meaning, numerous moral, religious, ethical, and legal issues remained to be addressed. Additional research and evaluation are necessary to determine the implications of the role of mental health workers in rational suicide.

Strategies for Clients with Substance-Abuse Problems

Substance abuse has become a major health problem in the United States as well as in many other countries. Alcoholism is considered to be the third most prevalent public-health problem in the United States (Pattison & Kaufman, 1982). For some cultures, such as Native American, alcoholism ranks first among all health problems (Herring, 1994). Illicit drug use is also widespread in American society and includes use among children and adolescents, as discussed in Chapter 11. A 1982 survey estimated that 32 million Americans smoke marijuana at least once a year, and 20 million use it once a month; over 12 million use cocaine once a year; and several million use a variety of drugs, such as tranquilizers and stimulants, without medical supervision (Polich, Ellickson, Reuter, & Kahan, 1984).

The result of the high prevalence of alcohol and drug use (not counting tobacco) is that approximately 40 percent of hospital admissions and 25 percent of deaths a year in the United States are related to substance abuse, costing society an excess of $300 billion a year in addition to human suffering and lack of productivity (American Psychiatric Association, 1995). The extensive cost and suffering generated by excessive use of alcohol and other drugs is not surprising when noting that approximately half of all highway fatalities involve alcohol; one-third of all new AIDS cases are related to intravenous drug users; and 7.5 to 15 percent of pregnant women have recently used a drug (not counting alcohol) just prior to their first prenatal exam (American Psychiatric Association, 1995).

Substance abuse permeates all levels of society: approximately one-fifth of all Americans have a problem with alcohol or drug abuse at some time in their lives, and one-third of all psychiatric patients have alcohol- or drug-abuse problems (Frances, 1988). Counselors can therefore expect to come into contact with problems relating to drug abuse regardless of the counseling setting where they work.

This section provides an overview of substance abuse, with information relating to diagnosis, special treatment issues, counseling goals, treatment strategies, and prevention of relapses. Since alcoholism is the most prevalent of these problems, particular attention is devoted to that issue.

Diagnosis

Counselors can diagnose substance-abuse problems using the DSM-IV-TR (American Psychiatric Association, 2000), which recognizes two mental disorders associated with substance abuse: substance abuse and substance dependence. A diagnosis of *substance abuse* applies to a client with an impairment in social or occupational functioning. *Substance dependence* is considered a more serious disorder and is diagnosed when a client shows evidence of physiological withdrawal or tolerance. It is important to note that use of a particular substance like marijuana does not constitute abuse. Instead, the use of the substance must result in impairment in functioning before it should be considered abuse or dependence, a recognized mental disorder.

Questionnaires can also be used as a part of the diagnostic process to determine whether a person is an alcoholic or has a substance-abuse problem. A commonly used questionnaire is the Michigan Alcohol Screening Test (Selzer, 1971). This test has 24 questions that require yes-or-no answers from the respondent.

Some dangers can result, however, from using the DSM-IV-TR system of diagnosis or a questionnaire to label a person as a substance abuser. These systems have either-or definitions of alcoholism in that they provide a result that a client either is or is not an alcoholic. This either-or definition could result in a counselor not providing needed services to a client with a borderline problem.

Pattison and Kaufman (1982) reject the either-or perspective and instead conceptualize alcoholism as a multivariant syndrome. This position suggests that no two alcoholics are alike. Instead, alcoholics represent multiple patterns of dysfunctional use, varying personalities, numerous possibilities for adverse consequences, and various prognoses, and each individual requires a different type of treatment (Pattison & Kaufman, 1982).

According to Lewis, Dana, and Blevins (2002), the multivariant position suggests that substance abuse should be conceptualized on a continuum from nonuse to dependence (see Figure 15.1). Lewis et al. (2002) note that the continuum model does not imply that people who develop problems will always move steadily along the continuum from left to right. The relationship to the continuum will vary from individual to individual. Some will stay at the same spot; others will move to the right, signifying more serious problems; and some will develop less severe problems, moving to the left on the continuum.

Lewis et al. (2002) suggest that counselors can estimate the place where a person is functioning on the continuum by determining the number of problems the person has experienced in relation to substance abuse. Valliant's (1983) Problem-Drinking Scale can be used to identify problems relating to drinking, including work-related problems, such as excessive tardiness or sick leave or being fired from work; family problems, such as complaints from family members or marital problems; legal problems, such as alcohol-related arrests; and health problems, such as medical disorders, blackouts, and tremors.

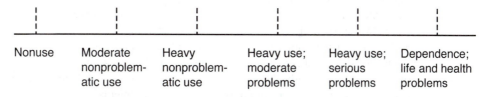

| Nonuse | Moderate nonproblematic use | Heavy nonproblematic use | Heavy use; moderate problems | Heavy use; serious problems | Dependence; life and health problems |

FIGURE 15.1 Substance-Abuse Continuum

Source: From *Substance Abuse Counseling: An Individual Approach* by J. A. Lewis, R. Q. Dana, and G. A. Blevins. Copyright © 2002, Brooks/Cole Publishing Company, Pacific Grove, CA 93950, a division of International Thomson Publishing, Inc. By permission of the publisher.

Special Treatment Issues

Most of the counseling theories and strategies described in this text can be applied to the treatment of clients with substance-abuse problems. At the same time, some special issues should be considered when working with this population. In this regard, Lewis et al. (2002) provide the following guidelines for substance-abuse counseling:

- Conceptualize substance-abuse problems on a continuum from nonproblematic to problematic rather than in dichotomous, either-or terms.
- Provide an individualized treatment program in terms of goals and methods.
- Incorporate a multidimensional treatment program that includes social and environmental aspects associated with long-term recovery.
- Select the least intrusive treatment for each client.
- Consider new methods and goals as research findings become available.
- Be sensitive to the individual differences and various needs of diverse client populations.

These guidelines provide a general theoretical framework for working with clients with substance-abuse issues. In addition, there are some unique counseling goals and treatment strategies associated with substance-abuse counseling.

Counseling Goals

Considerable debate exists in the literature as to whether the primary goal of alcohol-abuse counseling should be abstinence or controlled drinking (Fisher, 1982; Marlatt, 1983; Sobell & Sobell, 1984). Proponents of abstinence align themselves with the disease model of alcoholism, contending that alcoholism is a chronic and progressive disease and that abstinence is therefore the only solution. Alcoholics Anonymous (AA) and Narcotics Anonymous (NA) are among the proponents of this position. In contrast, supporters of controlled drinking conceptualize alcoholism from a behavioral perspective, believing that it results from maladaptive learning.

Miller and Munoz (1982) note that controlled drinking will be appropriate only for approximately 15 percent of all alcohol abusers. In addition, Miller and Munoz (1982) identify conditions that should preclude any consideration of controlled drinking as a treatment goal. These include clients who have a medical problem such as a disease of the gastrointestinal system (for example, liver disease), heart disease, or other condition that may be made worse by drinking; are pregnant or trying to become pregnant; tend to lose control of their behavior when they drink; have been physically addicted to alcohol; take medication that is dangerous when combined with alcohol, such as antidepressants or tranquilizers; or are currently abstaining successfully, particularly if there is a family history of alcoholism or a personal history of serious drinking problems.

Counselors who want to consider controlled drinking as a goal for a client should first receive specialized training. Behavioral self-control training is one approach that has received considerable attention, reporting a success rate between 60 and 80 percent (Miller, 1980). This program is educationally oriented and can be used in an outpatient setting. It involves a variety of behavioral techniques, including training the client to identify environmental cues that increase the frequency of drinking, to monitor drinking consumption, and to use self-reinforcement to control drinking rates.

Aside from the issue of abstinence versus controlled drinking, there are other, more specific goals that counselors should address in developing a comprehensive treatment program. Lewis et al. (2002) note that substance abuse tends to be associated with social, physiological, family, and financial problems. Considering these related problems, they identify the following goals that counselors could attempt to accomplish in substance-abuse counseling. The counselor can help clients to

- Resolve legal problems
- Attain stability in marriage and family
- Establish and meet educational and career goals
- Improve interpersonal and social skills
- Enhance physical fitness and health
- Develop effective coping mechanisms to deal with stress
- Learn how to recognize and express feelings
- Develop effective problem-solving and decision-making skills
- Establish a social support system
- Develop positive self-esteem and self-efficacy
- Deal effectively with psychological issues such as anxiety and depression
- Create recreational and social outlets

Treatment Strategies

Treatment approaches in substance-abuse counseling vary according to the counselor's theoretical orientation as well as the goals established by the counselor and client. The following overview presents some commonly used treatment approaches.

The Minnesota Model. The Minnesota model has been one of the most widely used forms of treatment for substance abuse. According to Gilliland and James (1997), there are two phases to the Minnesota model. The first phase involves a comprehensive treatment team to evaluate and provide initial treatment pertaining to the unique needs of the client. The second phase typically involves an intensive 28-day inpatient hospitalization directed at all aspects of the client's substance-abuse problem (for example, education, recovery, and relapse prevention). In an era of managed care, the 28-day hospitalization is in most instances not a realistic goal for treatment planning. Most managed-care organizations are shifting to an emphasis on outpatient substance-abuse treatment programs.

The Alcoholics Anonymous (AA) Model. Since AA was founded in 1935, it has developed into the most popular organization for the treatment of alcoholism and other substance-abuse problems (Lê, Ingvarson, & Page, 1995). AA incorporates the disease model of alcoholism and is based on the 12 steps of AA, which have a strong religious context. One of the strengths of AA is that it is run by individuals who have themselves struggled with substance dependence. In addition, it can be a place where people feel accepted, hope, and encouragement. It is also a highly accessible organization with outlets available in almost every major city in the world.

There has been some concern that the efficacy of AA has not been determined through empirical research and that the religiously oriented terms such as admitting power-lessness are inconsistent with counseling theory and practice (Bristow-Braitman, 1995; Lê et al., 1995). Bristow-Braitman (1995) suggests that cognitive-behavioral counseling could be used to help reframe some AA concepts to make them more compatible with traditional counseling approaches. Professional counselors may benefit from a deeper understanding of AA so they can become more sensitive to the spiritual aspects of counseling and be more supportive of their clients who are attending AA.

The Medical Model.   This approach also adheres to the disease model of alcoholism. Researchers are investigating the role of physiological factors (including brain function) in the etiology and treatment of substance-abuse disorders (Ruden & Byalick, 1997). Lewis, et al. (2002) suggest that there are a number of neurotransmitters that play important roles in the addiction process. For example, dopamine is believed to influence motor activity, reward, and reinforcement and has been associated with commonly used drugs such as cocaine, marijuana, and nicotine (Lewis et al., 2002). The dopamine hypothesis of addic-tion suggests that dopamine plays a key role in addiction by sending pleasure signals to the brain when it is stimulated by drugs such as cocaine (Volkow et al., 1997).

Ruden and Byalick (1997) identify medical approaches that can be used to treat substance-abuse problems. Antabuse is a form of aversive therapy that can be taken to pre-vent relapse in drinking alcohol. In antabuse treatment, a person experiences anxiety, vom-iting, nausea, and palpitations within minutes if alcohol is consumed. Methadone maintenance is another form of medical treatment for substance abuse. Methadone can be used to block the withdrawal symptoms associated with heroin, while not producing the euphoric effects. Detoxification centers can also play an important role in the treatment of substance-abuse problems. Detoxification allows for patients to overcome potentially life-threatening withdrawal effects of alcohol under medical supervision.

Cognitive-Behavioral Therapies.   Cognitive-behavioral therapies are effective treat-ments in substance-abuse counseling (especially alcohol-related problems). A number of research studies have focused on the role of cognitive-behavioral therapies in the acquisition of skills necessary to overcome alcohol abuse and dependence (American Psychiatric Asso-ciation, 1995). Some of these cognitive-behavioral–related skills are self-control, interper-sonal functioning, self-efficacy, alternative coping mechanisms, and relapse prevention.

Behavioral Therapies.   Behavioral therapies can be used in substance-abuse counseling. Some of the more common behavioral approaches are operant conditioning to reward and punish behaviors associated with abstaining and engaging in substance abuse and system-atic desensitization and aversion training to countercondition clients craving drugs (Ameri-can Psychiatric Association, 1995).

Individual Psychodynamic/Interpersonal Therapies.   The American Psychiatric Asso-ciation (1995) has provided some support for the use of psychodynamic and interpersonal therapies in substance-abuse counseling. The association notes that psychodynamic psy-chotherapy appears to help prevent relapse in substance abuse. In addition, newer, short-term forms of psychodynamic therapy (such as supportive-expressive therapy and interpersonal psychotherapy) are demonstrating efficacy in substance-abuse counseling (American Psychiatric Association, 1995). These newer approaches focus on formulating supportive counseling relationships in which clients can learn the social skills necessary to overcome negative patterns of interpersonal functioning, which in turn decreases problems with substance abuse (Ruden & Byalick, 1997).

Group Therapies.   Lewis et al. (2002) suggest that group counseling has many advantages over other methods of substance-abuse counseling. For example, it can provide an opportunity for group members to offer support and encouragement, generate problem-solving strategies, learn how to apply new skills such as assertiveness, and, when necessary, break through denial or other processes that interfere with recovery from substance-abuse problems.

Family Therapy.   Gilliland and James (1997) contend that it is critical to involve the family in the treatment of substance abuse. Family therapy recognizes that the behavior of each family member must be understood from the perspective of the family system. Drinking or the use of other drugs is therefore not an isolated event but an action that affects the overall functioning of the family.

Numerous concepts have emerged from family therapy literature that provide insight into the systemic nature of behavior of family members. For example, the concepts *enabling* and *codependency* imply that two individuals (one with a substance-abuse problem such as drinking) could be dependent on maintaining an adversarial relationship regarding the drinking. In this situation it is common for the drinker and the concerned family member to both get secondary gains from their codependency, thereby enabling the drinker to continue drinking (that is, drinkers feel they have an excuse to drink when they "get griped at" and concerned family members can get sympathy from others regarding having to put up with the drinking).

Family therapy can also be used to overcome one of the most difficult barriers to treatment in substance-abuse counseling: denial. It is very common for individuals to deny problems with alcohol or other drugs and resist treatment even when the problem is having a serious adverse effect on their health, family, social life, and work. When this occurs, Johnson's (1986) family-intervention model can be used to help a family confront a family member with the realities of his or her substance-abuse problem. This approach involves training family members to communicate in a clear, caring, and direct manner their concerns regarding how the substance abuse is affecting the individual and the family as a whole. The family-intervention model can be a powerful approach to overcoming denial and motivating the individual to seek help (Gilliland & James, 1997).

Stages of Change

Helping clients successfully engage in the change process is perhaps the most difficult yet important aspect of counseling. Unfortunately, little has been known about how the change process works. This bleak situation is being addressed by the pioneering work of Prochaska, DiClemente, and associates on how the change process relates to overcoming addictive behaviors (see Prochaska, 1984; Prochaska, DiClemente, & Norcross, 1992).

Prochaska et al.'s (1992) transtheoretical model of change posits that both the cessation of problematic behaviors and the acquisition of healthier behaviors involve five stages of change: precontemplation, contemplation, preparation, action, and maintenance. Prochaska et al. (1992) provide an overview of these five stages of change and the implications they have for developing intervention strategies.

Precontemplation.   During the first stage, clients have no serious plans to engage in the change process. Resistance and denial are common reactions in the precontemplation stage.

Contemplation.   The second stage is characterized by clients being aware that they have a problem and are thinking about making changes but have not quite reached the point of making a commitment to do something. During the contemplation stage, clients seriously consider resolving their problems. They tend to weigh the pros and cons associated with potential changes to help with decision making.

Preparation.   At the preparation stage, clients have unsuccessfully taken some action during the past year and plan to try to work on their problem during the next 30 days.

Action.   Clients have reached the action stage when they have made the necessary changes in their lives to successfully address a particular problem (for example, they have stopped drinking for one day to six months).

Maintenance.   The maintenance stage is characterized by clients attempting to prevent relapse and to stabilize their gains. In substance-abuse counseling, maintenance extends from six months to the rest of the client's life.

Change is like the tide. It moves forward and backward as clients progress and relapse. Prochaska et al. (1992) point out that since clients tend to relapse, it is common to regress back to earlier stages in the change process. Fortunately, people tend to learn from their mistakes and use this information to help them be more successful as they work their way back through the stages of change.

One of the most important implications of the change model is to identify where clients are in terms of the change process and match their position with the appropriate form of intervention. For example, there is some evidence that suggests that during the precontemplation and contemplation stages, experiential, cognitive, and psychoanalytic approaches are the most effective, whereas during the action and maintenance stages, existential and behavioral theories have the strongest efficacy (Prochaska et al., 1992).

Prevention of Relapses

A comprehensive treatment program for substance abuse should include strategies to prevent or deal with a client's relapse, or uncontrolled return to drug or alcohol use. The potential for relapse is a serious problem in substance-abuse counseling. Some estimates suggest that 90 percent of all clients have a relapse within four years following treatment (Polich, Armor, & Braiker, 1981).

Several factors have been related to substance-abuse relapse. Svanum and McAdoo (1989) note that differences in the outcome of a substance-abuse treatment program are related to the presence or absence of a mental disorder in addition to the substance-abuse disorder. These researchers found that clients with no additional disorders tended to avoid relapse as long as they complied with after-care treatment, especially an exercise program; had a satisfactory job; and had an adequate living arrangement. Clients with multiple mental disorders were more prone to relapse if their emotional disturbance continued after participation in a substance-abuse program. Other factors such as exercise, work, or living conditions do not appear to be related to relapse for these clients. Since a substantial minority of substance-abuse clients suffer from psychopathology such as anxiety and depression (Mirin, Weiss, Michael, & Griffin, 1988), substance-abuse programs should include careful screening and treatment for these disorders as part of relapse prevention.

A second factor related to substance-abuse relapse is the lifestyle imbalance that can result from certain life events. Cummings, Gordon, and Marlatt (1980) attempted to determine what types of events precipitated a relapse. They found that negative emotional states were associated with 35 percent of all relapses; interpersonal conflicts were related to 16 percent; and social pressures accounted for 20 percent.

Lewis et al. (2002) incorporated Marlatt and Gordon's (1985) model of the relapse process into the flowchart shown in Figure 15.2. The flowchart suggests that the relapse process can begin with a lifestyle imbalance, as shown at the left. This can occur when a client experiences a particular problem, such as a setback at work or a relationship problem. The imbalance may cause the client to feel the need for immediate stress release. The client may rationalize taking a drink by thinking, "I deserve a drink, with all that I'm going through." At this point the client may deny having a problem with alcohol and make apparently irrelevant decisions (AIDs). Without the necessary coping skills, the client will experience a decrease in self-efficacy, feeling unable to cope with the situation. This in turn will result in a slip—beginning to drink—creating an abstinence violation effect (AVE). The AVE further undermines the client's self-efficacy, reducing self-confidence. The client may

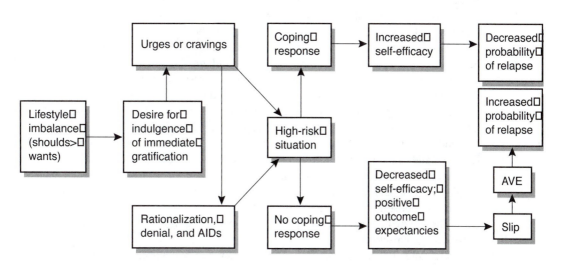

FIGURE 15.2 Relapse Process

Source: Relapse Prevention Maintenance Strategies in the Treatment of Addictive Behaviors, G. A. Marlatt and J. R. Gorden, Eds. New York: Guilford Press, 1985.

think, "I'm just a hopeless drunk." Such negative thinking can create a self-fulfilling prophecy, leading to an increased probability of a relapse. The flowchart in Figure 15.2 also shows how a substance-abuse counselor can help prevent relapse. The key to preventing a relapse is to teach effective coping skills, such as stress management, which can increase self-efficacy and decrease the probability of relapse.

Trends and Perspectives

Several trends affect all aspects of the profession of counseling, including mental health counseling. This section reviews three of these trends and perspectives: postmodernism, diversity issues, and issues relating to managed care.

Postmodern Trends

Postmodern trends are reshaping the manner in which mental health counseling is conceptualized and practiced (see the special issue of *Journal of Mental Health Counseling, 16*(1), 1994, on the constructivist and ecosystemic views) (D'Andrea, 2000; Gutterman, 1996a). These emerging trends can be understood by contrasting key concepts of modernism with postmodernism. Modernists view the "self" as autonomous and independent. It therefore follows from a modernist perspective that problems such as depression are caused by internal struggles (for example, intrapsychic conflicts). The modernist view of the world is objective, with a fixed understanding of knowledge and reality. Research methodology tends to be quantitative, focusing on testing observable, measurable hypotheses. The assessment of clients' problems are understood in terms of cause-and-effect relationships with a focus on content over process (for example, irrational and dysfunctional thinking causes depression and must therefore be analyzed in terms of its content). Goal setting and interventions are generated by mutual agreement between the counselor and client and are reflected in the major counseling theories and approaches.

Postmodern thought broadens the conceptualization of the self to include interpersonal, systemic, and sociocultural forces. Psychological problems, knowledge, and reality are viewed subjectively from a phenomenological perspective and are understood within the context they are presented (e.g., the sociocultural milieu). Assessment of clients' problems emphasizes process over content, with a focus on relational/contextual perspectives. Goal setting and intervention strategies often involve exploring clients' narratives and stories and working together to co-construct new stories that generate personal meaning. Research and evaluation methods tend to be qualitative, whereby the counselor and client function as coinvestigators interested in discovering patterns of meaning that can generate insight and understanding. Table 15.1 summarizes the major concepts that differentiate modern from postmodern perspectives.

The following *Personal Note* provides an example of how I engaged in a postmodern approach to counseling.

D'Andrea (2000) appears to be taking a community counseling/ecosystem perspective when he addresses several concerns regarding emerging trends in postmodernism and constructivism. He contends that postmodernism has overemphasized "internal meaning-making processes" and has overlooked the importance of ecosystemic factors that may

TABLE 15.1   **Comparison of Modern and Postmodern Views**

	Modern Views	**Postmodern Views**
View of the self	Autonomous, independent self	Relational/contextual self
View of knowledge and reality	Fixed-objective concept of knowledge and reality	Phenomenological perspective; subjective/relative concept of knowledge and reality
Assessment of client's problems	Etiology of problems is intrapsychic, with a focus on cause-effect and content (for example, how cognitions affect emotions)	Etiology of problems emphasizes process over content and is focused on relational/contextual perspectives
Goal setting and interventions	Goals are mutually agreed on between counselor and client as reflected in the major counseling theories	Goals and interventions evolve from exploring client's narratives resulting in co-construction of new stories that generate personal meaning
Research strategies	Quantitative research methodology	Qualitative research methodology

A Personal Note

I was a psychologist providing in-patient care in a hospital. My client was a 25-year-old Navajo woman, Martha, whose mother had died two months earlier. She was admitted into the hospital by an ER doctor with a diagnosis of major depression with psychotic features. The ER doctor utilized traditional diagnostic procedures that are by their nature grounded in modernism (e.g., a fixed-objective view of reality). The doctor gave Martha the diagnosis "with psychotic features" because she concluded that Martha was hearing voices and had lost contact with reality (i.e., she was conversing with her deceased mother). The ER doctor agreed to hold off on prescribing antipsychotic medication for Martha's voices until I could do a psychological consult.

At the time I saw Martha, I had been working on the Navajo reservation for two years as a psychologist with the Indian Health Service. By this time, I had become sensitized to some of the unique aspects of the Navajo culture, such as the role of medicine men in promoting mental health and healing. I was also aware of how attitudes, customs, and values shaped my clients' views of reality. I was, therefore, very open to Martha's story when she shared that she regularly conversed with her deceased mother. She asked me if I believed her when she said she often talked with her mother. I responded that it did not matter what *I* believed, it only mattered what made sense *to her.*

I worked with Martha, assisting her with her depression and grief, over a period of two weeks. With the support of her family, Martha was able to move on and let go of her sadness. In time, her story became one of hope and optimism versus one of sadness, despair, and loss. I believe that my relationship with her and the resulting therapeutic alliance was fostered by my openness to her experience. Clinical experiences such as this have made me aware of the importance of maintaining a postmodern phenomological perspective in counseling.

adversely affect clients' welfare (p. 14). D'Andrea also suggests that postmodernism should be more consistent with multiculturalism and that postmodernists should become advocates for social justice. Postmodern theories appear to offer much promise to counseling. Additional research must be done to evaluate their impact on the counseling process.

Mental Health Counseling and the Internet

Gutterman and Kirk (1999) identify a number of Internet tools and resources that can prove helpful to mental health counselors:

- *E-mail* can have numerous uses, including enabling practitioners to communicate. E-mail has also become a popular tool to provide mental health counseling to clients. Internet counseling has advantages and disadvantages. Advantages include easy access (e.g., clients can log on whenever they have time and are not restricted in terms of travel limitations). Disadvantages include difficulties reviewing a counselor's credentials, the limited opportunity to develop a personal relationship between counselor and client, and reduced control over confidentiality. The National Board for Certified Counselors (NBCC) Standards for the Ethical Practice of Web Counseling (1997) was created to address potential ethical-legal issues relating to Internet counseling.
- *Chat rooms* provide opportunities for two or more clients to share mental health information with each other. Chat rooms are especially popular as a self-help group format and are convenient for individuals to share information in that they are not restricted by time or distance limitations.
- *Web sites* can disseminate information regarding mental health services. For example, the American Counseling Association established its Web site in 1996 (http://www.counseling.org).
- *Search engines* can help clients and counselors locate information on the Internet. For instance, Mental Health Net (http://www.mentalhelp.net) has over 93,000 mental health listings as of 1999.
- *WebRings* have been created to facilitate interdisciplinary communication between laypeople and professionals.
- *Online communities* provide opportunities for individuals to visit sites that feature interactive services. Visitors are encouraged to visit often and get to know other users with common interests. Online communities developed for mental health professionals include the World Counseling Network (WCN) (http://www.counseling network.com); and Behavior Online: The Mental Health and Behavior Science Meeting Place (http://www.behavior.net).
- *Scholarly publications and professional newsletters* can be accessed through the Internet.
- *Education and training opportunities* are available on the Internet. Most professional organizations offer continuing education opportunities on the Internet, and many universities utilize the Internet for distance education programs that in some instances include graduate coursework in mental health counseling.

Gutterman and Kirk (1999) posit that the Internet reflects the tenets of postmodernism. From a postmodern perspective, the Internet has become a major sociocultural force in how people define their existence. The unique feature of the Internet is its capacity to link large numbers of people together in an easily accessible, open forum of communication, exploration, and discovery. With input from a multinational populous, ideas are constantly evolving on the Internet. The only constant is ongoing change.

The Internet represents an active versus passive form of communication, whereby all voices can be heard and can ultimately influence a field of endeavor. The resultant knowledge base for various professions, including mental health counseling, is now more fluid and diversified. Mental health professionals are using the Internet to address all aspects of professional activity from theory to research to practice. For example, Gutterman and Kirk (1999) used the Internet to solicit feedback regarding the evolution of an article that was subsequently published in the *Journal of Mental Health Counseling.* The possibilities seem limitless regarding the impact of the Internet on shaping professions such as mental health counseling and on influencing all other aspects of human existence.

Ecosystemic Mental Health Counseling

Ecosystemic mental health counseling appears to be an attempt to incorporate the major concepts from postmodern trends into a new way of conceptualizing the role and function of the mental health counselor. Sherrard and Amatea (1994) define *ecosystemic mental health counseling* as an approach that "enlarges the field of inquiry and intervention from the individual to the couple, the family, and the larger sociocultural contexts that constitute the individual's environment" (p. 3). Ecosystemic mental health counseling acknowledges the vital role that narrative psychology and counseling as storytelling play in the counseling process (Becvar & Becvar, 1994). In this regard, Daniels and White (1994) suggest that the role of the mental health counselor is directed at exploring the linguistic and language systems of the client, resulting in a shift from managing lives to managing conversations.

Mental health counseling recognizes the opportunity that postmodern thought poses for effective integration of theoretical positions. For example, Fong and Lease (1994) suggest that the ecosystemic perspective effectively translates systemic concepts (widely used in marriage and family counseling) into individual and group mental health counseling. Rigazio-DiGilio (1994) addresses the need to integrate theories of development into counseling theories. She provides an in-depth description of how Piaget's theory of cognitive development can be integrated into ecosystemic mental health counseling. Gutterman (1996a) provides another example of integration, noting that solution-focused counseling was derived from current trends in brief counseling and postmodernism/social constructionism. Gutterman contends that solution-focused counseling provides a theoretical framework that can crystallize and bring to focus the unique professional identity of mental health counselors.

Postmodern trends such as ecosystemic mental health counseling are exciting new dimensions of mental health counseling. They appear to offer considerable promise in terms of providing new paradigms for conceptualizing the counseling process. For example, postmodern trends can help create treatment programs that are more comprehensive and holistic in nature and that encourage awareness and sensitivity to issues of diversity, such as sociocultural forces and gender. Future research activities will need to be directed at the efficacy of postmodern trends as they are integrated into the role and function of mental health counselors.

Diversity Issues

Mental health counseling is attempting to embrace all aspects of diversity so that counselors can sensitively and effectively provide mental health services to clients. Culture, gender, individuals with disabilities, and spirituality are examples of diversity issues in mental health counseling. Locke (1993) suggests that mental health counselors need to increase their efforts to respond to the immense challenges that diversity issues pose in the delivery of mental health services. He suggests that mental health counselors can address these challenges in a number of ways, such as by being increasingly aware of cultural issues, providing improved assessment and diagnosis, developing intervention strategies that are more culturally relevant, and increasing awareness and utilization of political forces that have an impact on psychological functioning.

Cultural issues are critical in all phases of counseling. Substance-abuse counseling provides an illustration of the importance of cultural issues in mental health counseling. Terrell (1993) identifies acculturation, sources of stress, and beliefs and attitudes regarding substance use as important cultural factors that contribute to the development and treatment of substance abuse. Acculturation can play a role in the development of substance abuse in terms of the stress experienced during the acculturation process and as a result of conflicting cultural values regarding substance use. An example of acculturation stress could be Native Americans moving from the reservation to urban areas. Beliefs and attitudes regarding substance abuse can also play a role in treatment. For example, African Americans may resist investing themselves in substance-abuse treatment that adheres to the medical model, contending that substance abuse is not a disease but a condition based on personal choice (Terrell, 1993).

Gender is another important diversity consideration in mental health counseling. In this regard, McDonough and Russell (1994) note that most treatment modalities for substance-abuse counseling have been based on a male model of alcoholism. Research is beginning to suggest that women alcoholics have special needs relating to relationship expectations, development issues, and societal stigma. For example, Terrell (1993) notes that some Hispanic females feel a strong cultural sanction against alcohol use, which could make it difficult to admit to a problem and seek help from mental health services.

Gender and depression is another area of diversity for mental health services. Culberston (1997) provides an international review of the literature on the prevalence of depression in males and females. Culberston's study shows women have higher ratios of depression compared to men (2:1); women also suffer from more serious, profound depression at higher rates (between 3:1 and 4:1 for major depression) and the rates of bipolar (manic/depressive) disorders appear to be similar for men and women. Culberston (1997) identifies several factors that could contribute to the different rates of major depression for women and men. Women tend to seek out mental health services more than men, and there is some indication that men tend to "self-medicate" with alcohol and other drugs to deal with problems such as depression. There could also be biological differences in men and women that contribute to higher rates of depression in women. In addition, sociopolitical forces such as child-care demands and lower economic support could contribute to more depression in women than in men.

Helwig and Holicky (1994) note that clients with disabilities are an often neglected but important type of diversity that requires careful attention from mental health counselors. Their research suggests that clients with physical disabilities such as spinal cord injuries are also prone to having substance-abuse problems. Although approximately half of these individuals have symptomatology associated with substance abuse, rehabilitation counseling efforts tend to focus on helping the client adjust to the disability with little or no recognition and treatment of the substance abuse. Helwig and Holicky suggest that substance abuse problems should be addressed first to facilitate clients' ability to deal with the challenges of their disability.

Spirituality (which may or not include religion) is an emerging trend in the diversity literature (Bishop, 1995). Spirituality has been conceptualized as a developmental construct endemic to all people that is directed at addressing questions basic to one's existence (Ingersoll, 1995). Recent research has provided a proliferation of support for the positive role that spirituality and religion can play in mental and physical health (Koenig, 1997; Richards & Bergin, 1997; Witmer & Sweeney, 1995). Miranti and Burke (1995) note that people turn to spiritual values as an important source of strength and support in times of great need. This tendency is especially true as people get older. Richards and Bergin (1997) identify a number of other factors that make spirituality a particularly attractive dimension of the counseling process. Some of the inherent strengths promoted by religion and spirituality include the following:

- It fosters a secure sense of identity that promotes resiliency and helps alleviate stress and anxiety.
- It provides a sense of purpose and meaning to all phases of life, including death.
- It encourages positive feelings and thoughts such as hope, healing, optimism, and forgiveness.
- It provides a support system through activities such as church involvement.
- It fosters processes such as prayer and meditation, which promote healing through activities such as communion with the "higher power."
- It encourages healthy lifestyles.

Managed Care

Lawless, Ginter, and Kelly (1999) note that managed care is here to stay. They cite advantages and limitations associated with managed care. Some of the advantages include cost control for mental health services and establishment of mental health standards of practice to ensure quality control. Limitations of managed care include inadequate duration to treat disorders, overuse of medication in treatment programs, and reduced access to inpatient treatment.

It has become increasingly essential for mental health counselors and other health-care professionals to become providers for managed-care organizations in order to access clients' insurance programs, which are evolving in the health-care reform movement. Managed care is essentially an attempt by health organizations to control medical costs (Pipal, 1995). Its overall aim is to help clients achieve their premorbid levels of functioning and to obtain symptom relief with little interest in developmental or preventive enhancement (Pipal, 1995).

Two facets of managed care that have directly affected the delivery of mental health services are the emphasis on diagnosing and the utilization of time-limited, solution-focused sessions. In this regard, mental health counselors (and other practitioners) often feel under pressure to conform to managed care's expectations in order to remain providers. This can involve behaviors that are clearly ethical violations (Bachrach, 1995; Pipal, 1995). Examples of potential ethical problems are making improper diagnoses to gain authorization for services, not ensuring clients' confidentiality through communication with managed-care personnel, providing inadequate services owing to restriction of number of sessions (usually less than six), and providing services beyond the scope of one's practice.

Wagner and Gartner (1996) suggest that managed care necessitates changes in the counseling process and mental health delivery system. According to Wagner and Gartner, therapists need to function as coaches or teachers and act as catalysts for change. In this mode, clients learn skills from a variety of individuals and practice what they learn in their everyday life experiences. The working-through phase of counseling therefore occurs outside of counseling. In addition, counseling becomes more of an open-ended process involving intermittent or episodic care (Wagner & Gartner, 1996). In this regard, the therapist and client together work within the constraints of managed care to address the client's needs as efficiently as possible (for example, the client may sign up for a certain number of sessions to treat a substance-abuse problem and attempt to seek other assistance at a later date). One facet of counseling that does not appear to be in need of change is the nature of the therapeutic alliance. According to Wagner and Gartner (1996), it is essential for counselors to maintain a positive counseling relationship as advocated by Carl Rogers and others.

Managed care offers many challenges to the mental health counselor and other health practitioners. In an era of increasing pressures for cost containment, it appears to be becoming difficult to provide services that are consistent with the basic standards of practice and that are in the client's best welfare. Former Surgeon General C. Everett Koop voiced this concern when he noted that too much emphasis has been put on the economic/political pressures of health care with little attention to the ethical imperatives for health-care reform (Bachrach, 1995).

Summary

Mental health counseling is both an amorphous job role performed by various members of the helping profession and an emerging profession for individuals who identify themselves as mental health counselors.

Professional issues relating to mental health counselors include professional affiliation and certification requirements. The role and function of mental health counselors is to provide direct and indirect counseling services to clients who have either problems of living or mental disorders. Two mental health issues demanding increased attention by mental health counselors and other members of the helping profession are suicidal clients and clients with substance-abuse problems.

Personal Exploration

1. What do you think are the major challenges and opportunities associated with mental health counseling, and would you consider entering into this profession?
2. What do you believe are the key issues associated with substance abuse, and how should mental health counselors address these issues?
3. How can the concept of stages of change be useful in treating substance abuse and other mental health problems?
4. What is your opinion of rational (or physician-assisted) suicide?

Web Sites for Chapter 15

Burton, P. (1997). *A consumer's guide to mental health information.* Retrieved March 3, 2005, from http://www.vex.net/~madmagic/help/help.html
Provides an overview of the mental health profession from a consumer's perspective as well as numerous links to mental health–related sites.
The George Washington University. (2004). *Counseling.* Retrieved March 3, 2005, from http://www.gwu.edu/gelman/guides/social/counseling.html
Provides resources, links, and definitions of counseling.
Williams, D. (2003). *Peace and healing.* Retrieved March 3, 2005, from http://www.peaceandhealing.com/suicide/assessment.asp
Presents a partial summary of suicide assessment.

REFERENCES

Abelson, R., & Nielson, K. (1967). History of ethics. In P. Edwards (Ed.), *The encyclopedia of philosophy* (Vol. 3). New York: Macmillan.

Achenback, T. M., & Edelbrock, C. S. (1983). *Manual for the child behavior checklist and revised child behavior profile.* Burlington, VT: University of Vermont, Department of Psychiatry.

Ackerman, N. W. (1937). The family as a social and emotional unit. *Bulletin of the Kansas Mental Hygiene Society, 12*(2).

Ackerman, N. W. (1956). Interlocking pathology in family relationships. In S. Rado & G. Daniels (Eds.), *Changing conceptions of psychoanalytical medicine.* New York: Grune & Stratton.

Ackerman, N. W. (1966). *Treating the troubled family.* New York: Basic Books.

Ackerman, N. W. (1970). *Family therapy in transition.* Boston: Little, Brown.

Adams, J. H. (1997). *Perspectives of the oldest-old concerning resilience across the life span.* Unpublished doctoral dissertation, New Mexico State University, Las Cruces, NM.

Addington, J. (1992). Separation groups. *Journal for Specialists in Group Work, 17,* 20–28.

Adler, A. (1930). *The education of children.* South Bend, IN: Gateway Editions.

Adler, A. (1964). *Social interest: A challenge to mankind.* New York: Capricorn Books. (Original work published 1929)

Adler, A. (1969). *The practice and theory of individual psychology.* Patterson, NJ: Littlefield, Adams.

Adler, K. (1972). Techniques that shorten psychotherapy. *Journal of Individual Psychology, 28,* 155–168.

Adler, R. B., & Towne, N. (1996). *Looking out/Looking in* (8th ed.). New York: Holt, Rinehart & Winston, Inc.

Aiello, T. J. (1979). Short-term group therapy of the hospitalized psychotic. In P. Olsen & H. Grayson (Eds.), *Short-term approaches to psychotherapy.* New York: Human Sciences Press.

Ainsworth, M. D. S. (1989). Attachments beyond infancy. *American Psychologist, 44,* 709–716.

Ainsworth, M. D. S. (1991). Attachment and other affectional bonds across the life cycle. In C. M. Parkes, J. Stevenson-Hinde, & P. Marris (Eds.), *Attachment across the life cycle* (pp. 33–51). New York: Tavistock/Routledge.

Ainsworth, M. D. S., Blehar, M. C., Waters, E., & Wall, S. (1978). *Patterns of attachment: A psychological study of the strange situation.* Hillsdale, NJ: Lawrence Erlbaum.

Akos, P. (2000). Building empathic skills in elementary school children through group work. *Journal for Specialists in Group Work, 25,* 214–223.

Albee, G. W., & Ryan-Finn, K. D. (1993). An overview of primary prevention. *Journal of Counseling and Development, 72*(2), 115–123.

Al-Darmaki, F., & Kivlighan, D. M., Jr. (1993). Congruence in client-counselor expectations for relationship and the working alliance. *Journal of Counseling Psychology, 40*(4), 379–384.

Allan, J., & Brown, K. (1993). Jungian play therapy in elementary school. *Elementary School Guidance and Counseling, 28*(1), 30–41.

Allen, J., & Allen, B. (1989). Stroking: Biological underpinnings and direct observations. *Transactional Analysis Journal, 19,* 26–31.

Allen, S. F., & Stoltenberg, C. D. (1995). Psychological separation of older adolescents and young adults from their parents: An investigation of gender differences. *Journal of Counseling and Development, 73*(5), 542–546.

Allport, G. W. (1954). *The nature of prejudice.* Cambridge, MA: Addison-Wesley.

Allport, G. W., & Ross, J. M. (1967). Personal religious orientation and prejudice. *Journal of Personality and Social Psychology, 5,* 432–443.

Alper, J. (1986, May). Depression at an early age. *Science, 86,* 44–50.

Altmann, E. O., & Gotlib, I. H. (1988). The social behavior of depressed children: An observational study. *Journal of Abnormal Child Psychology, 16,* 29–44.

Alva, S. A. (1991). Academic invulnerability among Mexican-American students: The importance of protective resources and appraisals. *Hispanic Journal of Behavioral Sciences, 13*(1), 18–34.

American Association for Marriage and Family Therapy (AAMFT). (2001). *AAMFT code of ethical principles for marriage and family therapists.* Alexandria, VA: Author.

American Association of Suicidology. (1990). *Suicide postvention guidelines: Suggestions for dealing with the aftermath of suicide in the schools.* Denver, CO: Author.

American Counseling Association (ACA). (1995). *Code of ethics and standards of practice.* Alexandria, VA: Author.

American Counseling Association (ACA). (1997). *Code of ethics and standards of practice.* Alexandria, VA: Author.

American Counseling Association (ACA). (2003, March). *ACA governing council meeting minutes.* Alexandria, VA: Author.

American Psychiatric Association. (1980). *Diagnostic and statistical manual of mental disorders* (3rd ed.). Washington, DC: Author.

American Psychiatric Association. (1987). *Diagnostic and statistical manual of mental disorders* (3rd ed. Rev.). Washington, DC: Author.

American Psychiatric Association. (1995). Practice guidelines for the treatment of patients with substance use disorders: Alcohol, cocaine, opioids. *American Journal of Psychiatry (Supplement), 152*(11), 3–59.

American Psychiatric Association. (2000). *Diagnostic and statistical manual of mental disorders fourth edition-text revision (DSM-IV-TR).* Washington, DC: Author.

American Psychological Association (APA). (1997, July). *Terminal illness and hastened death requests: The important role of the mental health professional.* [Brochure]. Washington, DC: Author. (Reprinted as *Professional psychology: Research and practice, 28,* 544–547, by R. K. Farberman, 1997.)

American Psychological Association (APA). (2002). *Multicultural guidelines on education and training, research, practice and organizational development for psychologists.* Washington, DC: Author.

American Psychological Association (APA). (2003). *Ethical principles of psychologists and code of conduct.* Washington, DC: Author.

American School Counselor Association (ASCA). (1990). *American School Counselor Association role statement.* Alexandria, VA: Author.

American School Counselor Association (ASCA). (1998). *Ethical standards for school counselors.* Alexandria, VA: Author.

American School Counselor Association (ASCA). (2003). *The ASCA National Model: A framework for school counseling programs.* Alexandria, VA: Author.

Anastasi, A., & Urbina, S. (1997). *Psychological testing* (7th ed.). New York: Macmillan.

Andersen, B., & Andersen, W. (1985). Client perceptions of counselors using positive and negative self-involving statements. *Journal of Counseling Psychology, 32,* 462–465.

Andersen, T. (1991). *The reflecting team: Dialogues and dialogues about the dialogues.* New York: Norton.

Andersen, T. (1992). Reflections on reflecting with families. In S. McNamee & K. J. Gergen (Eds.), *Therapy as social construction* (pp. 54–68). Newbury Park, CA: Sage.

Anderson, H., & Goolishian, H. (1992). The client is the expert: A not-knowing approach to therapy. In S. McNamee & K. J. Gergen (Eds.), *Therapy as social construction* (pp. 25–39). Newbury Park, CA: Sage.

Angle, S. S., & Goodyear, R. K. (1984). Perception of counselors' qualities: Impact of subjects' self-concepts, counselor gender, and counselor introductions. *Journal of Counseling Psychology, 31,* 576–579.

Ansbacher, H. L. (1989). Adlerian psychology: The tradition of brief psychotherapy. *Individual Psychology: The Journal of Adlerian Theory, Research, and Practice, 45*(1/2), 26–33.

Ansbacher, H. L., & Ansbacher, R. R. (Eds.). (1956). *The individual psychology of Alfred Adler.* New York: Basic Books.

Ansbacher, H. L., & Ansbacher, R. R. (Eds.). (1964). *Superiority and social interest.* Evanston, IL: Northwestern University Press.

Ansell, C. A. (1987). *Ethical practices workbook.* Santa Monica, CA: Association for Advanced Training in the Behavioral Sciences.

Appelbaum, P. S. (1993). Legal liability and managed care. *American Psychologist, 48*(3), 251–257.

Arbona, C. (1996). Career theory and practice in a multicultural context. In M. L. Savickas & W. B. Walsh (Eds.), *Handbook of career theory and practice.* Palo Alto, CA: Davies-Black.

Arellano, A. R., & Padilla, A. M. (1996). Academic invulnerability among a select group of Latino university students. *Hispanic Journal of Behavioral Sciences, 18*(4), 485–507.

Argyle, M. (1981). The contribution of social interaction research to social skills training. In J. D. Wine & M. D. Syme (Eds.), *Social competence.* New York: Guilford.

Arlow, J. A. (2005). Psychoanalysis. In R. J. Corsini (Ed.), *Current psychoanalysis* (7th ed.) (pp. 15–51). Itasca, IL: F. E. Peacock.

Arredondo, P., Toporek, R., Brown, S., Jones, J., Locke, D. C., Sanchez, J., & Stadler, H. (1996). *Operationalization of the multicultural counseling competencies.* Alexandria, VA: Association for Multicultural Counseling and Development.

Arredondo, P., & Toporek, R. (2004). *Journal of Mental Health Counseling, 26,* 44–55.

Asarnow, J. R., & Calan, J. W. (1985). Boys with peer adjustment problems: Social cognitive processes. *Journal of Counseling and Clinical Psychology, 53,* 80–87.

Ascher, L. M. (1979). Paradoxical intention in the treatment of urinary retention. *Behavior Research and Therapy, 17,* 267–270.

Ascher, L. M., & Efran, J. S. (1978). The use of paradoxical intention in a behavioral program for sleep onset insomnia. *Journal of Consulting and Clinical Psychology, 46,* 547–550.

Association for Specialists in Group Work (ASGW). (1990). Ethical guidelines for group counselors. *Journal for Specialists in Group Work, 15*(2), 119–126.

Atkinson, D. R. (1993). Who speaks for cross-cultural counseling research? *The Counseling Psychologist, 21*(2), 218–224.

Atkinson, D. R., Morten, G., & Sue, D. W. (1998). *Counseling American minorities: A cross-cultural perspective* (5th ed.). Dubuque, IA: William C. Brown.

Atkinson, D. R., & Thompson, C. E. (1992). Racial, ethnic, and cultural variables in counseling. In S. D. Brown & R. W. Lent (Eds.), *Handbook of counseling psychology* (2nd ed.) (pp. 349–382). New York: John Wiley & Sons.

Aubrey, R. F. (1982). A house divided: Guidance and counseling in 20th century America. *The Personnel and Guidance Journal, 761,* 198–204.

Avis, J. M. (1986). Feminist issues in family therapy. In F. P. Piercy, D. H. Sprenkle, & Associates (Eds.), *Family therapy sourcebook* (pp. 213–242). New York: Guilford Press.

Axelson, J. A. (1999). *Counseling and development in a multicultural society* (3rd ed.). Belmont, CA: Wadsworth.

Axline, V. M. (1964). *Dibs: In search of self.* Boston: Houghton Mifflin.

Axline, V. M. (1974). *Play therapy.* New York: Houghton Mifflin.

Ayllon, T., & Azrin, N. (1968). *The token economy: A motivation system for therapy and rehabilitation.* New York: Appleton-Century-Crofts.

Bachrach, L. L. (1995). Managed care: I. Delimiting the concept. *Psychiatric Service, 46*(12), 1229–1230.

Baier, K. (1958). *The moral point of view.* Ithaca, NY: Cornell University.

Baker, E. L. (1985). Psychoanalysis and psychoanalytic psychotherapy. In S. J. Lynn & J. P. Garske (Eds.), *Contemporary psychotherapies: Models and methods.* Columbus, OH: Merrill/Macmillan.

Baker, S. (1995). Qualitative research has a place in the school counseling literature. *The School Counselor, 42*(5), 339–340.

Ball, F. L. J., & Harassy, B. E. (1984). A survey of the problems and needs of homeless consumers of acute psychiatric services. *Hospital and Community Psychiatry, 35,* 917–921.

Ballou, M. (1996). MCT theory and women. In D. W. Sue, A. E. Ivey, & P. B. Pedersen (Eds.), *A theory of multicultural counseling and therapy* (pp. 236–246). Pacific Grove, CA: Brooks/Cole.

Bandler, R., & Grinder, J. (1975). *The structure of magic* (Vol. 1). Palo Alto, CA: Science and Behavior Books.

Bandura, A. (1974). Behavior theory and the models of man. *American Psychologist, 29,* 859–869.

Bandura, A. (1977). *Social learning theory.* Englewood Cliffs, NJ: Prentice-Hall.

Bandura, A. (1982). Self-efficacy mechanism in human agency. *American Psychologist, 37*(2), 122–167.

Bandura, A. (1986). *Several foundations of thought and action: A social cognition theory.* Englewood Cliffs, NJ: Prentice-Hall.

Bandura, A. (1989). Human agency in social cognitive theory. *American Psychologist, 44*(9), 1175–1184.

Bandura, A., Reese, L., & Adams, N. E. (1982). Microanalysis of actions and fear arousal as a function of differential levels of perceived self-efficacy. *Journal of Personality and Social Psychology, 43*(1), 5–21.

Bangert-Drowns, R. L. (1988). The effects of school-based substance abuse education: A meta-analysis. *Journal of Drug Education, 18,* 243–264.

Bansberg, B., & Sklare, J. (1986). *The career decision diagnostic assessment.* Monterey, CA: CTB/McGraw-Hill.

Barclay, J. R. (1984, April). Primary prevention and assessment. *The Personnel and Guidance Journal,* 475–478.

Barlow, S. H., Burlingame, G. M., & Fuhriman, A. (2000). Therapeutic application of groups: From Pratt's "thought control classes" to modern group psychotherapy. *Group Dynamics: Theory, Research, and Practice, 4–1,* 115–134.

Barrett-Lennard, G. T. (1981). The empathy cycle: Refinement of a nuclear concept. *Journal of Counseling Psychology, 28,* 91–100.

Barrett-Lennard, G. T. (1997). The recovery of empathy—towards others and self. In A. C. Bohart & L. S. Greenberg (Eds.), *Empathy reconsidered: New directions in psychotherapy* (pp. 103–124). Washington, DC: American Psychological Association.

Barth, K., Nielson, G., Haver, B., Havik, O. E., Molstad, E., Rogge, H., & Statun, M. (1988). Comprehensive assessment of change in patients treated with short-term dynamic psychotherapy: An overview. *Psychotherapy Psychosomatic, 50,* 141–150.

Baruth, L. G., & Huber, C. H. (1985). *Counseling and psychotherapy: Theoretical analyses and skill application.* Columbus, OH: Merrill/Macmillan.

Baruth, L. G., & Manning, M. L. (1999). *Multicultural counseling and psychotherapy: A lifespan perspective* (2nd ed.). New York: Macmillan.

Baruth, L. G., & Robinson, E. H. (1987). *An introduction to the counseling profession.* Englewood Cliffs, NJ: Prentice-Hall.

Beale, A. V., & Scott, P. C. (2001). Bullybusters: Using drama to empower students to take a stand against bullying behavior. *Professional School Counseling, 4*(4), 300–305.

Bearden, L. J., Spencer, W. A., & Moracco, J. C. (1989). A study of high school dropouts. *The School Counselor, 37,* 113–120.

Beck, A. T. (1986). Hopelessness as a predictor of eventual suicide. In J. J. Mann & M. Stanley (Eds.), *Psychobiology.* New York: Academy of Sciences.

Beck, A. T. (1987). Cognitive therapy. In J. K. Zeig (Ed.), *The evolution of psychotherapy* (pp. 149–178). New York: Brunner/Mazel.

Beck, A. T. (1991). Cognitive therapy: A 30-year retrospective. *American Psychologist, 46*(4), 368–375.

Beck, A. T. (1993). Cognitive therapy: Past, present, and future. *Journal of Consulting and Clinical Psychology, 61*(2), 194–198.

Beck, A. T. (1996). Cognitive therapy of personality disorders. In P. M. Salkovskis (Ed.), *Frontiers of cognitive therapy* (pp. 165–181). New York: Guilford Press.

Beck, A. T., & Emery, G. (1985). *Anxiety disorders and phobias: A cognitive perspective.* New York: Basic Books.

Beck, A. T., Rush, A., Shaw, B., & Emery, G. (1979). *Cognitive therapy of depression.* New York: Guilford Press.

Beck, A. T., Sokol, L., Clark, D. A., Berchick, R., & Wright, F. (1992). A crossover study of focused cognitive therapy for panic disorder. *American Journal of Psychiatry, 149,* 778–783.

Beck, A. T., & Weishaar, M. E. (1989). Cognitive therapy. In R. J. Corsini (Ed.), *Current psychotherapies* (4th ed.) (pp. 285–320). Itasca, IL: F. E. Peacock.

Beck, A. T., & Weishaar, M. E. (2005). Cognitive therapy. In R. J. Corsini & D. Wedding (Eds.), *Current psychotherapies* (6th ed.) (pp. 241–272). Itasca, IL: F. E. Peacock.

Beck, A., Wright, F. D., Newman, C. F., & Liese, B. (1993). *Cognitive therapy of substance abuse.* New York: Guilford Press.

Becvar, R. J., & Becvar, D. S. (1994). The ecosystemic story: A story about stories. *Journal of Mental Health Counseling, 16*(1), 22–32.

Bednar, R. L., Bednar, S. C., Lambert, M. J., & Waite, D. R. (1991). *Psychotherapy with high-risk clients: Legal and professional standards.* Pacific Grove, CA: Brooks/Cole.

Bednar, R. L., Burlingame, G. M., & Masters, K. S. (1988). Systems of family treatment: Substance or semantics? *Annual Review of Psychology, 39,* 401–434.

Beers, C. (1908). *A mind that found itself.* New York: Longman Green.

Bello, G. A. (1989). Counseling handicapped students: A cognitive approach. *The School Counselor, 36,* 298–304.

Berenson, B., & Mitchell, K. (1968). Therapeutic conditions for therapist-initiated confrontation. *Journal of Clinical Psychology, 24,* 363–364.

Berger, K. S., & Thompson, R. A. (2000). *The developing person through childhood and adolescence* (5th ed.). New York: Worth Publishers.

Bergin, A. E. (1991). Values and religious issues in psychotherapy and mental health. *American Psychologist, 46,* 394–403.

Bergin, J. J., Miller, S. E., Bergin, J. W., & Koch, R. E. (1990). The effects of a comprehensive guidance model on a rural school's counseling program. *Elementary School Guidance & Counseling, 25*(1), 37–45.

Bergman, L. R., & Magnusson, D. (1997). A person-oriented approach in research on developmental psychopathology. *Development and Psychopathology, 9,* 291–319.

Berne, E. (1961). *Transactional analysis in psychotherapy.* New York: Grove Press.

Berne, E. (1964). *Games people play.* New York: Grove Press.

Bernstein, B. L., & Figioli, S. W. (1983). Gender and credibility introduction effects on perceived counselor characteristics. *Journal of Counseling Psychology, 30,* 506–513.

Bernstein, B. L., & Kerr, B. (1993). Counseling psychology and the scientist-practitioner model: Implementation and implications. *The Counseling Psychologist, 21*(1), 136–150.

Berrigan, L. P., & Garfield, S. L. (1981). Relationships of missed psychotherapy appointments to premature termination and social class. *British Journal of Clinical Psychology, 20,* 239–242.

Berry, G. W., & Sipps, G. J. (1991). Interactive effects of counselor-client similarity and client self-esteem on termination type and number of sessions. *Journal of Counseling Psychology, 38*(2), 120–125.

Bertoia, J., & Allan, J. (1988). Counseling seriously ill children: Use of spontaneous drawings. *Elementary School Guidance and Counseling, 22*(3), 206–221.

Betz, N. E. (1994). Self-concept theory in career development and counseling. *Career Development Quarterly, 43*(1), 32–42.

Betz, N. E., & Hackett, G. (1986). Applications of self-efficacy theory to understanding career choice behavior. *Journal of Social and Clinical Psychology, 4,* 279–289.

Beutler, L. (1983). *Eclectic psychotherapy: A systematic approach.* New York: Pergamon Press.

Beutler, L. E., Machado, P. P. P., & Neufeldt, S. A. (1994). Therapist variables. In A. E. Bergin & S. L. Garfield (Eds.), *Handbook of psychotherapy and behavior change* (4th ed.) (pp. 229–269). New York: John Wiley & Sons.

Beutler, L. E., Williams, R. E., Wakefield, P. J., & Entwistle, S. R. (1995). Bridging scientist and practitioner perspective in clinical psychology. *American Psychologist, 50*(12), 984–994.

Bigler, E. D., & Ehrfurth, J. W. (1981). The continued inappropriate singular use of the Bender Visual Motor Gestalt Test. *Professional Psychology, 12*, 562–569.

Birk, J. M., & Brooks, L. (1986). Required skills and training needs of recent counseling psychology graduates. *Journal of Counseling Psychology, 33*, 320–325.

Bishop, D. R. (1995). Religious values as cross-cultural issues in counseling. In M. T. Burke & J. G. Miranti (Eds.), *Counseling: The spiritual dimension* (pp. 59–72). Alexandria, VA: American Counseling Association.

Bitter, J. R., & Corey, G. (1996). Family systems therapy. In G. Corey (Ed.), *Theory and practice of counseling and psychotherapy* (5th ed.) (pp. 365–443). Pacific Grove, CA: Brooks/Cole.

Bitter, J. R., & Nicoll, W. G. (2004). Relational strategies: Two approaches to Adlerian brief therapy. *Journal of Individual Psychology, 60*, 42–66.

Black, J., & Underwood, J. (1998). Young, female, and gay: Lesbian students and the school environment. *Professional School Counseling, 1*(3), 15–20.

Blackburn, I. M., Bishop, S., Glen, A. I. M., Whalley, L. J., & Christie, J. E. (1981). The efficacy of cognitive therapy in depression: A treatment trial using cognitive therapy and pharmacotherapy, each alone and in combination. *British Journal of Psychiatry, 139*, 181–189.

Blackburn, I. M., Eunson, K. M., & Bishop, S. (1986). *A two-year naturalistic follow-up of depressed patients treated with cognitive therapy, pharmacotherapy, and a combination of both.* Unpublished manuscript, Royal Edinburgh Hospital, Scotland.

Blair, R. G. (2004). Helping older adolescents search for meaning in depression. *Journal of Mental Health Counseling, 26*, 333–348.

Blocher, D. H. (1974). *Developmental counseling* (2nd ed.). New York: Ronald Press.

Blocher, D. H. (1987). *The professional counselor.* New York: Macmillan.

Blustein, D. L. (1987). Integrating career counseling and psychotherapy: A comprehensive treatment strategy. *Psychotherapy, 24*, 794–799.

Blustein, D. L., Prezioso, M. S., & Schultheiss, D. P. (1995). *The Counseling Psychologist, 23*(3), 416–432.

Blustein, D. L., & Spengler, P. M. (1995). Personal adjustment: Career counseling and psychotherapy. In W. B. Walsh & S. H. Osipow (Eds.), *Handbook of vocational psychology* (2nd ed.) (pp. 295–329). Hillsdale, NJ: Erlbaum.

Boen, D. L. (1988). A practitioner looks at assessment in marital counseling. *Journal of Counseling and Development, 66*(10), 484–486.

Bonebrake, C. R., & Borgers, S. B. (1984, February). Counselor role as perceived by counselors and principals. *Elementary School Guidance & Counseling,* 194–199.

Bonett, R. M. (1994). Marital status and sex: Impact on self-efficacy. *Journal of Counseling and Development, 73*(2), 187–190.

Bonner, H. (1959). *Group dynamics.* New York: Ronald Press.

Bonnington, S. B. (1993). Solution-focused brief therapy: Helpful interventions for school counselors. *The School Counselor, 41*(2), 126–128.

Borders, D. L., & Drury, R. D. (1992). Comprehensive school counseling programs: A review for policy makers and practitioners. *Journal of Counseling and Development, 70*(4), 487–498.

Bordin, E. S. (1979). The generalizability of the psychoanalytic concept of the working alliance. *Psychotherapy: Theory, Research and Practice, 16*, 252–260.

Borg, W. B., & Gall, M. D. (1989). *Educational research: An introduction* (5th ed.). New York: Longman.

Borys, D. S. (1994). Maintaining therapeutic boundaries: The motive is therapeutic effectiveness, not defensive practice. *Ethics and Behavior, 4*, 267–273.

Boswell, B. (1983). Adapted dance for mentally retarded children: An experimental study (Doctoral dissertation, Texas Women's University, 1983). *Dissertation Abstracts International, 43*(9–A), 2925.

Bowker, M. (1982). Children of divorce: Being in between. *Elementary School Guidance & Counseling, 17*, 126–130.

Bowlby, J. (1969/1982). *Attachment and loss. Vol I: Attachment.* London: Tavistock.

Bowlby, J. (1973). *Attachment and loss. Vol. 2: Separation, anxiety and anger.* New York: Basic.

Bowlby, J. (1988a). *A secure base: Parent-child attachments and healthy human development.* New York: Basic Books.

Bowlby, J. (1988b). Developmental psychiatry comes of age. *American Journal of Psychiatry, 145*, 1–10.

Brabender, V. (1985). Time-limited inpatient group therapy: A developmental model. *International Journal of Group Psychotherapy, 35,* 373–390.

Brace, K. (1992). I and Thou in interpersonal psychotherapy. *The Humanistic Psychologist, 20*(1), 41–57.

Bradford, E., & Lyddon, W. J. (1994). Assessing adolescent and adult attachment: An update. *Journal of Counseling and Development, 73*(2), 215–219.

Brady, J. P. (1980). Some views on effective principles of psychotherapy. In M. Goldfried (Ed.), *Cognitive therapy and research, 4,* 271–306.

Brake, K. J. (1988). Counseling young children of alcoholics. *Elementary School Guidance & Counseling, 23,* 106–111.

Brammer, L. M. (2002). *The helping relationship: Process and skills* (8th ed.). Englewood Cliffs, NJ: Prentice-Hall.

Bray, D. W., Campbell, R. J., & Grant, D. L. (1974). *Formative years in business: A long-term AT&T study of managerial lives.* New York: John Wiley & Sons.

Bredehoft, D. (1990). Self-esteem: A family affair. *Transactional Analysis Journal, 20,* 111–116.

Brennan, K. A., Shaver, P. R., & Tobey, A. N. (1991). Attachment styles, gender, and parental problem drinking. *Journal of Social and Personal Relationships, 8,* 451–466.

Bristow-Braitman, A. (1995). Addiction recovery: 12-step programs and cognitive-behavioral psychology. *Journal of Counseling and Development, 73*(4), 414–418.

Brockman, M. P. (1987). Children and physical abuse. In A. Thomas & J. Grimes (Eds.), *Children's needs: Psychological perspectives* (pp. 418–427). Washington, DC: The National Association of School Psychologists.

Brooks, D. K., & Gerstein, L. H. (1990). Counselor credentialing and interprofessional collaboration. *Journal of Counseling and Development, 68,* 477–484.

Brooks, L. (2002). Recent developments in theory building. In D. Brown, L. Brooks, & Associates (Eds.), *Career choice and development* (4th ed.). San Francisco: Jossey-Bass.

Brooks-Gunn, J., McCormick, M. C., Gunn, R. W., Shorter, T., Wallace, C. Y., & Heagerty, M. C. (1989). Outreach as casefindings: The process of locating low-income pregnant women. *Medical Care, 27*(2), 95–102.

Brooks-Gunn, J., McCormick, M. C., & Heagerty, M. C. (1988). Preventing infant mortality and morbidity: Developmental perspectives. *American Journal of Orthopsychiatry, 58,* 288–296.

Brown, B. M. (1995). The bill of rights for people with disabilities in group work. *Journal for Specialists in Group Work, 20*(2), 71–75.

Brown, D. (1993). Training consultants: A call to action. *Journal of Counseling and Development, 72*(2), 139–143.

Brown, D. (1997). Implications of cultural values for cross-cultural consultation with families. *Journal of Counseling and Development, 76*(1), 29–35.

Brown, D., & Brooks, L. (2002). Introduction to career development: Origins, evolution and current approaches. In D. Brown & L. Brooks (Eds.), *Career choice and development* (4th ed.). San Francisco: Jossey-Bass.

Brown, G. W., & Harris, T. (1978). *Social origins of depression.* London: Tavistock.

Brown, K. S., & Parsons, R. D. (1998). Accurate identification of childhood aggression: A key to successful intervention. *Professional School Counseling, 2,* 135–140.

Brown, L. S. (1988). Feminist therapy with lesbians and gay men. In M. Dutton-Douglas & L. E. Walker (Eds.), *Feminist psychotherapies: Integration of therapeutic and feminist systems* (pp. 206–227). Norwood, NJ: Ablex.

Brown, L. S. (1997). The private practice of subversion: Psychology as tikkum olam. *American Psychologist, 52,* 449–462.

Brown, S. D., & Ryan Krane, N. E. (2000). Four (or five) session and a cloud of dust: Old assumptions and new observations about career counseling. In S. Brown & R. Lent (Eds.), *Handbook of counseling psychology* (3rd ed.) (pp. 740–766). New York: John Wiley.

Browning, C., Reynolds, A., & Dworkin, S. H. (1991). Affirmative psychotherapy with lesbian women. *The Counseling Psychologist, 19*(2), 177–196.

Bruce, M. A. (1995). Brief counseling: An effective model for change. *The School Counselor, 42*(5), 353–363.

Brunner, J. S. (1973). *Beyond the information given: Studies in the psychology of knowing.* New York: Norton.

Bruscia, K. E. (1987). *Improvisational models of music therapy.* Springfield, IL: Charles C. Thomas.

Buber, M. (1970). *I and thou* (W. Kaufmann, Trans.). New York: Scribner's. (Original work published 1958)

Buck, J. N. (1949). The H-T-P technique: A qualitative and scoring manual, Part 2. *Journal of Clinical Psychology, 5,* 37–76.

Bugental, J. (1976). *The search for existential identity.* San Francisco: Jossey-Bass.

Burke, D. M., & DeStreek, L. V. (1989). Children of divorce: An application of Hammond's group counseling for children. *Elementary School Guidance & Counseling, 24,* 112–118.

Burlingame, G. M., & Fuhriman, A. (1990). Time-limited group therapy. *The Counseling Psychologist, 18*(1), 93–118.

Burtnett, F. E. (1986). *Staffing patterns in mental health agencies and organizations.* Unpublished report. Alexandria, VA: American Association for Counseling and Development.

Butler, L., & Meichenbaum, D. (1981). The assessment of interpersonal problem solving skills. In P. C. Kendall & S. D. Hollen (Eds.), *Assessment strategies for cognitive behavioral interventions* (pp. 197–225). New York: Academic Press.

Campbell, C. A. (1993). Play, the fabric of elementary school counseling programs. *Elementary School Guidance and Counseling, 28*(1), 10–16.

Campbell, C. A., & Dahir, C. A. (1997). *The national standards for school counseling programs.* Alexandria, VA: American School Counselor Association.

Campbell, T. J., & Patterson, J. M. (1995). The effectiveness of family interventions in the treatment of physical illness. *Journal of Marital and Family Therapy, 21,* 545–584.

Caplan, G. (1964). *Principles of preventive psychiatry.* New York: Basic Books.

Caplan, G. (1970). *The theory and practice of mental health consultation.* New York: Basic Books.

Capuzzi, D. (1988). Personal and social competency: Developing skills for the future. In G. R. Walz & J. C. Bleuer (Eds.), *Building strong school counseling programs.* Alexandria, VA: American Association for Counseling and Development.

Capuzzi, D., & Nystul, M. S. (1986). The suicidal adolescent. In L. B. Golden & D. Capuzzi (Eds.), *Helping families help children: Family interventions with school-related problems* (pp. 23–32). Springfield, IL: Charles C. Thomas.

Carkhuff, R. R. (1969). *Helping and human relations* (Vols. 1–2). New York: Holt, Rinehart & Winston.

Carkhuff, R. R. (1971). *The development of human resources.* New York: Holt, Rinehart & Winston.

Carlsen, M. B. (1995). Meaning-making and creative aging. In R. A. Neimeyer & M. J. Mahoney (Eds.), *Constructivism in psychotherapy.* Washington, DC: American Psychological Association.

Carlson, G. A., & Cantwell, D. P. (1979). A survey of depressive symptoms in a child and adolescent psychiatric population. *Journal of the American Academy of Child Psychiatry, 18,* 587–599.

Carmichael, K. D. (1994). Sand play as an elementary school strategy. *Elementary School Guidance and Counseling, 28*(4), 302–307.

Carnelley, K. B., Pietromonaco, P. R., & Jaffe, K. (1994). Depression, working models of others, and relationship functioning. *Journal of Personality and Social Psychology, 66,* 127–140.

Carson, A., & Mowsesian, R. (1990). Some remarks on Gati's theory of career decision-making models. *Journal of Counseling Psychology, 37*(4), 502–507.

Carter, B., & McGoldrick, M. (1988). Overview: The changing family life cycle—A framework for family therapy. In B. Carter & M. McGoldrick (Eds.), *The changing family life cycle: A framework for family therapy* (2nd ed.). New York: Allyn & Bacon.

Carter, R. T., & Swanson, J. L. (1990). The validity of the Strong Interest Inventory with black Americans: A review of the literature. *Journal of Vocational Behavior, 36,* 195–209.

Casas, J. M., & Pytluk, S. D. (1995). Hispanic identity development: Implications for research and practice. In J. G. Ponterotto, J. M. Casas, L. A. Suzuki, & C. M. Alexander (Eds.), *Handbook of multicultural counseling* (pp. 155–180). Thousand Oaks, CA: Sage.

Casey, J. A. (1995). Developmental issues for school counselors using technology. *Elementary School Guidance and Counseling, 30*(1), 26–34.

Cashwell, C. S., Shcherbakova, J., & Cashwell, T. H. (2003). Effect of client and counselor ethnicity on preference for counselor disclosure. *Journal of Counseling and Development, 81,* 196–201.

Cashwell, C. S., & Vacc, N. A. (1996). Family functioning and risk behaviors: Influences on adolescent delinquency. *The School Counselor, 44*(2), 105–114.

Cass, V. C. (1979). Homosexual identity formation: A theoretical model. *Journal of Homosexuality, 4,* 219–235.

Cattell, R. B. (1949). *Culture-fair intelligence tests.* Champaign, IL: Institute for Personality and Ability Testing.

Cavanaugh, M. E. (1982). *The counseling experience.* Monterey, CA: Brooks/Cole.

Chambers, W. J., Puig-Antich, J., & Tabrizi, M. A. (1978, October). *The ongoing development of the Kiddie-SADS (schedule for affective disorders and schizophrenia for school-age children).* Paper presented at the meeting of the American Academy of Child Psychiatry, San Diego, CA.

Chambless, D. L., & Gillis, M. M. (1993). Cognitive therapy of anxiety disorders. *Journal of Consulting and Clinical Psychology, 61,* 248–260.

Chartrand, J. M. (1996). Linking theory and practice: A sociocognitive interactional model for career counseling. In M. L. Savickas & W. B. Walsh (Eds.), *Handbook of career counseling theory and practice* (pp. 121–134). Palo Alto, CA: Davies-Black.

Chesler, M. A. (1976). Contemporary sociological theories of racism. In P. A. Katz (Ed.), *Toward the elimination of racism* (pp. 21–72). New York: Pergamon.

Chiles, A., Miller, M. L., & Cox, G. B. (1980). Depression in an adolescent delinquent population. *Archives of General Psychiatry, 37,* 1179–1184.

Choney, S. K., Berryhill-Paapke, E., & Robbins, R. R. (1995). The acculturation of American Indians: Developing frameworks for research and practice. In J. G. Ponterotto, J. M. Casas, L. A. Suzuki, & C. M. Alexander (Eds.), *Handbook of multicultural counseling* (pp. 73–92). Thousand Oaks, CA: Sage.

Chu, L., & Powers, P. A. (1995). Synchrony in adolescence. *Adolescence, 30*(118), 453–461.

Chung, Y. B. (1995). Career decision making of lesbian, gay, and bisexual individuals. *Career Development Quarterly, 44*(2), 178–190.

Chwalisz, K. (2003). Evidence-based practice: A framework for twenty-first-century scientist-practitioner training. *The Counseling Psychologist, 31,* 497–528.

Cicchetti, D., Ackerman, B. P., & Izard, C. E. (1995). Emotions and emotion regulation in developmental psychopathology. *Development and Psychopathology, 7,* 1–10.

Ciechalski, J. C., & Schmidt, M. W. (1995). The effects of social skills training on students with exceptionalities. *Elementary School Guidance and Counseling, 29*(3), 217–222.

Claiborn, C. D. (1987). Science and practice: Reconsidering the Pepinskys. *Journal of Counseling and Development, 65*(6), 286–288.

Clair, D., & Genest, M. (1987). Variables associated with the adjustment of offspring of alcoholic fathers. *Journal of Studies on Alcohol, 48,* 345–356.

Clarizio, H. F., & McCoy, G. F. (1983). *Behavior disorders in children.* New York: Harper & Row.

Clark, A. J. (1995). Projective techniques in the counseling process. *Journal of Counseling and Development, 73*(3), 311–316.

Clarke, J., & Evans, E. (1973). Rhythmical intention as a method of treatment for cerebral-palsied patients. *Australia Journal of Physiotherapy, 19–20,* 57–64.

Clarke, K., & Breeberg, L. (1986). Differential effects of the Gestalt two chair intervention and problem solving in resolving decisional conflict. *Journal of Counseling Psychology, 33,* 48–53.

Clewell, B. C., Brooks-Gunn, J., & Benasich, A. A. (1989). Evaluating child-related outcomes of teenage parenting programs. *Family Relations, 38*(2), 201–209.

Cochran, J. L. (1996). Using play and art therapy to help culturally diverse students overcome barriers to school success. *The School Counselor, 43*(4), 287–298.

Coe, D. M., & Zimpfer, D. G. (1996). Infusing solution-oriented theory and techniques into group work. *Journal for Specialists in Group Work, 21*(1), 49–57.

Cohen, E. D. (1990). Confidentiality, counseling, and clients who have AIDS: Ethical foundations of a model rule. *Journal of Counseling and Development, 68,* 282–287.

Cohen, E. D. (2001). Permitted suicide: Model rules for mental health counseling. *Journal of Mental Health Counseling, 23*(4), 279–295.

Cole, C. G. (1988). The school counselor: Image and impact, counselor role and function, 1960s to 1980 and beyond. In G. R. Walz & J. C. Bleuer (Eds.), *Building strong school counseling programs.* Alexandria, VA: American Association for Counseling and Development.

Cole, I. (1982). Movement negotiations with an autistic child. *Arts in Psychotherapy, 9,* 49–53.

Cole, J. D., & Kupersmidt, J. B. (1983). A behavioral analysis of emerging social status in boys' groups. *Child Development, 54,* 1400–1416.

Cole, O. A., & Rehm, L. P. (1986). Family interaction patterns and childhood depression. *Journal of Abnormal Child Psychology, 14,* 297–314.

Coleman, S. (1985). *Failures in family therapy.* New York: Guilford Press.

College Entrance Examination Board. (1987). *Keeping options open: Recommendations, final reports of the commission on precollege guidance and counseling.* New York: Author.

Collins, B. G., & Collins, T. M. (1994). Child and adolescent mental health: Building a system of care. *Journal of Counseling and Development, 72*(3), 239–243.

Collins, N. L., & Miller, L. C. (1994). Self-disclosure and liking: A meta-analytic review. *Psychological Bulletin, 116*(3), 457–475.

Combs, A., Soper, D., Gooding, C., Benton, J., Dickman, J., & Usher, R. (1969). *Florida studies in the helping professions.* Gainesville: University of Florida Press.

Committee for Economic Development. (1991). *The unfinished agenda: A new vision for child development and education.* New York: Author.

Congdon, D. (1987). *Professional issues.* Santa Monica, CA: Association for Advanced Training in Behavioral Sciences.

Constantine, M. G., & Ladany, N. (2000). Self-report multicultural counseling competence scales: Their relation to social desirability attitudes and multicultural case conceptualization ability. *Journal of Counseling Psychology, 47,* 155–164.

Consumer Reports. (1995, November). Mental health: Does therapy help?, 734–739.

Cooley, J. J. (1998). Gay and lesbian adolescents: Presenting problems and the counselor's role. *Professional School Counseling, 1*(3), 30–34.

Corey, G. (2001). *Theory and practice of group counseling* (6th ed.). Pacific Grove, CA: Brooks/Cole.

Corey, G. (2005). *Theory and practice of counseling and psychotherapy* (7th ed.). Pacific Grove, CA: Brooks/Cole.

Corey, G., Corey, M., & Callanan, P. (2003). *Issues and ethics in the helping professions* (6th ed.). Pacific Grove, CA: Brooks/Cole.

Corey, G., Corey, M., Callanan, P., & Russell, J. M. (1982). Ethical considerations in using group techniques. *Journal for Specialists in Group Work, 7,* 140–148.

Corey, G., Williams, G. T., & Moline, M. E. (1995). Ethical and legal issues in group counseling. *Ethics and Behavior, 5*(2), 161–183.

Corey, M., & Corey, G. (2002). *Groups: Process and practice* (6th ed.). Pacific Grove, CA: Brooks/Cole.

Cormier, L. S., & Hackney, H. (1993). *The professional counselor: A process guide to helping* (2nd ed.). Englewood Cliffs, NJ: Prentice-Hall.

Cormier, W. H., & Cormier, L. S. (1998). *Interviewing strategies for helpers* (4th ed.). Monterey, CA: Brooks/Cole.

Corrigan, J. D., Dell, D. M., Lewis, K. N., & Schmidt, L. D. (1980). Counseling as a social influence process: A review [monograph]. *Journal of Counseling Psychology, 27,* 395–441.

Corsini, R. J. (1977). Individual education. *Journal of Individual Psychology, 33,* 295–349.

Corsini, R. J. (1979). Individual education. In E. Ignas & R. J. Corsini (Eds.), *Alternate educational systems* (pp. 200–256). Itasca, IL: F. E. Peacock.

Corsini, R. J., & Wedding, D. (2000). *Current psychotherapies* (6th ed.). Itasca, IL: F. E. Peacock.

Costello, A. J., Edelbrock, C. S., Dulcan, M. K., & Kalas, R. (1984). *Testing of the NIMH Diagnostic Interview Schedule for Children (DISC) in a clinical population* (Contract No. DB-81–0027, final report to the Center for Epidemiological Studies, National Institute for Mental Health). Pittsburgh: University of Pittsburgh.

Costello, A. J., Edelbrock, C., Kalas, R., Kessler, M. D., & Klaric, S. H. (1982). *The NIMH Diagnostic Interview Schedule for Children (DISC).* Unpublished interview schedule, Department of Psychiatry, University of Pittsburgh.

Cottone, R. R. (2001). A social constructivism model of ethical decision making in counseling. *Journal of Counseling and Development, 79*(1), 39–45.

Couch, R. D. (1994, February). Changes in the theory and practice of individual psychotherapy by the year 2003. *The Advocate, 6.*

Couch, R. D. (1995). Four steps for conducting a pregroup screening interview. *Journal for Specialists in Group Work, 20*(1), 18–25.

Couch, R. D., & Childers, J. H., Jr. (1989). A discussion of differences between group therapy and family therapy: Implications for counselor training and practice. *Journal for Specialists in Group Work, 14*(4), 226–231.

Cox, O. C. (1959). *Caste, class, and race.* New York: Monthly Review.

Craig, C. J. (2002). *Human development* (9th ed.). Englewood Cliffs, NJ: Prentice-Hall.

Cramer, D. (1994). Self-esteem and Rogers' core conditions in close friends: A latent variable path analysis of panel data. *Counseling Psychology Quarterly, 7*(3), 321–337.

Cripe, F. F. (1986). Rock music as therapy for children with attention deficit disorder: An exploratory study. *Journal of Music Therapy, 23,* 30–37.

Cronbach, L. J. (1984). *Essentials of psychological testing.* New York: Harper & Row.

Cross, W. E., Jr. (1995). The psychology of nigrescence: Revising the Cross model. In J. G. Ponterotto, J. M. Casas, L. A. Suzuki, & C. M. Alexander (Eds.), *Handbook of multicultural counseling* (pp. 93–122). Thousand Oaks, CA: Sage.

Culbertson, F. M. (1997). Depression and gender: An international review. *American Psychologist, 52*(1), 25–31.

Cummings, C., Gordon, J. R., & Marlatt, G. A. (1980). Relapse: Prevention and prediction. In W. R. Miller (Ed.), *The addictive behaviors.* New York: Pergamon Press.

Cummings, N. A. (1990). The credentialing of professional psychologists and its implication for other mental health disciplines. *Journal of Counseling and Development, 68,* 485–490.

Curran, J., & Loganbell, C. R. (1985). Factors affecting the attractiveness of a group leader. *Journal of College Student Personnel, 24,* 250–255.

D'Andrea, M. (2000). Postmodernism, constructivism, and multiculturalism: Three forces reshaping and expanding our thoughts about counseling. *Journal of Mental Health Counseling, 22*(1), 1–16.

D'Andrea, M. (2004). Comprehensive school-based violence prevention training: A developmental-ecological training model. *Journal of Counseling and Development, 82,* 277–286.

Dade County Public Schools. (1985). *Dropout prevention/reduction programs and activities,* 22. Miami, FL: Author.

Daigneault, S. D. (2000). Body talk: A school based group intervention for working with disordered eating behaviors. *Journal for Specialists in Group Work, 25,* 191–213.

Daly, M., & Wilson, M. (1983). *Sex, evolution, and behavior* (2nd ed.). Boston: Willard Grant Press.

Damon, L., & Waterman, J. (1986). Parallel group treatment of children and their mothers. In K. MacFarlane & J. Waterman (Eds.), *Sexual abuse of young children.* New York: Guilford Press.

Dana, R. H. (1993). *Multicultural assessment perspectives for professional psychology.* Boston: Allyn & Bacon.

Daniels, M. H., & White, L. J. (1994). Revisiting Auerswald's conundrum—A response to Fong, Lease, and Lanning. *Journal of Mental Health Counseling, 16*(2), 217–225.

Danish, S. J., D'Augelli, A. R., & Brock, G. W. (1976). An evaluation of helping skill training: Effects on helpers' verbal responses. *Journal of Counseling Psychology, 23,* 259–266.

Davanloo, H. (1978). *Basic principles and techniques in short-term dynamic psychotherapy.* New York: SP Medical and Scientific Books.

Davanloo, H. (1984). Intensive short-term dynamic psychotherapy. In H. Kaplan and B. Sadock (Eds.), *Comprehensive textbooks of psychiatry.* Baltimore: Williams & Wilkins.

Davis, J. L., & Mickelson, D. J. (1994). School counselors: Are you aware of ethical and legal aspects of counseling? *The School Counselor, 42*(1), 5–13.

Davis-Berman, J. (1988). Self-efficacy and depressive symptomatology in older adults: An exploratory study. *International Journal of Aging and Human Development, 27*(1), 35–43.

de Shazer, S. (1985). *Key solutions in brief therapy.* New York: Norton.

de Shazer, S. (1988). *Clues: Investigating solutions in brief therapy.* New York: Norton.

de Shazer, S. (1991). *Putting difference to work.* New York: Norton.

de Shazer, S. (1994). *Words were originally magic.* New York: Norton.

DeLucia-Waack, J. L. (1999). What makes an effective group leader? *Journal for Specialists in Group Work, 24,* 131–132.

DeLucia-Waack, J. L. (2000). Effective group work in the schools. *Journal for Specialists in Group Work, 25,* 131–132.

Denkowski, K. M., & Denkowski, G. C. (1982). Client-counselor confidentiality: An update. *Personnel and Guidance Journal, 60,* 371–375.

DePauw, M. E. (1986). Avoiding ethical relations: A time-line perspective for individual counseling. *Journal of Counseling and Development, 64*(5), 303–310.

Devine, D. A., & Fernald, P. S. (1973). Outcome effects of receiving a preferred, randomly assigned, or non-referred therapy. *Journal of Consulting and Clinical Psychology, 41,* 104–107.

Digdon, N., & Gotlib, I. H. (1985). Developmental considerations in the study of childhood depression. *Developmental Review, 5,* 162–199.

Dingman, R. L. (Ed.). (1988). *Licensure for mental health counselors.* Huntington, WV: Marshall University Press.

Dinkmeyer, D. (1971). The "C" group: Integrating knowledge and experience to change behavior. *The Counseling Psychologist, 3,* 63–72.

Dinkmeyer, D. (1973). The parent "C" group. *Personnel and Guidance Journal, 52,* 4.

Dinkmeyer, D., & Carlson, J. (1973). *Consultation: Facilitating human potential and processes.* Columbus, OH: Merrill/Macmillan.

Dinkmeyer, D., & Carlson, J. (1984). *Time for a better marriage.* Circle Pines, MN: American Guidance Service.

Dinkmeyer, D., & Dinkmeyer, D., Jr. (1982). *Developing understanding of self and others. DUSO-1 Revised, DUSO-2 Revised.* Circle Pines, MN: American Guidance Service.

Dinkmeyer, D., & Dinkmeyer, D., Jr. (1985). Adlerian psychotherapy and counseling. In S. Lynn & J. P. Garske (Eds.), *Contemporary psychotherapies: Models and methods.* Columbus, OH: Merrill/Macmillan.

Dinkmeyer, D., & Dreikurs, R. (1963). *Encouraging children to learn: The encouragement process.* Englewood Cliffs, NJ: Prentice-Hall.

Dinkmeyer, D., & Losoncy, L. E. (1980). *The encouragement book: Becoming a positive person.* Englewood Cliffs, NJ: Prentice-Hall.

Dinkmeyer, D., & McKay, G. (1990). *Systematic training for effective parenting of teens* (2nd ed.). Circle Pines, MN: American Guidance Service.

Dinkmeyer, D., & McKay, G., (1997). *Systemic training for effective parenting (STEP): The parent's handbook* (4th ed.). Circle Pines, MN: American Guidance Service.

Dinkmeyer, D., McKay, G., & Dinkmeyer, D., Jr. (1997). *Parent's handbook: Systemic training for effective parenting.* Circle Pines, MN: American Guidance Service.

Dinkmeyer, D., McKay, G., Dinkmeyer, D., Jr., Dinkmeyer, J. S., & Carlson, J. (1985). *PREP for effective family living: Student handbook.* Circle Pines, MN: American Guidance Service.

Dinkmeyer, D., Jr., & Sperry, L. (2000). *Counseling and psychotherapy: An integrated, individual psychological approach* (3rd ed.). Columbus, OH: Merrill/Macmillan.

Dixon, D. N., & Glover, J. A. (1984). *Counseling: A problem solving approach.* New York: John Wiley & Sons.

Dobson, K. S. (1989). A meta-analysis of the efficacy of cognitive therapy for depression. *Journal of Consulting and Clinical Psychology, 57*(3), 414–419.

Dodge, K. A. (1983). Behavioral antecedents of peer social station. *Child Development, 54,* 1386–1399.

Donne, J. (1952). *The complete poetry and selected prose of John Donne.* New York: Random House.

Dorn, F. J., & Day, B. J. (1985). Assessing change in self-concept: A social psychological approach. *American Mental Health Counselors Association Journal, 7,* 180–186.

Dougherty, A. M. (1995). *Consultation: Practice and perspectives in school and community settings* (2nd ed.). Pacific Grove, CA: Brooks/Cole.

Douglas, C. (2005). Analytical psychotherapy. In R. J. Corsini & D. Wedding (Eds.), *Current psychotherapies* (7th ed.) (pp. 96–129). Itasca, IL: F. E. Peacock.

Dowd, E. T., & Sanders, D. (1994). Resistance, reactance, and the difficult client. *Canadian Journal of Counseling, 28*(1), 13–24.

Dreikurs, R. (1949). The four goals of children's misbehavior. *Nervous Child, 6,* 3–11.

Dreikurs, R. (1971). *Social equality: The challenge of today.* Chicago: Henry Regnery.

Dreikurs, R., Corsini, R. J., Lowe, R., & Sonstegard, M. (1959). *Adlerian family counseling.* Eugene, OR: University of Oregon Press.

Dreikurs, R., & Soltz, V. (1964). *Children: The challenge.* New York: Hawthorn Books.

Drummond, R. J. (2000). *Appraisal procedures for counselors and helping professionals* (4th ed.). Columbus, OH: Merrill.

Dryden, W. (1987). Theoretically consistent eclecticism: Humanizing a computer "addict." In J. C. Norcross (Ed.), *Casebook of eclectic psychotherapy* (pp. 221–237). New York: Brunner/Mazel.

Duncan, B. L., & Moynihan, D. W. (1994). Applying outcome research: Intentional utilization of the client's frame of reference. *Psychotherapy, 31,* 294–301.

Dungy, G. (1984). Computer-assisted guidance: Determining who is ready. *Journal of College Student Personnel, 25,* 539–546.

Dunn, R. L., & Schwebel, A. I. (1995). Meta-analytic review of marital therapy outcome research. *Journal of Family Psychology, 9*(1), 58–68.

Durkheim, E. (1897). *Suicide: A study in sociology.* Glencoe, IL: Free Press.

Durlak, J. A., Fuhrman, T., & Lampman, C. (1991). Effectiveness of cognitive-behavioral therapy for maladapting children: A meta-analysis. *Psychological Bulletin, 110,* 204–214.

Durrant, M. (1995). *Creative strategies for school problems: Solutions for psychologists and teachers.* New York: Norton.

Dusay, J., & Dusay, K. M. (1989). Transactional analysis. In R. Corsini (Ed.), *Current psychotherapies* (4th ed.). Itasca, IL: F. E. Peacock.

Duvall, E. M. (1957). *Family development.* Philadelphia: Lippincott.

Duvall, E. M. (1977). *Marriage and family development* (5th ed.). Philadelphia: Lippincott.

Dworetzky, J. P. (1996). *Introduction to child development* (6th ed.). New York: ITP.

Dysinger, B. J. (1993). Conflict resolution for intermediate children. *The School Counselor, 40*(4), 301–308.

Ebert, B. (1978). The healthy family. *Family Therapy, 5*(3), 227–232.

Eccles, J. S., Midgley, C., Wigfield, A., Buchanan, C. M., Reuman, D., Flanagan, C., & Iver, D. M. (1993). Development during adolescence: The impact of stage-environment fit on young adolescents' experiences in schools and families. *American Psychologist, 48,* 90–101.

Edelbrock, C., & Costello, A. J. (1988). Structured psychiatric interviews for children. In M. Rutter, A. H. Tuma, & I. S. Lann (Eds.), *Assessment and diagnosis in child psychopathology* (pp. 82–112). New York: Guilford Press.

Edelson, M. (1994). Can psychotherapy research answer this psychotherapist's questions? In P. F. Tally, H. H. Strupp, & S. F. Butler (Eds.), *Psychotherapy research and practice: Bridging the gap.* New York: Basic Books.

The Education Trust. (1999). *Transforming school counseling.* Retrieved January 18, 2002, from http://www.edtrust.org/main/school_counseling.asp

Egan, G. (2002). *The skilled helper: A model for systematic helping and interpersonal relating* (7th ed.). Monterey, CA: Brooks/Cole.

Eggen, P., & Kauchak, D. (1994). *Educational psychology: Classroom connections* (2nd ed.). Columbus, OH: Merrill.

Eidson, C. E., Jr. (1989). The effects of behavioral music therapy on the generalization of interpersonal skills from sessions to the classroom by emotionally handicapped middle school students. *Journal of Music Therapy, 26*(4), 206–221.

Elkaim, M. (1982). From the family approach to the socio-political approach. In F. Kaslow (Ed.), *The international book of family therapy* (pp. 331–357). New York: Brunner/Mazel.

Elkin, I., Shea, M. T., Watkins, J. T., Imber, S. D., Sotsky, S. M., Collins, J. F., Glass, D. R., Pilkonis, P. A., Leber, W. R., Docherty, J. P., Fiester, S. J., & Parloff, M. B. (1989). NIMH Treatment of Depression Collaborative Research Program: I. General effectiveness of treatments. *Archives of General Psychiatry, 46,* 971–982.

Elkind, D. (1984). *All grown up and no place to go.* Reading, MA: Addison-Wesley.

Elliott, D. S., Huizinga, D., & Ageton, S. S. (1985). *Explaining delinquency and drug use.* Beverly Hills, CA: Sage.

Elliot, G. (1989). An interview with George M. Gazda. *Journal for Specialists in Group Work, 14*(3), 131–140.

Elliott, J. M. (1999). Feminist therapy. In C. Capuzzi & D. R. Gross (Eds.), *Counseling and psychotherapy: Theories and interventions* (2nd ed.) (pp. 201–230). Columbus, OH: Merrill.

Ellis, A. (1962). *Reason and emotion in psychotherapy.* New York: Lyle Stuart.

Ellis, A. (1977). The basic clinical theory of rational-emotive therapy. In A. Ellis & R. Grieger (Eds.), *RET handbook of rational-emotive therapy* (pp. 3–34). New York: Springer.

Ellis, A. (1986). Comments on Gloria. *Psychotherapy, 23,* 647–648.

Ellis, A. (1993, Summer). RET becomes REBT. *IRETletter, 1,* 4.

Ellis, A. (1994). *Reason and emotion in psychotherapy revised.* New York: Carol Publishing.

Ellis, A. (1996). *Better, deeper and more enduring brief therapy.* New York: Brunner/Mazel.

Ellis, A. (2000). A continuation of the dialogue on issues in counseling in the postmodern era. *Journal of Mental Health Counseling, 22*(2), 97–106.

Ellis, A. (2005). Rational emotive behavior therapy. In R. J. Corsini & D. Wedding (Eds.), *Current psychotherapies* (7th ed.) (pp. 166–201). Itasca, IL: F. E. Peacock.

Ellis, A., & Harper, R. (1975). *A new guide to rational living* (Rev. ed.). Hollywood: Wilshire Books.

Ellis, P. L. (1982). Empathy: A factor in antisocial behavior. *Journal of Abnormal Child Psychology, 10,* 123–133.

Elman, N. S., & Forrest, L. (2004). Psychotherapy in the remediation of psychology trainees: Exploratory interviews with training directors. *Professional Psychology: Research and Practice, 35*(2), 123–130.

Emmelkamp, P. M. G. (1994). Behavior therapy with adults. In A. E. Bergin & S. L. Garfield, *Handbook of psychotherapy and behavior change* (4th ed.) (pp. 379–427). New York: John Wiley & Sons.

Emmons, R., & Nystul, M. S. (1994). The effects of a prenatal course including PREP for effective family living on self-esteem and parenting attitudes of adolescents: A brief report. *Adolescence, 29,* 935–938.

Engels, D. W., Minor, C. W., Sampson, J. P., & Splete, H. H. (1995). Career counseling specialty: History, development, and prospect. *Journal of Counseling and Development, 74*(2), 134–138.

England, L. W., & Thompson, C. L. (1988). Counseling child sexual abuse victims: Myths and realities. *Journal of Counseling and Development, 66,* 370–373.

Enns, C. Z. (1988). Dilemmas of power and equality in marital and family counseling: Proposals for a feminist perspective. *Journal of Counseling and Development, 67*(4), 242–248.

Enns, C. Z. (1993). Twenty years of counseling and therapy: From naming biases to implementing multifaceted practice. *The Counseling Psychologist, 21*(1), 3–87.

Epstein, E. S., & Loos, V. E. (1989). Some irreverent thoughts on the limits of family therapy: Towards a language-based explanation of human systems. *Journal of Family Psychology, 2*(4), 405–421.

Erford, B. T., House, R., & Martin, P. (2003). Transforming the school counseling profession. In B. T. Erford (Ed.), *Transforming the school counseling profession* (pp. 1–20). Columbus, OH: Merrill.

Erickson, M. (1954a). Pseudo-orientation in time as a hypnotherapeutic procedure. *Journal of Clinical and Experimental Hypnosis, 2,* 261–283.

Erickson, M. (1954b). Special techniques on brief hypnotherapy. *Journal of Clinical and Experimental Hypnosis, 2,* 109–129.

Erikson, E. H. (1950). *Childhood and society.* New York: Norton.

Erikson, E. H. (1963). *Childhood and society* (2nd ed.). New York: Norton.

Erikson, E. H. (1968). *Identity, youth, and crisis.* New York: Norton.

Eron, J. B., & Lund, T. W. (1993). How problems evolve and dissolve: Integrating narrative and strategic concepts. *Family Process, 32,* 291–309.

Estes, C. P. (1992). *Women who run with the wolves.* New York: Ballantine Books.

Estrada, A. U., & Pinsof, W. M. (1995). The effectiveness of family therapies for selected behavioral disorders of childhood. *Journal of Marital and Family Therapy, 21,* 403–440.

Evans, K. M., Seem, S. R., & Kincade, E. A. (2005). In G. Corey (Ed.), *Case approach to counseling and psychotherapy* (6th ed.) (pp. 212–246). Belmont, CA: Wadsworth.

Everett, C. A. (1990a). The field of marital and family therapy. *Journal of Counseling and Development, 68,* 498–502.

Everett, C. A. (1990b). Where have all the "gypsies" gone? *Journal of Counseling and Development, 68,* 507–510.

Everstine, L., Everstine, D. S., Heymann, G. M., True, R. H., Frey, D. H., Johnson, H. G., & Seiden, R. H. (1980). Privacy and confidentiality in psychotherapy. *American Psychologist, 9,* 828–840.

Eysenck, H. J. (1965). The effects of psychotherapy. *Journal of Consulting Psychology, 16,* 319–324.

Fadiman, J., & Frager, R. (1976). *Personality and personal growth.* New York: Harper & Row.

Farren, C., Gray, J. D., & Kaye, B. C. (1984). Mentoring: A boom to career development. *The Personnel and Guidance Journal, 61,* 20–24.

Fassinger, R. E. (1991). The hidden minority: Issues and challenges in working with lesbian women and gay men. *The Counseling Psychologist, 19*(2), 157–176.

Fassinger, R. E. (1995). From invisibility to integration: Lesbian identity in the workplace. *The Career Development Quarterly, 44*(2), 148–167.

Feinauer, L. L. (1990). Relationship of treatment to adjustment in women sexually abused as children. *American Journal of Family Therapy, 17*(4), 326–334.

Feist, J. (1985). *Theories of personality.* New York: Holt, Rinehart & Winston.

Feldman, R. A., Caplinger, T. E., & Wodarski, S. S. (1981). *The St. Louis conundrum: Prosocial and antisocial boys together.* Unpublished manuscript.

Feller, R. W. (1995). Action planning for personal competitiveness in the "broken workplace." *Journal of Employment Counseling, 32,* 154–163.

Ferris, P. A. (1988). Future directions for elementary/middle school counseling. In G. R. Walz & J. C. Bleuer (Eds.), *Building strong school counseling programs.* Alexandria, VA: American Association for Counseling and Development.

Festinger, L. (1957). *A theory of cognitive dissonance.* Stanford, CA: Stanford University Press.

Field, T., Healy, B., Goldstein, S., Perry, S., Bendell, D., Schanberg, S., Zimmerman, E. A., & Kuhn, C. (1988). Infants of depressed mothers show "depressed" behavior even with nondepressed adults. *Child Development, 59,* 1569–1579.

Fisch, R., Weakland, J. H., & Segal, L. (1982). *The tactics of change: Doing therapy briefly.* San Francisco: Jossey-Bass.

Fischer, A. R., Jome, L. M., & Atkinson, D. R. (1998). Reconceptualizing multicultural counseling: Universal healing conditions in a culturally specific context. *The Counseling Psychologist, 26,* 525–588.

Fisher, B. L., & Sprenkle, D. H. (1978). Therapists' perceptions of healthy family functioning. *International Journal of Family Counseling, 19*(4) 9–18.

Fisher, K. (1982, November). Debate rages on 1973 Sonell study. *APA Monitor,* 8–9.

Fitzgerald, L. F., & Rounds, J. B. (1989). Vocational behavior, 1988: A critical analysis. *Journal of Vocational Behavior, 35,* 105–163.

Fleshman, B., & Fryrear, J. L. (1981). *The arts in therapy.* Chicago: Nelson-Hall.

Foa, E. B., Rothbaum, B. O., Riggs, D. S., & Murdock, T. B. (1991). Treatment of posttraumatic stress disorder in rape victims: A comparison between cognitive-behavioral procedures and counseling. *Journal of Consulting and Clinical Psychology, 59,* 715–723.

Fong, M. L., & Lease, S. H. (1994). Constructivist alternatives: The case for diversity and integration in mental health counseling. *Journal of Mental Health Counseling, 16*(1), 120–124.

Fontaine, J. H. (1998). Evidencing a need: School counselor's experiences with gay and lesbian students. *Professional School Counseling, 1*(3), 8–14.

Forester, J. R. (1977). What shall we do about credentialing? *Personnel and Guidance Journal, 55,* 573–576.

Forester-Miller, H. (1989). Dr. Irvin Yalom discusses group psychotherapy. *Journal for Specialists in Group Work, 14*(4), 196–201.

Forisha, B. L. (2001). Feminist psychotherapy. In R. J. Corsini (Ed.), *Handbook of innovative therapy* (2nd ed.) (pp. 242–254). New York: John Wiley & Sons.

Fosterling, F. (1980). Attributional aspects of cognitive behavior modification: A theoretical approach and suggestions for techniques. *Cognitive Therapy and Research, 24,* 27–37.

Foucault, M. (1980). *Power/knowledge: Selected interviews and other writings.* New York: Pantheon Books.

Framo, J. (1992). *Family of origin theory: An intergenerational approach.* New York: Brunner/Mazel.

Framo, J. L. (1981). The integration of marital therapy with family of origin sessions. In A. Gurman & D. Kniskern (Eds.), *Handbook of family therapy.* New York: Brunner/Mazel.

Frances, R. J. (1988). Update on alcohol and drug disorder treatment. *Journal of Clinical Psychiatry, 49*(9), 13–17.

Frankl, V. (1959). *From death-camp to existentialism.* Boston: Beacon.

Frankl, V. (1963). *Man's search for meaning.* New York: Washington Square Press.

Frankl, V. (1967). *Psychotherapy and existentialism: Selected papers on logotherapy.* New York: Simon & Schuster (Touchstone).

Frankl, V. (1971). *The doctor and the soul.* New York: Bantam.

Frankl, V. (1978). *The unheard cry for meaning.* New York: Simon & Schuster (Touchstone).

Frazier, S. H. (1985). Responding to the needs of the homeless mentally ill public. *Health Reports, 100,* 462–469.

Freeman, M. A. (1995). Behavioral at-risk contracting in a changing healthcare environment. In G. L. Zieman (Ed.), *The complete capitation handbook: How to design and implement at-risk contracts for behavioral healthcare* (pp. 11–27). Tiburon, CA: Centra-Link Publications.

Freud A. (1928). Introduction to the technique of child analysis. *Nervous and Mental Disease Monograph No. 48.* New York.

Freud, S. (1933). New introductory lectures on psychoanalyses. In J. Strachey (Ed. and Trans.), *The complete psychological works* (Vol. 22). New York: Norton.

Freud, S. (1953). Fragment of an analysis of a case of hysteria. In J. Strachey (Ed.), *The standard edition of the complete psychological works of Sigmund Freud* (Vol. 7) (pp. 3–122). London: Hogarth.

Freud, S. (1969). *A general introduction to psychoanalysis.* New York: Simon & Schuster.

Freud, S. (1900). *The interpretation of dreams.* New York: Avon Books.

Friedan, B. (1963). *The feminine mystique.* New York: Dell.

Friedlander, M. L., & Highlen, P. S. (1984). A spatial view of the interpersonal structure of family interviews: Similarities and differences across counselors. *Journal of Counseling Psychology, 31,* 477–487.

Friedlander, M. L., Highlen, P. S., & Lassiter, W. L. (1985). Content analytic comparison of four expert counselors' approach to family treatment: Ackerman, Bowen, Jackson, and Whitaker. *Journal of Counseling Psychology, 32*(2), 171–180.

Friedlander, M. L., & Tuason, M. T. (2000). Process and outcomes in couples and family therapy. In S. D. Brown & R. W. Lent (Eds.), *Handbook of counseling psychology* (3rd ed.) (pp. 797–824). New York: John Wiley & Sons.

Friedman, S. (1997). *Time-effective psychotherapy: Maximizing outcomes in an era of minimized resources.* Needham Heights, MA: Allyn & Bacon.

Frieman, B. B. (1993). Children of divorced parents: Action steps for the counselor to involve fathers. *Elementary School Guidance and Counseling, 28*(3), 197–205.

Fuhriman, A., & Burlingame, G. M. (1990). Consistency of matter: A comparative analysis of individual and group process variables. *The Counseling Psychologist, 18*(1), 6–63.

Furstenberg, F. F., Jr., Brooks-Gunn, J., & Chase-Lansdale, L. (1989). *Unplanned parenthood: The social consequences of teenage childbearing.* New York: Free Press.

Gabbard, G. O. (1994). Teetering on the precipice: A commentary on Lazarus's "How certain boundaries and ethics diminish therapeutic effectiveness." *Ethics and Behavior, 4,* 283–286.

Gardill, M. C., & Browder, D. M. (1995). Teaching stimulus classes to encourage independent purchasing by students with severe behavior disorders. *Education and Training in Mental Retardation and Developmental Disabilities, 30,* 254–269.

Garfield, J. C., Weiss, S. I., & Pollack, E. A. (1973). Effects of the child's social class on school counselors' decision-making. *Journal of Counseling Psychology, 20,* 166–168.

Garfield, S. L. (1983). *Clinical psychology. The study of personality and behavior* (2nd ed.). New York: Aldine.

Garfield, S. L. (1994). Research on client variables in psychotherapy. In A. E. Bergin & S. L. Garfield (Eds.), *Handbook of psychotherapy and behavior change* (4th ed.) (pp. 190–228). New York: John Wiley & Sons.

Garfield, S. L., & Bergin, A. E. (1971). Therapeutic conditions and outcome. *Journal of Abnormal Psychology, 77,* 108–114.

Garfield, S. L., & Bergin, A. E. (1994). Introduction and historical overview. In A. E. Bergin & S. L. Garfield (Eds.), *Handbook of psychotherapy and behavior change* (4th ed.) (pp. 3–18). New York: John Wiley & Sons.

Garland, A. F., & Zigler, E. (1993). Adolescent suicide prevention. *American Psychologist, 48*(2), 169–182.

Garrett, M. W. (1995). Between two worlds: Cultural discontinuity in the dropout of Native American youth. *The School Counselor, 42*(3), 186–195.

Garske, J. P., & Molteni, A. L. (1985). Brief psychodynamic psychotherapy: An integrative approach. In S. J. Lynn & J. P. Garske (Eds.), *Contemporary psychotherapies.* Columbus, OH: Merrill/Macmillan.

Gati, I. (1986). Making career decisions: A sequential elimination approach. *Journal of Counseling Psychology, 33,* 408–417.

Gati, I. (1990a). Interpreting and applying career decision-making models: Comments on Carson and Mowsesian. *Journal of Counseling Psychology, 32*(4), 508–514.

Gati, I. (1990b). Why, when, and how to take into account the uncertainty involved in career decisions. *Journal of Counseling Psychology, 37*(3), 277–280.

Gati, I. (1994). Computer-assisted career counseling: Dilemmas, problems, and possible solutions. *Journal of Counseling and Development, 73*(1), 51–56.

Gati, I., Fassa, N., & Houminer, D. (1995). Applying decision theory to career counseling practice: The sequential elimination approach. *Career Development Quarterly, 43,* 211–220.

Gati, I., & Tikotzki, Y. (1989). Strategies for collection and processing of occupational information in making career decisions. *Journal of Counseling Psychology, 35*(3), 430–439.

Gazda, G. M. (1989). *Group counseling: A developmental approach* (4th ed.). Boston: Allyn & Bacon.

Gazda, G. M., Asbury, F., Blazer, F., Childress, W., & Walters, R. (1979). *Human relations development: A manual for educators.* Boston: Allyn & Bacon.

Gelso, C. J., & Carter, J. A. (1985). The relationship in counseling and psychotherapy: Components, consequences, and theoretical antecedents. *The Counseling Psychologist, 13,* 155–243.

Gelso, C. J., & Fassinger, R. E. (1990). Counseling psychology: Theory and research on intervention. *American Review of Psychology, 41,* 355–386.

Gelso, C. J., & Fretz, B. R. (1992). *Counseling psychology.* Orlando, FL: Holt, Rinehart & Winston.

Gelso, C. J., & Fretz, B. R. (2001). *Counseling psychology* (2nd ed.). Orlando, FL: Holt, Rinehart & Winston.

Genia, V. (1994). Secular psychotherapists and religious clients: Professional considerations and recommendations. *Journal of Counseling and Development, 72*(4), 395–398.

George, R. L., & Cristiani, T. S. (1995). *Counseling: Theory and practice* (4th ed.). Englewood Cliffs, NJ: Prentice-Hall.

Geoseffi, D. (1993). *On prejudice: A global perspective.* New York: Doubleday.

Gerber, P. J. (1986). Counseling the learning disabled. In A. F. Rotatori, P. J. Gerber, F. W. Litton, & R. A. Fox (Eds.), *Counseling exceptional students.* New York: Human Sciences Press.

Gergen, K. (1982). *Toward transformation in social knowledge.* New York: Springer-Verlag.

Gergen, K. (1994a). Exploring the postmodern. *American Psychologist, 49*(5), 412–416.

Gergen, K. (1994b). *Realities and relationships.* Cambridge, MA: Harvard University Press.

Gerler, E. R., & Anderson, R. F. (1986). The effects of classroom guidance on children's success in school. *Journal of Counseling and Development, 65,* 78–81.

Gerler, E. R., Jr. (1995). Advancing elementary and middle school counseling through computer technology. *Elementary School Guidance and Counseling, 30*(1), 8–15.

Gibbons, A. C. (1984). A program for noninstitutionalized, mature adults: A description. *Activities, Adaptation, and Aging, 6,* 71–80.

Gibbons, A. C. (1988). A review of literature for music development/education and music therapy with the elderly. *Music Therapy Perspectives, 5,* 33–40.

Gibbs, N. (1995, October 2). The EQ factor. *Time,* 60–68.

Giblin, P., & Chan, J. (1995). A feminist perspective. *The Family Journal: Counseling and Therapy for Couples and Families, 3*(3), 234–238.

Gibran, K. (1965). *The prophet.* New York: Alfred A. Knopf.

Gibson, R. L. (1977). *Counseling and annual guidance committee report.* Unpublished manuscript, North Central Association of Colleges and Schools.

Gibson, R. L. (1989). Prevention and the elementary school counselor. *Elementary School Guidance & Counseling, 24,* 30–36.

Gilbert, L. A. (1992). Gender and counseling psychology: Current knowledge and directions for research and social action. In S. D. Brown & R. W. Lent (Eds.), *Handbook of counseling psychology* (2nd ed.) (pp. 383–418). New York: John Wiley & Sons.

Gilbert, L. A., & Scher, M. (1999). *Gender and sex in counseling and psychotherapy.* Needham Heights, MA: Allyn & Bacon.

Gilbert, N. (1982, July). Policy issues in primary prevention. *Social Work,* 293–296.

Gilligan, C. (1987). Adolescent development reconsidered. In C. Irwin (Ed.), *Adolescent social behavior and health.* San Francisco: Jossey-Bass.

Gilligan, C. (1990). Joining the resistance: Psychology, politics, girls, and women. *Michigan Quarterly Review, 29*(4), 501–536.

Gilligan, C. (1991). Women's psychological development: Implications for psychotherapy. *Women in Therapy, 11,* 5–31.

Gilligan, C. (1993). *In a different voice: Psychological theory and women's development* (2nd ed.). Cambridge, MA: Harvard University Press.

Gilliland, B. E., & James, R. K. (1997). *Crisis intervention strategies.* (3rd ed.). Pacific Grove, CA: Brooks/Cole.

Ginter, E. J. (1988). Stagnation in eclecticism: The need to recommit to a journey. *Journal of Mental Health Counseling, 10,* 3–8.

Ginter, E. J. (1996). Three pillars of mental health counseling: Watch in what you step. *Journal of Mental Health Counseling, 18*(2), 99–107.

Ginter, E. J., Scalise, J. J., & Presse, N. (1990). The elementary school counselor's role: Perceptions of teachers. *The School Counselor, 38,* 19–23.

Gintner, G. G., & Poret, M. K. (1987). Factors associated with maintenance and relapse following self-management training. *Journal of Psychology, 122*(1), 79–87.

Gladding, S. T., Remley, T. P., & Huber, C. (2001). *Ethical, legal, and professional issues in the practice of marriage and family therapy* (3rd ed.). Columbus, OH: Merrill.

Gladstein, G. (1983). Understanding empathy: Integrating counseling, developmental and social psychology perspectives. *Journal of Counseling Psychology, 30,* 467–482.

Glaser, B. G., & Strauss, A. (1967). *The discovery of grounded theory: Stategies for qualitative research.* Chicago: Aldine Publishing Co.

Glasser, W. (1961). *Mental health or mental illness?* New York: Harper & Row.

Glasser, W. (1965). *Reality therapy: A new approach to psychiatry.* New York: Harper & Row.

Glasser, W. (1969). *Schools without failure.* New York: Harper & Row.

Glasser, W. (1976). *Positive addiction.* New York: Harper & Row.

Glasser, W. (1980). Reality therapy: An explanation of the steps of reality therapy. In N. Glasser (Ed.), *What are you doing? How people are helped through reality therapy.* New York: Harper & Row.

Glasser, W. (1981). *Stations of the mind.* New York: Harper & Row.

Glasser, W. (1984). *Take effective control of your life.* New York: Harper & Row.

Glasser, W. (1985). *Control theory: A new explanation of how we control our lives.* New York: Harper & Row (Perennial Paperback).

Glasser, W. (1986). *Control theory in the classroom.* New York: Harper & Row.

Glasser, W. (1989). Control theory in the practice of reality therapy. In N. Glasser (Ed.), *Control theory in the practice of reality therapy: Case studies* (pp. 1–15). New York: Harper & Row.

Glasser, W. (1990). *The quality school.* New York: Harper & Row.

Glasser, W. (1998). *Choice theory: A new psychology of personal freedom.* New York: HarperCollins.

Glasser, W. (2000). *Counseling with choice theory: The new reality therapy.* New York: Quill.

Glasser, W., & Glasser, C. (1999). *The language of choice theory.* New York: HarperCollins.

Glasser, W., & Wubbolding, R. E. (1995). Reality therapy. In R. J. Corsini & D. Wedding (Eds.), *Current psychotherapies* (5th ed.) (pp. 293–321). Itasca, IL: F. E. Peacock.

Glauser, A. S., & Bozarth, J. D. (2001). Person-centered counseling: The culture within. *Journal of Counseling and Development, 79*(2), 142–147.

Glenn, E. E. (1998). Counseling children and adolescents with disabilities. *Professional School Counseling, 2*(1), iii.

Glick, I., Clarkin, J., & Kessler, D. (1987). *Marital and family therapy* (3rd ed.). Orlando, FL: Grune & Stratton.

Glover, E. (1950). *Freud or Jung.* New York: Norton.

Golann, S. (1987). On description of family therapy. *Family Process, 26,* 331–340.

Goldberg, R. T. (1974). Adjustment of children with invisible and visible handicaps. *Journal of Counseling Psychology, 21,* 428–432.

Goldenberg, I., & Goldenberg, H. (2004). *Family therapy: An overview* (6th ed.). Monterey, CA: Brooks/Cole.

Goldenberg, I., & Goldenberg, H. (2005). *Family therapy: An overview* (7th ed.). Monterey, CA: Brooks/Cole.

Goldfried, M. R., Greenberg, L. S., & Mormar, C. (1990). Individual psychotherapy: Process and outcome. *Annual Review of Psychology, 41,* 659–688.

Goldfried, M. R., & Wolfe, B. E. (1996). Psychotherapy practice and research: Repairing a strained alliance. *American Psychologist, 51*(10), 1007–1016.

Goldman, L. (1989). Moving counseling research into the 21st century. *The Counseling Psychologist, 17,* 81–85.

Goldman, L. (1990). Qualitative assessment. *The Counseling Psychologist, 18,* 205–213.

Goldman, S., & Beardslee, W. (1999). Suicide in children and adolescents. In D. Jacobs (Ed.), *The Harvard Medical School guide to assessment and intervention* (pp. 417–442). San Francisco: Jossey-Bass.

Goldner, V. (1985). Feminism and family therapy. *Family Process, 24,* 31–47.

Goldstein, A. P. (1999). *Low-level aggression: First steps on the ladder to violence.* Champaign, IL: Research Press.

Goldston, S. E., Yager, J., Heinicke, C. M., & Pynoos, R. S. (Eds.). (1990). *Preventing mental health disturbances in childhood.* Washington, DC: American Psychiatric Press.

Goleman, D. (1997). *Emotional intelligence.* New York: Bantam.

Good, G. E., Fischer, A. R., Johnston, J. A., Jr., & Heppner, P. P. (1994). Norman C. Gysbers: A proponent of comprehensive school guidance programs. *Journal of Counseling and Development, 73*(2), 115–120.

Good, G. E., Gilbert, L. A., & Scher, M. (1990). Gender aware therapy: A synthesis of feminist therapy and knowledge about gender. *Journal of Counseling and Development, 68,* 376–380.

Gooding, P. R., & Glasgow, R. E. (1985). Self-efficacy and outcome expectations as predictors of controlling smoking status. *Cognitive Therapy and Research, 9,* 583–590.

Goodman, J. (1994). Career adaptability in adults: A construct whose time has come. *The Career Development Quarterly, 43*(1), 74–84.

Goodyear, R. K. (1990). Research on the effects of test interpretation: A review. *The Counseling Psychologist, 18,* 240–257.

Gordon, J., & Shontz, F. (1990). Representative case research: A way of knowing. *Journal of Counseling and Development, 69,* 62–66.

Gottfredson, L. S. (1981). Circumscription and compromise: A developmental theory of occupational aspirations. *Journal of Counseling Psychology Monograph, 28,* 545–579.

Gottfredson, L. S. (1996). Gottfredson's theory of circumscription and compromise. In D. Brown & L. Brooks (Eds.), *Career choice and development* (3rd ed.) (pp. 179–232). San Francisco: Jossey-Bass.

Gottman, J. M. (1994). *Why marriages succeed or fail.* New York: Simon & Schuster.

Gottman, J. M., Coan, J., Carrere, S., & Swanson, C. (1998). Predicting marital happiness and stability from newlywed interactions. *Journal of Marriage and the Family, 60*(1), 5–22.

Gottman, J. M., & Notarius, C. I. (2000). Decade review: Observing marital interaction. *Journal of Marriage and the Family, 62,* 927–947.

Grant, B. (1992). The moral nature of psychotherapy. In M. T. Burke & J. G. Miranti (Eds.), *Ethical and spiritual values in counseling* (pp. 27–36). Alexandria, VA: American Counseling Association.

Gray, L. A., & Harding, A. K. (1988). Confidentiality limits with clients who have the AIDS virus. *Journal of Counseling and Development, 66*(5), 219–223.

Green, R. L. (1988). Image-building activities for the elementary school counselor. *Elementary School Guidance & Counseling, 22*(3), 186–191.

Greenberg, L., Elliott, R., & Lietaer, G. (1994). Research on experiential psychotherapies. In A. E. Bergin & S. L. Garfield (Eds.), *Handbook of psychotherapy and behavior change* (4th ed.). New York: John Wiley & Sons.

Greenberg, L. S., & Paivio, S. C. (1997). *Working with the emotions in psychotherapy.* New York: Guilford Press.

Greenson, R. R. (1967). *Technique and practice of psychoanalysis.* New York: International University Press.

Gregg, C. (1994). Group work with single fathers. *Journal for Specialists in Group Work, 19,* 95–101.

Griffin, H. C., Gerber, P. J., & Rotatori, A. F. (1986). Counseling the health impaired student. In A. F. Rotatori, P. J. Gerber, F. W. Litton, & R. A. Fox (Eds.), *Counseling exceptional students* (pp. 213–231). New York: Human Sciences Press.

Griffin, H. C., Sexton, D., Gerber, P. J., & Rotatori, A. F. (1986). Counseling the physically handicapped child. In A. F. Rotatori, P. J. Gerber, F. W. Litton, &

R. A. Fox (Eds.), *Counseling exceptional students* (pp. 197–212). New York: Human Sciences Press.

Griggs, S. A. (1988). The counselor as facilitator of learning. In G. R. Walz & J. C. Bleuer (Eds.), *Building strong school counseling programs.* Alexandria, VA: American Association for Counseling and Development.

Gross, D. R., & Robinson, S. E. (1987). Ethics, violence, and counseling: Hear no evil, see no evil, speak no evil? *Journal of Counseling and Development, 65*(7), 340–344.

Guinan, J., & Foulds, M. (1970). Marathon groups: Facilitator of personal growth? *Journal of Consulting Psychology, 17,* 145–149.

Gumper, L. L., & Sprenkle, D. H. (1981). Privileged communication in therapy: Special problems for the family and couples therapist. *Family Process, 20,* 11–23.

Gunning, S., & Holmes, T. (1973). Dance therapy with psychotic children. *Archives of General Psychiatry, 28,* 707–713.

Gurman, A. S., & Kniskern, D. P. (1981). Family therapy outcome research: Knowns and unknowns. In A. S. Gurman & D. P. Kniskern (Eds.), *Handbook of family therapy.* New York: Brunner/Mazel.

Gutterman, J. T. (1996a). Doing mental health counseling: A social constructionist re-vision. *Journal of Mental Health Counseling, 18*(3), 228–252.

Gutterman, J. T. (1996b). Farewell to families: Language systems in the postmodern era. *The Family Journal: Counseling and Therapy for Couples and Families, 4*(2), 139–142.

Gutterman, J. T., & Kirk, M. A. (1999). Mental health counseling and the Internet. *Journal of Mental Health Counseling, 21*(4), 309–325.

Gysbers, N. C. (1988). Career guidance: A professional heritage and future challenge. In G. R. Walz & J. C. Bleuer (Eds.), *Building strong school counseling programs.* Alexandria, VA: American Association for Counseling and Development.

Gysbers, N. C. (2004). Counseling psychology and school psychology partnership: Overlooked? Underutilized? But needed!, *The Counseling Psychologist, 32,* 235–244.

Gysbers, N. C., & Henderson, P. (1988). *Developing and managing your school guidance program.* Alexandria, VA: American Association for Counseling and Development.

Gysbers, N. C., & Henderson, P. (2000). *Developing and managing your school guidance program.* Alexandria, VA: American Counseling Association.

Gysbers, N. C., Heppner, M. J., & Johnson, J. A. (1998). *Career counseling: Process issues and techniques.* Needham Heights, MA: Allyn and Bacon.

Gysbers, N. C., & Moore, E. J. (1987). *Career counseling: Skills and techniques for practitioners.* Englewood Cliffs, NJ: Prentice-Hall.

Haase, J. E., Britt, T., Coward, D. D., Kline, N., & Penn, P. E. (1992). Simultaneous analysis of spiritual perspective, hope, acceptance and self-transcendence. *Images, 24*(2), 141–147.

Hackett, G., & Betz, N. E. (1981). A self-efficacy approach to the career development of women. *Journal of Vocational Behavior, 18,* 326–339.

Hackett, G., & Byars, A. M. (1996). Social cognitive theory and the career development of African American women. *Career Development Quarterly, 4*(4), 322–340.

Hackman, H. W., & Claiborn, C. D. (1982). An attributional approach to counselor attractiveness. *Journal of Counseling Psychology, 29,* 224–231.

Hale, S. (1990). Sitting on memory's lap. *The Arts in Psychotherapy, 17*(3), 269, 274.

Haley, J. (1963). *Strategies of psychotherapy.* New York: Grune & Stratton.

Haley, J. (1971). Approaches to family therapy. In J. Haley (Ed.), *Changing families: A family therapy reader.* New York: Grune & Stratton.

Haley, J. (1973). *Uncommon psychiatric techniques of Milton H. Erickson.* New York: Norton.

Haley, J. (1976). *Problem-solving therapy.* San Francisco: Jossey-Bass.

Haley, J. (1980). *Leaving home.* New York: McGraw-Hill.

Haley, J. (1984). *Ordeal therapy: Unusual ways to change behavior.* San Francisco: Jossey-Bass.

Haley, M. (2005). Technology and counseling. In D. Capuzzi & D. R. Gross (Eds.), *Introduction to the counseling profession* (4th ed.) (pp. 123–152). Boston: Allyn & Bacon.

Haley-Banez, L., Brown, S., & Molina, B. (1998). *Association for specialists in group work: Principles for diversity-competent group workers.* Alexandria, VA: American Counseling Association.

Hall, A. S., & Lin, M. J. (1994). An integrative consultation framework: A practical tool for elementary school counselors. *Elementary School Guidance and Counseling, 29*(1), 16–27.

Hall, C. S. (1954). *A primer of Freudian psychology.* New York: World Publishing.

Hall, C. S., & Lindzey, G. (1978). *Theories of personality* (3rd ed.). New York: John Wiley & Sons.

Hall, G. S. (1904). *Adolescence.* New York: Appleton.

Hamachek, D. (1995). Self-concept and school achievement: Interaction dynamics and a tool for assessing the self-concept component. *Journal of Counseling and Development, 73*(4), 419–425.

Hamann, E. E. (1994). Clinicians and diagnosis: Ethical concerns and clinician competence. *Journal of Counseling and Development, 72*(3), 259–260.

Hammen, C., & Rudolph, K. D. (2003). Childhood mood disorders. In E. R. Mash & R. A. Barkley (Eds.), *Child psychopathology* (pp. 233–278). New York: Guilford Press.

Hammer, C., & Zupan, B. A. (1984). Self-schemas, depression, and the processing of personal information in children. *Journal of Experimental Child Psychology, 37,* 598–608.

Hammond, J. (1981). *Group counseling for children of divorce: A guide for the elementary school.* Ann Arbor, MI: Cranbrook.

Hammond, W. R., & Yung, B. (1993). Psychology's role in the public health response to assaultive violence among young African-American men. *American Psychologist, 48*(2), 142–154.

Hannon, K. (1996, May 13). Upset? Try cybertherapy. *U.S. News and World Report, 120,* 81–83.

Hansen, J. C., & Campbell, D. P. (1985). *Manual for the SVIB-SCII* (4th ed.). Palo Alto, CA: Consulting Psychologists Press.

Hansen, J. C., Himes, B. S., & Meier, S. (1990). *Consultation: Concepts and practices.* Englewood Cliffs, NJ: Prentice-Hall.

Hansen, J. T. (2002). Postmodern implications for theoretical integration of counseling approaches. *Journal of Counseling and Development, 80,* 315–321.

Hardesty, P. H., & Dillard, J. M. (1994). The role of elementary school counselors compared with their middle and secondary school counterparts. *Elementary School Guidance and Counseling, 29*(2), 83–91.

Hardman, M. L., Drew, C. J., Egan, M. W., & Wolf, B. (2002). *Human exceptionality* (7th ed.). Boston: Allyn & Bacon.

Harmon, L. W. (1996). A moving target: The widening gap between theory and practice. In M. L. Savickas & W. B. Walsh (Eds.), *Handbook of career counseling theory and practice* (pp. 37–44). Palo Alto, CA: Davies-Black.

Harmon, L. W., Hansen, J. C., Borgen, F. H., & Hammer, A. L. (1994). *Strong Interest Inventory: Application and technical guide.* Palo Alto, CA: Consulting Psychologists Press.

Harrar, L. (Producer). (1984). *Make my people live: The crises in Indian health* [Television broadcast]. Boston: Public Broadcasting System, NOVA.

Harris, A. S. (1996). *Living with paradox: An introduction to Jungian psychology.* Pacific Grove, CA: Brooks/Cole.

Harris, D. E. (1963). *Children's drawings as measures of intellectual maturity: A revision and extension of*

Goodenough Draw-A-Man Test. San Diego, CA: Harcourt Brace Jovanovich.

Harris, T. (1967). *I'm OK—You're OK*. New York: Avon.

Hart, S. N., & Brassard, M. R. (1987). A major threat to children's mental health: Psychological maltreatment. *American Psychologist, 42,* 160–165.

Havens, L. (1994). Some suggestions for making research more applicable to clinical practice. In P. F. Talley, H. H. Strupp, & S. F. Butler (Eds.), *Psychotherapy research and practice: Bridging the gap* (pp. 88–98). New York: Basic Books.

Havighurst, R. J. (1972). *Developmental tasks and education* (3rd ed.). New York: David McKay.

Haviland, M. G., & Hansen, J. C. (1987). Criterion validity of the Strong-Campbell Interest Inventory for American Indian college students. *Measurement and Evaluation in Counseling and Development, 19,* 196–201.

Hawkins, J. D., Herrenkohl, T. I., Farrington, D. P., Brewer, D., Catalano, R. F., Harachi, T. W., & Cothern, L. (2000). Predictors of youth violence. *Juvenile Justice Bulletin, 32,* 1–11.

Hayes, S. G. (1995). Infusing diversity into family and couples counseling. *The Family Journal: Counseling and Therapy for Couples and Families, 3*(3), 231–233.

Hazan, C., & Shaver, P. R. (1990). Love and work: An attachment-theoretical perspective. *Journal of Personality and Social Psychology, 59,* 270–280.

Hazelrigg, M. D., Cooper, H. M., & Borduin, C. M. (1987). Evaluating the effectiveness of family therapies: An integrative review and analysis. *Psychological Bulletin, 101*(3), 428–442.

Hazzard, A., King, H. E., & Webb, C. (1986). Group therapy with sexually abused adolescent girls. *American Journal of Psychotherapy, 40*(2), 213–223.

Heinlen, K. T., Welfel, E. R., Richmond, E. N., & Rak, C. F. (2003). The scope of WebCounseling: A survey of services and compliance with NBCC Standards for the Ethical Practice of WebCounseling. *Journal of Counseling and Development, 81,* 61–69.

Heinze, A., & Rotatori, A. F. (1986). Counseling the visually handicapped child. In A. F. Rotatori, P. J. Gerber, F. W. Litton, & R. A. Fox (Eds.), *Counseling exceptional students* (pp. 179–196). New York: Human Sciences Press.

Helms, J. E. (1986). Expanding racial identity theory to cover the counseling process. *Journal of Counseling Psychology, 33,* 62–64.

Helms, J. E. (1989). At long last: Paradigms for cultural psychology research. *The Counseling Psychologist, 17,* 98–100.

Helms, J. E. (1995). An update of Helms's white and people of color racial identity models. In J. G. Ponterotto, J. M. Casas, L. A. Suzuki, & C. M. Alexander (Eds.), *Handbook of multicultural counseling* (pp. 181–198). Thousand Oaks, CA: Sage.

Helwig, A. A., & Holicky, R. (1994). Substance abuse in persons with disabilities: Treatment considerations. *Journal of Counseling and Development, 72*(3), 227–233.

Henderson, S., Hesketh, B., & Tuffin, K. (1988). A test of Gottfredson's theory of circumscription. *Journal of Vocational Behavior, 32,* 37–48.

Henry, W. P., Strupp, H. H., Schacht, T. E., & Gaston, L. (1994). Psychodynamic approaches. In A. E. Bergin & S. L. Garfield (Eds.), *Handbook of psychotherapy and behavior change* (4th ed.) (pp. 467–508). New York: John Wiley & Sons.

Heppner, M. J., & Johnston, J. A. (1985). Computerized career guidance and information systems: Guidelines for selection. *Journal of College Students Personnel, 26,* 156–163.

Heppner, P. P., Casas, J. M., Carter, J., & Stone, G. L. (2000). The maturation counseling psychology: Multifaceted perspectives, 1978–1998. In S. D. Brown & R. W. Lent (Eds.), *Handbook of counseling psychology* (3rd ed.) (pp. 3–49). New York: John Wiley & Sons.

Heppner, P. P., & Claiborn, C. D. (1989). Social influence research in counseling: A review and critique [monograph]. *Journal of Counseling Psychology, 36,* 365–387.

Heppner, P. P., & Dixon, D. N. (1981). A review of the interpersonal influence process in counseling. *Personnel and Guidance Journal, 59,* 542–550.

Heppner, P. P., & Heesacker, M. (1983). Perceived counselor characteristics, client expectations, and client satisfaction with counseling. *Journal of Counseling Psychology, 30,* 31–39.

Heppner, P. P., & Krauskopf, C. J. (1987). An information-processing approach to personal problem solving. *The Counseling Psychologist, 15,* 371–447.

Heppner, P. P., & Petersen, C. H. (1982). The development and implications of a personal problem-solving inventory. *Journal of Counseling Psychology, 29,* 66–75.

Heppner, P. P., Rogers, M. E., & Lee, L. A. (1984). Carl Rogers: Reflections on his life. *Journal of Counseling and Development, 63,* 14–20.

Heppner, P. P., Witty, T. E., & Dixon, W. A. (2004). Problem-solving appraisal and human adjustment: A review of 20 years of research using the problem-solving inventory. *The Counseling Psychologist, 32,* 344–428.

Herjanic, B., & Reich, W. (1982). Development of a structured psychiatric interview for children: Agreement between child and parent of individual symptoms. *Journal of Abnormal Child Psychology, 10,* 307–324.

Herlihy, B., & Sheeley, V. L. (1987). Privileged communication in selected helping professions: A comparison among statutes. *Journal of Counseling and Development, 65*(9), 479–483.

Herman, J. L. (1986). *Father-daughter incest.* Cambridge, MA: Harvard University Press.

Herman, K. C. (1993). Reassessing predictors of therapist competence. *Journal of Counseling and Development, 72,* 29–32.

Herr, E. L. (1996). Toward the convergence of career theory and practice: Mythology, issues, and possibilities. In M. L. Savickas & W. B. Walsh (Eds.), *Handbook of career counseling theory and practice* (pp. 13–36). Palo Alto, CA: Davies-Black.

Herring, R. D. (1990). Nonverbal communication: A necessary component of cross-cultural counseling. *Journal of Multicultural Counseling and Development, 18*(4), 172–179.

Herring, R. D. (1994). Substance use among Native American Indian Youth: A selected review of causality. *Journal of Counseling and Development, 72*(6), 578–584.

Herrington, B. S. (1979). Privilege denial in joint therapy. *Psychiatric News, 14*(1), 1–9.

Hershenson, D. B., & Power, P. W. (1987). *Mental health counseling.* New York: Pergamon Press.

Hershenson, D. B., Power, P. W., & Waldo, M. (1996). *Community counseling: Contemporary theory and practice.* Needham Heights, MA: Allyn & Bacon.

Hesketh, B., Elmslie, S., & Kaldor, W. (1990). Career compromises: An alternative account to Gottfredson's theory. *Journal of Counseling Psychology, 37*(1), 49–56.

Hill, C. E. (1992). An overview of four measures developed to test the Hill process model: Therapist intentions, therapist response modes, client reactions, and client behaviors. *Journal of Counseling and Development, 70,* 728–737.

Hill, C. E., & Corbett, M. M. (1993). A perspective on the history of process and outcome research in counseling psychology. *Journal of Counseling Psychology, 40*(1), 3–24.

Hill, C. E., Tanney, M. F., & Leonard, M. M. (1977). Counselor reactions to female clients: Type of problem, age of client, and sex of counselor. *Journal of Counseling Psychology, 24,* 60–65.

Hill, C. E., Thompson, B. J., & Williams, E. N. (1997). A guide to conducting consensual qualitative research. *The Counseling Psychologist, 25*(4), 517–572.

Hilton, T. L. (1962). Career decision making. *Journal of Counseling Psychology, 9,* 291–298.

Hines, M. (1988). Similarities and differences in group and family therapy. *Journal for Specialists in Group Work, 13*(4), 173–179.

Hines, P. L., & Fields, T. H. (2002). Pregroup screening issues for school counselors. *Journal for Specialists in Group Work, 27,* 358–376.

Hobson, S. M., & Kanitz, H. M. (1996). Multicultural counseling: An ethical issue for school counselors. *The School Counselor, 43*(4), 245–255.

Hoffmann, T., Dana, R., & Bolton, B. (1985). Measured acculturation and MMPI-168 performance of Native American adults. *Journal of Cross-Cultural Psychology, 16,* 243–256.

Hohenshil, T. H. (1996). Editorial: Role of assessment and diagnosis in counseling. *Journal of Counseling and Development, 75*(1), 64–67.

Holland, J. L. (1973). *Making vocational choices: A theory of careers.* Englewood Cliffs, NJ: Prentice-Hall.

Holland, J. L. (1985a). *Making vocational choices: A theory of vocational personalities and work environments* (2nd ed.). Englewood Cliffs, NJ: Prentice-Hall.

Holland, J. L. (1985b). *Manual for the vocational preference inventory.* Odessa, FL: Psychological Assessment Resources.

Holland, J. L. (1994). *Self-directed search.* Odessa, FL: Psychological Assessment Resources.

Holland, J. L. (1996). Exploring careers with a typology: What we have learned and some new directions. *American Psychologist, 51*(4), 397–406.

Holland, J. L. (1997). *Making vocational choices: A theory of vocational personalities and work environments* (3rd ed.). Odessa, FL: Psychological Assessment Resources.

Holland, J. L., Daieger, D. C., & Power, P. G. (1980). Some diagnostic scales for research in decision making and personality: Identity information and barriers. *Journal of Personality and Social Psychology, 39,* 1191–1200.

Holland, J. L., Johnston, J. A., & Asama, N. F. (1994). More evidence for the relationship between Holland's personality types and personality variables. *Journal of Career Assessment, 2,* 331–340.

Hollingdale, R. J. (1978). *Twilight of the idols and the anti-Christ.* New York: Penguin Books.

Hollon, S. D., & Beck, A. T. (1994). Cognitive and cognitive behavioral therapies. In A. E. Bergin & S. L. Garfield, *Handbook of psychotherapy and behavioral change* (4th ed.) (pp. 428–466). New York: John Wiley & Sons.

Hollon, S. D., DeRubeis, R. J., Evans, M. D., Wiemer, M. J., Garvey, M. J., Grove, W. M., & Tuason, V. B. (1992). Cognitive therapy and pharmacotherapy for depression: Singly and in combination. *Archives of General Psychiatry, 49,* 774–781.

Hollon, S. D., Evans, M. D., & DeRubeis, R. (1983). The cognitive-pharmacotherapy project: Study design, outcome, and clinical follow-up. Paper presented at the World Congress of Behavior Therapy, Washington, DC.

Holt, P. A. (1989). Differential effects of status and interest in the process of compromise. *Journal of Counseling Psychology, 36,* 42–47.

Homans, G. C. (1962). *Sentiments and activities.* New York: The Free Press of Glencoe.

Honeyman, A. (1990). Perceptual changes in addicts as a consequence of reality therapy based on group treatment. *Journal of Reality Therapy, 9*(2), 53–59.

hooks, b. (1995). *Killing rage: Ending racism.* New York: Henry Holt.

Horne, A. M. (1993). Telling stories: The ecosystem model (Editorial). *Journal for Specialists in Group Work, 18,* 98.

Horne, A. M. (1995). Changes and challenges in group work. *Journal for Specialists in Group Work, 20*(2), 67–68.

Horne, A. M. (1996). The changing world of group work. *Journal for Specialists in Group Work, 21*(1), 2–3.

Horne, A. M., & Ohlsen, M. M. (1982). Introduction: The family and family counseling. In M. Horne & M. M. Ohlsen (Eds.), *Family counseling and therapy.* Itasca, IL: F. E. Peacock.

Horst, E. A. (1995). Reexamining gender issues in Erikson's stages of identity and intimacy. *Journal of Counseling and Development, 73*(3), 271–278.

Hoshmand, L. L. S. (1989). Alternate research paradigms: A review and teaching proposal. *The Counseling Psychologist, 17,* 3–80.

Hoshmand, L. T. (1985). Phenomenological-based groups for developmentally disabled adults. *Journal of Counseling and Development, 64*(2), 147–148.

Hosie, T. W., West, J. D., & MacKey, J. A. (1988). Employment and roles of mental health counselors in substance-abuse centers. *Journal of Mental Health Counseling, 10*(3), 188–198.

Howard, G. S. (1991). Culture tales: A narrative approach to thinking, cross-cultural psychology, and psychotherapy. *American Psychologist, 46*(3), 187–197.

Huba, G. J., & Bentler, P. M. (1983). Causal models of the development of law abidance and its relationship to psychosocial factors and drug use. In W. S. Lauger & J. M. Day (Eds.), *Personality theory, moral development, and criminal behavior* (pp. 164–215). Lexington, MA: Lexington Books.

Hubbard, R. L., Brownlee, R. F., & Anderson, R. (1988). Initiation of alcohol and drug abuse in the middle school years. *Elementary School Guidance & Counseling, 23,* 118.

Hubble, M. A., Duncan, B. L., & Miller, S. D. (1999). *The heart and soul of change: What works in therapy.* Washington, DC: American Psychological Association.

Huebner, L. A. (1980). Interaction of student and campus. In E. Delworth, G. Hanson, & Associates (Eds.), *Student services: A handbook for the profession* (pp. 117–155). San Francisco: Jossey-Bass.

Huey, W. (1986). Ethical concerns in school counseling. *Journal of Counseling and Development, 64*(5), 321–322.

Hughey, K. F., Gysbers, N. C., & Starr, M. (1993). Evaluating comprehensive school guidance programs. *The School Counselor, 41*(1), 31–35.

Humphrey, F. G. (1983). *Marital therapy.* Englewood Cliffs, NJ: Prentice-Hall.

Hutchinson, R. L., Barrick, A. L., & Groves, M. (1986). Functions of secondary school counselors in the public schools: Ideal and actual. *The School Counselor, 34*(2), 87–91.

Ibrahim, F. A. (1991). Contribution of cultural worldview to generic counseling and development. *Journal of Counseling and Development, 70*(l), 13–19.

Ibrahim, F. A. (1993). Existential world view theory: Transcultural counseling. In J. McFadden (Ed.), *Transactional counseling* (pp. 23–57). Alexandria, VA: American Counseling Association.

Ibrahim, F. A., & Kahn, H. (1984). *Scale to assess world views.* Unpublished manuscript, University of Connecticut, Storrs, CT.

Ibrahim, F. A., & Kahn, H. (1987). Assessment of world views. *Psychological Reports, 60,* 163–176.

Ingersoll, R. E. (1995). Spirituality, religion, and counseling: Dimensions and relationships. In M. T. Burke & J. G. Miranti (Eds.), *Counseling: The spiritual dimension* (pp. 5–18). Alexandria, VA: American Counseling Association.

Irwin, E. C. (1987). Drama: The play's the thing. *Elementary School Guidance and Counseling,* 276–283.

Isenberg-Grzeda, C. (1988). Music therapy assessment: A reflection of professional identity. *Journal of Music Therapy, 25*(3), 156–169.

Ivey, A. (1971). *Microcounseling: Innovations in interviewing training.* Springfield, IL: Charles C. Thomas.

Ivey, A. (1986). *Developmental therapy: Theory and practice.* San Francisco: Jossey-Bass.

Ivey, A. (1989). Mental health counseling: A developmental process and profession. *Journal of Mental Health Counseling, 11*(1), 26–35.

Ivey, A. (1996, June). The spirit and the challenge: Postmodernity or reality? *Counseling Today,* p. 33.

Ivey, A. (1999). *Intentional interviewing and counseling: Facilitating client development* (4th ed.). Pacific Grove, CA: Brooks/Cole.

Jacobs, E. E., Harvill, R. L., & Masson, R. L. (2002). *Group counseling: Strategies and skills* (4th ed.). Pacific Grove, CA: Brooks/Cole.

James, M. R. (1988). Music therapy values clarification: A positive influence on perceived locus of control. *Journal of Music Therapy, 25*(4), 206–215.

Jepsen, D. A. (1996). Relationships between developmental career counseling theory and practice. In M. L. Savickas & W. B. Walsh (Eds.), *Handbook of career counseling theory and practice.* Palo Alto, CA: Davies-Black.

Jewell, D. A. (1989). Cultural and ethnic issues. In S. Wetzler & M. M. Katz (Eds.), *Contemporary approaches to psychological assessment* (pp. 299–309). New York: Brunner/Mazel.

Johnson, A. C. (1995). Resiliency mechanisms in culturally diverse families. *The Family Journal: Counseling and Therapy for Couples and Families, 3*(4), 316–324.

Johnson, D. R. (1984a). Establishing the creative arts therapies as an independent profession. *The Arts in Psychotherapy, 11,* 209–212.

Johnson, D. R. (1984b). Perspectives, projects, and training facilities. *Journal of Mental Imagery, 7*(1), 105–109.

Johnson, E., Baker, S. B., Kapola, M., Kiselica, M. S., & Thompson, E. C., III. (1989). Counseling self-efficacy and counseling competency in preparaticum training. *Counselor Education and Supervision, 28,* 205–218.

Johnson, I. H., Torres, J. S., Coleman, V. D., & Smith, M. C. (1995). Issues and strategies in leading cultural diverse counseling groups. *Journal for Specialists in Group Work, 20*(3), 143–150.

Johnson, V. E. (1986). *Intervention: A professional guide.* Minneapolis, MN: Johnson Institute.

Johnson, W. B., & Campbell, C. D. (2004). Character and fitness requirements for professional psychologists: Training directors' perspectives. *Professional Psychology: Research and Practice, 35*(4), 405–411.

Johnston, J. A., Buescher, K. L., & Heppner, M. J. (1988). Computerized career information and guidance systems: Caveat emptor. *Journal of Counseling and Development, 57*(1), 39–41.

Johnston, V. S., & Oliver-Rodriguez, J. C. (1997). Facial beauty and the late positive component of event-related potential. *Journal of Sex Research, 34*(2), 188–198.

Jones, A. S., & Gelso, C. J. (1988). Differential effects of style of interpretation: Another look. *Journal of Counseling Psychology, 35,* 363–369.

Jones, J. V., Jr. (1995). Constructivism and individual psychology: Common ground for dialogue. *Individual Psychology: The Journal of Adlerian Theory, Research, and Practice, 51*(3), 231–243.

Jongsma, A. E., & Petersen, L. M. (1995). *The complete psychotherapy treatment planner.* New York: John Wiley & Sons.

Josephson Institute of Ethics. (2001). Josephson Institute of Ethics report card on the ethics of American youth 2000. Report #1: Violence, guns, and alcohol. Marina del Rey, CA: Josephson Institute of Ethics.

Jourard, S. M. (1958). *Personal adjustment: An approach through the study of healthy personality.* New York: Macmillan.

Juhnke, G. A., & Osborne, W. L. (1997). The solution-focused debriefing group: An integrated post-violence group intervention for adults. *Journal for Specialists in Group Work, 22*(1), 66–76.

Jung, C. (1928). *Contributions to analytic psychology.* New York: Harcourt.

Jung, C. (1959). *The archetypes and the collective unconscious.* Princeton, NJ: Princeton University Press.

Kadushin, A., & Martin, J. A. (1981). *Child abuse: An interactional event.* New York: Columbia University Press.

Kandel, D. B. (1973). Adolescent marijuana use: Role of parents and peers. *Science, 181,* 1067–1081.

Kanfer, F. H., & Busemeyer, J. R. (1982). The use of problem solving and decision making in behavior therapy. *Clinical Psychology Review, 2,* 239–266.

Kanfer, F. H., & Goldstein, A. P. (1986). Introduction. In F. H. Kanfer & A. P. Goldstein (Eds.), *Helping people change: A textbook of methods* (3rd ed.) (pp. 1–18). New York: Pergamon.

Kanner, L. (1962). *Child psychiatry* (3rd ed.). Springfield, IL: Charles C. Thomas.

Kaplan, L. S., & Geoffroy, K. E. (1990). Enhancing the school climate: New opportunities for the counselor. *The School Counselor, 38,* 7–12.

Kaufmann, F. A., Castellanos, Z. F., & Rotatori, A. F. (1986). Counseling the gifted child. In A. F. Rotatori, P. J. Gerber, F. W. Litton, & R. A. Fox (Eds.), *Counseling exceptional students.* New York: Human Sciences Press.

Kaufmann, Y. (1989). Analytical psychotherapy. In R. J. Corsini (Ed.), *Current psychotherapies* (4th ed.). Itasca, IL: F. E. Peacock.

Kazdin, A. E. (1978). *History of behavior modification: Experimental foundations of contemporary research.* Baltimore: University Park Press.

Kazdin, A. E. (1985). *Treatment of antisocial behavior in children and adolescents.* Homewood, IL: Dorsey Press.

Kazdin, A. E. (1987). Treatment of antisocial behavior in children: Current status and future directions. *Psychological Bulletin, 102,* 187–203.

Kazdin, A. E. (1988). Childhood depression. In E. J. Mash & L. Terdal (Eds.), *Behavioral assessment of childhood disorders* (2nd ed.) (pp. 157–196). New York: Guilford Press.

Kazdin, A. E. (1989). Developmental psychopathology: Current research, issues, and directions. *American Psychologist, 44*(2), 180–187.

Kazdin, A. E. (1993). Adolescent mental health: Prevention and treatment programs. *American Psychologist, 48*(2), 127–141.

Kazdin, A. E. (2001). *Behavior modification in applied settings* (6th ed.). Pacific Grove, CA: Brooks/Cole.

Kazdin, A. E., Bass, D., Ayers, W. A., & Rodgers, A. (1990). Empirical and clinical focus of child and adolescent psychotherapy research. *Journal of Consulting and Clinical Psychology, 58,* 729–740.

Kazdin, A. E., Bass, D., Siegel, T., & Thomas, C. (1989). Cognitive-behavioral therapy and relationship therapy in the treatment of children referred for antisocial behavior. *Journal of Consulting and Clinical Psychology, 57*(4), 522–535.

Keeton, W. P. (1984). *Prosser and Keeton on the law of torts* (5th ed.). St. Paul, MN: West.

Kelley, R. H., & Rotatori, A. F. (1986). Counseling the language-disordered child. In A. F. Rotatori, P. J. Gerber, F. W. Litton, & R. A. Fox (Eds.), *Counseling exceptional students.* New York: Human Sciences Press.

Kelly, K. R. (1996). Looking to the future: Professional identity, accountability, and change. *Journal of Mental Health Counseling, 18*(3), 195–199.

Kelly, K. R. (1999). Coda: A contextual perspective on the future of mental health counseling. *Journal of Mental Health Counseling, 21*(3), 302–307.

Kemp, C. G. (1971). Existential counseling. *The Counseling Psychologist, 2,* 2–28.

Kennell, S. E., & Rotatori, A. F. (1986). Counseling the abused child. In A. F. Rotatori, P. J. Gerber, F. W. Litton, & R. A. Fox (Eds.), *Counseling exceptional students.* New York: Human Sciences Press.

Kenny, A. (1987). An arts activity approach: Counseling the gifted, creative, and talented. *The Gifted Child Today, 10*(3), 22–37.

Kenny, M. E., Waldo, M., Warter, E. H., & Barton, C. (2002). School-linked: Theory, science, and practice for enhancing the lives of children and youth. *The Counseling Psychologist, (30)*5, 726–748.

Kern, R., Gfroerer, K., Summers, Y., Curlette, W., & Matheny, K. (1996). Life-style, personality, and stress coping. *Individual Psychology: The Journal of Adlerian Theory, Research, and Practice, 52*(1), 42–53.

Kernberg, O. F. (1976). *Object-relations theory and clinical psychoanalysis.* New York: Jason Aronson.

Kerwin, C., & Ponterotto, J. G. (1995). Biracial identity development: Theory and research. In J. G. Ponterrotto, J. M. Casas, L. A. Suzuki, & C. M. Alexander (Eds.), *Handbook of multicultural counseling* (pp. 181–198). Thousand Oaks, CA: Sage.

Kessler, S. (1979, November). Counselor as mediator. *The Personnel and Guidance Journal,* 194–197.

Kidder, L. H., Judd, C. M., & Smith, E. R. (1986). *Research methods in social relations.* New York: Holt, Rinehart & Winston.

Kim, B. C. (1981). *New urban immigrants: The Korean community in New York.* Princeton, NJ: Princeton University Press.

Kim, B. S., Hill, C. E., Gelso, C. J., Goates, M. K., Asay, P. A., & Harbin, J. M. (2003). Counselor self-disclosure: East Asian American client adherence to Asian cultural values and counseling process. *Journal of Counseling Psychology, 50,* 324–332.

Kim, B. S., & Abreu, J. M. (2001). Acculturation measurement: Theory, current instruments, and future directions. In J. G. Ponterotto, J. M. Casas, L. A. Suzuki, and C. M. Alexander (Eds.), *Handbook of multicultural counseling* (2nd ed.) (pp. 394–424). Thousand Oaks, CA: Sage Publications.

Kirk, M. A. (1997, January). Current perceptions of counseling and counselor education in cyberspace. *Counseling Today, 39,* 17–18.

Kiselica, M. S., & Look, C. (1993). Mental health counseling and prevention: Disparity between philosophy and practice? *Journal of Mental Health Counseling, 15*(1), 3–14.

Kitchener, K. S. (1984). Ethics in counseling psychology: Distinctions and directions. *Counseling Psychologist, 12,* 15–18.

Kitchener, K. S. (1985). Ethical principles and ethical decisions in student affairs. In H. J. Canon & R. D. Brown (Eds.), *Applied ethics: Tools for practitioners.* San Francisco: Jossey-Bass.

Kitchener, K. S., & Anderson, S. K. (2000). Ethical issues in counseling psychology: Old themes–new problems. In S. D. Brown & R. W. Lent (Eds.), *Handbook of counseling psychology* (3rd ed.) (pp. 50–82). New York: John Wiley & Sons.

Kitchur, M., & Bell, R. (1989). Group psychotherapy with preadolescent sexual abuse victims: A literature review and description of an inner-city group. *International Journal of Group Psychotherapy, 39*(3), 285–310.

Kivlighan, D. M. (1990). Relation between counselors' use of intentions and clients' perception of working alliance. *Journal of Counseling Psychology, 37,* 27–32.

Kivlighan, D. M., Johnston, J. A., Hogan, R. S., & Mauer, E. (1994). Who benefits from computerized career counseling? *Journal of Counseling and Development, 27*(3), 289–292.

Kivlighan, D. M., Jr., & Shapiro, R. M. (1987). Holland type as a predictor of benefit from self-help career counseling. *Journal of Counseling Psychology, 34*(3), 326–329.

Kjos, D. (1995). Linking career counseling to personality disorders. *Journal of Counseling and Development, 73*(6), 592–597.

Klein, M. (1960). *The psychoanalysis of children.* New York: Grove Press.

Klerman, G. L., & Weissman, M. M. (Eds.) (1993). *New applications of interpersonal psychotherapy.* Washington, DC: American Psychiatric Press.

Kluger, J. (2001, June 18). How to manage teen drinking (the smart way). *Time,* 42–44.

Knapp, S. (1980). A primer on malpractice for psychologists. *Professional Psychology, 11,* 606–612.

Knoff, H. M., & Prout, H. T. (1985). *The kinetic drawing system for family and school.* Los Angeles: Western Psychological Services.

Kobak, R. R., & Hazan, C. (1991). Attachment in marriage: Effects of security and accuracy of working models. *Journal of Personality and Social Psychology, 60,* 861–869.

Koenig, H. G. (1997). *Is religion good for your health? The effects of religion on physical and mental health.* New York: Haworth Press.

Kohlberg, L. (1963). Development of children's orientation towards a moral order. 1. Sequence in the development of moral thought. *Vita Humana, 6,* 11–33.

Kohlberg, L. (1973). Continuities in childhood and adult moral development revisited. In P. B. Baltes & K. W. Schair (Eds.), *Life-span developmental psychology: Personality and socialization.* New York: Academic Press.

Kohlberg, L. (1981). *The philosophy of moral development.* New York: Harper & Row.

Kohut, H. (1971). *The analysis of the self.* New York: International University Press.

Kokotovic, A. M., & Tracey, T. J. (1990). Working alliance in the early phase of counseling. *Journal of Counseling Psychology, 37,* 16–21.

Koopman, E. J. (1985). The education and training of mediators. In S. Grebs (Ed.), *Divorce and family mediation.* Rockville, MD: Aspen Systems.

Kopp, S. B. (1971). *Guru: Metaphors from a psychotherapist.* Palo Alto, CA: Science and Behavior Books.

Koss, M. P., & Shiang, J. (1994). Research on brief psychotherapy. In A. E. Bergin & S. L. Garfield, *Handbook of psychotherapy and behavior change* (4th ed.). New York: John Wiley & Sons.

Kottler, J. A. (1994). Working with difficult group members. *Journal for Specialists in Group Work, 19*(1), 3–10.

Kottler, J. A. (2002). *Theories in counseling and therapy.* Needham Heights, MA: Allyn & Bacon.

Kottler, J. A., & Brown, R. W. (2000). *Introduction to therapeutic counseling* (4th ed.). Monterey, CA: Brooks/Cole.

Kottman, T., & Johnson, V. (1993). Adlerian play therapy: A tool for school counselors. *Elementary School Guidance and Counseling, 28*(1), 42–51.

Kottman, T., Lingg, M., & Tisdell, T. (1995). Gay and lesbian adolescents: Implications for Adlerian therapists. *Individual Psychology: The Journal of Adlerian Theory, Research, and Practice, 51*(2), 114–128.

Kovacs, L. (1988). Couple therapy: An integrated developmental and family system model. *Family Therapy, 15*(2), 133–155.

Kovacs, M. (1981). Rating scales to assess depression in school-aged children. *Acta Parlopsychiatrica, 46,* 305–315.

Kovacs, M. (1982). *The Interview Schedule for Children (ISC):* Unpublished interview schedule, Department of Psychiatry, University of Pittsburgh, Pennsylvania.

Kovacs, M. (1989). Affective disorders in children and adolescents. *American Psychologist, 44,* 209–215.

Kovacs, M., Gatsonis, C., Marsh, J., & Richards, C. (1988). *Intellectual and cognitive development in childhood-onset depressive disorders: A longitudinal study.* Manuscript submitted for publication.

Kovacs, M., Rush, A. J., Beck, A. T., & Hollon, S. D. (1981). Depressed outpatients treated with cognitive therapy or pharmacotherapy. *Archives of General Psychiatry, 38,* 33–39.

Kramer, E. (1987). Sublimation and art therapy. In J. A. Rubin (Ed.), *Approaches to art therapy: Theory and technique.* New York: Brunner/Mazel.

Krause, A. M., & Haverkamp, B. E. (1996). Attachment in adult child-older parent relationships: Research, theory, and practice. *Journal of Counseling and Development, 75*(2), 83–92.

Kroll, J., & Sheehan, W. (1989). Religious beliefs and practices among fifty-two psychiatric inpatients in Minnesota. *American Journal of Psychiatry, 67–72,* 146.

Krumboltz, J. D. (1979). A social learning theory of career decision making. In A. M. Mitchell, F. B. Jones, & J. D. Krumboltz (Eds.), *Social learning theory and career decision making.* Cranston, RI: Carroll.

Krumboltz, J. D. (1994). The career beliefs inventory. *Journal of Counseling and Development, 72*(4), 424–428.

Krumboltz, J. D. (1996). A learning theory of career counseling. In M. L. Savickas & W. B. Walsh (Eds.),

Handbook of career counseling theory and practice (pp. 55–80). Palo Alto, CA: Davies-Black.

Krupp, J. (1982). *Mentoring as a means to personnel growth and improved school climate: A research report.* Colchester, CT: Project Rise.

Kuder, G. F. (1964). *Kuder general interest survey: Manual.* Chicago: Science Research Associates.

Kupersmidt, J. B., & Patterson, C. J. (1991). Childhood peer rejection, aggression, withdrawal, and perceived competence as predictors of self-reported behavior problems in preadolescence. *Journal of Abnormal Child Psychology, 19,* 437–449.

Kurpius, D. (1978). Consultation theory and process: An integrated model. *Personnel and Guidance Journal, 56,* 335–378.

L'Abate, L. (1986). *Systematic family therapy.* New York: Brunner/Mazel.

Labi, N. (2001, April 2). Let bullies beware. *Time,* 46–47.

La Crosse, M. B. (1980). Perceived counselor social influence and counseling outcomes: Validity of the Counselor Rating Form. *Journal of Counseling Psychology, 27,* 320–327.

La Fromboise, T. D., & Dixon, D. N. (1981). American Indian perceptions of trustworthiness in a counseling interview. *Journal of Counseling Psychology, 28,* 135–139.

LaFountain, R. M., Garner, N. E., & Eliason, G. T. (1996). Solution-focused counseling groups: A key for school counselors. *The School Counselor, 43*(4), 256–267.

Lamb, D. H. (1985). A time-frame model of termination in psychotherapy. *Psychotherapy, 22,* 604–609.

Lamb, D. H., Catanzaro, S. J., & Moorman, A. S. (2004). A preliminary look at how psychologists identify, evaluate, and proceed when faced with possible multiple relationship dilemmas. *Professional Psychology: Research and Practice, 35*(3), 248–254.

Lambert, M. J. (1991). Introduction to psychotherapy research. In L. E. Beutler & M. Crago (Eds.), - *Psychotherapy research. An international review of programmatic studies* (pp. 1–11). Washington, DC: American Psychological Association.

Lambert, M. J., & Bergin, A. E. (1994). The effectiveness of psychotherapy. In A. E. Bergin & S. L. Garfield (Eds.), *Handbook of psychotherapy and behavior change* (4th ed.) (pp. 143–189). New York: John Wiley & Sons.

Landreth, G. L. (1993). Child-centered play therapy. *Elementary School Guidance and Counseling, 28*(1), 17–29.

Lang, M., & Tisher, M. (1978). *Children's depression scale.* Victoria, Australia: Australian Council for Educational Research.

Langs, R. (1985). *Madness and cure.* New York: Newconcept Press.

Lapan, R. T., Boggs, K. R., & Morrill, W. H. (1989). Self-efficacy as a mediator of investigative and realistic general occupational themes on the Strong-Campbell Interest Inventory. *Journal of Counseling Psychology, 36,* 176–182.

Larson, J. H., Busby, D. M., Wilson, S., Medora, N., & Allgood, S. (1994). The multidimensional assessment of career decision problems: The career decision diagnostic assessment. *Journal of Counseling and Development, 72*(3), 323–328.

Lasseter, J., Privette, G., Brown, C. G., & Duer, J. (1989). Dance as treatment approach with a multi-disabled child: Implications for school counseling. *The School Counselor, 36,* 310–315.

Lawless, L. L., Ginter, E. J., & Kelly, R. R. (1999). Managed care: What mental health counselors need to know. *Journal of Mental Health Counseling, 21*(1), 50–65.

Lawrence, G., & Kurpius, R. (2000). Legal and ethical issues involved when counseling minors in non-school settings. *Journal of Counseling and Development, 78*(2), 130–136.

Lazar, Z. (2001, February). Bullying: A serious business. *Child,* 79–84.

Lazarus, A. A. (1993). Tailoring the therapeutic relationship, or being an authentic chameleon. *Psychotherapy, 30*(3), 404–407.

Lazarus, A. A. (1997). *Brief but comprehensive psychotherapy.* New York: Springer.

Lazarus, A. A. (1998). How do you like these boundaries? *The Clinical Psychologist, 51,* 22–25.

Lazarus, A. A. (2000). Multimodal therapy. In R. J. Corsini & D. Wedding (Eds.), *Current psychotherapies* (6th ed.) (pp. 340–374). Itasca, IL: F. E. Peacock.

Lazarus, A. A. (2001). Not all "dual relationships" are taboo: Some tend to enhance treatment outcomes. *The National Psychologist, 10,* 16.

Lazarus, A. A., & Beutler, L. E. (1993). On technical eclecticism. *Journal of Counseling and Development, 71*(4), 381–385.

Lê, C., Ingvarson, E. P., & Page, R. C. (1995). Alcoholics Anonymous and the counseling profession: Philosophies in conflict. *Journal of Counseling and Development, 73*(6), 603–609.

Lebow, J. L., & Gurman, A. S. (1995). Research assessing couple and family therapy. *Annual Review of Psychology, 46,* 27–57.

Lee, C. (1982). Self-efficacy as a predictor of performance in competitive gymnastics. *Journal of Sports Psychology, 4,* 405–409.

Lee, C. C. (1991). Cultural dynamics: Their importance in multicultural counseling. In C. C. Lee & B. L. R. Richardson (Eds.), *Multicultural issues in counseling: New approaches to diversity.* Alexandria, VA:

American Association for Counseling and Development.

Lee, C. C., Oh, M. Y., & Mountcastle, A. R. (1992). Indigenous models of helping in nonwestern countries: Implications for multicultural counseling. *Journal of Multicultural Counseling and Development, 20,* 1–10.

Lee, D. (1984). Counseling and culture: Some issues. *Personnel and Guidance Journal, 62,* 592–597.

Lee, M. A., & Tolle, S. W. (1996). Oregon's assisted suicide vote: The silver lining. *Annals of Internal Medicine, 124,* 267–269.

Lee, S. D. (1968). *Social class bias in the diagnosis of mental illness.* Doctoral dissertation, University of Oklahoma. Ann Arbor, MI: University Microfilms No. 68–6959.

Lent, R. W., Brown, S. D., & Hackett, G. (1994). Toward a unifying social cognitive theory of career and academic interest, choice, and performance. *Journal of Vocational Behavior, 45,* 79–122.

Lent, R. W., & Hackett, G. (1987). Career self-efficacy: Empirical status and future divisions. *Journal of Vocational Behavior, 30,* 347–382.

Leong, F. T. L., & Chou, E. L. (1994). The role of ethnic identity and acculturation in the vocational behavior of Asian Americans: An integrative review. *Journal of Vocational Behavior, 44,* 155–172.

Lerner, H. G. (1988). *Women in therapy.* New York: Harper & Row.

Lerner, R., & Naiditch, B. (1985). *Children are people.* St. Paul, MN: Children Are People.

Leslie, R. (1991, July/August). Psychotherapist-patient privilege clarified. *The California Therapist,* 11–19.

Lester, D. (1993). The effectiveness of suicide prevention centers. *Suicide and Life-Threatening Behavior, 23,* 263–267.

Leung, S. A., & Plake, B. S. (1990). A choice dilemma approach for examining the relative importance of sex type and prestige preferences in the process of career choice compromise. *Journal of Counseling Psychology, 37*(4), 399–406.

LeVine, E., & Sallee, A. (1992). *Listen to our children: Clinical theory and practice* (2nd ed.). Dubuque, IA: Kendall/Hunt.

Levinson, E. M. (1994). Current vocational assessment models for students with disabilities. *Journal of Counseling and Development, 73*(1), 94–101.

Levitsky, A., & Simkin, J. S. (1972). Gestalt therapy. In L. N. Solomon & B. Berzon (Eds.), *New perspectives on encounter groups* (pp. 245–253). San Francisco: Jossey-Bass.

Levitt, E. E. (1957). The results of psychotherapy with children: An evaluation. *Journal of Consulting Psychology, 21,* 189–196.

Lewis, J. A., Dana, R. Q., & Blevins, G. A. (2002). *Substance abuse counseling: An individualized approach* (3rd ed.). Pacific Grove, CA: Brooks/Cole.

Lewis, S. Y. (1994). Cognitive-behavioral therapy. In L. Comas-Díaz & B. Greene (Eds.), *Women of color: Integrating ethnic and gender identities in psychotherapy* (pp. 223–238). New York: Guilford Press.

Lewis, T. F., & Osborn, C. J. (2004). Solution-focused counseling and motivational interviewing: A consideration of confluence. *Journal of Counseling and Development, 82,* 38–48.

Liddle, H. (1982). On the problems of eclecticism: A call for epistemological clarification and human-scale theories. *Family Process, 21,* 243–250.

Lincoln, Y. S., & Guba, E. G. (1985). *Naturalistic inquiry.* Beverly Hills, CA: Sage.

Linder, R. (1954). *The fifty-minute hour.* New York: Bantam Books.

Linehan, M., Armstrong, H., Suarez, A., Allmon, D., & Heard, H. (1991). Cognitive-behavioral treatment of chronically parasuicidal borderline patients. *Archives of General Psychiatry, 48,* 1060–1064.

Linehan, M., Goodstein, J., Nielsen, S., & Chiles, J. (1983). Reasons for staying alive when you are thinking of killing yourself: The Reasons for Living Inventory. *Journal of Consulting and Clinical Psychology, 51,* 276–286.

Litton, F. W. (1986). Counseling the mentally retarded clinic. In A. F. Rotatori, P. J. Gerber, F. W. Litton, & R. A. Fox (Eds.), *Counseling exceptional students* (pp. 78–98). New York: Human Sciences Press.

Littrell, J. M., Caffrey, P., & Hopper, G. C. (1987). Counselor's reputation: An important precounseling variable for adolescents. *Journal of Counseling Psychology, 34,* 228–231.

Littrell, J. M., Malia, J. A., & Vanderwood, M. (1995). Single-session brief counseling in a high school. *Journal of Counseling and Development, 73,* 451–458.

Livneh, H., & Wright, P. E. (1999). Rational-emotive theory. In D. Capuzzi & D. R. Gross (Eds.), *Counseling and psychotherapy: Theories and interventions* (2nd ed.) (pp. 325–350). Columbus, OH: Merrill.

Locke, D. C. (1993). Diversity in the practice of mental health counseling. *Journal of Mental Health Counseling, 15*(3), 228–231.

Loeber, R., & Schmaling, K. B. (1985). Empirical evidence for overt and covert patterns of antisocial conduct problems: A meta-analysis. *Journal of Abnormal Child Psychology, 13,* 337–352.

Lonner, W. J. (1985). Issues in testing and assessment in cross-cultural counseling. *The Counseling Psychologist, 13*(4), 599–614.

Lopez, F. G. (1995). Contemporary attachment theory: An introduction with implications for counseling psychology. *The Counseling Psychologist, 23*(3), 395–415.

Lopez, F. M., Jr. (1966). *Evaluating executive decision making.* New York: American Management Association.

Los Angeles Unified School District. (1985). Dropout prevention and recovery. Los Angeles, CA: Author.

Lowe, R. N. (1982). Adlerian/Dreikursian family counseling. In A. M. Horne & M. M. Ohlsen (Eds.), *Family counseling and therapy.* Itasca, IL: F. E. Peacock.

Lum, C. (1999). *A guide to state laws and regulations on professional school counseling.* Alexandria, VA: American Counseling Association.

Lundervold, D. A., & Belwood, M. F. (2000). The best kept secret in counseling: Single-case (N=1) experimental designs. *Journal of Counseling and Development, 78*(1) 92–102.

Luzzo, D. A. (1996). A psychometric evaluation of the career decision-making self-efficacy scale. *Journal of Counseling and Development, 74*(3), 276–279.

Lyddon, W. J. (1995). Cognitive therapy and theories of knowing: A social constructionist view. *Journal of Counseling and Development, 73,* 579–585.

Lyddon, W. J., Bradford, E., & Nelson, J. P. (1993). Assessing adolescent and adult attachment: A review of current self-report measures. *Journal of Counseling and Development, 71*(4), 390–395.

Lynch, S. (1980). The mentor link: Bridging education and employment. *Journal of College Placement, 40,* 44–47.

Lynn, S. J., & Frauman, D. (1985). Group psychotherapy. In S. J. Lynn & F. P. Garske (Eds.), *Contemporary psychotherapies: Model and methods* (pp. 419–458). Columbus, OH: Merrill.

Lynn, S. J., & Garske, J. P. (1985). *Contemporary psychotherapies: Models and methods.* Columbus, OH: Merrill/Macmillan.

Lyons, L. C., & Woods, P. J. (1991). The efficacy of rational-emotive therapy: A quantitative review of the outcome research. *Clinical Psychology Review, 11,* 357–369.

Mabe, A. R., & Rollin, S. A. (1986). The role of a code of ethical standards in counseling. *Journal of Counseling and Development, 64*(5), 294–297.

MacGregor, J., & Newlon, B. J. (1987). Description of a teenage pregnancy program. *Journal of Counseling and Development, 65,* 447.

Madanes, C. (1981). *Strategic family therapy.* San Francisco: Jossey-Bass.

Madanes, C. (1984). *Behind the one-way mirror: Advances in the practice of strategic therapy.* San Francisco: Jossey-Bass.

Mahoney, M. J. (1988). Constructive metatheory: 1. Basic features and historical foundations. *International Journal of Personal Construct Psychology, 1,* 1–35.

Mahoney, M. J. (1991). *Human change processes: The scientific foundations of psychotherapy.* New York: Basic Books.

Mahoney, M. J. (1995a). Continuing evolution of cognitive sciences and psychotherapies. In R. A. Neimeyer & M. J. Mahoney (Eds.), *Constructivism in psychotherapy* (pp. 39–68). Washington, DC: American Psychological Association.

Mahoney, M. J. (Ed.) (1995b). *Cognitive and constructive psychotherapies: Theory, research, and practice.* New York: Springer.

Mahoney, M. J., & Lyddon, W. J. (1988). Recent developments in cognitive approaches to counseling and psychotherapy. *The Counseling Psychologist, 16*(2), 190–234.

Mahrer, A. R. (1988). Discovery-oriented psychotherapy research: Rationale, aims, and methods. *American Psychologist, 43,* 694–702.

Makover, R. B. (1992). Training psychotherapists in hierarchical treatment planning. *Journal of Psychotherapy Practice and Research, 1*(4), 337–350.

Malan, D. (1976). *The frontier of brief psychotherapy.* New York: Basic Books.

Malan, D. H. (1980). The most important development since the discovery of the unconscious. In H. Davanloo (Ed.), *Short-term dynamic psychotherapy.* New York: Aronson.

Maldonado, A. (1982). Terapia de conducta y depresion: Un analisis experimental de los modelos conductal y cognitivo (Cognitive and behavioral therapy for depression. Its efficacy and interaction with pharmacological treatment). *Revista de psicologia general y aplicada, 37*(1), 31–56.

Maling, M. S., & Howard, K. I. (1994). From research to practice to research to. . . . In P. F. Talley, H. H. Strupp, & S. F. Butler (Eds.), *Psychotherapy research and practice: Bridging the gap.* New York: Basic Books.

Mallinckrodt, B., & Helms, J. E. (1986). Effect of disabled counselors' self-disclosure on clients' perceptions of the counselor. *Journal of Counseling Psychology, 33,* 343–348.

Maniacci, M. P. (1996). An introduction to brief therapy of the personality disorders. *Individual Psychology: The Journal of Adlerian Theory, Research, and Practice, 52*(2), 158–168.

Mann, J. (1973). *Time-limited psychotherapy.* Cambridge, MA: Harvard University Press.

Mann, J. (1981). The core of time-limited psychotherapy: Time and central issue. In S. H. Budman (Ed.), *Forms of brief therapy.* New York: Guilford Press.

Mardirosian, K., McGuire, J. M., Abbott, D. W., & Blau, B. I. (1990). The effects of enhanced informal consent in a profile pregnancy counseling center. *Journal of Counseling and Development, 69,* 39–41.

Margolin, G. (1982). Ethical and legal considerations in marriage and family therapy. *American Psychologist, 7,* 788–801.

Marinoble, R. M. (1998). Homosexuality: A blind spot in the school mirror. *Professional School Counseling, 1*(3), 4–7.

Markham, A. N. (2004). Internet communication as a tool for qualitative research. In D. Silverman (Ed.), *Qualitative research: Theory, method, and practice* (3rd. ed.) (pp. 95–124). Thousand Oaks, CA: Sage.

Marlatt, G. A. (1983). The controlled drinking controversy: A commentary. *American Psychologist, 38,* 1097–1110.

Marlatt, G. A., & Gordon, J. R. (Eds.). (1985). *Relapse prevention.* New York: Guilford Press.

Martin, D. G. (1989). *Counseling and therapy skills* (2nd ed.). Prospect Heights, IL: Therapy Press.

Marziali, E. (1984). Predictions of outcomes of brief psychotherapy from therapist interpretive interventions. *Archives of General Psychiatry, 41,* 301–304.

Maslow, A. H. (1968). *Toward the psychology of being* (2nd ed.). New York: Van Nostrand Reinhold.

Mason, M. J. (1996). Evaluation of an alcohol and other drug use prevention training program for school counselors in a predominantly Mexican American school district. *The School Counselor, 43*(4), 308–316.

Matsui, T., Ikeda, H., & Ohnishi, R. (1989). Relations of sex-typed socializations to career self-efficacy expectations of college students. *Journal of Vocational Behavior, 35,* 1–16.

Matsui, T., & Onglatco, M.-L. (1992). Career self-efficacy as a moderator of the relation between occupational stress and strain. *Journal of Vocational Behavior, 41,* 79–88.

Matus, R., & Neuhring, E. M. (1979). Social workers in primary prevention: Action and ideology in mental health. *Community Mental Health Journal, 15,* 33–38.

May, R. (1953). *Man's search for himself.* New York: Norton.

May, R. (1961). *Existential psychology.* New York: Random House.

May, R. (1977). *The meaning of anxiety* (Rev. ed.). New York: Norton.

May, R. & Yalom, I. (2005). Existential psychotherapy. In R. J. Corsini & D. Wedding (Eds.). *Current psychotherapies.* (7th ed.), Itasca IL: F. E. Peacock.

May, T. M. (1990). An evolving relationship. *The Counseling Psychologist, 18,* 266–270.

Mayer, J. D. (1999, September). Emotional intelligence: Popular or scientific psychology? *APA Monitor, 30,* 50.

Mayer, J. D. (2001). A field guide to emotional intelligence. In J. Ciarrochi, J. P. Forgas, & J. D. Mayer (Eds.), *Emotional intelligence in everyday life* (pp. 3–24). Philadelphia: Psychology Press.

Mayer, J. D., Caruso, D. R., & Salovey, P. (1999). Emotional intelligence meets traditional standards for intelligence. *Intelligence, 27*(4), 267–298.

Mayer, J. D., Dipaolo, M. T., & Salovey, P. (1990). Perceiving affective content in ambiguous visual stimuli: A component of emotional intelligence. *Journal of Personality Assessment, 54,* 772–781.

Mayer, J. D., & Geher, G. (1996). Emotional intelligence and the identification of emotion. *Intelligence, 22,* 89–113.

Mayer, J. D., & Salovey, P. (1997). What is emotional intelligence? In P. Salovey and D. Sluyter (Eds.), *Emotional development and emotional intelligence: Implications for educators* (pp. 3–31). New York: Basic Books.

Mayer, J. D., Salovey, P., & Caruso, D. R. (2000). Models of emotional intelligence. In R. J. Sternberg (Ed.), *Handbook of intelligence* (pp. 396–420). Cambridge, England: Cambridge University Press.

Maynard, R. A. (1996). *Kids having kids: A Robin Hood Foundation special report on the costs of adolescent childbearing.* New York: The Robin Hood Foundation.

Maze, M. (1984). How to select a computerized guidance system. *Journal of Counseling and Development, 63*(3), 158–162.

McAuley, E. (1985). Modeling and self-efficacy: A test of Bandura's model. *Journal of Sports Psychology, 7,* 283–295.

McBride, M. C., & Martin, G. E. (1990). A framework for eclecticism: The importance of theory to mental health counseling. *Journal of Mental Health Counseling, 12,* 495–505.

McCarthy, P. R. (1982). Differential effects of counselor self-disclosure versus self-involving counselor statements across counselor-client gender pairings. *Journal of Counseling Psychology, 26,* 538–541.

McCrae, R. R., & Costa, P. T., Jr. (1989). Reinterpreting the Myers-Briggs Type Indicator from the perspective of the Five-Factor model of personality. *Journal of Personality, 57*(1), 17–40.

McDonough, R. L., & Russell, L. (1994). Alcoholism in women: A holistic, comprehensive care model. *Journal of Mental Health Counseling, 16*(4), 459–474.

McDowell, W., Coven, A., & Eash, V. (1979). The handicapped: Special needs and strategies for counseling. *Personnel and Guidance Journal, 58,* 228–232.

McFadden, J. (1996). A transcultural perspective: Reaction to C. H. Patterson's "Multicultural counseling: From diversity to universality." *Journal of Counseling and Development, 74*(3), 232–235.

McFadden, J., & Brooks, D. K. (1983). *Counselor licensure action packet.* Alexandria, VA: American Association for Counseling and Development.

McGlothlin, J. M. (2003). Response to the mini special issue on technology and group work. *Journal for Specialists in Group Work, 28,* 42–47.

McIntire, M., Marion, S. F., & Quaglia, R. (1990). Rural school counselors: Their communities and schools. *The School Counselor, 37,* 166–172.

McKenzie, V. M. (1986). Ethnographic findings on West Indian–American clients. *Journal of Counseling and Development, 65,* 40–44.

McMahon, R. J., & Forehand, R. (1988). Conduct disorders. In E. J. Mash & L. G. Terdal (Eds.), *Behavioral assessment of childhood disorders* (2nd ed.) (pp. 105–156). New York: Guilford Press.

McMillan, J. H. (1984). Culture-fair tests. In R. Corsini (Ed.), *Encyclopedia of psychology* (pp. 335–336). New York: John Wiley & Sons.

McMurty, S. C. (1985, January–February). Secondary prevention of child maltreatment: A review. *Social Work, 42*–46.

McNair, L. D. (1992). African American women in therapy: An Afrocentric and feminist synthesis. *Women and Therapy, 12*(1/2), 5–19.

McNeill, B. W., May, R. J., & Lee, V. E. (1987). Perceptions of counselor source characteristics and successful terminators. *Journal of Counseling Psychology, 34,* 86–89.

McNeilly, C. L., & Howard, K. I. (1991). The effects of psychotherapy: A reevaluation based on dosage. *Psychotherapy Research, 1,* 74–78.

McRae, M. B. (1994). Interracial group dynamics: A new perspective. *Journal for Specialists in Group Work, 19*(3), 168–174.

McRoberts, C., Burlingame, G. M., & Hoag, M. J. (1998). Comparative efficacy of individual and group psychotherapy: A meta-analytic perspective. *Group Dynamics: Theory, Research, and Practice (2)2,* 101–117.

McWhirter, E. H. (1994). *Counseling for empowerment.* Alexandria, VA: American Counseling Association.

McWhirter, J. J., McWhirter, B. T., McWhirter, A. M., & McWhirter, E. H. (1994). High- and low-risk characteristics of youth: The five Cs of competencies. *Elementary School Guidance and Counseling, 28*(3), 188–196.

Meara, N. M., Schmidt, L. D., & Day, J. D. (1996). Principles and virtues: A foundation for ethical decisions, policies, and character. *The Counseling Psychologist, 24*(1), 4–77.

Meichenbaum, D. (1972). Cognitive modifications of test-anxious college students. *Journal of Consulting and Clinical Psychology, 39,* 370–390.

Meichenbaum, D. (1977). *Cognitive-behavior modification: An integrative approach.* New York: Plenum.

Meichenbaum, D. (1985). *Stress inoculation training.* New York: Pergamon.

Meichenbaum, D. (1986). Cognitive behavior modification. In F. H. Kanfer & A. P. Goldstein (Eds.), *Helping people change: A textbook of methods* (pp. 346–380). New York: Pergamon.

Meichenbaum, D., & Fitzpatrick, D. (1992). A constructivist narrative perspective on stress and coping: Stress inoculation applications. In L. Golderger & S. Breznitz (Eds.), *Handbook of stress.* New York: Free Press.

Melnick, R. R. (1975). Counseling responses as a function of method of problem presentation and type of problem. *Journal of Counseling Psychology, 22,* 108–112.

Melton, G. B. (1988). Ethical and legal issues in AIDS-related practice. *American Psychologist, 43*(11), 941–947.

Mendoza, R. H. (1989). An empirical scale to measure type and degree of acculturation in Mexican-American adolescents and adults. *Journal of Cross-Cultural Psychology, 20,* 372–385.

Mental disorders may affect 1 in 5. (1984, October 3). *Washington Post,* p. A1.

Mercer, J. R. (1977). *SOMPA: System of Multicultural Pluralistic Assessment.* New York: Psychological Corp.

Merluzzi, T. V., & Brischetto, C. S. (1983). Breach of confidentiality and perceived trustworthiness of counselors. *Journal of Counseling Psychology, 30,* 245–251.

Merrill, C., & Andersen, S. (1993). A content analysis of person-centered expressive therapy outcomes. *The Humanistic Psychologist, 21,* 354–363.

Messina, J. J. (1999). What's next for the profession of mental health counseling? *Journal of Mental Health Counseling, 21*(3), 285–294.

Meyer, A. (1957). *Psychobiology: A science of man.* Springfield, IL: Charles C Thomas.

Milich, R., & Dodge, K. A. (1984). Social information processing in child psychiatric population. *Journal of Abnormal Child Psychology, 12,* 471–490.

Miller, C. A., & Capuzzi, D. (1984). A review of transactional analysis outcome studies. *American Mental*

Health Counselors Association Journal, 6(1), 30–41.

Miller, D. R. (1995). The school counselor and Christian fundamentalist families. *The School Counselor, 42*(4), 317–320.

Miller, G. D. (1989). What roles and functions do elementary school counselors have? *Elementary School Guidance and Counseling, 24,* 77–88.

Miller, G. M. (1982). Deriving meaning from standardized tests: Interpreting test results to clients. *Measurement and Evaluation in Guidance, 15,* 87–94.

Miller, J. B. (1987). *Toward a new psychology of women* (2nd ed.). Boston: Houghton Mifflin.

Miller, M. J., & Cochran, J. R. (1979). Evaluating the use of technology in reporting SCII results to students. *Measurement and Evaluation in Guidance, 12,* 166–173.

Miller, W. R. (1980). Treating the problem drinker. In W. R. Miller (Ed.), *The addictive behaviors: Treatment of alcoholism, drug abuse, smoking, and obesity.* New York: Pergamon Press.

Miller, W. R., & Munoz, R. F. (1982). *How to control your drinking.* Albuquerque, NM: University of New Mexico Press.

Mills, J. A., Bauer, G. P., & Miars, R. D. (1989). Use of transference in short-term dynamic psychotherapy. *Psychotherapy, 26*(3), 112–119.

Milner, J. S. (1986). *The child abuse potential inventory: Manual* (Rev. ed.). Webster, NC: Psytec Corporation.

Minton, H. L., & McDonald, G. J. (1984). Homosexual identity formation as a developmental process. *Journal of Homosexuality, 9,* 91–104.

Minton, H. L., & Schneider, F. W. (1981). *Differential psychology.* Monterey, CA: Brooks/Cole.

Mintz, J., Luborsky, L., & Auerbach, A. (1971). Dimensions of psychotherapy: A factor-analytic study of ratings of psychotherapy sessions. *Journal of Consulting and Clinical Psychology, 36,* 106–120.

Minuchin, S. (1974). *Families and family therapy.* Cambridge, MA: Harvard University Press.

Minuchin, S. (1984). *Family kaleidoscope.* Cambridge, MA: Harvard University Press.

Mio, J. S., & Iwamasa, G. (1993). To do, or not to do: That is the question for white cross-cultural researchers. *The Counseling Psychologist, 21*(2), 197–212.

Miranti, J. G., & Burke, M. T. (1995). Spirituality: An integral component of the counseling process. In M. T. Burke & J. G. Miranti (Eds.), *Counseling: The spiritual dimension* (pp. 1–4). Alexandria, VA: American Counseling Association.

Mirin, S. M., Weiss, R. D., Michael, J., & Griffin, M. L. (1988). Psychopathology in substance abusers: Diagnosis and treatment. *American Journal of Drug and Alcohol Abuse, 14*(2), 139–157.

Mischel, W., Shoda, Y., & Rodriguez, M. L. (1989). Delay of gratification in children. *Science, 244,* 933–938.

Mitchell, J. T., & Everly, G. S. (1993). *Critical incident stress debriefing: An operations manual for the prevention of traumatic stress among emergency services and disaster workers.* Ellicott City, MD: Chevron.

Mitchell, L. K., & Krumboltz, J. D. (1987). The effects of cognitive restructuring and decision-making training on career indecision. *Journal of Counseling and Development, 66,* 171–174.

Mitchell, L. K., & Krumboltz, J. D. (2002). Social learning approach to career decision making: Krumboltz's theory. In D. Brown, L. Brooks, & Associates (Eds.), *Career choice and development* (4th ed.). San Francisco: Jossey-Bass.

Monahan, J. (1993). Limiting therapist exposure to Tarasoff liability: Guidelines for risk containment. *American Psychologist, 48*(3), 242–250.

Moon, S. M., Dillon, D. R., & Sprenkle, D. H. (1990). Family therapy and qualitative research. *Journal of Marital and Family Therapy, 16*(4), 357–373.

Moreno, J. (1988). Multicultural music therapy: The world music connection. *Journal of Music Therapy, 25*(1), 17–27.

Moreno, J. L. (1946). *Psychodrama* (Vol. 1). Beacon, NY: Beacon House.

Mormar, C. R., & Horowitz, M. J. (1988). Diagnosis and phase-oriented treatment of post-traumatic stress disorder. In J. F. Wilson, Z. Harel, & B. Kahana (Eds.), *Human adaption to extreme stress: From Holocaust to Viet Nam.* New York: Plenum.

Morrissette, P. J. (2000). The experiences of the rural school counselor. *Professional School Counseling, 3*(3), 197–207.

Morrow, D., Worthington, E. L., & McCullough, M. E. (1993). Observers' perceptions of a counselor's treatment of a religious issue. *Journal of Counseling and Development, 71*(4), 452–456.

Morrow, P. C., Mullen, E. J., & McElvoy, J. C. (1990). Vocational behavior, 1989: The year in review. *Journal of Vocational Behavior, 37,* 121–195.

Morse, C. L., & Russell, T. (1988). How elementary counselors see their role: An empirical study. *Elementary School Guidance & Counseling, 23*(1), 44–62.

Mosak, H. (1991). Where have all the normal people gone? *Individual Psychology: The Journal of Adlerian Theory, Research, and Practice, 47*(4), 437–446.

Mosak, H. (2005). Adlerian psychotherapy. In R. J. Corsini (Ed.), *Current psychotherapies* (7th ed.) (pp. 52–95). Itasca, IL: F. E. Peacock.

Moyerman, D. R., & Forman, B. D. (1992). Acculturation and adjustment: A meta-analytic study. *Hispanic Journal of Behavioral Sciences, 14,* 163–200.

Muller, L. E., & Hartman, J. (1998). Group counseling for sexual minority youth. *Professional School Counseling, 1*(3), 38–41.

Muro, J. J. (1981). On target—on top. *Elementary School Guidance and Counseling, 15,* 307–314.

Murphy, G. E., Simons, A. D., Wetzel, R. D., & Lustman, P. J. (1983). Cognitive therapy and pharmacotherapy: Singly and together in the treatment of depression. *Archives of General Psychiatry, 41,* 33–41.

Murphy, J. J. (1994). Working with what works: A solution-focused approach to school behavior problems. *The School Counselor, 42*(1), 59–65.

Myers, I. B., & McCaulley, M. H. (1985). *Manual: A guide to the development and use of the Myers-Briggs Type Indicator.* Palo Alto, CA: Consulting Psychologists Press.

Myers, J. E., Sweeney, T. J., & White, V. E. (2002). Advocacy for counseling and counselors: A professional imperative. *Journal of Counseling and Development, 80,* 394–402.

Myers, L. J. (1988). *Understanding an Afrocentric worldview: Introduction to optimal psychology.* Dubuque, IA: Kendall/Hunt.

Myers, L. J., Speight, S. L., Highlen, P. S., Cox, C. I., Reynolds, A. L., Adams, E. M., & Hanley, C. P. (1991). Identity development and worldview: Toward an optimal conceptualization. *Journal of Counseling and Development, 70*(1), 54–63.

Myrick, R. D. (1987). *Developmental guidance and counseling. A practical approach.* Minneapolis, MN: Educational Media.

Myrick, R. D., & Sabella, R. A. (1995). Cyberspace: New place for counselor supervision. *Elementary School Guidance and Counseling, 30*(1), 35–44.

Nansel, T. R., Overpeck, M., Pilla, R. S., Ruan, W. J., Simons-Morton, B., & Scheidt, P. (2001). Bullying behaviors among US youth: Prevalence and association with psychosocial adjustment. *JAMA, 285*(16), 2094–2100.

Nathan, P. E., & Harris, S. L. (1980). *Psychopathology and society* (2nd ed.). New York: McGraw-Hill.

National Board for Certified Counselors (NBCC). (1997, December 1). *The practice of Internet counseling.* Retrieved March 23, 2005 from http://www.nbcc.org/ethics/webethics.htm.

National Institute of Mental Health (NIMH). (1999). *Suicide fact sheet.* Retrieved March 23, 2005, from http://www.nimh.nih.gov/suicideprevention/suifact.cfm.

Neimeyer, R. A., & Mahoney, M. J. (1995). *Constructivism in psychotherapy.* Washington, DC: American Psychological Association.

NeJedlo, R. J., Arredondo, P., & Benjamin, L. (1985). *Imagine: A visionary model for the counselors of tomorrow.* Alexandria, VA: Association for Counselor Education and Supervision.

Nelson, M. D., Thomas, J. V., & Pierce, K. A. (1995). Inside-outside: A classroom discussion model for conflict resolution. *The School Counselor, 42*(5), 399–404.

Nelson, M. L., & Holloway, E. L. (1990). Relation of gender to power and involvement in supervision. *Journal of Counseling Psychology, 37,* 473–481.

Nelson-Jones, R. (1992). *Group leadership: A training approach.* Pacific Grove, CA: Brooks/Cole.

Nergaard, M. O., & Silberschatz, G. (1989). The effects of shame, guilt, and the negative reaction in brief dynamic psychotherapy. *Psychotherapy, 26,* 330–337.

Neukrug, E. S., Barr, C. G., Hoffman, L. R., & Kaplan, L. S. (1993). Developmental counseling and guidance: A model for use in your school. *The School Counselor, 40*(5), 356–362.

Newcomb, M. D., & Bentler, P. M. (1988). *Consequences of adolescent drug use: Impact on the lives of young adults.* Newbury Park, CA: Sage.

Newcomb, M. D., & Bentler, P. M. (1989). Substance use and abuse among children and teenagers. *American Psychologist, 44*(2), 242–248.

Newcomb, N. S. (1994). Music: A powerful resource for the elementary school counselor. *Elementary School Guidance and Counseling, 29*(2), 150–155.

Newmark, C. S. (1985). *Major psychological assessment instruments.* Boston: Allyn & Bacon.

Nicholas, D., Gerstein, L., & Keller, K. (1988). Behavioral medicine and the mental health counselor. Roles and interdisciplinary collaboration. *Journal of Mental Health Counseling, 10,* 79–94.

Nichols, M. (1984). *Family therapy: Concepts and methods.* New York: Gardner Press.

Nichols, M. (1987a). The individual in the system. *Family Therapy Networker, 11*(2), 33–38, 85.

Nichols, M. (1987b). *The self in the system: Expanding the limits of family therapy.* New York: Brunner/Mazel.

Nichols, W. (1988). *Marital therapy: An integrative approach.* New York: Brunner/Mazel.

Nichols, W. C., & Everett, C. A. (1986). *Systematic family therapy: An integrative approach.* New York: Guilford Press.

Nicki, R. M., Remington, R. M., & MacDonald, G. A. (1984). Self-efficacy, nicotine fading/self-monitoring and cigarette-smoking behavior. *Behavior Research and Therapy, 22,* 477–485.

Nielsen, S. L., Smart, D. W., Isakson, R. L., Worthen, V. E., Gregersen, A. T., & Lambert, M. J. (2004). The *Consumer Reports* effective score: What did consumers report? *Journal of Counseling Psychology, 51,* 25–37.

Nietzel, M. T., Russell, R. L., Hemmings, K. A., & Gretter, M. L. (1987). The clinical significance of psychotherapy for unipolar depression: A meta-analytic approach to social comparison. *Journal of Consulting and Clinical Psychology, 55,* 156–161.

Norcross, J. C., & Hill, C. E. (2003). Empirically supported (therapy) relationships: ESRs. *The Register Report, 29,* 22–27.

Norcross, J. C., & Newman, C. F. (1992). Psychotherapy integration: Setting the context. In J. C. Norcross & M. R. Goldfried (Eds.), *Handbook of psychotherapy integration* (pp. 3–45). New York: Basic Books.

Norcross, J. C., Prochaska, J. O., & Gallagher, K. M. (1989). Clinical psychologists in the 1980's: II. Theory research, and practice. *The Clinical Psychologist, 42,* 45–53.

Northcutt, N., & McCoy, D. (2004). *Interactive qualitative analysis.* Thousand Oaks, CA: Sage.

Nykodym, N., Rund, W., & Liverpool, P. (1986). Quality circles: Will transactional analysis improve their effectiveness? *Transactional Analysis Journal, 16,* 182–187.

Nystul, M. S. (1976). Identification and movement within three levels of social interest. *Journal of Individual Psychology, 30,* 211–215.

Nystul, M. S. (1978a). Adler as a Sherlockian. *The Individual Psychologist, 15*(1), 41–45.

Nystul, M. S. (1978b). The use of creative arts therapy within Adlerian psychotherapy. *The Individual Psychologist, 15,* 11–18.

Nystul, M. S. (1979a). Integrating current psychotherapies into Adlerian psychotherapy. *The Individual Psychologist, 16,* 23–29.

Nystul, M. S. (1979b). Three levels of a counseling relationship. *The School Counselor, 26,* 144–148.

Nystul, M. S. (1979c). The courage to be imperfect: Now more than ever. *Individual Psychologist, 26,* 15–19.

Nystul, M. S. (1980a). Nystulian play therapy: Applications of Adlerian psychology. *Elementary School Guidance and Counseling, 15,* 22–30.

Nystul, M. S. (1980b). Systematic training for effective parenting: STEP in Australia. *Australian Child and Family Welfare, 1–2,* 32–34.

Nystul, M. S. (1981). Avoiding roadblocks in counseling. *The Individual Psychologist, 18,* 21–28.

Nystul, M. S. (1982a). The effects of systematic training for effective parenting on parental attitudes. *The Journal of Psychology, 112,* 63–66.

Nystul, M. S. (1982b). Ten Adlerian parenting principles applied to the Navajos. *Individual Psychology: The Journal of Adlerian Theory, Research, and Practice, 38,* 183–198.

Nystul, M. S. (1984). Positive parenting leads to self-actualizing children. *Individual Psychology: The Journal of Adlerian Theory, Research, and Practice, 40,* 177–183.

Nystul, M. S. (1985a). An interview with Dr. Albert Ellis. *Individual Psychology: The Journal of Adlerian Theory, Research, and Practice, 41*(2), 243–254.

Nystul, M. S. (1985b). The use of motivation of modification techniques in Adlerian psychotherapy. *Individual Psychology: The Journal of Adlerian Theory, Research, and Practice, 44*(2), 199–209.

Nystul, M. S. (1986). Reaching in-reaching out: Treatment of an autistic child. *Mental Health Counselor's Association Journal, 8,* 18–26.

Nystul, M. S. (1987a). Creative arts therapy and the existential encounter. *The Creative Child and Adult Quarterly, 12*(3), 243–249.

Nystul, M. S. (1987b). Strategies of parent-centered counseling of the young. *The Creative Child and Adult Quarterly, 12*(2), 103–111.

Nystul, M. S. (1988). An interview with Dr. Shulman. *Individual Psychology: The Journal of Adlerian Theory, Research, and Practice, 44*(2), 210–216.

Nystul, M. S. (1991). An interview with Jon Carlson. *Individual Psychology: The Journal of Adlerian Theory, Research, and Practice, 47*(4), 498–503.

Nystul, M. S. (1994a). Increasing the positive orientation to Adlerian psychotherapy: Redefining the concept of "basic mistakes." *Individual Psychology: The Journal of Adlerian Theory, Research, and Practice, 50*(3), 271–278.

Nystul, M. S. (1994b). The use of normalizing and structuring in the counseling process. *Counseling and Human Development, 26*(8), 11–12.

Nystul, M. S. (1995). A problem solving approach to counseling: Integrating Adler's and Glasser's theories. *Elementary School Guidance and Counseling, 29*(4), 297–302.

Nystul, M. S. (1999). Problem solving counseling: Integrating Adler's and Glasser's theories. In R. E. Watts & J. Carlson (Eds.), *Interventions and strategies in counseling and psychotherapy* (pp. 31–42). Philadelphia: Accelerated Development.

Nystul, M. S. (2002a). Emotional balancing: A parenting technique to enhance parent-child relationships. In R. F. Watts (Ed.), *Techniques in marriage and family counseling* (Vol. 2) (pp. 125–132). Alexandria, VA: American Counseling Association.

Nystul, M. S. (2002b). The role of parental emotions in parenting. *New Zealand Journal of Counseling, 23,* 29–39.

Nystul, M. S., Emmons, R., & Cockrell, K. (1992). The use of pet therapy in counseling. *New Zealand Journal of Counseling, 14*(1), 32–35.

Nystul, M. S., & Musynska, E. (1976). Adlerian treatment of a classical case of stuttering. *Journal of Individual Psychology, 32*(2), 194–202.

O'Brien, S. (1983). *Child pornography*. Dubuque, IA: Kendall/Hunt.

O'Connor, M. (1992). Psychotherapy with gay and lesbian adolescents. In S. Dworkin & F. Gutierrez (Eds.), *Counseling gay men and lesbians: Journey to the end of the rainbow*. Alexandria, VA: American Association for Counseling and Development.

O'Hanlon, W. H., & Weiner-Davis, M. (1989). *In search of solutions: A new direction in psychotherapy*. New York: Norton.

O'Tolle, M. E. (1999). *The school shooter: A threat assessment perspective*. Quantico, VA: FBI.

Office of Strategic Services. (1948). *Assessment of men*. New York: Holt, Rinehart & Winston.

Ohlsen, M. M. (1970). *Group counseling*. New York: Holt, Rinehart & Winston.

Oklahoma State Department of Education. (1988). *Building skills for tomorrow: A developmental guidance model*. Oklahoma City: State Board of Affairs.

Okun, B. F. (2002). *Effective helping interviewing and counseling techniques* (6th ed.). Monterey, CA: Brooks/Cole.

Oliver, L. W. (1977). Evaluating career counseling outcome for three modes of test interpretation. *Measurement and Evaluation in Guidance, 10,* 153–161.

Oliver, L. W., & Spokane, A. R. (1983). Research integration: Approaches, problems and recommendations for research reporting. *Journal of Counseling Psychology, 30,* 252–257.

Oliver, L. W., & Spokane, A. R. (1988). Career-intervention outcome: What contributes to clients' gain? *Journal of Counseling Psychology, 35*(4), 447–462.

Olson, D. H., & DeFrain, J. (1997). *Marriage and family: Diversity and strengths* (2nd ed.). Mountain View, CA: Mayfield Press.

Orbach, I., Feshbach, S., Carlson, G., Glaubman, H., & Gross, Y. (1983) Attraction and repulsion by life and death in suicidal and in normal children. *Journal of Consulting and Clinical Psychology, 51,* 661–670.

Orenchuk-Tomiuk, N., Matthey, G., & Christensen, C. P. (1990). The resolution model: A comprehensive treatment framework in sexual abuse. *Child Welfare, 69*(5), 417–431.

Orlando, D. E., & Howard, K. I. (1986). Process and outcome in psychotherapy. In S. L. Garfield & A. E. Bergin (Eds.), *Handbook of psychotherapy and behavior change*. New York: John Wiley & Sons.

Orton, G. L. (1997). *Strategies for counseling with children and their parents*. Pacific Grove, CA: Brooks/Cole.

Osipow, S. H. (1990). Convergence in theories of career choice and development: Review and prospects. *Journal of Vocational Behavior, 36,* 122–131.

Osipow, S. H. (1996). *Theories of career development* (4th ed.). Englewood Cliffs, NJ: Prentice-Hall.

Othmer, E., & Othmer, S. C. (1989). *The clinical interview: Using DSM-III-R*. Washington, DC: American Psychiatric Press.

Page, B. J., Delmonico, D. L., Walsh, J., L'Amoreaux, N. A., Danninhirsh, C., Thompson, R. S., Ingram, A. I., & Evans, A. D. (2000). Setting up on-line support groups using the Palace software. *Journal for Specialists in Group Work, 25,* 133–145.

Page, B. J., Jencius, M. J., Rehfuss, M. C., Foss, L. L., Dean, E. P., Petruzzi, M. L., Olson, S. D., & Sager, D. E. (2003). PalTalk online groups: Process and reflections on students' experience. *Journal for Specialists in Group Work, 28,* 35–41.

Paisley, P. O., & Benshoff, J. M. (1996). Applying developmental principles to practice: Training issues for the professional development of school counselors. *Elementary School Guidance and Counseling, 30*(3), 163–169.

Paisley, P. O., & Borders, D. L. (1995). School counseling: An emerging specialty. *Journal of Counseling and Development, 74*(2), 150–153.

Paisley, P. O., & DeAngelis-Peace, S. (1995). Developmental principles: A framework for school counseling programs. *Elementary School Guidance and Counseling, 30*(2), 85–93.

Paivio, S., & Greenberg, L. (1992). *Resolving unfinished business: A study of effects*. Paper presented at the annual meeting of the Society for Psychotherapy Research, Berkeley, CA.

Palmatier, L. L. (1990). Reality therapy and brief strategic interactional therapy. *Journal of Reality Therapy, 9*(2), 3–17.

Palmo, A. J. (1986). Professional identity of the mental health counselor. In A. J. Palmo & W. J. Weikel (Eds.), *Foundations of mental health counseling*. Springfield, IL: Charles C Thomas.

Paniagua, F. A. (1996). Cross-cultural guidelines in family therapy practice. *The Family Journal: Counseling and Therapy for Couples and Families, 4*(2), 127–138.

Papalia, D. E., & Olds, S. W. (2001). *Human development* (8th ed.). New York: McGraw-Hill.

Paradise, L. V., & Kirby, P. C. (1990). Legal issues in group work: Some perspectives on the legal liability of group counseling in private practice. *The Journal for Specialists in Group Work, 15*(2), 114–118.

Paradise, L. V., Conway, B. S., & Zweig, J. (1986). Effects of expert and referent influence, physical attractiveness, and gender on perceptions of counselor attributes. *Journal of Counseling Psychology, 33,* 16–22.

Parette, H. P., & Hourcade, J. J. (1995). Disability etiquette and school counselors: A common sense approach toward compliance with the Americans with Disabilities Act. *The School Counselor, 52*(3), 224–233.

Parr, G. D., & Ostrovsky, M. (1991). The role of moral development in deciding how to counsel children and adolescents. *The School Counselor, 39,* 14–19.

Parsons, F. (1909). *Choosing a vocation.* Boston: Houghton Mifflin.

Passons, W. R. (1975). *Gestalt approaches in counseling.* New York: Holt, Rinehart & Winston.

Pate, R. H., & Bondi, A. M. (1992). Religious beliefs and practice: An integral aspect of multicultural awareness. *Counselor Education and Supervision, 32*(2), 108–115.

Pate, R. H., & Miller-Bondi, A. (1995). Religious beliefs and practice: An integral aspect of multicultural awareness. In M. T. Burke & J. G. Miranti (Eds.), *Counseling: The spiritual dimension.* Alexandria, VA: American Counseling Association.

Patterson, C. H. (1986). *Theories of counseling and psychology.* New York: Harper & Row.

Patterson, C. H. (1989). Eclecticism in psychotherapy: Is integration possible? *Psychotherapy, 26*(2), 157–161.

Patterson, C. H. (1992). Values in counseling and psychotherapy. In M. T. Burke & J. G. Miranti (Eds.), *Ethical and spiritual values in counseling* (pp. 107–120). Alexandria, VA: American Counseling Association.

Patterson, C. H. (1996). Multicultural counseling: From diversity to universality. *Journal of Counseling and Development, 74*(3), 227–231.

Patterson, C. H. (2004). Do we need multicultural counseling competencies? *Journal of Mental Health Counseling, 26,* 67–73.

Patterson, G. R. (1982). *Coercive family process.* Eugene, OR: Castalia.

Patterson, G. R., DeBaryshe, R. D., & Ramsey, E. (1989). A developmental perspective on antisocial behavior. *American Psychologist, 44*(2), 329–335.

Patterson, J. B., McKenzie, B., & Jenkins, J. (1995). Creating accessible groups for individuals with disabilities. *Journal for Specialists in Group Work, 20*(2), 76–82.

Pattison, E. M., & Kaufman, E. (1982). The alcoholism syndrome: Definitions and models. In E. M. Pattison & E. Kaufman (Eds.), *Encyclopedic handbook of alcoholism* (pp. 3–30). New York: Gardner Press.

Pavlov, I. P. (1906). The scientific investigation of the psychical faculties of processes in the higher animals. *Science, 24,* 613–619.

Pearson, J., Lunday, B., Rohrbach, L., & Whitney, D. (1985). *Project SMART: A social approach to drug abuse prevention.* Unpublished curriculum guide, University of Southern California, Health Behavior Research Institute, Los Angeles, CA.

Pedersen, P. (1987). Ten frequent assumptions of cultural bias in counseling. *Journal of Multicultural Counseling and Development, 15*(1), 16–24.

Pedersen, P. (1988). *A handbook for developing multicultural awareness.* Alexandria, VA: American Association for Counseling and Development.

Pedersen, P. (Ed.). (1991a). Multiculturalism as a fourth force in counseling (Special Issue). *Journal of Counseling and Development, 70.*

Pedersen, P. (1991b). Multiculturalism as a generic approach to counseling. *Journal of Counseling and Development, 70*(1), 6–12.

Pedersen, P. (1993). The multicultural dilemma of white cross-cultural researchers. *The Counseling Psychologist, 21*(2), 229–232.

Pedersen, P. (1997). The cultural context of the American Counseling Association Code of Ethics. *Journal of Counseling and Development, 76*(1), 23–28.

Peer, G. G. (1985). The status of secondary school guidance: A national survey. *The School Counselor, 32*(3), 181–189.

Peluso, P. R., Peluso, J. P., White, J. F., & Kern, R. (2004). A comparison of attachment theory and individual psychology: A review of the literature. *Journal of Counseling and Development, 82,* 139–145.

Penrose, L. S., & Raven, J. C. (1936). A new series of perceptual tasks: Preliminary communication. *British Journal of Medical Psychology, 16,* 97–104.

Pepinsky, H. B., & Pepinsky, P. N. (1954). *Counseling: Theory and practice.* New York: Ronald Press.

Perls, F. (1969a). *Gestalt therapy verbatim.* Moab, UT: Real People Press.

Perls, F. (1969b). *In and out of the garbage pail.* Moab, UT: Real People Press.

Petersen, A. C., Compas, B. E., Brooks/Gunn, J., Stemmler, M., Ey, S., & Grant, K. E. (1993). Depression in adolescence. *American Psychologist, 48*(2), 155–168.

Peterson, D. R. (1995). The reflective educator. *American Psychologist, 50*(12), 975–983.

Phillips, S. D., & Blustein, D. L. (1994). Readiness for career choices: Planning, exploring, and deciding. *Career Development Quarterly, 63*–73.

Phillips, S. D., Cairo, P. C., Blustein, D. L., & Myers, R. A. (1988). Career development and behavior, 1987: A review. *Journal of Vocational Behavior, 33,* 119–184.

Piaget, J. (1952). *The origins of intelligence in children* (M. Cook, Trans.). New York: Norton.

Piaget, J. (1955). *The language and thought of the child.* New York: New American Library. (Original work published 1923)

Piaget, J. (1965). *The moral judgment of the child* (M. Gabain, Trans.). New York: Free Press. (Original work published 1936)

Pincus, H. A., Goodwin, F. K., Barchas, J. D., Cohen, D. J., Judd, L. L., Meltzer, H. Y., & Vaillant, G. E. (1989). The future of the science of psychiatry. In J. A. Talbott (Ed.), *Future directions for psychiatry*. Washington, DC: American Psychiatric Press.

Pipal, J. E. (1995). Managed care: Is it the corpse in the living room? An expose. *Psychotherapy, 32*(2), 323–332.

Pistole, M. C. (1993). Attachment relationships: Self-disclosure and trust. *Journal of Mental Health Counseling, 15,* 94–106.

Poidevant, J. M., & Lewis, H. A. (1995). Transactional analysis theory. In D. Capuzzi and D. R. Gross (Eds.), *Counseling and psychotherapy: Theories and interventions*. Columbus, OH: Merrill.

Polansky, N., Chalmers, M., Buttenwieser, E., & Williams, D. (1981). *Damaged parents: An anatomy of child neglect*. Chicago: University of Chicago Press.

Polich, J. M., Armor, D. M., & Braiker, H. B. (1981). *The course of alcoholism: Four years after treatment*. New York: Wiley.

Polich, J. M., Ellickson, P. L., Reuter, P., & Kahan, J. P. (1984). *Strategies for controlling adolescent drug use*. Santa Monica, CA: Rand.

Polk, E. (1977). Dance therapy with special children. In K. Mason (Ed.), *Dance therapy: Focus on dance VII* (pp. 56–58). Washington, DC: American Alliance for Health, Physical Education, and Recreation.

Ponterotto, J. G., & Casas, J. M. (1991). *Handbook of racial/ethnic minority counseling research*. Springfield, IL: Charles C Thomas.

Pope, K. S., & Vetter, V. A. (1992). Ethical dilemmas encountered by members of the American Psychological Association. *American Psychologist, 47*(3), 397–411.

Pope-Davis, D. B., & Ottavi, T. M. (1994). Examining the association between self-reported multicultural counseling competencies and demographic variables among counselors. *Journal of Counseling and Development, 72,* 651–654.

Pope-Davis, D. B., Toporek, R. L., Ortega-Villalobos, L., Ligiero, D. P., Brittan-Powell, C. S., Liu, W. M., Bashshur, M. R., Codrington, J. N., & Liang, C. T. H. (2002). Client perspectives of multicultural counseling competence: A qualitative examination. *The Counseling Psychologist, 30,* 355–393.

Popkin, M. H. (2000). Youth violence in our communities—And what we can do. *The Journal of Individual Psychology, 56*(4), 395–410.

Prince, J. P. (1995). Influences on the career development of gay men. *Career Development Quarterly, 44*(2), 148–167.

Prochaska, J. O. (1984). *Systems of psychotherapy: A transtheoretical analysis*. Chicago: Dorsey Press.

Prochaska, J. O., DiClemente, C. C., & Norcross, J. C. (1992). In search of how people change: Applications to addictive behaviors. *American Psychologist, 47*(9), 1102–1114.

Prochaska, J. O., & Norcross, J. C. (2002). *Systems of psychotherapy: A transtheoretical analysis* (5th ed.). Pacific Grove, CA: Brooks/Cole.

Public Law 94-142, *The Education for All Handicapped Children Act of 1975* is coded at 20 U.S.C. Sec. 613 et. seq. and its implementing regulations at 45 C.F.R. Part 121a. (1975).

Puig-Antich, J., Perel, J. M., Lupatkins, W., Chambers, W. J., Tabrizi, M. A., King, J., Goetz, R., Davies, M., & Stiller, R. L. (1987). Imipramine in prepubertal major depressive disorders. *Archives of General Psychiatry, 44,* 81–89.

Puryear, D. A. (1979). *Helping people in crisis*. San Francisco: Jossey-Bass.

Quay, H. C., & Petersen, D. R. (1983). *Interim manual for the revised behavior problem checklist*. Unpublished manuscript, University of Miami.

Quintana, S. M., & Holahan, W. (1992). Termination in short-term counseling: Comparison of successful and unsuccessful cases. *Journal of Counseling Psychology, 39*(3), 299–305.

Radbill, S. X. (1980). Children in a world of violence: A history of child abuse. In C. H. Kempe & R. E. Helfer (Eds.), *The battered child*. Chicago: University of Chicago.

Raffa, H., Sypek, J., & Vogel, W. (1990). Commentary on reviews of "outcome" studies of family and marital psychotherapy. *Contemporary Family Therapy, 12*(1), 65–73.

Raiche, B. M., Fox, R., & Rotatori, A. F. (1986). Counseling the mildly behaviorally disordered child. In A. F. Rotatori, P. J. Gerber, F. W. Litton, & R. A. Fox (Eds.), *Counseling exceptional students* (pp. 123–143). New York: Human Sciences Press.

Raimy, V. (1950). *Training in clinical psychology*. Englewood Cliffs, NJ: Prentice-Hall.

Rak, C. F., & Patterson, L. E. (1996). Promoting resilience in at-risk children. *Journal of Counseling and Development, 74*(4), 368–373.

Rapaport, D. (1958). The theory of ego autonomy: A generalization. *Bulletin of Menninger Clinic, 22,* 13–35.

Rapin, L. S., & Keel, L. (1998). *Association for specialists in group work: Best practice guidelines*. Alexandria, VA: American Counseling Association.

Raskin, N. J., & Rogers, C. R. (2005). Person-centered therapy. In R. J. Corsini & D. Wedding (Eds.),

Current psychotherapies (7th ed.) (pp. 133–167). Itasca, IL: F. E. Peacock.

Raskin, P. A., & Israel, A. C. (1981). Sex role imitation in children: Effects of sex of child, sex of model, and sex role appropriateness of modeled behavior. *Sex Roles, 7*(11), 1067–1077.

Raskin, P. M. (1987). *Vocational counseling: A guide for the practitioner.* New York: Teachers College Press.

Rawlings, E. I. (1993). Reflections on "Twenty Years of Feminist Counseling and Therapy." *The Counseling Psychologist, 21*(1), 88–91.

Rawlins, M. E., Eberly, C. G., & Rawlins, L. D. (1991). Infusing counseling skills in test interpretation. *Counselor Education and Supervision, 31,* 109–120.

Read, H., Fordham, M., & Adler, G. (Eds.). (1953–1978). *Jung's collected works.* Princeton, NJ: Princeton University Press.

Reams, R., & Friedrich, W. N. (1983). *Play therapy: A review of outcome research.* Seattle: University of Washington, Department of Psychology.

Reddy, M., Borum, R., Berglund, J., Vossekuil, B., Fein, R., & Modzeleski, W. (2001). Evaluating risk for targeted violence in schools: Comparing risk assessment, threat assessment, and other approaches. *Psychology in the Schools, 38*(2), 152–172.

Reisetter, M., Korcuska, J. S., Yexley, M., Bonds, D., Nikels, H., & McHenry, W. (2004). Counselor educators and qualitative research: Affirming a research identity. *Counselor Education and Supervision, 44*(1), 2–16.

Remafedi, G. (1987). Homosexual youth: A challenge to contemporary society. *JAMA, 258,* pp. 222–225.

Remley, T. P. (1991). *Preparing for court appearances.* Alexandria, VA: American Association for Counseling and Development.

Reynolds, C. R. (1982). The problem of bias in psychological assessment. In C. R. Reynolds & T. B. Gutkin (Eds.), *The handbook of school psychology.* New York: John Wiley & Sons.

Reynolds, M. (1976). Threats to confidentiality. *Social Work, 21,* 108–113.

Reynolds, W. M., & Coats, K. I. (1986). A comparison of cognitive-behavioral therapy and relocation training for the treatment of depression in adolescents. *Journal of Counseling and Clinical Psychology, 54,* 653–660.

Rhyne, J. (1987). Gestalt art therapy. In J. A. Rubin (Ed.), *Approaches to art therapy: Theory and technique.* New York: Brunner/Mazel.

Ribak-Rosenthal, N., & Russell, T. T. (1994). Dealing with religious differences in December: A school counselor's role. *Elementary School Counseling and Guidance, 28*(4), 295–301.

Rice, K. G. (1990). Attachment in adolescence: A narrative and meta-analytic review. *Journal of Youth and Adolescence, 19,* 511–536.

Rice, K. G., & Meyer, A. L. (1994). Preventing depression among young adolescents: Preliminary process results of a psycho-educational program. *Journal of Counseling and Development, 73*(2), 145–152.

Richards, P. S., & Bergin, A. E. (1997). *Strategy for counseling and psychotherapy.* Washington, DC: American Psychological Association.

Richards, P. S., & Bergin, A. E. (2004). A theistic spiritual strategy for psychotherapy. In P. S. Richards & A. E. Bergin (Eds.), *Casebook for a spiritual strategy in counseling and psychotherapy* (pp. 3–32), Washington, DC: American Psychological Association.

Richardson, B. K., & Bradley, L. J. (1985). *Community agency counseling: An emerging specialty in counselor education programs.* Alexandria, VA: American Association for Counseling and Development.

Richardson, M. S. (1996). From career counseling to counseling/psychotherapy and work, job, and career. In M. L. Savickas & W. B. Walsh (Eds.), *Handbook of career counseling theory and practice* (pp. 347–360). Palo Alto, CA: Davies-Black.

Richardson, T. Q., & Molinaro, K. L. (1996). White counselor self-awareness: A prerequisite for developing multicultural competence. *Journal of Counseling and Development, 74*(3), 238–242.

Ricks, M. H. (1985). The social transmission of parental behavior: Attachment across generations. *Monograph of the Society for Research on Child Development, 50,* 211–227.

Ridley, C. R., & Kleiner, A. J. (2003). Multicultural counseling competence: History, themes, and issues. In D. B. Pope-Davis, H. L. K. Coleman, W. M. Liu, & R. L. Toporek (Eds.), *Handbook of multicultural competencies in counseling and psychology* (pp. 3–20), Thousand Oaks, CA: Sage.

Ridley, C. R., Li, L. C., & Hill, C. L. (1998). Multicultural assessment: Reexamination, reconceptualization, and practical application. *The Counseling Psychologist, 26,* 827–910.

Ridley, C. R., Mendoza, D. W., & Kanitz, B. E. (1994). Multicultural training: Reexamination, operationalization, and integration. *The Counseling Psychologist, 22*(2), 227–289.

Rigazio-DiGilio, S. A. (1994). A co-constructive-developmental approach. *Journal of Mental Health Counseling, 16*(1), 43–74.

Rimm, D. C., & Cunningham, H. M. (1985). Behavior therapies. In S. J. Lynn & J. P. Garske (Eds.), *Contemporary psychotherapies.* Columbus, OH: Merrill/Macmillan.

Riordan, R. J., & Wilson, L. S. (1989). Bibliotherapy: Does it work? *Journal of Counseling and Development, 67,* 506–508.

Ritchie, M. H., & Partin, R. L. (1994). Parent education and consultation activities of school counselors. *The School Counselor, 41*(3), 165–170.

Rittenhouse, J. A. (1997). Feminist principles in survivors' groups: Out-of-group contact. *Journal for Specialists in Group Work, 22*(2), 111–119.

Ritter, K. Y., & O'Neill, C. W. (1995). Moving through loss: The spiritual journey of gay men and lesbian women. In M. T. Burke & J. G. Miranti (Eds.), *Counseling: The spiritual dimension* (pp. 127–141). Alexandria, VA: American Counseling Association.

Robbins, A. (1985). Working towards the establishment of creative arts therapies as an independent profession. *The Arts in Psychotherapy, 12,* 67–70.

Robins, L., Helzer, J. E., Croughan, J., & Ratcliff, K. S. (1981). National Institute of Mental Health diagnostic interview schedule: Its history, characteristics, and validity. *Archives of General Psychiatry, 38,* 381–389.

Robson, B. E. (2002). Changing family patterns: Developmental impacts on children. In J. Carlson & J. Lewis (Eds.), *Counseling the adolescent: Individual, family and school interventions* (4th ed.) (pp. 261–278). Denver, CO: Love.

Roe, A. (1956). *The psychology of occupations.* New York: Wiley.

Roe, A., & Lunneborg, P. W. (2002). Personality development and career choice. In D. Brown, L. Brooks, & Associates (Eds.), *Career choice and development* (4th ed.). San Francisco: Jossey-Bass.

Rogers, C. (1939). *The clinical treatment of the problem child.* Boston: Houghton Mifflin.

Rogers, C. (1942). *Counseling and psychotherapy.* Boston: Houghton Mifflin.

Rogers, C. (1951). *Client-centered therapy.* Boston: Houghton Mifflin.

Rogers, C. (1957). The necessary and sufficient condition of therapeutic personality change. *Journal of Consulting Psychology, 21,* 95–103.

Rogers, C. (1961). *On becoming a person.* Boston: Houghton Mifflin.

Rogers, C. (1970). *On encounter groups.* New York: Harper & Row.

Rogers, C. (1981). *A way of being.* Boston: Houghton Mifflin.

Rogers, C., Gendlin, E. T., Kiesler, D. J., & Truax, C. B. (1967). *The therapeutic relationship and its impact: A study of psychotherapy with schizophrenics.* Madison: University of Wisconsin Press.

Rogers, C., & Wood, J. K. (1974). Client-centered theory: Carl R. Rogers. In A. Burton (Ed.), *Operational theories of personality* (pp. 211–258). New York: Bruner/Mazel.

Rogers, F., & Sharapan, H. (1993). Play. *Elementary School Guidance and Counseling, 28*(1), 10–16.

Roll, S. A., Crowley, M. A., & Rappl, L. E. (1985). Client perceptions of counselor's nonverbal behavior: A reevaluation. *Counselor Education and Supervision, 24,* 234–243.

Romano, J. L., & Kachgal, M. M. (2004). Counseling psychology and school counseling: An underutilized partnership. *The Counseling Psychologist, 32,* 184–215.

Rosenhan, D. L., & Seligman, M. E. P. (1995). *Abnormal psychology* (3rd ed.). New York: Norton.

Rotatori, A. F., Banbury, M., & Sisterhen, D. (1986). Overview of counseling exceptional students. In A. F. Rotatori, P. J. Gerber, F. W. Litton, & R. A. Fox (Eds.), *Counseling exceptional students* (pp. 21–38). New York: Human Sciences Press.

Rotatori, A. F., Gerber, P. J., Litton, F. W., & Fox, R. A. (Eds.). (1986). *Counseling exceptional students.* New York: Human Sciences Press.

Roth, E. A. (1987). A behavioral approach to art therapy. In J. A. Rubin (Ed.), *Approaches to art therapy: Theory and technique.* New York: Brunner/Mazel.

Rothenberg, P. S. (1995). *Race, class, and gender in the United States: An integrated study.* New York: St. Martin's Press.

Rowe, F. A. (1989). College students' perceptions of high school counselors. *The School Counselor, 36,* 260–264.

Rowe, W., Behrens, J. T., & Leach, M. M. (1995). Racial/ethnic identity and racial consciousness: Looking back and looking forward. In J. G. Ponterotto, J. M. Casas, L. A. Suzuki, & C. M. Alexander (Eds.), *Handbook of multicultural counseling* (pp. 218–235). Thousand Oaks, CA: Sage.

Ruben, A. M. (1989). Preventing school dropouts through classroom guidance. *Elementary School Guidance and Counseling, 24,* 21–29.

Rubin, J. A. (1987). Freudian psychoanalytic theory: Emphasis on uncovering and insight. In J. A. Rubin (Ed.), *Approaches to art therapy: Theory and technique.* New York: Brunner/Mazel.

Rubisch, J. C. (1995). Promoting postsecondary education in rural schools. *The School Counselor, 42*(5), 404–409.

Rudd, M. D. (1989). The prevalence of suicidal ideation among college students. *Suicide and Life-Threatening Behavior, 19,* 173–183.

Ruden, R. A., & Byalick, M. (1997). *The craving brain: The biobalance approach to controlling addiction.* New York: HarperCollins.

Rupert, P. A., & Baird, K. A. (2004). Managed care and the independent practice of psychology. *Professional Psychology: Research and Practice, 35*(2), 185–193.

Russell, R. L., & Lucariello, J. (1992). Narrative, yes; narrative ad infinitum, no! *American Psychologist, 47*(5), 671–672.

Russell, T., & Madsen, D. H. (1985). *Marriage counseling report user's guide.* Champaign, IL: Institute for Personality and Ability Testing.

Russo, T. J., & Kassera, W. (1989). A comprehensive needs-assessment package for secondary school guidance programs. *The School Counselor, 36,* 265–269.

Rutter, M. (1996). Transitions and turning points in developmental psychopathology: As applied to the age span between childhood and mid-adulthood. *International Journal of Behavioral Development, 19*(3), 603–626.

Rutter, M., Dunn, J., Plomin, R., Simonoff, E., Pickles, A., Maughan, B., Ormel, J., Meyer, J., & Eaves, L. (1997). Integrating nature and nurture: Implications of person-environment correlations and interactions for developmental psychopathology. *Development and Psychopathology, 9,* 335–364.

Ryan, N. E. (1999). *Career counseling and career choice goal attainment.* Unpublished doctoral dissertation, Loyola University, Chicago.

Saayman, G. S., Faber, P. A., & Saayman, R. V. (1988). Archetypal factors revealed in the study of marital breakdown: A Jungian perspective. *Journal of Analytical Psychology, 33,* 253–276.

Sager, C. (1976). *Marriage contracts and couple therapy.* New York: Brunner/Mazel.

Sakolske, D. H., & Janzen, H. L. (1987). Dependency. In A. Thomas & J. Grimes (Eds.), *Children's needs: Psychological perspectives* (pp. 157–166). Washington, DC: The National Association of School Psychologists.

Salkind, N. (1994). *Child development* (7th ed.). San Diego, CA: Harcourt Brace Jovanovich.

Salomone, P. R. (1988). Career counseling: Steps and stages beyond Parsons. *Career Development Quarterly, 36,* 218–221.

Salovey, P., & Mayer, J. D. (1990). Emotional intelligence. *Imagination, Cognition, and Personality, 9,* 185–211.

Sampson, J. P. (1990). Computer-assisted testing and the goals of counseling psychology. *The Counseling Psychologist, 18,* 227–239.

Sampson, J. P. (1994). Factors influencing the effective use of computer-assisted career guidance: The North American experience. *British Journal of Guidance and Counselling, 22*(1), 91–106.

Sampson, J. P., Jr., Shahnasarian, M., & Reardon, R. C. (1987). Computer-assisted career guidance: A national perspective on the use of DISCOVER and SIGI. *Journal of Counseling and Development, 65*(8), 416–419.

Samuels, A. (1985). *Jung and the post-Jungians.* London: Routledge & Kegan Paul.

Samuels, A. (1989). Analysis and pluralism: The politics of psyche. *Journal of Analytical Psychology, 34,* 33–51.

Sandhu, D. S., & Aspy, C. B. (1997). *Counseling for prejudice prevention and reduction.* Alexandria, VA: American Counseling Association.

Sandhu, D. S., & Portes, P. R. (1995). The proactive model of school counseling. *International Journal for the Advancement of Counselling, 18,* 11–20.

Satir, V. M. (1983). *Conjoint family therapy* (3rd ed.). Palo Alto, CA: Science and Behavior Books.

Satir, V. M. (1988). *The new peoplemaking.* Palo Alto, CA: Science and Behavior Books.

Savickas, M. L. (1994). A festschrift for Donald E. Super. *The Career Development Quarterly, 43*(1), 3.

Savickas, M. L. (1996). A framework for linking career theory and practice. In M. L. Savickas & W. B. Walsh (Eds.), *Handbook of career counseling theory and practice* (pp. 191–208). Palo Alto, CA: Davies-Black.

Savickas, M. L. (1997). Career adaptability: An integrative construct for life-span, life-space theory. *Career Development Quarterly, 45,* 247–259.

Savickas, M. L., & Walsh, W. B. (1996). Toward convergence between career theory and practice. In M. L. Savickas & W. B. Walsh (Eds.), *Handbook of career counseling theory and practice* (pp. xi–xvi). Palo Alto, CA: Davies-Black.

Sayger, T. V., Horne, A. M., & Glaser, B. A. (1993). Marital satisfaction and social learning family therapy for child conduct problems: Generalization of treatment effects. *Journal of Marital and Family Therapy, 19,* 393–402.

Schulte, J. M. (1992). The morality of influencing in counseling. In M. T. Burke & J. G. Miranti (Eds.), *Ethical and spiritual values in counseling* (pp. 107–120). Alexandria, VA: American Counseling Association.

Schultz, C., & Nystul, M. S. (1980). Mother-child interaction behavior as an outcome of theoretical models of parent group education. *Journal of Individual Psychology, 36,* 16–29.

Schultz, C., Nystul, M. S., & Law, H. (1980). Attitudinal outcomes of theoretical models of parent group education. *Journal of Individual Psychology, 37,* 107–112.

Schultz, W. C. (1977). *FIRO-B* (2nd ed.). Palo Alto, CA: Consulting Psychologists Press.

Scott, C. N., Kelly, F. D., & Tolbert, B. L. (1995). Realism, constructivism, and the individual psychology of Alfred Adler. *Individual Psychology: The Journal of Adlerian Theory, Research, and Practice, 51*(1), 5–20.

Schwartz, J. P., & Waldo, M. (2003). Interpersonal manifestations of lifestyle: Individual psychology integrated with interpersonal theory. *Journal of Mental Health Counseling, 25,* 101–111.

Seligman, L. (1986). The manuscript evaluation process used by AACD journals. *Journal of Counseling and Development, 65*(4), 189–192.

Seligman, L. (1994). *Developmental career counseling and assessment* (2nd. ed.). Thousand Oaks, CA: Sage.

Seligman, L. (1998). *Selecting effective treatments: A comprehensive, systematic guide to treating adult mental disorders* (2nd ed.). San Francisco: Jossey-Bass.

Seligman, M. (1991). *Learned optimism.* New York: Knopf.

Seligman, M. E. P. (1995). The effectiveness of psychotherapy: The consumer reports study. *American Psychologist, 50*(12), 965–974.

Selvini-Palazzoli, M. (1980). Why a long interval between sessions? The therapeutic control of the family-therapist suprasystem. In M. Andolfi & I. Zwerling (Eds.), *Dimensions of family therapy.* New York: Guilford Press.

Selzer, M. L. (1971). Michigan alcoholism screening test: The quest for a new diagnostic instrument. *American Journal of Psychiatry, 127,* 1653–1658.

Senge, P. M. (1990). *The fifth discipline: The art and practice of the learning organization.* New York: Doubleday/Currency.

Sexton, T. L., & Whiston, S. C. (1994). The status of the counseling relationship: An empirical review, theoretical implications and research directions. *The Counseling Psychologist, 22*(1), 6–78.

Shadish, W. R., Ragsdale, K., Glaser, R. R., & Montgomery, L. M. (1995). The efficacy and effectiveness of marital and family therapy: A perspective from meta-analysis. *Journal of Marital and Family Therapy, 21*(4), 345–360.

Shafranske, E. P. (Ed.). (1996). *Religion and clinical practice of psychology.* Washington, DC: American Psychological Association.

Shakespeare, W. (1938). *The works of William Shakespeare: Gathered into one volume.* New York: Oxford University Press.

Shannon, J. W., & Woods, W. J. (1991). Affirmative psychotherapy for gay men. *The Counseling Psychologist, 19*(2), 197–215.

Sharf, R. S. (2001). *Applying career development theory to counseling* (3rd ed.). Pacific Grove, CA: Brooks/Cole.

Shaver, P. R., & Brennan, K. A. (1992). Attachment styles and the "big five" personality traits: Their connections with each other and with romantic relationship outcomes. *Personality and Social Psychology Bulletin, 18,* 536–545.

Shaw, M. D., & Goodyear, R. K. (1984, April). Introduction to special issues on primary prevention. *The Personnel and Guidance Journal,* 444–445.

Shea, M. T., Pilkonis, P. A., Beckham, E., Collins, J. F., Elkin, I., Sotsky, S. M., & Docherty, J. P. (1990). Personality disorders and treatment outcome in the NIMH Treatment of Depression Collaborative Research Program. *American Journal of Psychiatry, 147,* 711–718.

Sherman, R., & Dinkmeyer, D. (1987). *Systems of family therapy: An Adlerian integration.* New York: Brunner/Mazel.

Sherrard, P. A. D., & Amatea, E. S. (1994). Looking through the looking glass: A preview. *Journal of Mental Health Counseling, 16*(1), 3–5.

Sherrard, P. A. D., & Amatea, E. S. (2003). Ecosystem theory. In D. Capuzzi & D. R. Gross (Eds.), *Counseling and psychotherapy: Theories and interventions* (3rd ed.). Columbus, OH: Merrill.

Sherwood-Hawes, A. (1995). Nontraditional approaches to counseling and psychotherapy. In D. Capuzzi & D. R. Douglas (Eds.), *Counseling and psychotherapy: Theories and interventions* (2nd ed.). Columbus, OH: Merrill.

Shields, C. G. (1986). Critiquing the new epistemologies: Towards minimum requirements for scientific theory of family therapy. *Journal of Marital and Family Therapy, 12,* 359–372.

Shneidman, E. S. (1976). A psychological theory of suicide. *Psychiatric Annals, 6,* 51–66.

Shneidman, E. S. (1984). Suicide. In R. Corsini (Ed.), *Encyclopedia of psychology* (Vol. 3) (pp. 383–386). New York: Wiley.

Shneidman, E. S., Farberow, N. L., & Litman, R. E. (1976). *The psychology of suicide.* New York: Aronson.

Shoda, Y., Mischel, W., & Peake, P. K. (1990). Predicting adolescent cognitive and self-regulatory competencies from preschool delay of gratification: Identifying diagnostic conditions. *Developmental Psychology, 26,* 978–986.

Sholevar, G. (1985). Marital therapy. In H. Kaplan & B. Sadock (Eds.), *Comprehensive textbook of psychiatry IV* (Vol. 2). Baltimore: Williams & Wilkins.

Shostrom, E. L. (Producer). (1965). *Three approaches to psychotherapy* (film). Orange, CA: Psychological Films.

Shulman, B. H. (1973). *Contributions to individual psychology.* Chicago: Alfred Adler Institute.

Sifneos, P. (1979). *Short-term dynamic psychotherapy.* New York: Plenum.

Sifneos, P. (1984). The current status of individual short-term dynamic psychotherapy and its future. *American Journal of Psychotherapy, 38*(4), 472–483.

Silver, R. A. (1987). A cognitive approach to art therapy. In J. A. Rubin (Ed.), *Approaches to art therapy: Theory and technique.* New York: Brunner/Mazel.

Silverman, D. (2001). *Interpreting qualitative data: Methods for analyzing talk, text, and interaction* (2nd ed.). London: Sage.

Silverman, D. (2004). Who cares about 'experience'? Missing issues in qualitative research. In D. Silverman (Ed.), *Qualitative research: Theory, method, and practice* (3rd ed.) (pp. 342–367). Thousand Oaks, CA: Sage.

Simons, A. D., Murphy, G. E., Levine, J. L., & Wetzel, R. D. (1986). Cognitive therapy and pharmacotherapy: Sustained improvement over one year. *Archives of General Psychiatry, 43,* 43–48.

Simpson, J. A., Rholes, W. S., & Nelligan, J. S. (1992). Support-seeking and support-giving within couples in an anxiety-provoking situation: The role of attachment styles. *Journal of Personality and Social Psychology, 62,* 434–446.

Sire, J. W. (1976). *The universe next door.* Downers, IL: Intervarsity.

Sisterhen, D., & Rotatori, A. F. (1986). Counseling the hearing-impaired child. In A. F. Rotatori, P. J. Gerber, F. W. Litton, & R. A. Fox (Eds.), *Counseling exceptional students* (pp. 162–178). New York: Human Sciences Press.

Skinner, B. F. (1938). *The behavior of organisms.* New York: Appleton-Century-Crofts.

Skinner, B. F. (1953). *Science and human behavior.* New York: Macmillan.

Skinner, B. F. (1961). *Cumulative record.* New York: Appleton-Century-Crofts.

Skinner, B. F. (1990). Can psychology be a science of mind? *American Psychologist, 45,* 1206–1210.

Sklare, G., Keener, R., & Mas, C. (1990). Preparing members for "here and now" group counseling. *Journal for Specialists in Group Work, 15*(3), 141–148.

Sloane, B., Staples, F., Cristol, A., Yorkston, N., & Whipple, K. (1975). *Psychotherapy versus behavior therapy.* Cambridge, MA: Harvard University Press.

Smart, D. W., & Smart, J. F. (1997). DSM-IV and culturally sensitive diagnosis: Some observations for counselors. *Journal of Counseling and Development, 75*(5), 392–398.

Smart, J. F., & Smart, D. W. (1995). Acculturative stress: The experience of the Hispanic immigrant. *The Counseling Psychologist, 23*(1), 25–42.

Smith, D. C. (1993). Exploring the religious-spiritual needs of the dying. *Journal of Counseling and Values, 37,* 71–77.

Smith, D. C., & Sandu, D. S. (2004). Toward a positive perspective on violence prevention in schools: Building connections. *Journal of Counseling and Development, 82*(3), 287–293.

Smith, H. B., & Robinson, G. P. (1995). Mental health counseling: Past, present, and future. *Journal of Counseling and Development, 74*(2), 158–162.

Smith, M. B. (1994). Selfhood at risk: Postmodern perils and the perils of postmodernism. *American Psychologist, 49*(5), 405–411.

Smith, M. L., & Glass, G. J. (1977). Meta-analysis of psychotherapy outcome studies. *American Psychologist, 32,* 752–760.

Smith, M. L., Glass, G. V., & Miller, T. I. (1980). *The benefits of psychotherapy.* Baltimore: Johns Hopkins University Press.

Smith, R. L. (1994). Directions in marriage and family graduate level training. *Counselor Education and Supervision, 34,* 180–183.

Smith, R. L., Carlson, J., Stevens-Smith, P., & Dennison, M. (1995). Marriage and family counseling. *Journal of Counseling and Development, 2*(74), 154–157.

Snell, W. E., Jr., Hampton, B. R., & McManus, P. (1992). The impact of counselor and participant gender on willingness to discuss relational topics: Development of the relationship disclosure scale. *Journal of Counseling and Development, 70,* 409–416.

Snyder, D. K. (1981). *Marital Satisfaction Inventory (MSI).* Los Angeles: Western Psychological Services.

Snyder, J. J. (1977). Reinforcement analysis of interaction in problem and nonproblem families. *Journal of Abnormal Psychology, 86,* 528–535.

Sobell, M. B., & Sobell, L. C. (1984). The aftermath of heresy: A response to Pendery et al.'s (1982) critique of "Individualized Behavior Therapy for Alcoholics." *Behavior Research and Therapy, 22,* 413–447.

Sodowsky, G. R., Kwan, K. L. K., & Pannu, R. (1995). Ethnic identity of Asians in the United States. In J. G. Ponterotto, J. M. Casas, L. A. Suzuki, & C. M.

Alexander (Eds.), *Handbook of multicultural counseling* (pp. 123–154). Thousand Oaks, CA: Sage.

Solomon, J. (1996, May 20). Breaking the silence. *Newsweek, 20–24.*

Solomon, M. A. (1973). A developmental, conceptual premise for family therapy. *Family Process, 12,* 179–188.

Sommers-Flanagan, R., Barrett-Hakanson, T. B., Clarke, C., & Sommers-Flanagan, J. (2000). A psychoeducational school-based coping and social skills group for depressed students. *Journal for Specialists in Group Work, 25,* 170–190.

Sonstegard, M. A., Hagerman, H., & Bitter, J. (1975). Motivation modification: An Adlerian approach. *The Individual Psychologist, 12,* 17–22.

Sparks, R. W., & Deck, J. W. (1994). Melodic intonation therapy. In R. Chapey (Ed.), *Language intervention strategies in adult aphasia* (pp. 368–379). Baltimore: Williams & Wilkins.

Spencer, G. (1977). Effectiveness of an introductory course in TA. *Transactional Analysis Journal, 7,* 346–349.

Spengler, P. M., Blustein, D. L., & Strohmer, D. C. (1990). Diagnostic and treatment overshadowing of vocational problems by personal problems. *Journal of Counseling Psychology, 37*(4), 372–381.

Sperry, L. (1987). ERIC: A cognitive map for guiding brief therapy and health care counseling. *Individual Psychology, 43*(2), 237–241.

Sperry, L. (1989a). Assessment in marital therapy: A couples-centered biopsychosocial approach. *Individual Psychology: The Journal of Adlerian Theory, Research, and Practice, 45,* 446–451.

Sperry, L. (1989b). Varieties of brief therapy: An introduction. *Individual Psychology: The Journal of Adlerian Theory, Research, and Practice, 45*(1/2), 1–2.

Sperry, L., & Carlson, J. (1991). *Marital therapy: Integrating theory and technique.* Denver, CO: Love.

Spiegelman, J. M. (1989). The one and the many: Jung and the post-Jungians. *Journal of Analytical Psychology, 34,* 53–71.

Spitz, R. (1946). Anaditic depression. *Psychoanalytic Study of the Child, 2,* 113–117.

Spitzer, R. L., Gibbon, M., Skodol, A. E., Williams, J. B., & First, M. B. (2002). *The DSM-IV-TR casebook.* Washington, DC: American Psychiatric Press.

Spivak, H., & Prothrow-Stith, D. (2001). The need to address bullying: An important component of violence prevention. *JAMA, 285*(16), 2131–2132.

Spruill, D. A., & Fong, M. L. (1990). Defining the domain of mental health counseling: From identity confusion to consensus. *Journal of Mental Health Counseling, 12*(1), 12–23.

Sroufe, L. A. (1997). Psychopathology as an outcome of development. *Development and Psychopathology, 9,* 251–268.

Sroufe, L. A., & Cooper, R. G. (1996). *Child development: Its nature and course* (3rd ed.). New York: McGraw-Hill.

Stabler, B. (1984). *Children's drawings.* Chapel Hill, NC: Health Science Consortium.

Stanard, R., & Hazler, R. (1995). Legal and ethical implications of HIV and duty to warn for counselors: Does Tarasoff apply? *Journal of Counseling and Development, 73*(4), 397–400.

Starker, S. (1988). Psychologists and self-help books: Attitudes and prescriptive practices of clinicians. *American Journal of Psychotherapy, 42,* 448–455.

Steenbarger, B. N. (1992). Toward science-practice integration in brief counseling and therapy. *The Counseling Psychologist, 20*(3), 403–450.

Stern, M., & Newland, L. M. (1994). Working with children: Providing a framework for the roles of counseling psychologist. *The Counseling Psychologist, 22*(3), 402–425.

Sternberg, R. J., Wagner, R. K., Williams, W. M., & Horvath, J. A. (1995). Testing common sense. *American Psychologist, 50*(11), 912–926.

Stile, S. W. (1993). *N=1 handbook: Designs for inquiry in special education and related services.* Dubuque, IA: Kendall/Hunt.

Stinnet, N., & DeFrain, J. (1985). *Secrets of strong families.* Boston: Little, Brown.

Stoltz-Loike, M. (1996). Annual review: Practice and research in career development and counseling—1995. *The Career Development Quarterly, 99–140.*

Strachey, J. (Ed.). (1953–1974). *The standard edition of the complete psychological works of Sigmund Freud.* London: Hogarth Press.

Strassberg, Z., Dodge, K. A., Pettit, G. S., & Bates, J. E. (1994). Spanking in the home and children's subsequent aggression toward kindergarten peers. *Development and Psychopathology, 6,* 445–462.

Straus, M. A., Gelles, R. J., & Steinmetz, S. (1980). *Behind closed doors: Violence in the American family.* Garden City, NY: Doubleday/Anchor.

Stricker, G., & Trierweiler, S. J. (1995). The local clinical scientist: A bridge between science and practice. *American Psychologist, 50*(12), 995–1002.

Strober, M., Hanna, G., & McCracken, J. (1989). Bipolar illness. In C. Last & M. Hersens (Eds.), *Handbook of child psychiatric diagnosis.* New York: Wiley.

Strohmer, D. C., & Biggs, D. A. (1983). Effects of counselor disability status on disabled subjects' perceptions of counselor attractiveness and expertness. *Journal of Counseling Psychology, 30,* 202–208.

Strong, S. R. (1968). Counseling: An interpersonal influence process. *Journal of Counseling Psychology, 15,* 215–224.

Strong, S. R., & Claiborn, C. D. (1982). *Change through interaction.* New York: John Wiley & Sons.

Strupp, H. H. (1992). The future of psychodynamic psychotherapy. *Psychotherapy, 29*(1), 21–27.

Stuart, R. B. (1983). *Couples' pre-counseling inventory, counselor's guide.* Champaign, IL: Research Press.

Sue, D. W. (1978). World views and counseling. *The Personnel and Guidance Journal, 56,* 458–462.

Sue, D. W. (1981). *Counseling the culturally different: Theory and practice.* New York: John Wiley & Sons.

Sue, D. W., Arredondo, P., & McDavis, R. J. (1992). Multicultural counseling competencies and standards: A call to the profession. *Journal of Counseling and Development, 70,* 477–486.

Sue, D. W., Bermier, T. E., Durran, A., Feinberg, L., Pedersen, P., Smith, E. T., & Vasquez-Nuttall, E. (1982). Position paper: Cross-cultural counseling competencies. *The Counseling Psychologist, 10*(2), 45–52.

Sue, D. W., Ivey, A. E., & Pedersen, P. B. (1996). *A theory of multicultural counseling and therapy.* Pacific Grove, CA: Brooks/Cole.

Sue, D. W., & Sue, D. (1977). Barriers to effective cross-cultural counseling. *Journal of Counseling Psychology, 24,* 420–429.

Sue, D. W., & Sue, D. (1999). *Counseling the culturally different* (3rd ed.). New York: John Wiley & Sons.

Sue, S. (1988). Psychotherapeutic services for ethnic minorities. *American Psychologist, 43*(4), 301–308.

Sue, S., Zane, N., & Young, K. (1994). Research on psychotherapy with culturally diverse populations. In A. E. Bergin & S. L. Garfield (Eds.), *Handbook of psychotherapy and behavior change* (4th ed.) (pp. 783–820). New York: John Wiley & Sons.

Suinn, R. M., Rickard-Figueroa, K., Lew, S., & Vigil, S. (1987). The Suinn-Lew Asian Self-Identity Acculturation Scale: An initial report. *Education and Psychological Measurement, 47,* 401–407.

Suit, J. L., & Paradise, L. V. (1985). Effects of metaphors and cognitive complexity on perceived counselor characteristics. *Journal of Counseling Psychology, 32,* 23–28.

Sullivan, B. F., & Schwebel, A. I. (1996). Birth-order position, gender, and irrational relationship beliefs. *Individual Psychology: The Journal of Adlerian Theory, Research, and Practice, 52*(1), 54–64.

Sullivan, H. S. (1968). *The interpersonal theory of psychiatry.* New York: Norton.

Sundberg, N. D. (1977). *Assessment of persons.* Englewood Cliffs, NJ: Prentice-Hall.

Super, D. E. (1957). *The psychology of careers.* New York: Harper & Row.

Super, D. E. (1970). *Work values inventory.* Boston: Houghton Mifflin.

Super, D. E. (1980). A life-span, life-space approach to career development. *Journal of Vocational Behavior, 16,* 282–298.

Super, D. E. (1990). A life-span, life-space approach to career development. In D. Brown & L. Brooks (Eds.), *Career choice and development: Applying contemporary theories to practice* (pp. 197–261). San Francisco: Jossey-Bass.

Super, D. E. (2002). A life-span, life-space approach. In D. Brown, L. Brooks, & Associates (Eds.), *Career choice and development* (4th ed.). San Francisco: Jossey-Bass.

Sutton, J. M., Jr., & Southworth, R. S. (1990). The effect of the rural setting on school counselors. *The School Counselor, 37,* 173–178.

Svanum, S., & McAdoo, W. G. (1989). Predicting rapid relapse following treatment for chemical dependence: A matched subjects design. *Journal of Consulting and Clinical Psychology, 57,* 222–226.

Swan, G. E., & MacDonald, M. D. (1978). Behavior therapy in practice: A national survey of behavior therapists. *Behavior Therapy, 9,* 799–807.

Swanson, J. L. (1992). Vocational behavior, 1989–1991: Life-span career development and reciprocal interaction of work and nonwork. *Journal of Vocational Behavior, 41,* 101–161.

Swanson, J. L., & Gore, P. A. (2000). Advances in vocational psychology, theory, and research. In S. Brown & R. Lent (Eds.), *Handbook of counseling psychology* (3rd ed.) (pp. 233–269). New York: John Wiley.

Sweeney, T. J. (1988). Building strong school counseling programs: Implications for counselor preparation. In G. R. Walz & J. C. Bleuer (Eds.), *Building strong school counseling programs.* Alexandria, VA: American Association for Counseling and Development.

Takanishi, R. (1993). The opportunities of adolescence—research, interventions, and policy. *American Psychologist, 48,* 85–87.

Talbutt, L. C. (1986). The abused child. In L. B. Golden & D. Capuzzi (Eds.), *Helping families help children* (pp. 45–58). Springfield, IL: Charles C Thomas.

Talerico, C. J. (1986). The expressive arts and creativity as a form of therapeutic experience in the field of mental health. *The Journal of Creative Behavior, 20*(4), 229–247.

Talkington, L. W., & Riley, J. B. (1971). Reduction diets and aggression in institutionalized mentally retarded patients. *American Journal of Mental Deficiency, 76,* 370–372.

Tanaka-Matsumi, J., & Higginbotham, H. N. (1994). Clinical application of behavior therapy across ethnic and cultural boundaries. *The Behavior Therapist, 17*(6), 123–126.

Tarasoff v. Board of Regents of the University of California, 13 Cal. 3d 177, 529 P.2d 553 (1974), vacated, 17 Cal. 3d 425, 551 P.2d 334 (1976).

Task Force on Promotion and Dissemination of Psychological Procedures. (1995). Training in and dissemination of empirically validated psychological treatments. *The Clinical Psychologist, 48,* 3–23.

Taylor, N. B., & Pryor, R. G. L. (1985). Exploring the process of compromise in career decision making. *Journal of Vocational Behavior, 27,* 171–190.

Taylor, R. (1979). *The gifted and the talented.* Englewood, CO: Educational Consultant Agency.

Taylor, R. M., & Morrison, L. P. (1984). *Taylor-Johnson temperament analysis manual.* Los Angeles: Psychological Publications.

Taylor, S. E., & Brown, J. D. (1988). Illusion and well-being: A social psychological perspective on mental health. *Psychological Bulletin, 103,* 193–210.

Teasdale, J. D., Fennell, M. J. V., Hibbert, G. A., & Amies, P. L. (1984). Cognitive therapy for major depressive disorder in primary care. *British Journal of Psychiatry, 144,* 400–406.

Tennyson, W. W., Miller, G. D., Skovholt, T. G., & Williams, R. C. (1989). Secondary school counselors: What do they do? What is important? *The School Counselor, 36,* 253–259.

Terrell, M. D. (1993). Ethnocultural factors and substance abuse: Toward culturally sensitive treatment models. *Psychology of Addictive Behaviors, 7*(3), 162–167.

Tesolowski, D. G., Rosenberg, H., & Stein, R. J. (1983, July, August, September). Advocacy intervention: A responsibility of human service professionals. *Journal of Rehabilitation,* 12–17.

Teyber, E. (2000). *Interpersonal process in psychotherapy: A relational approach* (4th ed.). Pacific Grove, CA: Brooks/Cole.

Thomas, K. R., & Weinrach, S. G. (2004). Mental health counseling and the AMCD multicultural counseling competencies: A debate. *Journal of Mental Health Counseling, 1,* 41–43.

Thomas, M. D. (1989). The role of the secondary school counselor: The counselor in effective schools. *The School Counselor, 36,* 249–252.

Thompson, C. E., & Neville, H. A. (1999). Racism, mental health, and mental health practices. *The Counseling Psychologist, 27*(2), 155–223.

Thompson, C. L., & Rudolph, L. B. (2003). *Counseling children* (6th ed.). Pacific Grove, CA: Brooks/Cole.

Thompson, J. M., Flynn, R. J., & Griffith, S. A. (1994). Congruence and coherence as predictors of congruent employment outcomes. *Career Development Quarterly, 42,* 271–281.

Thompson, L. W., Gallagher, D., & Breckenridge, J. S. (1987). Comparative effectiveness of psychotherapies for depressed elders. *Journal of Consulting and Clinical Psychology, 55,* 385–390.

Thompson, R. A. (1993). Posttraumatic stress and posttraumatic loss debriefing: Brief strategic intervention for survivors of sudden loss. *The School Counselor, 41,* 16–22.

Thompson, R. A. (1996). *Counseling techniques: Improving relationships with others, ourselves, our families, and our environment.* Washington, DC: Accelerated Development.

Thompson, R. A., & Wilcox, B. L. (1995). Child maltreatment research. *American Psychologist, 50*(9), 789–793.

Thorndike, E. L. (1920). Intelligence and its uses. *Harper's Magazine, 140,* 227–235.

Tobler, N. S. (1986). Meta-analysis of 143 adolescent drug prevention programs: Quantitative outcome results of program participants compared to a control or comparison group. *Journal of Drug Issues, 16,* 537–568.

Topper, M. D. (1985). Navajo "alcoholism": Drinking, alcohol abuse, and treatment in a changing cultural environment. In L. A. Bennett & G. M. Ames (Eds.), *The American experience with alcohol: Contrasting cultural perspectives.* New York: Plenum Press.

Towberman, D. B. (1992). Client-counselor similarity and the client's perception of the treatment environment. *Journal of Offender Rehabilitation, 18*(1/2), 159–171.

Tremblay, R. E., LeBlanc, M., & Schwartzman, A. E. (1988). The predictive power of first-grade peer and teacher ratings of behavior: Sex differences in antisocial behavior and personality at adolescence. *Journal of Abnormal Child Psychology, 16,* 571–583.

Trevino, J. G. (1996). Worldview and change in cross-cultural counseling. *The Counseling Psychologist, 24*(2), 198–215.

Truax, C. B., & Carkhuff, R. R. (1967). *Toward effective counseling and psychotherapy.* Chicago: Aldine.

Truax, C. B., & Mitchell, K. M. (1971). Research on certain therapist interpersonal skills in relation to process and outcome. In A. E. Bergin & S. L. Garfield (Eds.), *Handbook of psychotherapy and behavior change.* New York: John Wiley & Sons.

Trzepacz, P. T., & Baker, R. (1993). *The psychiatric mental status examination.* New York: Ford University Press.

Tuma, J. M. (1989). Mental health services in children: The state of the art. *American Psychologist, 44*(2), 188–199.

Turner, R. M., & Ascher, L. M. (1979). Controlled comparison of progressive relaxation, stimulus control, and paradoxical intention therapies for insomnia. *Journal of Consulting and Clinical Psychology, 47,* 500–508.

Tyrer, K., Catalan, J., Schmidt, U., Davidson, K., Dent, J., Tata, P., Thornton, S., Barber, J., & Thompson, S. (1999). Manual-assisted cognitive-behaviour therapy (MACT): A randomizied controlled trial of a brief intervention with bibliotherapy in the treatment of recurrent self-harm. *Psychological Medicine, 29,* 19–25.

Tyson, J. A., & Wall, S. M. (1983). Effect of inconsistency between counselor verbal and nonverbal behavior on perceptions of counselor attributes. *Journal of Counseling Psychology, 30,* 433–437.

Unger, R. (1989). Selection and composition criteria in group psychotherapy. *Journal for Specialists in Group Work, 14*(3), 151–157.

Usher, C. H. (1989). Recognizing cultural bias in counseling theory and practice: The case of Rogers. *Journal of Multicultural Counseling and Development, 17,* 62–71.

Vacc, N. A. (1989). Group counseling: C. H. Patterson— A personalized view. *Journal for Specialists in Group Work, 14*(1), 4–15.

Vacha-Haase, T., Davenport, D. S., & Kerewsky, S. D. (2004). Problematic students: Gatekeeping practices of academic professional psychology programs. *Professional Psychology: Research and Practice, 35*(2), 115–122.

Vail-Smith, K., Knight, S. M., & White, D. M. (1995). Children of substance abusers in the elementary school: A survey of counselor perceptions. *Elementary School Guidance and Counseling, 29*(3), 163–176.

Valliant, G. E. (1977). *Adaptation to life.* Boston: Little, Brown.

Valliant, G. E. (1983). *The natural history of alcoholism.* Cambridge, MA: Harvard University Press.

Van Hoose, W. H. (1980). Ethics in counseling. *Counseling and Human Development, 13*(1), 1–12.

Van Slyck, M., Stern, M., & Zak-Place, J. (1996). Promoting optimal adolescent development through conflict resolution education, training, and practice: An innovative approach for counseling psychologist. *The Counseling Psychologist, 24*(3), 433–461.

VandenBos, G. R. (1996). Outcome assessment of psychotherapy. *American Psychologist, 51*(10), 1005–1006.

Vera, E. M., & Speight, S. L. (2003). Multicultural competence, social justice, and counseling psychology. *The Counseling Psychologist, 31*(3), 253–272.

Vernon, A. (1995). Working with children, adolescents, and their parents: Practical application of developmental theory. *Counseling and Human Development, 27*(7), 1–12.

Vernon, P. E., & Parry, J. B. (1949). *Personnel selection in the British forces.* London: University of London Press.

Vinson, M. L. (1995). Employing family therapy in group counseling with college students: Similarities and a technique employed in both. *Journal for Specialists in Group Work, 20*(4), 240–252.

Volkow, N. D., Wong, G. J., Fischman, M. W., Foltin, R. W., Fowler, J. S., Abumrad, N. N., Vitkuns, S., Logan, J., Gatley, S. J., Poppas, N., Hitzemann, R., & Shea, C. E. (1997). Relationship between subjective effects of cocaine and dopamine transporter occupancy. *Nature, 386,* 827–833.

Von Bertalanffy, L. V. (1968). *General systems theory: Foundations, development, application.* New York: Braziller.

Vondracek, F. W., Lerner, R. M., & Schulenberg, J. M. (1986). *Career development: A lifespan approach.* Hillsdale, NJ: Lawrence Erlbaum.

Vontress, C. E. (1973). Counseling the racial and ethnic minorities. *Focus on Guidance, 5*(6), 1–10.

Vontress, C. E. (1988). An existential approach to cross-cultural counseling. *Journal of Multicultural Counseling and Development, 16,* 73–83.

Vossekuil, B., Reddy, M., & Fein R. (2001). The Secret Service's safe school initiative. *Education Digest, 66*(6), 410.

Wachtel, P. L. (1991). From eclecticism to synthesis: Towards a more seamless psychotherapeutic integration. *Journal of Psychotherapy Integration, 1*(1), 43–54.

Wadeson, H. (1980). *Art psychotherapy.* New York: John Wiley & Sons.

Wagner, E. (1971). Structural analysis: A theory of personality based on projective techniques. *Journal of Personality Assessment, 35,* 422–435.

Wagner, J., & Gartner, C. G. (1996). *Psychiatric Services, 47*(1), 15–20.

Wagner, W. G. (1994). Counseling with children: An opportunity for tomorrow. *The Counseling Psychologist, 22*(3), 381–401.

Wagner, W. G. (1996). Optimal development in adolescence: What it is and how it can be encouraged. *The Counseling Psychologist, 24*(3), 360–399.

Wahler, R. G., & Dumas, J. E. (1987). Family factors in childhood psychopathology: Toward a coercion neglect model. In T. Jacob (Ed.), *Family interaction and psychopathology.* New York: Plenum Press.

Wakefield, J. C. (1997). When is development disordered? Developmental psychopathology and the harmful dysfunction analysis of mental disorder. *Development and Psychopathology, 9,* 193–229.

Waldo, M., & Bauman, S. (1998). Regrouping the categorization of group work: A goals and process (GAP) matrix for groups. *Journal for Specialists in Group Work, 23*(2), 215–224.

Walsh, W. B. (1990). Putting assessment in context. *The Counseling Psychologist, 18,* 262–265.

Walsh, W. B., & Srsic, C. (1995). Annual review: Vocational behavior and career development—1994. *Career Development Quarterly, 44*(2), 98–145.

Walter, J., & Peller, J. (1992). *Becoming solution-focused in brief therapy.* New York: Brunner/Mazel.

Wampold, B. E., Lichtenberg, J. W., & Waehler, C. A. (2002). Principles of empirically supported interventions in counseling psychology. *The Counseling Psychologist, 30,* 197–217.

Wartik, N. (2001, February). Bullying: A serious business. *Child,* 78–84.

Warwar, S., & Greenberg, L. S. (2000). Advances in theories of change and counseling. In S. D. Brown & R. W. Lent (Eds.), *Handbook of counseling psychology* (3rd ed.) (pp. 571–600). New York: Wiley & Sons.

Wastell, C. A. (1996). Feminist developmental theory: Implications for counseling. *Journal of Counseling and Development, 74*(6), 575–581.

Watkins, C. E. (1993). Person-centered theory and the contemporary practice of psychological testing. *Counseling Psychology Quarterly, 6*(1), 59–67.

Watkins, C. E., & Campbell, V. L. (1990). Testing and assessment in counseling psychology. *The Counseling Psychologist, 18,* 189–197.

Watkins, C. E., Jr., Lopez, F. G., Campbell, V. L., & Himmell, C. D. (1986). Contemporary counseling psychology: Results of a national survey. *Journal of Counseling Psychology, 33,* 301–309.

Watkins, C. E., Jr., Schneider, L. J., Cox, J. R. H., & Reinberg, J. A. (1987). Clinical psychology and counseling psychology: On similarities and differences revisited. *Professional Psychology: Research and Practice, 18,* 530–535.

Watkins, C. E., Jr., & Subich, L. M. (1995). Annual review, 1992–1994: Career development, reciprocal work/non-work interaction, and women's workforce participation. *Journal of Vocational Behavior, 47,* 109–163.

Watkins, E. (1984). The individual psychology of Alfred Adler: Towards an Adlerian vocational theory. *Journal of Vocational Behavior, 24,* 27–48.

Watts, A. G. (1996). Toward a policy for lifelong career development: A transatlantic perspective. *Career Development Quarterly, 45*(1), 41–53.

Watts, R. E. (1993, Spring). Developing a personal theory of counseling: A brief guide for students. *Texas Counseling Association Journal,* 103–104.

Watts, R. E. (2000). Entering the new millennium: Is individual psychology still relevant? *Journal of Individual Psychology, 56,* 21–30.

Watts, R. E., & Pietrzak, D. (2000). Adlerian "encouragement" and the therapeutic process of solution-focused brief therapy. *Journal of Counseling and Development, 78,* 442–447.

Watts, R. E., Trusty, J., & Lim, M. (1996). Characteristics of healthy families as a model of systemic social interest. *Canadian Journal of Adlerian Psychology, 26*(1), 1–12.

Watzlawick, P., Weakland, J. H., & Fisch, R. (1974). *Change: Principles of problem formation and problem resolution.* New York: Norton.

Webster-Stratton, C. (1990). Long-term follow-up with young conduct problem children: From preschool to grade school. *Journal of Clinical Child Psychology, 19,* 144–149.

Weighill, V. E., Hodge, J., & Peck, D. F. (1983). Keeping appointments with clinical psychologists. *British Journal of Clinical Psychology, 22,* 143–144.

Weikel, W. J. (1985). The American Mental Health Counselors Association. *Journal of Counseling and Development, 63,* 457–460.

Weikel, W. J., & Taylor, S. S. (1979). AMHCA: Membership profile and five journal preferences. *AMHCA Journal, 1,* 89–94.

Weinberg, R. S., Hughes, H. H., Critelli, J. W., England, R., & Jackson, A. (1984). Effects of pre-existing and manipulated self-efficacy on weight loss in a self-control program. *Journal of Research in Personality, 18,* 352–358.

Weiner, I. B. (1992). *Psychological disturbance in adolescence.* New York: Wiley.

Weinrach, S. G. (1988). Cognitive therapist: A dialogue with Aaron Beck. *Journal of Counseling and Development, 67*(3), 159–164.

Weinrach, S. G. (1995). Rational emotive behavior therapy: A tough-minded therapy for a tender-minded profession. *Journal of Counseling and Development, 73*(3), 296–300.

Weinrach, S. G., & Srebalus, D. J. (2002). Holland's theory of careers. In D. Brown, L. Brooks, & Associates (Eds.), *Career choice and development* (4th ed.). San Francisco: Jossey-Bass.

Weinrach, S. G., & Thomas, K. R. (2002). A critical analysis of the multicultural counseling competencies: Implications for the practice of mental health counseling. *Journal of Mental Health Counseling, 24,* 20–35.

Weinrach, S. G. & Thomas K. R. (2004). The AMCD multicultural counseling competencies: A critically flowed initiative. *Journal of Mental Health Counseling, 26,* 81–93.

Weissberg, R. P., Caplan, M., & Harwood, R. L. (1991). Promoting competent, young people in competence-enhancing environments: A systems-based perspective on primary prevention. *Journal of Consulting and Clinical Psychology, 59,* 830–841.

Weisz, J. R., Weiss, B., & Donenberg, G. R. (1992). The lab versus the clinic: Effects of child and adolescent psychotherapy. *American Psychologist, 47*(12), 1578–1585.

Welch, I. D., & McCarroll, L. (1993). The future role of school counselors. *The School Counselor, 41*(1), 48–53.

Wells, N. F., & Stevens, T. (1984). Music as a stimulus for creative fantasy in group psychotherapy with young adolescents. *The Arts in Psychotherapy, 11,* 71–76.

Werner, E. E. (1986). Resident offspring of alcoholics: A longitudinal study from birth to age 18. *Journal of Studies on Alcoholism, 47,* 34–41.

Werner, E. E. (1992). The children of Kauai: Resiliency and recovery in adolescence and adulthood. *Journal of Adolescent Health, 13,* 262–268.

Werner, E. E., & Smith, R. S. (1982). *Vulnerable but not invincible: A longitudinal study of resilient children and youth.* New York: McGraw-Hill.

Werner, E. E. & Smith, R. S. (1992). *Overcoming the odds: High risk children from birth to adulthood.* Ithaca, NY: Cornell University Press.

West, J. D., Hosie, T. W., & Mackey, J. A. (1988). The counselor's role in mental health: An evaluation. *Counselor Education and Supervision, 27,* 233–239.

Westefeld, J. S., Range, L. M., Rogers, J. R., Maples, M. R., Bromley, J. L. & Alcorn, J. (2000). Suicide: An overview. *The Counseling Psychologist, 28,* 445–510.

Westgate, C. E. (1996). Spiritual wellness and depression. *Journal of Counseling and Development, 75*(1), 26–35.

Westwood, M. J., & Ishiyama, F. I. (1990). The communication process as a critical intervention for client change in cross-cultural counseling. *Journal of Multicultural Counseling and Development, 18*(4), 163–171.

Whiston, S. C., & Keller, B. K. (2004). The influence of family of origin on career development: A review and analysis. *The Counseling Psychologist, 32*(4), 493–568.

Whiston, S. C., Sexton, T. L., & Lasoff, D. L. (1998). Career-intervention outcome: A replication and extension of Oliver and Spokane (1988). *Journal of Counseling Psychology, 45,* 150–165.

Whitaker, C. A. (1976). The hindrance of theory in clinical work. In P. J. Guerin (Ed.), *Family therapy: Theory and practice.* New York: Gardner Press.

Whitaker, C. A. (1977). Process techniques of family therapy. *Interaction, 1,* 4–19.

Whitaker, C. A., & Bumberry, W. M. (1988). *Dancing with the family: A symbolic-experiential approach.* New York: Brunner/Mazel.

Whitaker, C. A., & Keith, D. V. (1981). Symbolic-experiential family therapy. In A. S. Gurman & D. P. Kniskern (Eds.), *Handbook of family therapy* (pp. 187–225). New York: Brunner/Mazel.

White, J. A., & Allers, C. T. (1994). Play therapy with abused children: A review of the literature. *Journal of Counseling and Development, 72*(4), 390–394.

White, M., & Epston, D. (1990). *Narrative means to therapeutic ends.* New York: Norton.

Whitledge, J. (1994). Cross-cultural counseling: Implications for school counselors in enhancing student learning. *The School Counselor, 41*(5), 314–318.

Wickman, S. A., & Campbell, C. (2003). An analysis of how Carl Rogers enacted client-centered conversations with Gloria. *Journal of Counseling and Development, 81,* 178–184.

Wickman, S. A., Daniels, M. H., White, L. J., & Fesmire, S. A. (1999). A "primer" in conceptual metaphor for counselors. *Journal of Counseling and Development, 77*(4), 389–394.

Wiggins, J. D. (1985). Six steps towards counseling program accountability. *NASSP Bulletin, 69*(485), 28–31.

Wiggins-Frame, M. (1998). The ethics of counseling via the Internet. *The Family Journal: Counseling and Therapy for Couples and Families, 5*(4), 328–330.

Wilcoxon, S. A. (1985). Healthy family functioning: The other side of family pathology. *Journal of Counseling and Development, 63,* 495–499.

Wilkerson, C. D. (1967). The effects of four methods of test score presentation to eighth-grade students. *Dissertation Abstracts International.* 1318A (order number 67–12661)

Wilkinson, W. K., & McNeil, K. (1996). *Research for the helping professions.* Pacific Grove, CA: Brooks/Cole.

Wilson, G. T. (2005). Behavior therapy. In R. J. Corsini (Ed.), *Current psychotherapies* (7th ed.). Itasca, IL: F. E. Peacock.

Wilson, G. T., & Fairburn, C. G. (1993). Cognitive treatments for eating disorders. *Journal of Consulting and Clinical Psychology, 61,* 261–269.

Wilson, J. Q., & Hernstein, R. J. (1985). *Crime and human nature.* New York: Simon & Schuster.

Wilson, L. (1987). Symbolism and art therapy: Theory and clinical practice. In J. A. Rubin (Ed.), *Approaches to art therapy: Theory and technique.* New York: Brunner/Mazel.

Wilson, R. E., Rapin, L. S., & Haley-Banez, L. (2000). *Association for specialists in group work: Professional standards for the training of group workers.* Alexandria, VA: American Counseling Association.

Wislocki, A. (1981). Movement is their medium: Dance movement methods in special education. *Milieu Therapy, 1,* 49–54.

Witmer, J. M., & Sweeney, T. J. (1995). A holistic model for wellness and prevention over the life span. In M. T. Burke & J. G. Miranti (Eds.), *Counseling: The spiritual dimension* (pp. 19–40). Alexandria, VA: American Counseling Association.

Witty, C. (1980). *Mediation and society: Conflict management in Lebanon.* New York: Academic.

Wogan, M., & Norcross, J. C. (1985). Dimensions of therapeutic skills and techniques: Empirical identification, therapist correlates, and predictive utility. *Psychotherapy, 22,* 63–74.

Wolfe, D. A. (1988). Child abuse and neglect. In E. J. Mash & L. G. Terdal (Eds.), *Behavioral assessment of childhood disorders* (2nd ed.) (pp. 627–679). New York: Guilford Press.

Wolpe, J. (1958). *Psychotherapy by reciprocal inhibition.* Stanford, CA: Stanford University Press.

Wolpe, J. (1973). *The practice of behavior therapy* (2nd ed.). New York: Pergamon Press.

Woody, R. H., Hansen, J. C., & Rossberg, R. H. (1989). *Counseling psychology: Strategies and services.* Pacific Grove, CA: Brooks/Cole.

Worthington, E. L., Jr. (1989). Religious faith across the life span: Implications for counseling and research. *The Counseling Psychologist, 17,* 555–612.

Wright, R. (1994). *The moral animal: The new science of evolutionary psychology.* New York: Pantheon Books.

Wubbolding, R. (1986). *Reality therapy training.* Cincinnati: Center for Reality Therapy.

Wubbolding, R. (1990). *Expanding reality therapy: Group counseling and multicultural dimensions.* Cincinnati, OH: Real World Publications.

Wubbolding, R. (2000). *Reality therapy for the 21st century.* Philadelphia: Taylor and Francis.

Wubbolding, R. (2003). Reality therapy theory. In D. Capuzzi & D. R. Douglas (Eds.), *Counseling and psychotherapy: Theories and interventions* (3rd ed.) (pp. 252–282). Columbus, OH: Merrill.

Yager, J. (1989). A futuristic view of psychiatry. In J. Yager (Ed.), *The future of psychiatry as a medical specialty.* Washington, DC: American Psychiatric Press.

Yalom, I. D. (1980). *Existenital psychotherapy.* New York: Basic Books.

Yalom, I. D. (1995). *The theory and practice of group psychotherapy* (4th ed.). New York: Basic Books.

Yalom, I. D., & Lieberman, M. (1971). A study of encounter group casualties. *Archives of General Psychiatry, 25,* 16–30.

Yontef, G., & Jacobs, L. (2005). Gestalt therapy. In R. J. Corsini & D. Wedding (Eds.), *Current psychotherapies* (7th ed.) (pp. 299–336). Itasca, IL: F. E. Peacock.

Yontef, G. M., & Simkin, J. S. (1989). Gestalt therapy. In R. J. Corsini (Ed.), *Current psychotherapies* (4th ed.) (pp. 323–361). Itasca, IL: F. E. Peacock.

Yost, E., & Corbishley, M. (1987). *Career counseling: A psychological approach.* San Francisco: Jossey-Bass.

Young, M. E. (1992). *Counseling methods and techniques: An eclectic approach.* Columbus, OH: Merrill.

Younggren, J. N., & Gottlieb, M. C. (2004). Managing risk when contemplating multiple relationships. *Professional Psychology: Research and Practice, 35,* 255–260.

Zaccaria, J. S., & Moses, J. A. (1968). *Facilitating human development through reading: The use of bibliotherapy through teaching and counseling.* Champaign, IL: Stipes.

Zerin, M. (1988). An application of the drama triangle to family therapy. *Transactional Analysis Journal, 18,* 94–101.

Zimmerman, M. A., & Arunkumar, R. (1994). Resiliency research: Implications for schools and policy. *Social policy report: Society for research in child development, 8*(4), 1–17.

Zinnbauer, B. J., & Pargament, K. I. (2000). Working with the sacred: Four approaches to religious and spiritual issues in counseling. *Journal of Counseling and Development, 78*(2), 162–171.

Zunker, V. G. (2002). *Career counseling: Applied concepts of life planning* (6th ed.). Monterey, CA: Brooks/Cole.

Zytowski, D. G. (1985). *Kuder Occupational Interest Survey Form DD Manual Supplement.* Chicago: Science Research Associates.

Zytowski, D. G. (1994). A super contribution to vocational theory: Work values. *Career Development Quarterly, 43*(1), 25–31.

Zytowski, D. G., & Warman, R. E. (1982). The changing use of tests in counseling. *Measurement and Evaluation in Guidance, 15,* 147–152.

NAME INDEX

SUBJECT INDEX

Note: *f* = figure; *t* = table

515

CREDITS

pages 106–107: Spitzer, R. L., Gibbon, M., Skodol, A. E., Williams, T. B., & First, M. B. (Eds.). (1900). In *Casebook: A learning companion to the D.S.M.IV*. Washington, DC: American Psychiatric Press.

pages 162–165: Sue, D. W., Bernier, T. E., Durran, A., Feinberg, L., Pedersen, P., Smith, E. T., & Vasquez-Nuhall, E. (1982). Position paper: Cross-cultural counseling competencies. *The Counseling Psychologist*, *10*, 45–52. Copyright © 1982 by Sage Publications. Reprinted by permission of Sage Publications, Inc.

page 344: Fuhriman, A., & Burlingame, G. M. (1990). Consistency of matter: A comparative analysis of individual and group process variables. *The Counseling Psychologist*, *18*, 6–63. Copyright © 1982 by Sage Publications. Reprinted by permission of Sage Publications, Inc.

page 349–350: Burlingame, G. M., & Fuhriman, A. (1990). Time-limited group therapy. *The Counseling Psychologist, 18*, 93–118. Copyright © 1982 by Sage Publications. Reprinted by permission of Sage Publications, Inc.

page 367: From Samuel H. Osipow & Louise F. Fitzgerald. *Theories of career development,* 4th ed. © 1996, Allyn & Bacon.